Insight into the Ancient Mysteries Internet the Ageless Mythologies

Insight into the Ancient Mysteries Internet the Ageless Mythologies

by

Christopher Saint
Master of Mythology

RIVERCROSS PUBLISHING, INC.
NEW YORK • ORLANDO

 For information address RIVERCROSS PUBLISHING. INC., 127 East 59th Street, New York, NY 10022

ISBN: 0-944957-95-1

Library of Congress Catalog Card Number: 97-36463

First Printing

Library of Congress Cataloging-in-Publication Data

Saint, Christopher.
Initiation into the ancient mysteries : that's who instruction in the ageless mythologies / by Christopher Saint.
p. cm.
ISBN 0-944957-95-1
1. Mythology, Egyptian—Miscellanea. 2. Religions—Miscellanea. I. Title.
BF1999.S3112 1998
291.1'3—dc21 97-36463
CIP

History, Theology, and Mytheology
{The Theology of Relativity}
Warning!

Do not attempt to read this book
without first asking God
for the spiritual gift of understanding.
Only those with strong hearts and open minds
should seek the unknown knowledge.
In the quest of truth
it takes courage to face the facts.
Now
Prepare for a voyage to the unknown.
Clear your mind of all preconceived ideas.
We shall travel where no (white) man has gone before.
In cracking the code that reveals the secret message
we must seek out the missing link in the Mystery of MyTheology.
The Mythos-Theos-Logos is our kinsman Redeemer
and the Key to unlocking the Mystery.
The Word of God is the Universal Truth
that comes from the Mouth (Myth) of God.
He is the one-way Door of the dual dimension,
in the House of the Living,
in the Kingdom of en-Light-enment.
By returning to the roots of religion,
we discover that all Theology is Related
and we are all relatives of the Redeemer
in the family of our Father in Heaven.

Contents

Mastering Mythology

I would like to dedicate this book to the memory of Joseph Campbell. Who dedicated his life to teaching the meaning of the universal myth. Myth does not mean fable. Mythology means My theology. Which is the study of My God. Mythology tells us how to relate to the natural and supernatural worlds.

Joseph Campbell said we westerners are at the 3rd "physical" level of the seven chokras, compared to the easterners who are at the upper levels of spiritual enlightenment. We are as children compared to the ancients.

Insight into the Ancient Mysteries
Internet the Ageless Mythologies

Myth in the Making

The origin of All myths

In the beginning God thought. God created the second heaven and earth. God dwells alone in the first heaven and the third heaven the earth's atmosphere was not created until the second day. This second heaven is the dark sphere of space void of life. The Egyptians call it Nun, as in non-existence. This is the matrix of creation. The Hindus call it Maya, mother of all living. She is NOT a goddess. God has No partners. It is the primordial watery womb from with all the suns of God were born.

The Spirit was hovering over the face of the waters. The earth was dark and void of life. God opened his mouth and the Word of God thundered "Let there be light." and the good sun of God or Morning star was formed from the virgin womb. This virgin called Maya is Mary in English. It was Thoth as Messenger of God who announced the original immaculate conception as well as the incarnation of Jesus. The Egyptians call the Word of God, Thoth. The firstborn Sun of God is Thom or Atom and is represented by the star Sirius. To the Egyptians, the second heaven filled with suns of God is called Nut. Then God the Father send his favorite sun to rule over the earth.

Now God sent his Spirit to move over mother earth producing life. All living things possess a piece of God's Spirit called the power on high. The Egyptians called it Shu. A tree has life, therefore, a tree has a piece of God's Spirit. In fact, the vegetation produces the atmosphere or breath of life necessary for all creatures. The water of life flows through the veins of the Tree of life which gives life. The laws that govern are mother nature. Distinctly different from supernatural laws that govern the spirit realm.

God created all things in duality. The good sun of God, archangel Michael, was made to rule over the earth. The earthlings are his bride to be. It was not until the fourth day that the bad sun of God and the other stars were created. Lucifer is the daystar and his consort is the moon. As the moon follows the sun across the sky. Just as moonday follows sunday. The Romans created the myth of the moon goddess Dianna and the sungod Apollo. Satan rules over the day and the darkness of night. The Egyptians call him Amen-Ra. The star of Hyades in the constellation of Taurus the bull. The Bull became Baal of the Canaanites. The suns of God created man in their image with a good and bad nature. This explains man's dark side. In the womb of mother earth, the earthlings were formed. The Spirit of God activated their growth.

Lucifer presented himself to Eve as the most beautiful being ever created. This smooth talking devil has a forked tongue like a serpent. He seduced Eve planting evil ideas in her head. The seeds took root and did bear bad fruits. Lucifer told her she was immortal and able to be like God. This is the first fable. Breaking the supernatural laws by attempting to trespass into the spiritual realm. Lucifer took her cherry. Eve shared her forbidden fruits with Adam. The fruits she did bear were the bad seed Cain and good son Abel. Eve became the mother of all living. The Romans called her Dianna. God's curse on her is the monthly curse that parallels the moon's 28 day cycle.

Adam and Eve were exiled from the garden of God where the Lord of the Sabbath ruled over the earthlings. Now they have entered the first day of the second week. Sunday is Satan's day as the sungod. The Egyptians call him Set which is an abbreviation of Satan. The Hindus call him Shiva the Destroyer or Indra the ruler of this wicked world. When Satan took control, time was put to motion. Mankind was given a limited lifetime. Each day they grew closer to the end. Adam lived just short of one divine day, which is a thousand years. Then he returned to the mother earth from which he came.

Two cherubim or archangels were placed at the gate to the garden to guard the way to the tree of life. The flaming sword which turns in every direction is the sun of God or Morning star. One of these angels or sons of God is Lucifer and the other is Michael the archangel. Zoroaster calls them the twin Morning stars who are diametrically opposite. Sinners are not able to get past Satan because he Accuses us of our evil to Michael. The Greek name for Satan is Hades. He is the ruler of the underworld. That means he is the sun who goes under the world not underground. Peter is Not guarding the gate.

It is God's desire to recreate the garden of Eden and place His good sons in that paradise to live forever. This will occur at the end of the Sabbatical Millennium. Which is the seven thousandth year of mans existence. The linear time will go full cycle, back to the beginning. The second Adam has made atonement for the sons of Adam. But sinners still will not be allowed to enter the Holy Land of God's kingdom.

The sons of God saw Lucifer's perversion and decided to follow his lead. These angels left their domain, mated with human women and produced infamous half-breeds who were giants mentally and physically. These giants became the legends of the Titans in Greek mythology. There was a battle of the Titans vs. the gods. These gods are sons of God. Michael and his angels fought against Satan and his angels and cast them into the

Lake of fire. The Lord brought the great flood to destroy these mutant freaks. This story is an universal theme in every nation and every religion.

Then the descendants of Noah built the Tower of Baal which was later called the Tower of Babel because the Lord caused the confused tongues. The followers of Baal wanted to ascend into heaven. They quoted Lucifer in saying, "I shall ascend into heaven, I will exalt my throne above the stars of God, I will also sit on the mount of the congregation on the farthest sides of the north;"

Satan's desires was to sit on the throne of monarchangel Michael and rule over the sons of God: both the angels and the humans. He did not consider it possible to overthrow God the Father. He wanted to sit at the right hand of God the Father instead of the Lord.

From here the myth of evolution was started by the writers of science fiction. Who tell the fable that man is evolving from a lower life form and is continually improving. Actually man has de-evolved from Adam. We are the descendants who are slowing going down hill with each new generation. Mankind gets worse and worse. We have entered the Dark Ages of the end times.

It was the Romans who worshipped the creation rather then the Creator. They worshipped the goddess Diana as queen of heaven and mother of all living. When the disciples of Christ came along, the Diana cult was killed off and buried. But when Christendom was created by emperor Constantine, the Diana cult was resurrected. She was rename Madonna or Ma-Diana queen of heaven and mother of God. Christendom worships Mary or Maya as the Creator who gave birth to their little god Jesus. They worship the Mother and Child rather than the Father.

The Romans are the bastard children of the Greeks and Aryans of Assyria. They are orphans without a Father in heaven. "You are of your father the devil, and the desires of your father you want to do. He was a murderer from the beginning, and does not stand in the truth, because there is no truth in him. When he speaks a lie, he speaks from his own resources, for he is a liar and the father of it." [John 8:44] "In this the children of God and the children of the devil are manifest: whoever does not practice righteousness is not of God, nor is he who does not love his brother. For this is the message that you heard from the beginning, that we should love one another, not as Cain who was of the wicked one and murdered his brother. And why did he murder him? Because his works were evil and his brother's righteous." [1 John 3:10-12] Cain and his mate escaped the flood by climbing aboard the ark as an unclean beast. He is the albino primate commonly called the Neanderthal man. He is tall, pale and hairy. The Roman empire is called the Beast in Daniel and Revelation. They are the body members of the blood-thirsty dragon. The head of state and church pretends to be Christ, but is really the Antichrist. The Lord with the Sword is coming on a white horse to slay the dragon. And that is no fairy tale. Even the Catholics confess that after two more Popes, the wrathful Judge is coming to destroy the unholy Roman Catholic empire.

The legend of the battles of Herackles and the Amazons is the Greek fighting and later mating with the Aryan women. This produced the Romans. The Romans boast that they are descendants of the gods. This is true. They are the bastard sons of the fallen son of God. The Devil is their dad.

Legend says the founders of Rome, Romulus and Remus, were born on the winter solstice (Dec.25th). They were suckled by a bitch or she-wolf. This is Not a fairy tale. It is a metaphor. As a wolf is of the canine family. Which is a metaphor for the eleven families of Canaanites and one family of Cainite. The children were taken to a cave where shepherds brought them gifts. Sound familiar? Saying that Christ was born on Dec.25th, placed in a cave, and visited by shepherds and wise men bearing gifts... is a fable. The spirit of Chrismas is the evil spirit of: merry-making, drunkenness, folly, selfishness, greed and deception. Giving to the poor is what the Lord taught, not exchanging gifts with friends and family.

All soldiers are dog-soldiers. That is why they wear dog-tags. They are trained to follow their leader-dog. Dog is a metaphor for humans who act like savage animals. The Jews called the Samarians dogs because they were half Assyrian. The Aryans are like their father Cain who shed the blood of his peace-loving brother. Satan puts his mark on all that are his. The mark of the Beast is the Satanic star the military puts on all that is theirs. Romulus murdered his brother Remus just as Cain killed Abel.

They created unrest, that is contrary of God's Rest. God's kingdom will be orderly and peaceful....the garden paradise restored. The Sabbath is the sign that shows you are God's children. When Adam and Eve decided to follow Satan out of the Sabbath day, Satan became ruler of the earth. He will rule six divine days which are six thousand years. Then the Lord will come on the beginning of the Seventh divine day to restore God's garden.

The Lord of the Earth decided to work with each of the three sons of Noah for 2,000 years. First he worked with Ham, who is the African nations. The Egyptian Delta became the center of true worship. But it was soon divided between those who worshipped the good Son of God in Lower Egypt. and those who worshipped the bad son of God in Upper Egypt.

The Egyptians call the good Sun of God, Atum-Ra and Horus of the Horizon. As Horus went beyond the western horizon to the darkside of the underworld. He returned to the constellation of Orion in the night sky. This represents the death of Christ on the cross. Who returns to the right hand of God in heaven.

They call the bad Sun of God Amon-Ra, Set. He is the sun that rules over the earth for the time being. The sun does rise and Set daily. Amon-Ra-Set means Sun-Set. When he rises and when he sets, he is red like the blood thirsty dragon of Revelation chapter 12. He is the fallen star and his symbol is the pentacle. Why do the translators put the Word of God in red ink when it is Satan's color? Why do they put a five pointed asterisk to mark the prophecies of Christ when five is Satan's number. Six is the number of man who was created on the sixth day and seven is the number of the Lord of the Sabbath.

When the people of Israel where in bondage to the Egyptians, they learned to worship the evil sun of God Amen. To this day they end their prayers with Amen. Then when the Greeks and Romans conquered Egypt, they studied the mythology of the Upper Egyptians who worshipped Amen. This obviously influenced their translation of the Bible, which was partially done in Egypt. As the Christians also praise Amen at the end of their prayers.

Later, the Roman Catholics took one of Amen's obelisks to the Vatican in Rome. The obelisk is both a phallic symbol of potency and a memorial for the countless unknown soldiers. Demonstrating the potency of the Papacy. The new Roman mythology was based on the myths of Upper Egypt where they worshipped Amen-Set who is Satan the Warlord. When Emperor Constantine created Christendom, he continued to worship the Invincible Sun for the remaining 40 years of his life. That Sun is Lucifer the Daystar.

Constantine saw a swastika superimposed over the sun and heard the words "By this conquer." So he took the hooked cross to be his sign and conquered the whole Roman empire. The state religion became his religion called Christendom and the blood red cross on a white flag was their logo. Later, Hitler used the very same cross of Christendom called swastika in German. Hitler wanted to create the third Reich or third rise of the Roman empire. Hitler took the name Nazi Germany from the Hebrew word Nasi Israel; Which means leader of Israel. Nazi Germany refers to Hitler as leader of Germany.

Constantine took the statue of Zeus to Constanople and worshipped it as Jesus. He built statues of Dianna and called them Madonna the blessed virgin. Madonna is Ma-Diana. Diana was the virgin sister of Apollo the sungod. She constantly chases him to mate with him under the moonlight. Just as the moon follows after the setting sun. The Babylonians and the Canaanites continued to worship Amen as Baal. From the Tower of Baal.

While the Hittites called him Helio. Helio means sun. He was the Warlord portrayed on a chariot and a sun burst or halo on his head. The halo is the symbol of Helio. The statue of Helio at the island of Rhodes is one of the infamous Seven Wonders of the Ancient world. The French made a replica of this sun-god in feminine form and gave it to the United States. Helio is now Shelio the sun-deva with a sun burst crown on her head. The infidels also built the Eiffel Tower in the skeleton shape of an obelisk.

Washington DC (District of Columbus) is Not one of the 50 states of United States, but a District owned by Columbus. Columbia is the Latin spelling for Columbus. Now the Romans can claim their property at any time. Once they control the capital, they control the country. The United States will have no choice but to join the New World Order or Neo-Roman Empire. Washington DC will fit right in with its Roman architecture and legislature.

Opposite the obelisk in Washington DC is the temple of Zeus. The so called Lincoln memorial is a replica of Zeus sitting on his throne in his temple at Olympus. Zeus like Jesus means Savior. They are insinuating that Lincoln is the savior of the nation. He is given credit for saving the Union. This is further proof that Satan is ruler of this wick world and that he appoints All heads of state. As stated in Luke 4:5,6. Just as he appointed the Caesars, Napoleon, Hitler, Stalin, etc.

Uncle Sam, believe it or not, originated in Egypt. It was Set and his minions, the Sami, who murdered Osiris. The kingdom of Egypt was divided. Horus ruled the northern kingdom. Set or Sat is the uncle of Horus and the ruler of the southern kingdom. Menes (Manes), the Scorpion King from the south, united the two lands (sam-taui) by military conquest. Sam, in Egyptian, means "Union". Therefore, Uncle Sam refers to the Warlords; Sat and his minion, Menes. Set can also be spelled Suth, as in south. Compare to Lincoln uniting the north and the rebels of the south; the 50 states of the United States. In Turkey, Uncle Sam was a circus clown that wore red and white stripped pants (the colors of the Viking warriors) with a blue hat with a Satanic star (his head in the stars). [Isaiah 14:12-15] There are 50 of these pentacles on the U.S. flag and the Pentagon is the headquarters of the military. Uncle Sam (Sat-aman) later became the icon of the United States military. He is "The Man" or A-man, the Warlord, who leads the flock to the slaughter. It is by no accident that he looks like a goat, one of the sacred animals of Sat-Aman (Satan). He is the shepherd of the goats. [Matthew 25:31-46] It is the Antichrist that worries about saving the state. While Christ is saving the individuals of the church. Ironically, Lincoln was obsessed with death. Not only the thousands of deaths he caused through the Civil War, but his own eminent death. Not to mention the attempted genocide of Indians before, during and after the Civil War. When Lincoln's son died at an early age, Lincoln exhumed the body of his son, not once, but twice. Trying to communicate with his dead son. Strange, since Christians are supposed to believe they go to heaven at death.

Trying to communicate with the dead is condemned by the Lord. The Bible says the dead return to the dust. The dead know nothing. They have no memory in the grave. The same happens to man as to the beasts. [Ecclesiastes 3:19,20 9:5,6,10 12:7] The dead lay dormant until the Lord returns on the Day of Resurrection. King David is yet in his grave. He has

NOT ascended to heaven. [Acts 2:29,34] The Lord says no one has ascended into heaven except himself. [John 3:13] Those who say they are going to heaven are quoting Satan. Who said "I shall ascend into heaven, as high as the stars of God".

Above the Capitol building is the Goddess of Freedom. Is it one nation under God? or One nation under the goddess? She rules over the men in politics. She is the warrior woman just as Dianna was the moon goddess armed with a bow for the battle. The bow comes from the shape of the crescent moon. She fights for the freedom of her white race by enslaving the other races. White supremacy is the strategy of the White House. Another Roman icon that symbolizes dominion and oppression. In India, she is Durga the warrior deva. Her consort is Shiva the destroyer. Both are attributes of Satan. Shiva is the evil sungod portrayed in a ring or halo of fire. He is the archenemy of Vishnu, the good son of God who set in the west and will return from the east.

In Washington, Lady Justice is blind. The balance of justice is tilted by the money bags of the wealthy and the poor are the ones to pay the penalty. Freedom is an illusion that can not be achieved in a world of people who are slaves to sin. Lady Libertine represents the promiscuous behavior of a society free to do as they please. She represents the secular society's "Freedom from Religion" not freedom of religion. Those not under God's law, are the lawless ones the Lord is coming to execute. Either he is your Savior or your Executioner. All shall by judged based on God's law.

God gave us freedom of choice: the freedom to sin vs. the freedom from sin. And with the freedom comes the responsibility for the consequences. Those who choose not to believe in the hereafter, will not be here, after all things are made new. Those who deny God's existence, God will deny their existence! Those who believe God is going to torment people in hell-fire forever, are the ones going in that Lake of fire. You receive what you believe in. Those who think they shall go to heaven will be disappointed when the heavens are consumed by God's awesome presence.

It was by no accident that the space ship that went to the moon was called Apollo. This is Roman mythology and science fiction. The Apollo ship shaped like a phallus rendezvoused and mated with the moon. The name of the ship remained the same for 13 missions just so they could use that name. Apollo and Dianna's mating has produced their sons the satellites that orbit the earth. Now they can broadcast the Roman dogma to every nation from heaven. The god of the space age is TV. The Bible says that Satan is prince of the power of the air waves. It is he who programs the minds of the masses with his propaganda. Now the state has a free hand to make enough Inter-ballistic missiles with nuclear warheads to destroy the enemy and ourselves.

Asherah is the Canaanite term for mother nature. Her mate is Baal. The Canaanites worship mother nature and her sun by going into a grove of trees and finding a phallic symbol to worship. Modern Canaanites cut down one of those trees and bring it into the house and decorate it with gold and silver. God condemns this pagan tradition. [Jeremiah 10:1-5] This is the Forbidden Fruit of the Tree of Carnal knowledge. The star on the top of the X-mas tree is Lucifer the fallen star. The angel is Satan the fallen angel. You must bow down to him to get your gift under the tree!

Christ died on a tree, an X-Mas tree or Roman Cross. Showing that Asherah had her hand in the death of Christ. Asherah is Satan's feminine side, as well as his dark side. She represents the life to death cycle of nature and the night that the moon rules over. The cross was the instrument of Christ's death. It was dark for three hours while the prince of darkness killed the Son of Man. The Roman's, like Constantine, had succeeded in conquering the King of the Jews by their Satanic symbol, the cross. But they did NOT conquer the Son of God called the King of kings. He had conquered death by transfiguring from a human-being to a spirit-being.

Modern Myth

Modern mythology is based on the old fables. The Roman gods have been replaced by Mother Mary and her saints. Saint Nickolas soon became a deity. He is worshipped as an immortal being who lives at the North Pole Star. The legend of Santa is past down generation to generation as if it is fact. In the same way and at the same time the story of Jesus Christ is told. The children can Not discern between the two. Either both are gospel or fable. In fact, Americans call Santa, Kris Kringle. Which is German for Christ Child. So they are saying Santa is the Christ Child and Krismas is his birthday.

Santa is an anagram for Satan. He is the Antichrist trying to steal Christ's glory. The children are never told that Santa is not real. Then when the children find out the truth, they realize they can never fully trust their parents ever again. This sick prank is the beginning of children starting to rebel against their lying parents. Parents teach their children that there is a tooth fairy, an Easter Bunny, and other fables as if they were facts. The fact is: The Easter bunny is Ishtar the sex deva who has sex with every Peter rabbit who comes along. Harem comes from the Hindu Hari (to pro-create) as the hare multiplies profusely.

Santa Claus has little or nothing to do with St. Nickolas. St. Nickolas lived and died in Europe, while Santa lives (in the minds of believers) at the North Pole Star. He rides a chariot pulled by flying creatures. The lead reindeer has a glowing nose like a fiery angel. Just as in the Barbarian mythology. Santa or Father Chrismas wears the crown of Amen-Ra, the evil sun-god of Upper Egypt. Even though he has no children of his own, he is a father figure to the masses. Just as the Pope and his priests are called father.

Santa is the sungod who comes on the eve of the winter solstice. The Vikings called it the Yule tide. When the sun wanes in power like the waves going out at low tide. This is the lowest point of the sun's power, yet the peak of the moon's. The sun is renewed at New Year (Sun's birthday) and regains its power in the spring at Valentine's day and Easter when the sun and the moon mate. Valentines day honors Venus the sex deva and Cupid. The spring is when men go blind and stupid because the wrong head is leading them astray. The head that has no mind or eyes to see the truth.

The sun returns to full strength at the summer solstice. June 22nd is the high day for the evil sun of God. His ship comes in on the high tide. This is the time most weddings occur, in honor of the Roman deva Juno. The Antichrist is rapturing away the June brides. for the time is short before the Lord will be coming in the autumn season. Autumn gets its name from the good Sun of God of Lower Egypt, Atum-Ra.

You are betrothed to one husband, therefore present yourself a virgin to Christ. Do not be like Eve who was seduced by that old serpent Satan. That smooth talking Devil who planted lies in her head and stold her innocence. She ate of the Tree of Carnal knowledge and Satan took her forbidden fruit, commonly called her Cherry. Then she shared the same with Adam. When the Antichrist comes many will be deceived by his lies. He will convince the masses that he is the Savior who will save the world. He will steal them from their first loved, who is Christ. He will take their virtue by getting them to live in sin with himself.

This will be no great feat since Satan has got most of the world believing they do not have to obey God's laws. Christendom claims they are saved by the magical word "grace". The Lord says calling upon his name will not save you if you practice lawlessness. No sinner shall enter God's kingdom. [Matthew 7:21-23]

Television is today's; baby-sitter, companion, comforter, teacher, preacher, advisor, counselor, and social conscience. Television programs the potential leaders of the future. Forget Big Brother, "Big Mother" is here. Television is the Mother who weans the kids. Big Brother is not watching you, you are watching it. And "it" controls every aspect of our lives.

Television is the voice box of modern mythology. The televangelists appear to be like Christ speaking the Word of God, when in reality they speak the words of the Devil. The audience can not discern the difference because they have not heard the Word of God. The preachers of Christendumb keep their masses dumb. They keep retelling the life and times of the man Jesus, but do not teach the Word of God. They feed the people baby food, never weaning them from the milk of God's Word onto the solid food. Those who are not growing spiritually, are spiritually dead.

Spiritual growth means learning the knowledge of God's kingdom. Maturing through discipline and correcting past mistakes. Repenting of sin, not repeating of sin, is the way to God's kingdom. God's Word is the instruction manual on how to stop sinning. Study the sacred scriptures and see what God has to say about man's traditions and pagan customs.

Television produces the images that people idolize. The masses follow what it says as if it were the Gospel truth. It is television that promotes the pagan holidays like Christmas and Easter so the merchants can profit from them. Modern people idolize movie stars, sports stars, and music stars. They all use the logo of the Satanic star. The mark of the beast is an universal symbol that is so common it is accepted as "our" symbol. At Hollywood Blvd. movie stars bow down to the satanic star to make their mark in the synthetic stone. Like shooting stars, they burn bright for a short time but they soon crash and burn. Movie "stars" promote astrology readings and psychic advisors. They seek psychic advisors and psychiatric advice for help in their unstable lives.

The circuits of the stars (celestial beings) obviously do influence the circus on earth. Spiritualism has been revived by the Psychic advisors of TV land. They claim to be in touch with the dead. The Word of God says that familiar spirits are the fallen angels pretending to be dead people you are familiar with. These angels are called spirits, demons, and poltergeist. The fact that these spiritualist and astrologers can predict the future is proof of the Devil and his demons. It is Satan who has social intercourse with those who live in sin with him. The Egyptians say the circumpolar stars (Ursa Major, Ursa Minor, and Draco) are the followers of Set (Satan). The caged animals of the zoo-diac.

The Word of God condemns: divination, spiritualism, monthly prognosticators, sorcerers, witches and pagan priests. Communicating with the dead is called necromancy and is an abomination to God. The dead do not turn into ghosts. The dead remain dormant in the dust of mother earth until the Lord resurrects them from the grave. You will notice the word Roman in the word necromancy because the Romans are the greatest pagans of all.

The Roman-Christian calendar is supposed to be based on the birth of Christ. Even this is fiction. Christ was born between 7 and 4 BC He was born at least four years before the Christians claim. Not to mention the fact that the Sun of God was the first born of the creation, at least 13,000 years ago. As Sun of God he rules over the Earth. Then on the Seventh divine day, he was made Lord of the Sabbath. The Sabbath is the Lord's day. Sunday is Satan's day. The day Adam and Eve were exiled from the garden of God.

Television is the most powerful medium in the world. Whoever controls it controls the world. It claims to broadcast "live", but that is merely an illusion of artificial lights and sounds. Television is a graven image. Satan is prince of the power of the air waves pretending to be the Angel of light. The evil spirit of error comes from the darkness of the black box. The black box is a metaphor for a coffin containing those who already died and those who shall die.

Luke Skywalker of Star Wars is an example of science fictional character who saves the world. He is the Savior of science fiction. He is an Aryan warrior intent on conquering the perceived enemy then conquering a mate. Sex and violence is the sick scenario of the American Dream. This is the Crusader syndrome of "manifest destiny". It is the slave master mentality. Superman, Batman, Spiderman, Heman are all demigods of science fiction. These are spurious saviors trying to take the place of the true Christ Savior. Satan's specialty is to subtly twist the truth and entwine truth with lies. He mixes pagan ideas with the Word of God. Satan is author of confusion. He is the ghost-writer behind the scenes who writes these science-fiction scripts.

In the Star Trek movie, Captain Kirk says to Captain John Luke, "I was out saving the galaxy while your grandfather was still in diapers." The name Kirk means Church. He is Captain of his Church. The Captain and his followers go on a voyage "where no man has gone before" in his star-ship (solar bark). Their mission: to prove there is no God in heaven. The Russian (Arian) cosmonaut boasted, "I have been up in the sky, and nowhere did I find God."

Like Ra in his solar bark, they battle their perceived enemies. Star-Wars is the war in heaven which Satan has brought down to earth. All aliens (foreigners) are potential enemies. They try to cloak their violence with self-righteous propaganda, while spreading colonialism. The Aryan-Anglo prime directive is to conquer and dominate all beings; terrestrial and extra-terrestrial (aliens). They want to convert everyone to their way of thinking. That is NOT science fiction.

President Nixon said, "We have ascended into the heavens and now they are ours." Quoting Satan who tried to storm the gates of heaven through force. Man fantasizes that he can have dominion in heaven. These delusions of grandeur shall be short lived. Just as Satan was cast down to the abyss for his insurrection. [Revelation 12:3-12] Interstellar travel is science fiction.

John and Luke are followers and scribes of Christ. John Luke is Luke-warm, neither hot nor cold in his believe in God. These names were not picked at random. In Star Trek the Next Generation, Deonna Troy has an immaculate conception and "virgin birth". Her son Eon (meaning infinite time) willingly dies in his prime and returns to being the Morning star. Dianna was the virgin goddess of Troy who was later converted to Madonna (Ma-dianna), Mother Mary of Christendom. Di-anna means second Anna, as the first was Anu, Egypt the nativity of the Son of God, Atum-Horus.

The secular world replaces the Word of God with the science fiction of UFOs. They believe in aliens from other planets who travel in flying saucers. This is part of television created mythology. Started by War of the Worlds a fictional radio broadcast that people believed to be true. The Marsians who invade earth are an allegory for the Romans who worship Mars, the god of war. They tried to conquer the world, but were stopped by mother nature: the weather, disease, etc... The neo-Romans (United States of Europe) are still trying to conquer the world and beyond with their technology, but shall be stopped by the Supernatural Extra-terrestrial (Horus/Jesus).

SETI is a department of the Aerospace program. SETI = Search for Extra-Terrestrial Intelligence. Seti or Set is the evil extra-terrestrial being. Are they searching for Satan and his fallen angels? Satan is one of the most intelligent beings ever. Beware for he is able to deceive even the elect. He is the alien in his Star-ship (Solar Bark). To his followers, he promises to transform them into beings of light who shall sail over heaven in the Solar Bark forever. [From Fetish to God in Ancient Egypt by Wallis Budge page 357] This is the same lie Satan told Eve. And the same lie Christendumb tells their children. Man is not going to heaven in the future nor in the hereafter!

Joseph Campbell said the problem with the Bible mythology is that it is thousands of years old and does not relate to modern culture. I beg to disagree. The problem is: the scholars have misinterpreted the Word of God. So that it does not relate to today. Because they do not understand it. The Word of God is eternal. It is a timeless truth that never grows old. It relates just as much today as yesterday. When translated properly, the mythology does relate to all ages including the space age. We don't new myths. We need to renew the ancient ones.

The false church of Christendom has twisted the Word of God to fit their misinterpretation. Man has made God in his own image. They claim that God did manifest in the flesh of Jesus. Jesus is their demi-god. They want God to have human weaknesses and a sinful nature so they can continue to sin and feel guilt-free. They could follow his example if he were a sinner like them. This is Satan's lie! Jesus is Son of God who was first of the creation. God created His good Sun on the first day. God did not, would not, and could not come in human form. God is Spirit. He transcends the physical. The Creator does not climb into the creation. The creation is but a minor part of the Infinite Creator that encompasses the creation. God is a consuming fire. When God does come, He is going to consume the darkness of outer space and all the stars that will not be refined in His fire. All evil will be consumed.

Christ's example to us was to be humble. Earthlings are to remain down to earth. We are to wait on the Lord, for the Lord's day when he comes to raise us from the dust of the earth. The Lord will exalt those who are lowly. You can't get much lower than the grave. When the Lord comes, we will hear his voice. Which means we will hear the Word of God and be enlightened. Those who prefer the darkness of ignorance will remain in the grave. This is rejection of the Holy Spirit and the only unforgivable sin.

Television-The Graven Image

TV is the window to the world. We see the world through that dark window. But windows go both ways. Uninvited and unwanted guests can climb in that window into your home. Thieves can come in and steal your money. Robbers can come in and steal your children's innocence. The evil spirits come through the dark window of TV in the form of evil thoughts. TV preachers, Charity organizations, and crooked merchants can take your money. But far worse, the TV medium can put evil ideas into the heads of your innocent children. They are programmed with sex and violence from an early age.

Television sets the standards on what is right or wrong. Television tells you how to raise your children. What to do on the holidays. What to eat. What to buy. What to do. Between tradition, television and peer pressure most people will conform to what is acceptable behavior. The Bible says, "Do not conform to the ways of the world, but transform your thoughts to be acceptable to God." God wants you to keep His holy days, not Satan's holidays.

Television sets the standards of what is good or evil. Television is slowly making homosexuality socially acceptable. Just as it was in the Roman empire. The Romans were bisexuals. Television promotes freedom of sex and violence. War is glamorized so the children will be ready to fight for their country. Physical fitness is programmed into the secular schools so the youth will be ready for boot camp at graduation. The brains behind the speaker is Satan. Satan is prince of the power of the air waves. TV is the most powerful medium in the world. The world is being 'sodomized' by Satan.

Television promotes sex and violence. They claim sex and violence sells. This is true since they are preying on people's carnal nature. The flesh is weak. Christ condemned Peter for allowing his flesh to overpower God's spirit. The Spirit is willing, but if you allow the flesh to overpower it, you are playing into the evil spirit's hand. God's spirit will overcome if you work with it and not against it. Do Not let television tell you what the Word of God says. Read it for yourself. Learn to separate the Spirit of Truth from the Spirit of Error.

It was Satan who created the theory of evolution. The strongest shall survive. The mighty men of war shall conquer the world. The prime-evil predator shall devour the prey and plunder their goods. Those driven by their animal instincts believe it is kill or be killed. The Satanic military service is Satan's brain-child. The logo of the Pentagon is the pentacle. The problem with this theory is that the Lord with the Sword is coming to slay all warriors. Their glory shall be short lived. No warriors shall enter God's kingdom. The so called animal instincts are the knowledge acquired from the Tree of Carnal knowledge. The beast within is the Devil. These immoral beasts shall not be given immortal life.

TV is the modern myth maker. Television sets the standards as who is the good guy and who is the bad. The character that John Wayne personified in his many movies was that of manifest destiny or making your own destiny. John Wayne's character was an atheist anarchist who rebels against God's authority. He broke all God's commandments. He was the outlaw who lived and died by his own laws. People idolize him as white man fighting for his right to dominate nature and the native people. He was the savage heathen lost in the Wilderness of Sin called the Wild West. This is the story of how the West was Won and Lost. The Lord is coming to save those who lost and destroy those who won the war for the west. All warriors will be slain by the Lord with the Sword. Change your evil ways now while there is still time. John Wayne was a strong supporter of MacCarthy's persecution of the 'alleged communists'. His paranoia and pro-pagan-da helped to ruin the lives of many innocent citizens. MacCarthyism proved to be far more dangerous than any perceived Communism! Ironically, the logo of Red Communism and of movie stars is one and the same Satanic star. It should come as no surprise to learn that it was the Pope who instigated the inquisitions of the perceived enemy of Communists, as proclaimed by the Lady phantom at Fatima.

Myth in the Making

Television will help to produce the living legends of the new age. Out of the darkness of doom and despair will rise a new ray of hope. A man will appear to have the solutions to saving the world from eminent destruction. People will believe him to be the worlds greatest leader. They will idolize him. He will work hand and hand with the Pope. Their miraculous discoveries will show signs of healing the worlds problems. The people will call him the Savior of the world. He is the one who comes instead of Christ as King of kings. He is the infamous Antichrist. The Pope is the false prophet who is head of the false church. He claims to be the Vicar of Christ or head of the church. Together they will unite the world and lead the masses astray.

The romantic Antichrist will rapture away those who dwell in fantasy. Just as Lucifer enchanted Eve with his beauty and charm. The smooth taking Devil talked her out of her innocence and into living in sin with him. He is the super star of stardom who will sweep them off their feet. He will lure the masses to his way of life. Those who love this world will be blessed with the luxuries of this world by this dashing Devil. Those who hate this wicked world and will not conform to their wicked ways, will be blessed with an inheritance in God's kingdom in the hereafter.

The neo Roman empire proclaim the gospel of: freedom of religion. Everyone will be free to worship all the Roman deities. Anyone claiming theirs is only one true God will be excommunicated and persecuted. Everyone will be pressured into believing in Santa, Mary mother of god, Madonna goddess of mother nature, Jesus the re-incarnated Zeus, Mars the god of war and blood-shed, Apollo the god of science and medicine, Venus the sex deva, Cupid the god of Romance and heartbreak, Hades the god of hellfire and lord of the living dead, etc... All souls shall cease from work on the Sun's day. Sunday is the day to honor the sun-god, Helio.

This new age religion will believe that humans turn into spirits when they die. They will believe the dead go to heaven. The psychics and mediums will claim to communicate with the dead. They will believe the predictions of the psychics. Halloween is the day they imitate the dead souls. They celebrate the Day of the Undead when witches, demons, ghosts, and evil spirits haunt the living. The celebrations continue through X-mas. For the Chrismas spirit is the evil spirit of lies and fables. They will also believe in Lady luck, the tooth-fairy and the Easter bunny. The problem is; there is no such thing as "undead".

The head of Christendom will persecute the Saints who keep God's law. Making martyrs of the true followers of Christ. Just as during the inquisition. The final Pope will be called Romulus Peter II. Named after the founder of Rome, Romulus. And the founder of their church, Peter Pan, head of the pantheon. It has nothing to do with Christ's disciple, Peter, as it was the Romans who murdered him. Peter may have founded the original church of God in Rome, but the Romans murdered them and the Catholics took their place. There is no church of Rome mentioned in the book of Revelations.

The Lord on the white horse is coming to slay the dragon. This bloodthirsty beast is the body of believes who follow the head of state and head of the church. This is the revived unholy Roman Catholic empire which is now called the United States of Europe. The body of believers include the Crusaders of Christendom and all who worship the Sun's day. The Wrath of the Lord of the Sabbath will be on the evil sun-god and his followers.

The Antichrist will not conquer through violent overthrow as Alexander, Caesar, Napoleon, and Hitler did. He will come in on a platform of peace and prosperity. He is the politician who will make promises he never intents to keep. Just as he deceived Eve. The future will look bright for all those who will accept the Mark of the Beast in their head and in their hand. The Mark is a trade Mark on items bought and sold. That trade-mark is the Satanic star. [Revelation 13:16] Many of those who will not buy items with the satanic trade-ark will die of starvation. Others will be murdered by the body members of Christendom. These martyrs will be greatly rewarded by the Lord at his coming.

Christ is called the Logos or Word. He is also the Morning Star and Lord of the Seventh day. Christ's logo is a seven pointed star, the symbol of the archangel. Six is the number of man. The six pointed star of David is man's logo. As man was created on the sixth day. Satan imitates everything of Christ. Satan is called the fallen star. He was Lucifer the archangel, but lost his wings and fell from God's favor. Therefore, Satan's logo is the five pointed star that fell from heaven. He is now the sun that rules over the earth. The sun that rises and falls daily.

Television and the computer will be linked through the telephone. This technological trinity will be the medium through which most transactions will take place. People will become more and more isolated and dependent on them. They will become vulnerable to the massive power and influence of technology. Divide and conquer is the Devil's motto. No one can stand alone against this evil spirit-being. Only the holy spirit gives us the power to stand against him and resist all the temptations of technology.

The Antichrist will create a league of nations. [Daniel 11:23,24] He will rule over all nations from his capital in Rome. The beast has seven heads. The seven heads are the seven hills of Rome from which the Antichrist will rule the seven continents. Satan will incarnate as the eighth head of state or Antichrist Jesus who will rule over the ten nations of Europe which were formerly the unholy Roman Catholic empire. This is Christendom (Chris ten dom). The ten dominions that became ten Christian nations: Germany, France, Spain, Portugal, Italy, Poland, Greece, Belgium, England and Turkey. Today they are the League of Nations called the United States of Europe. The Antichrist will rule the world for 4 years. The Romans will occupy Jerusalem for the same period of time.

Then Michael the great Prince shall deliver everyone who is written in the Book of Life. Those who sleep in the dust of the earth shall awake and arise. Some to everlasting life and some to shame and everlasting destruction. Those who are wise and righteous shall shine like stars or suns of God forever and ever. [Daniel 12:1-3] Just as God promised Abraham that some of his descendants will be like the dust of the seashore. Stardust consumed in the Lake of fire. Others will be like the Sun of God called the Morning star. Monarch-angel Michael shall rule as King of kings from his capital JeruSalem. Then the children of God will live happily forever after.

The board of directors of show business are predominately Jews. The story of the Holocaust horror is at home in Hollywood. They remake a new version every year. Yet they never tell the story of how the Jews massacred the Canaanites and took their land. Or how about a movie about the Jews murdering the people of Palestine and stealing their land again. Most movie and TV stars are blondes. Aryans and Aryan want to be's (bleach blondes) dominate the screen just as they dominated the scene when they were known as Danites; one of the 12 tribes of the Israelites. Are the Jews trying to make the point that the Aryan race is the Master race? They have convinced the masses that blondes are the beautiful people. That's quite a feat; to convince the masses that the colorless, paste-faced, white-eyed, albino-Aryans are beautiful!

In the movie 'The Last Temptation of Christ' He is portrayed as an Aryan! Jesus marries Mary. Mary is His mother. Compare this to Amen-Ra who does marry Ma, his mother. This is the Rosicrucian belief that the holy Grail (San Greal) means Royal Blood in a holy vessel (Sang real). That vessel is Mary and the thing in it is the Christ child, or as they believe, Christ's child?

Modern Man's Myth's

The myth of modern man is the Big Bang theory. In the beginning, there was a great explosion from the fiery furnace. This fire ball filled the universe. In fact, was the universe. All that was is inside that explosion of light. Astronomers can see the light from the edge of our universe 20 billion light years away. It is just now reaching us.

This theory parallels the Bible. Which says God is a consuming fire. In the beginning, God the Father was alone in the first heaven. He conceived and created the darkness of outer space from nothing. This is the second heaven. He created His Sun or Morning star to rule over the earth. Our atmosphere is the third heaven. God, the Creator, is not part of that creation. He is the light beyond the darkness of space. Which was void of life until He created all living things with His supernatural powers called His Spirit.

When God comes earth in the Last Day, He will consume all the darkness of outer space and all the stars will flee from His fiery presence. The darkness will be consumed by the light. The stars or suns of God will be refined in the fire or consumed. The first heaven will replace the second and third heavens and become our new heaven here on the renewed earth.

Christendom was founded on fables. It was the Catholics who claimed the earth was flat, not the Word of God. The Catholics claimed the earth was the center of the universe and the sun revolved around it. It was the Catholics who threatened Galieo with death for teaching otherwise. Galieo retracted the truth and still received a life sentence in prison. It was the heads of Christendom who killed anyone who translated the Bible into any language other than Latin. It was the beast of Christendom who killed William Tyndale for translating the Bible into vulgar English version from the venerated Vulgate version.

Christendom rejected the spirit of truth. They are filled with the spirit of error. 1 John 4:1-6 says: "Beloved, do not believe every spirit, but test the spirits, whether they are of God; because many false prophets have gone out into the world. But this you know the Spirit of God: every spirit that confesses that Jesus Christ has come in the flesh is of God, and every spirit that does not confess is not of God. This is the spirit of the Antichrist, which you have heard was coming, and is now already in the world. You are of God, little children, and have overcome them, because He who is in you is greater than he who is in the world. They are of the world. Therefore they speak as of the world, and the world hears them. We are of God. He who knows God hears us; he who is not of God does not hear us. By this we know the spirit of truth and the spirit of error."

The false prophets are the heads of the religious part of Christendom and the Antichrist is the head of the state of Christendom. This represents the Roman Catholic church united with the Roman state. This neo-Roman Catholic empire is now called the United States of Europe.

1 Timothy 4:1-3 says: "Now the Spirit expressly says that in latter times some will depart from the faith, giving heed to deceiving spirits and doctrines of demons, speaking lies in hypocrisy, having their own conscience seared with a hot iron, forbidding to marry, and commanding to abstain from foods which God created to be received with thanksgiving by those who believe and know the truth." The ones who teach that priests are not to marry and that you should not eat meat on Fridays is the false prophets of Christendom.

1 John 3:4-12 says: "Whoever commits sin also commits lawlessness, and sin is lawlessness. And you know that He who manifested to take away our sins, and in Him there is no sin. Whoever abides in Him does not sin. Whoever sins has neither seen Him nor known Him. Little children, let no one deceive you. He who practices righteousness is righteous, just as He is righteous. He who sins is of the devil, for the devil has sinned from the beginning. For this purpose the Son of God was manifested, that He might destroy the works of the devil. Whoever has been born of God does not sin, for His seed abides in him; and he cannot sin, because he has been born of God. In this the children of God and the children of the devil are manifest: whoever does not practice righteousness is not of God, nor is he who does not love his brother. For this is the message that you heard from the beginning, that we should love one another, not as Cain who was of the wicked one and murdered his brother. And why did he murder him? Because his works were evil and his brother's righteous."

John 8:44 says: "You are of your father the devil, and the desires of your father you want to do. He was a murderer from the beginning, and does not stand in the truth, because there is no truth in him. When he speaks a lie, he speaks from his own resources, for he is a liar and the father of it." The sons of Satan are the lawless ones who claim they are not under God's law. Ironically they shall be judged by God's law. Those that stand on the Word of God shall be saved. Their house is built on a foundation of God's supernatural laws. Those who built on the shifting sand (man's ever changing laws of the land) will lose their house and their lives.

John 5:25-30 says: "Most assuredly, I say to you, the hour is coming, and now is, when the dead will hear the voice of the Son of God; and those who hear will live. For as the Father has life in Himself, so He has granted the Son to have life in Himself, and has given him authority to execute judgment also, because he is the Son of Man. Do not marvel at this; for the hour is coming in which all who are in the graves will hear His voice and come forth-those who have done good, to the resurrection of life, and those who have done evil, to the resurrection of judgment. I can do nothing of Myself. As I hear, I judge; and My judgment is righteous, because I do not seek My own will but the will of the Father who sent Me."

1 John 5:1-3 says: "If you love God, you will do His commandments."

God's Kingdom in Egypt

Theology of Relativity

The key to unlocking the mystery of mythology is in understanding the theology of Lower Egypt. We must discern fable from eschatology. Eschatology is the study of; death, resurrection, immortality, the end of the world as we know it, final judgment, and the future state. The roots of religion are on earth, but God's Family Tree of the Living, receives its en-light-enment and water of life from heaven. Spiritual growth comes from God. Theology is not a theory. Theology is the study that shows all religions and races are relative.

The Afro-American movement of returning to their African roots covers a vague panarama of: Islam, Voodoo, paganism, cults, occults, etc. This Pan-African view is not the answer to the cultural or spiritual problem. It is necessary to focus on the roots of religion, which is the nativity of the Word of God. The birth-place is Annu, which the Greeks called Heliopolis (i.e. the City of the Sun). Annu is the location of the University of Theology; the school of higher learning.

Osiris of Orion

Eons ago, in the Age of Orion, a green skinned extra-terrestrial visited earth. This alien in a foreign land was Osiris and he became the first Pharaoh of Egypt. Osiris taught his laws, religious rites, farming, wine making, wood-working, metal-working, stone masonry, mathematics, science, architecture, astronomy, and magic. This magic is the same supernatural powers (called miracles) later used by Jesus. Osiris abolished cannibalism, just as Jesus abolished blood sacrifice at his Communion. Osiris became ruler of the known world. Osiris left Isis in charge of the Kingdom of Egypt while he traveled the world teaching the way of civilization and peace to all nations. He spread the "gospel" saying, "Repent, God's kingdom is here". It manifests wherever peace, love and harmony prevail. The essence of establishing God's kingdom is law and order. Everything in the universe obeys God's laws in an orderly fashion or perishes.

Diodorus Siculus agrees that the Egyptians sent forth many expeditions and established colonies in divers parts of the world, in times of the remotest antiquity. [A Book of the Beginnings part 2 by Gerald Massey page 590] When he died, the heir to the throne was Horus, who left the world to a human pharaoh. Just as Jesus left to go to his Father in heaven. Thoth remained as the Comforter and spiritual guide. Each reigning pharaoh was considered the Vicar of Horus or son of Osiris. Horus will return in the Age of Aquarius to regain his throne. Then he will rule as King and high priest according to the order of Melchizedek who is, "without father, without mother, without genealogy, having neither beginning of days nor end of life, but made like the Son of God." [Hebrews 7:1-3,21]

For over 2,000 years, Egypt was the greatest kingdom on earth. The Pharaoh's were the high priest's and sons of God. They built temples to God through-out the Nile delta. Heliopolis is the city built for the good Sun of God called the Sun of Righteousness. "In that day shall five cities in the land of Egypt speak the language of Canaan, and swear to the LORD of hosts; one shall be called Heliopolis. In that day shall there be an altar to the LORD in the midst of the land of Egypt, and a pillar at the border thereof to the LORD." [Isaiah 19:18-20] Heliopolis is the City of the Sun of Righteousness.

"Blessed is Egypt My people, and Assyria the work of My hands, and Israel My inheritance," says the LORD. [Isaiah 19:25] To anyone who has read the Word of God, it is abundantly clear that Egypt is God's people, NOT the Jews. To see this we must return to the beginning. Genesis chapter ten says Noah had three sons. These three sons make up the three races. Japheth was the father of the aboriginal Europeans. Shem is the father of the Asians. Both have dark skin, dark eyes and dark hair. Ham is the father of the African peoples.

Ham's sons are; Cush the Ethiopians, Mizraim the Egyptians, Put the Libyans, and Canaan the Canaanites. The Canaanites are the Caucasian Indo-Europeans who later migrated through the Caucasus mountains and into Europe. Canaan was born cursed from the womb because his father Ham had sex with Noah's wife. This sick act produced a sickly looking child. Canaan is the father of all the pale faced people. Mizraim means black, as the people of Egypt were dark brown in color with black eyes and hair. Egypt is the Greek word for black. The name for Ham's descendants is Khamet (Kemet) meaning "land of Ham."

Now it was these original black Egyptians who built this great kingdom dedicated to the good Sun of God. The modern Egyptians are a mix of Greek, Arabian, Jews, etc.. It was these black Egyptians who built the pyramids, stone roads and architecture, a ship able to sail around the world, waterways for crops and household use, etc... The other races "borrowed" these inventions from the dark race. The Greek-Romans are indebted to the Egyptians for everything from their mythology to the food on their table. As the Egyptians fed the known world for thousands of years. Today we consider ourselves the advanced, evolved civilization. Yet, it was us who built the Aswan dam. It is the biggest in the world and has produced nothing but problems. The Egyptian solution was to build canals to capture the excess water of the flooding Nile and the silt that they used as fertilizer. Their system worked, ours failed. Today the neo-Egyptians can bearly fed themselves. Who is more advanced?

Two Lands Divided

The Egyptians were divided between two separate kingdoms. The Upper Kingdom in the south, was ruled by the king who was head of state. He got his orders from the evil sungod, Amon-Ra. The Lower kingdom, in the north, was ruled by the Pharaoh who got his orders from the Good Sun of God called Atum-Ra. The Devil (Sut) ruled the south, while the Lord ruled the north. These are the two sons of the Father in heaven called Patah (Phat) in Egypt. Phat is the male principle. When added to the female principle we get Phat+her or Father. The female principle is the creation created by the Creator. It is the material matrix or womb from which the suns of God or stars were born. (This is who the Catholic church worships as Mary. Maya in India.)

The Upper Egyptians made real life statues, built great cities, were the first to use stone pillars, made warfare an art, used surgery successfully, perfected the art of working with gold and precious stones, worked with glass, women used make-up, created a written language in both hieroglyphic, letters and phonics, taught mathematics, kept an accurate 365 day solar calendar, etc.. All other nations imitated the dark-skinned Egyptians, the sons of Ham. The root of all advance civilizations is Africa. The Arabians learned much when they invaded Egypt. As did the Greeks, Romans, French, Americans, when they unearthed this highly advanced civilization.

The priests of Amen taught the black magic of the evil spirits. They gave offerings to appease the anger of Amen and his fallen angels. They caused confusion and chaos by changing the original stories. They sacrificed humans to their sun-god Amen-Ra. They told the masses that they could become immortal, like the fallen angels, by saying some magic spells and calling on the name of Amen. They made their malevolent sungod appear as if he were benevolent.

When the Greeks and Romans invaded Upper Egypt, they took back the mythology. They worshipped Amen-Ra as their sungod. The Pope, to this day, wears the crown of Amen-Ra which is called the Tiara. It is the doomed crown that makes the body of the wearer appear like a phallus or penis. Which meant he was a potent priest of Amen. Papal means father. It is were we get papa. Madonna is where we get mama. Ironically, the Popes are celibate and have no children, other then their members of the "mother church". The priests are the foster-fathers of these orphans.

The Roman Catholics stold an obelisk from Upper Egypt and set it up at the Vatican in Rome. The obelisk is a phallic symbol that points up to the sun-god Amen-Ra who is the Warlord. The records of victorious battles are inscribed on them. This is the same sungod that Constantine worshipped. He saw a cross superimposed over the sun and heard the words, "by this conquer." It was Constantine that decreed that Jesus is god and Mary is mother of god. It was Constantine who ended his prays, "we pray in his name, Amen." His name is Amen. The Greeks knew him as Zeus-Amen.

It was these Greeks and Romans influenced by the Upper Egyptians who translated the Bible. This influenced the wording. To this day, people end their prayers with, "we pray in his name, Amen." Is their Lord's name Amen??? Likewise, the people of Israel learned about Amen when in bondage under the Upper Egyptians like Rameses. In their traditions and customs, they continued praising Amen. The made the Golden Calf (Baby Bull) in honor of Baal, which is another name of the Devil. And the Old Testament was not written down until they were in captivity in Babylon where the people worshipped Baal (Amen), the evil sun-god. Amen and Baal worship is the Mystery Babylonian Religion.

The Canaanite deity called Baal also wears the crown of Amen-Ra. As does Teshub the deity of the Hittites, Freyr the deity of the Danites, Shiva the sex-deva of the Hindus, etc... To this day, the English soldiers were the high hats in honor of Amen-Ra the Warlord. The high hat makes them look taller and therefore more potent or powerful. Using fear to get the "little people" to submit. The fact that the English are tall is genic proof that they are descendants of the Cainites who were giants in the land of Canaan.

In most myths, the evil sun-god has his penis cut off by the good Sun of God. A deity with a severed sex organ is not able to have offspring. Satan is said to be neuter; neither male or female. Cain being his only son before he was castrated. Neteru is the Egyptian word for gods. The Shiva worshipers pray to his phallic symbol. Asherah is a tree shaped like a phallus. Representing Baal's family tree. Horus castrated Set in the battle to see who would be heir to the throne of Egypt. The begotten sons of God are asexual (angels). [Matthew 22:30] Fathered or begotten from above, they are reborn from within themselves, having no mother.

In the beginning, God the Father created the dark and void universe. Then from that darkness, He created light. That light is the good Sun of God called the Morning star or Atom-Ra. His consort is the earth. For he is betrothed to the earthlings who are enlightened by him. [John 1:1-13] It was not until the fourth day that God created Lucifer the Day star and his consort the moon to reflect his glory at night. For Satan rules over the day and night. He pretends to be the Angel of light so to rob the virgin of her cherry, the Forbidden fruit. [2 Corinthians 11:2,3, 13-15] He is the antichrist savior or fraud.

The Egyptians in Lower Egypt were not deceived by the evil sungod Amon-Ra. They did NOT look up to the sun for enlightenment. They were enlightened by Atum-Ra. The Book of the Dead was the Egyptian Bible of Death and Resurrection. The word Bible is Greek for Book. The Pyramid Texts are literally the Word of God written in stone. The priests of Heliopolis taught the Greeks and Asians all they knew about God's kingdom. It is a well known fact that Homer, Plato, Plutarch, Aristotle, Pythagoras, Philo and many others studied in Egypt. Justin Martyr (100-165 AD) referred to the gods of Egypt as sons of God. Egypt had always been the University of knowledge until the evil Romans conquered and burned the library at Alexandria. The Romans were envious of the dark race so they tried to exterminate all the evidence of the great past.

The Aryan Romans are the diabolical adversaries of the black race. The Romans are direct descendants of Cain who murdered Abel. These Kenites (Cainites) are the blond haired blue eyed race. They are one shade from total albinism. They later were known by many alias' including: Danites, Vikings, Romans, Norsemen, etc... It is well documented that they have always worshipped the Devil by many alias' including: Baal, Odan, Apollo, Helio, Sol, etc... The tribe of Dan made graven images of bulls and worshipped them as Baal. The two parts of the Beast of Revelations 13 is the Roman state and Catholic church. They are united in unholy matrimony to produce the Roman Catholic empire.

It was the Romans who tried to erase all memory of the Egyptian culture. It was Julius Caesar who burned the library of Alexander. The Library held rare scriptures from every culture in the known world. Irreplaceable books were turned to ashes by the Barbarians who were too ignorant to understand. The only thing the Romans know is conquering and plundering. They remained at war from their foundation, when Romulus murdered his brother Remus, to the fall of this evil empire when the Lord shall slay Romulus Peter II and all his followers. Likewise, it was Caesar Constantine who created Christendom and destroyed all scriptures that went against his decrees.

The Caucasian conspirators have been trying to cover up and bury any information that proves the dark race was more advanced and superior than the pale race. Like Set and his 72 conspirators, they want to conSeal Osiris in an air-tight coffin forever. They want to silence Osiris, just as they tried to silence the Lamb of God (Jesus).

Ante-Christ

The ancient Egyptians were ante-Christ or pre-Christ. Their mythology predates Christendom by thousands of years. The incarnation of Christ was just one of the many reincarnations of Horus. See the ten incarnations of Vishnu. Horus is the original King of kings, Lord of lords and Savior of the world. In the last days, Set-Amen (Satan) is going to incarnate as the AntiChrist. He will be a Judeo-Christian born in JeruSalem and will become the spurious savior of Christendom, the universal religion.

Egyptian Creation

In the Egyptian pantheon, Patah is the Eternal Creator who dwells in the first heaven alone. He created the second heaven which the Egyptians call Nut and earth which they call Geb. Patah is Phather or Father in heaven. Then Patah divided the waters of heaven from the waters of earth. Producing the third heaven, our atmosphere. Which the Egyptians call Shu. Then the sons of God created man from the earth. The Word of God says, "Then the Gods said, "Let us make man in our image, according to our likeness." The Hebrew word for gods is elohim which means sons of God. As man was made in the appearance of the sons of God. That is why angels appear in the likeness of man.

God the Father transcends all thought. He is all-knowing, yet beyond knowing. No one even knows His name. It is NOT YHWH! He created the lesser gods or angels and placed Atum as Lord of this host of gods. What we know of the Father is revealed by His Son, Atum. Who is sometimes called Horus the Elder. Horus the Younger is Jesus after resurrecting. The Father remains in His domain in the first heaven and left Atum in charge of the second and third heavens. The second heaven is outer space and the third is our atmosphere. [See E.A. Wallis Budge in "Osiris the Egyptian Religion of Resurrection"] The only begotten son of God is called Osiris. Begotten means fathered and born of a woman. Christ is the only Son of God ever born of a woman. Osiris is the Sun of God manifest in the flesh. He has become Son of Man or human. The Word of God calls him the second Adam (Atum). His consort is Isis who represents mother earth. This is the spiritual mating of the Sun and the earthlings (the bride). When Osiris is killed by Seth, son of Satan, he is resurrected by Isis, mother earth. It is the power of the Ankh or God's Spirit that reactivates him. Osiris is reborn Horus, the only begotten Son of God. Horus and Atum are one and the same. Adam was the first man fathered by God and born of mother earth.

Egypt was part of the original garden of Eden, the Egyptian Sekhet-hetep. The Greeks call it Elysian Fields. The Bible says, "Now a river went out of Eden to water the garden, and from there it parted and became four riverheads. The name of the first is Pishon; it is one which encompasses the whole land of Havilah, where there is gold....The name of the second river is Gihon; it is one which encompasses the whole land of Cush (Ethiopia). The name of the third river is Hiddekel (Tigris); it is the one which goes toward the east of Assyria. The fourth river is the Euphrates." [Genesis 2:10-14] Therefore the garden extended from Ethiopia to Assyria, with Egypt in the center. Egypt is famous for its vast resources of gold and precious stones. The Nile is the longest river is the world. The Bible says, "the Lord God had not caused it to rain on the earth....but a mist went up from the earth and watered the whole face of the ground."[Genesis 2:5,6] This place where it never rains, yet is watered and fertile describes the Fertile Crescent ruled by Egypt.

It was the first Adam or Man who caused the fall of Atum-Ra when he chose to be ruled over by Amon-Ra the evil sun-god. Just as the Jew chose to be ruled over by a-man. Mankind was exiled from God's kingdom and Satan has ruled over mankind ever since. Satan is the sun that rises and falls daily. Those who look up to him for enlightenment are doomed to dwell in darkness. Those who expose their naked skin to his ultra-violent red rays, shall burn! The Egyptians, like the Hebrews, looked forward to the good Sun of God to rise in the east and overthrow the bad sun-god. He will usher in the day that shall never end called the Lord's day. He will resurrect his body of believers. But those who follow Amon-Ra shall burn in the Lake of fire.

When the first parents were exiled from the garden of God, two angels were placed at the east gateway to keep man from taking of the Tree of life. The one angel was Lucifer (Amen-Set) who caused the fall of man and the other is Atum-Horus. The Great Sphinx represents Horus by the name Herakhty-Khepera, the guardian of the gateway, who continually faces east. He watches for the day when Horus will return to be King of God's kingdom. [Matthew 24:27-31] When Atum (the star Sirius) left to be with Orion, we were no longer a binary solar system. It was Amon-Ra who created linear time when the Earth start revolving around the his sun. From that point on, mankind was limited to a lifetime that shall end. The cycle of life to death. When Atum-Ra returns, he will put an end to time and to death. Those written in the Book of life will never grow old or die. It is the sun that causes the signs of aging; wrinkles, dark spots, etc... Amon-Ra is also creator of unrest. Man is plagued by violence and war because he is no longer in the Sabbath Rest of God's kingdom. Amon-Ra is the Warlord who will lead his followers to their own self-destruction. As all warriors will die in the war to end all wars.

On the back of the U.S. one dollar bill, is two great seals. The one on the left is the Egyptian seal showing the eye of Horus. He is the all-seeing Sun of God and head stone of the church. He rules from the holy Mt. Zion represented by the Great Pyramid. The seal to the right is the Roman seal. The eagle is the Roman bird of prey that has stolen the peace from Egypt. Horus is represented as the hawk who shall defeat that evil eagle in the last days. Then he shall rule the church and state as Atum-Horus. He shall be King of God's kingdom and the right-hand-man of God the Father. [1 Corinthians 15:20-28]

The stars do foresee the future! According to Egyptian mythology, the pyramids are copies of the prototypes in heaven. [Hebrews 9:24] They are temples to the Son of God. Osiris is represented by the constellation of Orion and Sirius is Isis his companion, the Mother with Child. The constellations of the zodiac say, when the time is right, the main star shall rise as the Morning star who shall rule over the earth. The star of Bethlehem shall return on the Lord's day. [Matthew 2:2] The fallen star, alias Lucifer, shall be cast into the abyss of outer space. The Upper Egyptians call Sirius, Sothis (or Seth) because they worship Amen-Ra-Set the evil sun of God. This is a lie! Sirius does NOT represent Set. The star Hades in the constellation Taurus is his star.

God's Garden Paradise

Where you came from is Not as important as your religious roots. God's family tree has branched out to all nations. But only those still connected to the source shall survive. The cult branches that have broken off from God's ways shall be cut off. The off-shoot sects shall be pruned and burned. Only the faithful, whether natural or grafted (adopted into God's family), shall receive the water of life that runs through the veins of God's Family Tree of Life. They shall receive en-light-enment from the Father and His Sun.

From the darkness of the underworld, the Sun of God shall rise in the East. The new born children of God shall be delivered from bondage to Amen. Coming forth from Amenta (Land of the Dead) into the day light, they shall exodus this evil land in the Wilderness of Sin ruled by Setamen (Satan). The Lord shall lead His people to the restored Promise land. The wind (holy Spirit) shall part the sea and they shall cross over on dry land. Or as the Egyptians put it: the breath of God shall blow the bark (ark) across the waters to Paradise. In their glorified bodies they shall enter God's kingdom on earth. This is God's garden of Eden restored. The Egyptians called it the Field of Peace (Sekhet-hetep) and the Greek's Elysian Fields. The heavenly New JeruSalem (Sekhet-aanru) will descend down on Mount Zion as the capital of God's kingdom. This is the primordial mount the Egyptians call Anu (Heliopolis).

In Mythology, it is the Dragon who protects the precious treasure. In the Bible, it is the Serpent who protects the Tree of Life by offering mankind the forbidden fruit from the Tree of False Knowledge. This fig tree is the family tree of the Jews. They cover up the truth with their version. We are told the way to salvation is through the family of Jacob. Jacob means Swindler! We are told that the Savior is a Caucasian Jew. Meanwhile, the Dragon (Roman Catholic kingdom) conceals the true Tree of Knowledge that leads to Life. It is the Northern nations of Christendom that hid the Ancient Mysteries. The Dragon possesses the countless scriptures at the Vatican. They have stolen the hidden Mysteries of Egypt and display them in museums, but conceal the key that unlocks the Mysteries. They tell us the Egyptians worshipped many gods including animals. This is a lie!

They tell us fables about the Devil living underground in Hellfire. The Word of God says, "So the great dragon was cast out, that serpent of old, called the Devil and Satan, who deceives the whole world; he was cast to the earth, and his angels was cast out with him." [Revelation 12:9] The Devil dwells on the earth and has deceived everyone! The Devil and his demons are the heads of Christendumb, which is just a Branch of Jewism. The Olive tree represents the Tree of life, not the fig tree. [Romans 11:16-24] The fruits (figs) of false knowledge was passed on to them. And they to try to cover up the truth with fables and false gospels of the white Messiah. "And I saw the second part of the Beast coming up out of the earth, and he had two horns like a lamb and spoke like a dragon." [Revelation 13:11] "For many will come in my name, saying, 'I am Christ-ian,' and deceive many." [Matthew 24:5] The heads of Christendumb have been deceiving the masses ever since they took over for the Jews.

The Dragon offers salvation; "eat of this fruit (fig) and your eyes will be opened and you will be like gods, knowing good and evil". Or the modified version: "eat of the bread and wine of the fruit, it is all you need to know to become immortal gods living in heaven". They claim you are saved by the blood of the white savior. But the Revealed Word of God says, "the dragon was enraged with the woman, and he went to make war with the rest of her offspring, who Keep the Commandments of God and have the testimony of Jesus." [Revelation 12:17] The Dragon was angry with the Saints who exposed the truth hidden under the fig leaf. The Saints knew the way to salvation is the Ten Commandments of God. [Revelation 14:12] The Dragon martyrs anyone attempting to solve the secret to salvation. [Rev.11:7] The Devil is here and the Christian Inquisitions are proof of that!

Righteousness is the road to God's kingdom and the key that unlocks death's Door. Life is given to those who possess the true knowledge of what is good. The truth is; salvation does NOT come through the Jews or a Jewish messiah. Salvation comes through trials and tribulations to is if you are worthy. Spectators will receive no reward. You must run the good race by the rules in order to receive the crown of life. You must go through the human life to death circuit and then be born again in order to enter God's kingdom. God's family tree of the living is root in Egypt with a dark skinned Messiah. Often he is depicted as a green skinned extra-terrestrial. He is the Judge on Judgment Day when everyone is resurrected to stand trial for their trespasses against God's law. [John 5:22-30] It is the Dragon who says you will be Raptured away before the tribulation and you will not have to face charges for your crimes (sins). Wake up you walking dead, the times of tribulation are upon us and you have NOT been raptured away. Repent (change your evil ways) while you still can. Judgment Day, the day of retribution, is near at hand. [Revelation 20:11-15] It is time to slay the Dragon with the Sword of Truth, so we can partake of the fruit of the Tree of Life. The translation of the Egyptians hieroglyphics has exposed the Dragon's deception. We now have access to the Sacred Scriptures written in stone. All roads do NOT lead to the Roman Beast. The righteous road is found in ancient Egypt. Following the Word of God is the holy high that leads to God's kingdom on earth. Learn how to transform your tomb into the womb of metaphysical rebirth.

Atlantis

There are many legends about the lost civilization of Atlantis. Many people are speculating that the Egyptians got their advance civilization from there. I believe many people accept this theory because they believe the Atlantians to be Aryans (white). They desperately want to credit the Caucasian race with being the first and the most advanced. In my search, I have reaped what others have sown. I have plowed through the fields of literature on this subject, line by line. I have sifted through the chaff to find the grains of truth. Here's what I discovered. "There is nothing new under the sun"....Solomon. What I present are not new. In fact, they are ancient. The thing I offer is perspective: the old way of looking at the timeless truths.

Let us stick to the facts. First: Atlantis is a Latin word. Second: The root of Atlantis is Atlas. Third: the dictionary defines Atlantean as pertaining to Atlas. Atlas is the Greek god who holds up the heavens. He is the counterpart to Shu in Egypt. It was Atlas who went into the garden of the gods to get the forbidden fruit while Herakles temporarily held up the heavens. Herakles is a demi-god and not able to take the fruit (golden apples?). The so-called Pillars of Herakles are the Pillars of Atlas. They are the four pillars that hold up heaven. When Herakles travels beyond the Pillars, he is going to heaven. The 3-7 Hesperides who guarded the fruit were the daughters of Atlas. Atlantides is the seven daughters of Atlas called Pleiades. They are the inhabitants of Atlantis (also known as the Hesperides). Hera had received the tree as a wedding present. It was then planted in the garden in the western extremity of the world. Atlantis is said to be in the west near or on the Atlantic ocean. Atlantic derives from Mt. Atlas in Africa. {From the World Scope Family Library Dictionary} All the evidence points to Atlas.

It is my belief that Atlantis was the garden of God east of Eden. The lost civilization of Atlantis is Paradise Lost. Atlantis will be found when Paradise is Found. The Mystery is solved. Atlantis sank during the Great Flood. I believe Christendumb got the idea that the forbidden fruit was an apple from the story of Hera's garden. The Egyptians say the gods ruled for thousands of years before man was created. The seven divine pharaohs were: Atum-Ra, Shu, Geb, Osiris, Set, Horus, and Thoth. Thoth hid the "Emerald Tablets" holding the universal knowledge, before the Great Flood came. After them was the rule of the followers of Horus. It was the tilt of the Earth's axis that precipitated the Flood. When the Earth rotation of 360 degrees in 360 days changed to 365 days. {See the Sirius Connection by Murry Hope}

Compare the seven daughters of Atlas to the seven gods descended from Shu: Geb, Nut, Osiris, Isis, Set, Nephthys and Horus. These extraterrestrials are the elohim (gods) of the Bible who ruled for six divine days (6000 years?) before man was made. Shu (Atlas) is the life force; the breath of life and the atmosphere. The Atum-o-shere (atmosphere) is ruled by the Sun of God and Lord of the earth. Geb is the Earth. Nut is the stars of heaven. The constellation of Orion represents Osiris, of which Sirius is part. Sirius represents Isis and child. The Egyptian name for Sirius is Sept; meaning Seven. Taurus represents Set of which the seven stars of Pleiades is a part. Nephthys was to be the consort of Set, but they were incompatible.

It was these Atlanteans; Geb and Nut who created mankind (Adam in Hebrew). Nut is the suns of God. The gods, lead by Atum, created the earthlings from the earth (Geb). The earth is brown, therefore, Adam was Brown. The Atlanteans are our ancestors. Then the elohim said, "Let us make man in our image, according to our likeness..." The first man was created perfect, but mankind has been descending from there ever since. Chronology chronicles man's descent as he slowly de-evolves into a primate acting on animal instincts. Compare Edgar Cayce's vision of centaurs and bird-headed gods at Atlantis to the Egyptian gods like Horus the Hawk and the other Zodiac illustrations.

Plato says the god Thamus (Thomas) is King of all Egypt. Thamas is Tem or Atum. He is the first and the last Adam. He is King of kings and Lord of lords. Thomas means Twins. Plato says Atlantis was ruled by 5 sets of twins. This is totally Egyptian. They are: Atum-Amen, Shu-Tefnut, Geb-Nut, Osiris-Isis, and Set-Nephthys. None were human-beings.

Plato says the Egyptian priest, Solon, told so and so who told so and so who told who told so and so who told him that Atlantis was larger than Asis Minor with Libya and situated beyond the Pillars of Herakles. Now let us compare this to what the Bible says about the garden of God. The Bible say the garden covers an area from the Tigris and Euphrates in the Middle East to Ethiopia (Cush). This area includes Egypt and possibly Libya. After the flood of Noah's day, Atlantis-Eden went beyond the Pillars of Herakles (to the sea of space). The garden of God is now with Horus in the Sirius star system. Just as New JeruSalem and the Temple of the Lord is in heaven. They shall return with the Sun of God. [Hebrew 9:23,24 Revelation 21:2,10]

Plato says at the time of Atlantis' flood, there was an volcanic eruption. Actually this was the eruption of the Lord's wrath. [Genesis 6:5-7]

After the flood, Noah's family repopulated the human race on earth. They built the Tower of Babel so as to ascend to heaven. And for this, were confounded and scattered to their lands. Including those in Egypt, Sumeria, Asia and ancient America. This explains why all mythologies are basically the same, since they all originated at the same source. In the cycle of time called the last days, the eruption of the Lord's wrath is going to rain the Lake of fire and brimstone from heaven, earthquakes, etc... [Revelation 16:17-21 20:9 Zechariah 14:1,5,12] Brimstone is sulfur and the source of sulfur is a volcano. The lava is blood-red, hell-fire. It would seem that it was Plato who was confounded!

Plato's story of the battle between the Atlanteans and the Athens (Atheists) is the same as the Olympian gods battling the Titans. Plato says it occurred 9,000 years before his time or 10,000 BC. This is the time the gods ruled the earth. The Titans being the fallen angels (who Edgar Cayce called sons of Belial) mated with human women and produced giants. Plato probably linked Crete with Atlantis because it was the home of the gods Zeus and Europa and the nativity of the Minoans, who the primitive Greeks considered highly advanced. Zeus and Europa became the father and mother of the Europeans.

Plato's Republic was a fabrication of a non-existent land. Maybe Atlantis was too. Compare Plato's great battle with Homer's Trojan wars. Where the gods joined in the battle along-side the humans. Where the war on earth mirrors the wars in heaven. Admittedly, there may have been many wars between Greece and Troy, but they were all mortals.

Another scenario: The Aztecs call North America, Atlan. Could Atlantis be the Aztecs crossing the Atlantic ocean and invading Europe and Africa? It is very likely that Plato's story tellers had mixed human history with pre-human history.

The Egyptians believe that the age of Leo the lion (10,000 BC) is when the gods were created. They call it the First Time. It started with the birth of the firstborn Sun of God, Atum, represented by the Bright Morning Star Sirius. Leo is his sign as King of the Kingdom and Lord of the Earth. Likewise, Zeus was called king of the gods. Jesus was called lion-king of Judah. Man was not created until six divine days later (6,000 years) or 4,000 BC. In the cycle of time (precession of the Zodiac), the dawning of Aquarius, is the time Sirius shall be reborn from the watery womb of the sea of space. The helical rising of Sirius is the sign in the heavens of the dawning of a new age of no end.

To the atheist archaeologists, 'conjecture' is the 'pillar' that supports their belief in the Theory of Evolution. They want to make the gods as historical men. They say men made god in their own image by worshipping their ancestors. This proves their ignorance! If our ancestors were these highly advance people of Atlantis who lived very long lives, then it makes the Theory that man is Evolving invalid! In fact, mankind is de-evolving. Man has become so ignorant, we don't even know our own origin. The sands of time do not speak of ancient "mortals" of Atlantis. Archaeologists can not even locate the site because it has gone beyond the Pillars of Herakles. It is beyond their grasp; mentally and physically! I have a puzzling question: why are scientists given credit and praise for discovering what God created?

There was no advanced Aryan civilization as the Caucasians wish.

Egyptian Mythology

In Egypt, Patah is Creator and Father of the gods. Ptah is the mind behind the creation. He created all things by thinking of them in his heart and speaking their names aloud. The creation is the matrix from which all things were born. Ptah has fathered two suns; Amon-Ra and Atum-Ra. Ra means sun as in Ray. Atum-Ra is the first of the creation and Lord of the earth. [Colossians 1:15-18] But Amon took over and has ruled over mankind for 6,000 years. Amon of No (called Thebes by the Greeks) is lord of the dead. Thebes was called necropolis meaning city of the dead. [Jeremiah 46:25] Atom became the setting sun that will, one day, rise to rule again. We know Amon as Satan and Atom as the second Adam or Christ. In Zoroasterism, the twin stars are known as Ahura Mazdah (Spirit + WiseLord) and Ahriman the evil one. [Job 38:7] The Egyptian religion is stellar, NOT solar!

The Pantheon-Paut-neteru

Pantheon is Pan-the-on. "Pan" means All. God (Patah) is All and All. Patah is Pan-Potent or All-Powerful. [1 Corinthians 15:28]

"The" means God in Greek. Theology is the study of God. Mythology means My theology or the study of My God. "On" is the Egyptian name of Heliopolis, the City of the Sun of Righteousness. It is the house of God and His sons. Just as Elohim in Hebrew means God and His sons. "On" is the birthplace of Atum-Horus (Jesus). Which was later conquered by the Upper Egyptians and changed to the temple of Amon (Satan). The Greeks call the gods, the Pantheon. Paut-neteru means Company of the gods in Egyptian. Ptah is Pa-Neteru (Father of the gods) or Pater (Paternal) or Peter. He is the God-head. [1 Cor.11:3] Phat (fat) + her = Father of Horus. Pater-noster (Our Father) is the Lord's prayer to his Father in heaven. Mythos, like Logos, means oral sayings. The root of Myth and Mouth are identical. Atum-Horus is called the living Word.

In the Book of the Dead, chapter 17, it says; "I am the Great God-self created, that is to say who made his names" "who created names for his members and these came into being in the form of the gods who are in the following of Ra'' ''that the cycle of the gods is his body.'' The Father is the God-head and his creations are the God-body.

Patah-Ta-Thu-Nun is Creator of Heaven (Nun) and Earth (Ta). Patah or Pater is depicted as seated at a potter's wheel shaping the cosmic egg with his hands. Patah's many attributes has names like: Shu is the atmosphere; Geb is the earth; Nun is the oceans or sea of outer-space; Nephthys is mother nature; Maat is law and order and truth and justice; etc... They are NOT gods or goddesses. Some of these positions are held by the sons of God called angels, while other are just natural laws. Seth is the adversary (Satan) of Horus. They are extra-terrestrial beings.

Nun is the non-existence described as void and darkness (the abyss). The Hindus call it Maya, the cosmic egg. It is the primordial plasma of empty space from which the suns (male) and planets (female) of God were created. The Morning star is the virgin birth of first of the creation. He is Atum-Ra or Sun of Righteousness (Jesus Christ). Nun is not an entity or goddess. God (Ptah) has no partners. Nun is the watery womb of creation that was created by the Creator. The Creator is Not part of the creation. Nut-ur (Neter) is the Great Mother. The Greek word Nectar, the milk of the gods, is rooted in Netaru. The Mother nurses the Suns.

The designated number for Nun is nine as the human pregnancy is nine months. Many religions worship her as the Great Mother or queen of heaven. Ma in hieroglyphic is nine. She is the matrix of the nine of the Ennead. From the Greek ''Ennea'' or ''Annea'' for Nine. The number ''nine'' is even found in the word ''femi-nine''. She is called Anna in Assyria, In-anna in Mesopotamia, Di-anna in Rome, and Madonna (MaDi-anna) of the Mother (Roman Catholic) Church. The number of Patah is ''8'' meaning infinite. The number for Atum (as Lord of the Sabbath) is seven. Six is the number of man who was created on the sixth day. Worship of the Great Mother is Whoreship.

From the primeval waters was born the primeval mound called earth. ''God created the heavens and the earth.'' Then God created the Lord of light (Sirius). The earth provided a place for the first deity to stand upon. He is the sun that rules over the earth and everything on the earth. He is called Atum-Horus, the good Sun of God who shall descend on On (Heliopolis). Compare this to the Sun of God standing on Mt. Zion from where he rules the kingdom of God. [Rev.14:1] Horus the Elder preceded Osiris, just as the Son of God preceded Christ. The Son of God was created in the beginning, whereas the Son of Man was made manifest much later.

Annu is the place of birth of the Sun of God. For Atum-Ra (Horus the Elder) it was Nun or Nut (the second heaven). For Horus the Younger, it was Heliopolis (i.e. Anu). Just as there is a earthly Jerusalem and a heavenly Jerusalem. The heavenly Annu (Aanru-Sekhet) gave birth to Sirius the star of Atum. The earthly Annu is Heliopolis, Egypt. Same as; Joshua (Jesus) son of Nun (Annu) who lead the people to the Promise land. The Promise land represents the Garden of God and nativity of mankind. ''Tem (or Atum) hath departed to Annu to satisfy his love of pleasure; he hath thrust his member into his hand, and hath performed his desire, and hath produced the two children Shu and Tefnut." From the word "desire" the Greeks got Eros. Tem desired to reproduce himself. Desire is De + sire or The Osiris, first begotten Son of God. To beget means "to father" or "to sire". Atum is the father of man.

Atum created Shu (air of life) and Tefnut (Tef+Nut = water of life). [Colossians 1:15-18] It was Shu and Tefnut who created Nut and Geb. Air and water of life are the holy Spirit. Nut represents the hosts of heaven (stars) and Geb is earth. Together they produced the atmosphere called Shu. Shu caused a division between the two (as a child between two parents). Shu is the third heaven. It is the Spirit of life that is the breath of life for the living creatures on earth. "God made the firmament, and divided the waters which were under the firmament from the waters which were above the firmament. God called the firmament Heaven." [Genesis 1:6-8,17] Tefnut is the water that comes from heaven. Shu is the O- Zone that protects us from the suns ultra-violent rays. Otherwise, Amen-Ra's red rays would be deadly. The word Atmosphere is Atum's sphere, as Lord of the Earth. Shu's Greek counterpart is Atlas who holds up the heavens (Nut).

God dwells alone in the first heaven beyond the creation. Nut is the second heaven called the sea of space. The Elohim are the hosts of heaven and suns of God. They are begotten by the Father and born of the watery womb (Nut). Nut (Nuter or Neter) is the matrix of the sons of God. Nut is the Night-Sky and Nu is the Day-sky (Yin/Yang). The Elohim (God's sons) of Nut created man from the earth (Geb). [Genesis 1:26] Atum of On rules the Nut (Night), while Set-Amen of No rules the Nu (Day). Tefnut is the third heaven. The sky where Horus the Hawk does fly.

Nut and Geb (Earth) gave birth to two sets of twins: Osiris, Isis, Seth, and Nephthys. The Word of God says the Earth (Isis) and the good Sun (Atum-Osiris) were created on the first day. The bad sun (Amen-Seth) and his mate the moon (Nephthys) were not created until the fourth day. Nephthys represents mother nature and the female's 28 day menstrual/ moon cycle. She represents fertility and the cycle of life to death. Isis represents spiritual rebirth and the cycle of death to life. Osiris is also the son of Geb (Earth) because he was an Earthling, like Adam. Atum was incarnate as Osiris at the end of the Egyptian year, just before the autumn equinox. This is our first day of Autumn.

Osiris and Seth are suns fathered (begotten) by God (Patah). Egypt was divided into Two Lands: Lower Egypt ruled by Osiris and Upper Egypt ruled by Seth. Osiris is also known as Atum-Ra and Seth is Amon-Ra. Ra refers to sun; as in sun-rays. Osiris is linked to the constellation Orion and Isis to Sirius, the companion star. Seth is linked to the red star Aldebaran in Hyades (Hades). Hyades is the head and horns of the constellation of Taurus the Bull (Baal). The two stars, Sirius and Aldebaran, were the two all-seeing eyes of Horus. That is until Set tore out one eye in the battle over Egypt. Thoth then restored the eye of Horus; meaning he restored the rule of the two lands to Horus and he was given rule over all of the constellation of Taurus. [Book of the Dead chapter 17,71] The Greek Hades is the head of Tartarus (Taurus) in the under-the-world. Likewise, Jesus is called the Bright Morning star [Revelation 22:16] and Satan is Lucifer the Daystar. [Isaiah 14:12] They are the two suns of God battling to rule the earth.

On the celestial level, Sirius is the Mother with child. It represents Isis and Horus the child. Yet Sirius is a binary solar system. Sirius B is a white dwarf star. It represents Nephthys and her child Anubis. Isis and Nephthys are twins. Many religions believe that ours was a binary solar system in the beginning. This was until Atum returned to the constellation of Orion as the star Sirius.

Anubis is the jackel headed one. From here is where Sirius got its name the Dog star. It is the brightest star in Canis Major (Great Canine). Sometimes Orion is portrayed as Hunter and Dog. Both Horus and Anubis are the sons of Osiris (Orion). Anubis, like Horus, is another attribute of Osiris, Lord of the living and the dead. In Egyptian, Wtw means both Jackal and the Eldest.

Set kills Osiris in order to possess the kingdom of God in Egypt. Just as Cain killed Abel. Isis gave birth to Horus the child in the papyrus marshes of Heliopolis (Anu), and hid him from the wrath of Seth. Horus was the rightful heir to the throne as son of Osiris. Sound familiar? Moses was placed in an ark in the reeds to hid him from the wrath of Seti. Yet, in the Bible, it was Ramoses, son of Seth (Seti), who inherited the throne. That is until the Lord destroyed the power of Egypt and gave the throne to Israel. The Lord Atom defeated Ramoses and his god Ra-Amon.

Likewise, the Christ child was hid in Egypt to escape the wrath of the evil King Herod. [Matthew 2:13-16] And the Word of God (including the Gospel of Thomas) was hid in Egypt from the evil Caesars like Julius and Constantine who wanted to destroy them. It was Julius Caesar who burned the great library at Alexandria, Egypt and Constantine who destroyed all scriptures that did not agree with his dictates; the canon of Christendom. Horus the child is protected by the hawk, which is the counterpart of the dove representing the holy Spirit.

Horus is the son of Osiris and heir to the kingdom. It is he who defeats Seth (Satan). The four sons of Horus are the four races that cover the four cardinal points of the earth. They are the three sons of Noah. Japheth became the Gentiles or original Europeans like Greeks. Shem became the Mongoloids or Asians; including the Arabians, Orientals and Israel. Ham became the Negroid race of Africa; including Egypt. Ham's son, Canaan, was the cursed one who became the Caucasoid (pale) race. [Genesis 10:25-27] Osiris is the counterpart to the first Adam and Horus is the second

Adam. [1 Corinthians 15:45-50] Set cut Osiris into 14 pieces; representing the body of Christ being scattered. [Matthew 26:31,56] It was Isis and Nephthys who searched for the body of Osiris. These twin sisters are represented by Mary the mother of Jesus and Mary Magdalene searching for Christ in the tomb. [Matthew 28:1 Mark 15:46 16:1] They came to embalm the dead body with spices. Just as Osiris was wrapped as a mummy. From the tomb or womb of mother earth and mother nature, the Son was raised alive in bodily form. Isis is the virgin who conceived from the power on high called Thoth. The Son of Man was reborn the Son of God (Horus). Osiris had two natures; one divine (supernatural) and one human (mortal). Atum-Osiris-Horus is the true triune of the Father-Son-and holy Spirit-being.

Anubis (Anpu) is the son of Osiris and Nephthys (mother nature's cycle of life to death). Anubis is a jackal headed god. Notice dog is an anagram of god. Canines bury and later dig up its dead dinner. It is his job to bring the dead from the land of the dead to stand before Osiris the great Judge. For Osiris was the first to live and die. Uniting with Nephthys (death) in the west, and then overcoming death by rising as Horus (Sun of God) in the east. Both Isis (mother earth) and Nephthys (mother nature), the twin sisters, stand behind Osiris' throne as he Judges the people.

Apuat or Upuat means Opener of the Ways. Apuat is the dog constellation at the north pole (Ursa Minor). Which would be the south pole to the Egyptians who see South as up. Southern Egypt is Upper Egypt. Anup (Anubis) is the Anti-upat. Anup is the dog star Sirius. Apuat is the spurious dog star and antithesis of Anup. From here is where the Greeks got Cerberus the three-headed dog who guards the gates of Hades.

The Two Lands

Lower Egypt is Uat and Lower heaven is Tuat. Tu is Atum and At is the ancient city of On, called Heliopolis by the Greeks. Upper Egypt is Amenta or Amen of Ta. Ta is the ancient city of No called Thebes by the Greeks. No is the Land of Seth or Suth in the South. Suth is an abbreviation for south. Notice that At is opposite of Ta and On is reverse of No. Just as the Land in the North is opposite of the Land in the South. The souls in Amenta, Land of the Dead, are deaf, dumb and blind. Western Thebes is the Valley of the Dead Kings. They are unconscious in the deep sleep of death. Amenta is underground (Necropolis). Tu-at is the Land of the Living and the Land of Atum. T-uat is the Promise Land.

The Tuat or Duat has dual meanings. Its heavenly equivalent is the region around Orion and Sirius. As above, so below. Am-Tuat is the Lower Heaven, birthplace of Atum. It is not the Other-World nor the Under-World. Ta-urt is the Upper Heaven the stars north of the Pole Star. Am-Smen is the stars of the Arctic circle, birthplace of Amen-Set. The North-Pole-star (Egyptian South) is the spurious Dog star in Ursa Minor. Am-Smen is Ursa Major (Arctaurus), Usra Minor and Draco.

Tuat is God's garden paradise restored on earth. A river (the Nile) runs through the Tuat. Uat means water and also blue-green. Uat-ur (Great Water) is the dual nature of the sea of space and the sea on earth. Ia, Ea, Yea (Yes) are the fresh waters, while Nu (No) and Nut (Not) are the seas. Man can Not live on or in the seas of space or earth. Ea is the fresh water god of Sumeria. Jes-us is the Latin counterpart. The 'us' was a common Roman suffix. Green vegetation is the basis of life and also the source of our breath of life (air). They are the spirit and water of life.

Uati represents the twins Nephthys and Isis mourning for Osiris. The Udjat or Utchat eye is the All seeing eye of Horus and promotes prosperity and fertility. Isis is the blue-green star Sirius who gives birth to Horus. She sacrifices herself so the star represents Horus alone. Sirius, the bright Morning star produces green gamma rays. Uta signifies salvation. The Ute Indians of Utah have one word for eye and seed. In other words, the Eye of Horus is the Seed or Son of Isis, the Savior.

The Egyptian word for eye is iris. Add a "s" and you have Siris the star of Isis and Horus. This star Sirius represents the right eye of Horus. The left eye, that was ripped out by Set, is Hyades. They represent Heliopolis in Lower Egypt and Thebes in Upper Egypt. Add an "O" to Siris and you get Osiris. Siris is feminine of the masculine Osiris. In Hebrew, Ish is male and ishah is female. Adam is translated Man and Adamah is mother earth. Orus = Horus = Osiris = Sirius. The two eyes represent the Yin/Yang or dualism as in wrong/right or evil/good. They are the two hemispheres of the brain.

Hathor

Hathor controls the life to death cycle as mother nature. As mother nature dies out in the winter and returns in the spring. Of which, God Patah set the laws of nature. She is the cow nurturing her children. Her consort is the Bull (Min or Baal) of the setting sun in the west where there is the darkness of death. It is the sun that controls the seasons. The Romans called them Apollo the sungod and Dianna the moon goddess. She chases after her intended mate across the horizon. The horns form the bow of the crescent moon and the sun produces the arrows of light. The difference is: the ancient Egyptians did not worship these attributes or powers of God, but the Romans did. Hathor's counterpart in Hinduism is Durga the Destroyer of mankind.

It is Hathor (House of Horus), in the form of Sekhmet, who destroys mankind for rebelling against Atum-Ra and "breaking his Covenant". She is pacified after drinking 7,000 vessels of "blood". This synthetic blood made of mandrake wine parallels the Harvest Judgment where the blood of men is compared to wine. [Rev.14:24-20 Zech.14:1-11] Compare this to the 7,000 men who are killed at JeruSalem at the Lord's coming. [Rev.11:13,15] Hathor's slaughter causes rivers of blood. Compare this to the so-called battle of Armageddon that takes place at JeruSalem. [Revelation 16:14-16 19:11-21] It shall be Atum who shall save the remnant or firstfruits from the wrath of Hathor (i.e. the Grim Reaper). "For Behold, the Day is coming burning like a oven, and all the proud, yes, all who do wickedly will be stubble. And the day which is coming shall burn them up...but to you who fear My name the Sun of Righteousness shall arise with healing in His wings, says the Lord of hosts." [Malachi 4:1-6] Obviously, the Sun of Righteousness is Atum-Ra the good Son of God.

Hathor represents vanity and violence; death and destruction. She is the dark side of nature: earthquakes, tornadoes, plagues, famines, etc... She is Neuter or Neutral (neither good or bad). As the avenger upon mankind, her counterpart is Greek Nemesis. Nemes is the Egyptian head-dress that resembles a cobra's hood. Nem (Num) is an attribute of the Upper Egyptian Khnemu; the rain-god who waters the groves of Asherah or the Wood of Nemi in Rome. Its a corruption of the water of life feeding the garden of God. Khnemu is the Greek Kronus. In the Tale of Two Brothers (Horus & Set?) the people unanimously conclude that Hathor's death will be caused by the knife. The Bible says those who live by the sword shall die by the Sword of the Lord. [Revelation 13:10] Hathor means House of Horus. It is Taurus, one of the twelve Houses of the Zodiac. As Sekhmet the lion-headed goddess, she represents the Power on High during the age of Leo the lion. Sekhmet is the Hebrew Shekinah. Sekhem means Power (Spirit) and Met, Mut or Nut is the heavens. As the cow goddess, Hathor represents the heavens in the age of Taurus the bull. She is often depicted as a cow with stars across her body. Atum-Ra climbs on the back of the cow representing that he rules over the age of Taurus the bull. The Ancient of Days is described as having a silver core, golden body and lapis-lazuli (blue) hair. He is Sirius, the blue-green star, in the constellation of Taurus.

One day Set saw Hathor bathing in a river. He transformed into a ram, the sacred animal of Amen, and tried to rape her under the moonlight. Just as Zeus transformed into bulls and other animals. But Set's animal desires backfired on him. The passion went to his head causing moon-madness or lunacy. The sun-god, Amen-Ra-Set, was forbidden to mate with Hathor because she is really Isis. Isis, as Mother of the Night Sun or Morning Star Sirius (Atum) and can only be impregnated by divine fire. She is not the moon that does rendezvous with the sun during an eclipse.

The council of the Gods (Elohim) decided Set was not worthy to have an Egyptian wife. Therefore, he was given foreign females as a consolation; Anat & Astarte the warrior & sex goddesses of Syria and Mesopotamia. This represents the spread of the Upper Egyptian version to the Middle East. As Ast-arte is a corruption of Ast (Isis). Set became their god (Baal). {From Fetish to God in Ancient Egypt p.446 and World Mythology p.51}

Astarte is Ast (Bast) and Art (Urt), the northern stars of Ursa Major. Ta-urt (Great Mother) is the antithesis of Tuat. Astarte's counterparts are: Ashtorah and Ishtar (Ash-taurus). Ashtorah is the sister and mistress of Baal (Set). Ishtar the goddess of sex and violence in Babylon. Her mate is Tammuz the sun-god. Artemis (Urt+Mot) is the Great Mother of the Great she Bear (Ursa Major). She is the sister and mate of her brother Apollo (Apollyon- Typhon). Bast is the female and Bes is the male dwarf deity of sex in Upper Egypt. They are the prototype for Cupid in Roman myth. Venus is his mother and mate. An illegitimate child is called a Bast-ard or son of Bast+urt. (As d and t are interchangeable.)

This story sounds a lot like David watching Bathsheba bathing. He is so love sick that he seduces her, committing adultery. Their firstborn dies as this was a forbidden union. The people of Israel were not to inbred with the Canaanites. To take a foreign mate is to follow in the ways of Set (Satan). The fallen angels mating with women produced bastard beings. Bath-Sheba was Solomon's mother. Sheba became is mate. Just as Mut was Amen's mother and later became his mate.

The Upper Egyptians replaced Isis (Ast) with Hathor (Apt). Hathor become both the mother (Mot) and mistress of Amen-Set. This cow-goddess is the mistress of merrymaking, dance, music, lust, and intoxication. Compare this to the making of the Golden Calf. [Exodus 32:1-6,19] The hieroglyph for Apt is two cow horns. The horns of Hades in the Bull of Taurus. From which we get the word 'horny'. The Greeks transformed Hathor into Aphrodite, the goddess of love, who is both lover and mother to Eros. The Romans worshipped Hathor as Mother of god and Queen of Heaven long before Mary acquired those titles. Hathor = Chathor or Cathedral (House of God). C-Hat-hor-al means House of the god Horus. Hathor is often portrayed with a men-at or phallus (dildo) for sexual pleasure. Men-at is obviously Amen-at, the dildo of the lord of the libido. Compare to Shiva's linga in Hinduism.

Apophis

The serpent Apophis or Apep is one of Typhon's many faces. It represents the creation in chaos (disorder) until the Lord transformed it into cosmos (order). The Lord of light (Atum) battles the cold blooded dragon of dark abyss. The Lord of the Sabbath created rest from the unrest caused by that Old Serpent Satan (Apollyon). Apollyon is the Destroyer. Within Apollyon is Apollo the sungod. The uraeus (Egyptian A-ra-t) is Ra inside a coiled cobra. The uraeus is the uterus of Ra. From out of the dark body of the sea serpent, comes the evil eye (Rem the sun) attacking Sirius at its dawn rising. The light of the sun tries to eclipse the Bright Morning Star, but the female feline comes to the rescue of her Child. The cat, Bast, cuts the A-rat serpent to pieces (the Cat kills a rat). This explains the blood-red sunrise. Bast is an aspect of Ast (Isis). In fact, Isis and Horus can be spelt Chat-hor, a form of Hat-hor. Chathor is Kathor. Kat and Hat meaning Womb and Heart; as in Sacred Heart. Sirius represents Mother and Child. The Egyptologist Selim Hassan says, "Orion and Sirius are swallowed up each morning in the increased glow of dawn." Re (Rem), the sun, is their enemy. The rivalry between Horus and Set is called Rehui (Re vs. Horus).

This sea serpent is also the Mother (Mut) of Amen-Ra-Set. Apollyon, Typhon and Apophis are the dark womb of the sun. Upon Set's premature birth, he violently ripped his way out of the womb of Mut. His face was white and his hair red as the sunrise. Typhon-Set is Mother and Sun; darkness and light. Ra vs. Apophis is the same as Marduk vs. Tiamat and Bel vs. the Dragon.

Compare the Cat by the Kat tree slaying the Serpent, to Eve by the Tree of carnal knowledge and the fiery Serpent (Lucifer) offering her false enlightenment. The Kat is also the Persea 'fig' tree. Per-sea is the House of Saa (knowledge of nature). Ked (Kat) is the English; Great Mother and her family Tree of forbidden fruits. Sata is the serpent with human legs. Asfet means Sin, Set is the evil one, Af means Carnal, and Khat means Corpse. Catacomb is tomb for the dead. The sun dies and is reborn daily. Mother Nature and her sun dies and revives annually.

The Sun of Righteousness is the Son of Isis, rising as the star Sirius, from the Tree of Life (Ashet) at Anu. Anu is the birthplace of Atum-Horus. He is the Branch of the Ashet: the Tree Asar (Osiris) died in and Horus rose from. [Jer.23:5 33:15,16] The Bennu (Son of Anu) perched in this tree. The old Phoenix died and the new rose from its ashes. The Ash is of the Olive tree family. Olive tree in Greek is El-ah-yah (Lord God). God's family tree. [Rom.11:17-24] Holy Oil is Olive oil. The garden of God is called Sekhet-Hetep. [Rev.2:7] Ash is Nun in Arabic, Nun in Hebrew, Nu in Greek, Nuin in Irish, and Nun in Egyptian. Nun is the womb from which the firstborn Son of God was born.

Ashtoreth, goddess of trees, as mother nature and consort of Baal; is a corruption of Ast (Isis) and the Ashet tree. They worshipped the oak tree, the symbol of the sun. Oak is Elah in Hebrew (El = God & iah = Lord). Baal also means Lord. Oak, being a hard wood, became the phallic symbol of potency. Ash is Hebrew for the Great Bear (Ursa Major) and the root of Ashtoreth. Within the word mist-letoe is Leto, the mother of Apollo (sun) and Artemis (moon). The mistletoe ascending up the oak, became the symbol of the moon chasing and embracing the sun. The tradition of a man kissing any woman under the mistletoe during the winter solstice (Dec.25) was a fertility ritual; mimicking the moon's night becoming equal with the sun's daylight, therein, the mating occurred. [Gogmagog; the buried gods by T.C. Lethbridge page 120]

In one story, Isis creates a serpent from the dust. The serpent bites Ra (the sun) and causes him to fall. Isis heals him with magic powers and he rises again. This explains why the sun rises and falls daily. Kat also means a cycle of time. The three Cyclopes; Atum (Sirius), Ra (Sun) and Amen (Hyades). The Cat is a metaphor for the metaphysical. The cat can see at night just as the eyes of the sky (i.e. the stars) can see in the darkness of the underworld. Cat in Egyptian is mau, which also means "to see". From mau, we get meow. {See Gerald Massey's Lectures} For her help, the name of Ra is given to Isis' son. He is now Atum-Ra-Horus, firstborn Sun of God. The Ut-chat (ut-cat) is the all-seeing Eye of Horus (Sirius). Es-chat-ology is the study of; death, resurrection, immortality, the hereafter and Judgment day. Isis did NOT use magic. The Words of Power are the Word of God (Spirit of Truth) which contain supernatural power.

In Lower Egypt, the Morning star Sirius travels through the body of Nut and is reborn from her womb. But in Upper Egypt, the sun (Ra the Rat) is swallowed by the serpent (Uraeus or A-rat) and travels through the body of Apophis. Both Nut and Apophis represent the sea of space surrounding the earth. Kat also means Womb, therefore, the Mother and Child are one. Ra, the Cat, claws its way out of the bloodied body of the serpent. Therein, Amen-Ra is reborn daily as the scarlet Day-star (Lucifer). [A Book of the Beginnings by Gerald Massey, page 232] Amen-Ra is called King of the gods, just as Herod was King of the Jews. Amen-Ra tries to swallow the sun of God (Sirius) at its birth, just as Herod failed in his attempt to kill Jesus. [Revelation 12:4, 5]

The Hebrew word for Ashet is Shittim. The Ark of the Covenant was made of Shittim; the Tree of life. The power of God (Sekhmet) was in the Ark. The word Shittaim means dual eyes; one open and one closed. When Sun rises, it blinds us to Sirius. Sh'ttaim also denotes the all seeing Eye of Horus and the mind's eye that sees (envisions) even though our eyes are closed.

The Chinese say the red sunset is the red dragon chasing his tail. The sun is Amen-Ra-Set who does rise and 'set' daily. The Upper Egyptians corrupted the story to make him the Angel of light. [2 Corinthians 13-15] But this great impostor is really the red dragon alias Lucifer the Daystar. [Revelation 12:3-9] The conquering Hyksos (Arabians), who ruled Egypt during the Middle kingdom, often took the name of King Apophis (Serpent-King) and bragged that they worshipped Seth. Likewise Pepi is Apepi. He is the pharaoh of the Theban version of the Book of the Dead. In which, he calls himself Peter! Apep and Apophis is also the origin of Pope and Papa (Papal). The Papacy is the Dragon that rises from the Great sea in Revelation 13. The head is the Antichrist Amen who appears like the Son of God, but speaks lies.

On the physical level, the Egyptians say Shu, the Lion-headed god, transformed into a cat and slayed the "abominable rat of the sun". The men of science say the atmosphere (Shu) caused the ultra-violent rays of the sun to appear red at sunrise and sunset! It is Shu (the O-zone) who protects us from the ultra-violent rays of Ra! Scientists say it is the sun that causes skin aging and cancers.

The serpent created time: as previously there was no lifetime that comes to an end. Everything went on without end. Just as in the Garden of God east of Eden. The exile of Eden was the beginning of time. When Adam and Eve chose to follow the evil Sun of God with the serpent's tongue. Turning the world upside down. The rebellion against God started the revolution of time as the earth rotates under the sun. With the illumination coming from the sun and his mate the moon. From the sun, man calculates the days and years and from the moon he calculates the month cycles. The Tree of Knowledge of good and evil became their source of carnal knowledge. They live in a cycle of life to death. When the good Sun of God rises in the east, he will put an end to time. Then the endless day will go on forever.

The Sata serpent walks on two human legs and is the enemy of Osiris. This is obviously the serpent in the garden of God who seduced Eve. Sata is Satan, but to the Egyptians he is one of the forms of Set. It was Set who invented Sex. For his transgression, the serpent shall crawl on his belly (legless) eating dust. And the sons of the serpent (Cain's descendants) shall be enemies of the sons of Eve (Seth's descendants). [Genesis 3:14,15] Sata is Son of the Earth (Seb) and the hieroglyph is the goose, one of the sacred animals of Set. Seba is also an attribute of Set. The sebau fiends are his angels who fell to earth (seb) called Sami.

Our clock is based on the sun (Ra) being the center of our solar system. As the earth rotates, we look up to Ra to calculate 24 hours. As we orbit around the sun, we count 365 days. Ra rules over our lives. When Ra (Sol) dies in the winter solstice, the year ends. When Ra revives, the new Solar year begins. The symbol for Ra is the sun disk encircled by a serpent. The same symbol used for Satan. The Egyptians used the cosmic clock. The dawn rising of Sirius occurs ever 365 days and is the only star to do that. Their lives rotated around the cosmic clock ruled by Sirius-Atum. This is the Sirius year. The Egyptian and Mayan calendars are the most accurate ever. Our pagan Roman-Christian calendar is base on Chronos (Saturn) and his cronies: Saturday is Saturn's day, Sunday is day of the sun-god, Monday is the day of the moon goddess, etc... For the Egyptians, there is two halves of the year and two heavens: the Upper (Nu-Day) ruled by Amen and the Lower (Nut-Night) ruled by Atum. Our word Annual comes from the Greek Annu (Year) which comes from the annual cycle of Anu (Sirius). The Hebrew Rosh-hash-anah means New Year (hash = ash & anah = anual). In Hebrew 'ash' means first & tree. Rosh-hash-anah is the first of the new year.

Modern man worships the sun (Ra) as the sustainer of life and creator of the life cycle (i.e. life-time). They praise the false light of the physical sun rather than the true light of the metaphysical Son of God. [2 Corinthians 11:14] Since God is so far away, they worship the one close at hand. The ancient Egyptian day went from sunset to sunset. They were night hawks, seeking Horus the Hawk in the night sky (i.e. star Sirius)! The constellations were their movie stars reenacting the history of the heavens through-out the (zodiac) ages. This is the cosmic cycle of creation. They were deeply saddened when the sun rose up and swallowed them. The sun blots out the super-stars with a white veil of day-light. Lucifer means Day-star and Covering Cherub. The time system that goes from 12 midnight to 12 noon honors Amen-Ra. Amen is the sun at noon. The Greek word gn-omon means sun-dial. It is also garden of Amon, as gn = garden in Hebrew. It was Amen-Ra who replaced the good Sun of God in the garden of Atem (Eden).

The Great Flood

Now going back in time. Chapter 17 of the Book of the Dead speaks of the time when Tem (Atum) existed by himself in Nu, the day sky. Atum-Ra-Horus grew tired of mankind rebelling against himself, therefore, he decided to destroy them with a flood. [Genesis 6:5-7] The eye of Horus shed tears because of the creation and necessary destruction of mankind. Only a remnant remained (Noah's family). Then Thoth, being the tongue of the Great God declares that, acting for the Lord Tem, he is going to make a Flood. He says, "They have fought fights, they have upheld strifes, they have caused trouble and oppression... <therefore> I am going to blot out everything which I have made. This earth shall enter into the watery abyss of Nu by means of a raging flood, and will become even as it was in primeval time. I myself shall remain together with Osiris, but I shall transform myself into a small serpent which can neither be apprehended or seen.' [Book of the Dead chapter 175] Compare this to the Lord blotting out names from the Book of Life. [Exodus 32:33,34 Revelation 3:5] Originally the twin stars of our binary solar system kept things in balance (Yin/Yang). Sirius (Atum) leaving our solar system is what caused the earth's axis to tilt 23 degrees and caused the flood.

Meanwhile, Atum-Ra climbed on the back of Nut (the stars of heaven) ascending as the Lord of Hosts or Ruler of the Stars and Archangel over all angels (suns of God). "Horus Beyond the Horizon" is the Morning star called Sirius. Now his domain is Nut, the night sky. Amen-Ra became the sun that rules over the earth. Horus was upset to tears that another <evil> eye had caused the fall of man and took his place in the face of the sky (Nut). This other eye is Rem (Re-Amen). It is interesting that the word Remth means Tears. It was Rem who created the cold-blooded reptiles: scorpions, serpents, crocodiles, dinosaurs and dragons. [from the History of the Creation of the Gods and of the World] The name Roma comes from Rema which means; aborigines or natives. These Romans worship the sun-god Rem (Remus and Romulus). Romul or Rom-ur means Rem the Great. {l=r and d=t} The wandering star, Remphan, moved from Thebes, Egypt to Thebes, Greece. Rem made his home in Rome. [Act 7:43] The Ram of Ares (Mars) the Warlord originated in Ludium, Upper Egypt. Ludum or

Rutum is language. Latin is the language of Latium which comes from Lud or Lydian; meaning Ruddy or Redden. As in Mars the red planet and parent of Romulus & Remus. Roman = Ra-amen.

It is the Ark of Horus, Herfhaf the Ferry-man, who saves the righteous from the Lake of fire raining down from heaven, NOT the solar Bark of Ra. If you book passage on the wrong boat, you are going to be unhappy with your destination. In the last day, the sun, moon and fallen stars will be consumed in the heavenly Lake of fire. God is a consuming fire that shall swallow all evil. Ra, the sun, Mut the outer space, and Khonsu, the moon, will be no more. Horus and his followers dwell on the Island in the midst of the Lake of Fire. [Revelation 20:9] This is the safe haven for the time when God will consume everything in the heavens. Only the righteous suns of God will survive. After being refined and purified in the heavenly fire. [2 Peter 3:10-12 Revelation 21:1,23] Book reservations on the Bark of Horus and be in the Book of life. Reserve your place in the here (on earth) for the time when all things are made new.

Thoth, Tehuti, Taht

It was Thoth, the ibis-headed-one who hovered over Isis, immaculately conceiving the child Horus. Just as God's Holy Spirit, in the form of a dove hovered over Mary, impregnating her with divine seed. Thuth is the Spirit of Truth that represents Ptah's supernatural power working in the natural world. The child begotten was not the Holy Spirit's son, but God's Son. The Spirit represents the life force coming from God the Father. Thoth is the Advocate or Comforter which came after Horus went to heaven, just as the Holy Spirit came after Jesus ascended to heaven.

Thoth (Taht) wrote The Four Books: "The Old Book", "The Book to Destroy Man", "The Great Book", and "The Book to be as God". These are the Torah; Genesis, Exodus, Numbers and Leviticus. Deuteronomy was not included. The Egyptians call this instruction manual Teruu (Torah). Thoth's mate is Maat; the Word of God unites with Truth. Both are concepts, not beings. The Book of the Laws is the Book of Maat, that was inspired by Shu-Horus (the Spirit of Horus). They were dictated by Patah (the Father in heaven), through Thoth (Spirit of Truth), and delivered by Ra-Atum-Huhi (Son of God or Word of God). [Rev.1:1] Atum-Horus is the authorized Author (Atu-Hor) and finisher of faith. [Hebrew 5:9 12:2]

These are the books Moses studied while in the Great University at Annu (On) in Egypt. "Moses was learned in the wisdom of the Egyptians." This included the ancient Mysteries. [The Companion Bible-Acts 7:22] The Greeks called it Heliopolis (City of the Sun of God). They are part of the so called "Old Testament" of the Bible. Bible means Book, therefore its "The Old Book". It is part of the spoils Moses took out of Egypt during the Exodus. Compare the Lamentations of Isis to the Lamentations in the Bible. [Read "Signs & Symbols of Primordial Man" by Albert

Churchward] Kheri Heb is Egyptian for "the Keeper of the book." Compare Heb-jew to Hebrew as the Jews are called "the people with the book."

Thoth writes the names of the sons of God on the leaves of the Tree of life. [Revelation 2:7 22:2,19] Which is the same as the Book of life written on paper made from the tree. [Revelation 20:15] A persons name is registered in heaven in the Book of Life. The person does not go to heaven. [Philipians 3:20 4:3 Hebrews 12:23] They have a place reserved in God's kingdom on earth. This is part of the so called New Testament or revised New Book. The idea that storks deliver babies comes from Thoth, the ibis, who announced the birth of Christ Child and shall announce the rebirth of the children of God. The 'root' of the word papyrus is paper and papa and paps that give the milk of God (Word of God). Here we have the written Word of God and the oral Word of God. Papyrus is the Logo of the Lower Egyptians. The lotus is the logo of the Upper Egyptians.

At the Judgment Hall, Thoth is keeper of the Balance. On the celestial level, he is keeper of the equilibrium of the universe. He is measurer of the earth and counter of the stars. [Revelation 11:1] THOTH is the personification of the supernatural THOugHTs of God working in this natural world. Thoth is not a being, but the Spirit of Truth.

The Greeks called him Hermes. Heru-mes means Horus reborn. Thoth is the holy Spirit of Truth and Heru is the holy Spirit being called the living Word of God. Maa-kheru means truth-speaker. Heru or Horus is the spoken word of truth. The Books of Thoth-Hermes are the written Word of God. There are three ages of Hermes. Hermes the Great was before the Flood, during the age of Taurus. Hermes the Twice Great was after the Flood during the age of Ares. And Hermes Trismegistus (Hermes Thrice Great) during the age of Pisces. This is when the Lord worked with the Greeks. Thoth hid the "Emerald Tablets" of the ancient knowledge before the Flood. The Egyptian Mysteries were converted, and perverted, by the Greeks into the Elysian Mysteries of Demeter (counterpart of Isis).

Warning!

Most texts are taken from temples, tombs and pyramids of Upper Egypt where they worship Amen. The thieves of Thebes stold and perverted the original scriptures to make Amon their god. They made god in their own image (Aman is A man). They masquerade the evil one in all the trappings of the only begotten Son of Man. He (Amen) may look like the Lamb, but he still speaks like the Devil. [Revelation 11:13] It is no coincidence that Ra-Amen's sacred animal is the Ram! [From Fetish to God in Ancient Egypt by Wallis Budge p.356 and 357]

The land where Amon rules as the evil sun-god

In Upper Egypt, Amon and his Pharaohs wear the domed crown; identical to that of Baal of the Canaanites and Freyr of the Vikings. Both Baal and Freyr mean "Lord". He is the Warlord. This is the same domed crown that the Pope wears called the Tiara. The potency of the Papacy shows he is worshipped as a fertility deity. The heretic priests of Amon carried the image of their god to show to the masses on their high day. The graven images were not able to move on their own. There are no images of God the Father or His good Son. There is only the Ark of the Covenant with its laws or Maat within.

The "ministers of Min" are the "minions of Amen". Minister: 'ster' means laying out the dead (Mortician or Undertaker) for Min. Amenta is the underground land of Amen. Egyptians do not have vowels in their words. They are added when pronounced. Min was worshipped as Minos at Crete and the Minotaur at Greece. The Minotaur was the mon-ster of the underground labyrinth who devoured the human sacrifices. Just as Ammet and Typhon, the three headed monster, devour the dead.

The Upper Egyptians worshipped Amen instead of Atum. 'Instead of' or 'in place of' is the meaning of Anti, as in AntiChrist. Amen and Mut are the parents of Khonsu (the fake Horus). Khonsu is the spurious savior. From Khansu we get Khan and Chan and Cain. Khansu means to conquer, kill, etc.. As Cain killed his good brother. Khan means Prince or Son of the King of this world (Set-amen or Satan). Cain was son of Satan. After Cain killed Abel, Seth replaced Abel. Khonsu became Kronus or Chronus, son of Uranus in the Greek myth. He is the evil sun of God. The hymns to Amen are plagiarism, forged by the priests of Thebes in an attempt to make him God.

THE Pharaoh's of Amen

In 3100 BC, Menes conquered Lower Egypt, uniting the two kingdoms of Egypt, and built Memphis. This era is called the Old Kingdom. Menes was known as the "scorpion king". Set, in the form of a scorpion, killed the Horus Child. Menes = Amen. The battle between Amen-Set and Atum-Horus is called Rehui (Re-Amen vs. Horus). The land of Sut is called the Red land (Deshret) as it is covered with blood and lifeless Desert land, except for scorpions and serpents. The Black land of Horus (Nile Delta) is fertile and peaceful.

The Pharaoh's of Amon lived in the city of Thebes (Luxor, Karnak) in Upper Egypt. Upper Egypt being in the south. Amon is the State god and his priests are called Amonites. They shaved off all the hair of their bodies. At Thebes, they worshipped the Am-Smen; the seven planets and the sun (Amen-Set). It is also called an Ogdoad (Eight). Smen is the Mother Goose (Great Cackler) who laid the Golden Egg or Sun. Amen is the head of their solar pantheon. Amen and Mut (Heaven) produced Khonsu (the moon). They make up the Satanic trinity. The temple of Karnak is the house of the Warlord. User-Ka-f was the first King of the fifth dynasty and first to call himself "Son of the Sun (Ra)". Just as the Aztecs did. [Fetish to God in Ancient Egypt by Wallis Budge and [Signs and Symbols of

Primordial Man page 269] About 2,000 BC, the Shepherd Kings (Hyksos or Heksos) conquered Egypt. Hek-sos means servants of Hek (Amen the king of the gods). This era is called the Middle Kingdom. According to the Tablet of San, over 400 years lapsed between Apophis king of the Hyksos, in the day of Joseph, and Rameses II, in the day of Moses. Confirming the Bible's 430 years of bondage. About 1587 BC the kings of Upper Egypt defeated and exiled these Shepherd Kings. This is the great Exodus of the Semitics (Jews and Arabs). [Exodus 12:38,40] These exiles were called Aati (Lepers). These outcasts were the unclean white sons of Ham called Canaanites, whose home was the land of Canaan. [Genesis 43:32 46:34] Hu or Hut means White. Human is White-man. White men are the sons of A-men. Hu is also the sun-god. Manes means the Dead in Amenta.

Plutarch and Tacitus say that when Horus defeated Sut-Typhon, he fled out of Egypt riding on an ass. The ass is the symbol of the sun. Sut, the white faced, red haired sun-god, had twin sons called Judaeus (Judah) and Hiero-solymus (Holy-Salem or Jeru-Salem). They settled in Judea and Jerusalem. Hiero-solymus could also mean Holy Solomon. The Sem priests (sinister ministers of Set-amen) became the Semitic priests of Simeonites and Levites. [Genesis 49:5-7] Sem (Sham) also means Fable or false gospel. Shaman is Sat-aman or Set-Amen.

This was era called the New Kingdom, when Amen was king of the gods (suten neteru or Set of the neteru). Just like Zeus-Amen, king of the gods, and Satan of the elohim, chief of the fallen angels. Some of the infamous kings of the New kingdom are : Amonhotep I (1525-1504 BC), Thutmose I, Thutmose III (1479-1425 BC), Amonhotep II (1427-1401 BC), Thutmose IV, Amonhotep III (1391-), Amonhotep IV (1353-1335 BC), Smenkhara, Tutankhamon, Vizier Ay (1323-1319 BC), General Horemheb, Rameses (1307-1196 BC), Seti I (AKA. Ra-men-ma), Rameses II (1290-1224BC), Merenptah (1234 BC), Rameses III (1194-1163 BC).

Rameses II is the Pharaoh who stood against Moses in the Bible. Rameses (or RaMoses) was one of the most vain and arrogant Pharaohs ever. He built hundreds of statutes of himself. He worshipped the Warlord and god of war, Amon. As Rameses the great was a conqueror who wanted to be king of the world. The Lord stood with Moses against the evil RaMoses and his sun-god, Amon-Ra. The Lord being Atum-Ra, the good Sun of God. Merenptah is the king of Egypt who exterminated the people of Israel about 1234 BC They have recently discovered the tomb built by Rameses II for his sons. This maybe proof that he was the pharaoh of the Exodus. Rameses II had hundreds of wives and mistresses. Each capable of producing a firstborn son. Rameses may have lost many sons on that fateful day of the death of the firstborn sons of Egypt. The tomb is shaped like a T. Possibly in honor of Atum (A-Tomb), the Angel of Death and Lord of life.

Rameses II married the princess of Hatti (Hittites) in order to create an alliance between the two warrior nations. The two arch enemies are united by a treaty and a diplomatic marriage. The one theme repeated over and over in the Bible is: God's people shall NOT inter-marry with the Canaanites. Abraham, Isaac, and Jacob were all told Not to marry these white race with the sickness of sin. [Genesis 24:3] They are cursed with leprosy (partial albinism). Which is passed on through the genes. The Hittites are the sons of Canaan called Heth. [Genesis 10:15]

In the movie "Ten Commandments" Rameses' famous last words were, "So let it be written, so let it be done." Today Christians say the word Amen means "so be it". The saying is inseparable from the source. Christians pray, "In Christ's name we pray, Amen". Is the Christ's name Amen??? God forbid!!! Amen is the spurious savior or antichrist. Christians give Amen the last word rather than the true Word of God. Others say Amen means: verily, assuredly, truly, etc... There is no definitive definition because it is a proper name that is always capitalized in the Bible.

The "doomed" kings of Upper Egypt wore the domed crown of Amen-Ra. The same crown wore by Baal of Babylon. The crown was later past on when Rome conquered Egypt. Now the Pope wears the crown as Vicar of Amen the Antichrist. The throne was moved from Thebes, Egypt to Thebes, Greece under Alexander and then to Rome under Julius Caesar. The crown of Amen was to make the wearer a living phallic (penis) symbol when standing erect. The Egyptians even show a foreskin around the head of the phallic crown, while the Catholic's have circumcised theirs. The crown demonstrates the "potency of the Papacy" even though the "holy father" is childless. He is a foster-father and all his "kids" are adopted into the "Mother-church". The Aati are the illegitimate sons of the Great Mother (Mot-ur) who have no Father in heaven. [John 8:41-44] The Atef crown of Upper Egypt has two ram's horns just as described in Revelation 13:11. Amen-Ra gave the war helmet to Osiris; 'But on the very first day that he wore it, Osiris had much suffering in his head, and when Ra returned in the evening he found Osiris with his head angry and swollen from the heat of the Atef crown. Then Ra proceeded to let out the pus and the blood' [Egyptian Book of the Dead chapter 175] What kind of evil hell-met is this? Keep in mind that all pictures of Osiris wearing the Atef or Tiara crowns of Upper Egypt, were drawn by the Upper Egyptians.

The kings of Upper Egypt built the obel-isks to Amen (AKA Baal). The word "O-Bel" is O-Baal just as the Vikings called their evil deity O-Dan. Like the Tower of Babel (Baal) that tried to reach to heaven. The Egyptians recorded their battle victories on them. The Roman Catholics took one of Rameses' obelisks to Rome for their worship of Mith-Ra the sun-god. Both the domed crown and the obelisks are phallic or fertility symbols pointing up to the potent sungod. An obelisk is "a monolith" or "stone to Amon". Lithos is Greek for Stone. He mimics the Chief corner stone, Christ the Rock of salvation. Amon is called King of the gods or Mon-arch. Mono means Solo just as solitary comes from Sol the solar-god. The word for King in Egyptian is Sutan or Sut, the evil one. Monotheism means "Mon (Amon) is the One god". Have you noticed that everything Christendumb teaches has a Satanic source?

You might ask, "How did the peaceful priests of Lower Egypt keep the warriors of Upper Egypt at bay?" Divine intervention. God's power is in the Great Pyramid just as it was in the Ark of the Covenant which protected Israel from her enemies. [Exodus 14:14 Joshua 3:6-10-17] The priests of God did NOT fight for freedom nor defend their nation! The Declaration of Independence is the antithesis of Declaration of Innocence. Those proclaiming Dependence on God have no blood on their hands. The Lord fights the battles for his people. He is all-powerful and does NOT need man's help. Faith is: waiting for the Lord to act.

The LORD says, "Behold, I will bring punishment on Amon of No (Thebes), and Pharaoh and Egypt, with their gods and their kings-Pharaoh and those who trust in him." [Jeremiah 46:25] Amon is Amen. To end your prayer with Amen is praising the enemy of the LORD. The Upper Egyptians exalted themselves, and for that they shall be brought down low. [Isaiah 14:12-15 Matthew 11:23 Ezekiel 31 & 32 Jer.46] The Greek word "Thebes" is The (God) + bes (fire) or the sun-god (AKA. Baal). [2 Kings 23:4-11] The min-isters of Min and his min-ions shall be the human sacrifice for sin. Minister means Mortician.

Mon-asteries are Mon's-stars. The houses of their gods on earth (Thebes, Karnak, Luxor) have counterparts in heaven; the houses of the Zodiac (Draco, Ursa Major and Ursa Minor). As in heaven, so on earth. Memphis, Dahshur and Meidum are the Monsters; Taurus, Aries, and Cetus.

Exception to every Rule

When Thothmose IV was young, he was hunting near the Sphinx in Gizah. He was tired so he laid in the shade against the cheek of the Sphinx and fell asleep.

As the Sphinx was buried up to its neck in sand. In a dream, the Sphinx said: "Thutmose, my child, I am your father, I am the Sun <of> God, I am Khep-Ra and Atum and Ra, I am Harmarchis!" Horus of the Horizon promised to give Thutmose the kingdom of the earth to rule if he swept away the sand that was smothering the Sphinx and if he would serve Atum-Ra. Thutmose fetched an army and dug out the Great Sphinx. Thutmose became Pharaoh, "ruled" a vast empire, and continued to serve Atum-Ra all his days. Thutmose is Thoth + Moses.

The land where Atum rules as the good Sun of God

In Lower Egypt, Isis represents mother earth and Nephthys represents mother nature. They are the sisters working hand and hand. In order for mother earth to give birth to man, mother nature must assist. They are portrayed with sun disks on their heads which means the Son (Atum-Ra-Horus) rules over them. Just as in Revelations 12:1. The Egyptians did not worship them as goddesses, but as parts of God the Father doing His commands, and obeying His laws of nature.

Osiris parallels the Son of Man in the Bible. Isis is his wife and sister. Just as Adam and Eve were blood relatives. Osiris is killed by Seth, but is resurrected or reborn as Horus, Son of God. Therefore Isis is now his mother. She is portrayed as the fertile Mother earth giving milk to her son. Osiris was resurrected from mother earth as Horus. He has defeated the powers of death represented by the setting sun in the west. The earth and moon are female while the suns are male. Horus being the Sun of God betrothed to the earthlings (church body members). Isis is the bride dressed in white linen garments. [Revelation 19:7-9]

The Greeks called him Harpocrates. He is portrayed with a falcon as he can fly in the sky. His arch-enemy or Adversary is Seth. Seth was portrayed as a canine (carnivorous predator). Seth is the evil one or Satan. Satan means Adversary. Horus means Savior just as does Jesus and Zeus, Iesus and Hesus. Horus (Osiris) is the one to Judge the nations. In the battle of good vs. evil, Seth tears out Horus' eye and Horus inturn ripped off Seth's testicles. So he was no longer able to have children. For it was Satan who seduced Eve and produced Cain the canine killer who murdered his brother Abel. Just as Seth killed Osiris.

Ra-Atum is the original Sun of God who ruled over God's kingdom on earth. The Pharaoh's of Atum lived in the cities in lower Egypt near the Mediterranean Sea called the Nile Delta. In cities like: Heliopolis, city of the Sun of Righteousness. The Great Pyramid is in Gizah only a few miles away from Cairo. Ra-Atum became the setting Sun as Amon (Satan) took over as the rising god of this world. The narrow minded Upper Egyptians had the solar religion centered around Set-Amen, the sungod. The Lower Egyptians saw all the stars as suns of God. This is stellar religion. God the Father created all His sons; some rebelled and some obeyed.

Hebrew Seder-Set's day

The Egyptian's celebrate the king's jubilee festival called Heb Sed (Festival of Set) counterpart to the Hebrew year of Jubliee. {the letters 'd' and 't' are interchangeable}. Sed is the root of Seder, which is the Jewish name for Pass-over (Pasach). The Greek Pascha is the Egyptian Pasht. Pasht and Sekhet are the twin-lions of the equinox facing north and south. Sekhet is the autumn equinox. Compare Seder to Seker (Death). It is the memorial of the death and resurrection of Pharaoh Osiris during the spring equinox (on Pass-over). Set (Sed) killed Osiris, the firstborn of Egypt, just as the firstborn of Egypt died during the Exodus. Pash means to cut in pieces. As Set had done to Osiris. Jesus was killed by Set (Satan) on the anniversary of Passover. [John 19:14] Pas-char is called the Passion of Christ (Karast). Heb Sed was celebrated every thirty years. Osiris died at 28, but by the time Isis located and re-assembled the body, plus the 9 months gestation, it was starting the 30th year when he was reborn as Horus. Compare this to the legend that Christ was thirty-three at death. The question is: why do the Jews insist on calling it Set's Festival? Are they celebrating Osiris' death ....or his resurrection?

Each house of the Zodiac is 30 degrees (12 signs = 360 degrees). The age of Orion was 30 degrees (or 2160 years). According to the Egyptians, Osiris-Orion rose again 70 days after Passover. The embalming process is said to take 70 days. The 7 weeks or 50 days of the Judeo-Christian Pentecost is a corruption. It should have been 7 (10 day) weeks or 10 (7 day) weeks that equal 70 days, not 50. This is 3 months in the grave, not 3 days.

The Egyptians also did a ritual of purification of baptism. Both represent the delivery from the slavery to sin and the rebirth with a new start on life. "I purify myself at the great stream where all my ills are made to cease; that which is wrong in me is pardoned, and the spots which were upon my body upon the earth are washed away." [Ritual chapter 86]

Alexander the great son of Satan

In 332 BC Alexander the Great (Hebrew Gibor) drove the Persians out of Egypt. He was hailed as son of Amon. For his mother, Olympias, claimed that Zeus-Ammon had sex with her. Zeus had transformed into a serpent and seduced her. Alexander, like Amon, was a Warlord and cold blooded killer. When Alexander died in 323 BC, the Greek empire was divided among his four generals. Egypt became a province under General Ptolemy. Ptolemy's daughter was Cleopatra who murdered her older sister and was at war with her brother. She was not Egyptian, but Greek. She was NOT a Pharaoh! She was high priestess of the prostitutes in the temple of Amon. She lived in sin with the Roman emperor, Julius Caesar. She gave birth to his son, Caesarian. Egypt united with Rome. The religion of Amen became the illegitimate offspring adopted by the unholy Roman empire. Rome is the serpent that encircles the Great Mediterranean Sea. [Revelation 13:1] Manetho the Egyptian was high priest and historian during Ptolemy I. He chronicled the order and dates of the Pharaohs of Egypt. Plutarch in the "Life of Alexander the Great" says the last native king of Egypt, Nectanebo II, changed into a snake (Zeus-Ammon) and mated with Olympia. In other words they became partners in crime. He became Hellenized and the two (Greece and Egypt) became united as one nation.

Christendom soon followed. The Romans burned the library at Alexander which held ancient writings and sacred scriptures from all over the world. The Gospel of Thomas was buried in Egypt to keep the Christians like Constantine, from burning it. The Roman Catholics beat the Egyptians into converting to Christianity or killed them trying. When the Christians learned the religion of Amen in Upper Egypt, they were appalled. They murdered the priests of Amen. St. Anthony said, "We do this in the name of Jesus Christ, our Lord Amen." So Amen had the last word. St. Anthony was the founder of Mon's Monks in Egypt. The Christian Crusaders became the new sons of Amen. Egyptians converted to Christendum are called Copts and their writings is Coptic. Copt comes from C-apt. Apt is the ancient name of the region of Thebes, Karnak and Luxor. Apt is the birthplace of the deity, Amen.

The Gospel of Thomas was buried in Egypt to keep it from being destroyed by Christendumb. It was resurrected in the 20th century. Thomas is Thoth or Tom (the Word of God) and mas or mes (to be reborn from the watery womb).

"For such are false apostles, deceitful workers, transforming themselves into the apostles of Christ. And no marvel; for Satan himself is transformed into an angel of light. Therefore it is no great thing if his ministers also be transferred as the ministers of righteousness; whose end shall be according to their works." [2 Corinthians 11:13-15] Amen-Ra is pretending to be Atem-Ra-Horus, just as Satan pretends to be Jesus. The priests of Amen-Ra say he is the good Sun of God or Angel of light, but in reality he is the angel of darkness.

The warriors who Destroy in the name of their god Apollyon (Apollo the sun-god), shall be destroyed. [Revelation 9:11] This is Amon. In Hebrew, he is Abaddon who leads the armies of the world to their death at Armageddon. [Revelation 16:12-16] He is the AntiChrist or ChristYin. Yin being the negative supernatural force against Christ.

The praying mantis is the ideal symbol of Christendom. It takes the position of praying just before it kills!!!! Sometimes the female devours her mate, just as the Romans who killed Christ later became the Roman Catholic church. The bride is the black widow cloaked in black. The Mother church is known to have devoured her mates and even her offspring (the Protestants). A true man of God would never prey upon others. He would sacrifice himself as a martyr before he would harm another human-being. The Bushmen believe the Mantis puts evil thoughts in the minds of men.

The Christians got their version from the Thebans. They tell the story of the sun-god (Amen-Ra) waning weak and dying in the winter season. Christians celebrate the renewal of the sun during the Yule tide winter solstice. Sol, the solar-god, is born new as the daylight hours increase by New Year. The solar-child waxes strong by Easter sun-day. At the summer solstice, he is at the peak of power. The Romans called him Mith-ra.

A new Luxor has been recreated in Las Vegas in the Wilderness of Sin. They honor the deity of the dollar. From Luxor we get Luxury and materialism. The root of materialism is mater or mother. "Love of materialism is the womb of many evils." "For our of your heart proceed evil thoughts, murders, adulteries, fornications, thefts, false witness, blasphemies." Matthew 15:19] From Thebes, we get the den of thieves who lie, cheat and steal in the name of Lady Luck. Who is the goddess of greed for the godless. These dare-devils are willing to gamble that there is no God and no Judgment. The new temple in Las Vegas even has priestess' of prostitution. Where the selling of feminine favors is legal.

The Pyramid Temples

The pyramid is a temple Not a tomb. No one has ever been buried in a pyramid. The Pharaohs were buried in the tombs of the Valley of the Kings far up the Nile River. The Great Pyramid at Giza was dedicated to Atum-Ra the Sun of God. In fact, Giza (Gizah) is Iesa in Phoenician, Yesu in early British, Joshua in Hebrew, Jeezah or Jeesas in Greek and Jesus in Latin. The cap stone or head stone is missing because it represents Christ who has not returned yet. The sphinx is the Lion of Judah. The lion's body means king. As the Lord is head of state and church. The Great Pyramid represents the tomb of Christ which was transformed into the holy mountain of God's kingdom. [Daniel 2:34,44,45] {Piazzi Smyth agrees that Christ is the head stone in his book "The Great Pyramid" on p.539.}

The stone box in the King's chamber is for the Ark of the Covenant. It is far too small for a fully dressed mummy. It would hold the Ark which is 27" X 27" X 45". The Pyramid Texts say Atum-Ra has a 'golden box' in which he deposited his 'rod', a lock of his hair (the Horus lock), and his uraeus (cobra head-dress). It was placed in a fortress on the eastern frontier of Egypt until a great many years after his ascent to heaven. When Geb came to power, he ordered that it be brought to him and unsealed in his presence. In the instant the box was opened a bolt of fire ushered from it, struck dead all Geb's companions and gravely burned Geb (the Earth). Compare this to the golden Ark of the Covenant that contained Aaron's rod that transformed into a serpent. The Ark that struck anyone dead who touched it and plagued all who illegally possessed it.

Imhetep (2630-2611 BC) was seal-bearer of the King of Lower Egypt, one who is near the head of the King [i.e. vizier], Director of the Great Mansion, Royal representative, High Priest of Heliopolis, Imhetep, the carpenter and the sculptor... He held the same titles as Joseph son of Jacob as vizier of Egypt. And he is a mason like Christ. Who represents the holy temple of God. The Lord said he would prepare a place for the Saints in the Great Mansion or House of the Lord. [John 14:2,3] That house of God on Earth is the Great Pyramid. Could Imhetep be the architect of all the pyramids that represent Orion on earth? Some say Imhetep is the Nefer-Tem, son of Ptah (God). He is one of the many incarnations of Horus.

Im-hetep is Bringer of Peace. Sekhet-hetep is Fields of Peace. Hetep (hept or sept) also means Seven (Sabbath), Ark and Covenant. The Lord of the Sabbath, the Prince of Peace, the Ark of the Covenant and the Garden of God are all linked by one word. Aanru-Sekhet is the heavenly Jeru-Salem, city of Peace. It is Anu, Egypt. Hiero-Salem is Horus-Prince of Peace. Imhetep or I'mouthes is the Word of God "Before Abraham, I am," said the Lord.

The Lord said, "I am going away, and you shall seek Me, and will die in your sin. Where I go you cannot come. You are from beneath (terrestrial); I am from above (extra-terrestrial). Your are of this world; I am not of this world." [Matthew 8:21-23] He is the Sun of God that makes the voyage through the sea of space and returns triumpetly as the rising Sun.[-Matthew 24:27-31] The place or mansion He has prepared for the Saints is called New JeruSalem, the House of the Lord. When He comes, He shall bring it to earth. It shall set upon Mt. Zion which is represented by the Great Pyramid which is missing the head stone. [Revelation 21:10]

Immaculate Conception

The shafts of the Great Pyramid point toward the constellation of Orion. The one from the Queens chambers points directly to Sirius. The one from the King's chamber points toward the Belt of Orion. The constellation of Orion, appearing as the Son of Man with a Staff in one hand and ankh in the other, represents Osirus. The star Sirius is his queen Isis. According to the Egyptian texts, Osirus is killed by Seth and torn in 14 pieces on the 14th day of the first month. Which is the full moon and Pass-over. Then six months later, at the Fall Feast (of Ingathering), the Queen Isis gathers together the parts of the king just long enough to impregnate her during the appearance of Orion in the heavens. Yet his penis is missing, so she is given a metaphysical phallus and the spiritual seed from heaven. She conceives during the peak of her cycle at the winter solstice. Nine months later, is the Dawn rising of Sirius; which it now represents Horus.

The Belt of Orion represents the pelvis and the place of potency. The Lord said, "girdle your loins." An erect phallus means power or potency. The man of God possesses the power to over come the natural and supernatural. That power from on high is God's Spirit. The power that makes it possible for us to be reborn. When the holy Spirit moved over Mary, she conceived a new life in her womb. The Buckle of Isis is the mate to the Belt of Orion. It represents the vagina & uterus (watery womb) of the sea of space called Nun. As the Morning star Sirius, Atum-Ra-Horus was Son of God long before Osiris became Son of Man (or human).

June 21-22 is the summer solstice and the helical rising of Aldebaran in the constellation of Hyades in the House of Taurus. The helical or dawn rising is the appearance of the star just before sunrise. Helio is the sun-god called Sol (as in Solar and solstice) by the Romans, Hades by the Greeks and Amon-Re by the Egyptians. This is Satan's high day. July 19-23: 28 days (one moon) later is the dawn rising of Rigel, the brightest star in Orion. Aug.16-20: 28 days (another moon or lunar month) is the dawn rising of Sirius the brightest star in the sky. The Son of God is the Bright Morning Star. [Revelation 22:16] Sept.18-22: one moon or month later is the autumn equinox. Which is the Day of Atonement and Feast of Ingathering.

Human gestation is 280 days or 10 (28 day) months (moons). After 9 months of pregnancy, she gives birth on the tenth month. Just as prophecies predict.

Aton Atones for Sin

On the spring equinox, is the death of Christ on Passover and his resurrection three days later. The three days is three months in the original Egyptian version. The Son of Man (Osiris) was reborn the Son of God (Horus). The Passover lamb was raised as the Lion-King or Sphinx. This is Horus' redemption of the body of Osiris. Father and Son were reconciled as One. The body of Osiris is the body of believers. Aton did atone for the sins of man. So they made be "at one" with God. At-one-men-t; means men at one with Aton. Who are the body of believers under one God. Who is the head or Godhead. The Word of God says, "We are in Christ" and "Christ is in Us." Aton-Re is the Son of God who died for our past sins. He will not die again for the future sins we commit on purpose. [Hebrews 6:4-6 10:26-29] The Egyptians confess: "I have not purposely sinned". Read the book "Orion Mystery" by Robert Bauval and Adrian Gilbert.

The Ascension of Jesus was forty days after his resurrection on Passover. Fifty days (seven weeks) after Passover is Pentecost; the coming of the Holy Spirit. According to the Egyptians, Orion-Osiris rose 70 days after Passover, not 50. The 7 weeks (sabbaths) should have been 7 (10 day) weeks or 10 (7 day) weeks. Orion ascends from the underworld in July/August. Thoth is the Comforter who is ever-present while Horus is in heaven. Thoth was present at Horus' immaculate conception.

The process of embalming a body takes 70 days. This is the same length of time that Orion is out of sight in the underworld. Osiris-Orion is not seen for 70 days and then he reappears. He is ready to impregnate Isis-Sirius with the divine seed. It is now the autumn equinox, the 17th day of the month of Hathor. Nine months later is the dawn rising of Sirius (70 days past spring equinox) and Osiris' rebirth as Horus. By the next autumn equinox (30 days), Sirius now represents Horus full-grown, the heir to the Kingdom of Osiris.

Horus' childhood lasted only 12 months; from conception to adulthood. The Bible records Jesus as 12 years old, then says nothing about the missing years until his adulthood. The explanation is; there was no lost years.

According to the book The Mystical Year, September 29th is the Festival of Michaelmas (Michael reborn). Michael is the Mon-archangel and the heavenly name of the only begotten Son of God. Sept.24th is the time of Osiris' birth, during the Feast of Ingathering (the autumn equinox).

The Egyptian word for Pyramid is "Meri" which means "Place of Ascension." Ta-meri is the ancient name of Egypt. Ta means Earth and Meri means rising or ascending. The inundation of the Nile brings fertile soil. Meri-ta is the root of the word Meridian, the imaginary line going around the earth through the north and south poles which runs parallel with the Nile. When Orion reaches the celestial Meridian, it is at its peak of potency. Mer means to Plough as Osiris ploughs through the sea of space and plants his Seed (Sirius). Just as the Nile ploughs through Egypt. Tamarisk is the Tam-Asar (Tree of Life). The tree Osiris died in and Tem rose from. Tamar is of the roots of Christ's family tree. As is Ruth (Root) and Mary (Meri). [Matthew 1:3,5,16] Mare is the watery womb in the sea of space. Same as the Egyptian Mut (Mother). In Latin, Mere means Eve, the Mother of all living.

The day of the Lord Atum is in the Autumn. Just as the Feast of Ingathering is in the autumn. The Day of Trumpets announces the Kings trumpet victory over evil and death. The Day of Atonement is his sacrifice for our sins so we can be reconciled to the Father in the heavens. The Feast of Tabernacles (or Ingathering) is when the Lord comes to gather together the Saints who he transforms into sons of God. The Lord Atum-Ra shall rise in the east as the Sun of God or Morning star and gather the Saints from the four corners of the earth. [Mat.24:27-31 Levi.23:1-44 Deu.16 Num.28 & 29 John 7:2] The constellation of Orion appears during the autumn equinox. It remains in the southern sky for nine months. Sirius represents Isis as Mother pregnant with Child. During the summer months it disappears from sight. May, June and July are the high days of Amen-Ra-Set. Who is the evil sun of God called Satan. He is at peak power at the summer solstice (June 22). Then just before the autumn equinox, Sirius reappears as the Dawn rising and rebirth of the good Sun of God. Isis, as Sirius, is spelt Sept in Egyptian. From which we got September. Isis sacrifices herself; dying in child birth for her Son's sake. Sirius now represents Horus, the Bright Morning star (AKA the star of Bethleham). [Revelation 22:16]

Kingdom of Lights

It has been discovered that the pyramid's size and position represent the stars of Orion. The pyramids were covered with highly polished limestone. So they shined like stars. The Egyptians were reproducing heaven on earth. A replica of the heavenly bodies. [Hebrew 9:24] The Milky-way was considered the celestial Nile river running beside Orion. As the annual rising of the fertile Nile, which gave life to the land, coincided with the rising of Orion in the heavens. [Jeremiah 46:8 Isaiah 19:5-8] The Nile's banks, seven miles wide, were the only fertile land in the midst of a desert. Just as Osirus fertilized Isis who represents mother earth. Who gave birth to the first man, Adam, and the second Adam, Christ. The first is an earthling (terrestrial) and the second an extra-terrestrial. [1 Cor. 15:40,41-49] The Nile floods after the summer solstice and then recedes in the Autumn, leaving the land fertile. The land is ready for the sowing of the seed and rebirth. Compare this to the Great Flood of Noah's day that washed away the evil seed and prepared the earth for the good seed.

The Nile's birth waters break and a Sun is born! The Delta triangle is the uterus (vulva) and nativity of the Messiah. Mes means born of water. The Nile is the navel or umbilical cord and the source is the rain from heaven. Hathor, the holy cow, nurses the Child Horus. The Delta triangle is the Lotus (Tree of life) rooted in the water of life, the symbol of rebirth: Atum to Osiris to Horus. Moses (Meses) was brought forth from the waters of the Nile as a type of the Messiah.

He is Sun of God and the Morning Star. [Rev. 22:16] Who shall rise in the east.[Matthew 24:27-31] The Nile has seven streams in its delta. [Isaiah 11:15] Seven is the number of the Lord of the Sabbath. The water represents the life force of God called the holy Spirit, which waters the Tree of life (God's family tree). [Rev. 22:1,2 John 7:37,38] Sirius is separate from the constellation of Orion, the dwelling place of Osiris. Orion represents Osiris, Lord of Lower Egypt and Sirius represents his bride. Sirius is Heliopolis. The counterpart is New JeruSalem, the bride of the Son of Man. [Revelation 21:2,9,10] The Son of Man shall come in His kingdom just as Horus was the child in the womb of Isis. [Matthew 16:27,28] The Book of Job mentions Orion, Pleiades and the Bear. [Job 9:9] The constellation of the Bear is what the shafts on the north side of the Pyramid point to when the southern shafts are aligned up to Orion. Orion means "Coming Prince". Pleiades means "the congregation to be judged". Pleiades is also called the Seven Sister Stars. Arcturus means the Great Bear. "He made the Bear, Orion, and the Pleiades, and the chambers of the south;" [Job 9:9] Where we see the Big Dipper, the Egyptians saw the tool for opening the mouth. Allowing the Breath of life (Spirit) to enter the dead Pharaoh. He would then resurrect or be reborn a son of God like Osiris. The Big Dipper is a seven star constellation. Orion is seven stars representing Osiris plus Sirius representing Isis. Seven is the number of the Lord of the Seventh day. Who is the coming Prince and Judge of mankind. "He made the Pleiades and Orion; He turns the shadow of death into the rising sun..." [Job 38:31,32 Amos 5:8]

The Great Pyramid's north shaft from the king's ante-chamber points to Draco the Dragon. The Dragon is Set-Typhon who sealed Osiris in the sarcophagus (ark) and sent it up river. The north shaft from the queen's ante-chamber points to Ursa Minor. As it was Queen Isis who found the body of Osiris and took him home. The Little Bear (Bar) is depicted as a bull's leg in the Egyptian zodiac; part of Taurus the bull. Just as Pleiades is part of Taurus as the Seven Hathors or Seven Sisters. Ursa Minor represents Baal the baby bull (and baby Bear) who tore Osiris to 14 pieces. Ursa Major (Urt) is the mother of Ursa Minor. The entrance of the Pyramid descends down to a deep dark pit. Draco, the Dragon, Typhon, Apollyon is cast into the abyss or bottomless pit for killing Osiris. [Revelation 20:1-3] The Lake of fire is reserved for the antichrist and the Beast (body members) will follow him.

The Zodiac of Denderah depicts Ursa Minor as a dog. Therefore, at the moment that the southern shaft points to Sirius the Dog star, the northern shaft points to the spurious dog in the circumpolar stars.

Upper Egypt is in the south. They perceived the Nile as the source of life coming from the summit of God. The water of life comes down river through Egypt, and empties in the Mediterranean Sea. [Revelation 22:1,2 Ezekiel 47:12] "The chambers of the south" would be the kings chambers or the throne from which the waters of life come. They observed the stars to the south. South meant up as in "up river" that continued past the horizon into the Sea of space. The Milky Way is the celestial Nile. It was the Romans who came along and turned the world upside down by saying they were the on top of the world. They redrew the maps with Europe up on top and Africa down. Even though the earth spins in space and has no up or down.

Pharaoh is king and high priest of Egypt. Per-aa means Great House of which he is head of the house of the Lord. From the same root word as Pharisee which means separated ones or sanctified ones. They are set apart as special men of God. Since Pharaoh = Great House and Osiris = Asrael, Pharaoh Osiris means House of Israel. The Pharaoh is the Sun of God here on Earth. In Greek, Pharaoh is Pharaus (Harus). As Pro-Tem, he stands in the place of the Sun of God called Tem-Horus. Until the day Sun of God (Atum) rises in the east to rule the earth. From the name Sirius we get 'iris' or the eye of Horus. The seal on the back of the U.S. one dollar bill pictures the "eye of Horus" on the pyramid as the all seeing Sun of God. [Revelation 5:6] Annuit means Temple of Anu, while Coeptis (Coptic) is the antithesis Christian Egyptians of Thebes (Apt). This is the Yin vs. Yang; Upper vs. Lower; Lie vs. Truth.

All Pharaohs, even the females, where portrayed with false beards because only sons of God the Father can enter God's kingdom. The beard is shape of the feather of Maat. It means the Pharaoh speaks the Truth or Word of God. In the Gospel of Thomas, the Lord says he will transform the daughters into sons of God. He speaks metaphysically, not physically.

The Creator and Godhead
Ptah (Phath) = God the Father
God dwells in the first heaven alone
Pa-Neter is Pater or Father of Neter

The Creation and Godbody
Nu or Nun = primeval watery womb or material matrix
The sea of space: dark and void of life
Neteru is Nut and her suns
Neter is mother Nature
Ennead == nine, the number of human gestation

Atum-Ra = Sun of God
Horus the Elder (a.k.a. Khepera)
Morning star and Light unto mankind

Shu = Holy Spirit + Tef-Nut
The cosmos or stars of heaven or suns of God
The sons of God dwell in the second heaven

Geb = Earth Nut = our solar system
Shu = Atmosphere or Sky: the air being the breath of life
The sons of Adam (Atum) dwell in the third heaven

Osiris	Isis	Nephthys	Seth (Amen-Ra)
Son of Man	Mother Earth	Mother Nature	evil Son of God

{Isis and Nephthys are twin sisters}

Horus = Son of God (Osiris reborn)
{Sun of Righteousness}
Horus the Younger

Seth is his evil brother
{i.e. Satan and Lucifer}

The Creator is part of all living things through His Spirit called the life force. Patah was the original mummy. His mind was active, but His body was lifeless. The Creator is the Master Mind. The creation is His mummified body. From His body, He created the cosmos. The virgin body of Nun gave birth to the first begotten Sun, Atum-Ra. In the macrocosm, His atoms are the solar systems moved by His Spirit. The suns are the sons of the Father in heaven. In the microcosm, His atoms are in all things. His Holy Spirit activates all living things. The Atom (Atum) is the quintessential element of everything in the material universe. [Romans 1:20-25]

E.A. Wallis Budge, late keeper of the Egyptian antiquities in the British Museum says, "Egyptians believed in One God, who was self-existent, immortal, invisible, eternal, omniscient, almighty, and inscrutable; the maker of heaven, earth, and the Other World; the creator of men and women, animals, birds, and creeping things, trees and plants, and the incorporeal beings who were the messengers that fulfilled his wish and word." The word "Pa-neter" means God the Father. The plural form "neteru" means "gods", "suns of God", "stars" or "Company of gods". Likewise, in Hebrew, "El" means God and "elohim" means "gods", "sons of God" or "hosts of heaven". Budge says, "The Egyptian "gods" formed a sort of court or council of the God of the Egyptians, and they are the equivalents of the Arch-angels and the Order of Angels which we find in other systems of religion." The Egyptians believed that these "gods" were manifestations of the One true God.

There are three companies of gods: 1) the Greater company of Ptah. 2) the company of Atum as Lord of Hosts. He is archangel of his one-third of the angels. 3) the Little company of Set-amen. Setan cause one-third of the angels to fall from God's favor. [Revelation 12:3-9] The Egyptians says: "One and Alone, without a second. One, the Maker of all things, the Spirit, the hidden spirit, the maker of spirits. He existed in the beginning, when nothing else was. What is he created after he came into being. Father of beginnings, eternal, infinite, everlasting. Hidden one, no man knoweth his form, or can search out his likeness; he is hidden to gods and men and is a mystery to his creatures. No man knows how to know Him; his name is a mystery and is hidden. His names are innumerable. He is truth, he lives on truth, he is the king of truth. He is life, through him man lives; he gave life to man, he breathed life into his nostrils. He is father and mother, the father of fathers, the mother of mothers. He begets, but was not begotten; he brings forth, but was not brought forth; he begat himself and gave birth to himself. He created, but was not created, he made his own form and body. He himself is existence; he neither increases nor diminishes. He made the universe, the world, what was, what is, and what shall be. What his heart conceived came to pass forthwith; when he speaks what results therefrom endures forever. He is the father of the gods. He is merciful to his worshiper, he hears him who calls on Him,

He rewards his servants, those who acknowledge Him He knows, he protects His follower."

God established the natural and supernatural laws and set them to motion. Then He appointed His favored Son, Horus (Jesus) as Lord of the Earth. Horus sits on a great throne at the side of God. Repa means Sun of Ptah or rightful heir. Since Atum-Horus created man, his Father (Patah) is our Grandfather. Our word "father" comes from the anagram of the Egyptian word for father (at-f). at-f or f-at + her (horus). Christ said, "Do not call anyone on earth your father; for One is your Father, He who is in heaven." [Matthew 23:9] From Pat-ra, we get patriarch and paternal. Pater or Peter is the Latin equivalent. He is Patah the Potter, at the wheel of time, creator of the cosmos. The Greeks identified him with He-phaistos the black-smith. Mut or Mot + her (Horus) = Mother. Mut is the Theban version of Nut; the watery womb that gave birth to Atum-Horus. Mut is NOT a goddess or even a being any more than "mother nature" (Mut nuter) is.

The Many Names of the Two Suns of God

Atum-Ra-Horus is God's ambassador from God's kingdom to earth. Ra means son or sun of God. As in sun Ray. All the stars are suns of God. - From Re; we get re-birth, re-surrection, re-deemed, etc...

Atum (Tem) is Archangel and Lord over all suns of God (angels). Atum is the ancient spelling. Atum was born in the Autumn. Isis is the Greek spelling for the Egyptian Aset, which is also spelt Sept. From Sept, we get September, the month Isis gave birth to Atum-Ra-Horus. He is also Horus of the Horizon as he is now in the night sky as Osiris in the constellation of Orion. Septet (Sirius) is the counterpart in heaven. Septet is Sirius; the star of Isis who sacrifices herself so her Son can take her place in the heavens. Anu is also the city of Heliopolis: one of the pyramid cities that make up the copy of Orion on earth. Just as there is a heavenly JeruSalem and an earthly JeruSalem. Jesus Christ is: Lord of the Sabbath, Sun of Righteousness (Atum-Ra), Bright Morning star (Sirius), Son of Man (Osiris) and Son of God (Horus).

Autum is an execution by hanging; to fall from a tree as a leaf in autumn. Christ was hanged on a tree. [Acts 5:30 10:39] Heru-ur (Har Wer) 'Horus the Elder' or 'Horus the Ancient'. The good Sun of God was created on the first day. Her-ur is depicted as a hawk-headed lion as he is Atum-Horus, the star Sirius, begotten in the age of Leo the Lion. He incarnated as Osiris or Son of Man. Then he died and resurrected as Heru-p-khart 'Horus the Younger', Son of God. The Greeks called him Harpocrates. Christ is called the second Adam. In Egypt, he is Atum-Horus 2nd or Younger.

Osiris is spelled Sar, Ser, Sir, Asar and Asir. Sir became a title of respect like; Caesar, Kaisar, T-Sar, etc. Sar-cophagus is the coffer or coffin of Sar. Nasarsert or Nazareth is the Nativity of Sar. It is the same as Ansar; Osiris of Anu (Heliopolis). Anher is Horus of the heavenly Anu. Nasert (Nut) is the mother of Horus. Nasarsert is the Cosmic Egg from which Horus the Hawk was born. From Nasarsert we get, "He shall be called a Nazarene." [Matthew 2:23] Soar (Sar) comes from Osiris who transformed into Horus the Hawk who soars in the sky. Herr is German for mister. Horus is the master. Her is "heir" in Latan. Horus is heir to the throne. Osiris' body members take on his sur-name (Sar-name). Simon was surnamed Peter (Pater). Pater is God the Father. The body of believers are part of his family with his family name. Sol is the Roman rendering of Sar. Surreal = Sar-real (supernatural). Isr is the Hebrew for Savior. Asr or Asar is the Egypt for Osiris.

Har-Pa-Neb-Taui 'Horus of two lands' He is ruler over Upper and Lower Egypt. This is the original garden of God or kingdom of God: Field of Reeds. Horticulture is Horus' garden.

Hor-khenti Irti 'Horus who rules the two eyes'. He has the all seeing eyes that oversee the two lands of Upper and Lower Egypt. Represented by the stars Sirius in Canis Major and Aldebaran the red star in Hyades. Hyades is the horns and head of Taurus the bull. It was Set who stold Upper Egypt from Horus by force. Represented by Aldebaran the red eye in the constellation of Taurus. In the battle, it is said, Set tears out one of the eyes of Horus while Horus castrates Set. Set (Satan) is now ruler of this wicked world outside of Orion's kingdom. Yet he not able to procreate. The two eyes of Horus are NOT the sun and the moon as many so-called scholars claim!

"O thou seer who beholds his Father! O keeper of the books of Thoth!" This refers to the Son of God who reveals his Father. [John 1:18 5:37] The books are the life story of every soul and the Book of life. [Revelation 20:12] Hor Nubti 'Horus conqueror of Set'. In the end Horus shall conquer all evil and unite Egypt. He is Lord of the Earth and King in God's kingdom.

Harakhty (Heraktes) 'Horus of the horizon'. Heraktes is obviously where the Greek's got the name Herakles. Horizon = Horus' zone or nome.

Heru-Tem-Akhuti (Harmakis of the Greeks) 'Horus-Tem is on the horizon'. Ra-Tem-Khepera-Heru-khuti is the name of the great Sphinx of at Gizeh, symbol of resurrection of the King of kings. The Sphinx (Khepera) faces the eastern horizon as it watches over the pyramids of the kings; Khufu, Khephre, and Menkaure. Kheper-a = Keeper of the Way.

Har-march-is is another name of the sphinx. Strangely within the name is the word "march". There is a famous saying "if March goes in like a lamb, it comes out like a lion." March is the spring equinox when the Passover Lamb of God was slain, yet rose again as the Lion of Judah. [Revelation 5:5,6] Horakhti is the heavenly image of Leo the Lion, where as Hor-Tem-akhuti is the earthly image of the Sphinx.

Har-Makheru = Word of Truth. Ma = Truth and Kheru or Heru = Word. Heresy = Horus says. Heresy is dogma contrary to what Horus says as the Word of God.

Heru-Pa-Khrat (Har-po-crates of the Greeks) is 'Horus the child'. This is the Madonna and Child. The Child has his index finger to his mouth as if in thought and a gesture of silence. The Quran says the new born Christ told his mother to remain silent while he answered all questions.

Karast (Krst) is Christ. It also means to anoint and embalm a mummy. Osiris-Karast is Christ wrapped in linen. [Mark 15:46 16:1 Matthew 27:59] He was previously anoint with oil. [Mat.26:12] The Greeks got Christos "to anoint" from the Egyptian Karast. Horus-Karast is Jesus the Christ Child wrapped in swaddling clothes. Which connects his birth with his death. Christ = hrs-t = Horus-Tem. The wooden coffin of Osiris becomes the cradle of Horus. The mummy in the mommy (mother earth); the Sarcophagus-Tomb becomes the womb of A-Tum. "I am coffined in an ark like Horus, to whom his cradle is brought." The Bark of Osiris is like the Ark that saved Noah and his family. Ark in hieroglyphics means the end of time. T-ark means Covenant as the Ark of the Covenant. Atum is the Word of God within. Metamorphosis of the butterfly is a metaphor of rebirth. The cocoon or chryssalis is Christ Saris (Karast Osiris). This is the metaphysical metamorphosis of the Son of Man into the Son of God.

Tem or Atem is the root of the word Temple. The Lord said, "destroy this temple", referring to his mortal body. Tem-ple is Tem + place or Tem's palace. Atom or Thom is Thoth, the Word of God or Word of Truth. Hathor is the Holy House or Temple of Tem. Isis is the house of Horus. Tem also means people gathered together (a congregation).

Mes means to be born again of water as in baptism. From this the Hebrews got Messiah. The "iah" means Lord. It is the root of the name Moses who was drawn from the water. Hermes means Horus born of water.

IHUH is the son of Ptah who later became the tetragramaton IHWH (Yahweh). The tet-ra-gramma-aton is four Egyptian words. Tet is the symbol of the tree or pillar of strength. Ra is the Sun of God. Gramma is writing (from grammar). Aton (Atom) is Horus the good Son of God. Combined, it means that Aton-Ra is the living Word of God born of God's family tree. Tetra-teuch is the four letters or books of Thoth (Genesis, Exodus, Leviticus, Numbers). Iusu became Iesus in Latin or Jesus in Greek.

Imhetep (Imhotep) is Horus. Hetep means Prince and Hepti (septi or septem in Latin) means Seven. The Lord of the Sabbath is the Prince of Peace. Imouthis is the Greek spelling. From the Mouth of God came the Word of God.

Shemsu Heru = Followers of Horus. During the age of Ares, the descendants of Shem, son of Noah, became followers of Horus. Abraham was a Shem-sa or son of Shem. [Gen.10] Sa means Son.

Bennu means Son of Nu. The Bennu bird is the same as the Phoenix. Heron is Horus of On (Annu or Heliopolis). Same as Horus the Hawk.

Amen-Ra-Set

Amen (Amon, Amun, Amen) means "the hidden one" just as the Greek "Hades" means "the Unseen". Amenta means hidden underground (ie. grave). Occult also means "hidden". Satan is invisible. Sheta means hidden or secret. The root of Sheta is Set. D'amon is daemon or demon just as D'evil is 'to do evil'.

Omni-potent = Omen-potent = Amen-potent or Amen all powerful. Omni = All = Pan. Ominous means ill-omened or portentous. Omniscient = All knowing. The root is Gnosis or Gnostic.

Min (aMin or Amen) means Moon. He/She is the counterpart of the sun-god Amen-Ra. She is his dark side that rules the nights. Hathor has cow horns on her head. The crescent moon and the cows horns are the same shape. They represent the life to death cycle of mother nature. Men is the root of Menstrual period which is equal to the moon's cycle of 28 days.

Mint or Menat is the post, stake or pole that Osiris was bound to (the crucifix). It is the mooring-post or mourning post which the women (Isis/Mary) sat around. On the celestial level, it is the North Pole.

Set (Seth, Seti, Sety) was born premature; he ripped his way out of the womb of Nut. He was a disgusting sight for his skin was white and his hair red. He is the white sun with the red ultra-violent rays at sunset. This is the red halo of Helio, the sun-god. Lucifer means Daystar or the sun that rises and sets daily. The curse of Cain, son of Satan, was to be turned white (leprosy).

Set-Typhon represents the monster hurricanes, twisters, and tornadoes that do massive destruction. This connects him to Amen, the Wind-god. The prince of the power of the air is Satan. [Ephesians 2:2] He is Baal, the storm-god. Nature is his mother. Likewise, Monsoon is Mon or Amon.

The Apis Bull and the Asp Serpent are his symbols. Bull is Baal or Beelzebub. Set is short for Satan the Serpent. Just as Satan is: that old serpent, the great dragon. [Revelation 12:9] Baal-Set (Shet) = Bull-Shit or to Lie (Beliel).

Uraeus 'the coiled cobra'. The sea serpent or sea of space that surrounds the sun (Ra). This is obviously where the Greeks got Uranus (Heaven).

The Apep (Apophis) serpent swallows the sun at sunset and it is reborn from its body at sunrise. This is Apollyon in the Bible. Who is the Serpent of Old and the blood-thirsty dragon of destruction.

King Apophis was a name used by the Hyksos kings who worshipped Seth. Pepi of the Theban Book of the Dead is Apepi (Apophis).

The Apis (Hapi in Egyptian) bull wears the royal uraeus (asp). The Apis and the Asp are attributes of Satan and Amen the Bull of heaven. Apis = Alpha in Greek and Amen calls himself the First One. This is Bull! C + alpha = calf; as in the Golden Calf.

Herodotus says the black Apis bull has a white triangular blaze on his forehead, the figure of an eagle on his back, the figure of a beetle on his tongue, and he had double hairs on his tail. There has never been a bull on earth to fit this description. But there is in heaven. Taurus the Bull is black, the stars of Hyades form the triangle of the bull's head and horns, Pleiades forms a mark on its back as the seven Hathors who wear vulture head-dresses and cow's horns. It has a forked tongue as well as a forked tail. Sar-apis is the Orion-Taurus constellation. Serapeum is the House of Taurus.

Set's star is Hades (Hyades) in the constellation of Taurus the Bull. The Setites are the followers of Set; the fallen stars (angels) who battle against the Horus child (Michael) and his angels (Shemsu-Heru). [Revelation 12:3-9]

Taueret (Ta-Urt) is the cow goddess of childbirth. From the word Taurus. Hat-kheb, the hippo-(water cow)-mother, is another aspect of Hathor the cow who gave birth to the baby Bull (Baal). The Northern stars of the Arctic circle (ArcTurus) are her suns. Taurus is Tartarus of the Greeks tale. As the Greeks came in at the tail end of the Egyptian kingdom. Ta-urt is the matrix of Ursa Minor the dog Up-uat, antithesis of Anup (Anubis) the dog star Sirius in Canis Major. Anup is Anti-upuat. Ursa Minor is also the Little Bear (Baal) and the Baby Bull (Golden Calf) of Taurus the Bull.

Sebek is the crocodile headed one. He is a cold blooded killer on land or in water. Sebau fiends are the angels who fell to earth. [Jude 6 Revelation 12:9] Both have Seb as root of the word. Seb means of the Earth. They are the evil powers on earth that cause: death, darkness, destruction, drought, or deluge. These fallen angels are called: demons, genies, jinns, evil spirits, familiar spirits, ghosts, etc...

The serpent Sa-ta (Son of the Earth) is obviously Satan. Sata is the serpent who stood upright on human legs until he fell from favor. Sata is Set, son of Seb (Earth) and Nut along with Osiris, Isis and Nephthys. [Genesis 3:14] The hippopotamus, crocodile, turtle, scorpion, hog, frog and dog are the unclean animals of Set. Sut took the form of a black pig when ripping the eye from Horus. Likewise, Attis was killed by a wild boar. Set, as the black pig, is banished by a baboon just as the Hebrew "scapegoat" called Azazel. Could this be Israel being banished from Egypt?

The animals sacrificed by the followers of Osiris were: the Bull representing Taurus, the antelope (spelt Ari or Aries in Egyptian), and the duck (Smennu). Smennu (duck) = S-amen-nu or Amen of Nu. Smen is goose. The duck and goose being symbols of Set-Amen who rules over the land, sea and air. The golden egg laid by Mother Goose (Geb) is the sun (Ra) reborn on Dec.25th. The yellow yoke is the sun in the primeval waters (plasma). At the crack of dawn, Set-Amen came forth from Am-Smen (Mother goose). Seb also means Five, the number of the Satanic star or Pentacle. Smen is also the minions of Set.

The names African-Americans use for white people; "cracker" and "honky" may have roots in Egypt. The goose is the sacred animal of Amen & Set (Satan). It is called the Great Cackler for its loud obnoxious honking. "Kaka" is to cackle like a goose (i.e. babble like an idiot). The Arabian "Raka". [Matthew 5:22] Part of the hieroglyphic for the serpent Sata is a goose. Sata is the evil spirit who possesses people. The serpent Sata had human legs until he deceived Eve and was cursed to creep in the dust. [Genesis 3:13,14] The term "foul play" may be derived from "fowl play" of that subtle serpent, Sata. A "quack" is someone pretending to be what he is not or claiming to do what he can not. This is Set, the charlatan, masquerading as Horus.

Goose is of the sub-species called Anserinae (Anti-Sar of Anu).

Monastery is Mon's stars. They are the houses of the Zodiac that belong to Amen. Amen's ministers are the fallen stars.

Khons or Khonsu the son of Amun and Mut. These three formed the Satanic trinity at Thebes in Upper Egypt. This is obviously Kronus of Greek mythology. Mut is both mother and wife to Amun. Chrons is the antiChrist. Khons Hor is the Great Impostor pretending to be Horus. Compare Khon-sut, the Dog star or Cainine, with Cain son of Satan. Khent means South, land of Sut. Khen means to be carried away as by an adversary. With the determinative of Sut, we have Khensu, the Antichrist who will rapture away the unsuspecting. In Polynesia, Kane (i.e. Sut) is the evil brother of Khoro (i.e. Horus).

Monday comes after Sunday. Amen, the sun, and Mut produce Khonsu the Moon. Khunsu is stationed in the zodiac of Denderah, in the sign of Pisces, figured with the pig (Amen's animal) and the full moon which is Easter (Sun's day), the sign of the solar revitalization. The solar revolution is an insurrection against Horus. [A Book of the Beginnings by Gerald Massey page 355] Khunsu is pretending to be the Angel of Light. [2 Corinthians 11:13-15] Sirius is the stellar resurrection of Horus on the equinox. Jesus is Horus reincarnated during the age of Pisces and resurrected at Passover (spring equinox).

Amun-Ra is called "king of the gods" which is "suten neteru" in Egyptian. The root of Suten is Sut or Set. Just as Zeus-Amon was the self proclaimed "king of the gods". Thebes, the city of Amen, was called Diospolis, the city of Zeus, by the Greeks.

Sut or Suth is Set the lord of the land in the South (Upper Egypt). Sut is an abbreviation of the word South.

Sutte or Sati is the ritual sacrifice of the widow upon the death of her husband. The evil kings of Upper Egypt performed this murder, in honor of Set. Re-Set is Rebel or Re-Baal. As it was the Devil who rebelled against the LORD.

Since Set is brother of Osiris, he is Uncle Set to Horus. Over time, Uncle Set-Amen was abbreviated to Uncle Sam. Sam means West where the sunsets in Amenta. The Sami are the united union of evil workers, who are Set's fishers of men. They set up "nets" to entrap the unsuspecting. Sam means to gather together for destruction. [Revelation 16:16 19:17-21] It also means to devour. As the Ammit beast, at the Judgment Hall, shall devour her own young, Smen. Samhi is the left hand in Egyptian. The lambs of God are at the right hand of God. The goats are on the left. Khnum is Amun as the bearded goat or serpent. Uncle Sam is depicted like a goat. [Matthew 25:31-33-46] Smen are the sons of Satan. Khnum is the Upper Egyptian corruption of Ptah as Creator.

Mentu or Montu is the great impostor from Upper Egypt. He was depicted as a falcon-headed sun-god, like Horus, but is not. Men-tu is hybrid name: Amen the Warrior combined with Tum (Atum). From Montu and Min (both depicted with erections) we get the Latin Mentula (Penis).

Names are often linked to show relationships between two or more entities. Ptah-Tem-Ra would be Tem Son of Ptah. Atum-Shu-Nun would be Atum the Spirit in Nun. The Hebrews did the same in combining El (God) or iah (Lord) with names to show their relationship to God. Michael and Gabriel were not God, but "of God". Isaiah and Zechariah are "of the Lord". Ra would be similar to Elohim in Hebrew which means "sons of God".

When Amen or Set uses the names; Ra, Osiris, Atum, and Horus, he is impersonating the good Son of God. This impostor is what the Bible calls the Antichrist who wants you to believe he is the real Christ. This is not difficult as Amen-Ra, like Lucifer, originally was a good Sun of God. The Upper Egyptians made Amen the Creator instead of Atum. Using names like Amen-Ra-Osiris would link Amen with Osiris. This is a corruption! In reality, he is the Anti-Christ pretending to be the Angel of Light. [2 Corinthians 11:13-15] The Upper Egyptian pharaohs were believed to be sons of Amun. While the Lower Egyptian pharaohs were sons of Osiris, like Horus.

Sometimes the name will show attributes or places. Such as: Amente or Amenta-the land of Amen called the Valley of the Dead Kings. Osiris-Khent-Amentet means Osiris Lord of the Land of the Dead. The deceased (manes) connects his name with Osiris (as in Osiris-Ani or Sir Ani), therein becoming part of the body of Osiris. The body of pyramids of Lower Egypt represent Osiris-Orion on earth. The Lord said, "Destroy this temple and in three days I will raise it up." [John 2:19] In Hebrew: Sheol (hell) means land of the dead or grave or cemetery. The word cemetery comes from Amente-re meaning Land of Amen-Ra. Manu or Amenu is the place where Amen-Ra sets in the west; representing death. Set-Amentet; the Valley of the dead Kings west of the Nile.

Amenta is translated as Hell in the Bible, from the Viking deity Hel. It also has a heavenly counterpart. The Greeks called it the Underworld of Hades. This is the place of Amen-Set in the constellation of Taurus where the main set of stars is Hyades. The heavenly place of Osiris is the constellation of Orion and its companion star, Sirius. Anu is the birthplace of Sirius (Atum-Horus) in heaven. The counterpart on earth is On (or An). The Greeks named it Heliopolis. As above, so below. [Hebrews 9:24] Amenta is under-the-ground, not under-the-world or the underworld of heaven. Amenta is land of the dead.

Tuat means the Land of the living. "at" means; land, region, place or abode. "Tu" is aTum or Tem. Amenta is the underground land of the dead. Amen = Death and the Manes are the Dead. On (An or Annu) is the birth place of Horus. No (Thebes) is the birth place of Set. Notice the letters are reverse for Set, the contrary one. Ham (Kham) is the father of all Africans. [Genesis 10:6-14] Khamat or Khemet or Kemet is the land of Ham. Uat is Lower Egypt, Mera-ta or Ta-Mera (land of Upper Egypt) and Ken-Set is Nubia. Wa-Set is Thebes (No). Deshret is the Desert or Red Land ruled by Set. It is the Barren land or land of Bar. Bar = Baal.

Tuat is also spelt Duat as it has Dual meanings. There is a heavenly as well as a earthly region. Uat is Lower Egypt. "As in heaven, so on earth." Tuat is the area around the constellation of Orion and its companion star Sirius. Tuat is the Lower Heaven in Nut (Heaven at night). Ta-urt is the Upper Heaven. All the stars south of the North-Pole-star are in the Tuat. All stars north of the North-Pole-star are in the Taurt. The stars Arctic circle; Ursa Major (Great Bear), Ursa Minor (Little Bear or Baal) and Draco are the Am-Smen.

Nu is the heavens in the day time which are ruled by Amen-Ra the sun-god and his son Khonsu the moon-god. In other words, Set-Amen rules the night and the day. That is until Atum returns from Orion to be our Sun of Righteousness. For us mortals, we must shield against the fiery darts of the evil sun-god and the arrows of Eros (Cupid). [Ephesians 6:16] The ancient Egyptians were night-hawks who watched the nightly heavens of Nut.

The Upper Egyptians changed many names; Tefnut & Bast the Cat became Sekhmet the lion who slayed the Apep serpent, Nephthys became Neith or Hathor, Atum-Horus became Amsu (Amen-Sut), Horus became Khonsu or Montu the moon god, Nut became Net, Mut or Mot (Great Mother), the mother and consort of Amun. Making Amun the father of all gods.

Nephthys, as Nebt-hat (Lady of the House), was replaced by Hathor (House of Horus). In the Zodiac, she is Sirius (along with her twin sister Isis) in the House of Taurus. Ast (Isis), mother of Horus, was perverted into mother of Seth (Apt or Ursa Minor). Apt means Crib or Manger. It is the birthplace of Sothis, the spurious Dog star, antithesis of Sirius. Apt also means four-corners as is this North pole star. Ta-Apt or Aptet is also the land of Thebes, where Amen was born (created by man) (in the image of man).

The real mother of Set is the Ammit beast of Am-Smen who devours the dead. Sothis or Sept (S-apt) means the Seven stars of Ursa Minor. They tried to change it so that Set was the firstborn Sun of God instead of Horus. Sirius (the Dog star) represents Isis, companion to Osiris-Orion and her child Horus. Horus came forth from Am-Tuat. Set came forth from Am-Smen.

The Pole-stars of Ursa Minor make up the spurious Dog star of Set, son of Ursa Major (Hat-Kheb). Khebt = Sept = Set of Apt. Together they make up the eight stars of the Smen (Set-amen). The Upper Egyptians corrupted the original just as the Romans corrupted the Greek mythology where Zeus became Jupiter, Hades became Pluto, etc. Satan mimics or mocks all that the Lord does.

Isis is Greek for Ast. Which the Canaanites corrupted into Astarte (Anat), the sister and wife of Baal. Astarte, Asherah and Ashtoreth are all connected to Ta-urt (Ammit), mother of the evil son. Isis was corrupted into Sati and her sister Nephthys into Anquet. Other names for Isis were; Amen-t, Men-at and Seth-at. The Upper Egyptians were creating new titles in order to connect Isis with Set-Amen. These corruptions wore the sun disk and cows horns of Hathor, which connects them to Taurus the Bull. Anubis is the Greek spelling for Anpu or Anup. Sothis is the Greek for Sirius. Sothis is Seth, the Upuat canine. Apis is the Greek for Hapi (bull). Apophis is Greek for the Egyptian Apep.

In the Theban Book of the Dead chapter 18, it says the first-born son of Osiris is Baba (Bebon) who was depicted as a Typhonic animal like Set. In fact, Baba is a form of Baal of Babylon. Baba = Apap. The priests of Thebes were trying to insert Set in the place of Horus under the alias of Baba. Horus is the firstborn and heir to the throne, not the bad baby, Baba. Compare Baba to Cain the firstborn of Eve and first murderer. Baba is Bar, the Little Bear constellation of Ursa Minor. He is the Great Impostor! It is he who tells his follows that they are going to heaven to be as stars in the Am-Smen. They claim the dog soldiers will become part of the dog heaven.

Amsu was a composite deity made by combining the attributes of Horus (Iusu) with those of Sut (Amen). Sometimes depicted as Siamese twins with one body and two heads (Horus & Set). Sami is the Egyptian word for United. Much like Hari-Hara (Vishnu and Shiva combined). Vishnu is the good and Shiva is the bad son of God. Ser (Osiris) and apis (bull) were combined to form Serapis or Sarapis. They united the good with the bad. Sometimes the American Indians combined the good with the bad in statues with a good side and a dark or evil side. Probably because they could not figure out if they were being punished by the good One or persecuted by the bad One. When prosperous, they did not know if they were being rewarded by the evil one or tested by the good one.

Originally, Hapi represented the Nile. During the inundation or annual flood, the Nile fertilized the earth. This was seen as Isis being fertile and ready for the divine seed to be planted. She is the watery womb of Horus just as Nut was the watery womb of Atum. Compare Apis to Apsu (Apsi) of the Sumerians which means Heavenly Water. Sar-apis would be Osiris-Isis in pro-creation. It was the perverted Upper Egyptians who corrupted Sar-apis into a horny bull. Osiris and Isis did not fornicate. Horus was the virgin birth. The union of Taurus the bull and the divine water cow (Mut, Ammit Hathor or Taurt) gave birth to Amen, the Bull of heaven or the Apis of the Nile. The Apis was conceived in heaven and born at Apt (Thebes).

The Isis-Set Connection

Set's primary attribute is darkness and chaos. The Apophis serpent represents the chaos within the darkness and fear of the unknown. Atum-Horus was born from the darkness of the watery womb of Nun. Horus the Child was born from the dark womb Isis or Ast. Therefore, the link of the dark watery womb and the firstborn Sun of God. Set and Aset represent that darkness from which the Light sprang forth. They share the same concept of Yin verses the Yang of Horus. Yin being female and darkness. Yang being male and light. Eve is Evening which is opposite of the Morning Sun. Since Sirius represents Ast or Isis, the Egyptians spelt it Sothis or Sethis; the light born of the darkness. The hieroglyph for goddess is a serpent! This explains why Hera was often portrayed as the antagonist or adversary of Herakles, her son. Much like Hathor is the dark side of mother nature (mut-neter). Hera is Hara (the Destroyer) of Hinduism. Heva is the serpent who deceived Eve. [Anacalypsis volume 2 page 113] Eve equates to Evening and Evil (mother nature's dark side). "Hell hath no fury like a woman scorned." Eve being maternal materialism (mother earth) or love of this materialistic world. The cycle of life to death. Nature's law says, kill or be killed and mother earth is the grave we return to. Mother nature produces earthquakes, hurricanes, and typhoons. Set is Typhon and Satan is prince of the power of the air. God's law says, "You shall NOT kill." and "Vengeance is Mine." God's gift is the cycle from death to life. Nature's law says, take what you want from the material world. God's law say don't take what is not yours. And the creation is His. Nature's law says, have sex with many partners. God's law says, have one partner for life. Nature's law says lie if it will get you ahead or save your butt. God says you shall not lie. Men of science say Mother Nature (Ma Neter) is the Creator. The Catholic agree, Mary is Mother of god. The laws of nature are contrary to God's spiritual laws. Atum represents creation and Hathor represents destruction, as does Set.

From the Egyptian Ma we get: maternal, matrix, matriarch, mare, madame, maiden, mammals with mammary glands, and Madonna. Mam-Mary (Mother Mary) has mam-mary glands to nurse the Child. Mary is just a matrix, not a goddess! She was the vessel that held the divine Child.

Parts of Being

Khat is the mortal soul or physical body including the mental. Ka is represented by a corpse that is brain dead. The hieroglyphic is a corpse with hands raised up anticipating resurrection. Ka also means Image; as in graven image. When the LORD breathed the breath of life (spirit) into the graven image of Adam, it became a living image or living soul. The Ka became a Sa, Son of Atum. Osiris is Sahu. Akh is the dead. The symbol of Ka combined with the Ankh represents rebirth at sunrise. Ankh is the Spirit of life. Khu or Shu is the breath of life, the oxygen in the O-zone. Ankh + Shu = Ankhu. Akhu is the spiritual knowledge or Spirit of Truth that comes from God. T-akh is to cross. When Sirius (Anu) crosses the horizon, Horus is reborn (ankh). It is the root of the T-cross. The Latin word spiritus means breath or to breathe. From spiritus we get spirit and re-spirat-ion. Akh = Death and Ankh = Anti-death. It is called the ansata cross or anti-Satan cross. Compare to: Than = Death and Athena = Anti-death or deathless. The ankh is the key of life that opens the door to the afterlife.

Khabti is dual. The shade or shadow is the dark side or shady side or shadowy side of our character. It is represented as a silhouette of the body. The khabti, like DNA, retains the shape or form of the deceased in memory. It stays in the grave with the corpse. The light side returns to God as the spirit of life. The Bible says there is a spirit of truth (Holy Spirit) and a spirit of error (unholy spirit). [1 John 4:1-6] The truth is Maat. The spirit of error is Amen-Set. Atum is enlightenment. Amen-Set is the darkness of ignorance. Khabti includes the spiritual gifts of God including the spirit of life or breath of life. [1 Corinthians 12]

Kha represents the duality of the terrestrial Osiris on earth and the celestial Osiris in Orion.

Ba is the spirit represented by a man-headed hawk. It holds the memory in the brain for the day it is recalled or reactivated. It is the identity of the entity. The Upper Egyptians portrayed Ba as a Ram (Ra-amen the evil-spirit). During the Age of Aries, the Ram was the sacred animal to be sacrificed. Similarly, the Greek word Alpha means First and Bull because man was first created during the age of Taurus when the Bull was the sacred animal to be sacrificed. Ram in computer language is memory, force fed. Without energy (spirit) the computer is brain-dead. The electricity activates it.

Saa is the spiritual knowledge. [1 Corinthians 12] Ba means to Be. Ben to beget, conscious conception of a child or a thought.

Ren is Name. The Egyptian put great significance on ones name. They believe the name exists in heaven. Compare this to the Bible that says your name is registered in heaven. [Hebrews 12:23 Philippians 3:20 4:3] And if your name is written in the Book of life, [Revelation 20:15 21:27 22:19] it reserves you a place in God's kingdom on earth. Those who have become one with Osiris, are of the body of the Lord and receive his name. For example: Osiris Ani or Sar Ani or Sir Ani. [Revelation 3:12] Compare this to Christ's followers being called Saints. Ani would be Saint Ani. Abuse of these sur-names is common.

Sah is the spirit-body as sun of God or star in heaven. This is the immortal soul or glorified body. Osiris is Sahu of Orion. Sa is Sar or Osiris and Hu is Hur or Horus. They are one and the same. [Romans 8:19-30] Sebu is the stars as heavenly bodies like the earth (Seb). The Sebau fiends are the fallen stars or fallen angels. [Revelation 12] They are the demons and evil spirits that inhabit the earth (seb).

"King Menes"

It is believed that Menes was the first pharaoh following Osiris. Menes, Warlord of Upper Egypt, conquered Lower Egypt and united the two kingdoms of Egypt during the age of Taurus (4,500-3100 BC). He set up his capital at Memphis. The Egyptian texts say that the one who usurped Osiris was Set. This means that Menes is aMen-set, the evil brother of Osiris. Memphis is the location where Set murdered Osiris upon his return from his world peace tour. Memphis is the White Wall that divides the two lands of Upper and Lower Egypt. Just as Romulus' wall separated him from his twin brother. Memphis is where Menes established the worship of Sar-apis in the place of Osiris. Anti means instead of or in place of. Therefore, the Sarapis is a type of Anti-Karast or Anti-Christ. They preached that Osiris reincarnated as the bull; that his spirit transmigrated into the Apis. This is Bull! The Apis was sacrificed before age 28, in imitation of Osiris who died at 28. Originally, Osiris-Apis represented Orion in the age of Taurus the Bull. Menes also set up the Bull Menvis (Men-apis) worship at Heliopolis. Set-Amen is the Bull of Heaven (Taurus). The Bull of Min and the Bull of Minos (Minotaur) is the same. He is the pied bull that shall be sacrificed at the Hall of Osiris on Judgment Day. In India, Menes became the Menu or Manu; the first Man after the flood.

Ironically, this is the period following Enoch. Enoch was born in 3382 BC. He lived 65 years and begot Methuselah in 3317 BC Enoch continued to walk with God for 300 years. The Turin Papyrus says Horus ruled for 300 years! Enoch was translated in 3017 BC at the age of 365. 365 is the number of days in a solar year. Methuselah died the year of the great Flood in 2347 BC 360 degrees is the cycle of life. Enoch went beyond the cycle of life into the great beyond. Could he have been the one who told the Egyptians how to build the Great Pyramid? Mene means Numbered. As in: his days are numbered. [Daniel 5:25,26] Could he be Nimrod? Menes is also known as Namer (Nmr); which is Nimrod (Nmrd). Nimrod built most of the capital cities of the ancient world. Could Menes be Amen incarnate in the flesh? Memphis is Men-Nefer which means Young Amen. Men-Nefer is arch-enemy of Tem-Nefer meaning Atem the Younger (Horus the son of Osiris).

Later they worshipped the Mendes Ram. This is the sacred animal of Amen the Ram-god during the age of Aries. The Romans identified it with Pan the goat-god who had intercourse with women. As a Ram is a male sheep or goat. The hieroglyphics for Mendes is Ba-Neb-Tet. The Ba is depicted as a Bull, not a Ram. Ba is obviously Baal the Bull. It is a residue of the Taurus age. In Hebrew, the word 'ram' means both bull and ram. The Hindu Avatar between the age of Taurus and Aries is Bala-Rama or Bull Ram. The Goat of Mendes is a goat's head superimposed in a Satanic star (Pentacle).

The Temple Time Tablet

The author of Orion Mystery concludes that the Great Pyramid was built in 2450 BC and the First time of Osiris or Orion was 10,500 BC. The Great Pyramid was a temple time tablet for calculating the precession of the stars. 10,500 BC was the lowest point marking the starting date of the Zodiac cycle. 2550 AD is the highest point marking the end date of the cycle. That is a total of over 13,000 years or half of a processional cycle of 25,920 years. In the year 2550 AD, Orion will start to descend for 13,000 years. In other words, Orion-Osiris will reach his peak in 2550 AD. It is his crowning day as King of the celestial mountain! Could this be the time the capstone (Rock of Ages) shall descend upon the summit of the Great Pyramid?

If we count backward in time by divine days. Each divine day is a thousand years. [2 Peter 3:8] Adam was created in the year 4004 BC during the sixth divine day (4000 -5000 BC). On the fifth day (5000 -6000 BC), God created the flying creatures and sea creatures. On the fourth day (6000 -7000 BC), God created the sun moon and stars. On the third day (7000 BC), God created the dry land. On the second day (8000 BC- 9000 BC), God created the third heaven or sky. On the first day (9000 BC- 10,000 BC), God created the earth and the Morning star or Sun of Righteousness to rule over the earthlings. Before the Creation (BC) God was alone!

Somewhere around 10,500 the Bright Morning star called Sirius did rise for the first time. This is the immaculate conception and virgin birth of the first begotten Sun of God. According to the Bible, the rest of the stars were not created until the fourth day. Atum (Horus the Elder) ruled over the earthlings.

The Great Pyramid

The dimensions of the Great Pyramid not only holds the distances around the earth, but the time of the processional cycle of the equinoxes of 25,920 years. The sign of the Zodiac is figured by the constellation visible during the spring equinox. Once again paralleling the Bible in holding the equinoxes in reverence. The Lord was born on the Autumn Equinox. He died on the spring equinox (Passover). He shall return on the Autumn equinox, during the Feast of Ingathering. The height of the Great Pyramid 5,813 inches x 1,000,000,000 is equal to the distance to the sun. The perimeter of the Great Pyramid is 365.2 inches x 1,000 which is the number of days in a solar year.

The inside dimensions of the so called "coffer" of the Great Pyramid is: 77.85 x 26.70 x 34.31. Compare this to the Ark of the Covenant which is 58.9 x 33.9 x 35.7. That is 2.5 cubits long, and 1.5 cubits wide, and 1.5 cubits high. The cubic capacity of the Ark is 71,213 cubic Pyramid inches. The cubic capacity of the coffer is 71,250 cubic Pyramid inches. The lid of the Ark is a separate part called the Mercy Seat. On the lid are two Angels facing each other. Likewise the coffer of the Pyramid is missing its lid, on which were two scarabs (cherubs) facing each other.

Orion's Mystery

1,000—2,000 AD	
0—1,000 AD	
1,000 BC—0	Christ's birth on 7 BC
2,000—1,000 BC	
3,000—2,000 BC	Great Pyramid
4,000—3,000 BC	7th day of creation
5,000—4,000 BC	6th day of creation—Adam's birth (4004 BC)
6,000—5,000 BC	5th day of creation
7,000—6,000 BC	4th day of creation
8,000—7,000 BC	3rd day of creation
9,000—8,000 BC	2nd day of creation
10,000—9,000 BC	1st day of creation
Infinity—10,000 BC	before the creation

Orion's first rising as the Morning Star Sirius in 10,500. The Egyptians called it Zep Tepi or First Time. Tepi means First but it also means Mouth. In the beginning, God opened His Mouth for the First Time and said, "Let there be light." And it was good. So the evening and the morning were the first day."

The first day followed the creating of the Sun of Righteousness. Each divine day is a thousand years. [2 Peter 3:8 Psalms 90:4]

The earth's axis is 23 degrees off true north. The earth spins like a top, but because of the earth's wobble, we see the 12 constellations through a 26,000 year cycle, as we orbit the sun. This is called the processional cycle. Through the cosmic window we see only a piece of the Zodiac at a time. It is believed that we once were a binary solar system. When Sirius left, it jilted the earth from its true north axis. Then Lucifer the Day star (sun) became the center of our solar system. I believe that when Sirius left our solar system, the gravitational pull of the sun caused the tilt, and therein, the Great Flood. [Book of Enoch and Anacalypsis by Godfrey Higgins, ESQ pages 29,30] When the Morning Star (Sirius) returns, the gravitational pull will cause global catastrophes, including the Great Earthquake. [Matt. 24:7,27-31 Zechariah 14:1-5 Malachi 4:2 Rev. 10:1 11:13-19 16:18]

The sun's cycle through the Zodiac is reverse of the precession we observe at each spring equinox. Ra's journey during the course of the solar year is Aquarius > Pisces > Aries > Taurus > Gemini > Cancer > Leo > Virgo, etc.. Yet the precession cycle of the Great year takes 25,920 solar years to complete. The direction is Virgo > Leo > Cancer > Gemini > Taurus > Aries > Pisces > Aquarius, etc... Anything contrary to God's plan is Satanic. Ra's solar bark runs backward through the cosmic clock. Ra's solar cycle is the one pseudo-astrologers (i.e. monthly pronosticators) use to connect the twelve Zodiac signs with the twelve months. Ra's solar cycle is further proof that he is the evil sun of God known as Lucifer. The Lower Egyptians did not follow the Way of Ra. Only the Upper Egyptian did.

The Sphinx-facing back in time or looking forward?

10,500 BC was the age of Leo the Lion. The constellation rose on the eastern horizon exactly in the direction that the Sphinx faces. Which itself is a lion with a man's head. The Sphinx faces due east toward the sun rise during the spring equinox. At the same time Orion is due south; on the cross roads of the horizon and the celestial Meridian. It is a constellation conjunction! The Egyptians called this the "First Time". The Lord says, "I am the First and the Last, the beginning and the end." [Revelation 1:8,11] The Sphinx symbolizes the Lord as King or Lion of Judah, [Revelation 5:5] whose zodiac sign is Leo the Lion. This means it has been 12,500 years since the birth of the firstborn Sun (Atum-Horus) of the creation. Which is mid-point of the 25,920 year cycle. The secrets or Mysteries of the Pyramid were sealed up till the end of time. [Daniel 12:1-4-13 Revelation 22:10,13,16] {Read "The Message of the Sphinx" by Hancock and Bauval.}

The celestial cross is formed when Orion's ecliptic path (east to west) crosses the celestial meridian (north to south). Once Orion crosses this threshold, it descends into the underworld. When that star crosses the western horizon, it 'dies'. Simultaneously, Osiris was placed underground in Amenta. This is the Christ on the Cross during the spring equinox. 'There was darkness through-out the land from the 6th hour to the 9th hour.' [Matthew 27:45] Obviously, it is dark, it is the 6th hour to the 9th hour at night (12 AM-3 AM). His voyage through the Underworld begins. While the Son of Man was three days in the tomb, the Son of God was three days in the underworld preaching to the fallen angels of Tartarus (Taurus). [1 Peter 3:18,19 2 Peter 2:4,5] Meanwhile, Orion and Taurus are not seen for three months while they are in the underworld. Once the Sun of God crosses the eastern horizon, he is reborn from the watery womb and ascends into the heavens as Sirius, the Morning star.

Sirius ascends from the autumn equinox to the spring equinox. At which time it starts its descent into the underworld. The sun, on the other hand, ascends from the winter solstice to the summer solstice. Then proceeds to descend into the underworld. Once again, the sun is the antithesis of Sirius. For the sun worshipers, (like Christendumb) the sun crossing the eastern horizon on Easter Sunday is the rebirth of their sun god, Amen-Ra.

It was Set and his 72 sebeau fiends (fallen stars) who pushed Osiris into the coffin. Likewise, 72 years push Orion one degree past the celestial meridian. He starts falling into the Underworld. Anubis, Isis and Nephthys follow as the companion star, Sirius. This is Cosmic Funeral Procession. Set is the Sun and the fallen angels are his minions. Saba in Hindu and Seba in Hebrew means the host of heaven or angels. The Sebau are the fallen angels or fallen stars.

The Signs in Heaven

1) In the beginning (13,100 -11,000 BC) was the age of Virgo the Virgin. God (Patah) created the heavens (Nun) void of life. This is the virgin ready to give birth of the firstborn Sun of God called the Morning star. Who shall descend down to the holy mountain. Represented by the eye of Horus descending on the Great Pyramid. This is the primordial Great Flood when Atum-Horus was all alone in his bark sailing through the sea of space (Nun). Compare to Noah and his seven family members saved from the Deluge. There were eight divine kings: Atum, Shu, Geb, Osiris, Isis, Set, Horus and Thoth.

2) 11,000-8,800 BC, was the age of Leo the Lion. The Lion-King rules over the earth. Represented by the Great Sphinx (Harmakhis). The Sphinx rests on the equinoctial sunrise. Pointing to the celestial equator where Leo did rise in its day. Simultaneously, Orion appeared, standing on the southern horizon.

3) Followed by the age of Cancer from 8,800-6,600 BC The scarab beetle pushing the dung ball represents the force behind the heavenly bodies. And God separated the dry land from the seas. The Scarab, not the

crab, represents Atum-Khepra standing on the "dry land" of the primeval mound. Just as Noah stood on dry land after the flood. Geb (Earth) ruled at this time. On the first divine day God said, "Let there be light" and there appeared Atum, the good Sun of God, ruling over the earth. This is when Sirius rose above the horizon for the first time. This is the true AD (Anno Domini) the divine birth-day of our Lord.

4) Then the age of Gemini was from 6,600-4,500 BC God separated the sea of space (Nun) from the waters on earth (Geb). The twins Shu and Tefnut became the atmosphere. They ruled the age of Gemini. On fourth divine day of creation, God created Lucifer, the Morning star. The Egyptians called him Ra-Amen or Rem. "When the Morning stars sang together, and all the sons of God shouted for joy?" [Job 38:7] Zoroaster says the good Sun of God and bad sun of God are twins. Gemini is the sign of twins. They represent the dualism of Yin/Yang. This is the time of the binary solar system. Thomas means Twins. Thom-mes is Atom-reborn from the water.

5) The Zodiac sign during the building of the Pyramid (2400 BC) was the age of Taurus (4,500 -2,300 BC). This is called the Old Kingdom age of Egypt. It is the time of Adam-Noah-Ham. The Lord worked with the African nations of the line of Ham. [Genesis 10:6-14] In the beginning of the age of Taurus, Osiris ruled over all of Egypt, but after his death it was divided between Lower and Upper Egypt. The constellation of Taurus the Bull represents Upper Egypt ruled over by Set-amen (Satan), the evil sun of God. While Orion represents Lower Egypt ruled by Osiris/Horus. Who is the good Sun of God called Atum-Ra. Satan is ruler of this wicked world as head of state, while the Lord is head of the Church of God. This is the universal Yin/Yang or battle of evil vs. Good. The Lord worked with the Egyptians for about 2,000 years.

6) 2,300-150 BC was the age of Aries. This is the time of Noah's son, Shem. Starting about the year 2,000 BC the Lord worked with Abraham and his family of shepherds. [Genesis 10:21-32] At this time, the priests at Thebes changed from worshipping the Apis Bull of Taurus to worshipping the Ram of Aries. Ra-Amen is the Ram god. The Hyksos who ruled Egypt from 2,000 to 1500 BC were shepherd kings from the Middle East. This is called the Middle kingdom age of Egypt. It is the time Joseph was sold into slavery and became the Viser of Egypt. From 1500 to 1,000 is when the Upper Egyptians ruled all Egypt. It is called the New Kingdom age. It included rulers like Ram-ses who worshipped Ra-Amen the Ram god. In the Bible, it says the Lord would come in on an ass's colt. [Zechariah 9:9 Matthew 21:1-10] The Hebrew word is "ayir". The symbol is "Y". Similar to the symbol of Aries. The symbol is called "ayin". Similar to "ayil" meaning Ram. It is the same symbol of the ass, Set and Typhon. The ass is a beast of burden just like the ox (bull). The Lord came riding in on the back of Aries the Ram into the age of Pisces. The bull, ram and ass are Set-Amen's animals. During this time, the Upper Egyptians

changed Horus into Khnemu-Ra who had the head of a Ram. But this is really Amen-Ra-Set, the wicked Warlord. The age of Aries is the time of the Warrior empires: Babylon, Assyria, Israel, and Persia. The Lord had worked with the Semitics for about 2,000 years. The time of Alexander the Greek was the end of the age of Ares and the dawning of Pisces. Each empire took their turn in conquering Egypt. The final blow was the Roman empire under Julius Caesar.

7) From 150 BC (Before Christ)-2,010 AD is the age of Pisces. This is the time the Lord is working with the Gentiles. They are the descendants of Noah's son, Japheth. [Genesis 10:1-5] The Gentiles are the: Greeks, Macedonians, Medes, Athenians, etc... The Lord is going to work with the Gentiles for 2,000 years. Man will have existed for 6,000 years or six divine days. The seventh divine day is the Day of the Lord. Seven is the number of the Lord of the Sabbath. He turned the fishermen into fishers of men who shall be priests of God's kingdom during the Sabbatical Millennium (Seventh divine day or seven thousandth year). Jesus the Christ was born under the age of Pisces according to the Zodiac's Precession calculated at the spring equinox. During the years' astrology cycle of the solar year, the sun entered into Virgo the Virgin. The Autumn equinox (Sept.22), is the month of the virgin birth. It is also the time he shall return to destroy the Devil. Then at the winter solstice (Dec.21) the sun entered Sagittarius. Representing the Lord on the white horse. Then at the spring equinox (March 21) the evil sun of God killed the Passover Lamb. Then the sun entered Taurus at the summer solstice (June 21). This is the most high day for the Bull, the adversary of Orion the bull-fighter. No doubt the Antichrist will take power at this time of year for three and a half years. When Jesus (Horus) left, he sent the Comforter (Thoth).

8) The dawning of the age of Aquarius will be about 2,010-4,200 AD. This is the time that God is going to rain down fire from heaven. Those who are not refined in the flames, will be consumed. Eight is the day of God's coming after the Lord Jesus has made all things new. [1 Corinthians 15:20-28] It is called the Last Great Day. [John 7:37 Revelation 21:3] Just as in the day of Noah when all but eight drowned in the flood. Only those reborn of the water of baptism and remain innocent and pure, shall be saved. [1 Peter 3:20,21] They shall drink of the water of life. In Egypt, Atum-Ra-Horus was born of the watery womb of Nun. It was, is and shall be the dawning of the Morning star, Sirius.

9) Capricorn is 4,200-6,300 AD. This is the time of plenty (cornucopia) when the Antichrist incarnates and bribes the masses to follow him. The 6th angel blows the 6th horn and pours out the 6th plague (6+6+6). Capri means Goat and Cornu means Horn. Carni is the turning rides at the Carnival. Like the turning of the Celestial cycles or Mill-enniums or Cosmic Ages or Divine Days.

10) Sagittarius is 6,300-8,500 AD. This is when the Lord with the Sword comes on his white horse. Horus on his horse. Did the Word of God make a play on words?

11) Scorpio is 17,400-15,300 BC and 8,500-10,600 AD. It is the battle of good vs. evil. [Rev.9:1-21] The army of scorpion men shall be slain. [Rev.19:11-21] It is Sagittarius that shoots the scorpion in the head. The same scorpion (or serpent) that stung Horus in the heal. [Genesis 3:15] The Egyptians, Sumerians, Babylonians and Mayans all portrayed the constellation of Scorpio as a Scorpion!

12) Libra is 15,300-13,100 BC (and 10,600-12,800 AD). This is the time that scientists call the Ice Age. Nun is "frigid". It was Passion that broke the ice and produced the Virgin Birth. Libra, the balances, represents Judgment day which is followed by the Lord's Divine Day, the Sabbatical Millennium. It is the time of new births for the children of God. The cycle of time is a continuum that never ends. The famous Rosetta stone was written in three languages: Egyptian hieroglyphics, hieratic or demotic (root of Aramaic & Hebrew), and Greek. These represent the three ages the Lord worked with Noah's three sons. The age of Taurus is the Egyptian era. The age of Ares is the Aramaic era (the sons of Shem through Aram through Abraham). The age of Pisces is the Gentiles era (Greeks, Macedonians, etc.). It seems curious that the ancient name for Giza is Rosetau. Almost the same as Rosetta, the place northeast of Alexandria, where the stone was found. It was part of the divine plan for Alexander and the other Gentiles to rule at this time. It is curious that the Greek and Roman history does not predate the eighth century BC. I believe the Egyptians created the Greek and Hebrew languages for these people who could not read and write.

Orion vs. Taurus

Astronomers say the Orion Nebula is a birth place for new stars. It is the place to go to become one with Osiris. The Word of God says the reformed Saints shall be reborn and transformed into suns of God. We will become One with the Lord when he unites heaven and earth. On the other hand, the Crab Nebula in Taurus is the grave site of dying stars. Ironically, one of the stars in Taurus is called Hyades (Hades). Hades is the deity of death. On July 4, 1054, one of the stars in Taurus went supernova. It burned bright for awhile then burned out. Becoming what we now call the Crab Nebula. Those who follow the Fallen Star will end up in the inferno called the Lake of Fire.

The original Egyptian calendar was 12 months with 30 days each or 360. Five days were added in honor of the gods (Osiris, Isis, Horus, Nephthys and Set). 360 degrees represents the cycle of life. To go beyond that is to enter into everlasting life. Osiris, with the help of Isis and Nephthys, overcame the death caused by Set, and was reborn as Horus. This calendar harmonized with the 12 Zodiacs, 30 degrees each and 36 decans. Built within the dimensions of the Great Pyramid is Pi (3.14...). The foundation of the circle and the cycle of time. Pi-Ra-mid is Ra in the midst of the celestial cycle.

Originally the time it took the earth to go 360 degrees may have been 360 days, but during the flood (2340 BC) the world was tilted 23.4^0 from true north. The wobble has slowed the earth. Now it takes 365 days to go around the sun. Therein, the Egyptians, Mayans, Greeks, Romans and Sumerians added five "extra" days to the year to make it coincide. Chronus represents time and space. It is the creation of chronological time from the sea of space. [see Book of Enoch] 12,000 years is called a Brahma day. 12,000 x 360 = 4,320,000 days in a divine year (almost half of a Zodiac cycle). [Anacalypsis volume 2 pages 315-326]

30 degrees x 12 ages = 360 degrees in one cycle. 360 x 2 = 720 x 3 = 2160 (years per age). 72 years x 30 degrees = 2160. 360 x 72 years per degree = 25,920 years of 12 Zodiac ages. All based on the 360 day-year. { 3+6+0=9 7+2=9 } { 360 + 72 = 432 } All the Zodiac ages not only add up to 9 but are also equally divided by 9. { 2160, 4320, 6480, 8640, 10800, 12960, 15120, 17280, 19440, 21600, 23760, 25920 } The square root of 9 is 3. In the 3 dimensional world all things are divided into 3 (solid, liquid or gas).

It has been calculated that the Great Pyramid is on a scale of 1:43,200 of the size of the northern hemisphere. The apex of the Pyramid representing the North pole and the perimeter the earth's equator. The perimeter is 2pi to the height. 4 is the four cardinal points. 4+3=7 the number of the Lord of creation who rested on the 7th day. 4+3+2=9 the number of the great mother creation. Joseph Campbell says 432 is a non-number. The Egyptians called it Nun, the watery womb from which all creation was born; the Cosmic Egg. The very word feminine is femi + nine. The 12 zodiacs represent the 12 hours of night, each 60 minutes. The precession of the equinoxes is 25,920 years. The length it takes to go through all 12 ages. 2+5+9+2+0=18 then 1+8=9. Divide 25,920 by 60 you get 432. 4+3+2=9. A man in perfect shape at rest, has one heart-beat per second, 60 per minute, 3600 per hour {3+6+0+0=9} and 43,200 in a 12 hour period. In India, the cycle of time is 432,000 years in which the cosmos dissolves and then is recreated.

In Mesopotamia, 432,000 years was the time the first 10 kings ruled up until the flood. This is the time from the first man to Utnapishtim (counterpart of Noah). In Genesis, there were 10 patriarchs from Adam to Noah. They totaled 1656 years made up of 86,400 weeks. Which is double of 43,200. 86,400 weeks = 604,800 days. {6+0+4+8+0+0=18 then 1+8=9} and 86,400 {8+6+4=18 1+8=9} and 43,200 {4+3+2=9} and 1656 {1+6+5+6=18 then 1+8=9} each add up to 9. The Vikings (Aryans) say that at the end of this age (Pisces), 800 warriors will walk through 540 doors of the Warrior Hall to battle the anti-gods. 540 x 800 = 43,200. 432 is obviously an universal "nun" number.

Manu, the Hindu Noah, was the seventh of a line of Manu who lived for 4,320,000 years. Just as Enoch was seventh from Adam. Adam means Man (Manu). Seven is the number of days in a week. Enoch lived 365 years which is the number of days in a year. Enoch the seventh from Adam walked with God for 300 years. 7 x 300 = 2100 the age of each house in the Zodiac. The Zodiac moves one degree every 72 years, 30 degrees every 2160 years, 60 degrees every 4320 years, 90 degrees every 6480 years and a full 360 degrees every 25,920 years. {7+2=9} {2+1+6+0=9} {4+3+2+0=9} {9+0=9} {6+4+8+0=18 then 1+8=9} {3+6+0=9} {2+5+9+2+0=18 then 1+8=9}. The Great Flood took place about 2340 BC, which is reverse of 4320.

The Chinese Imperial library consists of 4320 volumes which contain all the knowledge of the world. Could these be the sacred books of Thoth (Enoch)? Now the earth's axis is tilted off of true north by 23.4 degrees. 234 is reverse of 432 and both add up to 9. The number for mother earth and the great mother, Nun, is nine. The Egyptians did not view them as goddesses, but as aspects or attributes of God. They are the body of natural laws created by God. In fact, Nun represents chaos and Nut represents the law and order of the cosmos. When Atum was born from Nun, order was created in the form of Nut. Nut is the stars moving through the cosmic clock. For the time being, mother earth is in the hands of Father Time (Chronus/Kronus). Who is Khonsu, the son of Amen and Mut (the great mother). Who is an aspect of Satan. At the appointed time, Atum-Horus will take back what is his as Lord of the Earth.

Chaldean Chronology

In Babylon, the first king was appointed by God to be the Shepherd of the people. He reigned ten sari (36,000 years). The next king reigned three sari (10,800 years). The next king reigned 13 sari (46,800 years). At this time an extraterrestrial rose from the sea for the second time. The next king reigned twelve sari (43,200 years). The next king reigned eighteen sari (64,800 years). The next king reigned for ten sari (36,000 years). At this time, four aquatic aliens rose out of the sea. The next king reigned eighteen sari (64,800 years). The eighth king reigned ten sari (36,000). The ninth king reigned eight sari (28,800 years). The last was Sisithrus who reigned eighteen sari (64,800 years). The total number of kings was ten and the length of their reigns totaled 120 sari (432,000 years). A sarus is 3,600 years.

This is obviously a reference of Sirius rising from the sea of space after going 360 degrees around the earth. Sar = Osiris, the king of Egypt. Each of these numbers total "9". Nine is the sea of space called Nun. Each age of the Zodiac is 2160 years. Twelve ages are 25,920 years. 2160 x 2 Zodiac ages = 4320 (years from Adam to the second Adam?). Each of these years totals to 9. The Egyptian scribe, Manetho, says the 6 Gods ruled for 13,900 years and the 6 demigods for another 11,025 years before the mortal kings ruled Egypt. 13,900 + 11,025 = 24,925 years. I believe this was originally 25,920 years and got "mixed up" through the millenniums. The 6 gods + 6 demigods are the 12 Zodiac houses with 3 decans each, which equals 36. Each one is 10 degrees, giving a total of 360 degrees. 12 Zodiacs x 36 decans = 432.

After this, other kings ruled. Then Sisit-hrus (named after Osiris-Horus?) was king. The 'god' Cronus revealed to him that on the 15th day of the month Desius there would be a deluge (Noah's flood occurred on the 17th day) and commanded him to deposit all the writings whatever that he had, in the city of the Sun in Sippara (Just as Thoth had done in City of the Sun in Egypt). He then sailed to Armenia (near Mt. Ararat where Noah's ark rested). Noah was 600 years old. The Babylonians say a neros is six hundred. During the deluge, Sisithrus sent out birds like Noah. When Sisithrus asked Cronus where he should sail?, Cronus said, 'to the gods'. [See the Sirius Mystery by Robert Temple pages 248 & 249 & 252]

"God's will be done on earth as in heaven." Obviously, this is referring to the birth of Atum, as the star Sirius, from the sea of space. He is the amphibious being with dominion over water and land. [Revelation 10:1,2] Lord of Heaven and earth. [Matthew 28:18] The Babylonians called these extraterrestrial beings the Oannes. On (or Anu) is the birthplace of the Ones or Oannus, which Atum was the firstborn Sun of God. The Oannes taught the Babylonians by day; agriculture, astrology, architecture, and how to be civilized. But, they returned to the sea at night. Just as the sun appears to set in the sea at sunset. Compare this to the Sun of God [1 Corinthians 15:35-54 2 Peter 1:19] who rises from the sea as an antitype of the flood. The replacement ritual is baptism. [1 Peter 3:18-22] The Lion of Leo who became the Lamb slain from the foundation of the world is Atum-Osiris-Horus. [Revelation 5:5,6 13:8] The Hebrew Yod = 10 and the letter Y of YHWH. The Roman X = 10 and the Chi of Christ. The Egyptian Mid is 10 and Perfection. The Greek and Chaldean Jod is 10 symbolized by a triangle. Compare Pyra-Mid and the triangle. X in Greek is 600. A Nero is 600 years. The Hindus say a Avatar or Savior (Sar) comes every Nero. Compare this to the phoenix coming every 500 years. 10 Neros = 6000 years of man's existence. 600 divided into 25,920 = 43.2. Neros = Heroes. Everything keeps cycling back to Egypt.

Star-Avatar

Comet = Kemet, the name of the Africans. Khamet is Ham and his sons who discovered astronomy. There is a comet observed 40 years before Christ that cycles every 575½ years. {40 years before Christ is about 44 BC as He was born 4-6 BC) Four cycles are 2300 + 40 = 2340, the year of the Great Flood. This is the drowning of the age of Taurus and dawning of the age of Aries. The root of the word Cat-astro-phe is astro meaning fallen star. 75 cycles x 576 = 43200. The comet was sited in 44 BC, 532 AD, 1106 AD, and 1680 AD. It will appear for the fourth time since Christ, in the year 2256 AD, corresponding with the dawning of Aquarius. The four ages of man are Taurus, Aries, Pisces and Aquarius. Compare this to the Avatar, Savior or celestial body returning every 500-600 years.

It is self-evident that the ten neters of Egypt (Atum, Shu, Tefnut, Nut, Geb, Osiris, Isis, Set, Nephthys and Horus) became the ten neros. Adam, Abel, Enoch, Noah, Melchizedek, Elijah, the Angel of God may be incarnations. Jesus would be the eighth to manifest in the flesh, the Antichrist (Set-amen) would be the ninth and Atum incarnating as Horus is the tenth Avatar. But the eight millenniums comes from the eight divine kings: Atum, Shu, Geb, Osiris, Isis, Set, Horus and Thoth. Aquarius covers the seventh and eighth millenniums. Thoth is the pouring out of the holy spirit. The seventh being the Sabbatical Millennium ruled by the Son of God and called the Lord's day, [Revelation 1:10 20:3,6,7] The eighth is the divine day that never ends, when God the Father comes to live with His sons. [Revelation 21:1] The antithesis to this is the ten spurious saviors: Sargon the Great, Nebuchadnezzar, Cyrus, Alexander the Great, Ptolemy the Great, Julius Caesar, Nero, Napoleon, Charles the Great (Charlemagne), and Hitler. Just to name a few. There have been many antichrist neros in the world. Satan mimics everything that Jesus does.

The Death of Osiris

According to Plutarch's version: Set conspired with Aso, the queen of Ethiopia and 72 others against his brother Osiris because he coveted his kingdom and his wife, Isis. Set made a beautiful chest or coffin then invited some guests to a feast at Memphis in honor of Osiris returning home from his world peace tour. Set told them that whoever fit in the chest would possess it. The guest of honor, Osiris, climbed into the coffin which was a perfect fit. Set and his sebeau fiends slammed the lid closed and sealed it. They then threw it into the Nile. {Compare this to Moses in the ark.} The chest floated down the Nile to the Mediterranean Sea and rested at Byblos, Syria. A Tamarisk tree grew around it and became one with it. The wooden chest became part of the tree trunk. Osiris gave up his last breath in that tree just as Christ gave up his last breath on the tree or cross. Then the Tamarisk (Ever-green pine tree) was cut down to make a pillar in the palace of the King of Syria. The queen of Syria is none other than Astarte (a.k.a. Ishtar and Asherah, the goddess of groves). In other words, the Egyptian religion became firmly rooted in Syria.

Compare this to Jesus, who was from Galilee in northern Israel, who was killed by the priests of Judah in southern Israel. The two lands are divided. Just as Osiris is Lord of northern Egypt and Set ruler of southern Egypt. The Jewish priests "plotted to take Jesus by trickery and kill him." [Matthew 26:4] He was killed on the anniversary of the Festival of Osiris (Feast of Unleavened Bread). The Jewish Sanhedrin with its 71 members plus the high priest represents the 72 conspirators headed by Satan. The 72 followers of Set were called Sami. These are the Minions of Min (Amen).

Isis did "pine" away with grief. Meanwhile, she hears of the news, finds the location of the chest and goes there. She is hired as the nurse to Asherah's son. She decides to make him immortal. So she transforms into a bird and starts to purify him in fire. This is the baptism of the holy Spirit by fire. "I will refine them in fire" says the Lord. [Zechariah 13:9] John the Baptist said, "He will baptize you will the Holy Spirit and fire." [Matthew 3:11] But they are interrupted and must stop. Isis tells Asherah that the pillar is her husband Osiris. Isis is allowed to take the coffin out of the pine pillar. She anoints and wraps the pillar with linen. Then she gives the pillar back to the king. The pine tree trunk / pillar later became the Tet or Ded (Dead) symbol, representing death and resurrection. In Assyria, the sacred tree is associated with Ashur, the Sun of God. He is often sitting inside a hallow (holy) tree. Asshur is As-Horus, Son of Isis and the resurrected Osiris (Asar). [From Fetish to God in Ancient Egypt by Budge]

In Greek mythology, it is Demeter, the Great Mother, who nurses Demophoon the son of Metaneira. She decides to transform him into an immortal by feeding him ambrosia, breathing on him with her divine breath and placing him in the purifying fire. They are interrupted by Metaneira and he loses the opportunity to become immortal. The idea of actually burning a child in fire is pagan and condemned by the Lord. [Jeremiah 7:31 2 Kings 23:10,11] The Holy Spirit is supernatural fire and power that shall refine and purge of impurities. Likewise, the Lord never intended for there to be human sacrifice. Abraham offering his son was a test and a preview of God the Father sacrificing His Beloved Son.

Isis put the coffin on a boat and sailed home. Once there she hides it. But, Set locates it while hunting by the light of the moon. The sun-god is hunting by the light of the full moon? Compare to Apollo and Diana. Set-Typhon rips open the coffin and tears Osiris to 14 pieces and scattered throughout the land of Egypt. Set feeds Osiris' penis to the Lepidotus, Phagrus, and Oxyrhynchus fishes. The 14 pieces represent 14 cities of Egypt and the 14 stars that make up Orion. As in heaven, so on earth. Compare this to Christ's death at Passover. The Hebrew New Year is the first new moon after spring equinox. 14 days (or parts of a month) later is the full moon and Passover. Isis was impregnated with child on the 17th day of the month of Hathor. That's six months plus three days dead (like Jesus).

When Isis returns, she is horrified and immediately searches for the dismembered parts of his body. This represents the body members of the Lord who were scattered when Christ was crucified. Isis, with the help of Nephthys and her son, Anubis, find 13 parts. Anubis is a canine who can track buried bones. Nephthys is his mother nature (the life to death cycle). One part is missing, his penis. Christ never had any natural children. Isis laid on the mummified body of her husband and prayed to God for an heir to the throne of Egypt. She was given a metaphysical phallus and spiritual seed. She immaculately conceived from the power on high. This is the divine Child called Horus in Egypt and Jesus in JeruSalem. Osiris' body never saw corruption (decay) because he resurrected as Horus. [Acts 2:27,31 1 Corinthians 15:42-55] The body of Christ (or church), like the body of Osiris, were reassembled after his resurrection. The body members became united through the Spirit they shared in common. Resurrection = Re-Sar-erection or Osiris re-erected.

The Thieves of Thebes

The thieves of Upper Egypt stole then changed the sacred scriptures. The story continues... Horus had chained Set and handed him over to Isis. Isis could not stand to see her brother, Set, chained so she released him. Horus was so angry he tore off her crown (or head). Thoth immediately replaced it with the head of Hathor with the crown of cow horns. Isis became Aset a form of Set. Sirius became Sothis (Set's star) or Septet (region of Set). Set became the son or sun of the Mother Cow. Hathor is now the mother and mistress of Set. As the "Antichrist Savior" Set is trying to take the place of the Christ Child.

When Horus matured, he battled with Set for the throne of Egypt. In retaliation, he tore off the testicles of Set so he could not bear any children. Set, in turn, ripped out the left eye of Horus. This means Set forceful took half the two lands of Egypt. Set was ruler of Upper Egypt while Horus was ruler of Lower Egypt. Just as Satan is ruler of this wicked world for the time being, but Jesus is going to retake his rule as Lord of the Earth. The Two eyes of Horus in heaven are the stars Sirius (of Orion) and Hyades in the constellation of Taurus. Set is Lord of the Underworld which the Greek's call Hades. The word for "eye" is Iris, from which the Egyptians got Siris.

Horus is heir to the throne as Lord of the Earth, but he is not the son of Osiris. He is Osiris resurrected or re-incarnated. Set is not his uncle, but his brother. Osiris represents the Son of Man, Jesus, the human-being. Horus represents the Son of God as a spirit-being who existed before and after his incarnation in the flesh. Osiris was born from the Earth (Geb). Horus the Elder (Atum) was created on the first day of creation and is called the Morning Star. [Revelation 22:14] He is the star Sirius in the celestial womb of Nut. Horus the Younger is Jesus after his resurrection from the Earth and ascension to heaven. The Lord said, "I am the same yesterday, today and tomorrow." "Osiris is Yesterday, and Ra (Horus) is today". [Book of the Dead chapter 17:15] Osiris is past, Horus is present and Atum is future. The eulogy of Osiris is the same as the Eucharist of Christ. In fact, karast or charist is an Egyptian word meaning; to anoint or embalm the mummy.

Horus redeems the body of Osiris from the grave (Amenta). The Father and Son are reconciled as One. The body of believers make up the body of Osiris. Osiris ascends to heaven (Nu) as Horus with his long hair down to his shoulders. Compare this to Jesus the Nazarene with long hair. Osiris is in the terrestrial Orion: the body of pyramids stretched out on the sands of Lower Egypt. Horus is in the celestial Orion or Kingdom of Osiris.

"Horus is triumphant in the presence of the whole company of the gods, the sovereignty over the world hath been given unto him, and his dominion is in the uttermost parts of the earth. The throne of the Earth (god Seb) hath been adjudged unto him, along with the rank which hath been founded by the god Temu, and which hath been inscribed upon an iron tablet according to the command of the Father Ptah-Tanen, on the great throne..." Ptah-Ta-nen means Father of earth and heaven. [Book of the Dead chapter 183 pages 11 & 12] Horus has overcome the evil one and is now Lord of the heavens and earth. He is lord of the two lands; both upper and lower earth. He is Lord of God's kingdom on Earth. Sekhet-Aaru (the Field of Reeds) and Sekhet-Hetep (Field of Peace) is God's garden paradise restored. The Greeks called it the Elysian Fields. The earth will go full cycle from life to death to life (rebirth). Likewise, the Saints will die and be reborn in the garden of Eden as sons of God. [Rev.2:7] The old Earth will be made new: Amenta is transformed into Tuat (Land of the Living). The Land of the Dead is plowed and sowed with the seeds or sons of God. The Bible calls it God's Rest (Sabbath). [Hebrew 4] Which is the Sabbatical Millennium or 7,000th year of man's existence. It is also called the Lord's divine day (a day = a thousand years).

The root of Astarte is Ast, the Egyptian name for Isis. Astarte became Queen of heaven; Asherah of the Phoenicians, goddess of groves, Ashteroth of the Hebrews, Ishtar of the Babylonians, Artemis of the Greeks. They worshipped the Tamarisk trees (Asherah) as symbols of potency. The northern stars of Ursa Major became her stars as the Great Mother. They replaced Isis and Horus with Asherah and Baal. The North Pole star replaced Sirius as the Dog star, Sun of Astarte. When the sun reached its most northern point at the summer solstice, it was called the Dog Days of Summer. When it fell to its lowest point, it was the winter solstice. The sun was dying. The Evergreen replaced the Ash Tree of Life as the place where the Sun (Sirius) rose. Venus became the Morning star. The physical tree replaced the metaphysical tree. The cut down and dying Tamarisk (Pine) became the Eucharist (the Lord's Last Supper) and death on the tree. Asherah played her part, as Mother Nature, in the cycle of life to death. The people did Pine at the Passion of Christ, just as they did weep for Tammuz. The evergreen became the tree of X-mas, a custom condemned by God. Whorship of trees is idolatry (idol-tree). [Jeremiah 10:1-5 3:6-9] The cut down tree has no life in it! Osiris in not in the evergreen, nor is on the cross. The tree represents death. (akh) or to kill (akar). Horus rising from the dead tree (wooden ark or coffin) represents life (ankh). Sar-cophi-gus means Sar's coffin.

Santa lives at the North Pole with his mother and mate, Astarte. He rides his chariot of fire as the sun-god. Since he is in a weakened state he needs the aid of the red nosed reindeer to lead the way. The sun-god is born new on New Years day. Then the dead Tamarisk tree is thrown out with the trash or burned to Baal at Beltine. The whole story of Osiris is corrupted!

One version says Attis castrated himself and died under a pine tree. Attis' (Adonis') death by a boar and being changed into a pine-tree is an obvious corruption of the god of death and resurrection. Both we emasculated. The boar, bear and bull are some of the sacred animals Set transformed into. Just like Zeus-Amen. [The Golden Bough by James George Frazer p.405] Attis and Cybele, Adonis and Aphrodite (Venus), Tammuz and Ishtar (Venus), Bel-Marduk and Ishtar, Baal and Ashtorah, Adonis and Astarte, Bacchus, Dionysus and Athene, Odin; are all corruptions of the original story Osiris and Isis. The morning star of Isis is Sirius, not Venus. The birthday of the Sun of God is the autumn equinox, not the winter solstice. The one who mated with his mother was Amen.

At Byblos, Syria the passion of Adonis was commemorated by public morning just as at JeruSalem they held the passion of Lord Jesus. Lord is translated from Adonai; the same word as Adonis. Byblos is the Greek word for Bible and the nativity of Phoenician mythology.

Trees named for the divine: Elm = Elohim Ash = Tree of life Oak = Ankh Maple = May-pole Olive = El + iah or Lord God

Accusations of Set

Set charged Isis with playing the harlot after the death of Osiris, therefore, Horus was an illegitimate child and not the true heir to the throne of Osiris. This is the same as saying Jesus is not the Son of God. Joseph thought Mary had committed adultery when he found her 'with child'. The gods gathered together at the Great Hall of Heliopolis and determined to settle this matter. They listened to the evidence of the Accuser, Set. Satan is the great Accuser of the brethren. [Revelation 12:10] The gods found that Set was the father of lies and Horus is the rightful heir to the throne. The gods: elohim in Hebrew means God's sons. Translated "judges" in Psalms 82:6 and John 10:34-36

It was further decreed that Isis was impregnated by the power on high. This Spirit of life is represented by Thoth. This is the immaculate conception of the firstborn Son of God. Horus is Osiris resurrected. Atum-Ra-Horus is the Sun of God who incarnated as Osiris, Son of Man. The Word manifested in the flesh. [John 1:18] Horus the Younger is Osiris resurrected. Horus is the Sun of God ascending to heaven from where he originally came. [John 3:13] Then Set brought charges against Osiris. Thoth pleaded his case as Osiris' Advocate. [1 John 2:1] Advocate is translated from the same word as Comforter. Again Thoth represents the Spirit of Truth. It was found that Osiris is the Word of Truth and Set a liar. Set was dragged into the Great Hall and thrown to the ground before Osiris. Thoth (the Spirit) lead Osiris to where Set was lying and made him take his seat upon him as a sign of overcoming evil through righteousness. Compare this to 1 Corinthians 15:20-28. Osiris (Son of Man) was made the honorable Judge of the dead. [John 5:22-30]

Just as they brought false charges against Christ and even found false witnesses to accuse him. But they could not find anything to convict him of. He was innocent of all charges. In fact, he exposed their guilt. This is what makes him worthy to be Judge. He is either your Savior or your executioner depending on your karma (deeds done on earth). He shall rule mankind with an iron rod which is represented by the symbol of Maat. Justice shall prevail. Set then counter-sued. Claiming he should be king, 'I am Set, I am the strongest of the Nine Gods. As I am daily in front of the Boat of Millions of Years I slay the enemy of Ra daily, and no other god can do this. Therefore, I am entitled to the office of Osiris.' Set and Ra ride in the solar bark together. Ra (Amen) the sungod agreed. Once again Ra is the adversary of Isis and Horus.

Set convinced the council to hold a retrial without Isis' intervention. So they decided on a remote island. But Isis bribed the ferry-man and turned herself into a beautiful woman (like Lilith). She asked Set to help her, explaining that she was a widow of a herdsman (Osiris) and that her only son had been robbed of their cattle by a brutal stranger. Set declared that it was wicked for a son to be robbed of his inheritance. Isis transformed into a sparrow-hawk and flew up into a tree. She told Set that he had condemned himself out of his own mouth. Compare this to David condemning himself before his son, Nathan the prophet. [2 Samuel 12:1-12-23] The Lord strikes dead their firstborn son and potential heir to the throne for David and Bathsheba's adultery. Yet, it was their evil son Solomon who became king. Sol and Amon are sun-gods. Set-Amen-Ra (Satan) is King of this wicked world for the time being, but soon the rightful heir, Atum-Horus, will sit upon the throne of David and rule the world. [2 Samuel 7:12-16 Luke 1:31-33] As a consolation, Ra summons Set to live with him, and be as a son to him in the sky as the god of storms (Typhon). In the Middle East, Baal is the storm god, just like Zeus-Amen. Amen-Ra and Set are two of a kind, in fact, they are one and the same.

This is the time when the earth was a binary solar system. While the Company of God took 80 years to decide, two Suns ruled over the earth; Sirius in the north and Ra in the south hemisphere. Because of man's rebellion, Horus-Sirius chose to return to his place next to Orion and leave Set-amen (Satan) as sun-god of this wicked world.

Osiris the Seed

Osiris was called the grain god as he taught the Egyptians to make bread. Which is no simple process: finding and grinding the grain, finding and mixing exact ingredients, letting it rise, baking at proper temperature and time. Spiritually speaking, he sows the seed or plants Word of God in the minds. [Matt.13:36-43] Set (Satan) plants the evil thoughts in the minds of his kids. [Matthew 25:31-46 James 1:14,15] Osiris is the bread of life and manna (man) from heaven who was broken into 14 parts. [John 6:32-58] These parts are his partners or co-heirs. [Romans 8:15-17] Osiris died and was planted in the ground, therefore, he sowed the Seed of Eve [Genesis 3:15] and the Seed of Abraham which became the Son of God (Horus). [Galatians 3:16] Manna is Maat, the food of the gods. It is the living Word of God.

The Spirit is what holds the body of believers together as one body or family. [1 Cor.12:12-31 Eph.2:18-22] The body of laws (Maat) keeps peace and order within the household. The children of God do NOT purposely sin. He who sins is of the Devil. "when we love God, we do His Commandments. [1 John 3:4-12 5:1-3] This is the spirit of the law that motivates one to do it. [Hebrews 8:10 10:16] If one part of the body is infected with the sickness of sin, it must be cut out in order to save the body. [Matthew 5:29,30] When there is mold on the bread, you cut it off. Likewise, a little leaven (pride) rises up the whole lump (in insurrection). The body of Christ is to be lowly and humble not exalted.

One rotten apple ruins the bunch. Set gave the forbidden fruit to Eve. The by-product was Cain. The seed of the Serpent shall have his head bruised by the Seed of the Mother of all living (Eve or Isis). The only begotten (or fathered) Son of God born of a woman is Horus. Osiris, like Adam, was not born of a woman. Set, the evil son of God, was not born of a woman. Osiris, Isis, Nephthys, and Set were begotten in heaven.

"Hail, Osiris, first of those who are in the Other World! I am thy sister Isis. No god hath done what I have done, and no goddess. I made a man child, though I was a woman, because of my desire to make thy name to live upon the earth. Thy divine essence was in my body; I placed him on the earth. He pleaded they case, he healed thy suffering, he decreed the destruction of him that had caused it. Set hath fallen before his Sword and the Smamiu fiends of Set have followed him. The throne of Keb (Earth) is to thee, O thou who art His <God's> beloved Son!" [Rev.19:11-21] Lord of the Earth. [Revelation 11:4 Zechariah 4:2,3,11,14]

As the grain god, it was necessary for Osiris to die in the spring, before he 'went to seed', to show he was reborn supernaturally not naturally. Horus was not his seed or son. Horus is Osiris reincarnated. In the Mystery Play, the Seed represented Osiris. Bulls, donkeys and swine were brought in to trample or thresh the Seed. Horus would beat the animals which represent Set trampling on the body of Osiris. The Seed was planted in the earth (tomb) and was reborn as Horus. This is the regeneration; renewing the same generation.

It was Set who killed Osiris, just as Satan caused the death of Adam. And Cain murdered Abel, the first martyr, because Cain was born of the evil one. Since Osiris and Horus are one and the same being, it is impossible for both to co-exist in heaven. The mummified Osiris is in Amenta, the land of the dead or graveyard. Horus the Hawk is the spirit-being or sahu who ascended to heaven as the Morning star Sirius. It is he who shall return in the physical form of Osiris (Son of Man) to judge and rule the nations of the earth. The body of believers will remain in Amenta (sheol in Hebrew) with Osiris until Horus' return. [John 5:22-30] The tomb is the womb of Earth from which the sons of God are reborn in the hereafter; here on earth after all things are made new. The seeds born from the body of Osiris are called first-fruits or first-born.

Memorial of the Son of Man

The Egyptians performed an reenactment of the story of Osiris as a Memorial every year at the Feast of Osiris (Pass-over). [1 Corinthians 11:17-34] During the Procession, Osiris' coffin contained the sacred things and deep secrets of the holy religion, was carried by 'Paul-bearers'. Compare this to the Ark of the Covenant. [Hebrews 9:4,5] The Upper Egyptians got the story, the characters and the time all wrong. Just as the Christians celebrate Christ at the wrong times (i.e. Christmas and Easter). They follow in the ways of the erring Romans. Christ (Horus) was born at the autumn equinox and died at the spring equinox. Likewise, he shall return at the Feast of Ingathering to gather together the body members unto himself. The making of the mummy is part of the gospel story. It is necessary for the story, but not necessary for our resurrection. The Lord is able to reconstruct us from dust just as he created Adam. In fact, he could recreate us from nothing!

The Lord's last supper, Passover and Communion are all the same. They are annual events, not weekly. In fact, the word "annual" comes from Annu the birthplace of Horus. Horus' 12 Hours in the Underworld are actually 12 months. Horus the Morning star (Sirius) is reborn once a year, not every day or every week as the infidels do. Jesus died during Passover, then resurrected during the Feast of Unleaven Bread three days later. These ancient Holy Days are celebrated annually as ordained by the Lord. Just as the Sun of God will return on the annual celebration of the Feast of Ingathering in the autumn. The very time of year that Sirius returns from a three month absence.

Set challenges Horus to a competition. Set proposes that they transform into hippopatamus (amphibians) and cast themselves into the sea, and the one who comes out of the water before the end of three months is disqualified from the office of Osiris. This represents the birth of the firstborn son from the waters of Nun. Compare to the ritual of baptism. A premature birth disqualifies, as nine months is the proper time required. This is the three months Sirius is absent. Isis intervenes and ruins the test. The Sun (Set) and Sirius (Horus) rise out of the sea of space at the same time. This is the Helical or Dawn rising of Sirius. Horus is angry and cuts off the head of Isis. This represents the death of Isis and the birth of Horus at the dawn rising of Sirius. The star representing Mother and Child is now ruled over by just the Child. Nun is the mother of Atum, Horus the Elder and Isis is the mother of Horus the Younger. Both are Horus.

Finally, Thoth wrote a letter to Osiris asking his advice. Osiris dictated his Last Will and New Testament. He declared that his son Horus shall be heir to the throne of Egypt! The matter is settled once and for all. Horus shall one day return to reclaim the throne of the Kingdom of God.

The Feast of Unleavened Bread

Osiris is the god of grain, who is trampled by the bulls and cows of Set. Horus is the Seed of his Father in heaven. [Galatians 3:16] The grain is beaten or threshed so the followers can make and "break bread" in Communion. This is the "manna from heaven". "Horus speaks to Osiris: 'I have beaten for you those who have beaten you.'" Horus defeats the Bull of Amen-Ra-Set. The Bull is Taurus, and the donkey is the sun (ie. Set). At Christ's Communion, (remember or not) we break bread in remembrance of Osiris being broken to pieces.

The Egyptian year had 12 months with 29 days each. Following the cycle of the moon. There are 4 weeks with 7 days in each. They add a 13th month of 17 days to make 365 total. One day is add every four years as in "leap year". The Hebrew calendar, which came much later, is the same. The first month starts at the dawning of Sirius. Coinciding with the Hebrew new year which is calculated at the first new moon following the autumn equinox. Both the Egyptians and Hebrews had a civil and sacred calendar. The civil begins at the autumn equinox and the sacred at the spring equinox. Osiris died during Passover just as did Jesus. The Egyptian day goes from sunset to sunset just like the Hebrew. The Egyptian 24 hour day was 12 hours daylight (Nu) and 12 hours night (Nut) which varies through-out the year just as we calculated it.

Ten great Mysteries of Amenta

1st day) Was the night of the evening meal-the last supper and the laying of offerings on the altar-the night of provisioning the Lord's Table. Osiris had been overcome by Sut and the Sebau, and they had renewed their assault upon Un-Nefer (Horus), but were defeated and exterminated by the faithful followers; it was the night of the great battle, when the Moon God Taht, and the Children of Light, overcame and annihilated the Powers of Darkness.

This is obviously the Lord's last supper on Passover. Osiris is Son of Man whose body is the bread and whose blood is the wine. Sut had just torn his body into fourteen pieces. Just as Christ's body of believers were scattered on the night of his arrest.

2nd day) Is "the night of hiding the body of him who is supreme in attributes." The mystery is that of collecting the mutilated and scattered body of Osiris, and of hiding it.

3rd day) Is the Mystery of Anup, the Embalmer, the anointer of the mummy; this is Rusta, the place of resurrection from Amenta.

Anup is Anubis, bearer of the dead souls. He is produced from Osiris laying with Nephthys in the land of the dead. Nephthys is mother nature's cycle of life to death. Anubis is one of the aspects of Osiris just like Horus.

4th day) Is in the region of Rekhet, and the Mystery is that of the two sisters, with Isis watching in tears over her brother Osiris, and brooding above the dead body to give it the warmth of life. [John 20:11-15]

The two sisters Isis and Nephthys are Mary the mother of Christ and Mary Magdalene who came to anoint the mummy (Karast). [Mark 15:46,47 16:1]

5th day) On this night the overthrown Tat-Cross, with Osiris on it, was again erected by Horus-Prince of Sekhem, in the region of Tattu, when the Holy Spirit Ra descended upon the mummy, and the two became united for the resurrection.

The Tet is the Tree Osiris died in and Jesus died on. It has been over three days and nights since the death of Osiris-Christ. The Spirit is God's supernatural power working in the natural world.

6th day) Here the scene is in Sekhem, where the Mystery is that of the blind Horus, or Horus in the dark, who here receives his sight, and it is also the Mystery of dawn upon the coffin of Osiris-the Mystery of Horus, the Mortal, transfiguring into Horus the Immortal.

The Sun of God had risen from the darkness of death. [Mark 16:2 Matt. 28:3]

7th day) On the 7th night, the four Pillars are erected, with which the future Kingdom of God the Father is to be found; it is called "the night of erecting the flag staff of Horus," and of establishing him as the heir to his father's "property."

The flag is the sign of Leo the Lion. He is the Lion of Judah and heir to the Promise land or New Earth. The four pillars are the four races that shall become sons of God. The Father's property is the earth. He has regained his throne as Lord of Earth.

8th day) The Mystery of the 8th night, was that the Great Judgment on the highway of the damned, when the suit was closed against the rebels, who had failed and were defeated-the verdict of the avengement.

Judgment day is the Last Great day or 8th divine day following the Millennium. [Revelation 20:7,11-15] It is foreseen by the Last Great day of the Feast of Ingathering. [John 7:37] Those who will no conform to the will of God will be annihilated in the Lake of fire.

9th day) The great hoeing in Tattu, when the associates of Sut are massacred, and the fields are manured with the blood.

This is the gathering together of the military men for the battle of Armageddon. [Rev.16:14-16 19:11-21] It is also the dividing of the good fruits from the bad fruits. The juice is their blood. The rivers of blood with run as high as the horses bridle. [Rev.14:14-20 Ezekiel 38 & 39]

10th day) On the 10th day the glorious ones are judged, the evil dead are parted off, and joy goes its round in Thinnis. It is the great festival night, named Ha-k-er-a, or "Come you to me," in which the blending of the two souls is solemnized.

This is obviously the Feast of Ingathering or Tabernacles. [Mat.24:27-31] God's new year is ushered in with ten days of penitence, including the Day of Atonement. It is when the Lord will gather together the glorious elect from the four corners of the earth. The body of believers will be at-one with the Lord. All evil will be destroyed so the sons of God can live in peace. [Zechariah 14:12,16-21 Revelation 21:1-8]

Judgment Scene

In the Judgment scene, the jackal-headed Anubis digs up the corpse and escorts the soul from the land of the dead to stand before Lord Osiris (Son of Man). [John 5:22-30] The four sons of Horus the Elder stand on a lotus-flower before Osiris as He is Judge of mankind. The lotus represents rebirth. In the embalming process, the heart was removed from the mummy and saved in a vessel. Now that heart is weighed in the balances against the feather of Maat (the Law). You are judged according to the Lord's laws you have broken. If it is weighed down by the burden of sin, it will be off balance. Then the Beast Amemut (Amen of Mut) will devour the heart of guilty party. Amemut is an attribute of Amen son of Mut and Destroyer of Amenta (the land of the dead). Amemut is part: hippopotamus, crocodile, and lion. The Bible says, "your adversary the devil, as a roaring lion, walks about, seeking whom he may devour". [1 Peter 5:8] When the Ammit beast devours the heart, it represents being consumed by Mother Nature. This is the first death. The second death is to be consumed by the Lake of fire.

Set (Satan) is the accuser who accuses them before God. [Rev.12:10] All sins will be exposed. The Saints stand on the symbol of Maat (the Word of God). Thoth, Isis and Nephthys all have the feather of Maat as head-dresses. Meaning the Law of God rules over them. [Rev.12:17 14:12] The ibis-headed Thoth is the Advocate as well as recorder and scribe. He has the biography of everyone ever born written in a book. [Rev.20:11-15] He writes the names on the leaves of the Tree of Life of those who shall receive everlasting life in the kingdom of Osiris. The Truth (Maat) shall set you free (of Set). Those not written in the Book of life, shall be exterminated. [Revelation 20:15 21:27 22:19 Daniel 12:1-3]

This is the Weighing of Words. "for every idle word men may speak, they will give account of it in the Day of Judgment. For by your words you will be justified, and by your words you will be condemned." [Matthew 12:31-37] "Anyone who speaks a word against the Son of Man (Osiris), it will be forgiven him; but whoever speaks against the Holy Spirit (Word of Truth), it will not be forgiven him, either in this age or the age (Millennium) to come." The great masses of common people were deceived by the priests of Amen, into believing that they would be magically saved by calling upon the name of the Lord and writing the texts on their coffins. They believed they were not under the law of God! This is the false gospel of Amen.

The soul found righteous will make the confession that he has not purposely sinned. These are the Declarations of Innocence: 1) "I believe in the One True God and Creator." 2) Only the Upper Egyptians made graven images or statues of their gods. 3) "I have not cursed or opposed God." 4) They kept the holy days ordained by God. 5) Honor your Father in heaven and your mother earth. Maat is God's natural and supernatural laws. "Do Maat that you might live long upon the earth." 6) "I have not killed." "I have not commanded anyone to kill" (as in military). Deciding to join the armed forces is premeditated murder. 7) "I have not committed adultery." "I have not committed fornication." 8) "I have not stolen." 9) "I have not lied." "Do not bear witness with false words nor injure another with your tongue." 10) "I have not desired the property of others." Plus many more (78). These not only parallel the Ten Commandments plus the two Commandments of Christ, but include the Sermon on the mount. Reference: The Book of Coming Forth by Day.

Above them is the 12 jurors or assessors, Horus and Osisis. Just as the Lord told his twelve disciples they would judge the twelve nations of Israel. [Matthew 19:28] These are his body of believers. The 14 also represent the 14 parts of Osiris' body. Horus has a sun-disk over his head showing he is Son of God (Atum-Ra). Horus the son takes the righteous deceased before Osiris the father. Compare to Christ defending the saints before his Father. Osiris is wearing the crown of the King. Below this, Horus is now wearing the crown as king because he is heir to the throne of Osiris. Horus, Thoth, Anubis and others are wearing tunics with tails hanging down the back. From here modern man got the idea of wearing tuxedos with tails on special occasions. The Egyptians were fashionably ahead of their time. At the Marriage Feast, the virtuous bride of the Son of God will wear white linen garment just as Ani is portrayed wearing. [Revelations 19:7-9]

The throne is the coffer of Osiris who is inside a type of tomb built on a stone foundation made in the shape of the symbol of Maat. The Judge is in the sacred chamber, much like the king's chamber in the Great Pyramid or the Holy of Holies in the Temple of Jerusalem. The Maat symbol is the chief corner stone of the Great Pyramid. [Mark 12:10] The throne is the Mercy seat on the Ark of the Covenant. The Ark was made from the Acacia (Shittim) tree. Shet-tim is Ashet, the Tree of life. Inside the Ark is the Commandments of God called Maat. Maat is the Manna or Bread of life or Word of God given to those judged innocent. Osiris is holding Aaron's staff or rod as law giver. [Hebrews 9:4,5]

This is the rod that came to life and budded. Compare this to the golden box of Atum-Ra that contains his Rod, the Horus lock of hair and the Uraeus head-dress. Its Aaron's rod that turns into a serpent! The vessel contain the power of God able to destroy the earthlings (sons of Geb) with divine fire. Just like the Ark of the Covenant.

The four sons of Osiris: Tuamutef (Anubis or Atum of Mut), Qebhusnuf (Horus), Amset (Amen-Set) and Hapi (Amen the Apis-Bull) bear the Ark or Coffin. They are the sacred Chest-bearers (Christ-bearers not Paul-bearers). They are the lion (king), eagle (hawk), man (son of man) and bull (ox) that bear the Lord on his throne in Ezekiel 1:10,26-28 & Rev.4:2-8. The chest of Christ contains the law of life. [Hebrews 8:10 10:16] The heart of the Covenant is God's Commandments. [Deu.4:13 Exodus 34:28] The hieroglyphic for Maat is a 24 inch (1 cubit) ruler. The Ruler rises to his two feet, standing on the law which measures out justice for all. [Rev.10:1,2 Micah 4:1-3] Standing on Maat is the same as standing on the Word of God. Under the Ark (Throne of Osiris), flows the river of life (Nile) that feeds the lotus flower or Tree of life. Here is the origin of the Hindus' use of the lotus flower as a symbol of rebirth.

Osiris is high priest in the order of Melchizedek, King of God's kingdom, and Judge of the world. Osiris is the Emerald One on the throne. [Revelation 4:2,3] Behind Osiris is Isis (mother earth) and Nephthys (mother nature). From the mother earth the soul is resurrected in mortal form. Then if found innocent or having received mercy (grace) from the Judge, you are transformed into a spiritual son of God (sah). "I will make your descendants as the stars of heaven...because Abraham obeyed My voice and kept My charge (Maat), My Commandments (Maat), My statutes (Maat), and My laws (Maat)." [Genesis 26:4,5] Pardons may be possible to those with the potential to reform. The incorrigible infidels will be thrown into the inferno called the Lake of fire.

Anubis delivers the souls (mummies) from the land of the dead because he is son of Osiris (Lord of the dead) and Nephthys. She is the cycle of life to death and Anubis is the cycle of death to mortal life. Horus faces Osiris as if in a mirror. As Osiris died and was reborn Horus. Horus is not his son, but himself regenerated. Horus is in the Hawk form as He is Son of God who flies the heavens, over the earth, seeing who does good and who does evil. The all-seeing eye of Horus sees everything. The bird (hawk, dove, phoenix) represents God's supernatural power called the holy Spirit. It is the power that raised the soul from the dead and transforms it into an immortal soul. That spirit-being (Ba) is represented as a human-headed hawk and the cradle of rebirth.

The Day of Souls

All Soul's Day is on the autumn equinox, not the day after Halloween. It is the Feast of Ingathering when the Lord is coming to gather his Saints. The Roman Catholics have corrupted the Day of the Lord Osiris, into the Day of the Lord of Death (Amen-Ra-Satan). Those that rise from their graves are not evil spirits, ghosts, demons, ghouls, or poltergeist. These are the righteous souls that follow the example of the Lord who resurrected from the grave. Immediately following the great earthquake, they shall rise from the earth. [Matthew 27:51-54 Revelation 16:18 Zechariah 14:5] The Saints shall resurrect at the Lord's coming and the second death has no power over them. [Revelation 20:4-6] Judgment Day is not until after the Millennium. [Revelation 20:11-15]

The "Opening of the Mouth" ceremony parallels Ezekiel 37. The mortal body (Ka) is reformed then the mouth is open so the Breath of life or Spirit of life can enter the dead body and reactivate it. Just as the Lord activated Adam's lifeless corpse. His inert soul (represented by a dark silhouette of a body) became a living soul. This is called the Day of Resurrection and the Lord's Day. Next the mortal soul is transformed into an immortal soul or spirit-being (Sahu). This is the glorified body. [1 Corinthians 15:42-55] To be as Horus, the good Son of God. To be At-One with Lord Osiris (Great Spirit or Sahu), which is the body of Christ. Any part of the body that won't be healed from the sickness of sin, shall be cut off in order to save the body. Remission and recovery come from repentance (turning from sin). [Matthew 5:29,30]

When the deceased comes to consciousness on rising in Amenta (the grave) he is said to have broken his sleep forever which was in the dwelling of Sebau, Seb or Geb (the earth). Christ also referred to the deceased as sleeping. "Our friend Lazarus sleeps, but I go that I may wake him up." [John 11:11-14] Lazarus was dead and the Lord was going to awake him from his deep sleep. The masses will not be awakened until the Lord returns. [1 Thessalonians 4:13-18] In fact, Osiris is still a mummy lying in Amenta, breathless and without motion, awaiting to rise again. This represents the body of Christ remaining in hell (the grave) until his return. [2 Thes.1:4-10 2:1,2] "I am the soul of Osiris, and rest <in peace> in him." [chapter 127] Even Christ rested in hell (the underground grave) for three days before resurrecting. [Acts 2:31] He dwelled in the darkness of Amenta, the land of the dead, and then rose up to Tuat, the land of the living, as Sun of God (Atum-Ra-Horus). L'azarus is L' Asar-us. Asar is Osiris. Le in Frech is The as in Theo (God). El is God in Hebrew. Lazarus is Osiris.

The Egyptians would not have gone to all the trouble of making mummies (preserving the corpse) and building elaborate tombs filled with precious things, if they believed they were going to heaven. They believed in the hereafter: to be here on earth after Horus resurrects them from Amenta (the land of the dead or cemetery). The Field of Reeds (Sekhet-Aaru) and the Elysian Fields refer to the God's garden paradise here on earth. The Book of Pylons says Her-qenbet-f (Horus) calls the souls of the righteous and puts them in their dwellings by the corner of those who live near him. Compare this to those in the graves hearing the voice of the Son of God and resurrecting to life. [John 5:28,29] He is the chief corner stone in the House of the Lord. Osiris assigns estates in his kingdom to the righteous. [John 14:2,3] The Egyptians believe in the first resurrection for the priests of God to teach God's law for a Millennium. [Rev.20:4-6] As it is the priests' job to teach the law and the king's job to enforce it. Then following the Millennium, would be the second resurrection and Day of Judgment. They were well aware that only Osiris as Horus could ascend back to the heavens from which He came. [John 3:13] They remain in their tombs awaiting the day of the Lord, when they shall hear his voice and awake from the deep sleep. The mummy shall rise up from the dead to live on earth. [Matthew 27:51-53 John 5:22-30]

"Let the Way be open to my soul and my shade, that I may see the great god within His sanctuary on the day of the soul's reckoning, when all hearts and words are weighed." The Bible says, "I will put My laws in their mind and write them on their hearts; and I will be their God, and they shall be My people." [Hebrews 8:10 10:16] The sons of God shall know God's law by heart. The shade or shadow represents the substance or shape of the body to be resurrected. "A shadow of things to come, is the body of Christ (Osiris)." [Colossians 2:17] This is the body of believers to be raised in the last day.

The Egyptians also believe in the second death of nonexistence in the Lake of fire. They do not believe anyone is tormented forever. In fact, it parallels the Bible almost exactly. The enemies of Osiris (Orion) are thrown into the Lake of fire. These are Taurus the Bull (Min-otaur), Ares the Ram (Ra-Amen) and Cetus the sea beast (the Dragon, Amemit). The constellations in heaven represent those on earth. "The Devil, who deceived them, was cast into the Lake of fire and sulfur where the Beast and the false prophet are. And they will be tormented day and night forever and ever." [Rev.20:10] This is the Antichrist (Satan incarnated) and the priest of Amon. [Jeremiah 46:25] "Then Death (Amemut or Amentet) and Hades (the star or sun of God in the constellation of Taurus) were cast into the lake of fire. This is the second death." [Revelation 20:14] "I enter in and I come forth from the tank of flame on the day when the adversaries are annihilated at Sekhem." [Book of the Dead-Ritual chapter 1] "I have come from the lake of flame, from the lake of fire and from the field of flame." The Saints are purged and refined in the fire of purgatory (Meskat), while the lawless are incinerated in the inferno. Mes means to be born from water and khat is the physical body. Meskhat is the rebirth as a spiritual being like Sahu (Osiris). Mes is the root of Messiah.

The fallen stars of heaven will be consumed by the fire of God presence. [2 Peter 3:12 Rev.21:1] God in the first heaven is going to consume the second heaven of outer space. What the Egyptians called Nut. The evil suns of God will be consumed in the Lake of fire raining down from the first heaven. Only the righteous will survive by being refined in the fire. The first heaven will become our New Heaven on this reNewed Earth. We are not going to heaven to be with Osiris, heaven is coming here. Orion is Osiris as Son of Man returning to earth and Sirius is Horus the Sun of God that shall rule the New Earth. [Rev.21:23] Ptah is the Father who rules over the Sun. [1 Cor.15:20-28] The Annu bark parallels Noah's ark. Those who are to be saved shall board the boat-ark where the Lake of fire will not take away their breath of life. [Gen.7:22] These are the ones who are rescued from the second death. They have found grace in God's eyes because they are righteous. [Genesis 7:1 6:8,9] All evil shall be destroyed [Gen.6:5-7] and the earth shall be renewed. [Rev.21:1-8] New Jeru-Salem is the celestial city setting down on the summit of Mt. Zion. It is the capital of God's kingdom on earth. Within the gates are the river of life and Tree of life.

The Egyptians had no vicarious atonement, no imputed righteousness, no second-hand salvation, no justified by faith, no sacrifice could wash away sin, no absolution by the so-called vicar of Christ (Pope). Since the Egyptians did not purposely sin, they did not need to be redeemed. Horus is the justifier of the righteous, not the lawless. You are saved by faithful obedience to the Word of God. Only those who proved themselves worthy shall enter God's kingdom. [2 Thessalonians 1:4-10] Christ did NOT sacrifice himself so that you could continue to sin. Baptism represents spiritual rebirth and a chance to start clean. A chance to do it right this time. A chance to learn from your mistakes and make the corrections. You are to repent of sin, NOT repeat the sin. See "Egyptian Book of the Dead and the Ancient Mysteries of Amenta" by Gerald Massey.

With freedom, comes responsibility for the consequences. You cannot escape by placing the burden on the scapegoat of some sacrificial redeemer who will do all your dirty work. On Judgment day, the books shall be opened and YOU shall be held responsible for your actions. All your sins shall be uncovered and exposed to the world. The covering cherub will take the veil from your eyes and the world will see you for who you really are. [Ezekiel 28:14] Clean up you act now while there is still time. Those who are found innocent are given the small "conical" crown of righteousness that is later traded in for the Crown of Life. [2 Timothy 4:8 Revelation 2:11 1 Corinthians 9:25]

In the hereafter, Set and Horus will be reconciled. If God the Father can't redeem His prodigal son, what hope is there for mortal sinners like us? Likewise, in the Bible, Satan shall be purged in the Lake of fire and be restored to his pure self as Lucifer the archangel. Compare to the Hindu story. Vishnu shall pardon the demons that Shiva threw into the bottomless pit, after which they will dwell with the gods on Mount Meru. Mount Meru is the same as Mount Olympus and Mount Zion. It is the capital of God's kingdom on the holy Promise Land called the renewed Earth. Which is God's garden, Elysian fields, Fields of Peace, etc. [Deceptions and Myths of the Bible page 387]

Book of the Dead

(Bible of Death and Resurrection)

Tem is an extraterrestrial time traveler. The 12 scenarios are the 12 ages of the Zodiacs as the Sun of God (Sirius) travels through time. In each age there is a battle between the Lord of light and the lord of darkness. The Yin vs. the Yang. The setting of Sirius on the western horizon represents the Sun of God going to be the companion of Orion in the Tuat (southern night sky). He goes through 12 hours or houses before it goes into the 12 hours in the underworld. This is symbolic of Christ's death as Son of Man (or Osiris) and resurrection as Son of God (or Horus) when he returns to earth. Compare the 12 hours to the 12 labours of Herakles (Horus) who was reborn one of the gods.

The ancient astronomers of Lower Egypt tracked the multitude of stars in the universe as taught by Osiris, the extraterrestrial. They had little interest in the dwarf white star of our solar system. The Egyptians were aware that the sun and stars do not move, but appear to move as the earth revolves around the sun. The two horizons (east and west) and the two meridians (south to north) are the four points that make the celestial cross. They were used as markers on the Cosmic Clock called the precession of the equinoxes.

The Book of the Dead is really the Book of Coming Forth by Night (Per-T-em-Hru in Egyptian). Which can be translated as House of Tem-Horus. The Book of the Dead or Book of the Necro could also be called the Book of the Negro (which means Black in Greek). As it was the dark skies that intrigued the dark skinned star-gazers. On the heavenly plane, Hathor is the Holy Cow or heavenly cow. She is the sea of space that gave birth to the stars (i.e. Nut). Hathor means the House of Horus and refers to Sirius within the House of Taurus, one of the twelve houses of the Zodiac. Horus-Sirius was her firstborn of the age of Virgo the Virgin. He was the King during the age of Leo the Lion. He manifested as Osiris in the age of Taurus. Then from out of the watery womb (sea of space) came the fish-god, Jesus, in the age of Pisces. The fish being his logo. Tem, the time traveler, is expected to return at the dawning of the age of Aquarius. Besides the Book of the Dead, there is: the Book of Am-Tuat, the Book of

Gates, the Book of Two Ways, and the Coffin Texts. All written during the New Kingdom age after 1500 B.C.

The Book of Am-Tuat

The Book of Ame-Tuat (Who is in the Tuat?). The answer is: Amen is in the Tuat as the Lord of Death (Seker). It is the twelve hour voyage of the Sun of God (Sirius) across the lower heaven, starting at sunset (Amen-Set). The Tuat is the lower heaven south of the Tropic of Cancer. It is NOT the underworld. The Taurt is the upper heaven, north of the Tropic of Cancer. Both are in the night sky (Nut). The Am-Smen are the northern (Arctic) stars that never go into the underworld. The earthly counterpart of the heavenly Tuat is the two lands of Lower and Upper Egypt. The Sun (Ra) is contrary to Sirius. The sun has nothing to do with the Zodiac. The Egyptians observed the stars at night when the sun is under-the-world. When the sun (Ra) travels through the underworld, the underworld is in 12 hours of daylight (Nu) and the upperworld is in darkness (Nut). It is the sun (Amen-Ra) that swallows up the stars, including Sirius, at sunrise.

Jesus, as Son of Man, was underground in the grave (Amenta/Sheol/Hell) for three days and three nights. During this time, Jesus, the Son of God, went to the Tuat of Tartarus (Taurus) to preach to the fallen angels (spirits). [1 Peter 3:19 & 2 Peter 2:4,5] Hades is the head and horns of Taurus the bull. Then the Sun of God (Sirius) rises just before sunrise on the first day of the week. This is the dawn rising of Sirius and rebirth of Jesus/Horus after 3 months in the underworld.

1st hour: The Son of Man, Osiris, is flesh or a human being subject to death. He is filled with the Word of God which is the knowledge of God's kingdom. He is carried in a bark (boat-ark) as he embarks on his voyage. Those on the ship are saved like Noah's family. The others are swallowed by the Sea Serpent and buried at sea. Much like Jonah. The Sea serpent is the Leviathan in Isaiah 27:1.

2nd hour: The Lord of the Sabbath is Land-Lord of the Promise Land called the new Earth. [Revelation 11:4 Zechariah 4:2,3,11,14] The Land-Lord wills this garden of God to his co-heirs. [Hebrews 9:15-20] The adopted Sons of God are the firstfruits or firstborn of God. [1 Corinthians 15:20-28] Those of the body of Osiris shall rise again in the garden of God.

3rd hour: Osiris died and Horus resurrected in his place. They are one and the same. The power of the Holy Spirit (divine essence) caused the rebirth from Son of Man to Son of God. Both Horus and Jesus mean Savior. Flesh cannot enter God's kingdom, therefore, we must be transformed or born again from human beings to spiritual beings. We must shed our skins and shed ourselves of Satanic ways (sin).

4th hour: The Son of God is guided by the Word of God (Thoth). [-John 1:1-14 & 5:19-30 Matthew 4:4-10] He possesses the breath of life or

Holy Spirit of God. He has power over the serpent Satan through enlightenment or spiritual growth. Which comes through the holy Spirit (God's supernatural medium).

In the Book Ami Tuat (Who is in the Tuat), they travel through Restau (Region of Set). Re-setau or sebau fiends are the followers of Re-Set. Restau is the no man's land between Upper and Lower Egypt. Sakkara and Memphis are the major cities between Giza and Dahshur. Sakkara is not on the Nile so the pilgrims cross in a sledge. Seker is the god of death in Amenta (both underground and underworld). Seker is Sakar, Warlord of Karnak. Kar, Art, Akar, and Kart are names of the abode of the damned. Kar means Killed (as in a war). Necropolis is Seker's city called Valley of the dead Kings of Thebes. All warriors shall die at the Battle of Armageddon. Dahshur's heavenly counterpart is the constellation of Hades. The region of Taurus called the Hidden Circle of Amen, the Bull of heaven. Amen is the head and horns. His followers make up the body. Restau borders on Hades (Dahshur), the region filled with fire breathing serpents and gods. This is where Christendumb got the idea of souls being tormented in hellfire (Hades). It is the Lake of fire that they should fear, as that is the second death. Even Hades shall be consume by the heavenfire of God. [Revelation 20:14] No one is tormented forever!

5th hour: He overcomes the obstacles of nature through his supernatural powers of the Spirit of God. [Hebrew 5:8-14] He became Sun of Righteousness by learning to choose good over evil. [Isaiah 7:14,15] The Lord with the Sword separates good from the evil. [Matthew 25:31-46] God promised Abraham that some of his sons would be as the stars in heaven and some as the sands of the sea. [Genesis 13:16 26:4,5] The sands of the sea are the dead; dust to dust. The fallen stars shall become star dust. Those in the domain of the sea serpent will be raised, judged and thrown into the Lake of fire. [Revelation 20:11-15] The fifth day is Satan's day. He is ruler of the sea and prince of the power of the air. [Genesis 1:20-22] He is the five pointed star (pentacle) that fell into the sea. [Revelation 8:10]

6th hour: The Son of God comes face to face with his mortal existence or physical death on the cross. The powers of darkness overcome him. This is when Sirius-Orion crosses the western horizon into the underworld. Satan the serpent possesses the flesh but the spiritual-being shall be born new. The lamb of God sacrificed himself to become the Lion-King of God. The sixth day of creation is when man was created in the likeness of the sons of God (Elohim). [Genesis 1:26] On the seventh divine day, they shall be recreated.

7th hour: The Lord with the Sword decapitates the beast. [Revelation 13:3,14] The body of the beast are the body members who follow the head (Antichrist). They are thrown into the Lake of fire. This is permanent second death. [Rev.19:11-21] Apollyon (Apophis) shall be destroyed. [Rev.9:11] Death shall be destroyed. [Revelation 20:13] Hades shall be destroyed. Meanwhile, the head of the beast is incarcerated in the bottomless pit or abyss.[Rev.20:1,7-9] Later, to be released for a short time to lead his followers in an insurrection against the Sons of God (Saints). These lawless ones who rebel against God's authority are liquidated by God Himself. The body of Osiris on the Island in the Lake of fire is the same as the Lord in the camp of the saints surrounded by the fire raining down from heaven. [Revelation 20:9]

The day of Judgement: the grim reaper crushes the bad fruits while the good fruits are saved to be the firstfruits of God's garden paradise. [Rev. 14:14-20] The Lord of the Sabbath is the Lord of the Seventh Divine Day (7,000th year). The Day of the Lord is the day of His coming.

8th hour: The Saints who overcome the evil one have washed their robes white.[Revelation 7:13-17] Through their righteous acts. [Revelation 19:7-9] They shall hear the voice of the Lord and rise up from the grave. [1 Thessalonians 4:16 John 5:28,29 Matthew 24:27-31 Revelation 20:4,,5] They are the bride to be in the white wedding gown.

9th hour: The Son of God rebukes Satan for the body of believers. Who are soon to be Sons of God. Just as He did Moses. [Jude 9] Michael is his heavenly name. Just as Lucifer is Satan's heavenly name.

10th hour: The Sun of God (Sirius) is ready to resurrect just before dawn on the Eastern horizon. The evil Son of God, Satan, is trying to prevent the rise of the Sun of Righteousness. War breaks out in the heavens. [Revelation 12:7-9] Satan and his stars or angels are cast down to Earth as the Fallen Stars, by Michael the Mon-arch Angel. The sun of Satan (Amen-Ra-Set) will set for the final time and the Lord of light (Atum-Ra-Horus) will rise in his place.

11th hour: Satan is thrown into the Lake of fire. [Revelation 20:10] Consumed by the presence of God. The four creatures (serphim) announce the coming of the triumphant Lord. [Revelation 4:7 5:8] The shadow (khaibit), the double (ka), the body (khat), the mind (ba) and the spirit (khu or shu) of the incorrigible infidels are cremated in the Lake of Fire. He exists no more. This is the double-death.

12th hour: The beloved Son of God is born the watery womb of deep space. [1 Corinthians 15:35-55] This is Atum-Ra begotten of Ptah and born from Nun (Nonexistence). The heavenly body called the Morning Star (Sirius) is risen to life to enlighten the world. [Rev.22:16 John 1:9] "Death is swallowed up by victory." He set precedence for us to follow: that we can be sons of God like him. [Romans 8:19-29 John 1:12,13] If we become righteous like him. The Way to God is through the Word of God, including the Commandments of God. [Revelation 12:17 14:12] Those saved have their names in the Book of the Living, [Revelation 21:15,27] but the outlaws have their names blotted out of the Book of life. [Exodus 32:33,34]

The Book of Gates

The Book of Gates and Book of Ami Tuat were both composed by the priests of Amen-Ra at Thebes. They are written as science fiction horrors.

They depict the sun in its daily conquest through the underworld. The sun dies and is reborn daily. It also goes through the 12 Zodiac signs during 12 months of a solar year dying at the winter solstice (Dec.25) and reviving in the spring. The priests of Amen used it for astro-divination.

I have adapted it to the Heliopolis priests' way of thinking. Replacing Amen-Ra (the sun) with Atum-Ra (Sirius). The bark of Atum-Horus does not travel through the Zodiacs. He travels through time. The Zodiacs are ages that last 2160 years each. The story written in the heavens tells how we can die and be reborn like the good Son of God. It is the wicked priests of Amen who say the souls ascend to heaven at death.

The Sun (Sirius) that ruled over the earth in Adam's day, sets in the west. Horus of the Horizon ascends to his place as Sirius, companion to Orion. The Son enters the western gate that leads to the underworld. He is on his maiden voyage through the sea of space that encompasses the earth. The Egyptians call this Nut, the mother aspect, that swallows the Sun and then gives birth to Him at the eastern gate. At the dawn rising of Sirius, the Horus Child is begotten from the watery womb of Nut. This occurs annually at the autumn equinox.

He has distanced himself from us earthlings because we rebelled against him from the beginning. Rem (Re-amen), the evil eye in the sky, became the sun of our solar system because man choose to follow his evil ways. They still look up to the sun for enlightenment and they still consider the sun the source of all life on earth. Mankind sees the sun as "good".

The twelve gates are the twelve doors of the twelve houses of the Zodiac. Jesus said "I am the Door and the Way." It is through him that we can enter the House of God. "I shall return and receive you to Myself; that where I am (on earth), there you may be also." [John 10:9 14:2,6] Jesus entered earth during the age of Pisces. He shall return as Atum-Horus at the dawning of Aquarius.

First scenario: Atum-Re orders the deaths of the outlaws. Their sins are: blasphemy, perjury, and murder. These are the Commandments 1,6 & 9. [Exodus 20:3,13,16 Revelation 21:8 22:15] The gate guarded by the serpent is the one that leads to the garden of God. [Genesis 3:24] The flaming Sword which turned in every way is the Sun of God.

Second scenario: Atum-Re-Horus has the power to overcome all obstacles through the Word of God. Which is the Sword of the Spirit.

Third scenario: The Lake of Life or River of Life awaits the righteous, while the Lake of Fire awaits the lawless sinners. This is the river, Eridanus, that runs at the foot of Orion. [Revelation 20:14,15 22:1,17] This is the second death.

Forth scenario: "Your flesh shall rise up for you, your bones shall fuse themselves for you, your members shall collect themselves for you, your flesh shall reassemble for you! Sweet be the breath for your noses, unraveled be your mummy cloths, unveiled by your mummy masks! Sunlight for your divine eyes, that with them you shall see the Light! Lift yourselves from your weariness, that you may receive your fields!" The breath of life (Spirit) reactivates the soul to see the sunlight of the Sun of God rising in the east. This is the resurrection of the sons of God in the Promise land after all things are made new. This is the Fields of Peace (Elysian fields). [Ezekiel 37:1-14]

The Father's (Atum's) phallus (penis) sprays semen over those who died at sea in their voyage for life. The ankh is the Spirit that gives life. The Opening of the Mouth allows the Breath of life to re-enter the soul. The breath of life is in your mouth. The Word of God is in your mouth. The Spirit of God is in your mouth. All are one and the same. [Ephesians 4:4-6 Ezekiel 37:1-14] They shall hear the voice of the Son of God (Horus/Jesus) and rise from their graves. [John 5:22-30] Resurrecting the born again sons of God. They shall embark on the bark of Osiris, just as Noah's day when the righteous were saved on the ark. [Genesis 7:22]

Fifth scenario: Lord Osiris is the Judge and the 12 disciples are his jurors. [Matthew 19:28] Osiris is Son of Man who rises from Amenta (the grave). [John 5:22-30] Sheol (the grave) has no hold on him. He has the keys of the cemetery gate. [Revelation 1:18] Osiris is the Judge sitting on the Great White Throne. He either your Savior or your Executioner.

Sixth scenario: The 'flesh of Re' is the Son of God in his human form as Son of Man. Man must shed his carnal nature. Humans are compared to grain or first-fruits. The Grim reaper with a sickle will gather the bad fruits. The life juices will run like rivers of blood. Then the Lord will gather the good fruits during the Feast of Ingathering. [Rev.14:14-20 Mat.13:37-43 1 Corinthians 15:20-28] The Lake of fire is reserved for those condemned at the Judgment of the dead. It is a complete and final annihilation. Osiris is Judge. The scale balances the heart against the Maat (law and order established by God). Only the pure can enter the blessed life in the Hereafter (Here on earth after all is made new). The food grown in the Fields of Peace (Eden) is also called Maat. The Saints live on the Word of God, the Manna from heaven. [John 6:32-58] The Son of Man sowed the seed and from the dead body of Osiris sprout the seeds or sons of God. [Matthew 13:37-43] The dormant seed is activated by the holy spirit. Osiris' enemies, the sons of Set, are beneath his heels. Just as stated in the Word of God. [Genesis 3:15 1 Cor.15:20-25-28 Psalms 110:1] Satan and his followers shall be under the Lord's heel. The black pig (Set) is banished as the scapegoat.

Seventh scenario: Seven is the Lord's number as Lord of the Sabbath. Osiris is portrayed as the Green One seated as King and Judge. He holds the willowing fan and the shepherd's staff. The willowing fan separates the chaff from the seed; the bad from the good by the Judge. [Matthew 3:12 25:31-46] The good seed shall be planted in God's garden and the chaff (outer shell) shall be burned in the Lake of fire. The shepherd leads and instructs the lambs of God. [Matthew 10:1-18] The Egyptians recorded this thousands of years before Christ came and proclaimed the same thing. Melchizedek and Krishna are also called the Green One. Green is the color of life. Especially the vegetation that produces the breath of life.

Eighth scenario: "I am the son born of his Father, I am the father born from his son [i.e. Atum and Re are together in a continual cycle of renewal]. You are bound with strong ropes... Your bodies will be hacked up, your soul will become non-existent. You will not see Re in his manifestations as he journeys in the secret region'.

Atum-Re is both the father and the son. He incarnated as Osiris, Osiris died and rose again as Horus, son of Isis. Christ is the only begotten Son of God the Father. He formed Adam and then was born of the line of Israel. He is the forefather and descendant of David. [Revelation 22:16] He is the Lord with the Sword that shall slay the followers of the lawless one. The shall become a feast for the fowls. [Revelation 19:11-21]

Ninth scenario: shows the dualism of the Lord. He is portrayed with two faces. Horus is his good side and Seth his dark side. Likewise, the Incas made statues with the good sun of God on one side and the bad on the other side. The bad (prodigal) son is refined in the Lake of fire and Upper and Lower Egypt are united as one. Is there two opposing sons or just one playing both parts??? Are the twin suns sibling rivals as Zoroaster says? [Job 38:7] Lucifer the Daystar [Isaiah 14:12] and Michael the Morning star. The Truth vs. the lie. The truth leads to life while the lie leads to destruction. The Lord is both the Savior and Executioner. Either way; it is your choice to make. [1 John 4:1-6] Those who follow the good Son, keep God's Commandments (Maat). [1 John 5:1-3] That is the sign that you are God's. Many scientists and religions believe the earth was originally a binary solar system. On the first day, God said, "Let there be light." This was Atum-Ra-Horus represented as a Hawk headed lion because it is the age of Leo the lion. The eye of Horus is Sirius. On the forth day, God created the sun. This is Re-Amen or Lucifer the Day-Star. The two eyes in the sky. The eye of Rem is the sun. "When the Morning stars sang together and all the sons of God shouted for joy." [Job 38:7]

Tenth scenario: that old serpent called Apophis and the Dragon is chained up. Then on Judgment day, the sea serpent (leviathan) gives up the dead from the sea and from the earth (Geb). [Revelation 20:13] The dead rise from their graves in mother earth. The sons of Horus are the sons of God in the first resurrection. [Revelation 20:1-5] The Uamemti or fallen angels are also restrained.

Eleventh scenario: four baboons represent the four races and the carnal nature of man driven by his "animal instincts". The corrupt flesh cannot enter God's kingdom. [1 Corinthians 15:50-55] We must be born again sons of God. [1 Corinthians 15:42-49] They announce the coming of the victorious Lion-King. The sons of God shout for joy. [Revelation 5]
Twelfth scenario: Just as there are twelve hours of night that ends with

the sunrise. The Sun of Righteousness rises from the watery womb of Nut just before dawn. Atum-Re is the Morning star of Sirius resurrected and rising to power. [Malachi 4:2 Matthew 24:27-31] He rises from the Island of the Double Cave. One cave is the mouth of Nut as she swallows the Sun. The island on the opposite cave in the east is Nut's pubic region; the primordial mound where the Sun of God is reborn. The hieroglyphic for Nut or Mut is a vulture, a rising sun, an egg and a female. The fertile female vul-ture represents her vul-va.

Atum-Horus ends up back in the place he started; on earth. This is the cycle of time through the ages of the Zodiac. The Lord Jesus is coming back to earth to rule as Sun of God. Just as in the beginning when he was Lord over the Garden of Eden. This voyage through the heavens (Nut) is something only he can do. [John 3:13 8:21-23] For he must defeat death and the Devil (Amen-Set). But when he returns, his followers will receive a place or mansion in God's kingdom on the new Earth. [John 14:1-4] Osiris assigns the righteous an estate in his kingdom. Then God the Father is going to make His home here on earth after all things are made new. The Garden of God restored as the Promise land.

Compare this to Amen's empty promise to his followers; Millions of Years in his Boat as beings of light, sailing through the heavens forever. This is the same lie Satan told to Eve. "You will not die, you will be like God." The Lord says that those who exalt themselves will be brought down to the abyss. [Isaiah 14:12-15] A home in heaven was Never our promise. Christendumb has been deceived by the spurious Angel of light (Lucifer) into thinking they shall ascend to heaven and escape Judgment. [2 Corinthians 11:13-15] [From Fetish to God in Ancient Egypt by Budge page 357]

The Egyptian texts were to be used as an instruction manual on how to get to God's kingdom. Just as Torah means instruction manuel. The stories are to guide the potential son of God in the Way to lead a good life. The Pharaohs were used as an example just as Christ was the example to Israel. The world awaits the day of resurrection when the sons of man will be transformed into suns of God. [1 Cor.15:20-42-55] Just as the Angel of the LORD told Abraham, "I will make your descendants multiply as the stars of the heaven". [Genesis 26:4,5] If they keep the Laws. He did NOT say He would make them the stars in heaven.

Spell 17 of the Book of the Dead says: "I am yesterday, I am tomorrow what does this mean? Osiris is yesterday and Re (Ra) is tomorrow." What does this mean? Osiris is Son of Man or human being. Re is Son of God or spirit-being. The Son of Man died on the cross, but the Sun of God did rise again. The Lord said, "I am the same yesterday, today and forever." [Hebrews 13:8] "I am" is the Angel of the Lord God; meaning the Son of

God. [Exodus 3:2,14] He is Mon-arch-angel or Lord over all the other sons of God.

Book of the Two Ways

In the Book of the Two Ways; there is the path on the land and there is the path by way of the water. The water refers to the sea of space. The celestial Nile is the Milky Way. The Way that leads to the Duat or Kingdom of God where Osiris dwells. The boat or ark takes the sons of God like Horus to the constellation of Orion. This space-ship is all symbolic. For spirit-beings who are resurrected and transformed into immortal souls, do not need a space-ship. Enoch and Elijah was taken to this place. Elijah did NOT ride on the fiery chariot. He was caught up in the whirlwind or holy Spirit. The fiery chariot was Satan keeping Elisha from trying to enter the holy kingdom of lights. [2 Kings 2:1-15] Just as the fiery cherubim kept anyone from entering the garden of God. [Genesis 3:24] These angels guarded the Way to the Tree of life. The Romans call the one in the fiery chariot, Apollo and Helio. The Egyptians call him Amen-Re-Set.

The path on land refers to those who walk on earth and live the life cycle of life to death. These worldly souls are buried in the earth and remain there dormant until resurrection day. The Lord says, "Enter by the narrow gate; for wide is the gate and broad is the Way that leads to destruction, and there are many who go in by it. Because narrow is the gate and difficult is the Way which leads to life, and there are few who find it." [Matthew 7:13,14] Only those who lead a good life by following the Way of the Lord can defeat death. This includes keeping the Maat or Laws of God. No outlaws shall enter God kingdom.

For the Egyptians this journey is a reenactment of Isis traveling up and down the Nile searching for the parts of Osiris' body. This pilgrimage starts at Thebes. They voyage up the Nile through; Abydos, Sakarah, Sais, Giza, Letopolis, and then crossover the Great River (Nile) to Anu (Heliopolis). This is the same as Joshua crossing over the Jordan to the Promise Land. Anu is the Kingdom of Osiris on earth. The Lord said, 'The kingdom of God is near at hand.' Anu is also the birthplace of the Sun of God, both in heaven and on earth. When the Sun of God (Horus/Jesus) returns, heaven (Tuat) will be on earth. Am-Tuat also means born from the lower heavens.

Coming forth from Amenta (the underground Land of the Dead) into the day light refers to those who were asleep in the deep dark dust of mother earth. "Those who are asleep in the body of Osiris (Christ)" shall be awakened by the voice of the Archangel Michael followed by the seventh trumpet of God. [1 Thessalonians 4:13-18 Matthew 24:27-31 John 5:22-30 Revelation 11:15] This is the first resurrection of the first-born or first-fruits. [1 Cor.15:20-28 Revelation 20:4,5] The body of Osiris remains on earth, just as Adam returned to the dust. He is always depicted as a mummy. It was Osiris transformed into Horus who ascended to heaven. "No one has ascended to heaven but He who came down from heaven, that is, the Son of Man." "Where I go you can Not come. You are from beneath; I am from above. You are of this world (earthlings); I am not of this world." [John 3:13 8:22-24] "I will come again, and receive you to Myself; that where I am, there you may be also" [John 14:1,3] When the Lord returns, he shall appoint estates in the Kingdom of God to the righteous. The sacred scriptures are synonymous!

Noah and his family were saved from the flood by the bark (boat-ark). Now, because of Christ's death and resurrection, we have baptism. Baptism represents the death of our old self and the rebirth. Christ saves us from that watery grave by pulling us aboard the bark. [1 Peter 3:20,21] If we learn our lesson and follow him, we can escape the second death. [1 Peter 2:21] For there are Two Ways; one leads to annihilation and the other to life. Those who learn to chose to do good shall have life in the age to come. [Hebrews 5:8-14 Isaiah 7:15] The dawning of Aquarius is an appropriate age for the Son of God to return in the Ark to save us from drowning in the Lake of fire. This is the Ark of the Covenant that holds the conditions of our agreement; the Ten Commandments. Also in the Ark is Aaron's rod that blooms into the Tree of life and manna, food of the gods. We have gone full cycle to the garden of God. [Revelation 2:7]

There are many barks; Solar bark, bark of Henu, bark of Horus, etc... If you get on the wrong bark, you are going to end up in an unexpected destination. It is Amen the Antichrist who raptures the masses away before the Lord's return. [Matthew 24] Ra's solar bark is going to sink in the sea of space, in the last days. The sun and the stars shall fall from heaven. Only Horus can travel the round trip through the sea of space in his bark. Those with reservations on the bark of Osiris shall escape the destruction of the second death in the Lake of fire. Those who embark on Osiris' bark, go the round trip through the cycle of life: life to death to life everlasting in paradise on earth. They become one with Osiris, and therefore, one with Tem, the time traveler. As Osiris, Tem and Horus are One and the same. [From Fetish to God in Ancient Egypt by Wallis Budge page 356-357]

Hymn to Aton

This hymn is very much like Psalm 104 of the Old Testament. Pharaoh Akhenaten lived centuries before David, King of Israel.

The Word of God came to Akhnaton (Ikhnaton):

The Darkness of Death

When thou settest in the western horizon of the sky,
The Earth is in darkness like the dead;

they sleep in their chambers,
their heads are wrapped up,
their nostrils are stopped, {mummified}
and none seeth the other,
while all their things are stolen,
which are under their heads,
and they know it not. {Ecc.9:5,6,10}
Every lion cometh forth from his den,
{lion is king / the sphinx}
all serpents, they sting. {sting of death}Darkness . . .
The world is in silence,
he that made them resteth in his horizon.

Day and Man

Bright is the Earth when thou risest in the horizon.
When thou shinest as Aton by day
thou drivest away the darkness.
When thou sendest forth thy rays,
The Two Lands (Upper and Lower Egypt) are in daily festivity,
awake and standing upon their feet
when thou hast raised them up.
Their limbs bathed, they take their clothing,
their arms uplifted in adoration to thy dawning
(Then) in all the world they do their work.

Day and the animals and plants

All cattle rest upon their pasturage,
the trees and the plants flourish,
the birds flutter in their marshes,
their wings uplifted in adoration to thee.
All the sheep dance upon their feet, all winged things fly, they live when thou hast shone upon them.

Day and the waters

The barques sail up-stream and down-stream alike.
Every highway is open because thou dawnest,
the fish in the river leap up before thee.
Thy rays are in the midst of the great green sea.

Creation of Man

Creator of the *germ in woman,
Maker of seed in man,
giving life to the son in the body of his mother,

soothing him that he may not weep,
nurse (even) in the womb,
Giver of breath to animate every one that he maketh! [Gen.2:7]
When he cometh forth from the womb . . . on the day of his birth,
thou openest his mouth in speech, {legond says the Lord spoke at birth}
thou suppliest his necessities.

{Germ means seed as in germination.}

Creation of Animals

When the fledgling in the egg chirps in the shell
thou givest him *breath therein to preserve him alive.
When thou hast brought him together
to (the point of) bursting it in the egg,
he cometh forth from the egg
to chirp with all his might.
He goeth about upon his two feet
when he hath come forth therefrom.

{the breath of life is the Spirit of God Gen.7:22}

The Whole Creation

How manifold are thy works!
They are hidden from before (us),
O sole God, whose powers no other possesseth.
Thou didst create the Earth according to thy heart
while thou wast alone:
Men, all cattle, large and small,
all that are upon the Earth,
that go about upon their feet;
(all) that are on high,
that fly with their wings. [Gen.1:19-26]
The foreign countries, *Syria and Kush (Ethiopia / Nubia),
the land of Egypt,
thou settest every man into his place,
thou suppliest their possessions,
and his days are reckoned.
The tongues are diverse in speech, [Gen.11:6,7]
their forms likewise and their skins are distinguished. [Gen.10]
(For) thou makest different the strangers.

{Syrians were descendants of Aram of Shem of Noah. But at this time, 1400 BC., the Canaanites (white people) had overrun the area.} [Genesis

10:6-20] Akhnaton (born Amenhotep IV) was son of Amenhotep III. Amenhotep III worshipped Amon (Amen) the State god of Thebes. In fact, he proclaimed that he was the son of the sungod. Amon the Sun of God represented Satan, the evil Son of God. Lucifer the Day Star. [Isaiah 14:12] These were the materialistic people who built the great cities of the Egyptian Empire, waged war against other nations and reaped the riches. The egotistic kings built hundreds of statues of themselves out of vanity. Akhenaton was a peaceful Pharaoh not interested in "state affairs" or conquering lands.

Akhnaton rejected the worship of Amen of Thebes and his mother Mut. He moved to El-Amarna where he built a temple to the solar god, Aton. He created the first monotheism by claiming Aton to be the sole god. He forbid the worship of Osiris which upset the masses, including me. Aton is the same as Adon or Adonai, which is translated Lord in the Bible. Yet, Aton is NOT the good Son of God. Holy Bible in Greek is Helios Biblos which means Sun Books or Books of the Sun. Akhnation's worship of the sun disk obviously influenced his Hebrew contemporaries (Moses?).

The problem arises when we see that Akhnaton worshipped the sun of our solar system. Since our sun represents Amen, he was still worshipping the wrong Sun of God. Monotheism is Mon + god or the god Amon. Like his father, Akhnaton claimed to be son of the sun. Atum is represented by the Morning star called Sirius. Which is the companion star of the constellation Orion. Orion represents Osiris. Horus of the Horizon means Aton-Ra-Horus has gone beyond the horizon to the underworld of the night sky. Osiris has resurrected as Horus and ascended to heaven. While Amen appears to rise and fall daily.Akhenaten built his temple to Aten exactly in the middle of Egypt. He was the middle-man sitting on the fence half way between Atum and Amen.

Akhnaton's symbol is the sun disk with rays of light giving life. This is incorrect! The sun does not give life as represented by the ankh. Life in the hereafter comes from the Tree of life fed by the Water of Life, not the sun. The sun represents the sustaining of mortal life that ends in death. Same meaning as the Christian cross. The sun represents man suffering as he labors to make a living by the sweat of his brow. [Genesis 3:17-19] If it were not for the protective atmosphere (Atum-sphere), the sun would kill us all. The ankh, like the lotus, is the symbol of rebirth in the hereafter (here on earth after all things are made new).

Ankh is the life force or holy Spirit called the breath of life and includes the spiritual gifts from God. It represents being born again a son of God. [Romans 8:19-30 1 Corinthians 15:42-55] The Spirit being the binding force that holds the body of believers together. [Ephesians 2:18-22] The Ankh is the cross with a circle on top called 'shen' and represents infinity. The ankh represents re-creation, not procreation (or reproduction) as is the modern defination of the female symbol. It represents the supernatural rebirth as a son of God, not the natural birth as a son of man (human).

The American Egyptologist James Breasted called the priests of Amon the "Amonite papacy" and the pharaoh the pope. Joseph Campbell likened Akhnaton's sect to Christian Protestantism. As he protested against the state religion, yet remained part of the mother church (Christendom). Akhnaton's counterpart is Martin Luther, the father of Protestantism. Even so, all his work was in vain. His step-son Tutankh-aton changed his name to Tutankh-amen when he became king of Egypt and restored the solar cult of Amen. Akhnaton's reformation was short lived. The sun-disk was originally the hieroglyph for Ra the sun-god (ie. Amen-Ra).

When Ikhnaton was a baby, his head was wrapped to produce the dome shape of the crown of Amen-ra. The Christians called it a tiara. While a baby's head is soft it can be reshaped. The crown of the head would be egg shaped. From the portraits, it is clear that he continued this tradition on his children. Again he had not shakened the customs of the Amen cult. This custom was also practiced by the Mayans and other African tribes who worship the evil sun-god. An interesting fact: Akhnaton's skull is the largest crania ever found. Larger than any Caucasian skull including Einstein's. It is time to bring the skeletons out of the closet and unearth the truth. The Theory of Evolution is a Lie! Man is de-evolving ever since the time of the highly advanced Egyptian kingdom. A large percentage of people today can't even read, know little about nature and even less about their own history. So who is the primitive ones?

Proverbs 22:17-23:11 is nearly word for word of the Egyptian book, The Wisdom of Amenemope, written about 1000 B.C. Which is not so surprising when you realize that the Bible is a copy of the Books of Thoth and the ancient mysteries of Egypt.

"There's nothing new under the sun (Ra)." Solomon.

Hinduism

Hindu (indu) is a Persian word that means "Indian". They believe in One God with many attributes, just like the Muslims and many others. The Lord has many titles that describe the duties He is to perform. The so-called lesser gods are sons of God or angels. The Hindu's elaborate use of symbology in their story telling, makes it very difficult to translate. Much like Revelations of the Bible.

The Hindus, like the Jews and the Egyptians have many of the same customs. A man is to raise up seed for the deceased brother by marrying his widow (As found among the ancient Mexicans). They all had the ark that was a portable temple that was too sacred to touch except for the Priests. (Also in Ethiopia). Only the high priests can enter the Holy of Holies. All ate the flesh of the sacrifices of atonement and poured the blood of the sacrifice on the earth. They sprinkled it, marked persons with it and smeared it upon the walls and stones. All their temples faced the East.

In Hinduism, there are three sets of sacred scriptures: the Vedas written about 2000-1700 BC and the Upanishads written about the sixth century BC and the Brahamanas. This is a Rig Veda creation story.

1) Then even nothingness was not, nor existence. There was no air then, nor the heavens beyond it. What covered it? Where was it? In whose keeping? Was there then cosmic water, in depths unfathomed? {Compare this to the Egyptian Nun, the watery womb of Atum-Ra-Horus.}

2) Then there were neither death nor immortality, nor was there then the torch of night and day. The One breathed windlessly and self-sustaining. There was that One then, and there was no other.

3) At first there was only darkness wrapped in darkness. All this was only unillumined water. That One which came to be, enclosed in nothing, arose at last, born of the power of heat.

4) In the beginning desire descended on it-that was the primal seed, born of the mind. The sages who have searched their hearts with wisdom know that which is, is kin to that which is not.

5) And they have stretched their cord across the void, and know what was above, and what below. Seminal powers made fertile mighty forces. Below was strength, and over it was impulse.

6) But, after all, who knows, and who can say whence it all came, and how creation happened? The gods (angels) themselves are later than creation, so who knows truly whence it has risen?

7) Whence all creation had it origin, he, whether he fashioned it or whether he did not, he, who surveys it all from highest heaven, he knows- or maybe even he does not know.

Brahman or Brahmin is a priest of Brahma, the Creator God. 'A Brahma' comes from Abraham meaning Father. Abraham is the father of many Asians, including those of the Persian persuasion. They say Ibrahim was their founder. Abraham's children with, Keturah, became the dark skinned Asians. Likewise, Ishmael's mother, Hagar, was Egyptian. Their descendants are the dark Arabians.

Brahma, the Father, has a daughter called Earth. The Earth is the mate to the Sun of God (Christ). The Son is the male principle and the Earth is the female principle. The Earth mother gives birth to Manu, the first man. Adam was created from the Earth; therefore he is an Earthling. Brahman means sacred Word that activates. He who holds the breath of life. [Genesis 7:15,22] Atman is the breath of life or essence of the individual. Atman is also the supreme universal self or Brahma. In Old High German, Atum is breath. The Atum-o-sphere (atmosphere) is the domain of Atum as Sun of God and Lord of the Earth. In The Prophecies by Ramutsariar, it is he who gave the first man, Adama, and the first woman, Heva (Eve), their breath of life. The Hindus call him Vishnu son of Brahma. Compare Vishnu to Yoshua (Jesus) the second Adam.

Vishnu rests on the coils of the cosmic serpent Ananta (Satan) in the waters of chaos. Satan is the one who causes the chaos. But Vishnu rests on and rules over him, creating order in the cosmos. Vishnu is the Lord of the Sabbath (Rest). In many religions, the sea serpent or snake represents the seas and the sea of space (Apophis in Egypt). Compare to Quetzalcoatl of the Mayans riding on a raft of serpents. Vishnu rides an eagle called Garuda through the heavens, just as Horus is a hawk that flies the skies. It means they are spirit-beings.

Vishnu emits a lotus from his navel which open to reveal the Creator God Brahma. The umbilical cord is connected to Vishnu's navel meaning he is the one born of Brahma. It is the Son who reveals the Father. [John 5:37] From Brahma' meditation the world is created, His divine thoughts took material form, lasting an immense expanse of time before dissolving back into chaos, [Genesis 1:1,2] from which a new universe eventually emerges in exactly the same way. Egyptian myth also anticipates that the universe will eventually dissolve back into chaos, after which a new cycle of creation will begin. As do the myths of many Meso-American Indians. Brahma has four heads facing in the four directions. In the Judgment Hall of Osiris, the four sons of Horus rise from the lotus which is watered by the river of life.

The Amrita is the elixir of immortality, fountain of life or living waters. The Word of God calls it the Holy Spirit or river that feeds the Tree of life. In the end, the faithful are reabsorbed into Brahma. In the Word of God, the Faithful Few become One with God. Reconciled through at-one-ment. In Egypt, the righteous become one with Osiris.

The ten avatars are Vishnu's incarnations:

1) Matsya the Lord warns Manu (Adam-Noah) of the coming great flood. He provides Manu with a boat and instructs him to take a pair of each living species and the seed of every living plant.

2) Kurma is the tortoise-avatar. The mountain of God was built on the back of the Lord. The Lord is the Rock that transformed into the mountain or kingdom of God. [Daniel 3:34,44,45]

3) Varaha baptizes the mother earth and she is born again new. [Romans 8:22-29 1 Peter 3:20-22] The old earth passes away and the new is born. [Revelation 21:1 2 Peter 3:13]

4) Narasimha the man-lion or king is symbolic of the sphinx. The Lord is the Lion of Judah. [Revelation 5:5] Narasimha defeats the infidel lion-king, Hiranyakasipu, who devours his subjects (i.e. Satan). [1 Peter 5:8]

5) Vamana starts out as a dwarf (the lowly Son of Man) and he aquires much land (the Promise land) and later transformed into a giant (the exalted Son of God). He overcomes the devil, Bali (Baal). The giant is Orion. The little one is Horus the child.

6) Parashurama leaves the world in shame. Compare to Quetzalcoatl and Christ. When he returns, he shall exterminate all the warriors with his double headed ax. The Lord with the double-edged Sword slays all military men in the Satanic Military service. [Revelation 19:11-21] He beheads the head of state of mother earth who is the antichrist Satan. The Lord is the Commander of the Army of God. [Joshua 5:14,15]

7) Rama is king of the kingdom of God. Compare the story of Heracles battling the 9 headed Hydra, to Rama battling the 10 headed Ravana. Rama rescues his wife just as Christ saves his bride. Bala-Rama (Bull-Ram) is the Avatar between Taurus the Bull and Aries the Ram. Rama-Bala is also called Rama-deva.

8) Krishna (the Lord as Christ, the Messiah). Krishna was born August 26th of a virgin called Maya. Maya translated to English is Mary. This blue-baby was predestined to die. [Revelation 12:4,5] He escapes the massacre of the innocents, like Moses and Christ. This is the end of the age of Aries the Ram.

Krishna's bride to be is Radha. She represents the body of believers or church members of Christ. They are all Earthlings of the female principle.

Krishna is shot in the Achilles heel with a poison tipped arrow by the hunter Jara (Old Age). Krishna dies and returns to his divine nature. The Word of God says that the serpent would bruise the heel of Christ.

And the Roman soldier did pierce his side with a spear. After which he returned to being the Son of God.

Likewise, Horus was killed by a scorpion.

9) Buddha (Enlightened One) separates the sinners (goats or kids of Satan) from the saints (lambs of God). [Matthew 25:31-46] The people did not worship the man called Buddha who lived in the 5th century BC. They worshipped the Lord who enlightened him.

10) Kalkin, the warrior on the white horse who will establish a new era of the Millennium. [Revelation 19:11-21] He is the Lord with the Sword who slays the wicked. There are 10 avatars who come every 600 years; totaling 6,000 years. Compare to the phoenix that comes every 500 or 600 years.

The Hindus believe there are a series of four ages (yugas): Krita Yuga, Treta Yuga, Dvapara Yuga, and Kali Yuga (Age of Destruction). Kali Ma is Hathor (Cat-holi or holy cat), the dark side of Mother Nature. Kali or Cali is the Greek Callisto (Cali-sot). She is the calico cat or feline who sees in the dark. She is the arctic constellation of Ursa Major and her evil son is Arca (Arctaurus). Callisto, like Nemesis (Divine vengeance), is an aspect of Artemis (Urt-mis). [Larousse Encyclopedia of Mythology page 130] Compare this to the Egyptian Ta-Urt (Ursa Major) and her evil sun (Ursa Minor).

The descent of morals, righteousness and piety will lead to the final age called the Day of Brahma which is a thousandfold cycle. Compare this to the Day of the Lord. A divine day is a thousand years. [2 Peter 3:8] The Lord's day is called the Millennium. It is the seventh divine day or 7000th year since man's creation. The Hindu scriptures, like the Bible, say several plagues will lead up to the destruction of evil. Lawlessness will abound and love will grow cold. Kalkin will slay all the warriors of the world. This is commonly called the battle of Armageddon. Then (following the Millennium) the heavens will be consumed by (the Lake of) fire. [2 Peter 3:10-13] Nothing remains save the eternal and uncreated Brahman. Then it all repeats with a new series of new ages. In the Bible, the earth and the earthlings are refined in the fire, purged of all evil, and shall dwell with the Father forever. This is the eighth divine day called the Last Great Day when all things are made new. [Revelation 21:1-8] Eight means Eternal or Infinite.

If each stage represents 500 years, starting from 4004 BC; by the time of the 8th Krishna came in the flesh it would be year 4 BC. Krishna means Christ. Who is the only one who can reincarnate. Krishna is portrayed as a blue-green color. As green is the color of life. The plants produce the breath of life needed for survival. Krishna is born of Maya which is also the name of the creation. The suns of God where born from the virgin matrix or watery womb of heaven. Maya is NOT a goddess. God the Father has no partners. The bride of Christ (female principle) shall be recreated in His image in the male principle. They shall be sons of God like the stars of heaven (angels). [Romans 8:19-29 Gen.1:26] Krishna says, "I am the light, I am the Life, I am the Sacrifice." He told his disciples that they dwell in him and he dwells in them. [John 14:6 15:4] Krishna is the immaculate conception of the Father Brahma. He was conceived in the mind of God. He is the virgin birth from his surrogate mother. He was the eighth child of Devaki (Daveki) and Vasudeva (Basheva). Could this mean he was the eighth generation from David and Bathsheba? Chrishna was of the tribe of Yadus. Yadus is Yudah (Hebrew) or Judas (Greek) or Judah. The Yadus were doomed to destruction for their sins. His birth was heralded by a star. Just as Christ's birth. [Matthew 2:2] Krishna spoke to his mother soon after birth. Just as it says Christ did in the Qur'an [Surah 19:29-33 and 1 & 2 Infancy of the Apocryphal New Testament]. Krishna was born while his foster-father was in the city to pay his tax to the king. Jesus was born while is foster-father Joseph was in the city to pay his tax to the governor. [Luke 2:1-3,5] The babe Krishna was adored by cowherds. The Christ child was adored by shepherds. Krishna escapes the death of the firstborn sons as ordered by King Kamsa, just as Christ escaped king Herod's slaughter of the first born sons. [Matthew 2:16] Both foster-fathers were warned by a heavenly voice to flee. Krishna was born at Mathara. The Arabic edition of the Gospel of the Infancy says that Jesus went to Matarea, near Hermopolis, Egypt to escape the horrid hand of Herod, king of the Jews. The Egyptians say it was Matarea near Heliopolis. Heliopolis is the City of Horus and the naval of the world. King Kamsa (Amsu) was Krishna's uncle just as Amen-Set was Horus' uncle. [Anacalypsis by Godfrey Higgins, ESQ Volume 1 pages 128-151, 392]

Krishna was crucified. He is pictured in Indian art as hanging on a cross with arms extended. Krishna was pierced by an arrow while hanging on the cross, just as Jesus was pierced by a spear. The light of the sun was blotted out at noon on the day of Krishna's death. The sun was darkened from noon till three P.M. on the day of Christ's crucifixion. Krishna descended into hell to raise the dead before returning to the abode of the gods. When Christ resurrected from the grave (Hell) he resurrected many saints back to mortal life. [Matthew 27:51-53] Krishna ascended bodily to heaven in the presence of a multitude of spectators. Just as Christ ascended bodily 40 days after his resurrection. [Acts 1:9-11] They did not leave their bodies behind. Which is proof of an ascension. Krishna means "dark". From which we get the black Madonna. Pictures all over Europe portray the Madonna and child as being black (dark brown). Krist-na is the Egyptian Krast-Nun (anointed Son of Nun).

Krishna saves the cowherds from the evil serpent king Kaliya (aspect of Kali wife of Shiva). The serpent submitted to the child Krishna. Compare this to Herakles strangling two serpents as a baby. Then later defeating the sea monster Triton. Also Horus is depicted with one serpent in each hand while standing on two crocodiles. He later defeats the Apep serpent. Likewise, Christ overcame the same serpent who deceived Eve.

Incarnations of the Lord

About 3,000 BC, Enoch was born 7th from Adam. [Genesis 5:21-24] He walked with God for 300 years preaching the Word of God, God's kingdom coming, and judgment day. [Hebrews 11:5 Jude 14-16] After 365 years, God took him. 365 days is the cycle of a year. 360 is the degrees of a circle. Therefore he went beyond the cycle of life, to the after life. Immediately following, was the flood of Noah's day which killed the lawless ones. [Genesis 6:5-7]

About 2,000 BC, Melchizedek visited Abraham. [Genesis 14:18-20] He had no beginning and no end, no father or mother. [Hebrews 5 & 7] He is high priest and king of JeruSalem. This could only be the Lord coming in the order of Melchizedek. [Hebrews 7:1-3] The priests work is to teach the law. Melchizedek taught the law to Abraham. [Genesis 26:5] Immediately following the Lord rained down fire on the five Canaanite cities including Sodom and Gomorrah. [Jude 7 Genesis 19:24] The lawless were incinerated in the Lake of fire raining down from God.

About 1,000-850 BC, Elijah was born. Elijah could call fire down from heaven. [1 Kings 18:38 2 Kings 1:10-14] He was taken in a whirlwind, while Elisha was held back by the chariot of fire. [2 Kings 2:11] The one who rides the chariot of fire is Helios, the sun-god and warlord. He is Lucifer the cherub who keeps man out of God's garden so he can't take of the Tree of life. [Genesis 3:24] He does it through temptation and sin. For it is our personal sins that keep us out of God's kingdom and cause our death. We die from the sickness of sin.

About 7 BC, Christ was born or incarnated. [John 1:14] This is not the first advent of the avatar. He warned the people that those who break God's law faced permanent death in the Lake of fire. Soon after his resurrection and ascension, JeruSalem was completely destroyed by the Roman empire. On the Lord's day, He shall return as Judge to judge the nations according to the Law of God. [John 5:22-30 Revelation 20:11-15] To the evil ones, he shall be the Executioner. To the obedient ones, he shall be the Savior who pardons the unintentional sins.

The Lord says, "No one has ascended to heaven but He who came down from heaven, that is, the Son of Man." [John 3:13] Therefore, each of these men were incarnations of Christ. Every thousand years he comes to warn people of the impending destruction to all who break God's Commandments. The penalty for sin is death.

The Hindus created the concept of transmigration and re-incarnation so that we would have compassion toward our fellow creatures. After all, one of those creatures may be a friend or relation. Taking a life in order that we may live, was not part of God's original plan. The creatures in the garden of God did NOT eat each other. [Genesis 1:30] God's plan for us is to resurrect in that garden paradise of peace and harmony. [Isaiah 11:6-9] The Hindus do NOT worship the cow. All life is sacred to them. The idea that a person with a certain animal's characteristics would reincarnate as that animal was an empty threat, like burning in hell-fire forever. The Book of Manu says, "In whatsoever disposition a man accomplishes such and such an act, he shall reap the fruit in a body endowed with such and such a quality." "You shall reap what you sow." "What goes around, comes around."

Shiva (Satan)

Shiva is the Destroyer who sits on a bull. Bull is Baal and Shiva is Satan. The Devil is portrayed with two horns like the sacred Apis (bull). Shiva is the deity of dance and music. It was he the people of Israel were honoring with their merrymaking and crafting of the baby bull or "golden calf".. [Exodus 32:1-6] In Egypt he is Min and in Greece he is the Minotaur. Shiva's bull mount is Nandi. Nandi is the cow produced at the churning of the sea of milk. Nandi's counterpart in Egypt is Nun, the sea of space that gave birth to and nursed the suns of God. The Upper Egyptians called her Hathor. Shiva is portrayed with a trident (pitch-fork), like Poseidon, showing he commands the seas.

Shiva is the "ruddy one". The Aryans falsely claim Adam means ruddy complexion. Shiva is a white redneck paleface deity. Blushing from shame. The paleface is the face of death. The walking dead are haunted by the ghosts of the future because of the deeds of their past. For the Word of God says the pale horse is death followed by the grave. [Rev.6:8] As sun of God, he is the red sunset and the red dragon of destruction. [Rev.12] He is Set of Egypt. He is portrayed surrounded by a halo of fire. His counterpart is Helio the sun-god. Helio is the root of the word halo. Vishnu is portrayed as the Setting Sun in the west like Atum-Ra-Horus who dies in the west and rises again in the east as the dawn rising of Sirius. Shiva is portrayed as the noon-day sun, in the south, like Amen-Ra-Sut. In fact, Lucifer means Day star. The only star we see in the daytime is the blinding sun of our solar system.

One of Shiva's symbols is the crescent moon for his female consort is Durga the moon goddess and war goddess. Durga, like Athene, was born fully grown, fully armed and ready for war. The Romans called her Dianna and the Babylonians called her Ashtar, Ishtar or Ianna. Shiva is the Lord of fire as the sun-god. The Romans called him Apollo or Helio. The bad Sun of God is mated to the Moon (female principle). Shiva is honored on the night of February 24th as the god of destruction. Set between Valentine's (Venus') day and Easter (Ishtar's day), Sex and violence go hand and hand. Durga, Kali and Devi are Shiva's feminine Trinity. The words Devil, devas and deity are derived from Devi. A devi is a she-devil or Temptress. (like Lilith).

Another of Shiva's symbols is the third eye of illumination (and destruction). The so called "evil eye". Shiva sent woman a fig tree and prompted her to tempt her husband with the fruit. This she did, assuring the man it would make him immortal. When the man ate, Shiva cursed him. Just as Lucifer, sun of God, with a serpent's tongue, who deceived Eve and caused their destruction. 215 Pretending to be the Angel of enlight-enment, [2 Cor.11:13-15] and giver of immortality, he lead her into darkness of death. [Gen.3:1-5] She looked up to the sun-god for enlightenment, but was blinded by the light. She thought he was the fiery Angel in the midst of the bush who spoke to Moses. [Ex.3:2] She was not aware it was the evil sun of God. The fig tree is the Tree of carnal knowledge. To know a woman carnally is to have sex with her.

Shiva is "lord of cattle". Cain's sons, the Aryans, raised cattle. [Genesis 4:20] Cain was the illegitimate son of Satan and Eve. For he seduced her with his great beauty. [Ezekiel 28:12-19] To this day, the people who raise cattle are the descendants of Cain called Kenites. It was these Aryans who migrated to India and taught the Vedas. The horns are the shape of the crescent moon. From her we get the word "horny". In fact, Shiva is worshipped in the form of a lingam or sacred phallus (penis). That's why he wears the domed crown like Amen of Egypt, Baal of the Canaanites, and Freyr of the Vikings. His body becomes that sacred symbol the phallus. Menmen (Amen-Amen) is the Egyptian word for cattle. See New Larousse Encyclopedia of Mythology, page 371.

Some Hindus worship Shiva's lingam or penis. Even though his manhood was severed by some holy men (just as Horus emasculated Set). Shiva is still worshipped as a fertility deity. The temple dedicated to him is covered with every sexual position imaginable. A sex manuel called the Kama Sutra explains in detail how to find spiritual enlightenment through sex. This is nonsense! Kama was the deity of primal desire like sexual passion. Kama was the cause of the original sin; the subtle serpent seduced Eve. His counterparts are Eros of Greece and Cupid of Rome. Sutra is Sut + Ra, the evil sun of God in Upper Egypt. As fertility deity his is called Min. His penis is erect showing he is potent. Sex is carnal knowledge learned from mother nature. It is NOT spiritual knowledge from God.

Raising the Kundalini (coiled serpent in the base of the spine) in order to unite with Shiva is the serpent in the Tree of Carnal Knowledge. It is arousing the libido. This is contrary to raising spiritual awareness. Being lead by the wrong head. Sex in a religious ritual is always Satanic (witch-craft).

Sati, consort of Shiva, and aspect of Devi set herself on fire for Shiva's sake. She established the ritual of Suttee in India, where a widow threw herself on her husband's burning funeral pyre. This sick ritual originated in Upper Egypt in honor of Sut, the evil sun of God. Sati and Suttee are just different spellings of Set.

Both Vishnu's and Shiva's followers claimed their god reigned supreme. A compromise was made. They combined the two into a composite deity called Hari-Hara. Hari is Vishnu symbolizing creation and growth. Hara is Shiva symbolizing destruction and death. Hara-Kari is ritualized suicide committed by the followers of Shiva. Together they are the duality of Yang/Yin. This is paralleled in Egypt when the worshipers of Amen-Ra of Upper Egypt combined the attributes and titles of Lower Egypt with their deity. They combined Osiris and Horus with Amen-Ra-Sut and produced the hybrid, Amsu. This is the Antichrist Horus. Hari (Vishnu) is obviously Heru (Horus son of Nu). The Hebrew Shuvah and Egyptian Shefi is terrible and demon-like. Shiva in Hebrew is a Funeral.

Indra

Indra is the warrior god (Warlord) of the Aryans. The Egyptians call him Amon-Ra. The Vikings called him Odan. He later loses his luster, his strength, and his good looks. Which sounds much like Lucifer who became Satan. Indra gave form to the formless chaos and caused the sun to rise and fall daily. Lucifer is the Sun of God who tried to ascend into heaven as high as the Morning Star (Christ) but was cast down into the bottomless pit of darkness. [Isaiah 14:12-15 Revelation 8:10 12:3,4,7-9] The great star fell taking one third of the stars (sons of God or angels) with him. He is now ruler of darkness. [Ephesians 6:12] Indra is the Aryan who lords over the dark race. He rides the fiery chariot. The wheel symbolizing the sun. His counterparts are Helio, Apollo, and Baal. "Indra is the prototype of the Aryan race which invaded and subjugated India." says Richard Carlyon, in "A Guide to the gods".

Indra rides the bull elephant like Shiva who rides the bull. The bull is Baal, the Devil. He is the sun-god who rules over this wicked world. Just as Satan is called ruler of this world. [John 12:31 14:30 16:11] Indra seduces and has sex with a married woman, then her husband. Compare to Adam and Eve. Gautama, curses him to loose his testicles. Just as what happened to Set in Egypt. He is no longer able to produce children. Later the gods replaced his testicles with those of a ram. The ram is the animal of Amen-Set. Indra was crucified by the keepers of the garden of Paradise for having robbed it. Indra is the archenemy of Krishna just as Set is the adversary of Horus. Indra ousted Varuna (cosmic order) creating disorder and unrest. Set represents darkness and disorder.

The Rig Vedas

The Aryan sacred scriptures (Vedas) say: "once a man has become Brahman, with self serene he neither grieves nor desires; the same to all contingent beings he gains the highest love and loyalty to me (Krishna). By love and loyalty to me he comes to know me as I really am, how great I am and who; and once he knows me as I am, he enters me forthwith."

The Word of God says, "I am". It is the signature of the Lord Christ and Lord Osiris. [John 6:35 8:12,16,23,58 10:11 11:25 14:6,10,11 15:1 17:11] Once you enter the body of Christ, you become one with God (Brahma). "And if you love God, you will keep His commandments." [1 John 5:1-3] And as Vishnu he says; "for whenever the law of righteousness withers away and lawlessness arises, then do I generate myself on earth. For the protection of the good, for the destruction of evil-doers, for the setting up of the law of righteousness I come into being age after age." [Matthew 24:12 2 Thessalonians 2:2-7,8,9 Revelation 21:8,27 22:14,15] [John 5:22-30 Rom.2:133,26 7:12 1 Cor.6:9,10 7:19 Galatians 5:19-21]

According to the Upanishads,, there is a journey to Brahma, with the reward of perfect knowledge, a place of no return or a journey to heaven where after enjoying the reward deserved the soul returns to be reborn here below. Is this transmigration or a poor translation. The Word of God says the spirit returns to the Father in heaven, but the soul (body) lies dormant in the dust. Those who seek to be One with God will be reborn and enlightened with the knowledge of God's kingdom... here on earth.

The book of Hebrews leaves little doubt that MelchiZedek (MelchiZadok) was an earlier incarnation of Christ. [Hebrews 7:1-3] As only Christ is Lord of lords as the high priest of the royal line of the Zadok. And only Christ is king of JeruSalem as King of kings. In fact, when Melchizedek met up with Abraham, there was no earthy JeruSalem. The city was occupied by the Jebusites who called it Jebus. Melchizedek was king of the heavenly JeruSalem that is soon to descend to earth. [Heb.12:22 Rev.21:2,10] It wasn't until 2,000 years later, that He incarnated as Son of Man. [John 1:1-18] 2000 years after that, He will return as our Lord and Savior. Just as the Hindus say. They call him Kalkin.

The Old Testament speaks often of the Angel of the Lord. The Angel with the power to forgive sin. [Exodus 23:20-22] The Angel who redeems. [Genesis 48:16] The Angel of God's presence. Christ says only he has seen and heard God the Father. [John 1:18 5:37] As he is the Angel of God, Michael the mon-archangel. Who defeats the Devil and casts him out of heaven. [Rev.12:7-9] It is clear that the Christ child was born, died and ascended to heaven. [Revelation 12:5] Then he suddenly transfigures into a spirit-being and takes on his heavenly name of Michael (meaning He who is like God). For he is created in the image of God. [2 Cor.4:4-6 Col.1:15-18] He is the Angel with the Sword of the Lord coming to slay the evil-doers! [1 Chronicles 21:12,15,16,27,30 Rev.19:15]

Gandhi

The Lord defeated the United Kingdom with a little help from his servants. Gandhi was his right hand man and Hitler the left. Together they broke the yoke of the white slave-master. The Lord caused the fall of the evil English empire and India won her independence. Gandhi demonstrated Christ-like behavior through non-violent protest. Hitler demonstrated Satanic behavior through violent warfare. Hitler was the rod of the Lord's wrath on the Aryan race: the blond-haired, blue eyed race.

Because of World War II, the arrogant Anglo-Saxons were brought down low and the Barbaric British will never rule again. At World War III, the Lord with the Sword will slay all warrior nations. Including those Christian crusaders who fought for Hitler. For Germany is 85% Christians. Following the Millennium, the war to end all wars, will exterminate All the violent people. All those like the Warlord, Satan, will go into the Lake of fire. Only then can the non-violent children of God live in peace.

Gandhi's first act, was to free the Untouchables from a type of slavery. He proclaimed all people are children of God. Compare this to Christ liberating the lepers. But Gandhi's greatest accomplishment was keeping himself from corruption. He refused to take part in politics. He would not be a political leader in a wicked world ruled by the Devil. He believed in social reform through spiritual reform. Gandhi was well aquatinted with the words, "do not be conformed to this world, but be transformed by the renewing of your mind, that you may prove what is that good and acceptable and perfect will of God." [Romans 12:2] The reformed Saints shall become transformed sons of God.

Manu-HuMan

Manu was the seventh Manu (man) belonging to a line from the first Manu (Adam). Their dynasty lasted 4,320,000 years. The seventh Manu saved a tiny fish and was later saved by the fish when he warned him of the flood to come. Compare this to Enoch, seventh from Adam, warning the people of the destruction to come in Noah's day. [Jude 14,15] The fish is one of the symbols of Osiris and Christ as Savior. Manu (Noah) built a vessel (ark) and placed all the things to be saved inside. When the deluge came, Manu fastened a rope to the fish, who had grown huge, and it guided it to safety. Compare this to the stellar bark being pulled by a rope in Egyptian mythology. When the flood was over, Manu (Noah) offered a sacrifice. The fact that the flood story is universal proves it is true!

In Egypt, Manu is the place in the West where the stars descend into the underworld (sea of space). Bekha is the place in the east where they rise again. The three sons of Manu were Shama, Chama and Pra-Japati. Compare to Noah's sons; Shem, Ham and Japhat. Shem became Shamesh the sun-god of Asia. Ham became Amen the sun-god of Africa. Ja-phater became Jupiter of the Gentiles. The father of Jupiter is Chronus or Kronos. Khronas is an anagram for noah's ark. Remember vowels are optional. They are added when pronounced.

Festival of Huli

At the vernal equinox, the Hindoos celebrate the festival of Huli. They throw red powder on one another. The powder represents pollen that fertilizes the Seed. Compare this to the Sed festival of the Egyptians and Seder of the Hebrews. At the same time (vernal equinox) the Israelites were marking their door-posts with lambs blood, the Egyptians were marking their goods with red. This red powder had replaced the brutal blood sacrifice. Huli means Holy. It is also Hori (Horus). (l = r) To the Egyptians, the death of the firstborn was a memorial of Osiris' death and resurrection as Horus. Passover represents the death and birth of a new age. To pass-over to the new age. The Lamb of Aries must pass away in order to prepare the way for the age of Pisces.

The Undead?

Christians ridicule the belief in transmigration of souls. Yet, it is the Christians who believe in the immortal soul that goes to heaven at death then return to earth with the Lord. To the Christians; Near death "out of body" experiences, mediums speaking to spirits, and apparitions of "angels" are their proof of the immortal soul. A soul migrating from earth to heaven is the definition of transmigration. This is Spiritualism that is condemned by God. [Deuteronomy 18:10-12] The fact is, that Christendom got this idea from the ancient pagans of India who believe man can re-incarnate over and over.

The truth is; only the angels can manifest in human form over and over. It was Vishnu, the good Son of God, who incarnated ten times. Christ incarnated in the flesh. Atum incarnated as Osiris. No humans can do this. "Where I go you cannot come. You are from beneath; I am from above. You are of this world (an earthling); I am not of this world (extra-terrestrial)." [John 8:21-23] "No one has ascended to heaven but, He who came down from heaven, that is, the Son of Man." [John 3:13]

Christians also believe that the bad souls will transmigrate to Hades where they will torment forever. This is a Theban (Egyptian and Greek) fable. Both the Egyptian and Hebrew versions of "The Bible of Death and Resurrection" say the outlaws shall become non-existent when thrown in the volcanic Lake of fire and sulfur (brimstone). The God of love and mercy does NOT cause torture and misery. The sinners are put out of their misery, so that the law-abiding citizens can live in peace.

Indra and the Parade of Ants

Indra slew the dragon, a giant titan that had been couching on the mountains in the limbless shape of a cloud serpent, holding the waters of heaven captive in its belly. The god flung his thunderbolt into the midst of the ungainly coils; the monster shattered like a stack of withered rushes. The waters burst free and streamed in ribbons across the land, to circulate once more through the body of the world.

COMMENTARY: Indra is the ruler of this wicked world. Satan, sun of God, is the dragon and leader of the titans. Indra is also the Warlord who leads the warriors to conquer and plunder. The cloud serpent is merely the atmosphere that encircles the earth. Compare to Marduk defeating Tiamat in the Babylonian version.

This flood is the flood of life and belongs to all. It is the sap of field and forest, the blood coursing in the veins. The monster had appropriated the common benefit, massing his ambitious, selfish hulk between heaven and earth, but now was slain. The juices again were pouring. The titans were retreating to the underworlds; the gods were returning to the summit of the central mountain of the earth, there to reign from on high.

COMMENTARY: Like in Greek mythology, the titans are the fallen angels. The gods are the sons of God the Father.

During the period of the supremacy of the dragon, the majestic mansions of the lofty city of the gods had cracked and crumbled. The first act of Indra was to rebuild them. All divinities of the heavens were acclaiming him their savior. Greatly elated in his triumph and in the knowledge of his strength, he summoned Vishvakarman, the god of arts and crafts, and commanded him to erect such a palace as should befit the unequaled splendor of the king of the gods.

COMMENTARY: Zeus is also called king of the gods and savior. All who build great cities and monuments are Satanic. Black arts and witchcraft are the gifts of the Devil. It was Rameses who built Thebes to Amen-Ra. Alexander the Great built Olympus to Zeus-Amen. Caesar built Rome to their gods. They vainly try to create heaven on earth. So they can play god.

The miraculous genius, Vishvakarman, succeeded in constructing in a single year a shining residence, marvelous with palaces and gardens, lakes and towers. But as the work progressed, the demands of Indra became even more exacting and his unfolding visions vaster. He required additional terraces and pavilions, more ponds, groves, and pleasure grounds. Whenever Indra arrived to appraise the work, he developed vision beyond vision of marvels remaining to be contrived. Presently the divine craftsman, brought to despair, decided to seek succor from above. He would turn to the demiurgic creator, Brahma, the pristine embodiment of the Universal Spirit, who abides far above the troubled Olympian sphere of ambition, strife, and glory.

COMMENTARY: Again another word "Olympian" that the Greeks borrowed.

When Vishvakarman secretly resorted to the higher throne and presented his case, Brahma comforted the petitioner. "You will soon be relieved of your burden," he said, "Go home in peace." Then, while Vishvakarman was hurrying down again to the city of Indra, Brahma himself ascended to a still higher sphere. He came before Vishnu, the Supreme Being, of whom he himself, the Creator, was but an agent. In beatific silence Vishnu gave ear, and by a mere nod of the head let it be known that the request of Vishvakarman would be fulfilled.

COMMENTARY: This is reversed. Brahma is the Supreme being Vishnu is the son.

Early next morning a brahmin boy, carrying the staff of a pilgrim, made his appearance at the gate of Indra, bidding the porter announce his visit to the king. The gate-man hurried to the master, and the master hastened to the entrance to welcome in person the auspicious guest. The boy was slender, some ten years old, radiant with the luster of wisdom. Indra discovered him amidst a cluster of enraptured, staring children. The boy greeted the host with a gentle glance of his dark and brilliant eyes. The king bowed to the holy child and the boy cheerfully gave his blessing. The two retired to the hall of Indra, where the god ceremoniously proffered welcome to his guest with oblations of honey, milk, and fruits, then said: "O Venerable Boy, tell me of the purpose of your coming."

COMMENTARY: This is the Christ child, Sun of God.

The beautiful child replied with a voice that was as deep and soft as the slow thundering of auspicious rain clouds. "O King of the Gods, I have heard of the mighty palace you are building, and have come to refer to you the questions in my mind. How many years will it require to complete this rich and extensive residence? What further feats of engineering will Vishvakarman be expected to accomplish? O Highest of the gods,"-the boy's luminous features moved with a gentle, scarcely perceptible smile-"no Indra before you has ever succeeded in completing such a palace as yours is to be."

Full of the wine of triumph, the king of the gods was entertained by this mere boy's pretension to a knowledge of Indras earlier than himself. With a fatherly smile he put the question: "Tell me, Child! Are they then so very many, the Indras and Vishvakarmans whom you have seen-or at least, whom you have heard of?"

The wonderful guest calmly nodded. "Yes, indeed, many have I seen." The voice was as warm and sweet as milk fresh from the cow, but the words sent a slow chill through Indra's veins. "My dear child," the boy continued, "I knew your father, Kashyapa, the Old Tortoise Man, lord and progenitor of all the creatures of the earth. And I knew your grandfather, Marichi, Beam of Celestial Light, who was the son of Braha. Marichi was begotten of the god Brahma's pure spirit; his only wealth and glory were his sanctity and devotion. Also, I know Brahma, brought forth by Vishnu from the lotus calix growing from Vishnu's navel. And Vishnu himself-Supreme Being, supporting Brahma in his creative endeavor-him too I know.

COMMENTARY: "Brahma brought forth Vishnu." The child has the umbilical cord in its navel, not the father.

"O King of gods, I have known the dreadful dissolution of the universe. I have seen all perish, again and again, at the end of every cycle. At that terrible time, every single atom dissolves into the primal, pure waters of eternity, whence originally all arose. Everything then goes back into the fathomless, wild infinity of the ocean, which is covered with utter darkness and is empty of every thing of animate being. Ah, who will count the universes that have passed away, or the creations that have risen afresh, again and again, from the formless abyss of the vast waters? Who will number the passing ages of the world, as they follow each other endlessly? And who will search through the wide infinities of space to count the universes side by side, each containing its Brahma, its Vishnu, its Shiva? Who will count the Indras in them all-those Indras side by side, who reign at once in all the innumerable worlds; those others who passed away before them; or even the Indras who succeed each other in any given line, ascending to godly kingship, one by one, and one by one, passing away? King of gods, there are among your servants certain who maintain that it may be possible to number the grains of sand on earth and the drops of rain that fall from the sky, but no one will ever number all those Indras. This is what the Knowers know.

COMMENTARY: The primal waters of the sea of space are called Maya (Mary). It is dark and void of life. Yet all living beings are begotten from that water womb. It is God's Spirit that activates them.

"The life and kingship of an Indra endure seventy-one eons, and when twenty-eight Indras have expired, one Day and Night of Brahma has elapsed. But the existence of one Brahma, measured in such Brahma Days and Nights, is only one hundred and eight years. Brahma follows Brahma; one sinks, the next arises; the endless series cannot be told. There is no end to the number of those Brahmas-to say nothing of Indras.

COMMENTARY: King Osiris was killed at age 28 by Set and his 71 sebeau fiends. Or the 72 decans push Orion 30 degrees, into the next age.

As the cycle of precession goes on.

10800 years is 5 zodiac ages or 3 sari.

"But the universes side by side at any given moment, each harboring a Brahma and an Indra: who will estimate the number of these? Beyond the farthest vision, crowding outer space, the universes come and go, an innumerable host. Like delicate boats they float on the fathomless, pure waters that form the body of Vishnu. Out of every hair-pore of that body a universe bubbles and breaks. Will you presume to count them? Will you number the gods in all those worlds-the worlds present and the worlds past?"

A procession of ants had made its appearance in the hall during the discourse of the boy. In military array, in a column four yards wide, the tribe paraded across the floor. The boy noted them, paused, and stared, then suddenly laughed with an astonishing peal, but immediately subsided into a profoundly indrawn and thoughtful silence.

"Why do you laugh?" stammered Indra. "Who are you, mysterious being, under this deceiving guise of a boy?" The proud king's throat and lips had gone dry, and his voice continually broke. "Who are you, Ocean of Virtues, enshrouded in deluding mist?"

The magnificent boy resumed: "I laughed because of the ants. The reason is not to be told. Do not ask me to disclose it. The seed of woe and the fruit of wisdom are enclosed within this secret. It is the secret that smites with an ax the tree of worldly vanity, hews away its roots, and scatters its crown. This secret is a lamp to those groping in ignorance. This secret lies buried in the wisdom of the ages, and is rarely revealed even to saints. This secret is the living air of those ascetics who renounce and transcend mortal existence; but worldlings, deluded by desire and pride, it destroys."

The boy smiled and sank into silence. Indra regarded him, unable to move. "O Son of a Brahmin," the king pleaded presently, with a new and visible humility, "I do not know who you are. You would seem to be Wisdom Incarnate. Reveal to me this secret of the ages, this light that dispels the dark."

COMMENTARY: He is the Word of God incarnate, son of Brahma.

Thus requested to teach, the boy opened to the god the hidden wisdom. "I saw the ants, O Indra, filing in long parade. Each was once an Indra. Like you, each by virtue of pious deeds once ascended to the rank of a king of the gods. But now, through many rebirths, each has become again an ant. This army is an army of former Indras.

"Piety and high deeds elevate the inhabitants of the world to the glorious realm of the celestial mansions, or to the higher domains of Brahma and Shiva and to the highest sphere of Vishnu; but wicked acts sink them into the worlds beneath, into pits of pain and sorrow, involving reincarnation among birds and vermin, or out of the wombs of pigs and animals of the wild, or among trees, or among insects. It is by deeds that one merits happiness or anguish, and becomes a master or a serf. It is by deeds that one attains to the rank of a king or brahmin, or of some god, or of an Indra or a Brahma. And through deeds again, one contracts disease, acquires beauty and deformity, or is reborn in the condition of a monster.

COMMENTARY: Notice the word "ants" in "inhabitants." Karma is your good and bad deeds that will bless or curse you. The sickness of sin produces sick offspring.

"This is the whole substance of the secret. This wisdom is the ferry to beatitude across the ocean of hell. "Life in the cycle of the countless rebirths is like a vision in a dream. The gods on high, the mute trees and the stones, are alike apparitions in this phantasy (fantasy). But Death administers the law of time. Ordained by time, Death is the master of all. Perishable as bubbles are the good and the evil of the beings of the dream. In unending cycles the good and evil alternate. Hence, the wise are attached to neither, neither the evil nor the good. The wise are not attached to anything at all."

COMMENTARY: The Lord says death is like sleeping. Only Osiris in his bark can awake (or Resurrect) us from that unconscious state.

The boy concluded the appalling lesson and quietly regarded his host. The king of the gods, for all his celestial splendor, had been reduced in his own regard to insignificance. Meanwhile, another amazing apparition had entered the hall.

COMMENTARY: The exalted are brought down low.

The newcomer had the appearance of a kind of hermit. His head was piled with matted hair; he wore a black deerskin around his loins; on his forehead was painted a white mark; his head was shaded by a paltry parasol of grass; and a quaint, circular cluster of hair grew on his chest: it was intact at the circumference, but from the center many of the hairs, it seemed, had disappeared. This saintly figure strode directly to Indra and the boy, squatted between them on the floor, and there remained, motionless as a rock. The kingly Indra, somewhat recovering his hostly role, bowed and paid obeisance, offering sour milk with honey and other refreshments; then he inquired, falteringly but reverently, after the welfare of the stern guest, and bade him welcome. Whereupon the boy addressed the holy man, asked the very questions Indra himself would have proposed.

COMMENTARY: The boy sits in the immovable spot, like a Rock. Christ is the Rock. The boy could read their minds.

"Whence do you come, O Holy Man? What is your name and what brings you to this place? Where is your present home, and what is the meaning of this grass parasol? What is the portent of the circular hair-tuft on your chest: why is it dense at the circumference but at the center almost bare? Be kind enough, O Holy Man, to answer, in brief, these questions. I am anxious to understand."

Patiently the old saint smiled, and slowly began his rely. "I am a brahmin. Hairy is my name. And I have come here to behold Indra. Since I know that I am short-lived, I have decided to possess no home, to build no house, and neither to marry nor to seek a livelihood. I exist by begging alms. To shield myself from sun and rain I carry over my head this parasol of grass.

COMMENTARY: The Hindus like the Bible call the holy ones, "saints". They do not possess anything of this world including a wife. Saint means to be sanctified or set apart. This includes separating from your wife. [Exodus 19:10-15] The earthling shall soon return to the earth, under the grass.

"As to the circle of hair on my chest, it is a source of grief to the children of the world. Nevertheless, it teaches wisdom. With the fall of an Indra, one hair drops. That is why, in the center all the hairs have gone. When the other half of the period allotted to the present Brahma will have expired, I myself shall die. O Brahmin Boy, it follows that I am somewhat short of days; what, therefore, is the use of a wife and a son, or of a house? [1 Timothy 6:7–12]

"Each flicker of the eyelids of the great Vishnu registers the passing of a Brahma. Everything below that sphere of Brahma is as insubstantial as a cloud taking shape and again dissolving. That is why I devote myself exclusively to meditating on the incomparable lotus-feet of highest Vishnu. Faith in Vishnu is more than the bliss of redemption; for every joy, even the heavenly, is as fragile as a dream, and only interferes with the one-pointedness of our faith in Him Supreme.

"Shiva, the peace-bestowing, the highest spiritual guide, taught me this wonderful wisdom. I do not crave to experience the various blissful forms of redemption: to share the highest god's supernal mansions and enjoy his eternal presence, or to be like him in boy and apparel, or to become a part of his august substance, or even to be absorbed wholly in his ineffable essence."

Abruptly, the holy man ceased and immediately vanished. It had been the god Shiva himself; he had now returned to his supramundane abode. Simultaneously, the brahmin boy, who had been Vishnu, disappeared as well. The king was alone, baffled and amazed.

COMMENTARY: Shiva is the great impostor, Satan, pretending to be the highest spiritual guide. [2 Corinthians 11:2,3, 13-15]

He knows he only has a short time to rule the world. [Revelations 12:12] Amen-Ra and Zeus-Amen were called King of the gods.

The king, Indra, pondered; and the events seemed to him to have been a dream. But he no longer felt any desire to magnify his heavenly splendor or to go on with the construction of his palace. He summoned Visvakarman. Graciously greeting the craftsman with honeyed words, he heaped on him jewels and precious gifts, then with a sumptuous celebration sent him home.

The king, Indra, now desired redemption. He had acquired wisdom, and wished only to be free. He entrusted the pomp and burden of his office to his son, and prepared to retire to the hermit life of the wilderness. Whereupon his beautiful and passionate queen, Shachi, was overcome with grief.

COMMENTARY: She desired the things of this wicked world.

Weeping, in sorrow and utter despair, Shachi resorted to Indra's ingenious house-priest and spiritual advisor, the Lord of Magic and Wisdom, Brihaspati. Bowing at his feet, she implored him to divert her husband's mind from its stern resolve. The resourceful counselor of the gods, who by his spells and devices had helped the heavenly powers wrest the government of the universe from the hands of their titan rivals, listened thoughtfully to the complaint of the voluptuous, disconsolate goddess, and knowingly nodded assent. With a wizard's smile, he took her hand and conducted her to the presence of her spouse. In the role, then, of spiritual teacher, he discoursed sagely on the virtues of the spiritual life, but on the virtues also, of the secular. He gave to each its due. Very skillfully he developed his theme. The royal pupil was persuaded to relent in his extreme resolve. The queen was restored to radiant joy.

COMMENTARY: The coun-seller did sell him on the idea of remaining a worldly man. "Do not love the world or the things in the world. If anyone loves the world the love of the Father is not in him." 1 John 2:15

This Lord of Magic Wisdom, Brihaspati, once had composed a treatise on government, in order to teach Indra how to rule the world. He now issued a second work, a treatise on the polity and stratagems of married love. Demonstrating the sweet art of wooing ever anew, and of enchaining the beloved with enduring bonds, this priceless book established on sound foundation the married life of the reunited pair.

COMMENTARY: This is the Book of Carnal knowledge from the Tree of Carnal knowledge. The Romans called it Romance as taught by Cupid and Venus. The Hindu's who worship Shiva actually have a book on sex and a temple that displays hundreds of sex positions. They worship Shiva's severed phallus (penis). He is the impotent son of God.

Thus concludes the marvelous story of how the king of gods was humiliated in his boundless pride, cured of an excessive ambition, and through wisdom, both spiritual and secular, brought to a knowledge of his proper role in the wheeling play of unending life.

COMMENTARY: The turning of time = cosmic clock = celestial mill = Zodiac ages.

The Gospel of Buddha

Buddha means the Enlightened One. The man of God who taught Buddhism is the Enlightened One, but the Lord is the One who enlightens. The man who taught Buddhism was Siddhartha Gautama who was born about 563 BC. He was enlightened by the Lord of light called Jesus Christ, the Sun of God. Buddha is not a god. Nor do the followers of Guatama worship his statues. The statues didn't come until 600 years after the Buddha. The Buddha sitting in Yoga position represents the "immovable spot". Just as the Lord is called the immovable Rock. People have perverted his teachings just as Christianity has changed Christ's teachings and made their god in their own graven images.

Siddhartha was born from his mother's side near her heart. Just as Eve was born from Adam's side. The male is the flip side of the female: Yin/Yang. Seven days after his birth, his mother Maya died of joy. Just as Isis sacrificed herself for her son Horus. Shortly after birth, Siddhartha walked seven steps and said seven words. "Listen heaven, Listen earth, I am It." Just as the Lord of the seventh day spoke to Moses saying, "I am: that is who I am." When incarnate as Christ, the Word of God spoke from birth says the Qur'an. This is the sign of the Logos.

Siddhartha left his wife and son as all men of God do. Christ's disciples left their families to do God's work. [Matthew 10:36-37 19:29] After seven years, he sat under the Bodhi tree (Bodh Gaya) to resolve the problem of suffering. After forty days of fasting, he became a Buddha. Then for seven weeks he meditated. Seven is the number of the Lord of the Seventh day.

During the full moon of the month of May (Maya), Buddha was tested for seven weeks or 49 days. This is the same period of time from Passover to the Feast of seven weeks (i.e. Pentecost). For the first seven days, he remained seated motionless, realizing the bliss of Nirvana. For the second seven days he remained standing. For the third week he paced west to east. For the forth week, he reviewed the Books of knowledge. For the fifth week, he sat beneath the Nigrodha tree meditating on the doctrine. For the sixth week, he was undisturbed by the terrible storm that raged. For the seventh week, he sat beneath a Rajayatana tree. Then four Great

Kings of the four corners of the earth brought him offerings. Just as the wise men brought gifts to Christ.

The Buddha was sitting in the yoga position in the immovable spot. Which is the same as the Lord being the immovable Rock. [1 Corinthians 10:4] Which the water of life or spirit springs forth from. [Exodus 17:6] The Lord built his house on the bedrock foundation which is the Ten Commandments written in stone. While Guatama was sitting there, the Lord of this world came to test him with three temptations.

The Lord of this earth is Mara the deity of desire and death. Mara is aMan-Ra (Amen-Ra) the evil sun of God of Upper Egypt. Compare Mara to Maria (Mary). Mother Nature or Ma-Neter has a dark side. She gave birth to the dark son as well as the son of light. The darkness did not comprehend the light. [John 1:5] Mary did not understand Jesus. Mara is also Mars the Greek god of war and son of Hera. Hera is the Hara, the Destroyer, of her son Herakles. Mother Earth (Maia or Gaia) is the womb of birth and the tomb of death. To the Romans Maya was Venus and Mara was Cupid (deities of desire).

The first temptation was the physical desire of the three beautiful daughters of Mara. Of which, he rejected. Lucifer's daughters are beautiful like himself. [Ezekiel 28:12] The second test; the Devil threatened him with bodily harm. But the Buddha is not moved (by fear) to self-defense or self-preservation. The third is duty to society. He knew his place and could not be moved to worldly desires. He decided he did not want to be a king in Mara's kingdom.

Siddhartha was the son of King Rajah and Queen Maya. He was given the choice of being world emperor or a Buddha who would preach the Law. Just as Christ Jesus was given the choice of being Caesar Julius and Pope combined. He could have become both head of church and state of Christendom (unholy Roman Catholic empire). [Luke 4:5-7] But he declined saying, God's kingdom is not of this wicked world. The Lord is the Rock that shall destroy the evil empires of this world and establish God's kingdom on earth. [Daniel 2:34,44,45] Just like Melchizedek, he shall be Buddha (high priest) and King (Lord of the Earth). [Hebrew 7] In Egypt, Pharaoh Osiris-Horus is high priest and King.

It is an interesting point that Maya means deception or illusion. Maya represents the illusion of worldly things or materialism. Maya is Mare (Mary) and also Mara, the adversary. The maternal mother earth is as much our adversary as Mara. Compare this adversity with; Nun and Atum, Isis and Horus. It is the Yin/Yang. The light must battle to be born from the darkness of the watery womb and separate from it. The male must separate from the mother female. A man shall leave his family and become as one in the body of the Lord. When the maternal matrix bruises the head of the serpent fiend, she is slaying the evil within: Eve bruises the head of the serpent, Bast (Isis) cuts off the head of the Apophis serpent. Mara is the dark side of Mother Nature.

Buddha's Last Supper

Siddhartha died shortly after eating an indigestible meal with one of his disciples. He said, "O disciples, everything created must perish. A man must separate from everything he has loved. Say not, we no longer have a Master... When I am gone the doctrine I have preached will be your Master. Watch and pray without respite." After speaking these words, Buddha entered into meditation and then into ecstasy (rapture), and finally passed into nirvana.

Siddhartha predicted that the true Buddha would come 500 years after him. He died about 480 BC at eighty years of age. 500 years would be 20 AD. On this subject he said, "I am not the first Buddha who came upon the earth, nor shall I be the last. I came to teach you the truth. Gautama Siddhartha will die, but Buddha will live, for Buddha is the truth, and the truth cannot die. He who believes in the truth and lives it is my disciple, and I shall teach him. The truth will be propagated, and the kingdom of truth will increase for about five hundred years. Then for a while the clouds of error will darken the light, and in due time another Buddha will arise, and he will reveal to you the selfsame eternal truth which I have taught. His name is kindness." Since Siddhartha rightly predicted the Lord's coming about 7 BC, that makes him a prophet.

The future Buddha's name is Maitreya which corresponds with Mithra of Persia. According to the Armenian Eznik the final savior should be a reincarnation of Gayomart, the first man. The Bible says Christ is the last Adam or second Adam. [1 Corinthians 15:45-47 Romans 5:12-21] In Egypt, Osiris was the first martyr who shall return as the savior, Horu-s. There are ten incarnations of Buddha that parallel Vishnu. Buddha as Tur is Buddha in the age of Taurus. Krishna was the age of Aries. Dag Po was his 8th incarnation. Dag = Fish. Dag Po = Pisces. Compare Vish-nu to Fish-nu.

The Lord says "The Word of God is eternal". The armor of God is the shield of faith with which you will be able to quench all the fiery darts of the wicked one (Cupid). And take the helmet of salvation, and the Sword of the Spirit, which is the Word of God. Guatama warning against women said, "Take then the bow of earnest perseverance, and the sharp arrow-points of wisdom. Cover your head with the helmet of right thought." He also taught that the persistence of his religion in India would be shortened by five hundred years as a result of admitting women.

Beware of Venus the Roman goddess of Roman-ce (lust). Guatama left his wife and children in his higher calling to seek the truth. Just as Christ told his disciples to do the same. [Matthew 19:29 10:37-42] Ezek-iel's wife was taken by the Lord because she was so beautiful she was distracting Ezekiel from doing God's work. [Ezekiel 24:15-18] Cupidity is the obsession of coveting. The passion to possess. The Greeks called Cupid; Eros the deity of heart-break, envy and jealousy. Eros is the illegitimate son of Ares' (god of war) adulterous affair with Aphrodite (goddess of sex).

It was Lucifer who seduced Eve, who in turn seduced Adam. [Genesis 3:13 1 Timothy 2:11-15] Lucifer transforms himself into an angel of light so as to deceive the naive. [2 Corinthians 11:2,3,13-15] He is the evil sun of God. Women are not being tested. A woman's desire is for a human husband. [Genesis 3:16] They are part of man's test. Lust is man's greatest weakness and the cause of the fall of many good men.

Like Christ, Guatama fasted for a long time while he searched for truth and then he baptized himself in a river to start his rebirth. At this time, he was enlightened to the Way. He was 35 years old. Much like Christ who said, "I am the Way, the truth and the life." [John 14:6] and "I am the light." [Matthew 3:16] He fasted for forty days after his baptism and preached the Way to the Kingdom of light, from age 30-40 +/-.

Guatama's teachings basically paralleled the Word of God. He taught that self-denial of the things of the world was the way to overcome the temptations of this wicked world. Seeing them for the evils they are. [1 John 2:15-17] John the Baptist was called the greatest man on earth because he sacrificed all earthly pleasures. [Matthew 11:7-11 3:3] He realized that all life is suffering. Desire and fear are the two things that cause suffering. Including the fear of loosing your possessions. Karma means your deeds shall come back to either haunt or bless you. What you sow, you shall reap. What goes around, comes around. Do unto others as you would have them do to you.

Fear of loosing your life is the greatest fear. Those who cling to this world will remain in the dust of the earth. Those who release this world, not desiring the things or the ways of this wicked world, will enter the Other World in the here-after. Here on earth after all things are made new. The truth shall set you free from this wicked world.

Gautama believed that the soul died but was later born again in a new body. Entering into the perfect peace and Rest he called Nirvana (transfiguration). This is God's Rest. [Hebrews 4] Just as the Lord taught the resurrection of the same person in a new glorified or spiritual body in God's kingdom here on the renewed earth. Christ was the only one who could reincarnate. He pre-existed before his incarnation in the flesh. He came as Melchizedek, the Angel of the LORD and then as Son of Man. [Hebrews 7:1-3 John 1:14] "No one has ever ascended to heaven but He who came down from heaven, that is, the Son of Man." [John 3:13] The Buddha said, "I have attained rest, and now I give rest to others". Six hundred years later, the Lord Christ said, "Come to Me, all you who labor and are heavy laden, and I will give you rest. Take My yoke upon you and learn from Me, for I am meek and lowly in heart (humble), and you will find rest for your souls. For My yoke is easy and My burden is light." [Mat.11:28-30] Reincarnation is no different than thinking you can live vicariously through your children. Perpetuation of the human species does not give you life forever. That's nonsense. The idea of reincarnation was created to cause people to have respect for all life forms. The Commandment "You shall not kill" is not limited to "You shall not kill humans." What if you believed your mother reincarnated as a cow, would you eat it? Would you take the chance that it might be true? In God's garden paradise there was not and shall not be the shedding of blood. [Isaiah 11:6-10]

In Buddha's day, there was a plague of five diseases; leprosy, boils, dry leprosy, consumption, and fits. These are described in the Bible. Epilepsy (epi-lepsy) is a form of leprosy causing fits and convulsions. Boils are another symptom of the many types of leprosy. [Leviticus 13:18-22] Leprosy is the curse put on man that turns his skin and hair white. [Leviticus 13:4,32,41] Also causes baldness. It is the Pale face plague that started with Cain who killed Abel. In Egypt, five is the evil number. The five pointed star is Satan the fallen star who lost his wings. The sign of the Lord of the Sabbath is the seven pointed star.

The Problem and the Solution
The Problem:

1) All life is suffering; sickness, pain, death, grief and sorrow
2) because of desire or clinging to this world. Coveting the things of this world. The ego is evil. The self is selfish and self-centered.

The Solution:

3) release desire and ego. All is impermanent or temporary. [2 Peter 1:13,14] Deny yourself of the things of this world, including people. [Mat.16:4-26 19:29] The Lord is our first love.
4) Eight fold path;
    1) right belief-There is one body and one Spirit uniting the believers, one Lord Jesus Christ, one faith, one baptism, one God the Father of all who is above all, and through all and in all. [Eph.4:4-6 1 Cor.8:6 11:3 15:28]
    2) right change-(repent; turn from evil ways) [Mat.4:17]
    3) right speech-(judged by your words) [Mat.12:31-37] 'Refrain from lying speech, slanderous speech, harsh speech, gossip,'
    4) right conduct-(10 Commandments) [Matthew 19:17-21] 'Refrain from onslaught on creatures, taking what has not been given, and pleasures of the five senses.' Dharma or Right Behavior comes from the Egyptian word Maat which means righteousness, law, justice, etc.. Dhar-ma is Horus + Maat.
    5) right livelihood-(do God's work)
    6) right effort-(doing good works) [Matthew 25:34-46]

7) right mindfulness-(do not conform to this wicked world, but transform your thoughts to the will of God) [Romans 12:2] By controlling your mind, you control your actions. [Matthew 5:28]

8) right meditation-(meditate on the Word of God). [Psalms 119:97] Concentrate on rising above and overcoming all evil. Meditate on nothingness. All man's thoughts are evil and must be stilled and silenced, [Genesis 6:5 8:21] so you will be open to God's thoughts.

The Buddha rejected the teachings of the Brahmins just as Jesus was opposed to the hypocritical priests of JeruSalem. Both Jesus and Buddha taught all things in moderation. Extremes are usually harmful and fatal. For example; excessive fasting causes death (suicide). Excessive feasting causes obesity and death.

The Buddha promised salvation only to those who obeyed Buddhist law and lived a life of rising to a higher spiritual state by renouncing all worldly pleasures; liberation from slavery to sin. This meant renouncing all emotional ties to family and friends and living a monastic life. This is just the same as the Word of God. [1 John 2:15-17 5:1-3 Matthew 19:29 1 Corinthians 5:11 6:9,10] When Buddha transcended to Nirvana, it is the same as when the Lord ascended to his Father in heaven and said, "the Father and I are One". Buddha ascended to Brahma which is the same as Abraham: meaning Father of many nations. The family of God is our true family.

Buddha's third commandment is "Commit no adultery, the law is broken by even looking at the wife of another man with lust in the mind." Compare this to Matthew 5:28. Among Buddha's teachings was the story of the wheat and the tares. [Mat.13:24-30, 36-43] Another is the parable of the sower. Another is the hidden treasure which may be laid up by a man and kept securely where a thief cannot break in and steal; the treasure that a man may carry away with him when he goes. [Mat.6:19-21] Another is the story of the rich young man who was commanded to sell all he had and give it to the poor. [Matthew 19:16-26] When speaking of his departure, he promises to send the Holy Spirit of truth. [John 14:16-17] Buddha's transfiguration on the Mount is identical to that of the Lord. The heaven opened and a great light was in full flood around him and the glory of his person shone forth with double power. He shone as the brightness of the sun and moon. [Mat.17:1-13] See "Gerald Massey's Lectures".

Buddha taught that on the 1st and the 15th day of the month, the monks should fast and confess their sins. Compare this to God's Holy days. The Feast of Unleavened Bread and Feast of Ingathering both fall on the 15th. The Day of Atonement is the 10th day of the seventh month. It is the holy day of fasting and self-sacrifice. [Leviticus 23] The Lord said Faith comes through fasting and prayer. [Matthew 17:21 1 Corinthians 7:5 Philippians 4:6-8] Meditation on the Word of God produces spiritual growth. God is spirit and we can communicated with Him through thoughts (mental telepathy).

The idea of monks and nuns living in a community originated in India. Buddha said the four offenses deserving excommunication are: sexual intercourse (fornication), stealing, taking a life, or lying. Taking a life means to kill any living being. It includes killing anything that has a life-force or spirit. Lying includes telling gossip and spreading rumors. The worse offense is to bear false witness against someone. All are based on the intent of the person. If a man thinks about having sex with a woman he has lusted and it is as he has committed the sin. [Mat.5:27,28] The fornication rule includes, not playing Cupid. Anyone who causes division in the community will be banished. There shall be no denominations. [Jude 19 1 Corinthians 1:10 3:3 Titus 3:9,10]

The Spurious Buddha

In the first century AD, Buddha was represented by a solar wheel (sun chariot) or an empty throne (as the Sun of God ruling from heaven). The sungod riding the solar chariot is the Antichrist or spurious Sun of God. It wasn't until after the Christian era that he took human form. They portrayed him with an urna between his eyebrows. This is the Egyptian uraeus (serpent) or the Greek Uranus. He is shown wearing an ushnisha or domed crown of Amen-Ra. Originally the movement was called the Little Vehicle because only the faithful few could ride. In Egypt, the ferry boat is the ferry bark of Horus. Herfhaf ferries the souls of the righteous over to the Island of fire where Osiris reigns. Now it is called the Great Vehicle with many Saviors. These human Buddhas are called Manushi (Man-Shivas). This mass transit moves the masses to an unknown destination. They were warned to beware of these anti-christs of transmigration who claim to transport you to "heaven" and back again. Amen-Ra claims he will rapture you away in his solar bark. Amen-Ra is the captain of the cosmic Titanic sailing the sea of space. His crewmen are the Titans. In the end, it will sink in the sea.

However, the masses preferred to worship the manifestation of the Buddha called Amitabha who was said to reign in a Western Paradise. He vowed to give salvation to all those who repented their sins and called upon his name. The state of bliss could be achieved by faith rather then giving up the things of the world. The masses created a new god called Buddha! Who magically pardoned them all just for saying his name. Obviously, no one realizes that repent means to change your bad ways, because they rarely do. Sound familiar? Amitabha means Infinite Light. He is Lucifer pretending to be the Angel of Light. [2 Corinthians 11:13-15] Amitabha's color is red, just like the Roman empire and the blood-thirsty dragon of Revelation 12:3.

The Western Paradise obviously refers to; the garden of God, the Promise land, the Egyptian Fields of Peace, the Elysian Fields, and Hera's garden paradise. It is Christianity that claims they are going to heaven.

The Lord said the Way to salvation is through faith in God and obedience to God's laws. [Revelations 12:17 14:12] We must obey the laws of nature; the cycle of life to death. Then Christianity come along (three hundred years after Christ), took two verses and created a new diluted religion. Claiming you are saved if you call upon the name of the new manifestation of God called Jesus. Jesus is their God. They claim they shall detour death, escape judgment and go straight to heaven.

To the Egyptians, the West represents the Land of the Dead (Valley of the Kings). As all the heavenly bodies set in the west, it represents death. It is called Amenta; Land of Amen. Osiris is Lord of Amenta or the cemetery. He is Lord of the Dead. The sun rising in the east represents rebirth. It is called Tuat; Land of Atum. Atum-Horus is Lord of the Living. This is the Way to life in the hereafter. There are no short cuts by going east. We must die and resurrect from the earth. Only two people ever escaped death; Elijah and Enoch. And even they must return [Malachi 4:5] "as it is appointed for men to die once, and after this is the judgment." [Hebrews 9:27,28] Christ died to show us the Way. When Osiris is resurrected to life, he will judge mankind. This is the Day of the Lord, [John 5:22-30] when he redeems the firstfruits from the earth (grave). [1 Corinthians 15:20-28 42-55 Revelation 14:4]

The Lord said many shall call on his name, but He shall reject them for practicing lawlessness. [Mat.7:21-23] Calling on the name Jesus will NOT save you. Obeying the Word of God will. The Lord said many will come in His name saying, "I am Christian", but they shall be raptured away by the Antichrist Jesus. [Matthew 24:5,11,12] They will follow the first Jesus to come along because they are ignorant of the Word of God. [Matthew 24:23-26 36-44] The many Buddhas or Saviors are reminiscent of Mary and her Saints who supplanted the "Roman gods". The true Savior comes after the masses have had their hearts impregnated by the Antichrist. They live in sin with Satan. They must go to purgatory to be purged of sin. Either you are refined in the fire or incinerated. Only the Faithful Few, who are enlightened, can enter Paradise. [Zechariah 13:8,9] It is time to see that the Word of God is spread out across the seven seas to the seven continents. God is the Father of all nations and it is His desire that all shall be saved. All people are given the opportunity to hear the message and a chance to follow the Way of the Lord. Those that haven't, will be given that opportunity during the Millennium. For God is a just God who loves All people. The incorrigible infidels will incinerate in the Lake of fire. God's mercy is to put them our of their misery. The lawless, who will not repent, shall NOT enter God's kingdom. [Ephesians 5:5 Galatians 5:19-21 1 Corinthians 6:9,10]

Tibetan Buddhists

Tibet was the only nation in the 20th century to be ruled by a priest. Just the way the Lord told Israel they should be. But they demanded a man-King to rule over them. The Tibetan lived in peace for a thousand years, until their holy land was conquered and occupied by the red Chinese. The Chinese who wear the red Satanic star on their hats in their foreheads. These murdering infidels follow the way of the Warlord, Satan. And Satan has put the Mark of the Beast in their heads and in their hands. [Revelation 14:9-13] The prophecy was fulfilled that said he would be the last Priest-King to rule in Tibet.

Their Commandments are: Thou shalt not kill any human being or animal, Thou shalt not commit adultery, Thou shalt not steal, Thou shalt not speak ill of others, Thou shall not lie, Thou shalt honor thy father and mother.[Anacalypsis by Godfrey Higgins volume 1 page 789]

Shangri-La

Shangri-La is a legendary paradise in Tibet where the people live long lives in peace. These unworldly people are diametrically opposed to those of the world. Compare Shangri-La to the garden of Eden before the fall. This is the Promise land that the whole world would love to find, but would soon destroy by their evil ways. Only the peaceful, unworldly, God-fearing, God obeying people shall life long in the Promise land. Those who love the world the way it is and love the things of this world will not enter God's paradise. They have their reward. Nirvana is the rapture one feels at being accepted into God's family. On the other hand, Shambala is the home of Baal (Satan).

Serendib is the Hindu, Arabic and Jewish Paradise. It is the primeval mount and the mountain where Noah's ark came to rest. The birthplace of Adam is the birthplace of Atum. Ser is Sar (Osiris) and En is An and On (Heliopolis). Serdab is a secret cell within a tomb where images of the deceased were deposited. Serene is a place of rest. Ser also means Rock as in the absent capstone of the Great Pyramid. The Great Pyramid is the ceremonial tomb and womb of Osiris/Tum. On the celestial level Serendib is Taprobane, sign of Pisces. Which is the age of Jesus who taught his followers to be fishers of men. Beth-le-hem (House of Ham) was originally Beth-Sham-esh (House of the Sun) or Heliopolis, Egypt. [A Book of Beginnings by Gerald Massey pages 452 and 453] The Tibetans also worshipped Tara who was born from the sea of enlightenment. She is called Perfection of Understanding. This is obviously a feminine form of Tam-Ra (Atum) of Egypt. Tara is called the Mistress of the boats who leads her devotees across the river of experience to the shore of spiritual freedom. This is the bark of Horus that saves the righteous souls and delivers them to the Fields of the Blessed. She is often shown seated on a lion holding the sun in her hand or holding a lotus, the symbol of rebirth. This is Isis holding the Horus Child. The lion-seat is the throne of royalty. The twin-lions of the equinox are Pasht (Passover in spring) and Sekhet (autumn).

Lao—tze and Taoism

Lao-tze (Laocius) was around the same time as the prophet Jeremiah, Confucius and Buddha; about 600 BC.

Lao-tze wrote a book called Tao-Teh-King which means "The Book of the Way and of Virtue." Tao means the Way, Logos and Principle. The Word of God is the Logos. The Lord also taught the Way. "I am the Way, the truth and the life." [John 14:6,7] The Way that leads to God's kingdom is the Road of Righteousness. [Acts 9:2 16:17 18:25 19:9,23 24:14] Lao-tze taught that to do nothing is the Way. Flow with the laws of nature. Non-resistance prevails. The Lord of the Sabbath agreed. The most holy times are the Sabbath days which are days of Rest. After all God created the laws of nature as well as the supernatural laws. Rebelling against God's established Way is foolish.

Lao-tze teaches that the answers are within yourself. The Lord taught to transform your thoughts that you will not conform to the wicked world. [Romans 12:2] The spiritual knowledge of God is thought. Just as the Ten Commandments are spiritual laws. Worldly wisdom is foolishness. You must seek the knowledge from where you are. No one will go to heaven and bring the Word of God down and no one will go to Hell and bring the knowledge up from there. Neither is God limited to dwelling in temples, statues, or sacred places. God is everywhere all the time through His thoughts which is called God's Spirit. It is spiritual knowledge and truth. [1 John 4:1-6] The knowledge of God's kingdom is within reach.

Lao-tze believed there is One greater than the Jewish god of wrath, and he was right. The Lord of the Old Testament is the Son of God who was created by God the Father. The Father was the only One before the creation was set to motion. God created all the stars of heaven including the Morning Star, Jesus Christ. Who is the Sun of God. Likewise, Lucifer is another Son of God whose name means Day Star. [Isaiah 14:12-15]

The Father is Yang: masculine, light, knowledge, cosmos (order) etc... The Creation is Yin: feminine, chaos, darkness, etc... The suns of the Father were born from the watery womb of the Creation. The suns are Yang, like their Father, yet some have turned to Yins. The fallen angels dwell in darkness. Man also has fallen into darkness. Only through Tao can we find our Way out of the darkness. The logos or Word of God will reveal the unknown Father to us. The Lord of light will lead us out of the darkness of ignorance.

Both Lao-tze and the Lord taught to be content and do not fight against nature. [Matthew 6:34] The heavens are set in order and harmony, just as the law of nature on earth. The Creator takes cares and provides for all of His creatures. We are to Honor our Father in heaven and our mother earth. Lao-tze says: "Water is strong by being weak; the soft overcomes the hard and the weak the strong." The water bends around the rocks but eventually breaks the rocks to sand. The Lord is strong in us when we are weak. Lao-tze says: "He who overcomes others is strong; he who overcomes himself is mighty." The Lord teaches that Self-improved is our number one priority. By His example, we are to learn and demonstrate to others. "Be holy as I am Holy."

Lao-tze said do not fear anything in nature. Paul said "them that believe shall take up serpents, and if they drink any deadly thing, it shall in no wise hurt them." Nature shall be restored to its peaceful state when the Lord makes all things new. There will be no more predators or plagues. The harmony of the garden of God will be re-created.

Lao-tze and Confucius were contemporaries. On the Yin and Yang Lao-tze says: "The two states communicating together, a harmony ensued and things were produced. Some one regulated and controlled all this, but no one has seen his form." The Lord Christ agree: God created the creation and no one has ever seen His form or heard his voice. [John 1:18 5:37] God is a consuming fire at the edge of space. He is not part of the creation. The creation is created on the foundation of good (Yang) vs. evil (Yin). The battle of the Lord Christ and his Adversary, Satan. The good Son of God vs. the bad Son of God. Lord of Light vs. the lord of darkness.

The day we are born we are one with nature, but our ultimate goal is to become one with God. We must transform the balance of yin/yang into one whole yang. The positive must consume the negative. There will be no Yin (sin, evil, darkness, death) in the re-creation.

Lao-tze taught that by learning to be humble, you become exalted. The Lord agreed; those who humble themselves will be exalted by God. The proud and arrogant will be brought down low. [Isaiah 14:12-15] Learn the become like a child; innocence and pure. Without a guilty conscience. As Adam and Eve were before the fall. Both taught against fame and wealth.[1 John 2:15-17] Materialism is coveting; the Tenth Commandment.

Lao-tze says: "Recompense injury with kindness; to those who are good to me, I am good; to those who are not good to me, I am also good. And thus all get to be good." The Lord says: "love your enemies, and pray for those who persecute you." [Matthew 5:44] "Therefore, whatever you want men to do to you, do also to them, for this is the Law and the

Prophets." [Matthew 7:12] They both agree that war is an evil. The Lord says; "For all they that take the sword shall perish by the sword." [Matthew 26:52 Revelation 13:10] Tao-tze said: "Or fame or life, which do you hold more dear? Or life or wealth, to which would you adhere? Keep life and lose these other things; keep them and lose your life:-which brings sorrow and pain more near?" The Lord says: Sacrifice everything for Him and you will be more than compensated with everlasting life in paradise. [Revelation 12:11] The Lord said, "For whoever desires to save his life will lose it, and whoever loses his life for My sake will find it. For what is man profited it he gains the whole world, and loses his own soul? Or what will a man give in exchange for his soul?" [Mat.16:24-26 19:29] Man can not redeem or save himself. Only the Lord can. Like it or not, Lao-tze was very much Christ-like.

Chinese Pantheon

Heavenly Master of the First Origin is the transcendent Creator. Queen Mother the Lady Queen of the West (Hsi Wang Mu) are the creation. In Lower Egypt, they would be Nut (Mut). In Upper Egypt, it would be Hathor. In the Western world, she is Mother Mary, Queen of Heaven. West is where the sunsets and represents death. August Personage of Jade or Father-Heaven is the Son who created mankind from clay. He shall be succeeded or reincarnated as Heavenly Master of the Dawn of Jade of the Golden Door. This is the good Sun of God who said, "I am the Door" and the Way to God's kingdom. East is where the Morning Star rises and represents his rebirth. The Egyptians called him Atum.

Compare August Personage of Jade to: the Jade Buddha, the green Quetzalcoatl, the green Osiris, etc...He is the ambassador from God's kingdom in heaven to us on earth. They go to the west, place of death, and then return in the east, place of rebirth.

There is a palace built on top of K'un-lun mountain. It has nine stories and is built entirely of jade. Around the palace are magnificent gardens in which grows the Peach-tree of Immortality. Compare this to the apple tree of Hera's garden in the Greek version. And the Tree of life in the garden (gar-eden) of God. The Chinese believe everything in heaven has a counterpart on earth. The Forbidden City is a copy of its heavenly counterpart. The Emperor is the son of the August Personage of Jade and his vicar on earth, just like in Egypt where Pharaoh is son of Osiris. This is New JeruSalem, the celestial city, which shall descend down on Mount Zion, the holy mountain. Like Mt. Olympus of the Greeks, which is home of the gods and center of the earth. Just as the Egyptians built the great Pyramid in the true center. The missing head-stone represents Horus the Hawk headed Son of God, who shall descend from heaven unto his holy primordial mount. The nine stories represent the Mother whose number is nine, like the term of human pregnancy. All the Saints shall be begotten from above as suns of God. They will be reborn in the garden of God and eat of the Tree of Life.

Yama-king is Lord and Judge of the dead. This Sun of God has two satellites called Niu-t'ou (Bull-Head) and Ma-mien (Horse-Face). They bring the dead souls to the Judgment Court. The two Messengers (one black and one white) who seize the souls from Walls and Ditches (i.e. the grave) are Without-Duration. These are the four sons of Horus: Anubis the jackal-headed, Amen-Set the human-headed, Horus the hawk-headed, and Hapi the bull-headed (apis) who take the deceased before Osiris the Judge. Yama's counterpart is Hades of the Greeks. The dead must cross the river Vaitarani (Styx) to stand before the Judge. The river represents the Water of life or Spirit of life. This is the Day of resurrection and Judgment when Jesus in his human form will Judge mankind. [John 5:22-30]

The moon goddess Ch'ang-o is wife of I the Excellent Archer. This is the counterpart of Diana the huntress of Roman myth. She is the prima-donna or primordial mother Diana. It is not a goddess, but the concept of fertility during the moon's 28 day cycle. Compare to Nephthys, the Mother Nature of Egypt. The Feast of the Moon is the full moon of the autumn equinox. This synchronizes with the Feast of Ingathering, which is the time the Lord gathers his faithful few to become the priests of God's kingdom. The saints are reborn sons of God just as the moon goes through its cycle of new to full (full of age) to new born again. Kuan-yin is the Great Mother of mercy and compassion who carries a child in her arms. Compare to Mother Mary. Both are portrayed in red which is symbolic of blood, menstrual cycle and child birth. She is Isis of Egypt. Chang-o is Mother nature who Changes her mind because its her prerogative.

To the Chinese, the sea of space is portrayed as a Dragon as well as the watery womb of creation. Both are Yin (darkness and female) as compared to Yang (light and male). In Egypt, the chaos of dark space void of life is the female, Nun (Hathor). Sometimes Horus battles with his mother, just as Hera is the adversary of Herakles, her son. This is the powers of light battling the powers of darkness. The light is struggling to be born from the dark watery womb. Mother Nature's cycle is life to death. A fate no creature looks forward to. At the same time Set is said to be the darkness and the fear of the unknown. He also is Yin and is portrayed as a monster. The Apophis serpent is the counterpart of the Dragon.

The Chinese say the red sunrise and sunset is the red dragon chasing his tail. In Upper Egypt, it is the serpent battling Ra the sun. The four Dragon Kings control the rain in the four directions. In Hinduism, it is Shiva who controls the rain fall flowing into the rushing rivers. Likewise, Baal is the storm god. The Destroyer decides how much destruction he will do. So they make offerings to him to appease and pacify him.

These destructive powers of; flood, drought and tempest are held in check by the Arch-Angel until he gathers the saints of God. [Revelation

7:1-3] He is the Lord with the Sword who shall destroy the Dragon of Destruction. [Revelation 12:7-9] He shall also slay the body of the Beast which is the false church. [Rev.19:11-21] It is he that we should appease, not the forces of Yin.

Japanese

In Japan, Amatsu-Mikaboshi (the-August-Star-of-Heaven) or Ama-no-Kagaseo (the-Brilliant-Male) is the evil sun-god we call Lucifer the Day-star. Amaterasu is the sun goddess. It is obvious the names are derived from the Egyptian Aman-Sut or Amen-Set the evil sun-god and Warlord. This is more proof that all mythologies originated in Egypt. The stories of Hinduism, and later Buddhism, migrated through China and India to Japan. The true August Star of Heaven is Atum's star, Sirius.

The Samurai were homosexual warriors, like their Christian counterparts, the Janissaries. The root of Samurai is sami, the minions of Set! Semi are the priests of Set-Amen-ra.

Confucius

Confucius: Kung-fu-tze means Master Kung. He is the creator of the Kung-Fu technique of self-defense. He was not a prophet, but he did teach the ideas that came from the men of God. What upset the Chinese about Bruce Lee? He had harnessed the supernatural power of Chi (Holy Spirit) and was teaching it to the Barbarians in the West. Undoubtedly, the Barbarians would abuse such a power, as they always do.

Confucius' most famous contribution was the teaching of the Yin and Yang. Even though he did not originate the idea. Everything in the universe is based on the Negative force (either supernatural or natural) and the Positive force. It is the balance of good and evil in the creation. Learn to chose the good and refuse the evil.

The Word of God teaches the same thing. During the creation, God divided all things. [Genesis chapter 1]. Good vs. evil; light vs. darkness; male vs. female; wet vs. dry. The Creator is male principle. His creation called Maya or Gaia is female principle. Even the planets are female while the stars are Suns or Sons of God. The moon is of female principle with the 28 day cycle equal to the menstrual cycle. Satan was Lucifer the Day Star who fell and became the ruler of the powers of darkness. While Michael is the Sun of Righteousness who slays the Dragon. The red sunset represents the dragon chasing his tail and returning the begin with a red sunrise.

The Chinese sacred book called the Shu-king has some of the same stories as the Bible. Shu is Spirit in Egyptian. In the Shu-King, Noah is called Fu-hi. In the Shu-King is a terrestrial paradise, rivers, water of life, the trees, the fall of angels and man, the Sabbath, the confusion of tongues, manna in the Wilderness, the Holy One in the West who is one with Tien.

Only the Holy One can reveal Tien to man. This is Osiris who is one with Atum-Horus. Osiris died in the West and rose again as Atum-Horus in the east. Tien is Aten, a corruption of Tem.

The Chinese say that Fu-hi founded his kingdom and formed the language 200 years after the Great flood. This synchronizes with the time of the Tower of Babal, the dividing of the nations and tongues.

Mandate of Heaven

The Mandate of Heaven is taken from Egypt. Where the Creator of Heaven and earth set down a code of moral laws for man to live by. The Chinese were astrologers who studied the Zodiac just as the Egyptians did. They were aware the stars represent the suns of God (Yang) and the planets are feminine in nature (Ying). For example: Mother earth. The spirit of the lie is the adversary of the spirit of Truth just as the Devil is the enemy of the Lord. [1 John 4:1-6] This is the universal truth of the cosmos.

Confucius often thought of the ancient times when the people lived in peace and harmony. This was the time people followed the Great Tao or Way of the Ancestors. It was the Way of Kings; Yao, Shun, T'ang, Wen, Wu, Ch'eng, Emperor Yu and Duke of Chou who set a good example. In Egypt, the eight divine Kings are; Atum, Shu, Geb, Osiris, Isis, Set, Horus and Thoth. The Egyptians followed the divine teachings of Osiris, the first Pharaoh and lived in peace and harmony. The Chinese teach that when Yin and Yang are in balance, we have harmony. But Osiris taught that as long as Set, the evil one, ruled anywhere on earth, there would be no peace. Set is Yin (creator of sin) who must be destroyed by Yang so the rest can live in peace. In the Bible, Paul also taught the Way of righteousness that leads to God's kingdom. [Acts 18:25 19:9,23 24:14]

Confucius believed you could not force people to be good, but if taught, they will choose good over evil. Man's nature is good. Ignorance is the root of all evil. This is a naive outlook. Many people who know the Way, the truth and the Law purposely choose to do evil. We must distinguish between the carnal brain and the spiritual mind. A child is innocent, but soon learns "worldly knowledge". We must take on the mind of the Lord. [1 Corinthians 2:16 3:1-3] When you change a person's mind, you change his behavior.

Confucius' social teachings parallel the ordinances and statutes given to Moses by the Lord. Exodus, Leviticus and Numbers are basically laws on hygiene, civil laws, and social regulations. Although they do include rituals, holy days, and moral laws. Some of which the Chinese observe. [Romans 2:13-16] Honor of ancestors is merely an extension of "Honor your mother and father that you days may be long in the land."

Golden Rule

Tzu-kung asked 'Is there one word which can express the essence of right conduct in life?' K'ung replied: 'It is the word shu-reciprocity: Do not do to others what you do not want them to do to you.' Compare this to Christ's saying, "Therefore, whatever you want men to do to you, do also to them, for this is the Law and the Prophets." [Matthew 7:12] The word Shu in Egyptian is the Holy Spirit of Truth, Love and Life.

Working as a Community is the Way to world peace. Christ taught his disciples to share all things in common. Only by working together can we become one with the Lord. "By this we know that we love the children of God, when we love God and keep His Commandments. For this is the love of God, that we keep His Commandments. And His Commandments are not burdensome." [1 John 5:1-3] The Ten Commandments are guidelines to follow so we do not offend our fellowman.

One Chinese teacher said, "Though we speak of individuals, and distinguish one from the other, yet there is in reality but one breath that animates them all. My own breath (or spirit) is the identical breath of my ancestors." He is correct. There is One Holy Spirit that is the life force shared by All living creatures. [1 Corinthians 12:1-11] It is called the Spirit of life and breath of life. [Genesis 7:22] It is the source of spiritual knowledge, like a well of wisdom containing the Water of Life. "There is One body (of believers) and One Spirit (of God), just as you were called in One hope of your calling; One Lord (Jesus), one faith, one baptism; One God and Father of all, who is above all, and through all, and in all." [Ephesians 2:18-22 4:4] The Spirit is God's, not ours. The body is the temporary temple where God's spirit dwells.

When Temujin took the Mongolian emperor by conquest (khanquest), he took the title Genghis Khan (Universal Ruler). It is highly likely he took his name from Khansu, son of Amon. Khansu was the Egyptian Warlord who conquers. Mongol is obviously derived from Mon. Genghis Khan was considered to be an avatar and incarnation of god as son of Amon. [Anacalypsis by Godfrey Higgins volume 2 pages 343-345]

Mayan Indians

When Columbus sailed into the Caribbean, he recorded in his diary that the Mayans had trading ships as large as his own capable of sailing to Europe and back. The Mayan Indians knew of the flood story, rebirth, baptism, confession, penance's and pilgrimages to holy places before the Spanish got to America. The cross was the symbol of the four directions of the compass. Cortez thought Saint Thomas had come and taught them, but it was not so. They were aware of the virgin Mother with child. In fact, Maya means Mary. {See "Sacred Texts of the World; a Universal Anthology" P.36,37}

For the Mayan, (and their ancestors the Olmecs) time began Aug. 13, 3114 BC and will end on the winter solstice of December 23, 2012 AD. At that time man's technology will turn against him for the abuses of mother nature and mother earth. The things that man calls good will turn out bad in the long run. For every action is an equal and opposite reaction. Progress produce by-products. Nature shall no longer produce resources. The air, water and earth will be toxic from pollution. The total destruction will be followed by a re-creation of a new world and new age.

Compare the date, 3114 BC to the time of the Tower of Babel. The Lord dispersed the races by confounding their tongues (Languages). Following the Great Flood and the dividing of the people, the Mayans and others sailed to the New Land (AKA America). These Afro-Americans were of African descent.

The gods of creation are God the Father and His sons called Elohim in Hebrew. First man was created of mud but it was too flimsy so it was changed to wood from a tree. The spine of man is his backbone. This is the trunk of his family tree carved by the Sword of God. Man's arms are called limbs and his descendants branch out. Our ancestors are our roots. The Word of God (Holy Scriptures) often refers to men as different types of tree. See the book of Isaiah.

The Mayan creation story is called Popol Vuh. Ometecuhtli, Lord of Duality, is the supreme deity being both male and female. He created and holds the earth as a grain in a drop of water in his hand. Superior to all other gods, too elevated to be counted among their colorful ranks, he is a metaphysical concept of a totally different dimension. He lives in the first dimension alone. Unknowable, he had no temple for men could not expect any experience of Him; He is too remote, too far above and beyond the universe to be bothered by such trivial things as weather, food, life or death. That was His Son's job. One of the Creator's titles is Tepeu. Compare this to He-tepi one of the titles of Ptah, God the Father, in Egypt. [From Fetish to God in Ancient Egypt by Wallis Budge] Gucumatz (Ueuetcotl) is the watery womb or dark sea of space void of life (abyss) that gave birth to the firstborn Sun of God, Kukulcan (i.e. Huracan / Quetzalcoatl). In Egypt, this maternal matrix is Nun. Atum-Horus is begotten by the supernatural power of the Father called the holy Spirit or Shu. Shu is the spiritual sperm of life. Once Nun gives birth to the suns of God (stars), she is called Nut. In the metaphysical myths, she is the Great Mother (Mot or Mut). Sometimes she is represented as a sea serpent. In fact, the Mayan word for "serpent" and "sky" is the same. It is said that Quetzalcoatl sailed the seas on a raft of serpents.

Quetzalcoatl is Quetzal (a bird) + serpent. Compare that to Horus the falcan with the ureaus (serpent crown) on his head. "Behold I send you out as sheep in the midst of the wolves. Therefore, be wise as serpents and harmless as doves." [Matthew 10:16] Compare Kukulcan to falcan. Both mean a bird and both end in 'can' which means serpent. It is Horus the falcon hatching from the cosmic egg as Sirius. In the physical realm, she is Isis and the Horus child or Mary and Jesus.

Quetzalcoatl was crucified by Mictlantecuhtli at "place of the skull". [Compare this to Christ at Golgotha] Together with his dog-headed companion, Xolotl, they descend to Mictlan, the region of the dead. He says to Mictlantecuhtli, "I come in search of the precious bones in your possession. I have come for them." [Compare to Jude 9] Quetzalcoatl then rises back to life. Quetzalcoatl takes the bones to Tamoanchan (Tem Prince of Anu), Land of the Living. Then He circumcised himself and from his blood, people were reborn. It is he who recreates mankind from the dead. [Ezekiel 37:1-14] He is both the king and priest of the Mayan people. Compare to Jesus. [Hebrew 5:5,6 7:1-3] Quetzalcoatl is portrayed as a bird riding on (ruling over) the raft of serpents. This is obviously Horus the Hawk ruling over the Apophis serpent. Contrary to popular belief, Christendumb does Not have exclusive rights on the story of the Savior.

The Mayas understood the Egyptians story of Horus and Sut (Satan). When Osiris was killed by Set-Amen, he united with Neththys (mother nature's cycle of life to death). Their son, the dog-headed Anubis, helped to find the body parts and embalm Osiris. Mictlantecuhtli would be Amen and Mictlan would be Amenta, land of Amen (i.e. the grave). Neththys and Isis were twins who shared the same star (Sirius) as Mother with Child. Isis produced Horus the Lord of life and Neththys produced Anubis the lord of death. From there is were Sirius got the name the Dog star. Mayans call Anubis, pe'co-Xolo or the Lightning Dog. Horus and Anubis are twin suns. Both are attributes of Osiris, lord of the living and the dead. Orion is often depicted as Hunter and dog. As Heart of Heaven, he (Sirius) is called Huracan (Horus the king). Compare this to Jesus who is called the Sacred Heart of Heaven. Heaven referring to Mary (Mare). See "Origin of the Indians" (book 5, chapter 4) by Fra Gregoria Garcia.

Gucumatz, the plumed serpent is enveloped in green and azure (sky-blue). Gucumatz is the sea of space that gave birth to Quetzalcoatl (Huracan). The quetzal is a beautiful bird with metallic green feathers above and scarlet below. In Islam, Malachi is the Green one. In Egypt, Osiris is the Green one. In India, Krishna is the Blue-Green One and the Jade Buddha is green. The image of Quetzalcoatl is called the "Emerald Jewel". He is the eradicator of sins. Who bled his member in the ritual circumcision or blood sacrifice for; ratifying the Covenant, redeeming the lost and resurrection of mankind. They understood the whole story.

The Forbidden Fruit

According to the Mayans: The Lord of the underworld was a sun of God. He came to earth as man strong and tall like a tree. The girl touched of his fruit. The seed was planted in her belly (pregnant). Her offspring were twin suns. They were the fruit of her womb.

In the Word of God, the twin sons are Cain and Abel. Cain's roots are in the family tree of the Knowledge of good and evil. The forbidden fruit that Eve ate was knowledge of evil. Satan, son of God, planted evil ideas in her mind. They got to "know" each other. In Hebrew, to know a woman means to have sex with her. This is carnal knowledge or knowledge of the flesh. The serpent in the tree symbolizes his sexual potency (penis). So, Satan seduced Eve, planting his seed (son) in her belly. Abel was rooted in the Lord's family tree of life. The seed of Adam. In Egypt, Atum is the Sun of God who created two sets of twins; Osiris, Set, Isis, and Nephthys.

Ixchel is the moon-goddess crowned with a uraeus (serpent). Compare this to Hathor of Upper Egypt, ruled over by the serpent (Satan). She is the daughter of Mut and Amun-Set, the evil one. Their son Khonsu is also the moon god.

For one year, a mortal impersonates Tezcatlipoca. He is the embodiment of the sun-god, Tezcatlipoca. The man rules as a god-king for one year, then he is sacrificed. At the feast of Toxcatl his heart is cut out while it still beats and offered to the sungod. This is the reenactment of the death of the Sun at winter solstice (Dec.25th). Some say it ends at the spring equinox. Demonstrating that is a mockery of the death of Osiris, king of Egypt. Who resurrected as the Sun of God, Horus (Jesus). It was Osiris who put an end to human sacrifice in Egypt. Likewise, they also sacrificed a girl to the Maize Goddess Chicomecohuatl in September. This being a mockery of the Festival of Isis in September.

This Protem stands in the place of the divine leader for the time being. Just as the Pope is called Vicar of Christ. When the Pope dies, he is easily replaced by another. Ironically, this ritual was recorded by the Catholic crusaders who have an almost identical ritual; the Roman Saturnalia (festival of Saturn). Where a man stands in Saturn's place, as Lord of Misrule, for thirty days and then sacrifices himself. It ended at the winter solstice. Satan is the real Lord of Misrule. He has mis-ruled for 6,000 years. Satan is the great impostor who imitates all that the Lord does. [2 Corinthians 11:13-15] In the last days, he will manifest as the Antichrist and will rule for a short time, then the Lord will return as the rightful heir.

The Incas: Sons of the Sun

The Inca's lived in Peru, South America. The word Peru may come from Per-Heru meaning House of Horus. Peru in Egyptian means to go out or go around. As if saying they went out of their native land and around the world. Their ancestors, during the ages of Taurus and Ares, were likely followers of Horus. Later, beginning with the age of Pisces, the people became the bastard sons of Set in the Per-Set, House of Set-Amun the Warlord. Set-Amun is the evil sun of God.

The Inca's believe in One Incomprehensible Creator God who has no name. He is called by many titles like Viracocha. He delegates the affairs of everyday like to the lesser gods He created. The Father fathered His two Suns. The twin Suns are called Morning Stars. The two Sons of a duality. Opposites contrasting each other. Yin / Yang. To illustrate this the Indians made a statue of the good son on the front and the bad son on the back is his dark side. Like Siamese twins connected at the spine. Ironically, Christ said to Satan, "Get behind me." The back would be the dark side of the Sun of God. The front is the face that looks forward. In the Word of God, Satan is constantly mimicking the Lord Christ. Both are Morning Stars [Isaiah 14:12 Revelation 22:16], Lions [1 Peter 5:8 Revelation 5:5], Angels of Light, Princes of this world, Lord (adoni vs. Baal) etc... The christ Jesus vs. the antichrist Jesus. As Judge, the Lord is giver of life (Savior) or Angel of Death (Executioner).

Viracocha is the god who vanished in the sea of space. Like Quetzalcoatl who went beyond the seas to the underworld on a raft of snakes. Just as Osiris went to the underworld in the west and rose from the sea of space in the east as Atum-Ra-Horus. He sailed on a bark sometimes portrayed as a snake. He rides on the back of that old sea serpent. Pachacamac is the invisible one just as Amen-Ra is called the Hidden one. Since the Devil is a spirit-being, he can't be seen. Supai is the god of death like Seker of Egypt. Pachacamac and Supai are aspects of Satan.

The Inca's have an Holy Island of the sun. The primeval mound which is the birthplace of the sun of God. Compare this to the primeval mound or birthplace (Anu) of the Egyptian Sun of God, Atum. The great Creator God Viracocha made the heavens and earth. [Gen.1:1] He created the sun and moon and stars. Just like Atum! Yet both were sons begotten of the Father in heaven. Just like Jesus. [Colossians 1:15-18] Inti (Anti) is the evil sun of God and Mama Kilya is his consort, the moon of goddess. Compare to Shiva's consort Kali Ma. The moon is the female principle with a 28 day cycle just like the menstrual cycle of women. The lesser light or heavenly body is the weaker vessel. Inti would be Amen-Ra the evil sun god of Egypt and Enlil of Babylon and Lucifer of the Bible and the Anti-christ.

The Creator flooded the Earth mother to destroy the evil giants created from stone who were fighting among themselves. The Word of God calls them the sons of the fallen angels (sons of God). [Genesis 6:1-4-22] Later, they are called Canaanites. After the deluge, the creator appeared in human form from Lake Titicaca. [Genesis 1:14-19,26] One man and one woman survived the flood in a box (ark). The wind carried them to Tiahuanaco where they renewed the human population on earth. The Incas say Manco Capac was the first Inca and from whom they began to boast that they are children of the sun of God. They worshipped the Sun. The warriors are the children of the evil Sun of God, Inti. The peacemakers are the children of the good Sun of God, Viracocha. After the flood, Viracocha promised by the sign of the rainbow never to drown mankind again. Sound familiar?

The God and His sons (or Elohim) made man in their likeness. The Incas say the Spirit of life is in water and wind for nothing can live without the breath of life and water of life from God. The Word of God says the Spirit hovered over the waters and then gave life to them on the fifth day. [Genesis 1:2,20] All living things have a portion of God's Spirit. A tree has life in it until it becomes dead wood. Then that life force returns to God. The Incas say that the Tree of life bears every kind of fruits. The Word of God says the Tree of life bears twelve kinds of fruits. [Revelation 22:1,2]For the twelve tribes of Israel. The Incas believe the Amazon river is sacred just as the Egyptians believe the Nile is holy and the Indians revere the Ganges river.

To this day, the Incas hold a three day Festival honoring Manuel (Jesus). Immanuel is his God given name. [Matthew 1:23] Legend says the Lord of Qolloritti transformed into petrified rock. Rock in Aramaic is petra. Christ is the Rock of Salvation. [1 Corinthians 10:4] The Festival ends at sunrise when the Sun of God rises or resurrects. The Catholics respect the ancient Festival and fellowship along side the Incas.

The Nazca lines in southern Peru are giant pictures in the side of a mountain. A whale, monkey, fish, pelican, lizard, hummingbird, etc. These are the signs of the Zodiac. The condor may be the fallen eagle. The spider is the constellation of Orion. The man may be Persus with Medusa's head or Herakles with the lion's head. The heron may be Heru of On (Horus of Anu). [See "Finger Prints of the Gods" by Graham and Hancock] Could the so-called Pyramids of the Sun and Moon really be the stars of the Belt of Orion? Could it compare to the Giza Pyramids? Both are aligned to the four cardinal points and may have been used to calculate the cosmic clock. Or could they represent the Circumpolar stars?

The Incas built reed boats just like the Egyptians used to go up and down the Nile. Could the Egyptians have sailed to South America thousands of years ago? They had ships capable. Several were found buried at Giza. Compare the murder of Thunupa-Viracocha to that of Osiris. Both were sealed in a vessel and cast into the water, ending up in the sea. Maybe Thunupa-Viracocha-Quezalcoatl was returning to his home-land in Egypt?

The Moche priests of Peru wore the tiara crown of Amen. The warriors wore the domed war hellmet. They built pyramids and sacrificed humans just like the Upper Egyptians.

Teotihuacan

The Teotihuacans had build the largest city in the new world just northeast of Mexico. Larger than any found in Europe. Teotihuacan was constructed in the middle of a lake. Compare this to the Hindus in India who did likewise. The Aztecs called it the City of the gods and made pilgrimages there. The Aztecs and Mayans believed in a pantheon of nine deities just like the Egyptian Ennead of nine.

The Toltecs built pyramids like the Egyptians. They wrote hieroglyphics just like the Egyptians. Their calendar is very similar to the Egyptians, with five extra days added to make a total of 365 in one year. They embalmed mummies just like the Egyptians. They bound the heads of nobles like the Africans. Reshaping the "crown" of the head. Pharaoh Akhenaton had his done this way. This is the domed crown of Amen-Ra. All Indians believed that one seeking enlightenment must fast and abstain from sex. Meditating on the Great Spirit in solitude is the Way to the knowledge of the great beyond. The Great Festival of Quetzalcoatl was in October (the equinox), just as the Festival of Osiris-Horus and the Feast of Ingathering in the Bible.

Anyone with eyes not clouded with stigmatism, can see that the so-called Pyramid of Quetzalcoatl, Pyramid of the Sun and Pyramid of the Moon is the same as the three Pyramids of Giza that represent Orion's belt. The Street of the Dead is the Egyptian Nome of the Dead. The Pyramid of Quetzalcoatl has 91 steps on 4 sides which = 364 and the top step makes 365, the days in a Sirius year. It is designed so that a shadow of the feathered-serpent is upon the stairs during the spring and autumn equinox. The very time of year that the dead Pharaoh was reborn as the star Sirius, companion to the constellation of Orion. It was the Aztecs who named them after the Sun and the Moon when they arrived and found them already there. They did not build them. The Aztecs at this time were sun worshipers. Their pagan beliefs eclipsed the true meaning behind the pyramids.

The Aztecs

The down fall of the Aztecs came when they started worshipping the sun-god of war, Huitzilopochtli. They were well aware that this was the evil son of God who we call the Devil. They made a graven image to him. He told them if they would leave the land of Aztlan (U.S.A) and go south, he would make them world rulers and wealthy. Just as Satan tempted Christ. [Luke 4:5-7] They followed an eagle down to Mexico City, where they conquered the Toltecs and took over the great city of Teotihuacan. They accepted the Toltec gods along with their own. Then they set up a temple and sacrificed humans "daily" to their sun-god of war, Huitzilopochtli. His festivals were held on the winter and summer solstices.

Legend say the Aztecs were 60 years in the wilderness. Compare that to the Israelites 40 years in the Wilderness of Sin. Who then occupied a magnificent city built by the predecessors. The Aztecs offered blood sacrifices to their god just as did the priests of Zadek. Could Aztec mean Zadek? Aztec = aZatek = aZadek. Compare Quetzalcoatl to Melchizedok. It is an anagram (Que = chi, = d t = d, zal = ze, coat = kot, el = mel (god with m prefix). The Aztecs had a sacred ceremony every 52 weeks and another every 52 years. The Jews have a sacred ceremony every 52 weeks (Pentecost) and another every 50 years (Jubilee).

The Aztecs prospered for two hundred years, until Cortez came. At first Montezuma, the ruler of the Aztecs, thought Hernan Cortez was Quetzalcoatl returning from sea of space in the East, because it was the time prophesied he would return (1519 AD). And the myth said the last Avatar would come riding on a horse. The strange thing is; the name Her-nan is 'Heru of Ana' or Horus of Heliopolis, northern Egypt. Horus is the counterpart of Quetzalcoatl. And Monte-zuma is similar to Montu the Warlord of southern Egypt. Montu is the son of the Sun-god and anti-Horus. Montezuma even claimed to be son of the sun-god, just like the evil kings of southern Egypt claimed to be sons of Amen-Ra. Cortez was appalled by the massive human sacrifice and driven by greed for gold, so he slaughtered the Aztecs and pillaged the gold and silver. The Aztecs say gold is the secretions (sweat and urine) of the sun-god. The sun-god showers them with gold. Montezuma did not understand Cortez's obsession for gold. Cortez replied, "My people have a disease of the heart (gold fever) that only gold can cure." That is sick! The Egyptians say gold is the root of evil.

The god of war is Satan whose symbol is the eagle and the serpent. The same eagle used by the Danites, Vikings, Romans, Hittites, and Americans. The Spanish Christian crusaders were the Roman dog soldiers of

Meso-America. They destroyed the sacred scriptures of the ancient Indians, just as Julius Caesar had done in Egypt. They sacrificed humans to their Christian god, Hey-Zeus (Jesus), just as the Aztecs did for Huitzilopochtli. The Christians and Aztecs were two of a kind and both shall stand trial on Judgment Day for their evil deeds. War is the way to hell (the grave). Peace is the path to paradise. [Aztlan An Anthology of Mexican American Literature]

Toltec Pantheon

To the Toltecs and Aztecs, Ometechtli is Lord of Duality (both male and female) who created the creation. The world was created formless and dark. The Word of God confirms. [Genesis 1:1,2] The Aztecs believed in the sacrifice of the Son of Man (human-being) and rebirth of the Son of God (spirit-being). Quetzalcoatl was born of a virgin, tempted and fasted for forty days, and crucified on a cross. He died, his ashes immediately flew upwards and were transformed into birds of all kinds, but his heart flew up to heaven and became the Morning Star (Sirius). Just like the phoenix, he was recreated from the ashes. Which signifies the resurrection.

In Guatemala, Central America was found a picture of a man crucified between two poles; one north and one south. He has a crown of thorns on his head. A spear has pierced his side, and blood and water is falling on his Spiritual name Hacaxipectli. He is identified with Horus in Egyptian and Jesus in Greek and Iesus in Latin. The signs and symbols say he Lord of the north and the south. In the Mexican Codices his age is 33. In the hieroglyphics of Egypt he is 33 years old. He is Horus of the two lands; north and south Egypt who was born in the 30th year of Osiris.

They divided the four gods into four quarters. The north was the dwelling place of Tezcatlipoca, the south that of Huitzilopochtli, the east that of Tonatiuh, and the west that of Quetzalcoatl. Their counterparts in Egypt are: Amen-Ra of the north, Set or Sut of the south, Osiris set in the west and rose again in the west as Aten-Ra, the good Sun of God. Quetzalcoatl is Osiris who went to the land of the dead in the west and rose again in the east as Aton-Ra-Horus (Tonatiuh). North is up and south is down to the pit or abyss. Lucifer exalted himself to the Arctic circle in the north and was brought down low. [Isaiah 14:12-15] The circum-polar stars are the birthplace of the evil sun of God. Tezcatlipoca (Tez is Set reversed) (catli is cathor or Hathor the Great Mother).

Tezcatlipoca (Smoking Mirror) is the sun-god, god of music and dancing. He is depicted with a bear face and bells on his ankles; identifying him with Baal (ursa Minor) and Shiva. He is the enemy of Quetzalcoatl. According to legend the Aztecs thought that Tezcatlipoca wandered at night as a "giant" wrapped in an ash-colored veil and carried his head in his hand. When nervous people saw him, they died, but the brave man seized him, saying he would not let him go until sunrise. The "giant" begged to be released, and then cursed. If the man succeeded in holding the monster until daylight, he changed his tone and offered wealth and invincible power if he was set free before dawn. The victorious man received four thorns as a pledge of victory from the conquered. The brave man tore out his heart, and took it home; but when he unwrapped the cloth in which he had folded it he found nothing but white feathers or a thorn or ashes or an old rag. The Aztecs feared him more than any other god, and offered him blood sacrifices. Compare this to Jacob wrestling with the Angel. [Genesis 32:24-31]

Tez-cat-lipoca is like the large 'cat' (the Jaguar). The Aztecs say the sun is like a cat who can see in the dark as it (the sun) travels through the underworld. Compare this to the identical story of the Egyptians about Ra the Cat-eyed-one. The sun and the moon are the two eyes of Amen-Ra.

The Aztecs believed in a series of world ages like the Mayans. Each of which had so far ended in a cosmic catastrophe: famine, fire, hurricane and flood. This present age was expected to end on the completion of a 52 year cycle. Every 52 years preparations were made: all fires were extinguished and priests and people ascended a sacred mountain, waiting for the rise of the Pleiades. Compare this to Israel celebrating the Jubilee every 50 years. The dawn rising of Orion during the autumn equinox is their Feast of Ingathering. It is the day of liberty, when the Lord shall descend unto the holy Mt. Zion to free the children of God. [Leviticus 25:8-55] It is obvious that the Aztecs brought this ritual from the east.

The fifth Sun or world age is the face of Tonatiuh with a knife in his mouth. Compare that to the Lord with a sword in his mouth coming at the age of Aquarius. [Revelation 2:16] Tonatiuh is said to be old and wrinkled, just as Atum-Ra was ancient of days who tired of mankind's evil ways. The destruction of the sun (Lucifer) and rising of the Morning star Sirius as the reborn Sun of God and Lord over the earth is the universal theme. These world ages are obviously Zodiac ages: Gemini, Taurus, Aries, Pisces, and Aquarius. The Aztecs had the Great Bear and the goat-mermaid constellations in their Zodiac. [Stars and men by Steven and Margaret Ionides pages 261, 262]

The south, to the Egyptians, is the land of Amen-Ra-Sut, the evil son of God. Aztec high priests wore the very same domed crown as the Upper Egyptians (in the south) who worshipped Amen-Ra. Another coincidence??? Huitzilopchtli is the sungod reborn everyday. Just as Amen-Ra is the sun that does rise and "Set" daily. Lucifer is the Fallen Star (sun) that rules over the earth for this age. [Revelation 12] He is the red Dragon because the sunrise and sunset is blood red. The Word of God says the eagle is the symbol of a predator or warrior. Huitzilopochtli demanded human sacrifices daily. He is also the sun of our solar system that dies in the winter and is reborn in the spring. Just like Helios, Apollo and Mithra.

On the other hand, the good Sun of God is the Morning star, Sirius. Sirius is reborn at the Autumn equinox.

Legend says that Quetzatcotl was betrayed and disgraced by his brother and was banished. He sailed upon the sea, but promised one day to return, " to judge the living and the dead." He was the scapegoat or escapegoat who they place their sins upon. Compare this to Osiris being betrayed by his brother (Set), voyaging to the western horizon and returning from the east. Just as the sun sets in the sea of space to the west and rises again in the east. Osiris is reborn as Horus. Set wanted to rule instead of or in place of Osiris. Instead of or in place of is the meaning of Anti, as in AntiChrist. The evil sun of God has ruled over man for 6,000 years, but his time is running out.

The Mexican Tower of Babel

"In the beginning, before the light of the sun had been created, this place, Cholula (Chaldea?), was in obscurity and darkness; all was a plain, without hill or elevation, encircled in every part by water, without tree or created thing. Immediately after the light and the sun arose in the east there appeared gigantic men of deformed stature who possessed the land. Enamored of the light and beauty of the sun they determined to build a tower so high that its summit should reach the sky. Having collected materials for the purpose they found a very adhesive clay and bitumen with which they speedily commenced to build the tower.... And having reared it to the greatest possible altitude, so that it reached the sky, the Lord of the Heavens, enraged, said to the inhabitants of the sky, 'Have you observed how they of the earth have built a high and haughty tower to mount hither, being enamored of the light of the sun and his beauty? Come and confound them, because it is not right that they of the earth, living in the flesh, should mingle with us.' Immediately the inhabitants of the sky sallied forth like flashes of lightning; they destroyed the edifice and divided and scattered its builders to all parts of the earth." ["Fingerprints of the Gods" by Graham and Hancock]

No this is not a copy of the Bible. This is the story found in MesoAmerica. The sun that enamored them was none other than subtle Lucifer. [Ezekiel 28:1-19] Who they called Huitzilopochtli and who the Egyptians called Amen-Ra. The giants are the mutant children of the fallen angels and humans. [Genesis 6]

The Hopi

The Hopi say that extra-terrestrials from Sirius visited earth and revealed great knowledge to them. Compare this to the Egyptians and Dogon people. The Hope tell how twin deities first created the animals and then molded humans from clay, bringing them to life with a ritual chant. Compare to Genesis 1:26 & 2:7. Zoroaster says these twin suns of God are the angel of light (Michael) and the angel of darkness (Satan). We are created in the image of the sons of God.

In the beginning, Tawa, the Sun <of> God and Spider Woman, the Earth goddess said, "Now, let us make ones like us." "I am Tawa," sang the Sun <of> God, "I am Light, I am Life. I am Father of all that shall ever come." [John 1:1-3] The Bible agrees: the elohim (sons of God) said, "Let us make mankind in our likeness." [Genesis 1:26] The Lord Jehovah (Jesus) formed the earthlings from the womb of mother earth. The two sang the magic song of life over them and they breathed and became living souls. [Genesis 2:7] "Now, that was a good thing," said Tawa, "so now all this is finished. [Genesis 2:1] Those things we have made shall multiply, each one after its own kind. [Genesis 1:25] Spider Woman weaves the web of life, connecting all living things as one. She is mother nature and her threads of the world wide web hold all things together. When one thread is damaged, it send vibrations through-out the world. All life is inter-connected and dependent on each other. When we hurt others, we hurt ourselves. If the food chain is broken, everything along that chain will suffer. This is also a Hindu idea. In modern terminology, the "Computer Web" refers to world linked by strands of fiber-optics.

The Hopi Indians say there are four world ages. The first was destroyed by fire. The second world age ended when the earth toppled from its axis and turned the world to ice. The third world ended in an universal flood. The fourth world is dependent on whether mankind will behave in accordance with the Creator's plans. This coincides with the Creation stories, the ice age theory of the men of science, the great flood of Noah's day and the second coming of the Lord. When He shall judge the nations. This world age is called the Sabbatical Millennium or the Lord's Divine Day.

The Hopi say the twin gods, Poqanghoya and Palongawhoya are the guardians of the north and south axes of the Earth, whose task it is to keep the planet rotating properly. They were ordered by Sotuknang, nephew of the Creator, to leave their posts so the second world could be destroyed because its people had become evil. The world toppled from its axis and plunged into the ice age. The earth tilting 23 degrees off true north could very well explain the ice age and the Great flood during the age of Taurus. Sotuknang is Sot or Set the Destroyer of Egypt. Also known as Typhon by the Greeks. The Hopi say the beings from "Blue Star Kachina" (Sirius) came to earth 250,000 years ago and deposited time capsules which are triggered to go off at the advent of the next millennium. 2010 +/- is the dawning of Aquarius. We wait with bated breath.

The Lakota (Dakota) worship Nagk Tanka (the Great Mystery). The Great Spirit is a mystery. God is beyond all mortal thought; all-knowing, yet unknown. The transcendent Great Spirit they call "Grandfather". The aspects, attributes and manifestations they call "Father". These manifestations or sons of God fathered mankind and the creation. [Genesis 1:26

John 1:14] Wakan means Spirit. All living things have a wakan or spirit. A tree has life or spirit. In fact, the water of life runs through the veins of the Tree of life. The Wakan Tanka are the wakan (spirit) beings united as one family (klan). There are good and bad wakan beings (angels). The Bible calls them Elohim (God's sons). Compare wakan to waken. The Lord says death is like sleep and He shall come to awaken the sleeping saints by restoring their spirits. [1 Thessalonians 4:13–17 Ezekiel 37:1–14]

Wakan Tanka Kin is the chief wakan being which is the Sun (of Righteousness) or Morning Star. They say the Morning star spreads life on the earth. [John 1:1-5 Revelation 22:16] It is the good Son who reveals His Father to us. [John 1:18 5:37] Wakan Tanka Kin is their Kindred Redeemer and their closest kin.

Compare Anaszi to Nasi. Anaszi means Ancient Ones and Nasi means Leader, referring to the Ancient of Days, as in the Massiah (Messiah). Which is why Jesus was called a Nasarene and the Messiah.

The Lord is not prejudice. He works with all nations. If the Lord does not give everyone an equal chance, He is not a just God. "The Lord is long-suffering, not willing that any should perish, but that all should come to repentance." [2 Peter 3:9] God sends prophets to all peoples to teach them the Word of God.

The Ancient Aboriginals of America

The original people of America did not call themselves Indians. It was Columbus who coined that name because he was so dumb-founded, he thought he was in India. He may have been sick, but he was not stupid. These are the immigrants from the east who sailed to the west. The original people who pioneered this land were peace loving people in harmony with nature and their fellow man. In fact, Hopi means Peaceful. Quetzalcoatl taught them to live in peace. They did NOT learn the art of warfare until the Europeans taught it to them. The English were the first to scalp their enemies. The Indians idea of warfare was more like a game. They called it counting coo. The warrior courageous enough to touch his enemy and not harm him achieved the ultimate in bravery. Similar war games are played in Africa. The purpose is to show courage, not kill your enemy.

The European's idea of the counting coo was the coup-de-grace; to strike the fatal blow as an act of mercy. They justified their evil acts as converting the heathens to Christians by making them martyrs against the cause. Therefore, the paleface had freedom of religion and were saved by grace, but the savage red skin was not! Which is ridiculous since the palefaces have the red-necks from sunburn and their is no such thing as a red-skinned Indian. Indians are dark brown just like the people in India. That's why Columbus thought they were Indians. The Lord will have the final say in His coup-de-grace on the savage white warriors. They are the outlaws in the Lord's eyes. Both the Indian warriors and the Christian crusaders, by their own confession, worship the same god of war. They are the soldiers of Satan, the Warlord. All warriors shall die at the battle called Armageddon.

Quetzalcoatl, Kukulkan and Viracocha are all one and the same. He is the Son of God who civilized the South American people. He taught them to live in peace and not to sacrifice humans or animals. He taught them; law, architecture, agriculture, astrology, writing, mathematics, and metal working. Just like Osiris. Yet, during the age of Pisces, he was rejected in favor of the evil sun of God who taught warfare and bloodshed. The good Son of God promised he shall return one day and exterminate evil.

Both the Tibet Indians and American Indians do sand paintings to explain their myths. Both wear feathers in their hair. The Hindus believe in a series of four ages: Krita Yuga, Treta Yuga, Dvapara Yuga and Kali Yuga. It will be a gradual descent of morals, righteousness and piety. On the Day of Brahma (a thousandfold cycle) there shall be total destruction by fire. Followed by a new age and new cycle. Compare this to the Day of the Lord which is a divine day lasting a thousand years. Some tribes believe in transmigration or reincarnation just like the Hindu brothers in India. Their numerous similarities prove the American Indians are originally from India. The predecessors of the Mayans and Aztecs built 9 pyramids like the 9 pyramids at Giza, Egypt. The ancient Indians wrote hieroglyphics similar, if not the same, as the Egyptians. Their stories are almost identical. Proof that they originated in the East. Also verifying that God has worked with people of every nation. The dark skinned Mayans and Incas were probably originally from Africa.

The Eskimos called themselves Inuit. It is easy to see the similarity to Annuit, Egypt; the birthplace of Horus. His birthplace in heaven is Nuit and his birthplace on earth Annu or On. The Greeks called it Heliopolis; City of the Sun. Obviously, the Innuit believed they were children of mother land, Egypt.

The Vision of Black Elk

Black Elk was of the Oglala Sioux. His vision includes 4 sets of horses; blacks, whites, sorrels, and buckskins. Compare this to the vision of Zechariah chapter 6 where the horses are; black, white, red and dappled. And the four horses of Revelation chapter 6 that are white, red, black and pale. They represent the plagues. Black Elk also speaks of the Morning star (Sirius) that is a relative that enlightens His family, the other suns of God. [Revelation 22:16]

In Black Elks vision he hears a Voice saying, "Behold a good nation walking in a sacred manner in a good land." These are those who walk the righteous road to the Promise Land. They and the bison must die, in the Promise land there will be no shedding of blood. The resurrected people will eat of the Tree of life (sacred herb). Just as the first man did in the garden of God. [Gen.1:29,30] See 'Sacred Texts of the World, an Universal Anthology' pages 359-365.

The Ghost Dance and Wounded Knee

The Paiute prophet Wovoka had a vision in 1889. "When the sun died [that is, was eclipsed, probably Jan.1,1889], I went up to heaven and saw God and all the people who had died a long time ago. God told me to come back and tell my people they must be good and love one another, and not fight, or steal, or lie. He gave me this dance to give you people.

Grandfather (referring to a messiah) says, when your friends die you must not cry. You must not hurt anybody or do harm to anyone. You must not fight. Do right always. It will give you satisfaction in life.... Do not tell the white people about this. Jesus is now upon the earth. He appears like a cloud. The dead are alive all again. I do not know when they will be here; maybe this fall or in the spring. When the time comes there will be no more sickness and everyone will be young again. Do not refuse to work for the whites and do not make any trouble with them until you leave them. When the earth shakes (at the coming of the new age) do not be afraid. It will not hurt you. I want you to dance every six weeks. Make a feast at the dance and have food that everybody may eat. Then bathe in the water. That is all. You will receive good words again from me some time. Do not tell lies." Compare this to the Revelation of John, seeing the future.

This sounds very much like the Day of Atonement followed by the Feast of Ingathering. They immerse in the water as a baptism of rebirth. In fact, the Word of God infers that Christ will come in the clouds during this time of year (autumn). At that time, the earth will quake and the dead will rise from their graves. [Matthew 24:27-31 27:51-53 John 5:22-30] This is also the time of the battle of Armageddon when the Lord with the Sword slays All warriors, white, red and brown.

This dance is called the Ghost Dance. They believed that White Man would be exterminated by a great flood while the Indians would be safe high in the mountains. Then the buffalo and all the Indian dead would return to the land. The naive native Americans also believed that their shirts would make them bullet-proof. The palefaces became paranoid and panicked. White Man's reaction was to massacre 300 men, women and children at Wounded Knee. These martyrs for Jesus will surely be resurrected in the last days to live in the Promise land.

The first settlers on this land, the Indians, kept God's Commandments. They honored their Father in heaven called the Great Spirit, who created mother earth and father sky (Sun of God). They revered the Father in heaven and never used His name in vain. They did not lie, cheat, steal, or covet. They didn't even claim to own the land. Which would be coveting. They shared with all who were in need. They even shared with the feeble white exploiters, creating the tradition of Thanksgiving day. Most of their bad traits they learned from the paleface pirates who came to plunder the land, natural resources, and their souls. If Christians were really God fearing and Christ like, they would return this land to the aboriginals.

The American Indians believe in the harmony of man in nature. The balance of Yin and Yang; just like their Hindu counterparts in India. White man believes in the division of man vs. nature and man's dominion over the creation. He uses it as an excuse to possess the land, animals and everything he can put his hands on. White man fears death, therefore, he tries to dominate the forces of mother nature and the life to death cycle. Trying to conquer death and ascend to be as God by his own power. This is the same Satanic rebellion of Adam and Eve. [Genesis 3:4,5] The Lord of the earth shall return to claim his land (the earth). He will gather together the children of God or sons like the Sun of God. They shall be co-heirs with the Lord of the Sabbath in the garden of God.

The eloquent letter Chief Seattle sent to the President of the United States in 1855.

"The President in Washington sends word that he wishes to buy our land. But how can you buy or sell the sky? The land? The idea is strange to us. If we do not own the freshness of the air and the sparkle of the water, how can you buy them?

"Every part of this earth is sacred to my people. Every shining pine needle, every sandy shore, every mist in the dark woods, every meadow, every humming insect. All are holy in the memory and experience of my people.

"We know the sap which courses through the trees as we know the blood that courses through our veins. We are part of the earth and it is part of us. The perfumed flowers are our sisters. The bear, the deer, the great eagle, these are our brothers. The rocky crests, the juices in the meadow, the body heat of the pony, and man, all belong to the same family. "The shining water that moves in the streams and rivers is not just water, but the blood of our ancestors. If we sell you our land, you must remember that it is sacred. Each ghostly reflection in the clear water of the lakes tells of events and memories in the life of my people. The water's murmur is the voice of my father's father.

"The rivers are our brothers. They quench our thirst. They carry our canoes and feed our children. So you must give to the rivers the kindness you would give any brother.

"If we sell you our land, remember that the air is precious to us, that the air shares its spirit with all the life it supports. The wind that gave our grandfather his first breath also receives his last sign. The wind also gives our children that spirit of life. So if we sell you our land, you must keep it apart and sacred, as a place where man can go to taste the wind that is sweetened by the meadow flowers.

COMMENTARY: The plants produce the air or breath of life needed to sustain life. In Hebrew, Ruach means both air and spirit.

"Will you teach your children what we have taught our children? That the earth is our mother? What befalls the earth, befalls all the sons of the earth. [us earthlings]

"This we know: The earth does not belong to man, man belongs to the earth. All things are connected like the blood which unites us all. Man did not weave the web of life, he is merely a strand in it. Whatever he does to the web, he does to himself.

"One thing we know: Our God is also your God. The earth is precious to Him and to harm the earth is to heap contempt on its Creator. {some translations say, "your God is not my God." They misinterpret, "Is not your God, our God?"}

"Your destiny is a mystery to us. What will happen when the buffalo are all slaughtered? The wild horses tamed? What will happen when the secret corners of the forest are heavy with the scent of many men and the view of the ripe hills is blotted by talking wires? Where will the thicket be? Gone! Where will the eagle be? Gone! And what is it to say goodbye to the swift pony and the hunt? The end of living and the beginning of survival.

"When the last Red <Brown> Man has vanished with his wilderness and his memory is only the shadow of a cloud moving across the prairie, will these shores and forests still be here? Will there be any of the spirit of my people left?

"We love this earth as a newborn loves its mother's heartbeat. So, if we sell you our land, love it as we have loved it. Care for it as we have cared for it. Hold in your mind the memory of the land as it is when you receive it. Preserve the land for all children and love it, as God loves us all.

"As we are part of the land, you too are part of the land. This earth is precious to us. It is also precious to you. One thing we know: There is only one God. No man, be he Red Man or White Man can be apart. We are brothers after all."

COMMENTARY: We are all a part of the same creation formed from mother earth. We are earthlings. [John 8:23] The Lord says those who destroy the earth, shall be destroyed. "Honor your Father in heaven and your mother earth". Now tell me; who is the savage heathens? God is Spirit. God is the Great Spirit. He transcends all thought. [John 4:24] The Spirit of God is His supernatural force working in the natural world. It is called the breath of life that all living things possess. [Genesis 7:22] A tree possess a piece of God's Spirit. God's Spirit is likened to rivers and to wind [John 7:38,39 3:8]. Christ gave up the Spirit of life with his last breath. [John 19:30 Mark 15:37] He then returned to being a spiritual-being or Son of God. We, on the other hand, are mere mortal human-beings. Only those who prove themselves worthy shall be transformed into spirit-beings. Therefore, White Man, you had better change your evil ways while there is time. Stop the self-destruction of the Creator's creations!

Twin Sons

The Indians in many myths about the twin hero and the sibling rivalry between the good son and the bad son. Here is one legend.

The elder of the brothers molded mud into a shape, set it down, and asked, "Can you jump?" It didn't move. He blew on it, and it jumped. It was a grasshopper. Then he thought to make something to go higher, took red clay, and made the cherry bird, which flew and lighted on a bough. He shaped a deer, blew on it, pushed it, and it ran off. Then he thought, "Maybe I can make something like myself." Out of mud he fashioned such a thing and, wanting to give it a spirit like his own, bent down and blew into its mouth. It moved. He stood it on its feet and told it to whoop. The new man whooped. He had a fine voice. {Compare to Genesis 2:7}

Secretly watching, the younger brother thought, "I will make a man too." He went away and made something as like himself as he could, but it was deformed and strange. Another of his productions was a frog as large as a man. Others were man-eaters. One was known as Shagodyowag, or False Face. Its maker said, "Go and eat all the creatures my brother has made."

{Compare to Revelations 16:12-16}

The elder brother, meanwhile, thought: "Let me make something like my grandmother." He made it of mud, breathed into it, brought it to the man he had made, and said: "This one I give to you. Be always together. You will have children like yourselves and will hunt the animals I have made for food. But you will not live forever. I now, go above the Blue <Sky>. When you die, your spirit also will go above the Blue." Then he departed.

{The grandmother refers to Maya, the watery womb of creation from which all things were born. Maya is the feminine aspect of God the Father just as the bride is to God's Son, Jesus. When you die, you return to the dust and the spirit of breath of life returns to God. Ecclesiastes 12:7}

But when, from the Blue <Sky>, he saw the creatures that his brother had made, he came down, put the man-eaters into the ground, and told them to remain there as long as the earth endured. Shagodyowag, however, spoke to him first: "Do not destroy me! I want to live on the earth and be your servant," he said. "I will inhabit the woods. The ashes of fire will be my medicine for men. I will scatter ashes over the sich and they will be well." Since he had spoken first, he could not be put into the ground; so the brother let him stay on earth. The true meaning of his name, Shagodyowag, is the Great One who Protects Mankind. {All creatures, including man, lay dormant in the dust until the end. Ecclesiastes 3:19,20. Notice the bad brother becomes the medicine man or physician.}

The elder brother returned to the Blue <Heaven>, and the younger said to their grandmother, "I have tried to make a man, but have failed. Now I shall cause <allow> those that my brother has made to do evil." {Compare to Genesis 6:5-7}

The Creeks say man was originally formed by the Great Spirit from fired clay; but the first batch was overbaked and came out black: these are the Negroes; the second was underbaked and came out pale: these are the Whites; the third came out just right in both color and form: and are, of course, the native Indian tribes. {The White man is the red-skin still raw inside and out} Compare this to God purging and refining the people in the fire of His presence. [Zechariah 13:9 2 Peter 3:12,13 Revelation 20:9] Christ was of medium color like the Indians and Asians. He was not a pale-face.

The Bighorn wheel in Wyoming

June 21,22 (the summer solstice) is the helical rising of Aldebaran and Hyades in the constellation Taurus. Helical or dawn rising is the appearance of the star just before sunrise. Helio is the sungod also known as Sol (Solar or Solstice) by the Romans. This is Satan's high day.

On July 19-23, 28 days (one moon) later, is the dawn rising of Rigel the brightest star in Orion. Aug.16-20, 28 days (another moon or lunar month) is the dawn rising of Sirius the brightest star in the sky. Sept.18-22, one moon or month later is the fall equinox and the Feast of Ingathering.

The Sun that ruled over the garden of God was Atum-Ra. From him we get the name for the season called autumn. He was born in the autumn and shall return in the autumn. His other name is Horus of the Horizon. When Adam and Eve chose to follow the evil sun of God, Horus went beyond the horizon to the dark underworld and returned to the constellation of Orion in the night sky. Then a new sun rose to rule over the earth. His name is Amen-Ra- Set. Amen-Ra rises and Sets daily. From him we get the name of the SunSet. Amen-Ra has been ruling over the earth ever since. He is commonly known as Satan the devil. Son of God.

The Serpent Mound

The serpent mound was made by the Adena in Locust Grove, Ohio. The serpent represents the sea of space. The golden egg in its mouth is the darkness swallowing the sun at sunset. The Egyptians call this sea of space, the Sea Serpent, Apophis. The sun is called Set (i.e. Amen-Ra), the evil sun of God. The bloody battle causes a blood-red sun-Set. The Sun then travels through the body of the sea serpent through the night time hours. The Sun violently rips its way out the dark watery womb and is reborn at sunrise. The bloody birth causes the red sunrise. This myth originated in Egypt. The symbol is the uraeus, a serpent surrounding the sun (Ra). It is now part of the Chinese, and Hindus of India mythology. The Chinese say the red dragon is chasing his tail causing the red sunset. [Revelation 12:3]

What is the difference between a Totem pole and Christ on the Cross? Paul says they hung Christ on a tree. [Acts 5:30] { tree = cross = pole} The Indian Totem has an impression of a man with a sacred bird hovering over-head. Christ is Son of Man who is portrayed with a dove hovering over-head. If the Totem is a graven image then so is Christ on the cross. Being double-minded and two-faced is condemned by the Word of God. The Indians see the Totem as a family tree, which is the idea behind the death and rebirth into God's family. Christendumb believes that the Crucifix wards off evil, therefore, it is a talisman or lucky charm. An amulet (Amun-little) is a little graven image of Amen, the god of Christendumb. The Totem originated in Egypt as the Tet, the tree that encased the coffin of Osiris and was made into a pillar in the palace of the king of Syria. It represents his resurrection (tet = tree & am = birth). Some Indians actually split a tree then passed through it, representing rebirth. The crucifix is a symbol that bears no magical powers. The cross did not save Christ, in fact, it killed him. Is the lamb the totem animal of Christendom? Is the fish? Saying an object or an animal possesses powers is animism or animal fetish. Christenddumb holds sacred the spurious spear said to have slayed their savior. They saved and venerate the very instruments that were supposed to caused the death of their god!

The Assyrians corrupted the story of Osiris and made the tree sacred and called it Asherah (Mother Nature). They were saying the life force within the tree is Baal the sun of mother nature. In other words, the sun gives the tree the power to grow. The Canaanites held the tree so sacred that they cut it down, set it up in their house, decorated it with gold and silver (the colors of the sun and moon). [Jeremiah 10:1-5] This festival was the winter solstice (Dec.25th). Then they watch the tree weaken and die just as mother nature and her evil sun dies in winter. The Druids, Greeks and Romans held sacred the oak and mistletoe with are symbols of the sun and the moon mating on X-mas Eve. Mistletoe produces its berries or seeds in the winter. The red Christ-mis tree lights are the red berries of the mis-t-leto-e. Leto was the mother of Apollo the sun-god and Artemis the moon-goddess. Artemis is an anagram of mistleto (l = r a = o) In the garden of God, the Tree of Mother Nature had a good Son (Jesus) and an evil sun (Satan). Just as Eve had two sons; one good & one evil. Mistletoe is a vine like Ivy-and Ivy = Eve, the one Satan did deci-eve. The Jews built a pole with a serpent and worshipped it. [Numbers 21:6-9]

The Indians of Northern America believed the people who killed the sacred white buffalo would never go hungry. Compare this to Mithra slaying the bull to provide the people with food from heaven. The bull and the white buffalo represent the Devil. It was, of course, white man who purposely tried to exterminated the buffalo and caused massive starvation among the Indians. If the great white beast had been killed, there would be prosperity. This is the same Roman-Beast of Revelation chapter 13, that makes war with the Saints. And the Ram with two horns is the worship of Amen, the Ram god, that was forced down everyone's throats. It later became known as the Lamb-god of Christendumb. Then the bread (flesh) and the wine (blood) sacrament (sac-Ram-ent) were forced down peoples throats. If you are saved by grace, why do you sacrifice the Lamb daily? [Hebrews 10:26-29 6:4-6]

Americans have food fetishes. Snakes, dogs, rats, donkeys, horses and sharks are taboo because they represent unclean or evil animals. Dolphins, whales, monkeys are not eaten because they are seen as good sentient animals. Yet, Americans are quick to ridicule others for their fetishes. Hypocrites!

Christendom: what will you do when the Lord of the Earth comes to take your land???? Will you fight for freedom? Will you give your life for your country? Will you give your immortal life for vanity?

Age of the Gentiles

The Lord worked with the three sons of Noah, one at a time. [Genesis 10] He worked with Ham's descendants, the Africans including the Egyptians, during the age of Taurus (4000-2000 BC). Egypt was God's people. [Isaiah 19:25] Then the Lord worked with the Shemites during the age of Aries (2000-0 AD). The descendants of Abraham became God's people. Jesus was a so-called Jew. The sacrifice of the Ram of God meant the end age of Israel as God's people. The Jews are no longer God's people. Then the Lord worked with the Gentiles (Greeks, Germans, Macedonians) during the age of Pisces (0-2000 AD). These are the dark aboriginal Europeans not the white Indo-Europeans from the Caucasian mountains. The Gentiles became heirs to the Ancient Mysteries of Egypt. The great Library of Alexandra, Egypt held sacred and rare scriptures from all over the world. It was built by Alexander the Greek. It wasn't until the 19th century that the Indo-Europeans translated the original Egyptian Pyramid Texts, including the Bible of Death and Resurrection. Which is mistakenly called the Book of the Dead. The Rosetta stone was written in Egyptian, Aramaic, and Greek! The three languages of the three sons of Noah. It was the Greeks and Romans who became heirs to the Hebrew Bible and the newly written New Testament. Which, by the way, was written in Greek. They canonized and pieced together the Bible. The Word of God went to the Gentiles, and will continue until the dawning of the age of Aquarius in about 2010 AD. The divine day of the Lord is the time when the children of God shall be born again from the watery womb of Aquarius.

Greek Mythology

Mythology is Not fiction, fable or a fairy tale. Mythology, by definition, is the study of God. My-theology is "my theology". It is the study of my God. As "The" or "Theo" means "God" in Greek. The Greeks got their pantheon from the cult in Upper Egypt where they worshipped Amen (Satan). The problem is: they did not fully understand the stories. Therefore, the Greeks created chaos from the Egyptian cosmos. Because of these confusing "myths" we get the saying, "It's all Greek to me."

In the beginning there was Chaos and Gaia (earth). Chaos is void of life. [Genesis 1:1-5] Chaos is obviously taken from the Egyptian Nun, the Cosmic Egg containing the dark primordial waters from which the suns of God and other heavenly bodies are born. Uranus was created from Chaos. Uranus is the Egyptian Urnas (Celestial sea) and Uraeus. Uraeus is the head-dress with the serpent worn on the forehead. Meaning the sea of space was on the forefront of the Creator's mind. In Greek, Uranus means Heaven with stars. The Egyptians called it Nut. Uranology is the study of the stars. Firstborn from Chaos was Light (Phanes) who separated from the darkness and created the Cosmos (Order). Some say Phanes (Egyptian Horus) fathered Zeus. Uranus, the heavenly bodies, were not created until the fourth day. [Gen.1:14-19]

Diodorus Siculus says that Uranus and Titea had two daughters, one called Basilea (Queen). Uranus is Anu within Nun and Titea is Geb (Earth). Their daughters are Isis and Nephthys. He says, "Basilea being the eldest, brought up her brothers with the care and affection of a mother, whence she was called the Great Mother." She married Hyp-erion (Orion), one of her brothers, by whom she had Helio (Horus) and Selene (Sirius B). Helio being Sirius A. Her other brothers assassinated Hyperion (Osiris), and drowned the child Helio in the river Eridanus. Eridanus is the river at the foot of Orion. Eridanus is the Jordan and means River of Adonis (Lord).

From the darkness of empty space is created the Cyclopes. This single eyed being is none other than the all-seeing Eye of Horus. This is the firstborn Sun of God, Horus the Hawk hatched from the Cosmic Egg. Horus lost his eye in the battle with the evil sun of God, Amen-Ra-Seth. Cronus is that evil sun of Uranus. He is the sun that swallows his suns, the stars of heaven. The stars can't be seen in the day time because they are consumed by his bright day-light. The root of Cycl-opes is cycle. It is the annual cycle of the star Sirius. The "opes" is "optic" or the all-seeing Eye of Horus. [The Sirius Mystery by Robert Temple page 130]

The Bible says Jesus called James and John Boanerges meaning "sons of Thunder". [Mark 3:17] It was the Cyclopes, Brontes (Thunder) and Arges (Lightning) who forged the lightning and thunder for Zeus (Jesus). The names are an anagram. Combine the letters of: Brontes + Arges = Boanerges. James and John could call down fire from heaven. [Luke 9:54] Eros is the force of attraction that causes things to come together.

Eros (divine love) is Heros or Horus. Uranus mates with Gaia. Uranus is Nun of Egypt. Gaia is mother Earth (Geb in Egypt). They produce the three monsters called Cottus, Briareus, and Gyges. These are the constellations of Cetus, Taurus and Ares. Then Uranus sires the twelve Titans, a race of paleface giants. One of the sons was Oceanus and his mate Tethys. Oceanus is Shu and Tethys is Tefnut of Egypt. They make up the O-zone or atmosphere. Cronus, the youngest of his Titan sons, emasculates his father with a sickle and seizes power. Uranus is now impotent (powerless) just as Seth was castrated by Horus and Shiva was castrated in the Hindu version. The Word of God says, "the kingdom of heaven suffers violence, and the violent take it by force." [Matthew 11:12] This is the story of Satan seducing Eve and producing Cain. Then the fallen stars (Titans), seeing what Satan did, followed suit. They mated with human women and produced the giants or demi-gods. [Genesis 6] In Upper Egypt, Khonsu is the son of Amun and Mut (Uranus). This is the Satanic trinity. Kronsu is thought of as the placenta or afterbirth of the king. Amun, like Zeus-Ammon, is called king of the gods. The Greeks identified Kronos with Baal-Hammon of the Canaanites.

In Greek mythology, Lucifer is personified as a male figure bearing a torch. As in the Statue of Helios at Rhodes. The transliteration of his name is Teitan or Titan, which means sungod. Also spelled Setan by combining Set and Satan. The twelve Titans are: Helios or Sol (Sun), Selene (Moon), Oceanos (O-zone), Rhea, Kronos, Eos (Dawn), Atlas, Prometheus, Themis (orderly cosmos), Hyperion, Theia, and Iapetus. Prometheus took fire from the sun and handed it to mankind. He is originator of the Olympic torch. The Sun is Amen-Ra-Set of Upper Egypt. His mate is Hathor the moon deity. These are the attributes of Satan. Who imitates everything of the Lord, the Morning star Sirius. There are twelve months in the solar year, yet thirteen moons (months) in the lunar year. Sun-day is the sacred day of the solar and the Sabbaths in the lunar year. Themis is the Egyptian Tehuti or Thoth who created an orderly cosmos from the chaos.

Kronos is father of six children with his sister and wife Rhea: Zeus, Poseidon, Hades; Hera, Hestia, Demeter (3 male and 3 female). Kronos was swallowing each one as they were born, fearing they would depose him. Rhea, the mother, was pregnant with Zeus when she went to a secret cave in Crete to give birth. She gave Kronos a stone wrapped in swaddling clothes, which he devoured, believing it to be Zeus. This is the Rock of Salvation. When Zeus grew up, he overthrew his evil father and freed his siblings. Zeus eclipses Chronus (Sun), leaving only his Corona (Coronus). At the final battle, the Olympian gods cast Kronos and the Titans into Tartarus. Compare this to Isis hiding her Son from Set and Mary hiding her Son from Herod. Both Sons are heirs to the throne of the earth who shall return to depose the Ruler of this wicked world (Satan). Hestia the vestal virgin is Ast (Isis).

The Olympians parallel the twelve tribes of Israel. To the Romans, Zeus is Jupiter (Ju-Peter), Jove or Jehud (Judah). Jesus was born of the line of Judah. Jupiter represents Zeus-Amon (the spurious Savior). Jove is Jehovah. In Greece, Zeus is the king of the gods who overthrew his father Cronus. He was not consumed by the brightness of his light. In fact, Zeus took his place. He is the sun ruling over the sky and earth instead of his father, Cronus. Cronus (the sun) represents Jacob who was over-shadowed by his good son Joseph. [Genesis 37:9,10] Joseph is the Morning star, Sirius. Selene (the moon) is Rachel, Joseph's mother. Hermes (Mercury) is the Messenger of Zeus. [Acts 14:11-13] He is the Angel of God speaking through the prophets of Israel. Poseidon is the Danites, lords of the sea. Aphrodite is Zebulunites, the lovers of the sea. [Genesis 49]

The number 12 means family. The 12 houses of Israel is a continuing theme in the Bible. The 12 disciples were the 12 brothers of Jesus. 12 houses in the Zodiac. The 12 houses of Israel also correspond with the signs of the Zodiac. Judah is Leo the Lion-King (Zeus). Gad is Aries the warrior. Dan is Scorpio the sea serpent and eagle; the symbols of Zeus. Benjamin is Gemini; the she-wolf who suckled the twins; Romulus and Remus. Apollo and Artemis are also twins. Reuben is Aquarius (Poseidon). Simeon is Pisces. Ephraim and Manasseh are the two horns of Taurus the Bull. One of Zeus transformations is the Bull. Hades is the head and horns in the constellation of Taurus. Levi is Libra the Altar; Hestia the hearth. Issachar is Cancer the Crab. Naphtali is Capricornus the goat (Pan). Asher is Sagittarius the Archer (Eros/Cupid). Zebulun is Virgo the Virgin (Artemis/Diana). See the Companion Bible: Numbers chapter 2.

Chronus is Father Time with his sickle. It is where we get the word Chronology. Chronos is the father of Hades. Therefore each mortal is given a "lifetime" to live, followed by death. Just as Satan caused the fall of Adam and Eve. He is the Grim Reaper that harvests the bad fruits. Cronos' Roman name is Saturn. Saturnalia (Dec.25th) is his day. This is the Yule tide or winter solstice when the sun dies and then starts again at New Years. The stopping of time and starting again. Mas or Mes means rebirth. Chronus+mas is the rebirth of Chronus at Chrismas. Saturn (Cronus) is the (spurious) star of the god Remphan. [Acts 7:43] Sat+ur = Set the Great in Egyptian. Saturn = Satan.

Zeus battles with Typhon (Kronus), just as Osiris had with Set. Typhon had defeated Zeus, but he is revived by Hermes (Horus) and goes on to drive the monster into exile. Just as Osiris died at the hand of Set, then resurrected as Horus who defeated and banished Set to Upper Egypt. Typhon means fallen star. "I saw Satan fall like lightning from heaven. I give you the authority to trample on serpents and scorpions, and over all the power of the enemy, and nothing shall by any means hurt you." [Revelation 12:3,4,9,12 Luke 10:18-20] Satan was cast down from the stars of Hyades to rule over the earth.

Zeus is the sky god or god of heaven. Zeus means Savior just as Jesus means Savior. Zeus was the one who ruled from Mt. Olympus. Just as the Lord dwelled on Mt. Sinai for a time. And shall return to rule from Mt. Zion. Actually Zeus is Jesus. But the story seems to have been corrupted over time. The Viking stories of Odin is almost the same. In fact, the reason why Jesus Christ was accepted in Greece and Roman was that they were already familiar with Je-Zeus. Jesus is the Latin spelling. Just as Christ is a Roman word meaning Anointed in English and Messiah in Hebrew.

In the Roman version, Zeus-Amon transforms himself into a white bull. Zeus-Amon appears at the Canaanite port of Tyre and seduces Europa (Europe), the Asian princess. She climbs on his back and is carried away to Crete, where she gives birth to; Minos, Rhad-amanthys (Ra-Amam) and Sarpedon (Sarapeum). Minos became king of Crete. His wife, Pasiphae, has intercourse with the Devil (Zeus-Min) in the form of a white bull and produces the Minotaur. The taur or bull within the labyrinth represents the devil within Minos' house or age of Taurus. The bull is the sacred animal of Baal in Babylon and Min (Menuis or Apis) in the Egyptian worship. Legend says that after his death Minos became judge of the underworld. This is BULL! He is not judge. It was the evil Upper Egyptians who mated bull worship with Osiris, the Judge of the underworld and produced Serapis (Zeus-Amon).

The story continues: Cadmus, the brother of Europa, went searching for her in Greece. He stumbled upon a dragon which he slayed. He planted its teeth and up sprouted the Greek nations. This shows that the Europeans are seeds or sons of the Dragon. And that all nations started at the Tower of Babylon. C-Adum-us is Atum with the Greek suffix and prefix. Atum-Osiris taught the Greeks to read and write the new 16 letter language he had created for them.

The Bible says Satan is the Prince of Tyre who seduced Eve. [Ezekiel 28:1-19] Compare to the harlot on the Beast. [Revelation 17:1-6] Europe being lead astray by Zeus Amon, the Antichrist Jesus, pretending to be the Christ Jesus. [2 Corinthians 11:3,13-15] This represents the social and sexual intercourse of the Asians and Greeks. Legend says Pythagoras took the Eleusinian Mysteries from Crete to Greece. These Great Mysteries originated in Egypt. Crete is the middle road between the advance Egyptians and the primitive Greeks. Serapis worship was carried from Thebes, Egypt to Thebes, Greece. Compare this to Helen (of Troy) being carried off by different suitors and spreading Helenism through the world. Zeus mates with mortals to produce human kings in Greece and Rome, just as Amon did in Upper Egypt. The kings were 'sons of the Sun'. Just as Lucifer mated with Eve and produced Cain. Since Zeus-Amon mates with mortals, he is a fallen god, like the fallen angels who left heaven to mate with mortals.

Zeus-Amon also transforms himself into a white swan and seduces Leda the wife of Tyndareus producing two sets of twins; Pollux and Helen fathered by Zeus and Castor and Clytemnestra fathered by Tyndareus. This is a corruption of Atum-Horus the Hawk who created Osiris and Isis, Set and Nephthys. Likewise, it is Adam (Atum) and Eve (Nun) producing Seth and his wife and Cain and his wife.

Zeus and Hera (his sister / consort) correspond to Amon-Ra (sun-god) and Hathor (moon deity) in Upper Egypt. Hathor means House of Horus. Hera is mother of Herakles. It is a corrupt version of Isis, wife of Osiris and mother of Horus. Both are depicted as cows nursing the child and mated to the Bull of Heaven. Hera is called cow-eyed and dog-eyed. She is the counterpart of Hathor, mother of Set as well as Horus. Set is the eye in Taurus, while Horus is the dog star Sirius. Hera, like Hathor, represents the Great Mother Nature. As the Roman Juno, she is the Yoni or Matrix of the Hindus. (J = Y and vowel interchange) Her horns are shaped as the quarter moon. Compare to the Canaanite sun god, Baal, and his moon mistress, Ashtaroth (Astarte). Ast is the Egyptians spelling of Isis. In Babylon, they are Tammuz and Ishtar. [Ezekiel 8:14] Also in Rome with Apollo and his moon mate, Diana. The female represents the fertility of mother nature and the 29 day (menstrual) cycle of the moon. Hera is Juno in Roman myth. Juno is deva of June, the summer solstice. Zeus rides a celestial chariot. The god who rides on the chariot is Baal, Helio, Apollo and Amon. [2 Kings 23:11] All are the Devil, the master of deception.

Hera's symbol is the green peacock feather. The end of which appears very much like the emerald eye of Horus. In Egypt, the symbol of Maat is the ostrich feather used to judge if the person is telling the truth. Hera would be the counterpart of the Maat goddess of Upper Egypt.

Alexander the Great

The Trojans, like the Persians, were the enemies of the Greeks. The Trojan war was just a part of the Persian wars. Helen represents Helenism. After the Persians conquered the Middle East and Egypt, they became a major threat to Greece. Troy is in Asia Minor (Turkey) on the border of Greece. Constantinople was the Christian border in Asia Minor. Then one day, the Greek soter was born. They say soter means savior, yet it is Set-ur (Set the great). Soter is the spurious savior. Esoteric is the secret service of Set.

Alexander the Great considered himself the son of Jupiter Ammon or Zeus-Amon, who had the two horns of a ram. His image on his coins shows two horns on his head (as the devil is portrayed). The ram is the symbol of Ra-Amon, the evil sun of God. This is the age of Aries the Ram god of war. When Alexander was born, a serpent was seen near his mother's bed. The truth is: he was an Aryan with long blond hair. He died at 33, the age they say Christ died at, but the Word of God gives no age. The Christians made Alexander a saint. Others declared him a deity. Claiming he ascended to Mt. Olympus to live with the gods. Actually he was son of Amen-Ra-Satan. The word "great" means "mighty" or "terrible" like a Titan. All killers are sons of Satan. [John 8:44 1 John 3:12] The Greeks were obsessed with the idea that the king will be killed by his son and take the throne. Their mythology is filled with this scenario over and over again. In fact, their creation story begins with Chronos usurping Uranos and then Zeus usurping Chronos and becoming king of the gods. It is not surprising to learn that Alexander had a hand in the assassination of his father King Philip II. Compare this to Amen-Ra usurping Atum-Osiris-Horus.

When Alexander died in 323 BC, General Ptolemy I became ruler of the province that included Egypt. Ptolemy I (323-285 BC.) created a hybrid religion that worshipped Sarapis (Asar = Osiris & apis = bull). This is like combining the Lord with Baal the Bull. Sarapis was much like the Minotaur (man-bull) of the subterranean Labyrinth at Crete. Both were sacrificed "because of" man's sins. The Labyrinth (or Catacombs) represents the grave from which there is no escape. Ptolemy I was called Soter or Savior by his followers, but he is a spurious or false savior, Setian, with delusions of deity. The Greek and Roman rulers who sat on the throne of Egypt were called the Vicar of Serapis.

Ptolemy's son was Ptolemy II Philadelphus who commissioned the first Greek translation of the Old Testament, known to this day as the Septuagint. The Greeks saved the Book of the Jews from obscurity by translating it into Greek. This is appropriate as this is the age the Lord was working with the sons of Japheth (the Gentiles). Philadelphus means 'lover of his sister' as he married his sister, just like Osiris and Jupiter (Zeus). Legend says seventy-two scholars completed the septuagint in seventy-two days. Ironically, the Jewish Sanhedrin has 72 members including the high priest. The Greeks call the Jewish Torah 'the Pentateuch' which means 5 books. They claim Moses wrote the first five books of the Bible. This is a lie. Moses wrote the first four books, the Tetrateuch. 5 (penta-cle) is Satan's number.

The words 'Holy Bible' are Hieros Biblos in Greek. It is also spelt Helios Biblos; meaning Sun Book. (r and l are interchangeable) Both words Helios and Hieros come from Heros (Horus) the Sun of Righteousness. Heliopolis, Egypt is the City of the Sun Righteousness (Horus). Heriopolis is Holy City and HieroSalem is Holy Salem.

In 240 BC, Ptolemy III, Euergetes I built the Serapeum Temple in Alexandria, Egypt. In Memphis, he built the Dionysus Temple to honor Serapis. He also built the Great Library which Julius Caesar burned to the ground. At Alexandria, Sarapis was molded in the image of Zeus. By the time the Romans came in 30 BC., Sarapis had grown into a Catholic (or Universal) god. Constantine the Great worshipped the statue of Zeus as Jesus (Iesus). They pronounced Jesus as Hay-Zeus. In 325 AD, Caesar Constantine became the Vicar of Serapis and proceeded to combine; the bull or Apis worship, the legends of Zeus, the bishops of the papacy, and Mithra religion from the Middle East. The main Mithreum Temple was in Antioch. Constantine went on to create Christendom and made Sylvester his first Pope. He unite the church and state in the unholy Roman Catholic empire. Christendom became the state religion.

From the Sarapis worship came the titles; Caesar (C-Asar), Tsar (T-Sar), Czar (C-Sar), and Kaiser (K-Aser). The Romans corrupted the Kingship of Osiris (i.e. Sar or Asar) into the evil emperor Julius Caesar and all his heirs through-out the dark-ages of Roman rule. The Russians and Germans consider themselves descendants of the Roman empire. Sargon (Sar-gon) also means King. Sargon the Great was first King of Assyria following the fall of the kingdom of Egypt. The Pharaohs were successors of Osiris, the first King of Egypt. After Sargon, came Nebuchadnez-zar (Sar) king of Babylon. Followed by Cyrus (Siris) king of Persia. Cyrus means Sun-throne. Referring to Horus as the heir apparent to the throne. They all "took" their titles from Egypt! Julius Caesar was high priest of the church of Rome before he became head of state. Compare to Jesus and Osiris who were both high priests and kings.

Octavianus Augustus Caesar was the first Roman Emperor. He was born Sept.23,63 BC and died August 19, 14 AD. Octavian means eight, yet August is the eight month, not October. In fact, August is the time of the august equinox when Atum-Osiris was born. Augustus was considered destine to be a deity. In the year 12 BC, Augustus Caesar was declared head of the Roman religion and given the title of Pontifex Maximus-a title later to be taken by the Catholic pontiffs or Popes of Rome. Proving the title has pagan roots.

Christ was born during his rule and oppression of Israel. Caesar Augustus was credited with creating 30 years of peace called the neo-Golden Age. But at what price? The price of 30 pieces of silver for the head of Jesus. Compare this peace to the temporary peace of the Antichrist in the end times. Who also will be world leader or Caesar. The heads of state have always been adversaries of the head of the church (Jesus) and his followers. Osiris' day lasted 30 years and the age of Orion lasted 30 degrees (2160 years)!

Constantine the Great (Caesar Constantine) became the father of Christendom. As king and priest, he anointed himself and united the church and state. He burned all writings contrary to his dogma. Later, Charlemagne (Charles the Great) became the founder of the unHoly Roman Catholic empire. {Great = Terrible} He was crowned emperor by Pope Leo III on Dec.25th, 800. Then the Pope and Charlemagne ruled hand and hand in uniting east and west Rome. The two halves of the Beast (church & state) united in unholy matrimony. [Revelation 13]

Hades-Judge of the Dead

Hades (Pluto in Roman) is god of the underworld called Tartarus and Poseidon (Neptune) is god of the sea. Both are attributes of Satan. Who is the Leviathan or sea Serpent. In fact, they are Zeus' evil brothers, just as Lucifer is the bad brother of the Lord Christ. They are sibling rivals and sons of God the Father. [Job 38:7 Isaiah 14:12-15] Zeus, Poseidon and Hades are all attributes of Cronos-Saturn (i.e. Satan). They make up the neo-Satanic trinity that rule over; the land of the living, the sea and the land of the dead. When Christ returns, he shall be Lord of the Earth.

"What in Tar-nation is going on." is slang that means "What in Tartarus region, is going on."

Hades was banished to Tartarus, the sunless region beyond the great river Ocean (Okeanus) which surrounds the earth. The Upper Egyptians called it Knum. This is the sea of space that surrounds the world with nine loops. Nine is the number of Nun, the Great Maternal Mother (watery womb). Sometimes Nun is refereed to as the sea of space containing a serpent. Typhon is an anagram of Python. Hyades is part of the constellation of Taurus the bull, that rises at night, then sets in the west into the dark underworld. Hades means "the Unseen" and Amun of Egypt means "the Hidden one". Satan is prince of darkness.

Now let's get down to earth. Styx is the daughter of Oceanus (Egyptian: Nut) and Tethys. Tethys is the Egyptian Tefnut (Rain). Oceanus is the sea of space that gave birth to all waters and all the stars, except the Great Bear (Ammit Beast). The ferryboat must cross the river Styx to get to the Tartarus. The old ferryman Charon is Herfhaf (Horus) in his bark who carries the dead souls across the river of life (Nile). It is the same as crossing the Jordan to get to the Promise land or Elysian Fields. But this will not occur until Horus gets in his bark and crosses the celestial Styx (Milky Way) and returns to earth to regain his throne as Lord of the earth. The earthly Tartarus is Turkey, where the Tartars live.

Actually, Hades is a distorted version, from Upper Egypt, of Osiris Khenti Amenta (lord of the dead in the grave). After the death of Osiris, the kingdom of Egypt was divided into Lower and Upper. Hades is called Aidoneus or Adonis (Lord). Hades = Hathes or Hathor (House of Horus). Horus is rightful heir of the House of Taurus and two kingdoms of Egypt. Thaurus = Hurus. But during the on going battle of Yin vs. Yang, Horus is lord of Lower Egypt and Set is lord of Upper Egypt. Horus heads the church and Set heads the state. On the heavenly level, Set is the head of the Constellation of Hyades in the House of Taurus. Tar-taurus = sTar in taurus. Tartarus is the dark abyss where Satan and his fallen angels are held awaiting judgment. "God did not spare the angels who sinned, but cast them down to Tartarus and delivered them into chains of darkness, to be reserved for judgment." [2 Peter 2:4 Jude 1:6 Revelation 9:1 20:1] According to Greek mythology; Hades, like Osiris, is Judge of the dead and Lord of the living. Hades, not Zeus, is either your Savior or your Executioner. The Greeks have confused the attributes of Osiris with Set and produced Hades. Just as the Hindus combined Krishna and Shiva to produce Hari-Hara.

What does the Word of God say about the ruler of the Underworld? Is Satan the ruler of a place called Hell? The Word of God says Satan is ruler of this wicked world. [Rev.12:12 John 12:31 14:30 16:11] Satan is god of this age. [2 Corinthians 4:4] Satan appoints the rulers of this wicked world. [Luke 4:5-7] Hell comes from the Hebrew sHeol which means Grave. The Hebrew religions have no place of torment (i.e. Hellfire). Christ is the Lord of the living and the dead, not Satan. The Sun of God (Sirius) is the one who goes into the Underworld of outer space and shall one day rise again as the Morning Star. Mortals do not go into space at death.

Demeter is De or Ge meaning Earth and Meter or Mater meaning Mother. She is Geb or Ta-neter (Earth-mother) of Egypt. Also known as Gaia and Maia. Demeter's daughter is Persephone. Who Hades kidnaps in his chariot of iron drawn by black steeds. They cross the celestial Styx to the rustic star, Hyades in the UnderWorld. Styx is the celestial river (the Milky way). Demeter searches for her for nine days. Nine is the number of the Great Mother of maternity. Hades gives her a pomegranate seed to eat just as Satan gave Eve the forbidden fruit. Planting the seed of sin in her mind. She falls for her capturer. Since she tasted the forbidden fruit of the underworld, she consequently became the consort of the Lord of the underworld. Before Eve ate the forbidden fruit, there was no darkness nor cold season of death called winter. But in the spring, nature is reborn. Compare this to Minos, lord of the underworld, and his wife Pasiphae (Persephone). The carnivorous Minotaur is the Ammit beast of Egypt who devours those found guilty.

Demeter searching for her dearly departed Persephone parallels Isis searching for Osiris. Demeter is goddess of corn-mills. Osiris is god of grain who taught the Egyptians how to grow grain and Isis taught them how to grind it and make bread. The 'Seed' is planted in 'mother earth'. The Son must die in order to be reborn. The Eleusinian Mysteries of Demeter was originally called the Mysteries of Isis and Osiris (the Bible of Death and Resurrection). The initiates learned the Lesser Mysteries at the spring equinox, but only the devoted can learn the Greater Mysteries at the autumn equinox. The first step is purification (baptism) in the river. Demeter's nine day festival is in September just like Isis' festival. The Key to unlocking the Mystery is Sirius.

Hades' part time mate is Persephone. She represents mother nature and her Sun that dies in the fall and winter. The time (6 months) she spends in Hades. Then her warmth and fertility returns in the spring and stays until fall. She divides her time between the Underworld and the Upperworld with her mother, Demeter. Tar-tarus is Terra-terra or land of the Dead. The Egyptians call it Amenta meaning land of Amen (i.e. cemetery). Persephone is Proserpine in Latin. Proserpine means Abode of Osiris (Ser) in the Pine. As Osiris died in the Pine tree. Persephone, like Asherah and Nephthys, rules the west as the cycle of life to death. The negative or dark side of nature. Those who die are buried in mother earth, awaiting resurrection when the good Sun of God returns from theeast. Persephone is the Persea tree from which the Sun of God is reborn. Isis (Ast) represents the death to life cycle. The Two Goddesses Demeter and Persephone are the Twin Goddesses Isis and Nephthys. De-meter is the Egyptian Ti-neter (dual nature of Mother Nature).

Hades decides if you go to the Field of Asphodel or Field of Elysium. The Field of Asphodel is the place to wait for nothing (Limbo?). It is the deep dark sleep of death in the grave where they await judgment. The twin brothers are Hypnos (Sleep) and Thanatos (Death). Elysian Fields is the Garden of God of which few are allowed. And then only after Judgment day. The Field of Elysium is the Promise land of the Elohim. The Greeks believed the dead only retain a shadow of their former personality. Their courage and intelligence had disappeared. The Bible says the dead know nothing and there is no knowledge or wisdom in the grave. [Ecclesiastes 9:5,6,10] The Egyptians believed that the good go to the Fields of the Blessed. The Greek, Isles of the Blest, is the New Earth floating in the sea of space.

The Word of God says Hades shall be thrown into the Lake of fire. [Revelation 20:14] Hades refers to the dead mortals in the grave, as well as the fallen angels in Tartarus. All the stars shall be consumed by the fiery presence of God. The sun shall also be consumed. The second heaven (outer space) shall be consumed by the first heaven. There will be no more dark void space or fallen stars to rebel against Gods' authority. Then the first heaven, where God dwells, will be our new heaven on earth. [Revelation 21:1 2 Peter 3:12,13]

Dante wrote his Divine Comedy as a fictional satyr. Where the bad people are tormented forever. Anyone crazy enough to believe this satyr, gets what they believe. The Hellfire is his! The joke is on him. Just as those who believe in the fable of Evolution shall die just as they believe. Those that believe the Word of God will have everlasting life. Hel is the Viking god of the underworld. Do you worship that pagan god?

Lethe, the river of forgetfulness runs through Hades. Dante says drinking the waters of Lethe enables "Christian" souls to be freed from the memory of their past sins. The Bible says there is no memory in the grave (Sheol in Hebrew). [Ecclesiastes 9:5,6,10] The soul that sins shall die! He returns to the dust from which he was created. Christ compared death to sleep. We sleep until the Lord returns to awake us from the deep sleep of death. [John 5:22-30 1 Thessalonians 4:13-17] Then we resurrect from the grave to face Judgment. This is another Advent of the Avatar Atum-Horus; the Savior Jesus.

Hermes

Hermes means Horus born of water. Maia (Maya) is the mother of Hermes. Just as Mary is mother of Christ. He is wrapped in swaddling clothes and laid on a winnowing fan. A winnowing fan is used to separate the useless chaff from the good seed. Both Osiris and Christ used it. [Matthew 3:12] Hermes spoke from birth. It is said that the Christ child is the Word of God who spoke at birth. Hermes is the Messenger of the gods and framer of Covenants. Just as the Lord is Messenger of the Word of

God and testor of the Covenant. Hermes is Horus of Egypt, who wrote the 42 sacred Books. The Emerald Tables of Hermes are the Egyptian Pyramid texts.

Hermes is the conductor of the souls of the dead to their final dwelling place. Anubis, as Herm-Anubis of Egypt, is bearer of the souls from the grave (Amenta) to the Judgment Hall of Osiris. The word Soul is Psyche in Greek. Psyche means Consciousness; as in psychology or psychological. The men of science agree with the Word of God in that the soul goes brain dead when you give up your last breath of life. The breath of life or spirit returns to God, but the dead know nothing (unconsciousness). A soul that sins shall die. A soul is mortal. [Ecclesiastes 9:5,6,10 12:7] Hermes steals some of Apollo's cows. Apollo takes him before Zeus. Apollo is the Accuser saying Hermes is a thief. [Revelation 12:10] Actually, the cows and everything on the earth belong to the rightful heir, Hermes. Just as Horus is heir to the Two Kingdoms of Egypt. Hermes trades a musical instrument (pipe) for Apollo's shepherd's staff or rod and a lyre for the cows. Just as Christ was shepherd who shall rule with a rod of iron. Hermes sacrificed a cow to God just as Abel offered a blood sacrifice. [Genesis 4:4] Apollo became god of music. It was he who taught it to Cain's descendants. [Genesis 4:21] Likewise, the stories of Dionysos and Adonis (Lord) are remakes of the Osiris/Horus story. The Greeks made Hermes the patron of thieves. This was Horus corrupted as Khonsu, son of Amen, and patron of Thebes.

Dionysus

The conception of Dionysus is said to take place in Thebes, Greece but, the origin of the cult was Thebes, Egypt. The fables traveled from Egypt to Greece, via Crete. The cult consisted of a dying and rising god associated with bulls and wine. In other words, Dionysus is the cult of horny satyrs (goat-men) and maenads (mad maidens). Fornication and intoxication was the satanic rituals of this sadistic cult. Dionysus is the deity of rapture; getting his followers worked "up" into a frenzy. Baal is the intoxicating spirit that causes you to loose your inhabitations. Bar is the house of Baal, a place to get drunk on Beer. {l & r interchange, as do vowels} Dionysus is also identified with Baachus.

This dying-savior, originated from the worship of Min (Amen). These Minions of Min often would commit savage animal and human sacrifice. On Crete, he is associated with the Minotaur (Bull of Minos). The bull cult of the Minoans is obviously connected to the Serapis cult in Egypt which gave birth to the cult of Dionysus. At Rome, Dionysus is known as Liber. From which we get libertine (licentious and promiscuous behavior).

One version says Dionysis (Dion-Isis) tried to escape by transforming into a serpent, a bull and a goat, but was torn apart by the Titans at Thebes.

Another version says his Maidens the Maenades (Aids of Amen) tore him apart. Compare to the Menevis bull and Mendes goat being sacrificed. His sister, Minerva, saved one part (his heart) and gave it to Zeus, who stitched it into his thigh. Then Dionysis was reborn from the loins of Zeus-Amon. In Egypt, the constellation of Ursa Major is a cow's thigh. Semen are the northern stars and Semele is said to be Dionysis' mother. Semele is the niece of Europea who mated with Zeus and produced Minos. Minos' wife mated with Zeus, in the form of a bull, and produced the Minotaur. When Semele died, Dionysis was nursed by many nymphs who were later changed into stars of the constellation Hyades (the horns and head of Taurus the bull). Zeus would be Amon the bull of heaven (Taurus). That means Dionysis (AKA. Baachus) is Baal, the baby bull or babe bear (Ursa Minor). [Larousse Encyclopedia of Mythology p.179] These plagiarists stold and then perverted the story of Osiris torn to pieces by Set (Sut) and reconstructed by Isis. Dionysis impersonates Horus, son of Isis, reborn as Horus-Atum. Dionysis (Dion-Iesus or Dion-Hey-Zeus) is part of Zeus just as Horus is part of Atum. The fake Horus is Khonsu (Honsu), son of Amen and Mot (Mother Neter). The priests of Thebes, Egypt depicted him with the crescent moon on his head like horns. Khonsu (or Chansu) is Cain-Sut, the first farmer and the first to sacrifice humans. [Genesis 4:3-12] When they called Jesus a wine-bibbler they were referring to Dionysus stories. It is well known that the drunken followers of Dionysus sacrificed human victims by savagely ripping them to pieces and using the parts as fertilizer in their fields. Human sacrifice is practiced by all religions who worship Mother Nature (AKA. Mother Earth) and her sun who die in the winter. They mistakenly believe it guarantees a good crop. Dionysis was worshipped as a god and Semele (Se-Marie) as Mother of god. Compare this to Mother Mary. [The Golden Bough by James George Frazer chapter 47]

Coupling

Aphrodite the goddess of physical love represents the maternal instincts of a woman, while Eros her son, represents the man's sex drive (lust). "Your desire shall be for your husband, and he shall rule over you." [Genesis 3:16] In Rome, they are Venus and Cupid. To this day they are honored with Valentine's day. Cupidity is the passion for possession. Eros learned first hand that all love ends in heart break when he lost his lover. Physical and emotional love is illusive at best. Spiritual love, as a father or mother has for their son, is enduring. This is agape (love) that our Father in heaven has for His children.

Eros represents the romance of both homosexual and heterosexual types. It is well known that the Greeks & Romans were bisexuals. Eros was often a dangerous force that could move men and women to self-sacrifice (suicide). Aphrodite (the lover), Artemis (the mother), and

Athene (the fighter) are the triplets connected at the heart. Sex and violence go hand and hand in the roller coaster of emotions. Heartbreak, jealousy, and envy are often the cause of suicide and/or homicide. Hephaistos (Roman god Vulcan) was the husband of Aphrodite, but she was an unfaithful wife. Ares, the Warlord, committed adultery with Aphrodite. As did Adonis. Adonis is the same as Adonai (the Jewish word for Lord). Love is blind, deaf and dumb. It makes men act like fools. It is by no accident that April fool's day coincides with spring fever and the rutting season. Hermaphrodite comes from coupling Hermes with Aphrodite.

He who burns with desire... shall end in the Lake of Fire!

The moral of the Greek stories is that all desire to couple, whether it be of mortal or immortals, ends in tragedy. The Heroes were distracted from their divine missions by tempting maidens and seductive nymphs. Almost every religion says that sex defiles the man of God. [See "The Golden Fleece and the Heroes Who Lived Before Achilles."]

The Greeks made their gods in their own image—lacking in morals.

Apollo

Zeus and a nymph named Leto had a son named Apollo. Apollo could not have the woman he loved, so he had her killed and gave her son Aesculapius, to Chiron, the centaur (half man and half horse) who taught him diagnostics, surgery, herbology, and hunting. Aesculapius became the healing god. Apollo is the sun god of the black arts and witch crafts. He is father of medicine. The Hippocratic oath says, "I swear to Apollo..." All Priests of Apollo (doctors) take this oath. These physicians practice their religion by playing god; taking life and death in their hands. The serpent on the staff is his sign called the Caduceus or Aesculapius magical wand used by the medical profession to this day. The snake on a pole comes from the plague of the people of Israel. [Numbers 21';7-9 2 Kings 18:4,6] That serpent on the tree represents Satan in the Tree of carnal knowledge. Knowledge of good and evil: able to heal or kill. These hypocrites swear to Apollo that they will not do abortions or euthanasia, yet they do. They think they are above the law; both man's and God's.

During the Dark Ages, doctors had midwives executed as witches because they were cutting into their profits by delivering babies for free. Physicians are the witch-doctors who shall burning in the last days. The Rx on prescriptions is Rex meaning King. Rex Mundi is King of this World (Satan). Apollyon is the Destroyer who gets people hooked on pharmaceutical drugs. [Companion Bible-Revelation 9:11,21] Apollo is the ruddy (red) light of the setting sun and Artemis is the silvery moon reflecting his light. In Egypt, Set was also white faced and red haired. He is the Sun that does rise and Set daily. Artemis represents the fertility cycle or menstrual cycle that coincides with the moon's monthly cycle. It is also blood-red. The Romans call her Diana the huntress who chases after her intended mate, the sun-god. Just as the moon chases the sun across the horizon. Apollo rides his fiery chariot across the sky. This is the chariots of the sun dedicated to Baal (AKA. Satan, the evil sun of God. [2 Kings 23:11]

Another of the sons of Apollo was Phaethon. He had golden yellow hair like his father the sun-god. For Apollo is the father of the Roman race. The Greeks had mated with Aryans (Cainites) and produced the blond haired, blue-eyed Romans. The Romans were warriors who rode in chariots like their sun-god, Apollo. These are called the Titans or Giants. They are the by-produces of the fallen angels mating with human women. [Genesis 6:1-4] The sons of Cain: Jubal is Apollo god of music, Jabal is Mercury god of pasturage, Tubal-Cain is Vulcan the god of smithing. [Genesis 4:20-22] Notice Bal (Baal) is in all their names. Phaethon crashed Apollo's sun-chariot which represents the end of the Age of Aries and the Arian warriors. The word Phaethon comes from Pharaoh. The Pharaohs of Amon claimed to be sons of the Sun (Aton or Aethon). Phaethon's mortal mother was Clymene (Cly-Men) a member of the family of Amen.

Apollo's oracle at Delphi was a spiritualist woman possessed with the spirit of the python-serpent. {python is an anagram of typhon} After becoming intoxicated with evil spirits, she would give omens and tell fortunes. Later this evolved into seances that sometimes connected with spirits of the other world. Necromancy or communicating with the dead is condemned by God. Today it has evolved into psychic advisors who can communicate with the familiar spirits at will. This familiar spirit are evil spirits or fallen angels pretending to be familiar dead people. Of which, Apollo is the head and ringleader of the circus of stars (circumpolar suns of God). Apollo uses women because they are easier to manipulate and men are less likely to retaliate against females for bad readings. Vatican means Oracle (Vati) of the Serpent (can).

Four Races

Some believe there to be four races; gold, silver, bronze and iron. The Golden Race was when mankind lived in paradise of peace, lived long lives, with all things provided. The season was always spring. When they died it was like a deep sleep in the dust. Compare to Adam and Eve in Eden. The Silver Race had to toil for their needs. They lived under the four seasons; summer, spring, autumn and winter. The cold made their hearts grow cold. They lived long lives, but not long enough to learn wisdom. Compare Adam and Eve exiled from the garden. The third race of Bronze were mighty men of war. Compare to Cain and his descendants. The fourth Iron Race is our own race. We grow old very quickly. Zeus decided to destroy the third Bronze race with a great flood. The Titan Prometheus warn his son, Deucalion and his wife Pyrrha of the flood and instructed them on how to build a ship to save them. Zeus saw that the only two survivors were just, kindly and had right reverence for the gods so he spared them. They were allowed to repopulate the world. Prometheus brought them fire to warm them.

Hesiod was a Greek writer. In his book Works and Days, he tells of five ages; gold, silver, bronze, heroes, and iron. He says man will descend from joy and innocence to guile misery and corruption. Compare this to the Book of Daniel. The gold is Babylon, silver is Persia, bronze is Greece and iron is Rome. Who shall return as iron and clay. This neo-Roman empire is now called the United States of Europe. [Daniel 2:32-45 7:4-8,23-27] The New World Order is built on iron and concrete, but the Chief Corner Stone shall break it to pieces. Of course, these represent the ages of the Zodiac. The old must fall so the new can rise.

Heraclitus believed in a cosmic fire into which the world is periodically dissolved and from which is born anew. This sounds much like the Phoenix on a cosmic scale. The Phoenix burns up on the altar fire and then is reborn from the ashes. The idea of the Lake of fire and the second death originated in Egypt. The recycling of the ages is an Indian idea.

Fire from Heaven

Prometheus was a Titan. It is said that he created man from clay and Athene gave them life. Which is corruption of Atem's creation of man in Egypt. Prometheus went before Zeus and asked, "Why do you leave mankind in the darkness of ignorance?" "Why do you not give him fire?" Zeus answered this is not ignorance, it is innocence. {There was no fire in God's garden paradise. Who's fault is it he got banished?} Prometheus disagreed but left. Early the next morning, he climbed Mt. Olympus and grabbed a piece of the suns fire. He brought his Olympic torch down to mankind to illuminate them. {Just as Lucifer claimed he would illuminate Adam and Eve.} [Genesis 3:1-5] The Titan, Prometheus, took fire from Helio, the sun god, and relayed it on to man. Soon mankind started to use the fire as an instrument of destruction, just as Zeus foretold. They started making weapons of war. Firepower is the Devil's instrument. Apollo, the sun god, also had his own "games" at Delphi. These "war-games" where played between times of war to prepare for war. [2 Kings 23:5-11]

Zeus decided to watch these war games as amusement, but would later destroy them in the very fire they desired. [2 Peter 3:10-12] The infidels dedicated their horses and chariots to the sungod (Satan) by burning them in fire. [2 Kings 23:11] As for Prometheus, Zeus chained him on top of Caucasus mountain. Just as the Lord chained Satan. [Revelation 9:1 20:1-3] The Caucasian mountains is the cradle of the Caucasian race. A thousand years later, it was Heracles who released him. This parallels the release of Satan after the Millennium and the war to end all wars. As all the follows of the Warlord shall die in the Lake of fire raining down from heaven. [Revelation 20:7-9]

Pandora

Zeus creates Pandora, the first woman. She was sent to Epimetheus (Afterthought) the brother of Prometheus (Forethought). She was given a sealed gift of which she was told not to open. But out of curiosity, she opened it and released all the evils onto the world. Only hope remained inside. She represents Eve who opened herself to the seduction of the Serpent. She took of the forbidden fruit by allowing Satan to place his seed in her womb. Satan took her cherry or virginity and supplanted evil in her heart. Their son was Cain, the evil one who murdered his brother Abel. Eve caused the "curses" to be released on mankind. The fallen angels saw what Satan did and imitated their leader.

Zeus is angered and sends a flood to destroy the giants created by Prometheus. This was the Bronze Race. Prometheus' son, Deucalion, builds an ark and survive the deluge. He and his wife, Pyrrha, the red-blonde daughter of Epimetheus and Pandora, repopulate the human race. Then begins the Race of Heroes. This parallels Genesis chapters 6 and 7. The Bible says the Lord sent the deluge because the fallen angels exchanged social and sexual intercourse with the humans. Planting evil thoughts in their heads. The Titans are the spirit-beings (angels) who mated with female human-beings and produced the giants. Heroes comes from Heru or Horus the hero who saved the Kingdom of Osiris.

Before the Millennium: time of UnRest

In the last days, the men of science will claim they (under supervision of Apollo) will save the world. [Revelation 9:11] But their illusion will not last for it is the same lie Satan told Eve in the garden. She did Not become like God and she soon died. Apollo is the incarnate Antichrist and his followers are Apollians. He will claim they can escape the earth's tribulations by flying away in an Apollo spacecraft. But it is all fantasy. The Apollo moon landing was named in honor of the mating of the sun-god and moon goddess. The Antichrist Savior will claim to have the powers of life and death. Which is true. He will kill untolled millions of unborn children through ABORTION!!! And millions more with the weapons of war developed by mental giants of Apollo. It is the Antichrist who leads the United Nations of Infidels into the battle known as Armageddon.

Zeus, wishing to have a son who should be the powerful protector of the people, descended one night to the city of Thebes where he assumed the appearance of the mortal Amphitryon and did lay with his wife, Alcmene. Shortly afterwards Amphitryon himself returned from a victorious expedition and did lay with his wife. From the two unions Alcmene conceived twins: Hercules and Iphicles. Compare this to Lucifer seducing Eve and producing their son Cain then Adam and Eve produce their son Abel. Zeus-Amen used deception and darkness as his allies. Also Thebes has a counterpart in Egypt, where they worship Set-Amen.

Herakles (Hercules in Roman) is the story of Samson the Danite. A Danite is a Cainite (son of Cain). Hercules battles the Amazon women then later mates with his mortal enemies, just like Samson. Sex and violence go hand and hand. This was his ninth Labour of the 12 Labours he was to perform. He was to get the golden girdle of Ares worn by the Amazon queen Hippolyte. The Amazon women were daughters of Aries, the Warlord. They are Aryans of Assyria, who are descendants of the Caucasian Cainites (Kenites). The modern name is Indo-European. This mixing with the white women is what produced the blond haired, blue eyed Romans. Amazons are still found in Albania. Albania means White from the root Albino. Leprous is a city founded by lepers. These lepers had vitiligo: the lack of skin pigment causing White skin and hair.

Hippolyte was also known as Antiope or Anti-cyclope. The Cyclope being the cycling Eye of Heru (i.e. Sirius). {See Greek Myth by Robert Graves 138.h & 138.2} Amazon is Ma + son. This is the Great Mother (Ursa Major) and her son Ursa Minor. For the Egyptians she was Ta-Urt the Hippo-beast (Hippo-lyte). These circumpolar stars that cycle the Pole star are called Smen or Samon stars. Sami are the fallen stars that follow Set. 'Amasons' is an anagram of 'Samson'.

According to the Roman versions, Hercules was a savage Barbarian like Samson. Samson is the mindless brute force of the sun. The gods caused a madness to overcome Hercules who killed his own wife and three children. After he repented, he was called Heracles. He was formerly known as Paleamon (Pale-Amon). Amon is the evil son of God. He was spiritually reborn and renamed like Abraham, Jacob, Solomon etc...H-eracles was named after Hera which is the feminine of Heru (Horus). As a penance he is to do the 12 Labours. This is an inaccurate rendering of the 12 Hours of the Egyptian Book of the Dead. Horus was the original Heracles who Never sinned.

Herakles' wife was Deianeira. Samson's wife was Delilah. Now if you combine Lilith and Deianeirah you get Delilah. Lilith in the Jewish Talmud is the evil wife of Adam, before Eve. In Jewish legend, she is the beautiful woman from the dark side (nymph), who seduces and destroys men. Samson means "sun-like". He is the sungod, Shamosh, whose golden hair is the sun rays. He is Apollo and Amen-Ra-Set who loose their power in the winter when the deva of darkness shaves his hair. He sleeps as his eyes (the sun and moon) are blinded (burned out). Samson at the mill represents the turning of time. In time, his hair grows and his power returns. He springs to power and returns to full strength in the summer. He slays the enemy with a jawbone of an ass and fiery foxes.

The ass and the fox are ancient symbols of the sun. [see Deceptions and Myths of the Bible by Lloyd M. Graham page 205-207]

Herakles is a demi-god; half man and half god just like Jesus. Both are sons of God with mortal mothers. Actually they were surrogate mothers. They were begotten by the Father in heaven who has no partners. Hera is the watery womb of creation and the tomb of destruction. In the Roman version, he also has a dark side just like Satan. In Hinduism, they created a new god by combining Vishnu (the Sustainer) and Shiva (the Destroyer) into a composite deity. This new god is Hari-Hara. Hari-krisna is Herakles and Hara-crisna is Hercules (r = l). Change the H to a M and drop the s in Hercules and you have Mercury, the Roman god who is identified with the Greek Hermes. The Greeks confess that Herakles was originally Egyptian. They got the idea from Upper Egypt where they combined Horus (Hari) and Amen-Set in Amsu. To the Orientals, this symbolizes the harmony of evil and good (Yin/Yang) rather than the rivalry of evil against good. We must fight against our evil nature. On Judgment day, we can't transfer the blame to our carnal nature or to the Devil. We are responsible for our actions.

There once was a king of Egypt named Busiris who sacrificed humans to Zeus-Amen to insure a good crop. When he tried to sacrifice Herakles, he burst the bonds and slew Busiris and his son. Bu-siris would be Bull-siris or the Ser-apis worship. Compare to Samson slaying the Philistines in their own temple. Compare Hercules with a club to Menes with his mace. It was Osiris who put an end to human sacrifice in Egypt.

The twelve Labours of Herakles coincide with the twelve signs of the Zodiac. In the first labor, Herakles kills a lion, Nemean, that was eating the sheep. Nemean is none other than N-Amen King of the gods. It is said to be the offspring of Typhon (Set). It is Satan devouring the sheep of the good Shepherd. [1 Peter 5:8] This is the sign of Leo. In the second labor, Herakles slays the 9 headed Hydra. This is similar to Hindu story of Rama battling the 10 headed Ravana. The Hydra is the offspring of Typhon (Set). The 10 headed Beast rising out of the sea is also in the Bible. [Rev.13:1] Hydro means Water. The beast represents the ten nations of the neo-Roman empire. Which is now known as the United States of Europe. The many heads represent the many faces of Satan. In the third labour, Herakles captures the golden-horned hind of Ceryneia, which is sacred to Artemis. This is Rudolph the reindeer, sacred to Santa. Hind is a red deer. The horns are crescent moon. Artemis is the Great Mother Urt and Santa is her sun at the North Pole star. In the fourth Labour, Herakles captures the Erymanthian boar. The pig is one is Set's animals. In the fifth Labor, Herakles cleans the stalls of the twelve white bulls sacred to Helios by diverting a river and washing away the "bull-shit". Just as Christ cleaned the Temple of the scum of the earth. This is Aquarius. In the Zodiac, Herakles is standing next to the Milky Way, the celestial river. In the sixth labor, he routed the Stymphalion birds which had iron wings, feed on human flesh and were sacred to Ares. Compare this to the fowls who shall feast on human flesh following the battle of Armageddon. [Revelation 19:11-21] The seventh labor, Herakles tames King Mino's bull at Crete is the counterpart of Horus defeating Amen the Bull of heaven. Mithra slaying the bull is his counterpart in Asia. This is house of Taurus. The eighth labour, he captures the man-eating mares of Diomedes, son of Ares. Mares are female horses. Urt is the water-horse (hippo) who eats her children. The ninth labor, he obtains the girdle of Hippolyte, queen of the Amazons.

At Joppa, Herakles is swallowed by a great fish. He is in the belly of a fish for three days. Compare this to Jonah, Jesus and the sign of the fish Pisces. In Egypt, two fishes swallowed Osiris' penis (sperm or seed). This Seed is Horus. Pisces swallowed up the age of Aries.

Herakles' tenth Labour is to get the cattle of Helios. Helio, the golden haired sun-god, tried to stop Herakles with the intense heat of the day. So Herakles shot an arrow at the sun. Helios submitted and sent Herakles a golden goblet (golden grail) shaped like a water lily, which he used as a ship to cross the Great Sea. Compare this to Horus riding in the his bark made from the serpent through the sea of space. The lotus (a water-lily) is the Egyptian symbol of birth from water, not from the earth. [John 3:5] Herakles sails past the pillars of Hermes that hold up heaven. In other words, Herakles voyaged into the underworld and brought back the cattle of Helio (Ra). In the end, the cattle were sacrificed to Hera. The cattle represent the followers of Taurus the bull. It was Cain, son of the Sun (Satan), who raised cattle. [Genesis 4:20] The Egyptian word "Menmen" means Cattle. It comes from the word Amen-Amen, the evil sun-god. Amnun means Amun born of Nun in the constellation of Taurus.

The eleventh labour, was to capture Cerberus the three-headed watchdog of Tartarus. Tartarus is Taurus the constellation in the underworld. Hades is the stars of the bull head and horns. The three heads of Cerberus are the constellations: Cetus-Ares-Bear-Taurus (Ce-re-ber-rus). The Great Bear is Ursa Major. Add to that the Egyptian dog-god, Anubus, who digs up the dead and escorts them to the Judgment Hall. In Tartarus, Hades is the Judge who decided where you go after death. In Egypt, Osiris is the Judge and Ammet is the Eater of the Dead at Amenta (underground land of Amen). Ammet is a triune composite of; a crocodile, hippopotamus and lion. In the Gospel of Bartholomew, Jesus drags the Beast Beliar up from the abyss.

Herakles, in his twelveth and final hour, goes to the Garden of Hesperides that Zeus created for Hera. This is the garden of Eden. Herakles can not enter because he is a demi-god, so he holds up the heavens while Atlas fetches the fruit of the gods. Herakles takes of the golden apples of the immortals. This is the Tree of life with the fruit forbidden to mortals. [Genesis 3:22] When he exits, he is thirsty, so he strikes the Great Rock and a river of water flows out. Compare this to Moses and the Rock. [Exodus 17:6 1 Corinthians 10:4] Christ is the Rock that shall break down the kingdoms of this world and give the water of life to those who thirst after righteousness. [Revelation 22:1,2,14,15 Daniel 2:31-45] They shall live as immortals in God's garden. [Revelation 2:7] This is the Egyptian Fields of Peace.

According to Lucian, "He (Herakles) sought not to subjugate nations by force, but by divine wisdom and persuasion." According to Bart, "His voluntary immolation betokened an eternal new birth of man... Through the release of Prometheus and the erection of altars we behold in him the mediator between the old and the new faiths... He abolished human sacrifice wherever he found it practiced. He descended into the somber realms of Pluto (Hades), as a shade... He ascended as a spirit to his father Zeus in Olympus." This is exactly what the Egyptians say about Osiris-Horus! Herakles, like Dionysis, was 'adopted' into the Greek pantheon from overseas.

Most of Greek myth is taken from Egypt and the Tower of Babel. As all the nations were present at the Tower following the Flood. They were all aware of the Creation and Flood and each had his story to tell. But the stories got tainted from telling them generation to generation. The symbology got more and more complex. The battle of the gods vs. the giants for instance. The gods are the elohim in Hebrew. Which are the good sons of God. The giants are the children produced when the disobedient sons of God (angels) mated with human women. [Genesis 6:2] These giants of the land are the Kenites (sons of Cain) and the Canaanites. The white race has always been taller than the other races. Tall as oak trees and hard to the core.

Battle of the gods

Zeus, with the help of the Cyclopes, defeated the Titans (fallen angels), who were bound in chains and cast into the abyss (Tartarus). Where they await Judgment day. [1 Peter 3:19,20 2 Peter 2:4,5 Jude 6] The Cyclopes is Horus as Son of God. Then Zeus slays the three monsters; Cottus, Briareus, and Gyges. This is Orion battling the monsters; Cetus, Taurus and Ares. Typhoeus (Typhon) is the son of Tartarus, which is the constellation of Taurus. The stars of Hades are the head that leads the rebellion. This is the Dragon of Revelation 12:3,4 & 20:1-3 with many heads. He is known as Amen-Set in Egypt. During the battle, Zeus commands Helios (the sun) not to shine. Therein the moon will darken. Compare this to the sun darkening in Matthew 24:27-31 and Revelations 6:12 & 16:10. Then the giants or mighty military men of every nation, will attack Zeus at Olympus. The Bible says this is Jesus at Jerusalem. [Zechariah 14:1-5] Zeus with the help of a human, Herakles, defeats the giants. [Revelation 19:11-21] Herakles is Horus as Son of Man. Then following a thousand year reign, the giants will surround the camp of Zeus once again. The Lake of Fire will rain down on them from heaven. This is the second death. [Revelation 20:7-10] This is the War to end all wars.

The Hindus have a story of extra-terrestrials (Titans) battling the gods with supernatural weapons. Mankind is saved by the gods. The Bible says, "War broke out in heaven." Satan and his angels battled with Michael and his angels. [Revelation 12]

Herakles was burned alive and then reborn from the ashes. Just like the Phoenix. Herakles then ascended Mt. Olympus to be with the Company of the gods. Compare to the Lord and Savior who died, resurrected and ascended to heaven. Who shall soon descend to rule the earth from New JeruSalem on Mt. Zion. [Revelation 21:2,10]

The Anti-God

Athene was the goddess of Athens. From Athene we get the word atheist. For they believed in her and not God the Father. The godless worship of the goddess of war is whorship. Americans have recreated her here in America! They have placed this pagan goddess in a temple in Nashville, Tenn. They even reconstructed a copy of the Parthenon. A temple to worship her in. She has found a home here with the other pagan goddess: the goddess of Freedom on the top of the White House, the Statue of Liberty (sister of the Statue of Rhodes), goddess of Justice, etc.... The Statue of Rhodes is Helio the evil sun-god. The Statue of Liberty is SHelio, his twin. She welcomes the alien immigrants (foreign gods) to America. Athene became the idolized goddess of the Women's Liberation Movement and Wicca. Athen in Egyptian means Sun. Athen in Greek means Deathless.

Athene is a perversion of the virgin birth of Aten-Re. She is the brother of Hermes, and therefore, a feminine form of Aten-Horus (Heru). Parthenon is the Temple of the Virgin as parthenos means virgin or maiden. Aten-Re was the virgin born Son who sprang from the mind of his Father in heaven. Just as Athene sprang from the head of Zeus armed for battle. [Ephesians 6:10-20] The He-man Heru became the She-woman, "Her". Athene-Hera took the place of Aten-Heru. In the Egyptian ritual chapter 78 the deceased says, "Horus has come to me out of my father Osiris? He has come to me out of the brains of his head!" On Athene's helmet was a Sphinx! Athene battles at the side of Herakles, just as Aten and Horus are inseparable. For they are one and the same. God shouted, "Let there be light" and the first begotten Sun of God was born out of the darkness. Aten (Atem) is that Bright Morning star (Sirius) preconceived in the mind of God.

On the other hand, Athene-Nike connects her with the Egyptian Neka the Devil-serpent. Her sacred animal is the serpent. The Roman deva, Minerva, is the female counterpart of Min-Ra or Amen-Ra, the Great Impostor pretending to be the Angel of En-light-enment. Athena is an anagram of Neitha, the goddess of war and wisdom in Upper Egypt. [The Book of the Dead by Sir Wallis Budge page 186] The Greek word for God is Theon, which comes from Aten (aThen). Theon is the singular and Theos is plural "gods". We say "the hat" instead of just saying "hat" to show God's possession. The French say "le hat" for the same reason. Le is the reverse of El which is Hebrew for God. Everything belongs to God. In French, "le" is masculine and "la" is feminine because they have gods and goddesses. The Europeans prefer to worship women like Helen, Hera and Mother Mary. Catholicism is the "mother church". They are Matriarchal by nature; worshipping the creation, not the Creator. [Roman 1:25] Helen was probably the original Greek Queen of Heaven (En or An) and Hel (Earth). Even the Statue of Helios became the Statue of Liberty (Statue of Shelios) in the hands of the French infidels.

Artemis is the counterpart to Diana the virgin. Diana was the great hunter like Orion. In fact, in the Greek version, Artemis slayed Orion at the instigation of her brother Apollo, and took his place. Apollo-Diana (Apollyon) would be Set-Typhon who had a hand in killing Osiris. Artemis is Urt-Mut (Great Mother) and Ursa Major (Great Bear) who tore Osiris to pieces. Artemis is counterpart of the Ashterah tree that crucified Christ. With her many breasts, she is Mother of Little Bar (Baal-Set) and the other fallen ones (Am-Smen). She is really Ammit, the composite beast; hippop-atemis, crocodile and lioness. Ammit devours her own young. Artemis' consort is Hippolytus. Hippo + poly (many) = the composite Beast. He later was canonized by the Roman Catholics as St. Hippolytus. Astarte is Ast-urt. Di-Ana is a counterfeit counterpart of the Virgin Mothers; Anu and Isis. In Egypt, Ana or Anu is the birthplace of Atum. Artemis is adversary and antithesis of the matrix that gave birth to Atum. The Son of Adam (Atum) who became a life-giving spirit-being is Osiris reborn as Horus. [2 Corinthians 15:45] Artemis hunting with her dog is a corruption of Orion and the Dog star, Sirius, that represents Isis, the Virgin Mother.

Homer's Iliad

Helen was the Greek Mother goddess. The Trojans are accused of stealing their matriarchal mythology of Helenism. These Persians of Troy were patriarchal religion who worship God the Father and His son. After 9 years the Greeks create the so-called Trojan Horse. This mare (female horse) was pregnant with the sons of Greece. Nine is the number of human gestation. Compare this mare to Marie, the mother of god in Rome. Helen + mare = Hera { l = r }. The sons of Japheth (Jupiter) were constantly at war with the sons of Shem (Asians) and sons of Ham (Africans).

Greek Philosophy

Sophia was the goddess of wisdom. Philosophy = philo + sophia which means the love of wisdom. This is worldly wisdom as philo is the root of philanthropy (brotherly love). "Greeks seek after wisdom." [1

Corinthians 1:22] Compare Sophia to Solomon's wisdom which he refers to in the feminine as "she". [Proverbs 1:20] Likewise, the Jews refer to the She-chi-nah (Holy Spirit) in the feminine. Yet, the Word of God is always masculine. In Egypt, both Shu (the Breath of Life) and Thoth (the Spirit of Truth) are masculine. Yin is feminine and darkness, Yang is masculine and light. Chi is the Spirit in China.

It was Plato and Socrates who said man has a immortal soul within. That man pre-existed before he was born human. And therefore, the good shall live forever in the Islands of the Blessed (to be like gods) and the bad shall be tormented forever in hellfire. Plato even believed in reincarnation of the soul over and over (transmigration). He attempts to take away the Promise of the Lord, who says He is the giver and taker of life. Dante's Divine Comedy further emphasized this idea. But the fact is; that the originator of the idea of the immortal soul was Satan. [Genesis 3:4,5] "You will not die. You will be like God", says the Serpent Satan. The one who first desired to ascend to heaven was Satan. [Isaiah 14:13] Man has desired to follow in this self-destruction ever since. If you are already immortal, why would you need a Savior?????

The Word of God says the soul shall die and the life force (Spirit) shall return to God. The personality is in the dead soul which is in a state of unconsciousness called the deep sleep of death. You are brain dead! Adam returned to the dust of mother earth and is awaiting the day of resurrection. [Ezekiel 37:1-14] The Lord said he is the only Son of Man that came from heaven and shall return there. [John 3:13 8:21-24] The earthlings shall return to the dust of the earth. No human is tormented forever in hellfire. The Lake of fire is total extermination (nonexistence). The person is turned to smoke. Which is reserved for those who have been judged and found worth of the death penalty. [Revelation 20:11-15]

Only the spirit-beings like Satan and the fallen angels can torment forever in the consuming fire of God's presence. And only the Saints transformed into spirit-beings can survive it. [Revelation 20:6] All the lawless ones will be turned to ashes and smoke. That is where we get the term: Ashes to ashes, dust to dust. We are not born with an immortal soul, it is a gift of God called the glorified body.

The Roman Catholics created the Purgatory fable for the unbaptized who died so they could be purged of the Original Sin inherited from Mother Eve. Since they believe in the immortal soul, a place was needed for all those not saved by grace, so they would not be tormented forever in hellfire. The truth is: Lies are compounded to cover-up the original lie. Christians are Spiritualists who believe you can communicate with the dead (ghosts). Spiritualism and nec-roman-cy (speaking with the dead) is condemned by God. [Deuteronomy 18:11] The pagan Pythagoras believed that the fall of man happened when he fell from heaven and became imprisoned in a human body on earth. He believes men are immortal souls who need no savior. Man can save himself and return to his celestial home. He taught that man acquired his vices during his fall through the heavens. Acquiring aggression from Mars, greed from Mercury, lust from Venus, etc... At death man will shed these characteristics as the soul retraces its path in its ascension through the heavens. This is astro-divination. The idea of immortal souls became the fundamental doctrine of Christendumb. An immoral soul can become an immortal soul by saying "grace". That's the "Saved by Grace" theory. The Lord Never said you are saved by grace!

Pythagoras was a student who studied at Egypt and Babylon. He was well aware the earth was round. In fact, everyone for thouands of years previous to Columbus was aware of this. Atlas is depicted with the globe on his shoulders. Not only was the earth a sphere, but the heavens too. If the stars, and planets are spheres that go in spherical orbits than so is the earth. The perfect shape in nature is a sphere. Only those of Christendumb believed the earth was flat with four corners. Pythagoras believed the cosmos was created by a single governing intelligence that expressed itself in numbers. According the Greeks; astronomy, mathematics, geometry, and writing did not originate in Greece or the Middle East, but in Egypt. Math-matics is Maat-Maat (The Two Truths). The Egyptians believed in the cycle of time, not linear time. We shall go full circle, back to the beginning and then the righteous shall enter God's garden (Elysian fields). PS Atlas is the counterpart to the Egyptian Shu who holds up the heavens.

The Pythagoras theorem comes from the Pyramid builders. Pythagoras was an amateur architect and mathematician. Why is Pythagoras given credit for things invented by Egyptians like Imhotep, designer of the pyramids? Mathematics is an Egyptian word based on Maat; the instrument used to measure or ruler. It is strange that the Greek word 'theo-rem' is 'god-Rem'. Rem is Re-amen, the evil sun-god. Compare to theory (theo-ray) or god-Ra.

It was Aristotle who blindly lead the masses through the Dark Ages. He claimed the earth was the center of the universe and everything, including the sun, revolved around it. He said everything in heaven, including the stars and planets, were perfect. Again he was proven wrong. He could not explain fallen stars and meterites crashing into planets, if they were so perfect. Philosophy is the theory of theology that is lacking in divine revelation. Their interpretation is mere speculation. Just as the Assumption of the Catholics that Mary ascended to heaven. If the earth is a heavenly body moving through space, we are already in heaven!

Plato and Pythagoras both claimed to be virgin births, foretold by prophesy and fathered by their god (Apollo in the form of a serpent). Socrates, Plato and Aristotle were the Greek Trinity. Plato says; at Socrates birth, three magi brought gifts of gold, frankincense and myrrh. [Anacalypsis by Godfrey Higgins vol. 2 page 96]

Plato believed that the eight independently revolving planets will return to the place they started. The planets will revolve in reverse and history will go in reverse. Many modern scientists believe that the universe is expanding like a balloon. It will reach a point where it will stop and start to go in reverse. At that time, time will reverse. This is the time that God consumes the cosmos. The fallen stars will either be refined or consumed in the Heaven-Fire (not Hell-fire) of God's presence. The surviving saints shall transform into sons of God to replace those fallen angels. It is called the Last Day or Eighth Divine Day.

Plato's Timaeus is identified with the god of the Jews (Yahweh). Timaeus is Tem (Atum) of Egypt. Timaeus means Craftsman. Timaeus, Tem, Jehovah and Jesus are all names of the Son of God who created the Cosmos. [Col.1:15-18] Herodotus was called the Father of History as there was no Greek history before the 5th century BC. He says the Egyptians discovered the solar year and invented the twelve signs of the Zodiac. While the Greek philosophers were debating the nature of the universe, the Egyptians had already mapped it out. Herodotus, Aristotle and Plato all agree that the Greeks "borrowed" their knowledge of the stars from Egypt. It took the Europeans 4,000 years to discover the true workings of our solar system. In 1600's, Copernicus rediscovered what the Egyptians already knew ages ago. Eusebius, Plato, and Tacitus all state that the Phoenicians did not claim to be the inventors of the art of writing, but admitted that it was obtained by them from Egypt. It is very likely that the Egyptians created the Greek language for them because they did not know how. See the Rosetta stone written in three languages by an Egyptian scribe. [Signs and Symbols of Primordial Man by Albert Churchward page 43]

The Americans discovered the world was round in 1492 AD, the Greeks in 500 BC, the Egyptians before 3,500 BC! So who's the backward ones? Who still dwells in the dark ages? Certainly not the dark people of the dark continent.

Rene Descartes was a Deist. Deism is the belief that God is entirely apart from the creation. God created the universe then established the natural and supernatural laws. Nature's laws operate automatically without God's interference. The supernatural laws are the universal moral laws that guide man to overcome his animal nature. The spiritual are above the carnal. It was Decartes who said, "I think, therefore, I am." He did not think there was a hellfire. If the fear of hellfire makes you a servant of God, you are really a slave to fear. "God's love knows no fear." We are free to choose life or death. Eternal torment is not one of the choices.

Sigmund Freud was a Jew living in Austria. He was the mentor and foster father of Carl Jung. Sigmund was a warrior in Aryan mythology. He had much in common with King Arthur, including a supernatural sword. Freud based his theories on Greek mythology. a) Oedipus is the desire of the son to kill his father and take his place. b) Thanatos (Death) is the impulse to kill. c) Eros is the sex drive. Venus is the violent side of the libido.

Cosmic Clock - Wheel of Time

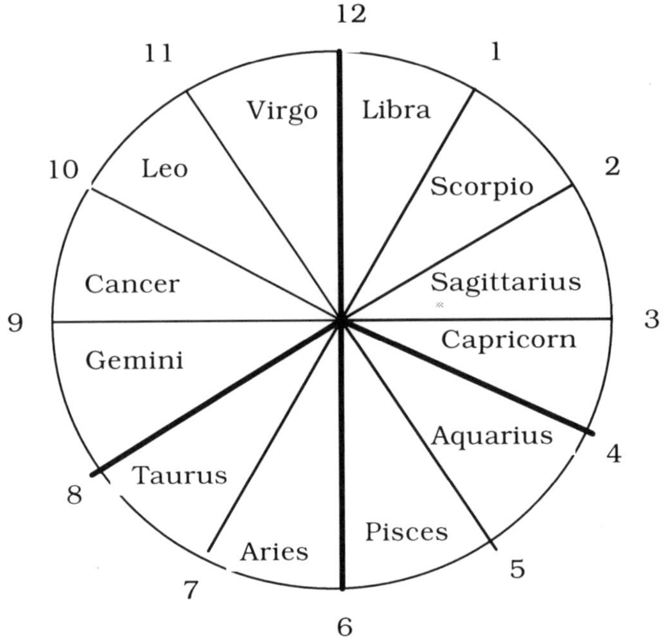

12 signs x 30 degrees = 360 degrees with 3 parts 120 degrees each.

The sign of Pisces = the Peace sign

Pisces is one of twelve Pieces of the Pie.

Jesus is the Prince of Peace born in the age of Pisces.

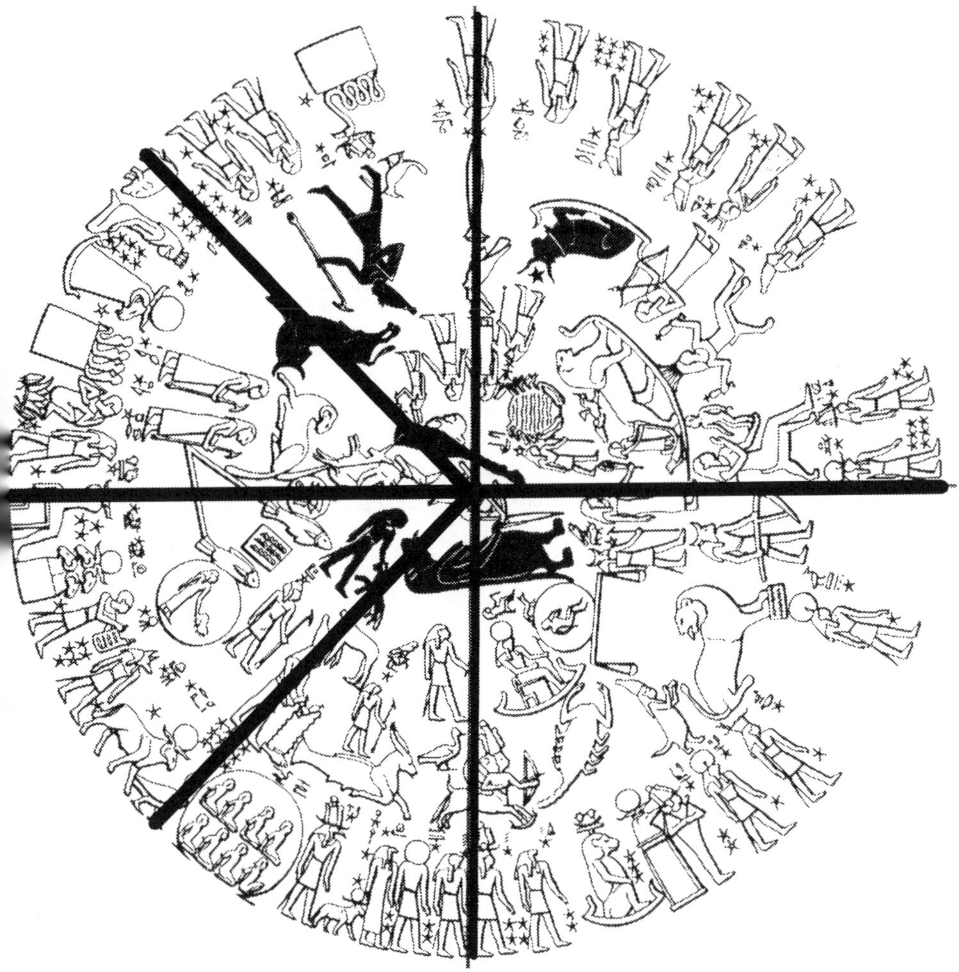

The Egyptians divided the 360 degrees of the Zodiac circle into 12 equal parts (30° each). Each Zodiac age is 30° or 2160 years. Each degree is 72 years. They also divided the Zodiac into halves (180° each), thirds (120°) and quarters (90°). This produced the familiar Peace sign. Since Jesus, Prince of Peace, was born during the age of Pisces - the Pisces sign became the Peace sign. Besides all people born since 150 BC are born under the age or sign of Pisces.

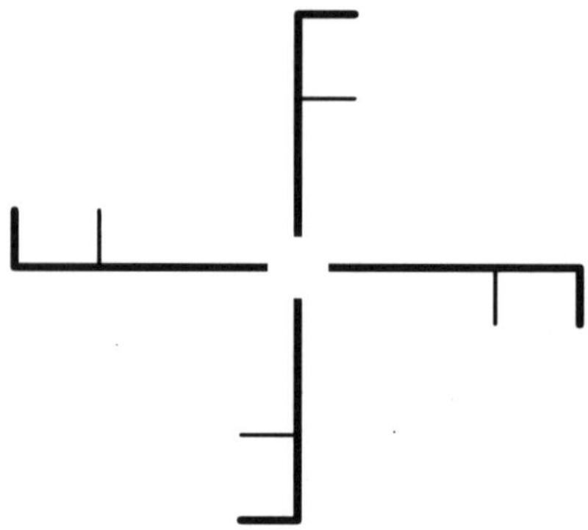

The Swastika represents Ursa Minor the Little Dipper turning around the Pole Star.

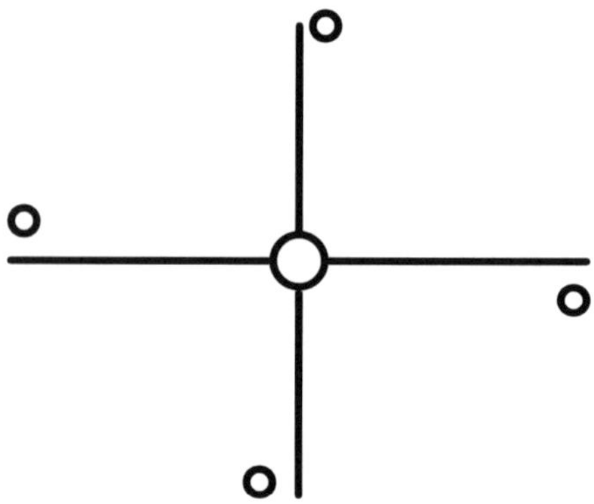

Likewise the earth rotates around the sun. At the summer solstice, the sun reaches its summit on the celestial meridian. The earth, sun and the North Pole star line up in conjunction. This represents the Satanic trinity of Amen, Ra, & Set.

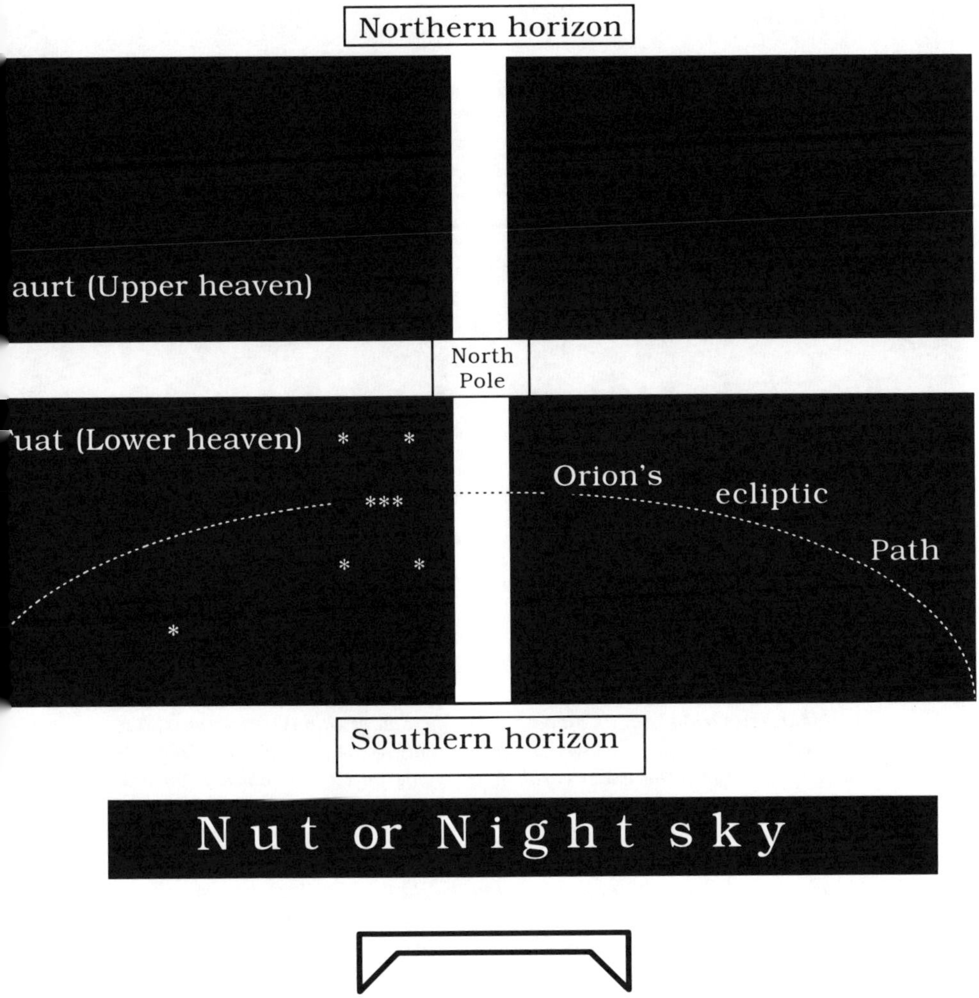
Northern horizon
aurt (Upper heaven)
North Pole
'uat (Lower heaven)
Orion's
ecliptic
Path
Southern horizon
Nut or Night sky

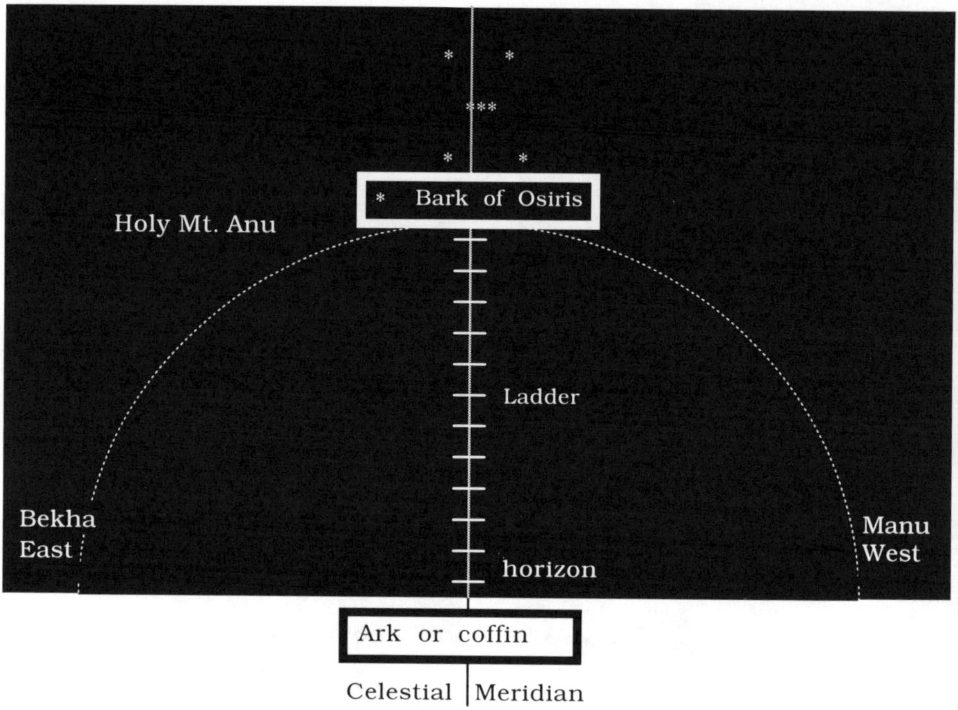

2000 AD; Orion is at its highest point, the Son of God (Osiris-Horus) has ascended Mt. Anu into the heavens. Compare this to the heavenly Mt. Zion. M-anu is the gate into the underworld. It is counterpart to the earthly Amenta. Ark is an anagram of Akar (killed). Bekha is the east gate into the upper world. It is the place of Birth. It takes Osiris 12,960 years to climb the ladder of the celestial meridian. There are 13 rungs, each representing thousand years.

The Ark of Osiris is transformed into the Bark of Osiris so he can sail the sea of space in his space-ship. The Ark is in heaven. [Revelation 11:19] Compare this to Noah's Ark. The animals are the Zodiac cosmic creatures. The Ark landed on Mt. Ararat. Ararat is an anagram of Aarru (with the feminine suffix). Aarru-Hetep is new Jeru-Salem the celestial city of peace. Hetep and Salem both mean Peace. Aarru-Hetep shall descend into Sekhet-Hetep, the garden of God. [Revelation 21:10] The eight in the Ark are; Nut & Geb, Tefnut & Shu, Osiris & Isis, Set & Nephthys (4 pairs).

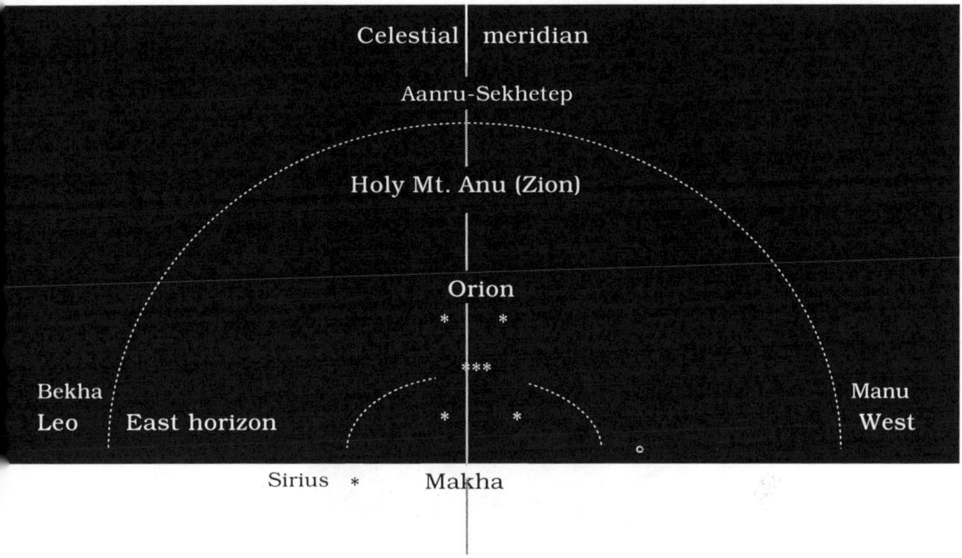

10,500 BC; Orion is at its lowest point, the Son of Man (Osiris) has descended onto the earth. It is changing from the age of Virgo the Virgin to the age of Leo and the Dawn rising of Sirius (Horus). The Virgin is ready to give birth to the Sun of God; Sirius is just below the horizon. Bekha is Bethlehem the birth place of David and Jesus. Aanru-Sek-hetep is Jeru-Salem, the holy city. Compare Mt. Anu to the holy Mt. Zion (Sion). Sion = Sirius-Orion. Si-on is the Son born of On (Anu). Likewise Mt. Sinai is Si-anu. Which is also called Horeb - Mt. of Horus. Makha is the Balance between Bekha (Birth) and Manu (Death).

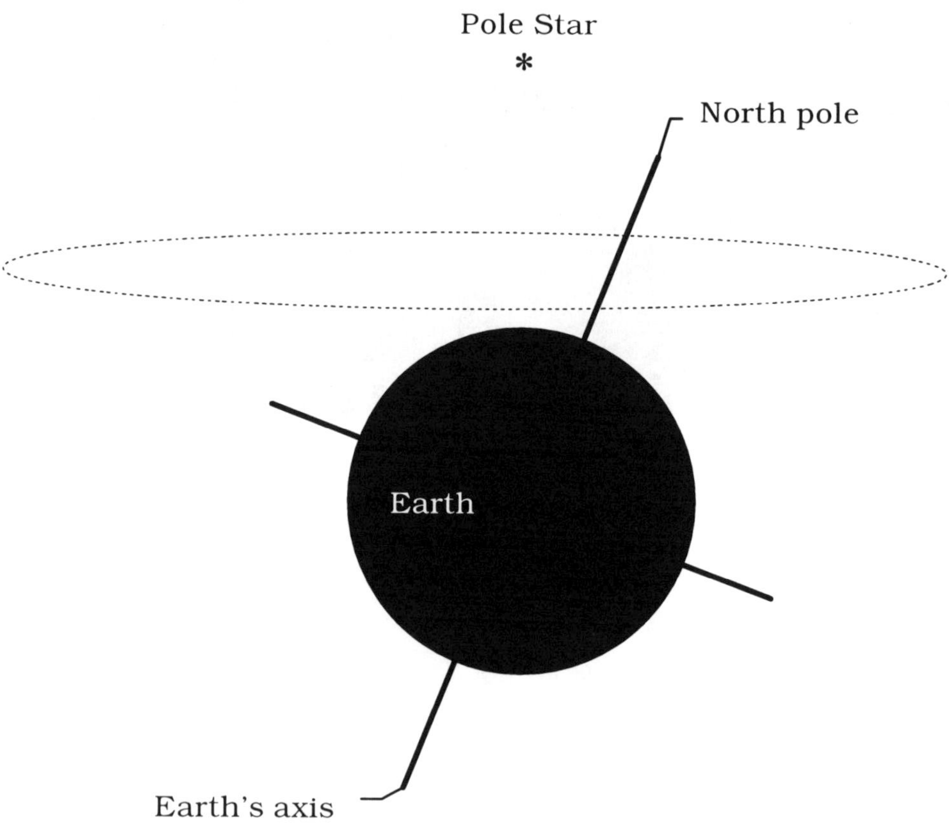

Precession of the Equinoxes is caused by the earth's wobble. Much like a spinning top that has slowed down and started to wobble. The slow down occurred in about 2300 BC, during the change from Taurus to Aries. The shift in the earth's axis caused the Great Flood. The rotation of the earth's wobble takes 25,920 years.

Seven Cakras

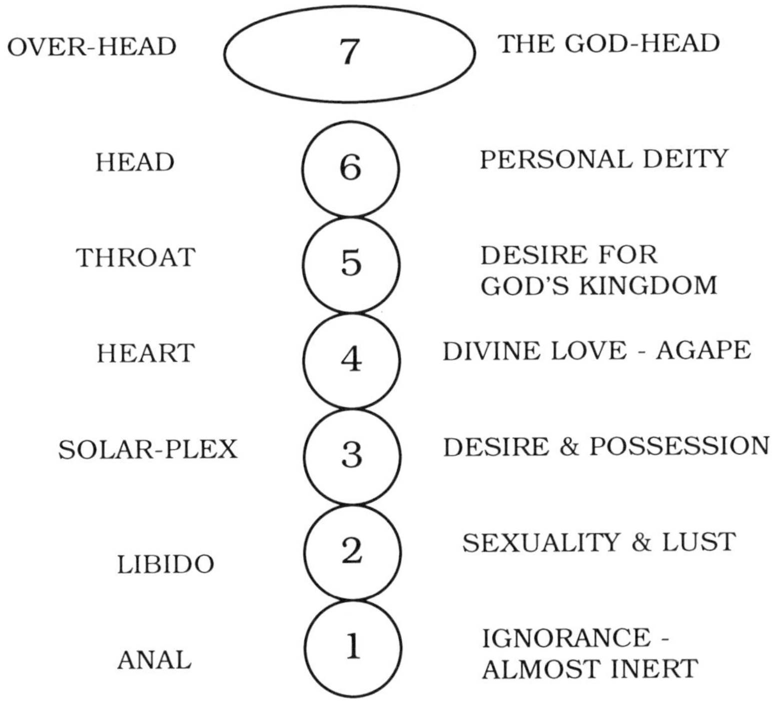

Cakra means Wheel as in Wheel of time. Upon death its time to meet your maker (Brahma). If you are fearful and draw back, you will drop to the 6th cakra. Here you concentrate on your god, whoever it may be (Yahweh, Allah, Vishnu, etc.). Notice your god is placed below Brahma. Brahma, the Father, transcends all thought so think of your god. If you can't hold on to that, you drop to cakra 5. The 5th cakra is the opening of the mouth ritual of Egypt. The 4th cakra is the place of Judgment, where everyone is weighed in the scales. The Judge is Osiris, Lord of Death. Cakra 3 is the love of this world. Those who love this world will not have life in the hereafter. Cakra 5 is the counterpart to 3. Cakra 2, physical lust is the counterpart of cakra 4. The kundilini is a corruption of the cakras. The serpent in the spine is sexual NOT spiritual.

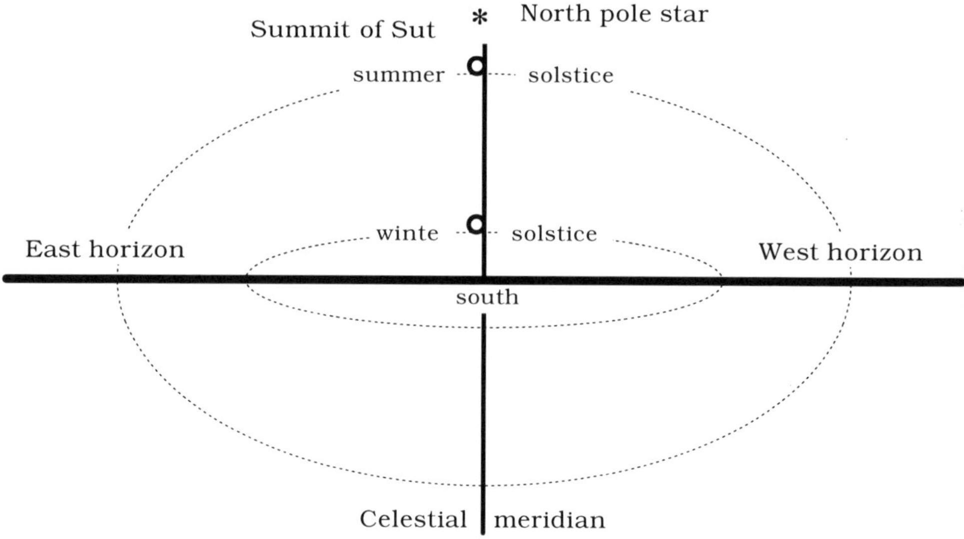

During the winter solstice, the sun has descended to its lowest point on the celestial meridian. It remains there for three days (Dec. 22-25). Solstice means 'to stand still'. When the sun crosses the celestial meridian, it descends into the underworld. When it rises in the east, it is reborn. Then the sun starts to ascend up the celestial meridian. Compare to the sun of God dying, descending for three days, resurrecting, and ascending to heaven.

During the summer solstice (June 21st), the sun culminates with the North Pole star. This is the Solar-Polar conjunction. The Polar star, Polaris, was the Dog star of the Egyptians. The summer solstice became known as the Dog Days of Summer. This is what Caesar Constantine saw when he looked up to the mid-day sun and saw a cross. The Egyptians call this the Apet (Apex). The Dog or Wolf is Apuat. Ironically, the wild dog or wolf is the symbol of the Romans. The she-wolf nursed the twins Romulus and Remus.

During the summer, Santa lives at the North Pole star. In the winter (Dec. 24th at sunset). Santa comes down to earth. Rudolph's red nose is the moonlight.

The sailors who embark in the solar bark shall end up in unexpected destination. They become carrion for the carnivorous Polar Bear. Ursa Major. The lost sailors sail into the Lake of fire. The ones saved sail into the River of Life. [Revelation 20:13-15]

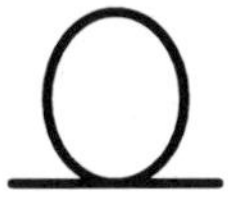

Eternity

Death & Rebirth
life everlasting

Infinity

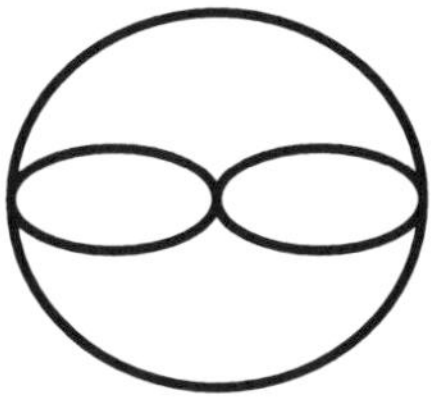

The symbol of eternity
within the world.

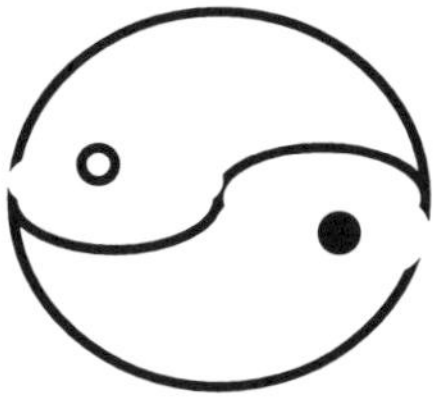

Yang = Life, Light, Love
Yin = Death, Darkness, Hatred

Universal symbol of Death

Death destroyed
no more death

No - Stop - End

Compare Pisces or Fishes to the
sign for Infinity and Eternity

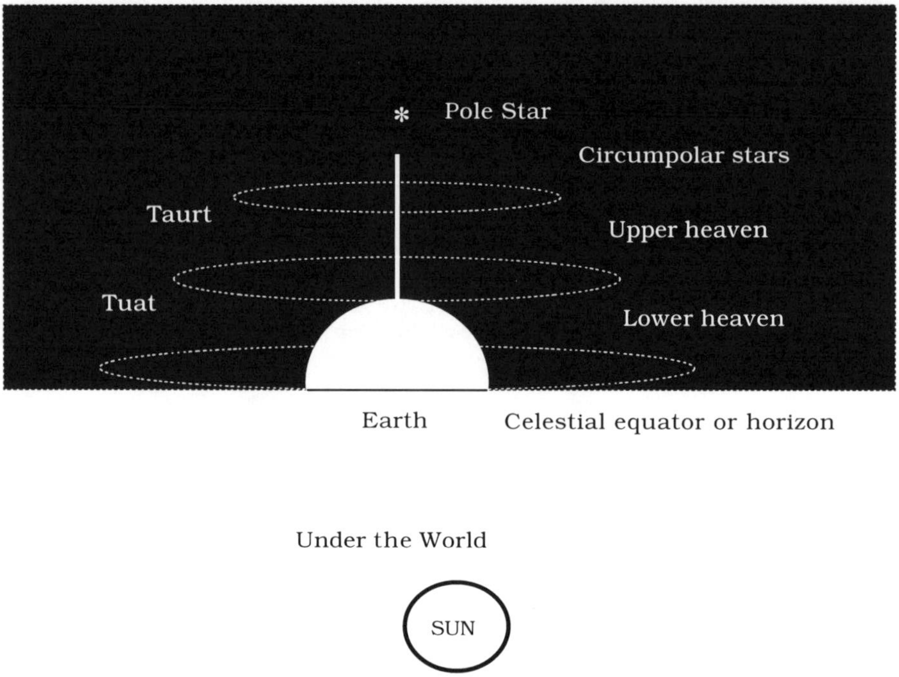

Tuat is the lower heaven where Orion cross the sea of space. Taurt is the upper heaven where the circumpolar stars are. They are called the imperishable stars because they never set.

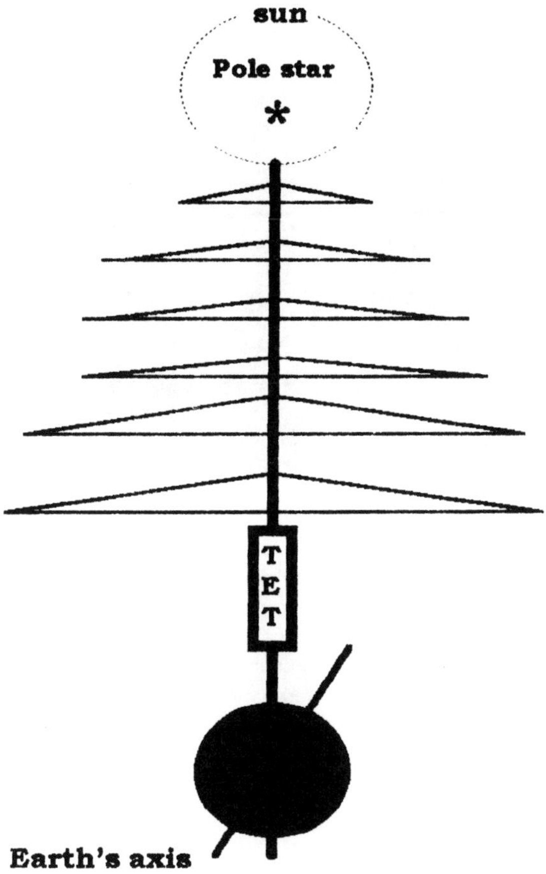

Sut is the South Pole star - born from the celestial Pole or Shittim Tree. Sut = South = Set = Sit = Shit. The sun and pole star are in alignment at the summer solstice. This is the nativity of the X-mas tree with the star on summit. Satan is the fallen star and fallen angel. His mother is the Ammit beast, Urt. This is the Asherah tree that crucified Christ. The Tet 'Pillar' is Osiris' coffin in the tree. Both Mayan and Viking mythologies speak of the World Tree that reaches into the sky and into the underworld. The Indians called the celestial pole - the hitching post of the sun. This link keeps the sun turning around the earth or the earth turning around the sun (depending on your perspective). This central point is also called the navel of Mother earth.
Likewise, the Little Dipper is hitched to the Mooring post to keep it on track. As the pole star, Polaris, was considered the most stable thing in the universe.

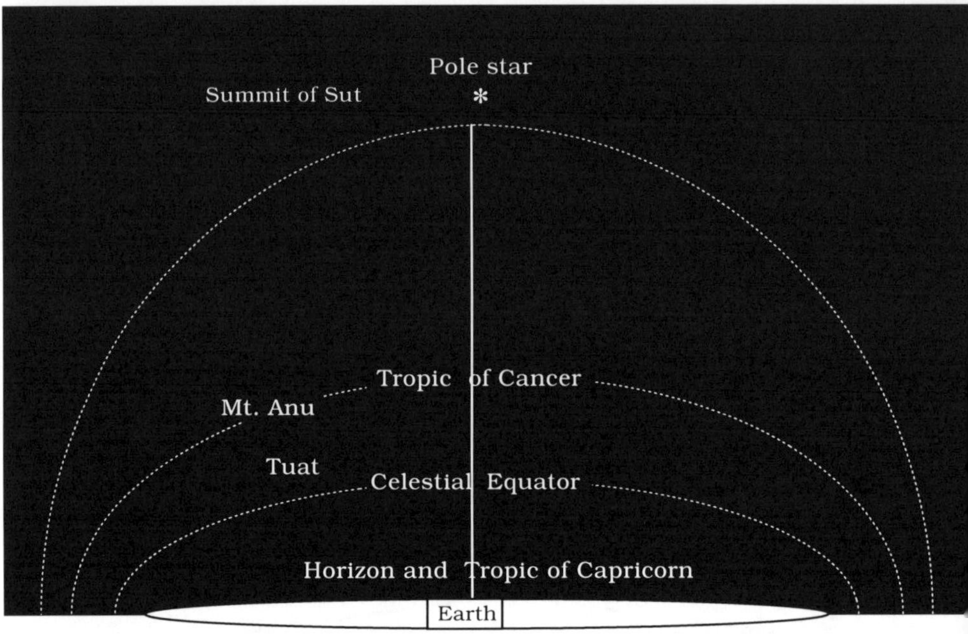

The Tropic of Cancer is 23.4° 30' north of the equator. The Tropic of Capricorn is 23.4° 30' south of the equator. Since the earth is tilted 23.4°, the horizon is level with the Tropic of Capricorn. From the horizon to the Tropic of Cancer is the Tuat. It is about 45 degrees. From there to the Pole star is Taurt. It also is about 45 degrees. From the horizon to the Pole star is 90 degrees.

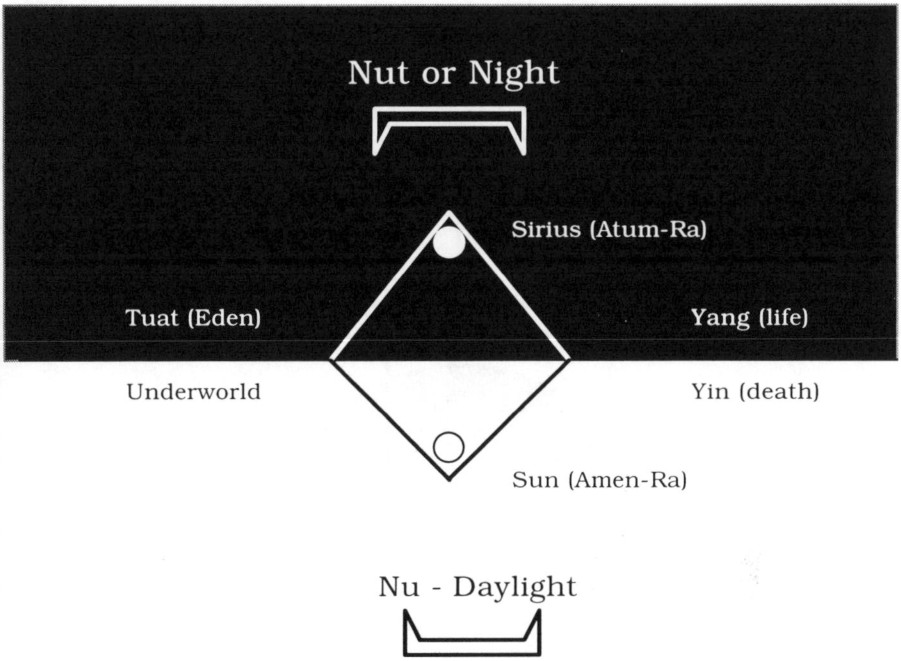
Nut or Night
Sirius (Atum-Ra)
Tuat (Eden)
Yang (life)
Underworld
Yin (death)
Sun (Amen-Ra)
Nu - Daylight

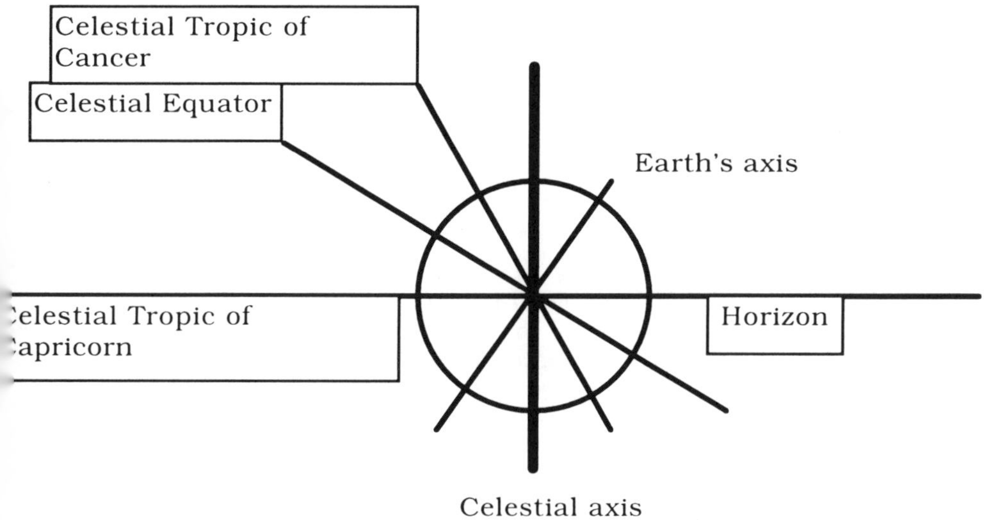
Celestial Tropic of Cancer
Celestial Equator
Earth's axis
elestial Tropic of
apricorn
Horizon
Celestial axis

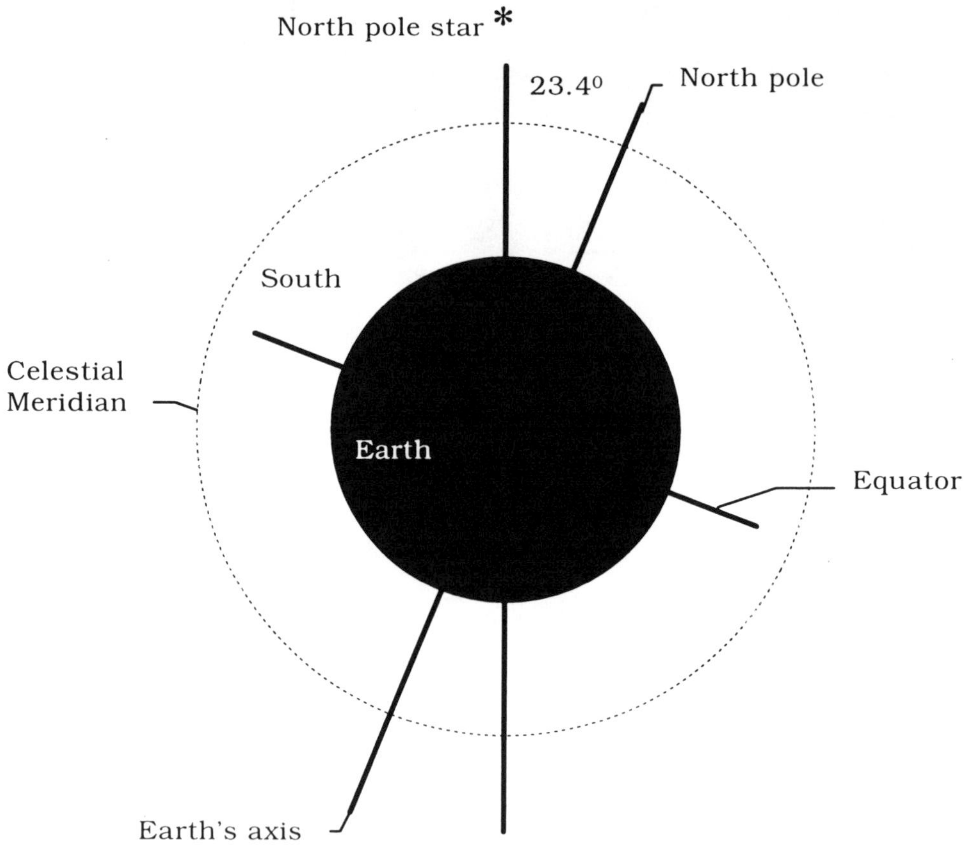

The eath's axis is 23.4 degrees off true north. The Tropic of Cancer is 23.4 degrees north of the equator. The Tropic of Capricorn is 23.4 degrees south of the equator.

The North Pole star the Egyptians called the South Pole star or the star of Sut (Set). Sut is the abbreviation for South. They depicted the Dog star (Upaut of Apt) in the place of our Ursa Minor. This is the antithesis of the Dog star. Sirius in Anu. It was the Europeans who 'turned the world upside down' so they would be on top of the world. In doing so, they would appear to be heavenly appointed to rule over the world. Our maps to this day put Europe at the top even though the earth is flowing in space with no apparent up or down.

The celestial meridian goes around the earth; north and south. The celestial pole goes through the earth; north and south.

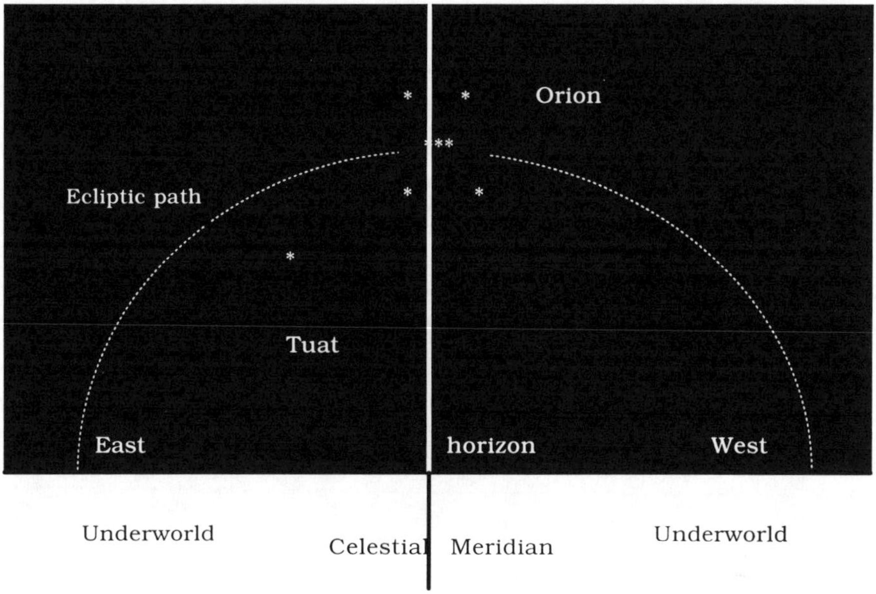

When Orion crosses the Celestial Meridian, it is Christ Crucified in the heavens. He then descends into the underworld. The two crooks on crosses beside him are places where the Ecliptic line crosses the two horizons (equinoxes). One is descending into the underworld, the other is ascending into paradise (Tuat). The celestial scale is kept in balance. Osiris shall return to Judge us mortals.

Sirius following Orion is the Funeral Procession. Sirius represents Isis, Nephthys, Anubis and Horus. Just as Mother Mary, Mary Magdalene, Joseph, and John were the Paul bearers at Jesus' funeral.

God's domain the 1st heaven
Egyptian; home of Patah (the Father).

God the Father's domain is the 1st heaven beyond outer space. The 2nd heaven is the domain of the sons of God (stars). The 3rd heaven is the Earth's Atmosphere (Atum's sphere). When God comes to earth. He shall swallow up the darkness of outer space. The glory of God will be our new heaven. Darkness will be no more.

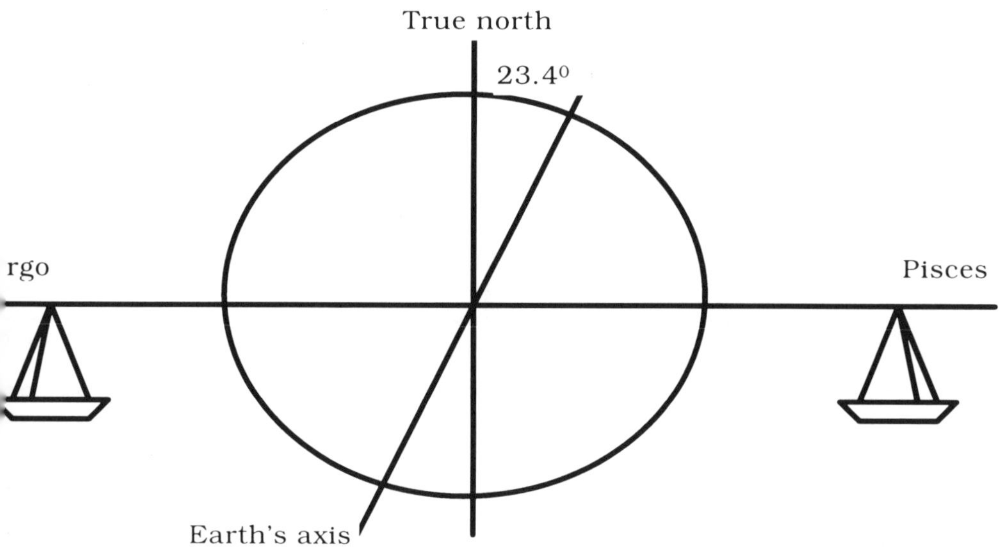

Atum-Horus was the first-begotten Son of God during the age of Virgo. Jesus was the first-begotten Son of God during the age of Pisces. They are one and the same; separated by 12,000 years which is one-half of the precession cycle. Horus of the two Horizons means he is Lord of the Earth.

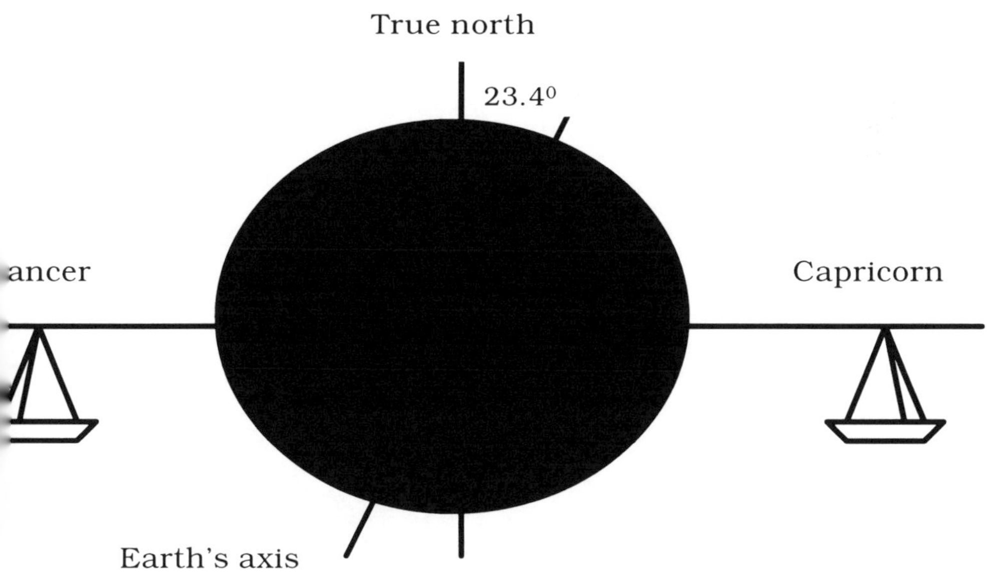

When Cancer ascends. Capricorn descends. Cancer the Scarab (not crab) represents Osiris-Jesus sitting on the great white judgment throne. The one sitting on the Mercy seat, between the two cherubs (scarabs), shall separate the lambs of God from the goats of Capricorn. [Matthew 25:31-34,46].

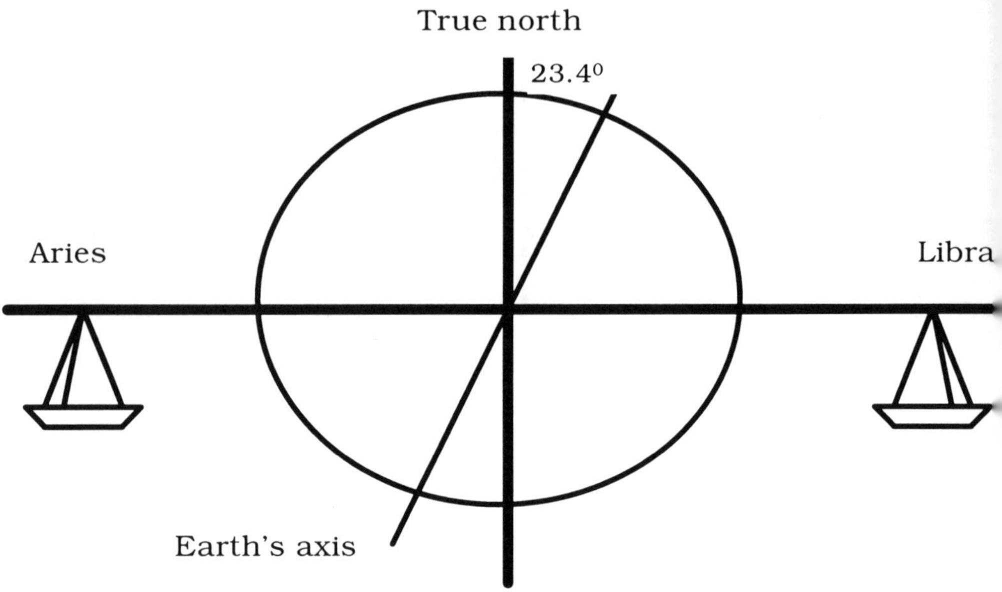

When Aries was ascending in 2300 BC, Libra was descending. The earth was thrown off balance and the Great Flood occurred.

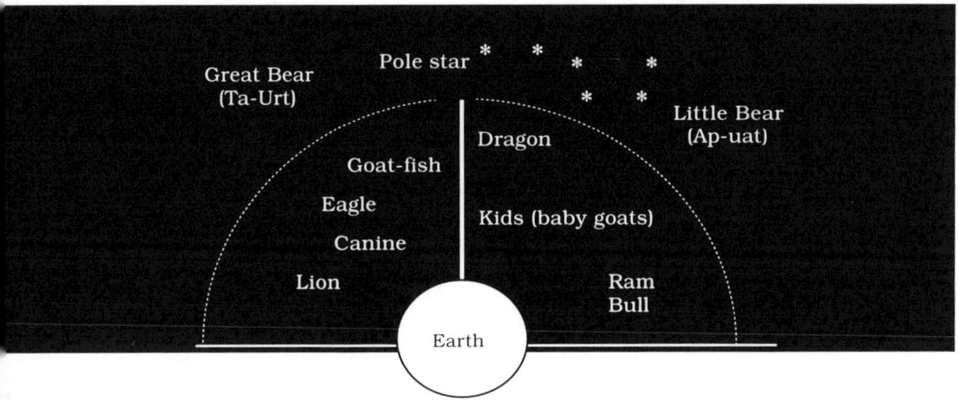

THE CIRCUS OF THE STARS

The ancients saw the Zodiac as a mount. The root of Zodiac is zoo or circuit of animals. The Great Mother and her flocks were on the summit. The celestial pole represents the Asherah (world tree). The Lord says the goats of Baal go to the top of the mount, while the lambs of God remain in the low lands. The goats attempt to ascend to heaven while the lambs remain down to earth.

At the summit is Ammit (Urt or Ursa Major). This is the summit of Sut (Ursa Minor). The Egyptians depicted it as the Dog star (Up-uat or Apuat). Apt is the abbreviation for Apuat.

The Christmas candy cane is Santa's crook, as shepherd of the kids (baby goats). The stripped cane is the celestial May pole turning round and round. Ursa Minor is the crooked handle of the Kane.

The corrupt Theban version of Noah's Ark says that Mt. Ararat is Mt. Rerit; the Great mother as a sow or Mt. Rurt as a female hippopotamus. Rerit = Lilith in Hebrew. It is the primordial mount from which the evil sun was born. When the Pole star Alpha Draco shifted to Polaris (2500 BC), Set was thrown off his mountain into the sea of space. The eight saved, from the sea of space, are the seven stars of Ursa Major and the Pole star of Set. The two unclean animals aboard Noah's ark are; Rerit the sow and her son Baal the boar. The celestial pole is called the mooring post (menat). The Ark is Ursa Minor tied to this celestial tree of Great Mother (Hathor). Ararat is the great harlot that sits on many waters. Arat is Egyptian for Uraeus (the serpent in the tree or cobra crown). Ark in Hebrew is TBS or Thebes. 'No' is the ancient Egyptian name of Thebes and is the root of Noah. Moses was obviously influenced by the corrupt version. The same Moses who was saved in an ark and raised by an Egyptian woman!

[Ancient Egypt the Light of the World by Gerald Massey - volume 2]

Originally we were in a binary solar system. Sirius in the Lower hemisphere and Ra in the Upper hemisphere.

The Bark of Osiris
Osiris defeats Taurus the bull. Osiris travels through the ages of Virgo the Virgin, Leo the Lion, Libra the Scales and Pisces the fishes. Behind Osiris is Madonna and Child (Isis and Horus). Behind them is Nephthys the twin sister of Isis. Together they represent the star Sirius following Orion (Osiris). Above is Horus the Hawk watching over them. Below is the Apophis serpent or the deep, dark sea of space. Osiris rules over Land and Sea. Just as Jesus in Revelation 10:1.

The Egyptians sailed the seven seas thousands of years before anyone else. Two 250 foot ships were found next to the pyramids at Giza. The same size as Columbus' ship. In fact, the Viking ship is a copy of the ships of the Nile that sail in shallow waters.

The Sata serpent has human legs, just like the one in the garden of Eden. The subtle serpent seduced Eve. Subtle and subtile both refer to a meta-physical being. The serpent sheds its skin (flesh). Sata is that spirit-being know as Satan. In Egypt, Sata is an aspect of Set.

Ta-Urt; a.k.a. Hathor, Mut, Nut, Ammit, Rerit, etc. Ta-Urt is the darkside of Mother Nature (Ma Neter). The circumpolar stars are hers (Ursa Major and Draco). She wears the horns of Hathor the heavenly heifer. She is a composite beast (hippopotamus, lion and crocodile) like the Ammit beast (devourer of the dead). The Bible calls her the Behemoth (Great Beast). She touches the Mooring Post which is the celestial North Pole. The Europeans call it the May Pole in honor of Maya, the Hindu Great Mother. The Greeks called her Artemis (Urt-emis). As Am-Semen she is the Great Matrix or primordial mound. As Rerit she is the celestial sow. As Sekhmet, she is the lioness. As Apt, she is the Apap serpent or Levithan (Draco). This explains why dragons have crocodile heads

The Zodiac

The stars are divided into different 'nomes' or regions. From this Egyptian word we get astro-nome (astronomy) which means star-naming. Astrology means Study of the stars. Egypt was also divided into nomes.

The Tuat is the lower heavens which represents Lower Egypt. The Taurt is the upper heavens which represent Upper Egypt. The circumpolar stars (Ursa Major, Ursa Minor and Draco) are the region called Apt. Apt means four corners. Apt is the abbreviation for Apartment or houses of the Zodiac. It is the home of Ta-Urt the great Mother and her evil suns. The North Pole star is the Dog star of Set. Taur-us the bull is the mate of Taurt the cow. The 'us' is a Roman suffix equal to the Egyptian 'ur' which means great. The 't' at the end of Taurt makes it feminine.

Anu in the heavens is the area of Sirius. Anu on earth was called Heliopolis (City of Horus, Sun of God) by the Greeks. Hathor means House of Horus and refers to Sirius in the House of Taurus.

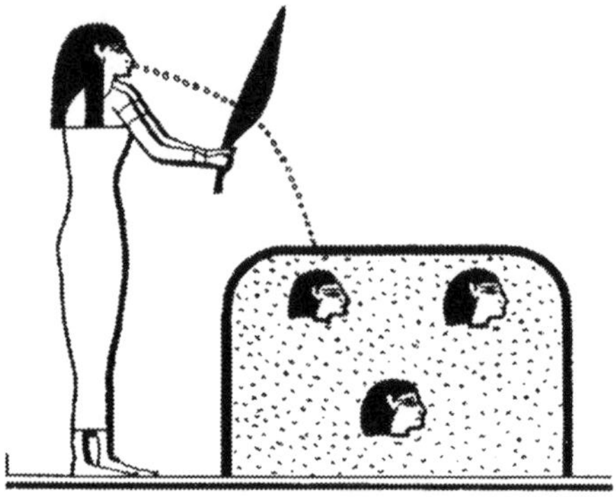

The damned immersed in the pits of fire up to their necks.

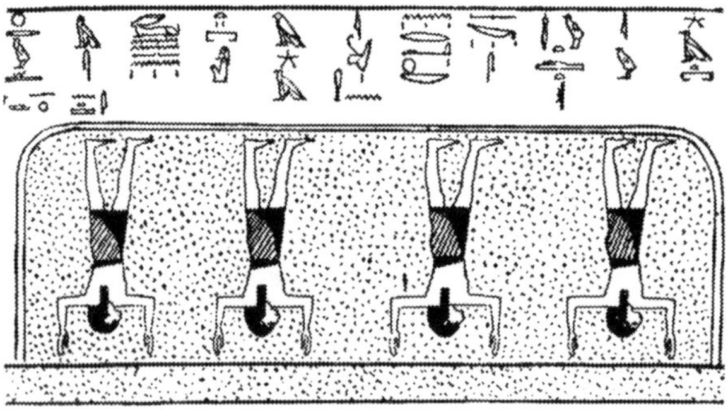

The damned immersed head downwards in the pits of fire.

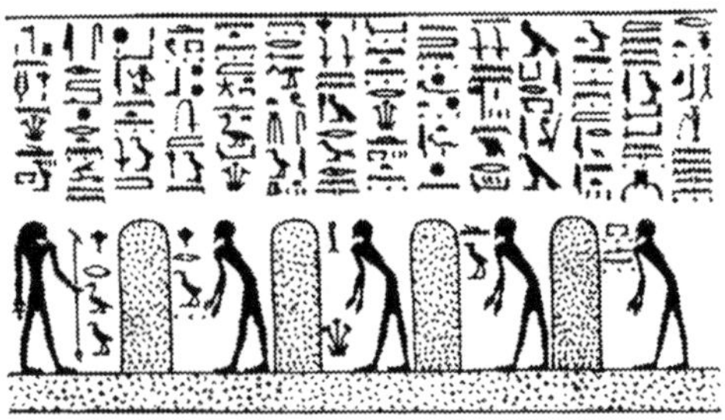

The pits of fire in which the damned are cremated.

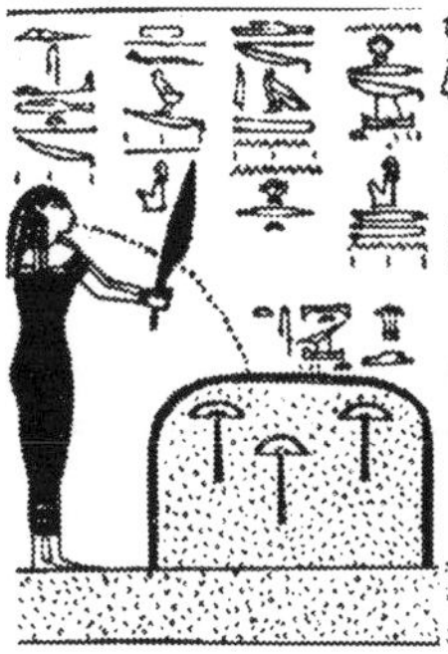

The shadows of the damned being burned in the pits of fire.

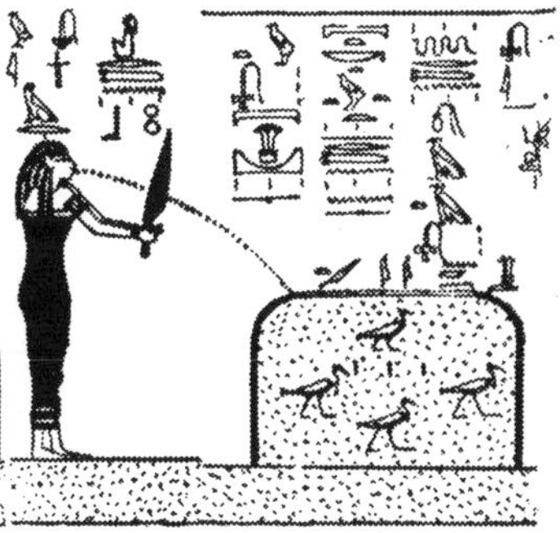

The souls of the damned being burned in the pits of fire.

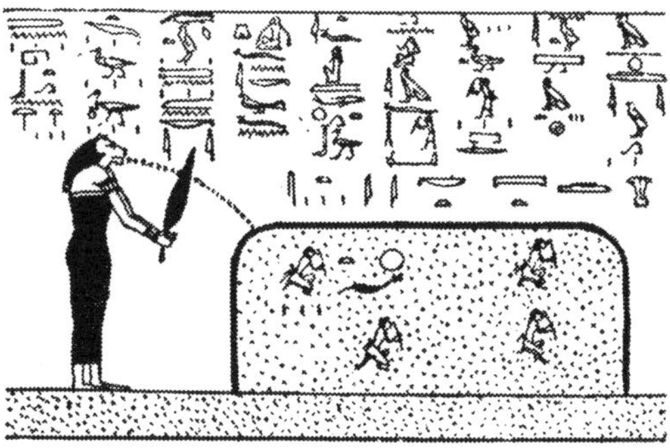

The bodies of the damned being burned in the pits of fire.

The Lake of fire.
Everyone experiences the cycle of life to death within Ma Neter (Mother Nature). But those found guilty on Judgment day, are condemned to suffer the second death in the Lake of fire. The brain, body, shadow, spirit, and all the soul of the infidel is incinerated in the presence of God. God is the all consuming Lake of fire. Nothing is left to suffer or to cause others to suffer. The Bible says only Satan and his fallen angels will torment in the flames [Revelation 20:10]

The Roman Pantheon

The Romans got most of their mythology from Greece. As Romans are half-breeds. They are half original European like the Greeks and half Indo-European (Aryans / Assyrians). According to the Aeneas' legend, the Trojans united with the Latins, producing the Roman race. Troy was a city in the Hittite empire (modern Turkey in Asia Minor). Zeus promised Aeneas to be the father of the Great Roman empire just as the Lord promised Abraham to be father of many nations. Yet it was named after Romulus, just as Israel was name after Jacob. Roman history doesn't start until 734 BC when Romulus was born.

The Romans worshipped the Pantheon of Planets which were ruled over by the Sun. They believed the planets controlled their fates which they called Astrology. Astrology; because they thought the planets were astros or stars (suns of God). To them: Jupiter was Zeus, Uranus was Uranos, Neptune was Poseidon, Pluto was Hades, Mars was Ares, Venus was Aphrodite, Mercury was Hermes, Saturn was Kronos, the Sun was Apollo and the Moon was Diana. In front of the Pantheon is an obelisk to the sun-god. The question is: Who decided that certain planets ruled over certain attributes? Was it divinely inspired? The Romans calculated the movements of Mars to predict the best day to wage war. The Mayans used the helical rising of Venus for the same reason. This pseudo-astrology was a perversion of Egyptian astrology; the history of the heavens. These are the followers of Ra in his solar bark or chariot of fire sailing through the heavens.

The Roman Circus or hippodrome had a pyramid of the sun in the center with altars of Saturn, Jupiter, Mars, Venus, Mercury and the moon as satellites. Seven circuits in all. The word Hippodrome may come from the Egyptian Urt (Ursa Major), the composite beast (hippo, crocodile, lion) that turns around her son, the North Pole star. Just as the planets make a circuit around the sun. Compare this to the MesoAmericans.

Under the Roman rule, Zeus became Jupiter Lucetius, the light-bearer. The Word of God says the light-bearer is Lucifer (the Devil). [Isaiah 14:12] Sol is the sungod. From which we get the word solar and Sunday. Sol was honored on the two solstices. The winter solstice (Dec.22th) and the summer solstice (June 22nd). From here we get the June bride betrothed to Sol the sun-god. She is called Juno. She is the body of believers who live in sin with Zeus-Amen (Satan). Also known as Helio. The statute at Rhodes, one of the seven great wonders according to Alexender the Greek, is of Helio. He was the proto-type for the statue of Liberty, crowned with a sun-burst. The Romans, who created the word, Romance, loved their goddess. If you find solace in Sol, you are seeking the spurious Comforter; the spirit of error. [1 John 4:1-6]

Janus is the two-faced or double minded or bisexual deity. Janus = Juno, mate of Jupiter. Juno is queen of heaven and Janus is queer of heaven. Janus is the Door that swings both ways. Janus (Anus) is the gay god of fairies and fairy-tales. The bisexual Romans produced a god in their own image! At the Olympics, the contestants competed naked as foreplay for fornication following the games. No females were allowed. From Janus, we got the month January, the beginning and end (anal) of the annual year. The Janissaries (Janus-Aries) were homosexual Christian warriors. They were slaves forced to convert to Islam and fight in the army of the Ottoman Empire. Aries, of course, is the god of war.

Mars is the red planet that the Roman's saw as a Bull who "sees red". Mars is the Lord of War of the Arian dog soldiers, who could only be seduced by Venus the symbol of lust. Sex and Violence go hand and hand. This horny red bull with a pointed tail was called Min in Egypt and Minotaur at Crete. Min's mate is Hathor the cow. The Roman's honored Mars more than any other because they loved conquering both the males and females. The Roman's were bisexuals. It was said that Julius Caesar was the wife to every husband and the husband to every wife. And that's no fairy's tail. He was a homosexual, homicidal maniac. The ritual of athletic competition (like the Olympics) was in honor of blood-red Mars to prepare the young men for war. Men competed naked as foreplay to sex. Women were not allowed. This "queer" behavior explains the sexual perversions of the Roman Catholic priests.

The Minotaur is half man and half bull. Minotaurus means Moon + Taurus. Taurus is the sign of the Bull. The bulls horns are the shape of the crescent moon. They show it has power or potency. This is where we get our word "horny". Romancing in the moon light. In the red light district. The bull is Baal the Devil. The Devil has two horns and a tail. He speaks like the red, blood thirsty dragon. [Rev.13:11] This reptile is cold blooded. Mino comes from Min (Amin, Amen) the evil sun god.

Valentine's Day

Diana is the moon-goddess and mistress of Apollo the sun-god. She is also his sister. She is the hunter, as the moon is constantly chasing after the sun. The Greeks called her Artemis, mother of all living. Which is the name of Eve. Eve for evening, as she is the lesser light of the moon at night. With its 29 day menstrual cycle. The color of Valentine's day is red like the flow of blood. To bleed = to breed. The planets are considered female and the stars are male. The suns are sons. When Eve mated with the evil sun of God, she became his consort, the moon goddess. Part of her curse is to desire for a man and the suffering of child birth. [Gen.3:16]

Romance is a Roman word for lust and passion. Venus is the sex goddess and her son Cupid is the match maker. She is the harlot, deva, nymph. Valentine's day (Valentinus) was created in honor of Venus. Men give red roses to their lovers in honor of Eros, the Greek god of love. EROS is an anagram of ROSE. The Romans celebrated Lupercalia, the fertility festival, on February 15th. In Babylon, she is called Ishtar, the deva of sex and war. As men go to war for the women they lust for. Easter is the holiday created for her. The bunnies represent sexual reproduction. The colored Easter Eggs represent fertility and variety. "The more the merrier." Easter always falls on Sunday in honor of the sun-god. Sunday sunrise services is worshipping the sun god. (Ra the Easter Rabbit). April Fool's day was originally the Festival of Fools in honor of Venus. It's when the love sick got spring fever and made fools of themselves. May was the month of the Maiden Maia (mother earth) which was converted to the month of Mary the virgin mother. No marriages were allowed at this time. By June, the females are pregnant. Therefore they marry in honor the Roman goddess of fertility, Juno (Hera).

The Romans, like the Babylonians, call Venus the Morning star. Actually, it is not a star, but a barren planet. Their symbol of sexuality is sterile. The true bright Morning star is Sirius; representing Mother with Child. The pattern produced by Venus' orbit is a pentacle or Satanic star. Which is the logo for the "Movie stars" and "sex goddesses" of TV land. Sex and violence makes money in the show business. Satan is prince of the power of the air waves and television is one of the mediums through which he works. Venus is the only planet that rotates contrary to all the others. Representing those going contrary to God's laws. Repent means to change your wrong ways and go in the right direction, guided by God.

The Passion of Beltine

Beltine means fire to Baal. The Europeans worshipped Baal and his mate by building Bonfires from May-June (summer solstice). Bonfires comes from bone fires. As after the sacrifice was passed through the fire, nothing was left but the bones. The kids of Baal (i.e. Pan the goat) climbed up a hill to build a fire. These are the high places where the Canaanites and Jews burned their children in fire to Baal and Ashtorah, his mother and mate. They bake hot-cross buns to the queen of heaven as her sun crosses the celestial summit aligning with the North Pole star. [Jeremiah 7:9,18,31-34 2 Kings 23:4-11]

Later they combined Baltine and Venus and got Valentine. The passionate fire of lust and orgies took the place of sacrifice. The females go in heat in the spring. The animal instincts rule the beastly behavior. Those so called animal instincts are evil spirits causing people to act like the Beast. During the Dark ages, Christendumb burned fire to Baal. The fuel of their hell-fires was the sacred scriptures of the world, including; the Hebrew Bible and the original Gospels. Even today they burn the Yule log in honor of the dying sun on Dec.25th. The evergreen Fir (Fire) tree represents the sun burning out at the winter solstice (waning of the Yule tide). The X-mas tree is lit-up as if burning. It is the Tree of Carnal knowledge giving artificial illumination. [2 Cor.11:13-15 Genesis 3:5] [Deceptions and Myths of the Bible by Lloyd M. Graham page 444]

May day is the time of May-poles and May-trees. These phallic symbols where set up in honor of Sathan, prince of Hel and Bess, queen of the Wood at Nemi (i.e. the Asherah/groves). Diana in the Arician grove is Ana in Africa. Nem is the Upper Egyptian water-neter (god?) that feds the garden. Nim-bus means rain-cloud. Bes is the Egyptian Eros or Cupid, deity of fertility. The drunken orgy lasted the month up to Whitesunday. The evergreen trees were burned at Beltine. [The Golden Bough by James George Frazer] This is another obvious corruption of the deceased Osiris in the tree/pillar during the spring equinox. They make-merry that Seth-aman assassinated Osiris, who exposed their evils. Compare to the Passion of Christ at the spring equinox. The Lord who exposed the evils of the Jews! Nimbus is also the aura of light or cloud of glory surrounding the Lord. Beltine coincides with the Jewish Shavuoth (Shivah) when 'tongues of fire sat upon each one of them'. [Acts 2:3] Shiva is god of fire and the Destroyer. Pentecost means 50, 5 is Shatan's number and the pentacle is Satan's star.

The celestial May-Pole is the sun reaching its summit at the North Pole star at the Summer solstice. The circumpolar stars circle around this spurious dog star (Ap-uat), antithesis of Sirius. Ursa Minor forms the Apt-cross or swastika used by the Romans and Germans.

May is the 5th month. On 5-5-2000 AD, the astronomers predict there will be a 5 planet conjunction; Venus, Mars, Earth, Jupiter, Saturn. This alignment will have a strong gravitational pull on the earth which may cause major catastrophes like earthquakes and tidal waves. The Great Plagues precede the coming of the antichrist (during the summer solstice). Followed by Armageddon and finally the Lord's coming. [Matthew 24:3-31]

Romulus and Remus-sibling rivals

The Romans worshipped their Pantheon of gods on their high day Dec.25 birthday of the sun-god Sol. Legend says that Mars Silvanus (Mars of the Woods), god of grain, mated with Rhea Silvia, a vestal virgin and daughter of King Numitor. Compare to Osiris, god of the Seed, Horus. Sil = Sir (i.e. Osiris). She gave birth to Romulus and Remus on Dec.25th in the year 753 BC. This was the age of Ares. {M-ars is Ares with the M prefix.} The twins were placed in a container and cast into the river by the usurper, Amulius. They were rescued by a she-wolf or wild dog and taken to a cave at Palatine Hill where she suckled them until they were found by shepherds. Then wise men came to worship and bring them gifts. Romulus later became founder of Rome and restored Numitor to his throne. Then Romulus, the son of god, mated with the Sabeans to produce the Romans. Sabeans is the Egyptian Seb (Earth) and Sebean (Earthlings) . The Sebeu fiends helped Set to murder Osiris.

At death, Romulus was venerated as Quirinus (Osiris). His evil brother was Bacchus the sun-god and antichrist. Quirinus, like Osiris, was torn to pieces. He then ascended to heaven and eclipsed or darkened the sun, like Jesus. Quirinus is the same name as his father Mars Quirinus (Horus Osiris). Therefore, Mars incarnated as Romulus and then after his death, he return to being Mars-pater, the son of God. The month of Mars is March, the spring equinox. His festivals are the full moon of March and October. This is a corruption of the Horus-Osiris-Horus story. Mardi Gras is a corruption of Mars Gradivus (to march or parade). The followers of Osiris did a pantomime of his murder every March. Keep in mind that Mars/Ares is the evil brother of Herakles (Horus). Mars is the Great Impostor pretending to be Horus!

In Egypt, the celestial river is the Milky Way. Osiris was placed in a vessel and cast into the Nile by the usurper, Set. The female dog who saved Romulus and Remus would be the Dog star. To the Romans, the star Sirius is the Dog star in the constellation of Canis Major (Great Canine). The Shepherd would be Orion and his companion Dog. This would symbolize that the Romans were followers of Osiris. The twin sisters sharing the star Sirius are Isis and Nephthys. Osiris-Orion and Isis-Sirius produced Horus. Osiris-Orion and Nephthys-Sirius produced the dog-headed Anubis. In Egypt, the heavens is sometimes pictured as a cow with its body lined with stars. The cow's milk feeds the earthlings. In Greek mythology Rhea is sister and wife of Chronus, the parents of the gods of Olympus. Rhea would be the counterpart of Hathor the cow deity. Rhea would be the virgin mother nature who nurses the demi-gods Romulus and Remus. In Egypt, Rem (Re Amen) is the evil eye in the sky or evil sun god. The Romans even built a temple to Isis in the Field of Mars.

Now compare this with the Roman Catholic version of the nativity that says Christ was born in Palestine (Palatine) in a cave or stable with cows, other animals, and shepherds! Could this be the unconscious reason mothers give their babies cow's milk in place of their own? In Egypt, Hathor, the holy cow, is the wet-nurse of the divine child. The cave represents the womb of mother earth; the primordial mound from which the Sun of God was born. Jesus is Hey-seus and Hesus is Horus. Obviously, they cribbed (plagiarized) the nativity scenario from Egypt.

Romulus yokes two bulls and plows a furrow for a border. Just as Osiris yoked the Taurus bull and Jason yoked the bulls of Ares. Romulus kills Remus when he crossed the border between them and become the first of seven legendary kings of Rome. In Egypt, Set killed his brother Osiris. Osiris resurrects as Horus and takes back the throne of Lower Egypt while Set rules Upper Egypt. When Horus returns he will cross the border and take all Egypt. In Egypt, seven divine Pharaohs ruled; Atum, Shu, Geb, Osiris, Set, Horus, and Thoth. [New Larousse Encyclopaedia of Mythology] Thoth represents the Holy Spirit or Comforter that has been present ever since Horus-Jesus ascended to heaven. The story is the same, but the deviant Romans have reversed the roles to make Romulus play the part of the hero and savior.

Romulus was taken to heaven in a chariot of fire just like Mithra. The chariot of fire is the evil sun of god. Elijah was taken up by a whirlwind (Holy Spirit) while this chariot of fire kept Elisha from entering God's kingdom in heaven. [2 Kings 2:1-11 Genesis 3:24] Later, King Josiah destroyed the idols of the chariots of fire dedicated to the evil sun god Baal, which Solomon (Sol-Amon) had made. [2 Kings 23:11] The chariot of Sol is the same as the solar bark of Ra, the sungod of Egypt. The golden chariot is the sun. Compare Rem-us' crossing the border, to the sun crossing the celestial meridian. At high noon (Nun) the sun is at its culmination. After that it slowly descends into the underworld. In winter, Mother Nature and her Sun dies.

The sacred tree of Romulus is the fig tree, as he needed to cover his sins with the fig leaf, like Adam and Eve. Sinners try to hid their shame. Likewise, the sacred tree of the Jews is the fig. [Hosea 9:10] The fig being the family tree of the Covering Cherub (Satan). [Ezekiel 28:12-19] The fig is the Tree of Carnal Knowledge. This demonstrates that Judism and Roman Catholicism sprouted from the same root. The family tree from their Trojan side is the oak.

The cradle of Christianity is in Rome, not JeruSalem. Christ did not create Christianity. Caesar Constantine did. The mother church of Christendom is the Catholic cult. Whereas, the Church of God is called the House of the Lord. The holy city is JeruSalem. [Revelation 21:10] The Catholic holy city is Rome. Rome is the Maternal city, not the eternal city. The children of God make up the body of believers in the family of God. The church of God started with Abel the first martyr. They Never called themselves Christyins, Jews or Muslims.

The infamous icon of the Romans is the she-wolf suckling Romulus and Remus. It is the symbol Rome was founded upon. Later they took on the cloak of Christianity and became the Roman Catholic empire. These are the Wolves in sheep's clothing pretending to be sheep of the good shepherd. [Matthew 7:15] The pope is the false shepherd masquerading as the Lamb of God. [Rev.13:11] When, in fact, it was they who killed Christ and then tortured and murdered the children of God for the past

1600 years. [Revelation 12:4,5,13,17 13:7 Matthew 10:16,17] The pope claims to be the one in place of Christ called the Vicar. Yet he does nothing the Word of God says. They purposely break all the Commandments of God. They even removed the second Commandment in the Catholic version so they could worship Mother Mary and her saints through graven images (statues) just as their ancestors worshipped their many gods through statues. The Roman Catholics replaced worship of the gods with worship of the dead 'Saints'. Nec-roman-cy, worship of the dead, is condemned by the Word of God. Pontiff is the pagan title of high priest.

[Anacalypsis by Godfrey Higgins-volume 2 chapter 1 section 3]

The Mother church of Christendom

The Romans worship the Great Mother or Magnificent Mater (Magna Mater). Who is the Material universe that the Hindus call Maya (Mary). This Magnificent Mater is the matrix from which all matter was born. She is not a goddess, but the universal uterus, the watery womb of space and placenta of proto-plasma. Mare (Mary) means Sea of space. From which the suns of God were born. Marie is the root of our word Marine. She is Black Madonna or Mary-diana, the virgin. In Babylon she is Inanna. In Egypt, she is Annu (Nun), the dark primordial watery womb that gave birth to the first born Sun of God. Matrimony comes from matrix+Amon or the Great Mother and her evil son. For it was Amon who mated with his mother (Ma). The Oedipus syndrome; who killed his father and married his mother. The Word of God condemns goddess worship as whorship and idolatry.

The Roman priests of the Great Mother would castrate themselves, just as the Roman Catholic priests are chaste (cut off from sex). Probably mimicking Amon being immasulated by Horus. Likewise, the priests of Attis castrated themselves. The Jew cut only the tip in Circumcision. The virgin priestess' of the Great Mother became the virgin nuns of Mother Mary. The pagan temples were merely converted to Catholic cathedrals. The Pope is the powerful "father" of the Mother church, yet is impotent: not producing children of his own.

Hail Mary in Latin is Ave (Eve) Mary. Eve is mother of all living. Just as the Greek Artemis and Roman Dianna were called mother of all living. Madonna is Ma-Dianna the virgin. Eve was the mother of the human race. While Mary is the mother of the One who gives life. [1 Corinthians 15:45] The Bible says to remain a chaste virgin to Christ, not as Eve who was seduced by the serpent. [2 Corinthians 11:2,3,14] Anna is the virgin mother of Mary who was impregnated by a Ghost in the form of a serpent (a python phantom). Compare this to the Egyptian Anun (Nun) who was the virgin mother of Isis.

Isis is the original virgin Mother of the good Son of God. The phonics for the hieroglyphic of Isis is "Cat". Kat means Womb in Egyptian. Hathor

(Womb of Horus) is Chathor or Cathedral (House of God). Hat-hor-al is the House of the god Horus (Hat = House hor = Horus al or el = god). Chateau is House in French. The problem is; they honor the Mother rather than the Father in Heaven. They worship the creation rather than the Creator. The Father has no partners!

The Queen of Heaven is Mother of God and top dog. Catholicism is the mother church of Christendom. [Jeremiah 7:18-34] The denominations are her daughters. This is the Mystery of the Great Mother; mother of harlots. [Revelation 17:4,5] The Bible calls this whoreship of the Mother Goddess, whoredom. Mary is almost always painted wearing red, like the great harlot. She is a d'eva (the Eva). Her son is the pseudo Dog star (North pole star) known as Baal, the Warlord who leads the dog-soldiers of Christendumb. The Catholics, like the Masons, conceal their Mysteries in the dead Latin Language. Free Mason = Phre-Mason or House of Ma and her evil son. Compare to the Temple of Hathor.

Caesar is the self made deity of state. The Pope is father of the church and self appointed Vicar of Christ. Vicar means instead of or in place of Christ. Antichrist means the same thing. From Papal, we get our slang for papa. Deo Patre Natus is Latin for Deity Peter Natal or Born of the Father. Paternoster is Latin for 'Peter's prayer', but is translated as the 'Lord's prayer' in the Bible. Pater is Patah (God the Father) of Egypt. Theopater is Greek for Son of God the Father. Christ never appointed anyone to take his place. In fact, he taught that the ones desiring to be the head would become the tail. [Matthew 20:25-28] Peter Romulus II will be the tail "end" of the Catholics.

The Catholics have corrupted Hos-anna to Hail Anna. Anna is the ancient name of the Great Mother (Magna Mater). Dianna is her name in Asia minor where the first "Christian churches" were established. Madonna comes from MaDianna and from there they get Hail Mary. Just as they say, "Hail Caesar" and "Hail Hitler". Mary can save no one. Nor is she to be praised. All praise goes to God the Father who has no (female) partners. In Egypt, Anu (Nun) is the birthplace and time of the Sun of God. It is the water womb of the sea of space, not a goddess. Pollyanna is Polly and Anna. Polly means Mary. Polyannas would mean Many Annas. In most religions the Great Mother is a form of the name Anna. Diana or Ti-ana means Two-anas or two equinoxes annu-ally. This is the dualism of Yin / Yang. The Magna Matrix gave birth to both the good son and bad. A.D. (Anno Domini) means 'in the year of our Lord'. In Egypt, it is the year Tom (Atom) was born of Anu. It is the birth-day and birthplace of Atum.

Mary or Ma-re = Mother of Re. Re is the good Sun of God (Atum-Re) and the evil sun god (Amen-Re). The Romans got their mythology from Upper Egypt. Where they worshipped Amen-Ra, the evil sun god. Amen-Ra and his men wore the domed crown, symbol of Upper Egypt. This domed crown or Tiara was passed down to the successor, the Pope. Therefore, the Pope is the vicar of the antichrist. Compare 'Mary' to 'Mars'. The Bible says the priests who wear black are priests of Baal. They continue to mourn their 'dead god'. [Ezekiel 8:14] [Companion Bible-Hosea 10:5 Zephaniah 1:4 2 Kings 23:5]

It was by no accident that the initials of the first Caesar was J.C. (Julius Caesar and Jesus Christ). Jesus Christ means Savior Anointed. It is purposely written backwards. It should be the Christ Jesus: Anointed Savior. The Christ is the Messiah and the Savior is the king who executes or pardons. Just as Caesar means king and savior of Rome. Julius Caesar ruled Rome from 46-44 BC. Augustus Caesar succeeded him. [Luke 2:1]

The Roman devils have deified themselves as gods. The word deity is rooted in the same word as devil, devas, etc.....Rome is the Evil Empire of Revelation called the Beast. The Roman color is red. [Rev.17:3] The red Beast that ruled the world in Christ's day and shall once again in the Lord's day. The revived Roman Catholic Empire is now called the United States of Europe. The pope is the false prophet and the Catholic cult is the false church of Rome. It is the seat of Satan who imitates everything the Lord does. [Matthew 24:24 Revelation 13:11] 'The Beast came out of the Sea.' The Roman empire completely encompassed the Mediterranean Sea. Mare is the Great Sea just as Mary is the Great Matrix or Matriarch. Mari is the root of Marine. The two parts of the Beast are the Head of state and head of church. When united in unholy matrimony, they produce the resurrected unholy Roman Catholic empire. It is the Pope who anoints the king.

Even the popes confess that the final pope will be the Antichrist. Pope John Paul II says there will be two more popes after him as predicted by their prophet Saint Malachy. John Paul I (1978) was called "from the half moon". John Paul II (1978-) is called "the labor of the sun". This is a direct reference to Diane the moon deva and Apollo the sun god. The deities Constantine worshipped. Two more popes are left. Leo XIV will be called "glory of the olive tree". The final Pope will be Romulus Peter II. When the Lord was asked who shall be the head of the church he said, "But many who are first shall be last, and the last first." [Matthew 19:30 20:21-27]

What they fail to tell us is that Peter or Pater means God the Father in Latin, Greek and Egypt! Dis Pater is Hades or Pluto, Ju Pater is Zeus. Who is Simon Pater? Is he Posiden, the final son of Pater? Jesus calls him Simon Bar Jonah, connecting him to the sea. He says, "I shall make you fishers of men." Then the Lord called him, Satan, who has the keys of hell. [Mat.16:17,23 Rev.9:1] Bar = Baal. Is he good or bad? The name Baal-Shalisha means lord of the trinity. Baal or Satan is the lord and his mistress is the Queen of heaven. Cybele (CyBaal or Sybil) was mother goddess of Attis who gave the oracles or prophecies. The new Catholic trinity is the Pope (Father), Mother Mary and their Son.

Nostradamus, a Jewish-Catholic-astrol diviner, predicts the Antichrist will come in June of 1999, the summer solstice. The summer solstice is the Devil's high day. The last pope will be called Romulus Peter II in honor of the founder of Rome and the disciple the Romans crucified. Then the Catholic church, who built their foundation on the grave of Peter, will be no more. "The City of the Seven Hills {Rome} shall be utterly destroyed and the awful (lawful) Judge will judge the people." This wrathful Judge is Jesus Christ. Who is coming in the fall equinox to destroy the false prophet and his body members. [Revelation 13:11] The Catholic parish shall perish. Rome shall fall once and for all.

Constantine: Confounding Father of Christendom

Constantine: confounding father of Christendom Constantine moved the statue of Zeus from the temple at Olympus to Constantinople (Turkey). He proceeded to worship it as Jesus (Je-Zeus). The Roman Catholics have returned to the homeland of Troy. In 325 AD, the Christian council of Nicaean (Ephesus) decreed: 1) Jesus to be God just as the Greeks worshipped Zeus as God. 2) There was a Trinity: God the Father, God the Son and God the Ghost. 3) Mary is Mother of God.

Under Christendumb, woman is head of the household in honor of Mary. Under this matriarchal system, the matrix or womb called Maya (Mary) gave birth to god. The Catholics worship the creation rather than the Creator. [Romans 1:25] The Bible says God is the Father who has no partners. He is head of His Son, who is the head of every man, who is the head of woman. [2 Corinthians 11:3] It is a patriarchal system; the Father and His sons rule the heavens. In Egypt, Mut or Mot (Mother) is not a being.

Ironically, Ephesus is the location of Dianna worship. She is called Mother of all living and Queen of Heaven. Her new Roman name is now Mary, Madonna, and Rosemarie. She is goddess of the Mother church (the Catholic). Ma-donna is Ma-dianna or Mother Dianna. The early Christians buried the statue of Dianna. Later, some Christians raised her from the grave and revived the Queen of Heaven worship. They Christened her Mary, Mother of God. The autumn festival of the Assumption of the Virgin Mary replaced the festival of Diana, which had replaced the annual festival of Isis! For the Rosecrucians, RoseMary is an perennial (per-annual) evergreen that never dies out. Solomon's Rose of Sharon is the Rose of Sar (Osiris of Anu). Both it and the Lily of the Valley are rooted in Egypt. The Water Lily or Lotus reproduces from the water, not from the earth. Rose is an anagram of Asar (Osiris) and Eros (divine love) and Horus. Nazir means Flower, Jesus was a Nazirite or Nazarene-from the flower rose the Seed.

The statue of Rhodes, statue of Dianna at Ephesus and the statue of Mary at Constantinople are all in the former land of the Hittites (modern

Turkey). Which was absorbed into the Roman Empire. And Pergamos is where Satan's throne is. [Rev.2:13] Also located in the same area. They honored Aesculapius, the god of healing, as their savior. Who was given the gift of healing by Apollo. The serpent entwined around his staff was his emblem that is still used today by the medical profession. To this day, all physicians swear an oath to the god Apollo in the Hippocratic oath. Hippocrates, son of Ta-urt, is the antithesis of Harpocrates, Horus the Child. The child of Ta-urt is Typhon/Set/Baal. Ta-urt is the composite beast; hippopotamus-crocodile-lioness (hippo-crod-es). The Rx on drugs is Rex. Rex Mundi means King of this World (i.e. Satan).

The Cross

Constantine saw a flaming cross superimposed on the sun and heard the words, "By this conquer". So he went out and murdered many people in honor of his sun god the Warlord of death and destruction. The cross is the symbol of death. It not only killed Christ, but thousands of others were crucified by the Romans. And the Germans under the "hooked cross" called the Swastika. To put an image of Christ on a cross is a graven or dead image which is breaking the second commandment. The commandment the Roman Catholics removed from the Bible. If Christ were hanged from a tree, [Acts 5:30 10:39] would you wear a noose around your neck???? The Roman Cross is part of the Asherah, tree worship. [Jeremiah 10:1-5 Galatians 3:13 Deuteronomy 12:3 16:21 Judges 3:7 Exodus 34:13 1 Kings 15:13 16:32,33 18:19 2 Kings 21:7 23:4,6,7] Their symbol is a red cross on a white banner. The place where the north/south meridian and east/west meridian cross is the North Pole star. It is the birthplace of the evil sun of God.

For the Romans, the cross was the symbol of Apollo. This cross was imported from the Middle East where Tammuz used it as his symbol. He was the sun who dies and rises daily as it crosses the western horizon. [Ezekiel 8:14-16] It is Lucifer the Day-star. The cross has long been used as a grave marker, a sign of the dead.

The infamous Chi-Rho cross (X+P) is Christ+Pan or Christian. In Egypt, 'ian' means Pan (i.e. Baal). Pan is the Greek goat-man (satyrs) and counterpart to Set-Typhon and Baal. Christ-Pan is the same as Antichrist. The ian is also the negative Yin of the Yin/Yang. Christian crusatyrs conquer for their god. The Chro (X) is the monogram of Chronus or Kronus. Kronus is an anagram of Khonsu, the anti-Horus, of the Egyptians. Likewise, Satian is Set + ian the Adversary of Horus. [Signs and Symbols of Primordial Man by Albert Churchward p.368-374] Christians are not followers of Christ. They never do the things he told them to do. They crucify him daily by continuing to purposely sin. [Hebrews 6:4-6 10:26-29] If you love God, you will keep His Commandments. [1 John 5:1-3] The Christyin motto: "Do onto others before they do it to you." They pervert the Word of God just as Satan does. Compare: [Genesis 2:17 & 3:4,5] Today the Maltese cross (cross of Patee) is given as a medal of honor to the men of war who are most proficient at manslaughter. As a military symbol, it is second only to the Satanic (five pointed) star.

The Romans sacrificed humans to their gods during unholy wars, in the Coliseum and on every hill where they left their unwanted children to die. Just as the Christian crusatyrs sacrifice humans during their Christian crusades, in honor of the gods made in their image. They sacrificed humans during the Inquisition in the name of their god. They even killed their own god; as Jesus dies daily because of their continual sins. [Hebrews 6:4-6 10:26-29] Christendumb was divided (east and west) under Constantine the Great, but was united under Charlemagne (Charles the Great). Great always refers to Greatly Evil. Charlemagne united the Roman Empire just as the Antichrist will in the end times. Today, Great Britain is part of the neo-Roman empire.

The Devil's Day

Halloween originally was the Day of the Dead. When the dead came back alive to haunt the living. The Christians would dress up as the ghosts, witches and demons so as to "trick" them into believing they were one of them. They became one with them. They would leave treats to appease the dead. The night before is fittingly called Devil's night. As the e'en on the end of Halloween means evening. For Satan is Ruler of the Darkness. Devil's night and Halloween are high days for witches and Satanists to honor the lord of darkness. The favorite color for Halloween is blood red. As the Devil is imagined as red with horns and a pitch-fork (trident). [Revelation 12:3] The Druids called it Samhain day. Samhain is the kids of Pan the satyr (Satan). Being haunted by ghosts is a heathen heresy.

Santa's Day

Legend says that Dec.25 is the birthday of Mithra the sun god (also known as Sol, Apollo, Baal, Lucifer and Satan). Santa is an anagram for Satan. Just move the "n" to the end and find Satan. This Festival of Lights is in honor of the Light Bearer, Lucifer. Pretending to be the angel of light. [2 Corinthians 11:14] Whose solar power dwindles as it nears the winter solstice (Dec.25th) and is born new a week later on New Years day (Sun-day). Santa riding in his sleigh is the sun god riding in his chariot of fire. [2 Kings 23:11] He transformed from St. Nicolas of the Roman Catholic church to Santa the Roman deity. Old Nick is the Devil according the Charles Dickenson. Kris Kringle, on the other hand, is a German name meaning Christ Child. From kringle we get kinder (kin); as in kindergarten. To say Kris Kringle is Santa is an abomination. Nicolas is the Latin spelling for Nimrod! In Egyptian, Neka is the evil one.

The Romans called it Saturnalia or day of Saturn (Cronus). It is a time of merry-making, feasting (satur means stuffed), drunkenness and chaos. All government departments, schools and businesses were closed. Even wars ceased. The twelve days of Christmas was originally the Roman Twelve Days of Chaos. The Lord of Misrule leads the revelry. Just as he shall in the last days. "And those who dwell on the earth will rejoice over them (God's witness), make merry, and send gifts to one another, because these two prophets tormented those who dwell on the earth." [Revelation 11:10] Merry eX-Mass! Saturn is Sat-urn (Set or Satan).

The color of Krismas is blood-red like the sunset. The meat of choice for X-mas is the (unclean) pink pig. The sacred animal of Zeus-Amen and Set is sacrificed in honor of their birthday. Cakes with crosses [Jeremiah 7:18] and a number of candles burning. The hot cross buns represent the sun crossing the threshold into the darkness and his days are numbered. The candles are blown out to represent the darkening of the sun and a wish is made hoping the sun will return. This is sun worship!

Easter Sunday: Istar's day

Easter is the celebration of the rebirth of the Eastern star, Venus, as the sun revives in the spring. Easter is calculated as the first Sunday following the first full moon after the equinox, as authorized by Constantine. The bunnies and eggs represent the fertility of Ishtar the goddess of sex. The Jack rabbit jumping from hole to hole in a mad frenzy and egg fertilizing orgy. In Egypt, the Ra-bbit is the sacred animal of Ra, the sun. Hare or Hara means the Destroyer. Easter has nothing to do with Christ's death and resurrection. He died on Passover and resurrected during the Feast of Unleavened Bread. Passover is the first full moon following the spring equinox, as authorized by the LORD. Easter Sunday has to do with the eastern sun-rise services to honor the sun god known as Satan and his mother, the Great Mother goddess. The Roman Catholics call her Mother Mary, the mother of god. The Catholics observe the Great Mother's Day (Ash-ur) in honor of Isis finding the body of Osiris and the miracle of the Immaculate Conception. This is a miscarriage of God's command.

The golden Easter egg laid by Mother Goose is the rebirth of the sun in spring. The color of Easter is red like the sunrise. The goose is Mot and her sun is Set, the Great Cackler. The witches of Wicca celebrate it as the feast of Eostre. The Lord says not to weep for Tammuz, the sun god rising in the east. [Ezek.8:14-16] Paul says you shall not eat food sacrifice to pagan idols. This includes foods prepared for Santa, the Easter bunny and any other pagan idols. [Acts 15:20 21:25] This is not a law that Paul created. It is God's law found in Deuteronomy 12:29-32. Paul was very upset that they called him Mercury, the deity of Merchants. [Acts 14:12] The merchants (Canaanites) are the ones who profit from the merchandise they sell on man-made holidays. Mercury is the heralder of "Santa is coming", not "the Lord is coming". In fact, they dread the Lord's coming.At Easter, the Greek Orthodox high priest goes into the holy of holies and gets fire from the Lord (Baal) and distributes it to the masses. Compare to Prometheus who gives fire to mankind. Lucifer is the light-bearer who gives artificial illumination. Christians insinuate that the sun of God died on Easter (March 25) and was born (or reborn) nine months (280 days) later at Christmas (Dec.25). Lucifer is the angel of the 'white light'.

Holy days vs. unholy days

The original Feast of Ast-ra (Isis-Ra) was the memorial of the death of Osiris as Son of Man and his rebirth as Horus-Ra, Son of God. It was celebrated at the spring equinox (Passover). Easter is a corruption! Michaelmas is celebrated at the autumn equinox. Michaelmes is the birth of the Morning star, Sirius. Michael is the god of scales who weighs the souls of the dead. He presides over the equinoctial scales at Michaelmas (Judgment Day). This is Horus. Sirius is the Bright Morning Star of Jesus. [Revelation 22:16] Venus is the Death star that guides the Crusatyrs of Christendumb. The Mayan's used Venus as an omen or sign that it was time for human sacrifice. The luminaries where created for signs, seasons, days and years. [Genesis 1:14] Some use them for good, some for evil.

Fifty days after Easter is WhitSunday or Christian Pentecost (June 4). It is no coincidence that it is shortly before the summer solstice, the high day of the sun-god. It is the time the sun rises to its summit and unites with the North Pole star. The pentacle is his five pointed star. White-sunday describes the white-faced sun-god (Set) of Egypt. June 15th is called Corpus Christi. It is when the Christians consume the Corpse of Christ. This is cannibalism! Celebrating the victory of Satan over Christ. It is deviation (devil-ation) from the original Feast of Sabbaths celebrated 7 Sabbaths after Passover. The Jewish Pentecost (Shavuos) falls on the month of Sivan (i.e. Shiva).

The Roman-Christian calendar

The calendar was redone in honor of the birth of their god. The months were named for the other gods. January for Janus, May for Maia (mother earth), August for Augustus Caesar, October for Octavius, June for Juno, July for Julius Caesar, etc... March for Mars, the Warlord, who commanded his soldiers to "march" into battle. The days of the week were named for the Aryan or Viking gods: Wednesday for Wodan's day, Thursday for Thor's day, Friday for Frig's day, Saturday for Saturn's day, Sunday for the sun-god's day (Mithra), etc...

The calendar is based on heathen holidays authorized by the state. The misconception is that the calendar was based on the Lord Jesus. Wrong! The Roman Christian calendar was calculated from the birth of Rome. Christ was born anywhere from 7-4 BC And it was in the fall, not in the winter. Sol, the sun-god was reborn on New Year (Jan.1). The Satanic day goes from 12:00 mid-night to 12:00 mid-day in honor of the sungod. Just like the winter darkness and summer brightness of the solstice. In honor of Sol, the solar deity. The Lord's day goes from sunset to sunset like the equinox. The setting Sun of God shall rise again to overthrow the evil sun god.

The Roman-Christians set the birth of Christ at 1 AD and death at 33 AD so it would fit their fable of "Good Friday" and "Easter Sunday". Passover fell on Friday in the year 33 AD. The fact is Christ died on Wednesday, April 25th (Passover) of 31 AD. The Word of God says that the Beast "shall persecute the Saints of the Most High and shall intend to change times and law." [Daniel 7:25 Revelation 13:7 17:6] This was fulfilled when Christendom changed God's holy calendar and Holy Days.

Many superstitious people believe Full Moons and Friday 13s are unlucky days. Actually, Christ was killed on the full moon of Passover (Wednesday, Nisan 14, 28 AD). 28 BC. Christians corrupted the day to Good Friday the 13, 33 AD. The Lord's Day of Judgment shall be an ominous day for these liars! The root of ominous is amen: as in a bad omen. Compare to Osiris' death on the full moon of Passover at age 28.

Under the original Roman calendar, March was the first month in honor of Mars. This made the Roman calendar synchronize with the Hebrew and Egyptian. Sept-ember became the seventh month as Sept means Seven, October became the eighth month as Octo means Eight, November the ninth as Novem is Nine, and December the tenth as Deca means Ten. King Numa revised the Roman calendar, making January the first month. Likewise, the calendar authorized by Julius Caesar and the Gregorian calendar created by Pope Geogory follow Numa's lead. This is our chaotic calendar of Christen-dumb where October is the tenth month. Ironically, Julius Caesar was killed on the Ides of March (March 15th), the same time of year Jesus Christ was killed.

Black Magic

Latin is the language of preference for witches and sorcery. Some say that the language of Latin is Lucifer's tongue. Lucifer + Satan = Latin. It is the pagans who vainly repeat their chants over and over. [Matthew 6:7] The Catholics teach their converts to say "Hail Mary's" over and over. Their heathen ways have worked their way into modern traditions and customs. The word Heathen = Shatan (sh = s & th = t). Through the arts and crafts; black arts and witch craft. Halloween is high day for the witches. Followed by Yule (Dec.22) and then Candlemas (Feb.2). Could this be the origins of Chrismas? God condemns this heathen holiday.

[Jer.10:1-5] May 1 is Beltane, which means fire to Baal. The Greeks called it May Day in honor of the Great Mother Earth (Gaia or Maia).

Juno: Bride of Sol

The Romans and Germans authorized Juno as the day of Solidarity. Sol is the solar deity or sun-god. When they all unite under the evil sun of God, just as they did at the Tower of Babel (Baal). Then June 21 is their summer solstice in honor of the sun god. The day he is at peak power. The tradition of the June bride comes from the Roman goddess Juno. The custom of wearing black all winter in mourning of the death of the sun god (Adon or S-atan). [Ezekiel 8:14] Which occurs Dec.25 on the winter solstice. They are not allowed to wear white until after May 31st. As it is at this time of year that the Antichrist will come to full power and rapture away his harem before the Lord comes for his bride in the fall. [Matthew 24:32-44] The Word of God says, the bride of Christ wears a white gown representing virtue earned by righteous acts. [Rev.19:7-9] The whores of Satan will be striped naked as their sins are exposed. [Revelation 2:20-23 3:18] Juno in Greece is Hera, the wife of Zeus. Zeus is the Antichrist or Spurious Savior and Hera (Juno) is the false church that has fallen away. She is the Mother church and Christendom are her daughters. She is the Harlot who rides on the Roman Beast. She lives in sin with Caesar Satan.

In conclusion, the Christian cult is the counterfeit church. Separate from these sinners before it is too late! The fact that Christendom is universal is proof that they are the false church of the end times. God's church is but a remnant of the Faithful Few. [Isaiah 1:9 10:22 28:22 Joel 2:32 Romans 9:27 Zechariah 8:11 13:7-9] The great masses of Christendom have not even read the Word of God, so how could they possibly know what God wants them to do? They listen to their false shepherds who teach lies! Those charlatans shall be held accountable for all those sheep they have lead to the slaughter. Come out of the Roman Beast before Roman falls again. Do not play the harlot of Babylon, who lives in sin with Satan, for they too shall fall. [Revelation 18:2]

Last Rights

The Roman Catholics give a dying person their last rights. "You have the right to remain silent." The dead do not speak. "You have the right to an attorney," says the arresting officer before incarcerating you. Satan is the Accuser, but Christ is our Advocate. "Anything you say may be held against you." The Word of God says; "But I say to you that for every idle word men may speak, they will give account of it in the day of Judgment. For by your words you will be justified, and by your words you will be condemned.'' [Matthew 12:36,37] The Lord says you shall not pray for the dead. That is necromancy. You are to pray for the living.

Sotterranna: Subterranean tombs

Sotterranna is the Roman name of the so-called Christian catacombs. These subterranean tombs were named after Set. Sot-terrain tombs originated at the necropolis (city of the dead) in Egypt. It is the same as Amenta (Land of the Dead). The catacombs in Rome contain no Christians. The Saints were Christophers (followers of Christ), not Christians. They were martyrs who died rather than conform. They did not love their lives and would not kill to save themselves. [Revelation 12:11 13:7-9] They believed in the bodily resurrection, like the Egyptians. For them, Cat is both the tomb and womb of rebirth. Unlike the Christians who believe they turn into ghosts and fly off to heaven. The Roman Catholics are the followers of Set (Satan) who persecuted the followers of Christ.

The Catholic Bull or Congressional Bill comes from the Code of Baal. As there is no vowels; Bull, Bill and Baal are the same. These man-made laws are inspired by the spirit of error. The words of Amen, the Bull of heaven, became the Papal Bull. They try to replace the Commandments of God with Constitutions of man. But God's Commandments are spiritual and eternal. No one can abolish or amend the Word of God. The Pope claims he can perform absolution. This is a Lie! Confession does Not = Salvation. Only God can forgive sin and even He will not blot out your sins. You shall be judged for All your actions and words. Only the Judge (Osiris-Christ) can pardon those he sees are rehabilitated. The Pope is an immoral mortal with no divine powers! [Revelation 20:11-15 21:8,27 22:15]

It was popes like Sylvester II, in the 10th century, who proclaimed the earth is the center of the universe and all the seven planets, the sun and the moon, revolve around it. Galileo was imprisoned for life for saying otherwise. In 1616, Pope Urban VIII threatened to execute him if he didn't retract his beliefs. Galileo told them what they wanted to hear and died a prisoner to Catholic lies. They believed the earth is flat because the Bible says it has four corners (north, south, east and west)!!!!

Luc Gauric (1476-1558) was the astrologer to Popes Julius II, Leo X, Clement VII and Paul III. Who tried to foresee their future. Pope Leo X's personal astrologer, Franciscus Priulus, saw something that caused Leo X to attempt suicide by drowning, jumping into fire, slashing his throat with a scythe, and jumping out of a window. He finally succeeded by starving himself. Is this the act of a sane man? The Catholic cult believed the spurious stars controlled their every move (astro-divination). They never understood that the Zodiac foretells mankind's future, not the individual man's. The twelve ages of the Zodiac is the story of Salvation. The planets have nothing to do with it. There is not sufficient room to speak of All the evils done by the Popes and their followers.

The Pope, in his arrogance, divided the world between the English Protestants and the Portuguese/Spanish-Catholics. He "gave" them land that did not belong to him. Who the hell does he think he is? He seems to think he is Lord of the Earth! This is the act of an antichrist! They called America the new Promise Land, of which, it was a garden paradise... until they took control of it. Paradise is Lost because of people with evil intent!

The Pope claims that the fall of USSR is fulfillment of prophesy. At Fatima, the three children saw a poltergeist appearing as Mary. This apparition told them communism would be conquered, followed by capitalism. The Pope's job is to establish the New World Order and its state Religion of Christendom. This is the revival of the Unholy Roman Catholic republic. Both the Russians and Germans consider themselves part of the original Roman empire. Both will join the neo-Roman empire. The Bible says Satan will incarnate as the Antichrist and head of the evil kingdom. This spurious Savior will promise the world, but will not deliver. Capitalism will fall. [Revelation 18] At Fatima, the people saw the sun dancing in the sky. This is their sun-god (i.e. Shiva or Set-Ra), the son of the Queen of Heaven (Ma or Mary). Shiva is often pictured as dancing.

The Fall of Rome

Historians have been debating for years as to what caused "the fall of the Roman empire." Well here is your answer; "the Beast who was mortally wounded by the Sword <of the Lord> and was revived." [Revelation 13:3,14] The same Roman Beast who murdered Jesus the Christ. [Revelation 12:3-5] The same Roman Catholic Beast who persecuted the Jews as well as the Saints of God. [Revelation 12:6,12-17] The Catholic half of the unholy union healed the Roman-Catholic partnership. They make up the two halves of the Beast in Revelation 13:1 & 13:11. "He who kills with the sword shall be killed with the Sword." [Revelation 13:10] Sin, breaking God's Commandments, caused the fall of the infidels. Just as they shall receive the final coup-de-Grace at the so-called battle of Armageddon. The revived unholy Roman Catholic empire, called the United States of Europe, and all other militant nations will be slain by the Sword of the Lord. The Catholic parish shall perish once and for all!

Simon Peter: founder of the Roman church

Simon Bar-Jonah was a disciple of Christ. Christ gave him the surname of Peter. [Matthew 16:16-19] It is highly unlikely that he ever went to Rome, except by force. The Lord said, "when you are old, you will stretch out your hands, and another will gird you and carry you where you do not wish." [John 21:18] It was the Romans who dragged him off in chains and crucified him upside down. The Roman Catholics built their cathedral on the bones of Peter. Simon Peter is not even mentioned in the book of Romans!

So who did found the Roman church? In the book of Acts, we find a Simon the Magnificent Magician. [Acts 8:9-25] Simon saw the miracles of Peter and John and desired that power. He thought he could buy the supernatural power of God called the holy Spirit. Because of his evil intent, he never received the power from on high. He never received the Spirit of truth because he possessed the spirit of error. [1 John 4:1-6] Justin Martyr, Irenaeus, and Eusebius are the secular historians who tell of Simon Magus (Simon the Great).

In 45 AD, Simon Magus (the Great) traveled from Samaria to Rome to start a new movement. His followers were first called Christian in Antioch. [Acts 11:26] Antioch means Anti-christ. It is on route to Rome. One of his disciples was Menander who also was a magician from Samaria. Simon taught that he was the Son of God to the Jews and the Father to the Samaritans. He changed his name to Simon Peter and later became the first Pope. Papal is where we get Papa. He even claimed that he had created the angels.

He said that a prostitute named Helen was 'mother of all things'. Which is the title of Eve. [Genesis 3:20] Mary in Latin is Eve. Dianna was also mother of all living. [Acts 19:23-35] The Helenists liked that Mother goddess religion. In fact, the Catholic church is called the Mother church and Mary is called Mother of god. She is called Madonna (Ma-Diana), the Great Mother (Mater-Magus).

Simon Magus taught a lawless religion full of sexual promiscuity. His followers were told they were saved by grace. He claimed they were not required to keep God's law. They lived in sin with Satan. [Rev.2:20-23] He taught another gospel; full of his heresies. [Galatians 1:6,7] Both the Lord and Paul taught that the Ten Commandments are the conditions of our Covenant. [Romans 2:13,26 3:31] The Ten Commandments were written on two tablets of stone by the finger of God. These tablets are called "the tablets of the Covenant". [Hebrews 9:4 Deu.4:13] The lawless ones are the ones the Lord is coming to destroy. [2 Thes.2:2-12]

In Rome, Simon Magus was respected by Claudius Caesar, the Roman Senate and the people. He was worshipped as a demi-god, like Julius Caesar. Claudius honored him with a graven image. Magus means Magusty (Majesty). He soon became known as Simon Peter. In the pagan religion of Rome, the name Peter was used for certain gods and idolatrous objects of worship. This spurious Simon Peter became the founder of the Roman Catholic church. Soon Simon Peter's movement became the accepted state religion called Christendom or Christianity.

Justin Martyr said, "Simon came to Rome in the day of Claudius Caesar and made such an impression by his magical powers, that he was honored as a god, a statue being erected to him on the Tiber, between the two bridges, bearing the inscription: Simon's deosancto (the holy deity of Simon)." The pagan deities were known as Peters or Paters. From there we get Peter Pan and others. Dis Pater is the Roman name of the Greek god Hades. Simon Peter became one of the Roman Pantheon. In Egypt, Pater means Father. Simon Peter would mean Simon son of God the Father. Which is just was he claimed: to be Son of God.

Did Simon Magus convince Nero Caesar to blame the followers of Christ for the burning of Rome? Both would benefit. The heat would be taken off Nero and Simon would be rid of his rival religion. Peter said, 'your adversary the devil walks about like a roaring lion, seeking whom he may devour.' [1 Peter 5:8] The followers of Christ were fed to the lions, while the Christians celebrated. [Revelation 11:10] So Simon Magus became the anti-Simon Peter (or in place of Simon Peter) just as the antichrist savior will come in the place of the Christ Jesus. The Romans killed the members of the church of God in Rome and took their place. These counterfeits became the Roman Catholic church. These are the wolves in sheep's clothing. The symbol of Roman is the she-wolf suckling Romulus, the founder of Rome. They are the Ram who appears to be like the Lamb of God but speaks the word of the Devil. [Rev.13:11] Lawlessness is their dogma. Paul warned about false apostles. "For such are false apostles, deceitful workers, transforming themselves into apostles of Christ. And no wonder! For Satan himself transforms himself into an angel of light. Therefore it is no great thing if his ministers also transform themselves into ministers of righteousness, whose end will be according to their works." [2 Corinthians 11:13-15] This Angel of light, that Lucifer is impersonating, is Archangel Michael, Sun of Righteousness. His counterfeit church pretends to be Christ-like, but do nothing the Lord says. [Matthew 24:1-23] The infamous saying, "Simon says....." comes from his followers saying, "Simon says we do this and don't do that." Whatever Simon says...goes. The sheep follow the shepherd to the slaughter.

The true church of God Never called themselves Christians. From the beginning to the end of the Bible, they are called Saints. In fact, both Christ and Paul are called Nazarenes. It was prophesied about the Messiah: "He shall be called a Nazarene." [Matthew 2:23 Judges 13:5] Then the Jews said of Paul; "For we have found this man a plague, a creator of dissension among all the Jews throughout the world, and a ringleader of the sect of the Nazarenes." [Acts 24:5] It is the reformed Saints who shall be transformed into sons of God. [Rev.12:17 14:12] Simon (pseudo Peter) later was adopted into the Druid religion. Simon became Samhain. Remember there are no vowels in the original languages, double vowels are redundant, and the 'h' is silent. Smn = Simon or Samhain. Samhain's high day is Halloween. He is the evil Set-amon of Upper Egypt. In Egypt, Semen is the northern circumpolar stars that fell to earth as fallen angels.

In the end, Simon claimed to be the Son of God. He tried to re-enact the miracles of Jesus. The Bible says; the Devil took Jesus to the pinnacle of the temple at Jerusalem and said, "If you are the Son of God, throw yourself down. . . ." saying God would not allow him to be hurt. [Matthew 4:5–7] Simon, in his delusion, jumped off a tower and fell to his death. St. Peter's Basilica was built upon his "Stone" cold body.

Mithra

Mithra was the rival religion of Christianity in Rome, and more successful than Christianity for the first four centuries of the "Christian" era. Neither were based on the Messiah. In 307 AD, the emperor officially designated Mithra "Protector of the Empire." Even St. Augustine declared the priests of Mithra worshipped the same deity as he did. In 323 AD, Caesar Constantine worshipped the "Invincible Sun" and called his cult Christendom. His deity was the blood-thirsty Warlord who rose every morning to do battle in his chariot. The wheel representing the sun.

Mithra was born on the 25th of December, called "Birthday of the Unconquered Sun," which was finally taken over by Christians in the 4th century AD as the birthday of Christ. Christians worship the dying sun who is reborn every year at the winter solstice. Lucifer is the Daystar or sun of our solar system that is reborn on Dec.25th. This is Not Christ who died once for mankind, not every year. The memorial of his death is the spring equinox at a Holy day called Passover.

Some claimed Mithra's mother was a mortal virgin. Christians claim Mary died a virgin. Ignoring the fact that the Bible says she had at least four other children. Others said Mithra had no mother, but was miraculously born of a female Rock, the petra genetrix which was fertilized by the Heavenly Father's phallic and potent lightning. Compare to Melchizedek. [Hebrew 7:3] Mithra's birth was witnessed by shepherds and by Magi who brought gifts to his sacred birth-cave of the Rock.

It was Romulus and Remus who was born on Dec.25th. They were placed in a vessel and thrown into the Tiber river. Shepherds found them in a cave being suckled by a she wolf (canine-ite or white woman). They were said to be sons of the Warlord called Mars and a vestal virgin Rhea Silvia. Romulus was venerated as Quirinus, the sun-god of the winter solstice. Christ was neither born in a cave nor was it in the winter. He was born in a house in the city of David where almost everyone was a relative. Besides God's law of hospitality says all people of Israel must take in the homeless.

Mithra performed the usual assortment of miracles: raising the dead, healing the sick, making the blind see and the lame walk, casting out devils. As a Peter, son of the petra, he carried the keys of the kingdom of heaven. His triumph and ascension to heaven were celebrated at the spring equinox. The death and resurrection story is taken from Egypt. Osiris is murdered by Set and resurrects as Horus during the spring equinox (Passover).

Before returning to heaven, Mithra celebrated a Last Supper with his twelve disciples, who represented the twelve signs of the zodiac. In memory of this, his worshipers partook of a sacramental meal of bread marked with a cross. This was one of the seven Mithraic sacraments, the prototype for the Christians' seven sacraments. It was called mizd, Latin missa, English mass. Mithra's image was buried in a rock tomb, the same sacred cave that represents his Mother's womb. He was raised from this tomb/ womb and said to live again.

Like early Christianity, Mithraism was anti-female religion. Its priesthood consisted of celibate men only. Women were forbidden to enter Mithraic temples. Like the Christians, they believed that because of Eve's sin, no woman could enter the kingdom of God. [1 Tim.2:13-15] The women of Mithraic families had nothing to do with the men's cult, but attended services of the Great Mother in their own temples of Isis, Diana (Artemis), or Juno (Hera). The irony is; that Catholicism became the mother church of all Christendom. They worship Mother Mary as Queen of Heaven and Mother of god. The canonized Saints are her chaste servants.

The Mithraists replaced the Mother of All Living in the primal garden of paradise with the bull named Sole-Created. Instead of Eve, this bull was the partner of the first man. All creatures were born from the bull's blood. The bull was castrated and sacrificed, and its blood was delivered to the moon for magical seed bearing, the moon being the source of women's magic lunar "blood of life" that produced real children on earth. The moon's monthly cycle parallels the woman's fertility period. The bull is Baal, the Devil and the moon is his consort. In Egypt, he is Serapis bull that was sacrificed every 28 years.

One of the most famous pictures is that of Mithra slaying the Bull. This bull is Zeus in disguise. Zeus took the form of a bull in order to intimidate the women he wished to have sex with. Zeus took the form of a bull to rape Europa. In other words, Zeus handed the Europeans a line of bull. Zeus was master of deception. The bull, like the serpent, represents the evil force. Mithra slaying the Bull is the same as Herakles defeating the Minotaur.

This story obviously originated thousands of years previous in Egypt. In Egypt, one of the faces of evil is Min. He has bulls horns and an erect phallus. This represents that he is "horny". Sex and violence are his characteristics. In one of the depictions of Orion, he is the Hunter holding the head of the bull with his left hand and is about to club it with the mace, held in his right hand. The head of the celestial bull is the Hyades cluster of stars in the constellation of Taurus. Min + Taurus = Minotaur. Who, like Hades, rules over the dead in the underworld. This is the region of Amen-Ra who is the sacred Apis or Bull deity who is the enemy of Orion-Osiris. He rules over the living and the dead in the underworld.

Persians have been called the Puritans of the heathen world. They developed Mithraism out of an earlier Aryan religion that was not so puritanical or so exclusively male-oriented. Mithra seems to have been the Indo-Iranian sun god Mitra, or Mitra Varuna, one of the twelve zodiacal sons of the goddess Aditi. Another of Aditi's sons was Aryaman, ancestor of "Aryans," whom the Persians transformed into Ahriman, the Great Serpent of Darkness, Mithra's enemy. As well as Ahura Mazdah's enemy in Zoroasterism. Ahura Mazdah and Ahriman are twin Suns diametrically opposed. Ahura Mazdah is the sun or star Sirius in the constellation of Orion. Ahriman is the star Hyades in the constellation of Taurus and Cetus the sea-monster. The Aryans or Assyrians are the blond-haired, blue-eyed, pale race.

Early on , there seems to have been a feminine Mithra. Herodotus said the Persians used to have a sky-goddess Mitra, the same as Mylitta, Assyria's Great Mother. Lydians combined Mithra with his consort Anahita as an androgynous Mithra-Anahita, identified with Sabazius-Anaitis, the Serpent and Dove of Anatolian (modern Turkey) mystery cults. Aditi is the counterpart of Nut, Mut or Mot of Egypt. It is the watery womb (Magna Mater) from which the suns of God were born. It is the chaotic abyss of the primordial waters or sea of space. It was Amen-Ra who mated with his mother, Mut.

Anahita was the Mother of Waters, traditional spouse of the solar god whom she bore, loved, and swallowed up. She was identified with the Analolian Great Mother, Ma. Mithra was naturally coupled with her, as her opposite, a spirit of fire, light, and the sun. Her "element," water, over-whelmed the world in the primordial flood, when one man built an ark and saved himself, together with his cattle, according to Mithraic myth. The story seems to have been based on the Hindu Flood of Manu, transmitted through Persian and Babylonian scriptures to appear in a late, rather corrupt version in the Old Testament.

The primordial waters from which the Sun was begotten is called Maya (Mary). The immaculate conception and virgin birth of the first begotten of the creation. The Egyptians call this watery womb, Nun. Which gave birth to Atem-Ra and Amen-Ra (Mith-Ra). Once she gives birth, she is called Nut or Mot (Mother). As the sea of space void of life, Nun is called the Apopis Sea Serpent who attempts to swallow the sun as it is rising. It is the red Dragon of Revelation chapter 12. For every action there is an equal but opposite reaction. God said, "Let there be light." "And the light shines in the darkness; and the darkness did not comprehend it." [John 1:5]

This sea of space (the second heaven) will be consumed by the lake of fire raining down from God in the first heaven. God is going to consume the darkness of outer space. Then the first heaven where God dwells will become our heaven. The Christian soldiers and all other military men will be slain by the Sword of the Lord in the battle commonly called Armageddon. Then after the Millennium, Satan will gather the lawless ones in a final attack on the Lord and his saints at JeruSalem. This is when the Lake of fire rains down on them.

What began in water would end in fire, according to Mithraic eschatology. The great battle between the forces of light and darkness in the Last Days would destroy the earth with its upheavals and burnings. Virtuous ones who followed the teachings of the Mithraic priesthood would join the sons of light and be saved. Sinful ones who followed other teachings would be cast into hell with Ahriman and the fallen angels. The Christian notion of salvation was almost wholly a product of this Persian eschatology. Roman military men thought the rigid discipline and vivid battle imagery of Mithraiam appropriate for warriors. Mithra became the supreme patron of Roman armies.

After extensive contact with Mithraism, Christians also began to describe themselves as soldiers for Christ; to call their savior Light of the World, Helios the Rising Sun, and Sun of Righteousness; to celebrate their feasts on Sun-day rather than the Jewish Sabbath; to claim their savior's death was marked by an eclipse of the sun; and to adopt the seven Mithraic sacraments. Helios is the evil sungod or son of God called Lucifer in the Bible and Amen-Ra by the Egyptians. His day is Sun-day. Like Mithraists, Christians practiced baptism in the belief that they would ascend after death through the planetary spheres to the highest heaven, while the lawless (unbaptized) would be dragged down to darkness (the grave). The Lord NEVER promised an ascension, but only a resurrection.

Mithra's cave-temple on the Vatican Hill was seized by Christians in 376 AD Christian bishops of Rome even took the Mithraic high priest's title of Pater Patrum, which became Papa, Papal or Pope. The Mithraic festival of Epiphany, marking the arrival of sun-priests or Magi at the Savior's birth place, was adopted by the Christian church only as late as 813 AD But the birth of Christendom has nothing to do with Christ. Neither was Peter, the disciple of Christ, the first pope. Dis Pater (Rich Peter) is the counterpart of the Greek god of the dead, Pluto. In the Roman fable, St. Peter became the Roman deity of the dead (Hades) who escorts the dead to Elysian Fields.

When the Lord used the term keys to God's kingdom, he meant that he gave Peter the key to unlocking the grave and resurrecting in the hereafter. It was not a physical key, but a secret. Christ showed him the key or missing piece of the puzzle to solving the mystery of death. This Key was: do God's Commandments and keep the testimony of Jesus. [Revelation 12:17 14:12] With the help of the Spirit of Truth and Love, we are able to fulfill God's Will.

The Aryans

The Aryan stories of folk heroes are all fables. Robin Hood and his merry men is a "fairy-tail". A woman was added to make the "gay" men more acceptable. Maid Marion is a corruption of Virgin Mary the maiden. Robin is a Hoodlum who robs and belongs in jail for armed robbery. These fables and fairy-tales are not mythology. They have no redeeming value and no morals to teach. Chivilry, like etiquette, is social dogma that has nothing to do with God. Any primate in a monkey suit can mimic good manners. Many savage tyrants have put on the airs of civilized gentlemen, while committing abominations in the name of God. Richard, the lion-hearted, was a homosexual maniac who wanted to commit genocide on all Semitics (Jews and Muslims). Of the dual lions; one of light and one of darkness, he is the knight. Chivalry (Shiva + rivalry) is dead, thank God! Mythology is the theology of my God. It is not fairy-tales of blood-thirsty warriors in search of nonexistent treasures like the Holy Grail.

The King Arthur character is an obvious corruption of Egyptian mythology. Art-hur is the Little Bear (Ursa Minor) son of the Great Bear (Ursa Major) and Uther Pen-Dragon (Draco). In Egypt, Urt is the Great She Bear and mother of babe Bar (Baal). Her Greek counterpart is Arte-mis (Great Mot-her). The Dragon is Set, Typhon, Satan, etc... The Egyptians saw them as Ammit (Eater of the Dead), the composite beast (hippopotamus, crocodile, and lioness) that gave birth to Set-Amen. The Latin, Arcturus (Bear) is the Polar Bear of the Arctic circle. Arth is Bear in the Welsh language. [Stars and men by S.A. and M.L. Ionides page 262]

These constellations, like Europe, are in the north. [Revelation 12:3 13:1] The kingdom of the north, the composite Beast (United States of Europe) shall attack the kingdom of the south (Egypt and her allies). [Daniel 12] These twelve United States are the neo-Roman empire. Their flag is twelve stars in a circle. The United Nations of the northern hemisphere.

The twelve knights of the Round Table is the time table of the Zodiac written on the night sky. Each age or house tells a story of the battle of good vs. evil. The Hero is Heru (Horus) represented by the star Sirius in the house of Taurus. He is the bull fighter and the dragon slayer. Urt is also Ta-urt. Taurt, consort of Taurus and mother of the baby bull (Baal), is the antithesis of Hathor, mother of Horus. When the Zodiac turns full cycle, the table will turn on the Warlord of this wicked world and all his warriors. The Lord with the Sword is returning to slay Arthur, the antichrist, and his Christian Crusaders (Cruel-satyrs). [Rev.19:11-21] Arthur (Urt-Hur) in his chariot is Anhur (Amen-Ra, the evil sun of God, in his solar bark). Chariot is Art in Egyptian. Anhur is the Anti-Horus or the Antichrist who raptures the masses away. He appears like Horus, but is an impostor. [2 Cor.11:13-15] Those who 'bear' bad fruit shall be taken by the Grim-reaper. [Rev.14:14-20] In Egypt, Art or Kart is the abode of the damned.

Sir Lancelot committed adultery with the king's wife. The fall of Camelot was caused by the infidelity of Guin-Eve-re. Just as Adam and Eve fell from God's favor and were exiled from God's kingdom (Eden). Afterwards they repented. Lancelot became a hermit (heru of Mut or follower of Horus). Guinevere became a nun (Virgin like Nun of Egypt). Compare Guinevere to Nephthys who left her intended, Set, to be with Osiris. Lancelot's son Sir Galahad, King of Sarras (King Osiris) was the only good one. Is Lancelot Osiris and Galahad Horus?

Legend says: Arthur was conceived out of wedlock and brought up by the wizard Merlin. Merlin made Urther to appear as a man so he could mate with his wife. Their child was Arthur. Compare this to Zeus impersonating Amphitryon and mating with Alcmene. Their child was Herakles, who was raised by Chiron the centaur. Compare to Horus, son of a widow. Or Christ conceived out of wedlock. The Holy Grail (Sangrail) means Vessel of Royal Blood or son of the King. Arthur and his bloodthirsty knights were lost because they did NOT have the blood of Christ. Nor did they follow his ways.

As a child, Arthur removes the Sword from the stone. Compare to Herakles killing two serpents as a child. The Sword set in the Rock are two obvious symbols of the Word of God; the Lord with the Sword riding the white horse. Arthur has an illegitimate son by his sister, just as Osiris and his sister, Nephthys, produce Anubis. In Egypt, Ursa Minor is depicted as the Dog Up-uat (antithesis of the Dog star Sirius). Arthur and his seven companions (stars of Ursa Major) escape the deluge just like Noah. Mer-lin means rising waters in Egyptian. His body is covered in stars as if he is the northern stars that gave birth to Arthur. To the Egyptians, Ta-Urt (Ursa Major) is a bull's thigh, representing the Golden Calf (the Sun) sired by Taurus, the Bull of heaven. Bear, Boar, Bull and Baal are the same root as r and l are interchangeable (as are all vowels).

Arthur fights with his son and both die. Compare this to Osiris being killed by his brother. The seven companion stars of Ursa Minor are Arthur's Paw-Bearers. Arthur is placed on his funeral boat with his two queens (Ammit and Ursa Major). Compare this to Osiris on the bark with his queens and sisters, Isis and Nephthys. In Glastonbury, Arthur's epitaph says, "Here lies Arthur, king that was, king that shall be." Compare it to "I am yesterday, today and unto the ages". Arthur spent three days in the cycle of death and rebirth, just like Jesus. Camelot means shrine of the dead; tomb of Arthur. It is his town-ship or bark of his town that carries him through the sea of space.

This is reproduction of the Upper Egyptian version where the Warlord ruled and his right hand man is the priest of Amen (i.e. Merlin the Magician). Compare to Simon the Sorcerer who masqueraded as Simon Peter. It is said that Merlin was the son of Satan. His magic wand had a Satanic star on the end. And he wears the domed crown of Amen. In the end, the Beast, the false prophet and their warriors shall go into the Lake of fire. [Revelation 19:11-21 Jeremiah 46:25 Ezekiel 38 & 39]

The Assyrian "Fight of Bel and the Dragon" and the Egyptian Ra battling the Apophis serpent are both corruption's of Horus: enLightenment battling against the darkness of deception and ignorance. Bel the Bull and Amen-Ra-Set the Bull of heaven are the evil ones. Arthur did not slay the dragon, he is the diabolical dragon. These are twisted tales told by serpentine tongues. In Britain, Artor was the boar god. Compare that to Set taking the form of a boar and attacking Horus. [A Book of Beginnings by Gerald Massey pages 358-359 and Larousse Encyclopedia of Mythology page 241]

The Aryans

The Aryans are the blond haired, blue eyed, pale race. They are of the line of Cain who murdered his brother Abel. The sons of Cain are called Kenites. A name used to cover their identity. The Aryans spread their religion throughout the Middle East and then moved on to India and China about 2000-1500 BC. Spreading their dogma through social and sexual intercourse. For they interbred with all nations trying to improve their genetic pool. Assyrians assimilated other races. The direct descendants of the Cainites are: the Danites, the Romans, the Vikings, the English, the white Russians, etc. The Zodiac age of Aries was 2,300 B.C. to 150 BC. This was the time of the Arians. Aries is also the god of war; that the Romans called Mars. M + ares = Mars. The Romans are remnants of the Aries age. The symbol of Aries is the conquering cross. The sacred animal is the predatory eagle.

Besides the Kenites, there are the Canaanites. The sons of Canaan, who was the son of Ham (father of the black race). Ham was the son of Noah who had sex with his mother (Noah's wife). Noah cursed Ham's son to be and Canaan was born white. The eleven tribes of Canaan are called the Canaanites. While all the other sons of Ham are black. [Genesis 10] Between the 11 tribes of Canaanites and the one tribe of Kenites, they pulled off the greatest charade in history. They pretended to be the 12 tribes of Israel after the people of Israel died in the wilderness of sin. These impostors took on the identity and called themselves Israelites (Israel + ite). Nobody noticed that the colored people had suddenly turned white.

Ham's descendants are called Khamats or Kemetes. Cain's descendants are called Kenites. The word Arian is within the word African. Just as Aryans are genetic mutants from the Kemet family. They are kin.

The Canaanite God is El, Father of the gods. Identical to the Hebrew beliefs. Baal is the bad lord and evil sun of God. [Jeremiah 7:9] The only way to tell the good Sun of God (Christ) from the bad sun of God is by his words. The good Son of God teaches the Word of God including the Ten Commandments of God. The bad son of God teaches to fight for freedom, fight for what is right, fight, fight, fight.... He says you are not under any law. He appears like a lamb of God but is a dragon-devil. A cold-blooded killer. A wolf (canine) in sheep's clothing. He is the god of violence (war) and sex. The Lord warned the people of Israel not to have social or sexual intercourse with them. Christianity inherited the Canaanite pantheon from the Israelites who inherited the land and culture of Canaan. See "The MacMillan Illustrated Encyopedia of Myths & Legends" by Arthur Cotterell-Page 188.

The Hittites are descendants of the Canaanites. Whose evil sun of God is called Tammaz (Baal). Tammaz feeds grapes to goats. In the Word of God, the goats are the kids of the Devil. [Matthew 25:31-46] Tammaz (or Shemach) is the sun god of the Assyrians who the Israelites started to worship. [Ezekiel 8:14,15] They worshipped on Sunday and held sunrise services in honor of the Devil, Satan. The Greeks called him Adonis (lord), and Helio (sun god), and the Romans called him Apollo who is mated to his sister the moon goddess Diana. Sin is the Assyrian and Anna is the Babylonian name for the moon goddess, mistress of the sun god. She gets her en-light-ment or illumination from him. Notice the Anna in DiAnna. "Weeping for Tammaz" is when the evil sungod is slain and cast into the abyss. He is also called Dumuzi. [Revelation 8:10-13 9:1 12:3,4,7-9 20:1]

Ishtar (Inanna / Ashtaroth) is the goddess of sex and war who is mated to Marduk (M-artuk) dragon god of magic. She is called Queen of heaven. [Jeremiah.7:18] Compare to Arthur and his Ma. The Israelites sacrificed their children to them. [Jeremiah 7:31-34] The Romans called her Venus. The Greeks called her Aphrodite. From which we get the word aphrodisiac (love potion). Baal is the Bull as in "golden calf" or "baby bull". The crescent moon compliments the bull's horns. The Gateway of Ishtar in Babylon is lined with bulls. Compare it to the gateway of Ra-Amen at Karnak lined with rams.

The Canaanite god of the Bible is Moloch (King) who is also called Baal-Hammon. He is depicted as an old man with ram's horns. This is Ra-Amon of Upper Egypt. He is called king of the gods, but he is Satan, the ruler of this wicked world for the time being. The Canaanites claim that Baal was the one who died and resurrected as heir to the earth. Baal defeated Yamm, the Lord of the Sea just like Tammuz of Babylon. Then he went to the land of the dead where Mot was Lord. Mot would not release him so Baal's wife Anat (Astarte) kills Mot and resurrects Baal. The problem is: they have reversed the characters. Yam is the Egyptian word for Sea. Mot is the Egyptian word for Mother (i.e. Mother earth). Man returns to the dust of "mother earth" at death. Astarte is a corruption of Ast (Isis) who helped in resurrecting her husband Osiris.

All family names that end in "ite" are white people. The Israelites, Canaanites, Hittites, Amorites, etc... The Assyrians were interbred with the Canaanites. The name Aryan or Arian comes from A-ssy-rian. Today Assyria is Iran which are the last four letters of Assyrian. Likewise, Syrian is within the word Assyrian. As they are all of the same family of white people who later crossed through the Caucasus mountains and acquired the name Caucasian. The Romans called Assyria; Syria.

The land of Shinar (Middle East) became home to many civilizations including; the Summerian (Hittites), Mesopotamian, Assyrian people. The Sumerian, Akkadian, Assyrian, Babylonian, and Mesopotamian myths are almost identical. Originating at the Tower of Babel. The stories of the Savior come from Egypt, but they make the Devil (Baal, Tammuz, Marduk) the hero as lord or ruler of this wicked world.

Story of Sargon the Great

"My mother was a priestess. I did not know my father. The priestess, my mother, conceived me and gave birth to me in hiding. She placed me in a basket made of reeds and closed the lid with pitch. She put the basket in the river with was not high. The river carried me away and brought me to Akki who was a man responsible for libations. Akki looked upon me with kindness and drew me from the river. He adopted me as his child and brought me up. He made me his gardener. It was while I was his gardener that the goddess Ishtar loved me. Then I became king." This is the same story of Isis and her child Horus; Moses and his mother of the Levi priests. Even Romulus and Remus have a similar story. On the celestial level, this is the Sun of God, in the bark, sailing through the sea of space. In fact, Sar of Sar-gon is the Egyptian spelling of Osiris.

About 2750 B.C., Sargon the Great produced 70 tablets summarizing all the elements of astrological knowledge of his era. This compilation was known as the Namman-Bel. Namman is the counterpart of Nun in Lower Egypt and Mut (Mother of Amen-Set) in Upper Egypt. Namman or Nammu is Mother of Amen-Bel, the evil one. On the terrestrial level, Sargon was son of Satan pretending to be king and savior. There are many Anti-Christ's and impostors. The laws of Sargon, code of Hammurabi (1750 B.C.), and laws of Moses (1500 BC) were all taken from Egypt.

Asshur is the king of gods in Assyria. This is a combination of ancestor worship and borrowing from Egypt. Asshur was the father of the Assyrians. [Genesis 10:22] But the god who says he 'is maker of the sky Anu and the underworld' is taken from Egypt. Anu is the heavenly birthplace of Horus. Ashur maybe Anhur (Anshar of Babylon) the Anti-Horus. He is born from, not maker of Anu. Asshur's consort is Ninlil (Nun-lilith), the consort of Enlil (Baal). Enlil is god of the wind, just like Typhoon-Set and Satan. Ashur is the Warlord that rides upon a bull, just like Shiva, and his attribute is a female goat (Set's animal). It sounds like they got their corrupt version of Anhur from Upper Egypt.

Lost Ten Tribes of Israelites

The Israelites were conquered and taken captive by the Assyrians. Israel was absorbed into Assyria. It is a well known fact that the Aryans assimilated people to try to improve their gene pool. When they were released, they did not go back to Israel. Therefore, they are called the Lost Ten Tribes. This Ten tribes went north through the Caucasus Mts., into USSR and into Europe. Once there the Romans called them the Barbarians. [Romans 1:14] Ironically, there are ten tribes of Barbarians: Celts, Franks, Gauls, Anglos, Saxons, Goths, Vis-goths, Slavs, Vandals, Langbards (Long-beards), etc... The modern name is Indo-Europeans as they were not the original Europeans, but immigrants from Indo (Asia). Or more precisely, the Middle East. These Ten tribes later became the Christian Crusaders who invaded the Middle East. The same Barbarians who barbecued babies over an open fire and ate them, just as the Israelite cannibals had sacrificed their children to Baal. [Deuteronomy 18:10 28:46-57] They are Israelites returning to their "homeland".

Conan the Barbarian was one of them. Conan is Canaan father of the Canaanites. Since the Hebrew has no vowels, they substituted an "o" for the "a". Conan means "little hound" just as canine is a dog. The Canaanites are the ones who domesticated and named the wild dog. His people called him Conan the Bald. One of the symptoms of the Curse of Canaan (leprosy) is baldness. [Leviticus 13:42,43] The Celt god Lugus means "the shining One." The Romans called him Mercury the messenger of God. This is NOT Hermes or Thoth! The Bible says Lucifer is the "Shining One" who deceived Eve with his false message. The planet Mercury is Set's planet. Statues of the Norse god Frey looks identical to those of the Canaanite god Baal and the Egyptian god Amon. All wear the same domed crown.

They also had a holiday called Beltane (May 1) which means "fire to Baal". Baal is the evil sungod or sun of God. He is represented by our sun that rises and falls daily. His most high day is the summer solstice (June 21). Followed by Halloween (Devil's day) and then the Yule Candlemas. Yule tide is the winter solstice (Dec.25). This is also the time of the Druid tree worship. [Jeremiah 10:1-5] The Jews have their Festival of Lights called Hanukkah and the Christians have Chrismas, or Santa-mas which comes from the Barbarian's pagan rituals. The Romans worshipped all their gods on Dec.25. Most important is the sun god with his mother the Queen of Heaven. Satan, the state, controls the holidays. God appoints the Holy Days.

Stone Henge is not a mystery. Pillars of wood and stone were dedicated to Baal the sun god. It is a monolith to Amon. It tracks the days of the summer and winter solstice so they could celebrate the renewal of the sun. Just as the Assyrians did.

Odan, god of the Danites

The Viking god of the dead was Odin or Odan. Who was named after the tribe of Dan (O-Dan). The great white god of the Aryans. Just as the Assyrians worshipped Asshur, their forefather. Asshur = Ass (Set) + hur (Horus) is a composite deity as well as being ancestor worship. Asshur is Anhur the Anti-Horus of Thebes. Odan would also be Adon, Adonai or Adonis; all meaning Lord. Odon is Aton the sun god of Egypt. Odan's legends are a mixed up blend of Satan and Christ. For Odan was the god of war like Satan. Yet the legend says he was hanged from a tree and pierced in the side like Christ. [Acts 5:30 10:39 John 19:34] Odin was hung as a sacrifice on the World Ash Tree in order to gain knowledge. He also gave one of his eyes for the sake of enlightenment from the Well of Wisdom. Just like Horus of Egypt who lost one eye in a battle against darkness (Set-Typhon). Except they hanged him for being evil.

The earth is a circle of land surrounded by ocean called Midgard (Egyptian Nut). The Aryans learned from the Egyptians that the world is round. In the ocean depths lies the World Serpent. This is Satan the Serpent of Old. [Rev.12:9] Who is also the Leviathan in the sea of space (Egyptian Apophis). The World Serpent and Hel, ruler of the underworld (Helheim) were his companions. Hel would be Hades of the Greek mythology. Also ruler of the underworld. It is obvious where Christendumb got its fables about Hell and Hades. Ideas foreign to the Word of God. The Lake of fire does not come until after the Millennium. When God, the consuming fire, comes to exterminate all evil. No one torments except the Devil and his fallen angels. [Revelation 20:10]

Yggdrasil, the World Tree, grows in many domains. An underground spring feeds the tree and is the source of hidden wisdom. [Revelation 22:1,2] It is the celestial pole. Svartalfheim the underground home of the dark elves, in the roots of the World Tree. Jotunnheim is land of the frost giants located under the first giant root of the Tree. Mannheim is land of mankind. Vannaheim is home of the Vanir. Ljosalfaheim is the land of the righteous. Niflheim (Niflhel) is the subterranean land of the dead (grave). Heim and Hel mean Land. Where the giants are kept "on ice". In the Bible, Nephilim are the giant sons of the fallen angels doomed to destruction. Niflhel is guarded by a monstrous dog named Garm. Compare it to the Greek Cerberus. Godheim is heaven (Nut in Egypt) and home of the Aesir. This is where we get the word God. Muspellheim is the realm of fire. It is inhabited by the descendants of Muspell, the fire giant, and guarded by Surt and his flaming sword, which will bring the fire of destruction to the gods at Ragnarok, the predestined day of destruction. [Gen.3:24] Sur-t is Osiris-Tum (Horus).

Odan sits on a throne; staff in hand with an eagle on top, and his 2 wild dogs at his side. Canaanites go nowhere without their canines. Odin is top dog. The eagle is counterpart of the Egyptian vulture which represents the Great Matrix (Mut). Her son is the dog star (Ursa Minor). Odin looks suspiciously like Zeus. In fact, it all sounds like Greek mythology. The Christianized Romans made a few changes and called their new god JeZeus or Jesus. Constantine, emperor of Rome established the dogma of his religion. They worship on Sunday in honor of the Venerable sun god as it crosses the celestial meridian (and North Pole star) during the summer solstice. Oden is the Egyptian sun-god, Aten. The Roman symbols are the eagle and the hooked cross or swastika. The swastika represents the turning of the Pole stars (Ursa Minor). The symbols of the god of war. Hitler used these same symbols as the past Christian crusaders who murdered millions. Christians, like Hitler, have been murdering Jews, Muslims, pagans, and other Christians for over 1900 years.

There are two races of gods: the Aesir and the Vanir. The Aesir is lead by Odin and Thor. Aesir is obviously Asir or Asar (Osiris) and Thor is Tem-Horus of Lower Egypt. Thor is the firstborn Son and mediator between God and men. Vanir is the Upper Egyptians. The two joined forces against the frost giants in the north (Europe). This is the counterpart of the Greek gods of Olympus battling the Titan giants.

Ymir was father of the giants just like Chronus. Ymir suckled from Adumla, the heavenly heifer. She is the counterpart of Hathor. Adumla is the matrix and wet-nurse of Atum-Ra as well as Amen-Ra (Ymir). Odan and his siblings usurped his father just as Zeus and his siblings overthrew their father, Chronos. As Horus overthrew his father's brother, Set.

Loki, like Lucifer, is handsome and good looking. [Ezekiel 28:12] He is the Trickster and Deceiver. Loki is chained to a rock like Prometheus. Compare to Revelation 20:1-3 where the Beast is chained. Loki is released from confinement and leads the giants against the gods in the last great battle at Ragnarok. This sounds just like Armageddon. [Revelation 19:11-21] The strange thing is that the Vikings are the evil giants. Descendants of the giants of the land of Canaan. The gods or sons of God are the angels who follow the Lord with the Sword in the battle against Satan and his Titans.[Revelation 12:3-9 Matthew 16:27] They slay all the warrior giants. Loki's son the Wolf Fennrir devours Odan. A wolf is also a canine, meaning a Canaanite. Romulus and Remus was suckled by a wolf or Canaanite woman. Romulus later became founder of Rome. The Romans are half Canaanite. Vidar, the son of Odin, thrusts his Sword into the heart of the Wolf Fenrir. Compare this to Set (a canine) killing Osiris and then Horus, his son, taking revenge. Meanwhile, Thor slays the World Serpent but is killed by its poison. Compare this to Tem-Horus (Thor) slaying the Apophis serpent, yet as the Christ Child is killed by the Scorpion, another attribute of Set. Herakles killed the Hydra, yet its poison later killed him. All the gods and Titans died.

In one version, Loki caused the blind Hodr (Hothor) to kill his brother, Balder with his sword. Balder goes to NiflHel. Hel is the daughter of Loki and ruler of Niflhel. Hermod (Hermes in Greek), another brother of Balder, volunteers to ride to Hel and bring him back, but it is decided that he can't return. Balder's wife, Nanna died from grief. Nanna is Mother Nature. Nanna's counterpart would be Persephone, consort of Hades, or Isthar of Babylon or Nephthys of Egypt. One version says Hothor killed his brother with an arrow made of mistletoe. He was then burned in a Beltine (Baal's pyre). At Christmas, Mother Nature and her sun dies. Balder (Baal-oak) is the sacred family tree of the Aryans that dies in the winter, while the parasite of the oak, mistletoe, lives on. Balder is described as "so fair of face and so shining that a light went forth from him." Just like the sun god, Set of Egypt. [The Golden Bough by James George Frazer page 819]

The Vikings believe, like the Christian crusaders, that all good warriors to Valhalla, the Hall of Val (the slain). Just as the Manes are the dead minions of Amen. They combined the ideas of the Greek Elysium fields and Roman Coliseum. Where they rise every morning to do mock battle, in preparation for Ragnarok, the day of destruction. Ragnarok is the same as Armageddon. Then return to the Hall of Valor to feast on food (swine) and drink (mead). They pig out on swine snout, pig feet, pork belly, boar brains, mountain oysters (hog testicles), etc... Following Ragnarok, a new world is created and populated with the people reborn from the World Tree of life.

It is true that everyone gets what they believe in. Not everyone gets what they want, not everyone gets what they need, but everyone will get what they deserve. Those who shed blood, their blood shall be shed. The warriors shall go to Hall or Hell where Amen-Baal rules (Amenta the Cemetery). Hell merely means the grave. On Judgment day, if they don't repent, they go into the Lake of fire.

The fire giant Surf, sets the earth ablaze, the sky falls, and the world is engulfed in the rising sea. This is the Lake of fire raining down from God. [Matthew 24:27-31 Revelation 20:9 2 Peter 3:10-13] Yet all is well that ends well. For the earth re-emerges green and fair and a new Sun rises as the old sun god falls. The new Sun is the son of that which a wolf had once devoured. In other words, the son of Odin. And the sons are born again from the Tree of life and everyone lives happily ever after in the Fields of Peace (Sekhet-hetep of Egypt and Elysian Fields of the Greeks). This Morning Star is Christ. Who defeats that Old Serpent, Lucifer. Satan and his followers are thrown into the Lake of fire by the good Sun of God. The sons of Odin; Balder and his twin brother Hodr shall repopulate the earth. Hodr is the blind Horus. The right Eye of Horus is Sirius and the left is Hyades. The twin Morning Stars shall be restored as the two all-seeing eyes of Horus. Only those purged in the fire shall enter God's kingdom and partake of the Tree of life.

Aryans follow the zodiac sign of Aries, the Roman god of war. The followers of Aries are called Arians. The constellation is a goat or ram, the animal that represents Satan. [Revelation 13:11] The symbol of Rameses II was a ram. The ram is the false lamb who shepherds his sheep to the slaughter. [Rev.13:11] Adolf Hitler was born under the sign of Aries. Just below Aries, is the star of Hyades in the constellation of Taurus. Hades (kingdom of Set) is the enemy of Orion (kingdom of Osiris). Taurus is the bull (Baal). They wore the domed crown of Amen with the horns of the bull. It is the helmet of the Warlord, Hel.

Don Quixote is a satire about a "madman" who battles a wind-mill. This is the ancient story of the Hero who battles the beasts of the Zodiac. The mill is the turning or precession of the constellations. The sea of space turns the wind or water mill. The mill is the wheel of time through the ages (mill-enniums). Don would be Odan. This is a corruption of the story of Orion. The beast is the dragon (Draco). [Hamlet's Mill] Compare Quixote to Coyote; a canine similar to Anubis the Jackal. Anubis being related to the Dog star (Sirius) and to Osiris.

Dracula means "son of Draco, the Dragon" or "son of the devil". Dracula was a real person, Vlad the Impaler. He was a Christian king who murdered thousands of his own people. 30,000 he impaled on poles and sometimes he drank their blood. This bloodthirsty, paleface was sick, yet the people have made him infamous. King Arthur was also son of the Pen-dragon. Likewise, he too lead the Christian crusader on conquests to kill Muslims in Palestine. King Arthur's right hand man was Merlin the Magician. Who did sorcery by the power of Satan the dragon. His magic wand did bear a satanic star at the point. These heads of state are the heads of the dragon that the Lord with the Sword is coming to slay.

It all started with Cain who murdered his brother Abel. Cain's mark was leprosy or albinism. [Leviticus 13 Numbers 12:10] He was the first white man. He was so pale and sickly looking, no one, including Adam, would dare go near him to take revenge on him for killing Abel. Cain looked like the walking dead. Cain's sons were called Cainites or Kenites. They were craftsmen in bronze and iron who made weapons for war. [Genesis 4:22] These Kenites (Cainites) later became the Danites and Vikings. They have fair skin, blond hair and blue eyes. The Indians called them 'White-eyes'. If they lacked any more pigment, they would be pink eyed albinos. I am sure they are seeing red right now. The 'dumb blond' stigma does not just pertain to the females. Most Aryans are ignorant of their 'white roots'.

"Leprosy was indigenous to Egypt and Africa; it has even been conjectured that the white Negroes were produced by it, as the Albinos of the Black race." [Gerald Massey in A Book of the Beginnings page 9] These Kenites are white Kamites (Khamet). Ham is father of the Khamet (Africans). Canaan was the white son cursed because of his father, Ham. [Genesis 9:25 10:6,15-20] Canaan is father of the Caucasians with dark hair and eyes. Scientists agree that the first man was a black African.

Let's look at the facts. People with the blood type O are dark skinned, and dark eyed. I believe the O stands for descendants of Osiris. People with the blood type "A" belong to the group of blond haired, blue-eyed type. I believe "A" stands for Albino, which means White in Latin. [See The Sirius Connection by Murry Hope page 39] The Bible calls this blood type "Leprosy". It is hereditary disorder. [See Numbers 12:10 Leviticus 13:2,4,10 2 Chronicles 26:19-23 2 Kings 5:27 2 Samuel 3:29]

The Indians called them "White eyes" and "pale face" because of lack of color or melanin pigments. Melanin or melanoid is Greek word meaning the Black or Negroid race. On the other hand, the lack of color is found in the white (Caucasian or Caucasoid race). Albinism is a genetic disorder just like Downs syndrome. [Grolier Encyclopedia of Knowledge; see Genetic diseases, Vitiligo, and Albinism] Venus Melainis is the Black Venus. Jupiter, Bacchus, Herakles, Apollo, Ammon, Hecati, Artemis, Diana, Juno, Metis, Ceres, Cybile, Krishna and Buddha were all Black. Not to mention the Black Madonna of the Catholics. [Anacalypsis by Godfrey Higgins, ESQ page 138] Dr. Herman Hoeh in his book "Germany in Prophecy?" wrote: "When the ancient Greek writers wanted to distinguish the Assyrians from the Arameans or Syrians, the Greeks called the Assyrians, 'Leucosyri'-meaning 'whites' or 'blondes' as distinct from the very brunette Syrians who still live in Mesopotamia." These Syrians are Arabians (Semitics).

The legend of Yeti, the Abominable Snow-Man, is universal. The roots of it are found in Egypt. Yeti is Seti (Satan) the abomination of God. In Egypt, Ab = "heart" + omin (Amin) "evil one". Therefore, Abomin means "evil heart". In Hebrew, it is "father" + "evil one". The Bible says Cain is the son of Satan and cursed from both heaven and earth for killing Abel. [1 John 3:12] Therefore, he could not ascend nor descend and die. His curse is to live on while suffering. This "Abominable Snow-Man" is an albino. Christ called the Jews, sons of the Devil through Cain. Cain, like Cronus, is father of the Titan (Giants) called the Kenites. [John 8:44]

It was Cain's descendants who worked iron and raised cattle. [Genesis 4:20,22] Sound familiar? Cowboys with their shooting irons! And branding irons to put the Mark of Cain on all that is theirs. Cowboys are famous for "raising Cain" in the Wild West. The modern Wilderness of Sin. The industrial age was crafted by the iron-workers. [Genesis 4:22]

They built their empire from iron and concrete. [Daniel 2:31-34-45] They honor the god of fortresses and self-defense that always takes the stand of offense. [Daniel 11:38-40] The American department of defense is the Pentagon. Which is built in the shape of a Pentagram or Satanic star. The Egyptian word Menmen means Cattle. It comes from Amen+Min, the Bull-god (i.e. Baal). Kine or Kain is the old English word for cattle.

America was called the new Promise land of the "new Canaan". But the Wild West soon became the new Wilderness of Sin. As the Palefaces slaughtered the people of color from the east coast to the west. In the tradition of their forefather Cain. And the survivors became their slaves. Who were forced to worship the Christian cult's pagan practices. The religion of the Aryan race places white supremacy at the top. The Pope is always a Paleface. The Romans were blond haired and blue eyed. Strangely, they portrayed Satan, in their art, as blond haired and blue eyed. The great white god of the Anglo-Saxons is the Warlord, Satan.

Christopher Columbus was a blond haired, hooked nosed Aryan. He was a Jew of the tribe of Dan who converted to Christianity. He returned to America in 1493 with 2,000 Christian crusaders to enslave the Indians. Those who would not dig for gold had their hands cut off or were executed.

The immigrants left Europe to escape the Catholic oppression. Then, in turn, they oppressed everyone who was different from them. The Christian inquisitions crossed the Atlantic ocean under the Protestant banner. The persecuted was now the persecutors. Those who would not conform to Christian dogma, were executed. Their propaganda is "love it or leave it." 'Love It' is referring to their idea of the way things should be. 'Leave it' refers to an early departure (death).

The Germans are NOT Aryans. Frankly, I don't understand why they would want to be. The ancient name for Germany is Gomer son of Japheth. [Genesis 10:1-5] Germany, like the Greeks (Javan), are the original Europeans called the Gentiles. All Gentiles are dark skinned, dark eyed, and dark haired. The Aryans are blond haired and blue eyed. The Aryans settled in Denmark, Sweden, England, Russia, Iceland, and North America. The Germans may have bred with the Hittites when the ten Canaanite tribes invades Europe. These ten tribes are better known as the Barbarians. They were Caucasians, but not blond haired and blue eyed. Only the Danites (Cainites) are pure Aryans. 85% of the Germans belong to the cult of Christendom founded by Caesar Constantine.

It was the Aryans who transformed mythology into fables and fairytales. The hero is on his conquest. The white knight slays the dragon and saves the damsel in distress. But should he marry the damsel, his adventures are over. He must choose between the quest or the confining institution of marriage. He must sacrifice his freedom to please his wife or start out on a new conquest. He-man, Superman, Batman, Spider-man are all single, celibate, super heroes who abstain from the physical pleasures of this wicked world.

The problem starts when a mortal man fantasies that he is the Savior who battles against the ones who he perceives as evil. Killing his chances for immorality. Cain was the first crusader who did shed the blood of Abel the first martyr. He who makes enemies, makes himself the Adversary (Satan). The Lord said, "You shall love your enemies." There is but One Judge who is the Savior of the law-abiding and Executioner of the outlaws. Anyone who takes the law into his own hands is an outlaw following in the ways of the Devil. The Romans learned their evil ways from the Egyptians of Upper Egypt who worshipped Amon-Ra, the evil son of God. Romulus, the crusader, shed the blood of his brother Remus because he (Romulus) was evil like his forefather Cain. [1 John 3:12]

Why were the Christian crusaders obsessed with possessing Israel and Jerusalem? It was Not because they thought JeruSalem was the holy city. They believe Rome is the holy city. The real reason was that they want to possess the land of Canaan, the home of the Canaanites. As you may recall, Israel was called Canaan before the Israelites took their land. This is one more proof that the Caucasian Christians are Canaanite giants.

Both the statue of Zeus at Olympus and Athene of Athens had faces of white ivory. Which is strange since the Greeks and Athenans were dark skinned. Yet, white is the color of their sun god (Lucifer / Ra). Caesar Constantine took the graven image of Zeus to Constantinople and worshipped it as Jesus. A replica of Athene was erected in Nashville, Tennessee. She is the prototype of the Goddess of Freedom on the Capitol building at Washington DC.

The militant mentality was carried over from the Europeans along with their icons they idolize. By Fighting for Freedom, they become Slaves to Sin. Compare the Aryan Declaration of Independence to the Egyptian Declaration of Innocence! "I have not killed. I have not commanded to kill." The declaration of Independence causes the division of a nation. The scriptures say to share all things in common. Common is the root of community and communion. The body members of Christ (Osiris) declare their dependence upon the head that unites them as one. [Ephesians 2:18-22] Osiris united the kingdom of Egypt on the platform of peace and brotherly love. Being a follower of Christ means dying (Not killing) for what you believe in. [Matthew 16:24-26 Revelation 6:9] Osiris, Abel, Christ, Stephen and Peter were martyrs not murders.

The New World Order

The Aryan conquest quickly spread their dogma and the sickness of sin soon followed. In the Americas, the paleface pilgrims invaded and occupied the new land. Millions of native Indians died from the various strains of the white plague. As the Canaanites and Cainites are carriers of the many diseases linked with leprosy. Leprosy being the curse of albinism. [2 Chronicles 26:19-23 Leviticus 13:2,4,10 Numbers 12:10 2 Kings 5:27] The natives have no immunities because they had none of these sickness.

The Inuit Indians (Eskimos) combine Thanksgiving with Halloween. The Day of the Dead is a memorial of the day white man massacred the very Indians who saved them from starvation on that first Thanksgiving day. The Indians were hospitable and charitable. The paleface pioneers were the selfish, savage, heathens. The startling thing is that white man documented this sick history. Often even bragging about his cruelties.

It is common knowledge that the Mormons hired the Danites (Kenites) as mercenaries. Mercen-aries are minions of Aries the Warlord. These hired guns murdered in the name of Christianity. Compare this to the blood money or bounty money the Jews offered to Judas for the capture of Jesus, dead or alive. In fact, the Mormon history is almost as bloody as the Jewish history. How dare these sinners call themselves Saints! Saint means sanctified or set apart from sin. The pilgrims of Christendumb claim that God promised the land of America to the Caucasian Canaanites as compensation for giving the land of Canaan to the Israelites.

The Christian Conspiracy: World Domination

The Christian colonies of the conquering Caucasian Canaanites now cover the planet. It has gone beyond the unholy Roman empire and the evil English empire. Few people realize that (white) Russia is a colony of the English empire. Lenin was trained in England and financially backed by the Capitalists (Rothschilds) for the purpose of starting the Russian revelation in order to gain huge profits off the poor 'communist'. The Rothschilds are a family of Jews who now possess one of the richest banks in the world in Moscow. Their god is Mammon. The people in the state of Russia are direct descendants of the Danites just like the English. Their official state religion is Christianity. Likewise, China, India and the African continent were conquered and oppressed by the Caucasian Christians. The mother religion, Catholicism, which means Universal, is true to its name. Christendom now covers the planet like the white plague. They teach their white lies of the white god. This is irrefutable proof that they are the universal state religion of the last days.

The Pope has succeeded the high priest of the Jewish temple after its destruction by the Romans. "There shall not lack one to sit on the throne of David until the Lord comes." The Pope is the successor who sits on that throne in the so-called Eternal City. Christendum is a sect of Judaism and continues on the rule of the royal religion of Thebes, Egypt. The throne, scepter, tiara or miter crown, and obelisk of Amen moved to Solomon's temple and then on to the Vatican. In the last days, the Anti-christ or Vicar of Christ will sit on the throne of Rome. When the Lord comes, he will depose these despots! [2 Thessalonians 2:2-8]

In London, England is an obelisk called Big Ben dedicated to Amen-Ra-Set. The whole world does "Set" their time according to the obelisk. In Ottawa's Parliament Hill, Canada is the so called Peace Tower. It is merely a copy of the obelisk in London. They have nothing to do with peace. Obelisks are used to record military victories. Just as the so called "peace sign" is really a victory sign that originated in the Victorian days. These Anglos are Aryans (partial albinos). Albion is the ancient name of Britian. The Romans assumed it to have derived from albus (white). The Washington monument is an obelisk 555 feet and 5 inches high. Its base is 55 feet square and the windows are 500 feet from the base. 5 is the number of Satan. The Satanic star is a pentacle. The word "monument" comes from Monu + Ament, the Warlord Montu and devil of Egypt. Amenta is the underground land of the dead (cemetery). The infamous Eiffel Tower is the skeleton of an obelisk.

Part of the Aryan dogma says that the warriors who fight the good battle shall turn into angels and go to heaven. Those who are your enemies go to hellfire to torment forever. This propaganda (pro-pagan-dogma) has a direct link to spiritualism or channeling. A seance is supposed to prove there is life after death by manifesting the ghost of a dead person (friend or relative) from the spirit world. The Word of God says these "familiar spirits" are the fallen angels pretending to be people familiar to you. The only three to have escaped the confines of death were: Enoch, Elijah, and Christ. Their human bodies were translated when they were taken, as proof.

It is absolutely amazing to me that Americans know every little detail of the life and death of Princess Diana, yet they know absolutely nothing about England joining the United States of Europe, as prophesied. Americans are ignorant of the greatest news in our lifetime. This is the Dark Age of Ignorance when Americans will read the gossip newspapers, but will not read the gospel's good news! I think the masses wait with bated breath for Diana's ascension to her throne as Queen of Heaven.

The Word of God says there are two parts to the Beast in Revelation 13. The first half is the state run by head of state who is the antichrist. The second half is the religion run by the head of the church (Pope). This false prophet looks like the Lamb of God (Christ) but speaks like the dragon (Devil). He is teaching little white lies to the masses. This church and state union fits the Roman Catholic Empire to a tee. In fact, it was that same Beast who crucified Christ. [Revelation 12:5] And that same Beast is described in the book of Daniel. [Daniel 2:31-45 7:1-7-27] There is no doubt that John and Daniel are speaking of the resurrection of the Roman Empire after it was mortally wounded at the Fall of the Roman empire. The Catholic church miraculously heals that wound and the neo-Rome rises again. [Revelation 13:3,12]

The Antichrist will be an Aryan. The fiery serpent (Satan) will incarnate in the flesh as the secular savior and ruler of the world. His white face shall be as the sun and his hair as golden rays. He will be a handsome blond haired, blue eyed, smooth talking devil. Just as Lucifer was the most beautiful being ever created. [Ezekiel 28:11,12] In the garden of God, his beauty and charm seduced Eve. Now he is turning his charm towards the masses. Christendom will conquer the world for a short time. Christians are attracted to the light of the sun-god like a moth to the flame. [2 Corinthians 11:2,3,13-15]

It would seem that Satan has won the war of good vs. evil. The dark age of the antichrist savior ruling the world from his home in Rome. His religion Christ-anti dominates the world. Those that won't submit are sacrificed to the Christian god. All rivals are crucified by the Christian crusaders. Just as the southern Baptist K.K.K. did to the African Americans and the Christian cavalry did to the American Indians. There was no freedom of religion for them. America was founded on Christian values and men like Gen. Custer was their heroes. The white warriors fight the unholy war for their Warlord. It has been estimated that the 'Christian Crusatyrs' killed between 200,000,000 and 400,000,000 people! The corpses, they claimed, to be converts to Christendumb!

All this was a necessary evil to prove that Satan is not able to rule the world. He has caused nothing but chaos in his attempt to have his people destroy the Lord's people. The Lord with the Sword shall soon return to take vengeance on those who shed innocent blood. He shall be victorious as the LORD of the Earth. [2 Peter 3:3-14] All warriors, white and colored, shall be exterminated! The peacemakers shall be called the sons of God and the meek shall inherit the earth. The warriors are the sons of Satan who shall inherit the beach front property on the Lake of fire. [1 John 3:12 John 8:44] In fact, they shall be the sands of the sea shore. "From dust to dust, ashes to ashes."

Paleface Predators

It was the white man who cut the trees of Europe, then Africa, then America and now the tropical rain forest of south America. It was the white man who hunted many animals to extinction and more are in danger of extinction: alligators, whales, rhinos, elephants, lions and other wild cats, birds, beavers, bears, buffalo, wolves, gorillas, seals, etc. They even nearly caused the extinction of their national symbol the bald eagle. The eagle is the ancient symbol of the Aryan race. It is the white man who polluted the land, water and air. They strip mined the land, spilled oil in the water, and put acid in the rain. It is white man who threatens all mankind with his destructive weapons of war. The Bible says that those who hurt mother earth shall be destroyed.

Man was created in the likeness of both the good and bad sons of God, therefore, he possesses the power to create as well as destroy. Each individual must choose whether to do good or evil. [Hebrews 5:8-14] With freedom and power comes the responsibility for the consequences. Man is a part of nature, yet apart from nature. Man has the ability to change his carnal nature. He can rise above his animal instincts.

The Bible says animals communicate with the Lord. Some African tribes communicate with clicks similar to dolphins. Dolphins and primates can learn human sign language, yet we can not learn their language. The Lord is aware when even a sparrow falls. Animals have a piece of God's Spirit (life force). At death, the same happens to man as to all beasts. [Ecclesiastes 3:19,20] Animals feel pain, make conscious decisions, and remember their enemies; including the human ones. Animals of the same species can be good or evil. They can be loving or hateful. In almost all aspects, animals are superior to homosapiens. Compared to animals, man is slow both mentally and physically. A hummingbird flaps its wings faster than our eyes can see. Its ability to hover and maneuver at high speeds boggles our minds. The only real difference in man is the ability to change nature. All other animals must adopt to nature's changes.

The Jews were so evil, they needed to sacrifice animals vicariously for their daily sins. The Semitic priests (Sem of Egypt) were no better than kosher butchers. Likewise, Christians sin purposely and impute their sin onto the spotless Lamb of God (their Scape-goat). They sacrifice their savior to make Atonement for past, present and future sins they plan on committing. The Pope claims to be Vicar of God who can Vicariously absolve you of sin. He exchanges Absolution for Confession and a Contribution ($$$) to the kitty (Catholic collection). Do the people of Christendumb really buy into this scam??? Only God can forgive sin. They continue to sacrifice a tithe (tenth) of their wages as an offering for their debts (sins). Paying penance for sin. At one time it was pentance (one fifth). The Bible says, 'The wages of sin is death.'

Sacrificing the animal for the benefit of the crops-means giving up being carnivorous for becoming vegetarian. The Hindus and Egyptians offered bread and wine instead of flesh and blood. The Lamb's blood and flesh were replaced by the bread and wine. In God's kingdom, just as in Eden, all (man and animal) will be nonviolent vegetarians. There will be no blood-shed. [Isaiah 11] Man can live in harmony with nature without worshipping mother nature (which is whorship). Saying Mother Nature gave animals their instincts is confessing her existence. The Theory of Evolution is the Theology of the Evil men of science who honor the Mother goddess. These priests of Mother Nature are fickle like their Mother. They think it is their prerogative to change their theories frequently.

God created mother nature (ma-neteru). God does not intervene (with few exceptions to this rule). Why? When you see a dying animal, do you intervene? No. You allow nature to run its course. We can't protect all the animals from the cycle of life to death. They must be free. God created the laws of nature and set them to run automatically. Mother nature controls the sun-god (Ra) and the rain-god (Baal). The heat of the sun evaporates the water and returns it as rain. This is not to say nature is a goddess. Nature is a self-contained system.

In Indian mythology, the great white (albino) buffalo represents the white man. Compare to the Beast of Revelation. Legend says that, if it is sacrificed there will be prosperity for the Indian. There are many stories of visions of the white buffalo, but no man can kill a vision or forestall fate. The Indian warrior shall not survive. Only the peacemakers have prospered.

It was the paleface race who tried to exterminate the Indians. The pilgrims (Puritans and pioneers alike) rejoiced at the death of the so called "heathens". Notice the "grim" in pilgrim as in "grim reaper". They also did exploit the naive natives. It was the paleface race who did the slave trade of Indians and Africans. [Revelation 18:13] They got wealthy from the plantations in America where the slaves did all the work. Caucasian Canaanites are capitalists who will do anything for a profit. These Southern Rebels even went to war to protect their luxurious lifestyles. Their god is Mammon or Materialism. Mammon is a perversion of Ammon or Amon of Upper Egypt. It is similar to Menmen (Amen-Amen). These slave masters broke all of God's laws on the subject. [Exodus 21] "Do onto others as you would want them to do for you." How would they like 200 years of white slavery?

Who did the Lord say it was OK to kill? He said, "You shall love your enemy." "You shall love your neighbor." "You shall love God." "If you love God, you will do His Commandments." [1 John 5:1-3] Obviously, Christians are not followers of Christ. They are followers of Cain, the first murderer. [1 John 3:4-12] The children of God do NOT purposely break God's laws. Christendom has slandered the Savior and misquoted the Messiah. They have sacrificed the Word of God in order to justify their evil deeds. Christ did NOT give his life so that people could continue to sin in his name. Christ blood does NOT cover your future sins done purposely. [Hebrews 10:26-29 6:4-6] Everyone's criminal records will be revealed on Judgment Day. [Revelation 20:11-15] The incorrigible sinners will receive the death penalty. [Revelation 9:20,21]

The English and American colonies are the drug dealers who sold opium around the world. Washington built the transcontinental railroad with drug money. Anyone who can't see that it is the government running the drugs today is blind. The Bible says drugs (legal and illegal) are the concoctions of witch-doctors (sorcerers). Who are Apollyons or followers of Apollo. [Rev.9:11,21] The evil English empire even went to war against the Chinese who refuse to buy anymore opium. The so-called Boxer Rebellion was the Buddhists attempting to banish the Christian devils. Christians who say God took the form of a bird and mated with a mortal. (Compare this to Zeus). The illegitimate son they worship as a lamb or a dead man on a cross (Totemism), while the maiden is raised to goddess status and called Queen of Heaven. Tragically, the Chinese are defeated and forced to buy the addictive drug and pay damages to the bloody British Barbarians. This is neither fiction nor fable. It is a fact of history.

Manifest Destiny?

Christyins are in possession of stolen property! The land that their forefathers stoled from the Indians. The land given to them to use by the Lord of the earth. Confess your sins and return the property your ancestors plundered from the aboriginal (ab-original) peoples. No thief shall enter the Promise land of God's kingdom. [1 Corinthians 6:9,10 Ephesians 5:3-5] The question is: Are you a citizen of Christendom or God's Kingdom? When Christ is made manifest, he will take back what is his. Satan's eminent domain of the earth and the earthlings, has been redeemed. The Lord shall re-incarnate as King of God's kingdom on earth. The peacemakers shall be his co-heirs of the Promise land. The warriors shall be disinherited. The Destiny of the Christian crusaders will manifest in a man-feast. The fouls shall feast on their carcasses. [Rev.19:11-21]

Eminent means exalted. The root of the word is Amen (AKA Satan). Satan exalted himself as ruler of this world, but he shall be brought down low. [Ezekiel 28:1-19 Isaiah 14:12-15] When Satan was cast out of heaven, he did Not go down to rule over a domain called Hell. His domain was earth. [Rev.12:12] For six thousand years he has ruled over the earth. Satan appoints all heads of state. Just as Amen was the state god of Egypt and the power behind the throne. Christendom was the state religion of the Unholy Roman Catholic Empire where evil rules.

To the Egyptians, the flag is the hieroglyph for god. To the Americans, the flag symbolizes their god of war. "Old glory" leads the way to conquer and plunder. This is a flag fetish. The red and white stripes are from the Viking pirates. The fifty stars of the northern circumpolar stars (Draco, Great Bear and Little Bear) representing north America. To the Egyptians, the Arctic stars represent the Devil, the Great Mother and their evil suns. They are called the Samen (the United). The kingdoms of the northern hemisphere are; United States of America, United States of Europe, and the United States of Russia.

The Caucasians teach the theory of evolution as a theology. They misquote by saying, "the strongest shall survive". Using that as an excuse for genocide. But the original is, "The fittest shall survive". Those who are found fit or worthy shall be saved. [2 Thessalonians 1:1-11] The meek shall inherit the earth, not the strong. The peace makers shall be sons of God. The warriors are sons of Satan. [John 8:44] In the end, the sons of light will have victory over the sons of darkness without striking a blow. The Lord with the Sword shall fight for us.

God has allowed the Caucasian Canaanites to rule the world to prove that Satan is a bad ruler. His people have produced chaos, anarchy and destruction. But for every action there is an equal and opposite reaction. The Aryans are the Yin or negative force in the world. The Lord is the positive force. The Lord with the Sword is coming for the coup de grace: a mortal stroke of mercy to put the evil ones out of their misery. Those who claim they are under grace and not God's law, will be eliminated! So that the children of God can live in peace.

Limited space does not allow me to speak of the horrors done by the Secret White Societies like: K.K.K., Rosicrucians, Masons, Illumini, Christian Knights Templar, etc... White man's mission is to put the colored people in submission. May God have mercy on all the sick souls with exalted egos, who think their race is better than the rest. Destruction follows the proud. We All belong to the same human race. Adam was the father of us all.

Strangely, the Christians claim the forbidden fruit was an apple, yet children are taught to take an apple to the teacher. Are they admitting that this is carnal knowledge from the Tree of good and evil? Are the children returning the forbidden fruit to the original trickster? It is obvious that Christendumb gets their knowledge from the Worldly Tree of good and evil. Most Christians can't read at an advance level, so they couldn't even read the Bible and understand it! They go by what others, who don't understand it either, misinterpret what it says. Yet they read Greek mythology that says the fruit of Hera's garden was an apple. Likewise, Aphordite's passion fruit is a 'love apple'.

The Christian conversion prayer says; "Dear Lord forgive us sinners. . . . In Your name. Amen." Question: is His name, Amen? Why does Christendumb use this standardized prayer that gives Amen the last Word? Why is Amen capitalized? Do they know it is the name of the evil Egyptian sun of God? The witches, Satanists, and others translated 'Amen' to 'So be it', just as Rameses II did.

The Church Bell

Jingle Bells herald the death of the sun at the winter solstice on Dec.25th for those who worship the sun-god. Likewise, the church bells of Christendumb herald the human deaths. "For whom the bell tolls" means someone has died! When Christendom dies, the bells will have been silenced. Christians believe a bell rings everytime a fallen angel gets his wings. How heathen! The word bell is from Baal, as in the Tower of Baal (AKA the Tower of Babel). From here is were we get church steeples and bell towers raised up the evil sun-god.

The Liberty bell is Not what it is "cracked" up to be. It does Not ring true. It heralds liberty for the Caucasian, Christian, capitalist, males only. The slave-masters are deaf to the cries of the oppressed. [Exodus 3:7] Hell's bells are the lies forged in hell-fire! A bell was converted into the first cannon, which became the Catholic canon. It spread the word that those who rebel against their canon, would be put to death. Heed the canon bull (Papal law, as in congressional bill) or feel the gun-fire of the cannon ball. Bellum is the Latin word for "War". Bull means to lie; as in fable (fa-bull). Tinker Bell is a fairy tale or lying spirit. Christendumb teaches the Papal-bull, not the Word of God. In 970 AD, Pope John XIV issued a bull for baptizing of Bells, 'to cleanse the air of devils.' Obviously, the air between his ears was full of devils, the dumb-bell!

The Assyrian custom of assimilating other races in order to improve the gene pool has produced America, the great melting pot. The dominant white race chooses natural selection to produce hybrids. Those who don't fit in, are crushed under the pressure and melted down (in their Hellfire) and forced to fit their mold. They will convert, one way or the other, dead or alive. This is the 'after-Birth of a Nation'. The documentary of America is written in blood! From the blood beginning, to the blood end. The Bible says, "Do not conform to the ways of the world..." [Romans 12:2] Their religion is watered down to appeal to the masses within Christendom, the immoral majority. The blood of Christ is diluted and polluted just as the people are. The corruption of Communion shall be their Last Supper. In the last days, the bad fruits will be crushed in the wine press, producing a bad vintage of vinegar, that will be hard to swallow. This time the rivers of blood will be theirs. What the prejudice sow, the Grim reaper shall reap. "Do onto others as shall be done to you." The arrogant (Aryan + ignorant) shall be brought down low.

The Egyptian word Ingle means parasite as the Anglo-Saxon pirates plundered Eng-land and other lands. The Vikings lived off the bounty of the land, reaping what they did not sow. Britain was once called Island of Beli (i.e. Baal, Set, Saturn, Satan). Both the Protestant and Papal pilgrims have pillaged around the world in reverence of their god. [A Book of Beginnings page 450]

I will neither apologize nor defend my white brotherhood. I've divorced the hueless humans, just as the Lord divorced the Israelites. [Jeremiah 3:8] The colorful children of God are now my family. The Lord's ex-wife is excommunicated. He neither hears their prayers nor answers them. They have a Covenant with death. [Isaiah 28:15-18 22:14] If this all seems very negative, it is because the truth hurts! I will not tell you the White Lies you are accustom to. Ignorance is NOT innocence!

Judaism

The Fable

The people of Israel did NOT build the pyramids nor any other structure in Egypt. When in the land of Goshen, Egypt, they were brick makers. They were not brick layers or masons. In fact, they had to hire foreigners to build the holy temple because they did not know how. Their custom was to live in tents or tabernacles or caves just like the Arabian nomads.

The people of Israel did exodus from Egypt during the reign of Rameses II. They wandered in the Wilderness of Sin for forty years, according to the Word of God. According to the Encyclopedia Britannica, Pharaoh Merenptah, the son of Rameses, became king of Egypt. He says he exterminated the people of Israel in 1234 BC. Verifying the fact that the Lord says only Jacob, Caleb and Eleazar will enter the promise land. [Numbers 14:29,30 26:65 32:11,12 Deuteronomy 1:34-38] Eleazar is son of Aaron and acting high priest of the House of Israel.

Here the mystery begins. The people of Israel were replaced with impostors. The eleven tribes of Canaanites and one tribe of Cainites became the 12 tribes of Israelites. [Genesis 10:15-20 15:18-21] For the first time they use the "ite" on their name. The original Hebrews were colored people, but the new Israelites are white. Looking more like the hooked nosed Hittites than the dark skinned Arabian descendants of Abraham. In fact, the Danites (Kenites/Cainites) are blond haired and blue eyed. The Canaanites are the white people from the Caucasian Mountains. Israelites are Canaanites. [Hosea 12:7,8 Ezekiel 16:3, 44-63]

The Curse of Canaan is to dwell in the tents of Shem. [Genesis 9:25,26] They accomplished this when they took on their identify. As tents refer to the body. [2 Peter 1:13,14] They also entered into the tent or tabernacle of God as servants and worked themselves up to being priests. The Nethinim are Canaanites working in the temple of God. [Ezra 8:20] They are associated with the Nephilim or sons of the fallen angels. [Genesis 6:4 Numbers 13:28-33] Also known as Rephaim (Giants). [Isaiah 26:14]

Chedorlaomer king of Persia (Elam) fought against the five nations of Rephaim: Sodom, Gomorrah, Admah, Zeboiim and Bela (Baal). [Genesis 14:1-9] These are Canaanites: Sodomites, Horites, Amalekites, Amorites.[-Genesis 15:18-21 Amos 2:9] Who are tall giants who lived in or around the land of Israel. [Deuteronomy 2:10,11,21,22,23 9:2 Joshua 11:21 15:13 21:11] They are the same five cities that God rain down fire from heaven upon. The Rephaim is often translated as "the dead" as they have no part in the resurrection. [Job 26:5 Psalms 88:10 Proverbs 2:18 21:16 Isaiah 14:8,9 26:19] Suspiciously, the Canaanites speak the same language as the Israelites. While the original people of Israel spoke Hebrew. Abraham, Isaac, Jacob and his sons all spoke Hebrew. When Christ spoke Hebrew from the cross, the people did not understand his words. [Matthew 27:46,47] They were foreign words to these foreign people.

Once in the Promise Land, the Covenant had to be renewed with these new people. [Joshua 24:1-13] And Deuteronomy was written by Joshua to teach the new people the laws. As Moses was dead and could not have written it. Deuteronomy means 'second law or copy of the law' as it is a repeat of Moses' books. The Jews claim that Moses wrote the first five books called the Torah (Greek Pentateuch) is a blatant lie! The root of Pentateuch and Pentecost is Penta (Five). Pentacle the five pointed star. 5 is Satan's number. The Word of God would not be based on Satan's number. Tetrateuch (four books) is correct. They make up the Tetragrammaton.

It is more than mere coincidence that the terms of the Canaanites are the same as the Israelites: El is God, Adonai YHWH is Lord Yahweh, and Baal is the bad lord known as Satan. The Tetragramaton YHWH comes from the Egyptian IHUH. Adonay or Adonai is Aton (Adon-Ra) the sun-god of Egypt. You will notice Ra and Aton are two of the names in Tet-Ra-gram-Aton. Adonai is also the dying god Adonis of Phoenicia. Adonai is translated Lord. [A Book of the Beginnings by Gerald Massey page 314]

Actually, Joshua, Caleb and Eleazar are the only survivors and the true line of Israel. Joshua and Eleazar settled in northern part of the Promised land called Israel. While Caleb went south to the other half called Judah. Rightly so, as he was of the line of Judah. [1 Chronicles 2:1-18-50-55 4:1-15] Christ had to come out of this line of Caleb. But the records are so chaotic, they are nearly impossible to discipher. John the Baptist, cousin of Christ, was of the line of Eleazar the son of Aaron. As his father, Zacharias, was a priest. [Luke 1] Therefore, Christ, was half Judah and half Levi priest of the order of Zadok.

The Jewish tradition where the boy grows a pony-tail on one side of his head until the time of his barmitzvah is borrowed from the Horus-lock in Egypt. The boy cuts it off the lock of hair as a rite of passage into manhood at puberty. The Jews say Minim means Heretics and Min is Heretic. Ironically, Min is one of the names of Amen, the evil sun of God, who mimics all that the good Son of God does.

The Sadducees were the priests in charge of the temple. Supplying the demands for blood sacrifices to the people for their sins. They perpetuate the continuous cycle of sin...sacrifice, sin...sacrifice, etc.... These aristocrats were appointed by the Romans. They do not believe in the resurrection of the dead. [Mark 12:18-27] The Word of God says the Lamb of God (Christ) was the final sacrifice that ended the slaughter of the innocents. The temple was destroyed shortly after his death and resurrection. [John 2:19-21] He re-erected the House of God in his body of believers. [Ephesians 2:18-22] Now he is the temple and the saints shall be the priests of God. [Hebrews 9 & 10:1-18 Revelation 20:6] The Sadducees made up the 72 members of the Sanhedron that conspired to kill Christ. [John 18:14 Matthew 26:3,4] Compare that to the 72 followers of Set (Satan) who conspired and kill Lord Osiris.

The Pharisees are a sect or cult separate from the temple priests. These Lawyers are called the legalists because they are sticklers for the minute details, yet loose the meaning of the original Commandments. [Matthew 23:23] The Lord calls them hypocrites for telling the people what they should do, but not doing it themselves. [Matthew 23:3 Romans 2:13-26] They go out of their way to find a convert and then teach him lies so they will not enter God's kingdom. [Matthew 23:13-15] They love prestige, power and wealth just like the Sadducees. [Matthew 23:5,6,16] Mammon is Amon the god of wealth (Pluto in Roman). Ma is the Maternalistic, Materialistic, Matrix of Amon. The Pharisees have become the modern Rabbis. [Matthew 23:7]

Jesus was neither Pharisee nor Sadducee. He was a Nazarene. [Matthew 2:23] His followers, like Paul, were called Nazarenes. [Acts 24:5] John the Baptist was probably a Nazarene or Essene. Their beliefs may have been similar. A Nazarene is the same as a Nazirite. Who take the vow of celibacy. They abstain from sex, wine, shaving, touching the dead. The law of separation is to set the Saint apart from all sin. [Numbers 6:1-21] The Saint becomes sanctified in the sight of the Lord. Just as the Sabbath is sanctified as the Lord's day. [Genesis 2:3] Keeping the Sabbath is the sign that you are God's people. [Exodus 31:12-17]

Judaism is not the religion of God. The Old Testament does not even use the word. The Lord Christ constantly condemned the high priests, Pharisees, and scribes of Judaism. He called them Serpents, the sons of Cain, and dogs. Which is a slang word for Canaanite (canine). [Matthew 15:21-28 23:33 John 8:44] The church of God is the House of the Lord. The bride of Christ is the saints who keep God's Commandments. [Revelation 12:17 14:12] The Israelites were divorced for spiritual adultery. [Jeremiah 3:8] They were a stiff-necked people. Meaning "bull-headed". A head like Baal. The ones who crafted the Golden Calf or Baby Bull for Baal. The lawless are the illegitimate sons. [2 Thessalonians 2:1-10] The outlaws are sons of Satan. The root of Judaism is Judas who betrayed the Messiah.

Plutarch says that following the fight between Horus and Set-Typhon, Typhon did take flight for seven days, and having escaped, begot two sons, Hierosolymus (Holy Salem) and Judaeus (Judah). In other words, the religion of Set settled in Israel the divided kingdom (Israel/Judas). Their family tree is the Fig tree which contains the Serpent. The Jewish exodus is a rerun of Adam and Eve's exile from Eden (Egypt). The sinners are banished from God's presence. The sem priests of Amen became the Semitics. [A Book of Beginnings by Gerald Massey page 189]

The Lord God told Israel He would be King, but they rebelled and demanded a human king like all the pagan nations. [1 Samuel 8:6-9] They got the likes of Saul, David and Solomon. When the Jews demanded that the Lord Jesus become king of the Jews, he flatly refused. [John 6:15] God's kingdom is not of this world. Satan is lord of this world. Christ is head of the church until God's kingdom comes to unite church and state. Meanwhile, Satan is head of state. As Antichrist, he will rule the world in person. When Horus (Jesus) comes, he shall slay the kings and, as Osiris, he shall judge the nations.

Why do Christians defend the Jews who the Lord divorced and condemned?? It was the Christian nations that went to war against the Muslim nations in order to give the Israelis (Israelites) the land that the Lord himself had banished them from! The Lord used the Romans to scatter the stiff-necked Jews. Then the Romans renamed the land Palestine after their own Paletine Hill. It was called Palestine for 2,000 years. The Jews are merely committing suicide, since one third will die in the battle called Armageddon and one third will die from the plagues. [Zechariah 13 & 14]

The Jews make up their own traditions against God's commands. Hanukkah or Festival of Lights is man made holiday celebrating the Maccabean war. It is not God's Holy Day. The nine candle Menorah represents Ma, the Mother whose number is nine, and her son Men (Amen-Ra). Men or Min is the Warlord from Upper Egypt. The Jews were warriors. Hanukah or Chanukah is Cain, the first murderer + nuka or neka, the deceiving serpent. The Lord said the peacemakers shall be called sons of God and the warriors sons of Satan. [1 John 3:12] You shall love your enemy and convert through example. These Jewish warriors along with the Roman warriors crucified Christ. And then celebrated his death. [Zechariah 11:10-13] The Jews don't believe in the resurrection from death or the hereafter. Even though all the Old Testament prophets spoke of it often. [Ezekiel 37:1-14] The reason: they have a "Covenant with Death." [Isaiah 28:15-18]

In 70 AD, the Jews rebelled against the tyranny of Rome and was totally destroyed. They fought for freedom and lost their lives. They rejected the Lord Jehovah of the Old Testament and the Lord Jesus of the New; and have lost their eternal lives. They have no savior.

God did NOT tell David to kill Goliath even though he claim to do it in the name of God. God did NOT tell Abraham to kill in order to rescue

Lot. God did NOT tell Israel to kill the Canaanites. God did NOT tell Samson to kill the Philistines. God did NOT tell Cain to kill Abel. God did NOT tell Paul (Saul) to assist in the murder Stephen, even though he claimed he was doing God's work. God did NOT tell the Jews to be involved in the murder of Christ, even though they claim to do it in the name of God. The Lord is able to defeat any enemy. He does NOT need man's help.

In fact, God said that those who shed the blood of others, their blood shall be shed. For all those who live by the sword shall die by the Lord with the Sword. [Revelation 13:10 19:11-21 Matthew 26:52] Samson broke his Nazirite vow by killing. The Israelites polluted the Promise Land with the blood shed upon it. All these mighty men were punished by God. As all are dead in their graves. [Acts 2:29,34] None where translated like Enoch and Elijah. They all must stand before the judgment Throne with the charge of premeditated murder. [Revelation 20:11-15 21:8]

Cabalists

The Cabala (Kabbalah) originated in Babylon during the Jewish captivity. The Cabalist's bible called the Zohar was published in the 13th century by Moses de Leon. It included the doctrines of the Gnostics and Neo-platonists. It is based on Hindu concepts. The idea of a spiritual rapture comes from Babylon, who got it from the heretic Hindus. It is based on nirvana (emotional ecstasy).

The Cabalists believe in the ten emanations of the one God. These aspects or manifestations are the ten incarnations of Vishnu in Hinduism. They parallel with the incarnations of the Lord, of which, Christ was just one. [John 1:14] The Lord's return as Son of Man will be another. The Cabalists say that the ten Sefiroth (Avatars or Incarnations) represent the Tree of life. This is the Lord who died on a tree and is worthy to be the giver of life. The tree represents God's family tree (God's sons). Compare to Osiris who died in a tree and rose again as Horus.

The name of Adam Kadmon is clearly rooted in Egypt. Adam is Atum the first being created. Kad or Ked is the Anglo name of the Mother goddess. Kad is Kat; a form of Hathor. Mon is Amon the second evil being created (Satan). Combining the two demonstrated the dualism. Just as Hari-Hara is Vishnu the creator and Shiva the destroyer. Adam Kadmon was replaced by Adam Beliyya'al (Ba'al) as lord of the earth.

The Cabalists say man has spiritual intercourse with God through the Shekhinah (God's Spirit or presence). This is the telepathic communication that some call inspiration. The Shechinah is the feminine umbilical cord from the Father to His new born. Gnostic means "to Know" or seeking to learn the knowledge of the mysteries of God. Where as agnostic means "not to know" any absolute truths or to believe it is not possible to know God.

Shekhinah and Shekhitah (to sacrifice) both come from the Egyptian Shekhmet. Shekhmet is the feminine Yin (destructive) and masculine Yang (creative) of God's supernatural power working in the natural world. Shekinah is the bride of the Lord and Shechitah is the sacrificed Lamb of God. [Revelation 5:5 21:9-11] Zion represents the primordial mount where the Sun of God was born. The heavenly JeruSalem (Aaru-Sekhet in Egyptian) is God's Shechinah descending to earth. Likewise, the Hebrew Meshken is the Egyptian Meskhenet, the spiritual midwife. She presides over the birth and rebirth (resurrection). Shekhmet is a form of Hathor, Mut and Isis as the Great Mother. The earth is laboring to give birth to the new earthlings who were once sacrificed (martyred). [Romans 8:18-29 Rev. 6:9-11] The tomb is now the womb.

Cabalists claim that God spoke Hebrew. They say God spelt out the names of things with the 22 Hebrew letters and they were created. Through spelling them in reverse, they would be uncreated. This is nonsense. The Word of God was originally spoken and written in hieroglyphics which means; holy writings & sacred scriptures. Atum (Adam) named all the creation in his native language. Osiris predated Abraham and Moses by many Millennium. Hebrew was not created until the confusion of languages at the Tower of Babel. Many Hebrew words are derived from the Egyptian. The Cabalists call upon the many names of God in prayer. This is rooted in Upper Egypt where there are many gods with many names. A master of the divine names is called Ba'al Shem. In other words, a magician of Baal. Scholars translate El Shaddai as God Almighty, yet it is God Shet-tai; Set, god of the earth (ta means earth in Egyptian). Set is the evil one (AKA Shatan). Cabalists say the Sun is the rising and Fallen Angel of light. [Isaiah 14:12-15]

The Jews claim God has a name, but it is so holy that nobody is allowed to say it. Therefore, if you ask a Jew, "Who is your god?" they have no reply. This is insane. If God has a name, He would want us to identify Him with that name.

The Roman Religion

At Rome, Judaism was reformed into Catholicism. The rituals remain the same. They both wear black, the color of the evil priests. Those in mourning because their Savior is dead. Ka-Marim are the priests of Baal or the priests of Mary, Queen of Heaven. [2 Kings 23:5 Zephaniah 1:4 Hosea 10:5] In Egypt, Hathor is Queen of heaven. Cathor is a feline form of Hathor. The letter r is interchangeable with l, therefore, we get Catholic. The worship the creation rather than the Creator. [Romans 1:25] They both wear those silly beanies and their priests were the crown of Amen. They both build extravagant temples trying to out do each other. They both conceal the truth. [Mat.23:13-15] and teach fables. [1 Timothy 4:1-5] Christendumb killed anyone who tried to translate the Word of God into English. They burned sacred scriptures that went against their dogma, yet, they taught the fables of Dante's Hellfire.

The Jews and the Catholics came to the New Land and created the new religion called Capitalism. They declared their freedom to worship any god or goddess they pleased. (Yet, the Indians were not allow to worship their way.) Lady Liberty was their graven goddess. They worshipped the god of greed. "In God we trust" they inscribed for prosperity. [Matthew 6:24] They worship wealth. They love their god of greed and gluttony. Their god was not mute, as "money talks". These "gold diggers" came from Europe to get rich quick. Judeo-Christian capitalists and exploiters, like Columbus, sent most of the gold to the Pope in Rome so they could build another extravagant cathedral.

These Canaanites called the new land "new Canaan". A Canaanite is a Capitalist. Who specializes in taking advantage of the less fortunate and less crafty. The paleface pilgrims sacrificed the Indians to their bloody god of war and plundered the riches. They make their war heroes their heads of state and place their image on their money. [Matthew 22:18-21] They placed the graven image of the new Caesar's (like Washington and Lincoln) on their money. And built monuments to their neo-deities. Compare Washington DC (District of Columbus) to the Vatican. Both are independent sovereign states within a country.

These lazy Caucasian Canaanites imported slaves from Africa to do their dirty work. They steal ideas from other nations just as the ignorant Romans did from the Egyptians, Greeks and Asians. Then put those ideas to an evil use. They exported drugs around the world. Drug money from Opium financed the U.S. government in its first years. Who built a railroad to make it more expedient in the acquisition of Indian land.

The Judicial system is from Judaism, while democracy is a Roman idea. Lady Justice, a Roman goddess, oversees the system. Lady Justice is blind, deaf, and dumb. A graven image is unable to do anything. They turn a blind eye to white collar crime and another blind eye to the injustices of the minorities. The power is divided into a trinity; Judicial (judges as Israel had), Legislative (Roman senators), and Executive (Caesar). The Caesar was elected. He was not a king or dictator. The legislators write the new laws, replacing the Levi priests who formerly had dispensed the Laws of God. It was this democratic system that ended Caesar's rein! Of which, there were 12 Caesars just as 12 tribes of Israel.

Under Roman Catholic government, state and church were united. Separation of church and state came from the Protestant and secular society. The Word of God is not allowed in the secular (state) schools. Man-made heathen holidays are taught in the state schools, but never God's Holy Days. The Capitalists take advantage of working hand and hand with the state by making huge sales during these heathen holidays. The state benefited through increased tax revenues and subliminal loyalty to the state. And the Capitalists merchants reap 50% of their profit from the holiday seasons. This is Babylon at work.

The Wild West was/is the Wilderness of Sin. Sex education is taught in state schools to prepare them for life and physical education is taught to prepare the boys for death. As they are fully expected to die for their government. History repeats the tragedy of war after war. They never learn from their mistakes. Clearly, the Warlord rules this world. The Way of Peace is not taught by Christians or Jews. To them, Love is a four letter word meaning lust. As you must reproduce sons to fight your wars for you. Only in the Wild West could killer and thief, Jesse James, become a martyr murdered by an oppressive government. To this day, he is idolized as a hero. Strangely: Jesse = Jesus and James was Jesus' brother.

The man-made Constitution has replaced God's Ten Commandments as the law of the land. The sacred spiritual law of order has be substituted with the secular laws of disorder. A government based on the rule of the masses is anarchy. The government decides which are days to celebrate and which to worship on. The Blue Laws forbid businesses to open on Sunday, the Christian day of sun-worship. As Constantine ordained it the "Venerable day of the Sun" while he continued to worship the sun-god for forty years after his so called conversion to Christianity. Actually, he created Christendom as the new religion of the Roman kingdom. Who decided that the American forefathers were infallible? and the Constitution is sacred? This is ancestor worship! Not to mention its anti-evolution.

They built their capital on Capital Hill just like Rome. Jupiter's temple is on Capitol Hill, Rome. He is also known as Jove (Jehovah). They placed their Roman goddess above the White House. The House of White Supremacy. The White supremist groups are allowed to do as they please. They have even made god in their own image. To them, 'freedom of religion' means 'freedom from religion'. During the French Revolution, the revolutionaries burned Bibles, forbid the worship of God, and worshipped the goddess of Reason and of Liberty. It was these same French who built the Statue of Liberty and gave this graven image to the U.S. The word Liberty comes from Liber-di, the deity Liber (i.e. Baachus). [Anacalypsis by Godfrey Higgins volume 2 page 265]

When Abraham Lincoln died, they declared him a deity, built a replica of the Partheon and placed him in it. He sits on his throne as if he were Zeus in his temple. Not because he freed the slaves, but because he Saved the Union. He is their savior. The Lincoln memorial is a temple and temple is the place you worship your god. This is ancestor worship! The Lord says you shall keep his death as a memorial, NOT Lincoln's. [1 Corinthians 11:23-26] Pres. Lincoln was a blood-thirsty Christian crusatyr who sent troops to massacre the Indians who would not submit to slavery in the reservations, at the same time as he was signing the Emancipation declaration.

The new Union is coming. The New World Order under the unholy Roman Catholic empire called the European Union or United States of Europe. The United Nations of the World will submit to the antichrist savior who sits in Rome. He will claim to be able to save the world. He will unite the world just as at the Tower of Babel.

Christianity is the worst oppressors of religious freedom ever! Christendumb is forced down the throats of innocent children from the time of birth. Babies are Christened and circumcised against their will. How many babies volunteer for this mutilation of circumcision? The idea that a "god-father" saves the child by Christening them with a new name is pagan. Just as Christening a boat is a pagan custom of the Vikings. Circumcision is the "Jewish" law that Paul says is done away with. The sacrifice of the flesh is nailed to the cross. The followers of Christ are to circumcise their hearts not the head of their penis'. Which means to cut away carnal knowledge; to be severed from the love of the things of this world. The Christian "healers" are working on the wrong heads, as usual.

Paul repeats twice that we are to abstain from; blood, things polluted to idols, things strangled with the blood still in them, and sexual immorality. [Acts 15:20 21:25] Circumcision is the cutting of the foreskin and letting of blood, condemned by God. The covenant validated by the law (or requirement) of circumcision is voided in favor of the Covenant written in the blood of the Lamb of God. The old is obsolete. [Galatians 3:15-18] So why do Christians, Jews, and Muslims continue to circumcise when it's been fulfilled and ended by Christ????????

Israel; God's people?

The nation of Israel had two great purposes. The first was to be the keepers of the Book. It was the scribes job to preserve the written Word of God called the Holy Scriptures. They faithfully reproduced them from generation to generation. The second was to be the inheritance. [Isaiah 19:25] From Israel would come the living Word of God. The Messiah who would be Savior. The Seed promised to Eve [Genesis 3:15] to Abraham [Galatians 3:16] and to David. [1 Chronicles 17:11-15] The Holy One of Israel would be born of the line of Israel. He would come to save the people from their evil selves and stop the self-destruction of the sickness of sin. From the living Word of God, the sons of God would be reborn. [John 1:1-12,13] He would teach the true Meaning of Life and lead the Way to the Tree of life in God's kingdom. As Lord of the Sabbath, he will restore God's garden paradise on the new Earth. Re-creating the original plan as conceived by God. [Revelation 2:7 21:2-7]

The Israelite Insurrectionists

The book of Maccabees of the Apocrypha is a historical record of the belligerent, blood-thirsty Jews rebelling against the Romans. They were quickly put down and JeruSalem was razed to the ground. They were following the Warlord Baal for God did NOT tell them to rebel. Just as in the book of Esther. Where it is recorded that the Jews murdered seventy-five thousand of the Persians and then had a party to celebrate their victory. [Esther 9:5,16,19] The blood-thirsty Jews are sons of the first murderer, Cain, and liars from the beginning. [John 8:44]

Hitler got the name Nazi Germany from the term Nasi Israel. Which means Leader of Israel. Hitler, like all leaders of Christendom, considered it his duty to exterminate the Jews who crucified Christ, the true Leader of Israel. Germany is 85% Christian. When the truth is that the Romans, who later became the Christians, killed Christ. And these Christians have murdered millions of Jews ever since. These blond haired, blue eyed Christians are the Aryans Hitler spoke of: the Romans, English, Danites, and Vikings. It was Hitler who broke the back of the evil English empire who oppressed the world.

Following World War II, the United Nations decided to give Palestine to the Jews so that Christendom would have a foothold in the Holyland. The Jews murdered thousands of Muslims and took their land. The land that the LORD God had banished the Israelites from. It is NOT their land. And for this they shall pay. In the last days there shall be another World War. It is known as Armageddon. The battle actually takes place in JeruSalem. One third of all Israelites shall die in this war before the Lord with the Sword comes and slays all warriors. Every military man of every nation shall die. The Christian Crusaders shall be no more! The Zionists shall be no more! No warrior shall enter God's kingdom.

2500 years ago, Socrates said on his deathbed, "I am not an Athenian or a Greek, but a citizen of the world." We are all children of Adam. The Saints are striving to be sons of God like the second Adam. We are citizens of God's kingdom. [Ephesians 2:18-22] You cannot divide you loyalty between a worldly nation and God's kingdom. [Matthew 6:24] Who is your Commander-n-Chief? Jesus was not king of the Jews, nor did He become the Caesar of Christendom. He is King of God's kingdom over the whole earth. He shall put all nations into submission. [1 Corinthians 15:20-28] The vultures and eagles shall eat the flesh of the kings of every nation. [Revelation 19:17-19] Then who will lead the masses?

Holy Land

Where is the Holy Land? It is wherever the Lord is standing. [Exodus 3:5 Joshua 5:15] When the Lord returns to JeruSalem, it will be holy, but not a moment sooner. The so called Holy of holies in the old Temple is NOT sacred. It is merely an archaeological ruins. The Lord said He will build His temple, not man. Is a graveyard hallowed ground? NO! A Hebrew priest is defiled if he goes near the dead. [Numbers 6:6-7] The Lord said let the spiritually dead bury the physically dead; since they have nothing to lose. The corpse even defiles the land, leaching poisons and diseases. The blood of man pollutes the land. Therefore, the earth, like the earthlings, must be born again. The restored earth will be the holy Promise land and God's garden paradise. Israel is Isarel in Phoenician. The land of Asar-el (Osiris-el) is the is holy land, not Palestine. The Catholic church is built on the corpse of Peter, therefore, it is built on Unholy ground.

The original Holy Land was the garden of God east of Eden. The Bible clearly describes this as Africa. What the Bible calls new JeruSalem, the ancient Egyptians called Aanru-Sekhet (Anu). The Greeks called it Heliopolis (City of the Sun), which is a corruption of City of Heru (Horus). {the letters l and r are interchangeable}. Anu (i.e. On) is the birthplace of Horus, the Messiah. The Great Pyramid is the temple and holy mountain of the Righteous Sun of God. The location of his return. [Revelation 21:10] Zion or Sion is Si-On (City of the Sun). The Aramaic spelling of Jerusalem is IheruSalem or Heru-Salem (Horus-Peace). The Egyptians called it Heru-hetep (Horus-prince of peace) or Sekhet-hetep (Fields of Peace). Compare this to the Greek-Elysian Fields. The Holy Land is NOT in Palestine! Solomon's Jerusalem was built on Mt. Moriah. Moriah is Maria, but it is also called Zion or Sion. In other words, the Son of God was to rise again and rule from the primordial mount. [Psalms 1:6-9] The Hindus call it Mt. Meru.

The Talmud says that Jesus Ben Panther was his full name. Panther is the combination of Pan and Patah (Phather). In Egypt, Patah is God the Father. Jesus Ben Pather was the Son of the Father. He took on God's family name. Pantheon, like Elohim, are the Sons of God. Pan-the-on is All the gods of On (Anu). Paut-neteru is 'the Company of the gods,' or as the Hebrews say, 'the host of heaven.' In one of the apocryphal Gospels, Jesus is said to be the son of a Painter and in another he is son of a Potter. Clearly these are corruptions of Pater, Peter, etc.

Mystery, Babylon Mythology

From the Tower of Babel, came all the peoples of the world. It was Nimrod's idea to build a Tower to Baal that would reach into the heavens as high as God. Baal is the bad lord known as Satan. Who implanted that idea in his head. [Isaiah 7:12-15] Nimrod took his followers to the land of Shinar and built Babylon. [Genesis 10:8-10] There a new belief was started. The Babylonians changed the creation and flood stories so that Marduk was the King of gods. Bel-Marduk is represented as the horned serpent or serpent-headed dragon. The Word of God says the horned serpent is Satan. [Revelation 12:3-9 13:1,11] Nimrod also built Nineveh in the land of Assyria. Nineveh is where Jonah went to preach the Word of God. There the people believed and repented. [Jonah 3] They destroyed their temple of Ishtar and Nabu (Nebo) god of arts and crafts.

An interesting note: the Sumerians were not Semitics (sons of Shem). They were the descendants of Nimrod. The Sumerians call themselves "Black-heads". They call the Egyptians "Black-feet". These are the sons of Ham (Khamet). They were implying that were the leaders (heads) and the Egyptians were the followers (feet). The gods are depicted with blue eyes because they were all-seeing and dwell in the blue skies, not because they were Caucasian!

The Creation

In the beginning, God created two sons from the water womb called Inanna; Ea (the good one) and Enlil (the evil one). Enlil caused the fall of the angels. Ea, the father of mankind, granted forgiveness to the conspiring gods, for whose redemption did he create mankind. These are the fallen angels or sons of God who left their home in heaven to mated with earth women. [Genesis 6:1-4] Of course, Ea is Jesus and Atum-Ra-Horus of Egypt. Inanna is Nun of Egypt. Enlil is Amen-Ra-Set. The fact that everyone has their version of the Creation and Flood stories verifies they are true. Ea or Enki comes from An meaning heaven and ki meaning earth. Anki is Lord of the heavens and earth. He is Lord of the Anunnaki (gods). Khenti-Ankh is the Lord of the Living in Egypt.

In the Babylonian version of the Flood story: The gods <elohim> decide to send a Flood upon the earth. One of the gods, Ea (Enki), decides to save King Utnapishtim (Noah of the Bible). He warns him of the coming danger and commands him to build a ship. When questioned why he is building a ship Utnapishtim is to tell a lie of omission. So no one else will be saved. When the ship is finished, he loads his possessions, family, dependents, including artisans, together with domestic and wild animals. Then he enters in and closes the door behind him. The storm rages for six days and nights, till all mankind are destroyed and the very gods <fallen angels?> cowered in terror like dogs. The boat grounded on a tall mountain. On the seventh day, the storm rests and he sends out a dove, which comes back to him. And then he lets go a raven, which does not return. On this, Utnapishtim released all the animals; and leaving the ship, offered a sacrifice. The gods gathered like flies over the sacrifice. <Baal-zebub means Lord of the Flies> [Matthew 12:26,27] The deities then began to quarrel; but eventually Utnapishtum is blessed, and is received into the society of the gods.

The story is so close to the Word of God, that is verifies it as true. The fact that the Babylonians have perverted the story is obvious. But it demonstrates that all races were present at the Tower of Babel and have passed down stories of the Creation and the Flood. The sons of God (elohim) did come down and make babies with the earth women. [Genesis 6:1-4] Their half-breed children where destroyed in the Flood and those Fallen Angels did tremble like canines (Cainites) for fear of God.

In one version, Ea warns Utnapishtim of the coming Flood; "Tear down your house and build a boat, abandon possessions and look for life, despise worldly goods and save your soul...Tear down your house, I say, and build a boat with her dimensions in proportion-her width and length in harmony. Put aboard the seed of all living things, into the boat." Compare this to "Do not love the world or the things in the world. If anyone love the world, the love of the Father is not in him. For all that is in the world-the lust of the flesh, the lust of the eyes, and the pride of life-is not of the Father but is of the world. And the world is passing away, and the lust of it; but he who does the will of God abides through the ages." [1 John 2:15-17] This is asceticism!

Utnapishtim was instructed by Ea 'to take the beginning, the middle and the end of whatever was consigned to writing and then to bury it in the City of the Sun at Sippara'. After the waters of the flood had subsided, survivors were instructed to make their way to the site of the City of the Sun to search for the writings, which would be found to contain knowledge of benefit to future generations of mankind. This City of the Sun is Anu called Heliopolis by the Greeks and On in the Bible. These sacred scriptures are the Great Mysteries or the Books of Thoth. [Berossus Fragments cited in the Sirius Mystery]

Gilgamesh

Gilgamesh parallels many of the stories of Heracles. Both are of divine parentage. Both kill lions and wear its pelt. Both overcame divine bulls. Ishtar tries to seduce Gilgamesh. Ishtar is Hathor the Great Cow of Egypt. When he spurs Ishtar, she sends the Bull of Heaven (Taurus) to ravage the city of Uruk. Gilgamesh seizes the Bull by its horns and slays it with his Sword. This Bull is Min of Egypt and the Minotaur of Greece. The Sumerians portrayed King Gilgamesh as Orion and the Bull as Taurus, just as in Egypt. Ishtar is the Sumerian Ianna. Both Herakles and Gilgamesh kill a seven headed (Hydra) monster. Both find the supernatural herb of immortality. Utnapishtim tells Gilgamesh where to find the plant of life, but a serpent (Satan) swallows it before he can use it. Both Gilgamesh and Horus battle the Scorpions (Scorpio). Both harrow hell (Western Island of Death). Gilgamesh and Herakles 12 Labors coincide with the 12 Hours of Horus through the houses of the Zodiac. Which is the voyage of the Sun of God to the UnderWorld via the Western Land of the Dead then reborn in the east. Both Gilgamesh and Heracles use his garment for a sail.

In the Babylonian version, Gilgamesh travels to the Mountains of Mashu to meet Utnapishtim. In Egypt, Manu is the mount in the west were the sun sets. West represents the place of death. Utnapishtim in his ark is Ra in his bark. Because of Gilgamesh's carnal nature, he can not achieve immortality. A serpent has stold his chance for immortality. Compare to Adam and Eve. That serpent being Set-Amen-Ra (ie. Satan).

One version says: Gilgamesh is reborn from the wood of the mes-tree. The New Way is opened for him. Compare to Osiris' rebirth from the 'tree of life'. "After his life on earth, Gilgamesh became king of the underworld, a Babylonian Osiris." He becomes "supreme king, judge of Anunnaki...-you stand in the underworld and give the final verdict." Osiris is Lord of the living and the dead in Amenta. [Hamlet's Mill by Santillana & Dechend pages 448,449]

The Lord with the Sword is coming to destroy Babylon and her followers because they teach lies. [Revelation 18:1-24] While the Jews were held captive by Babylon, they learned their evil ways. Like divination, spiritualism, and all forms of magic. Then when Israel was taken by Assyria, they lost their identity. The lost 10 tribes of Israel are called Mystery because it is a mystery to them as to who they are. [Revelation 17:5]

Nebuchadnezzar, king of Babylon, was warned by God through the prophet Daniel, that Babylon will fall if they don't repent. [Daniel 2:31-45] Yet, he still turned around and made a graven image of himself. [Daniel 3:1-7] Therefore, God punished the king of Babylon by making him eat grass like a bull. [Daniel 4:28-33] For he was acting like Baal. The king then repented (changed his evil ways). But his son returned to doing evil. [Daniel 5:1-4] Therefore, God gave the kingdom over to the Persians. [Daniel 5:30,31] Darius of Media and Cyrus of Persia were God fearing kings. [Daniel 6:25-28 2 Chronicles 36:22,23] They accepted the teachings of Daniel and Zoroaster, the prophets of God.

The Babylonians have corrupted the story of Christ. They claim Tammuz was born of a virgin, died a cruel death, descended into hell, arose from the tomb and ascended to heaven. The Word of God says you shall not weep for Tammuz nor watch the sun rise in the east in the hope of seeing him rise again or resurrect. [Ezekiel 8:14-16] Tammuz was the sun that died in the winter solstice (Dec.25th) and revived to full power in the summer solstice. In a mid-summer festival, the worshipers of Adonis wept over an effigy of the dead god which was washed with water, anointed with oil and clothed in red robes, amid clouds of incense. This sungod is Satan. The sun is clothed red at sunrise and sunset. Tammuz fell because of his love for Ishtar, just as with Aphrodite and Adonis in Greece; Venus and Eros in Rome; Attis and Cybele in Asia Minor; Adonis and Astarte of Phoenicia. Dumuzi and Ianna of Summeria. Ishtar is goddess of sex and violence.

It is a corruption of the story of Osiris and Isis of Egypt. Tammuz is a corruption of Tem-mes (or Atum reborn). Ishtar is a cribbed (plagiarized) version of Isis (Ast) and the virgin birth of Horus. But the Babylonians perverted the story by making Ishtar the mother and mistress of Tammuz. Atum (Horus) did NOT commit incest with his mother; anymore than Jesus did with Mary. The Babylonians are spiritually sick! It was Amen who mated with his mother!

The month that the Jews went into captivity to Babylon, they name Tammuz. [Jeremiah 39:1,2 2 Kings 25:1-12] It is called Tammuz to this day. It falls in the month of June during the summer solstice in honor of the evil sun of God. In fact, the month before this is called Shivan. It is named after Shiva the Destroyer (Devil) according to Hinduism. Shivan is called Shatan by the Arabians. Exactly on the anniversary, the month of Tammuz, the Romans destroyed the temple at Jerusalem. The Jews were dispersed though-out the Roman empire. Not to return for 1900 years.

At the city of Babylon, there is the Gateway of Ishtar lined with Bulls. Asht is a corrupt spelling of Ast (Isis). The Upper Egyptians called her Hathor the cow deity. From Ast came Astarte, Asherah and Ishtar (Ashtar). Asherah is consort of Baal the Bull. Ishtar is queen of heaven and goddess of sex and war; who identifies with Venus of Rome. They also worshipped the Winged Bull (the Greek Griffin) which is the Fallen Angel Baal. Who we know as Satan. From the crescent shape of the horns we get horny. Ishtar is the mistress of Marduk, dragon god of magic. Ishtar is the planet Venus and Marduk is the planet Mars, god of war.

Inanna, Anu, Anna or An is the Sea of Space, and Nanna is the full moon in the Sea of Space. Enlil raped Ninlil and produced Nanna. Compare to Set raping Hathor. Or Amen mating with Mut and producing Khonsu the moon-god. The crescent moon represents Sin, the moon goddess, who is mated to Shamash the sun god. Nanna is identified with Dianna the moon goddess of Rome (Luna in Latin). Inanna is the fertility goddess mated to Tammuz (Dumuzi in Sumerian). The story of Inanna and Dumuzi in the underworld for six month periods parallels Persephone in Hades. This represents the seasons. Notice the Anna in all the spellings of the moon goddess.

Milton says Satan conceived Sin, his daughter. She sprang forth full-grown from his forehead just like Athene from the head of Zeus. When Satan united with his daughter, Sin, they produced Death. "when lust has conceived, it gives birth to sin; and sin, when it is full-grown, brings forth death." [James 1:15] Satan = sun & Sin = moon in conjunction.

The Sumerian story of Inanna going through the 12 gates of the underworld is the Egyptian Book of the Dead. Inanna is counterpart of Isis who searched for Osiris in the land of the dead. The root of In-anna is Anu, the annual birthplace of Atum-Horus.

The Sham of Shamesh

It was the sun-god Shamash who dictated his laws to King Hammurabi in the year 2000 B.C. Around the same period that the LORD gave His Laws to Abraham descendant of Shem. [Genesis 26:5] Shamash (Shatan) rides the fiery chariot as his counterpart Apollo. He is Judge of the Heavens and the Earth. Sublime Judge of the Anunnaki (House of Anu). Beth Shamesh (House of the Sun) is the Hebrew name for Anu (Heliopolis). He is seated on a throne holding a scepter in his right hand. Shamash is the Great Impostor pretending to be the Angel of Light or Sun of God. [2 Corinthians 11:13-15] He is trying to destroy man through confusion. Babel, the root of Babylon, means confusion. The true Morning Star is represented by Sirius. Satan is the sun of our solar system. The Egyptians called him Amen-Ra-Set.

Shemash is Chemosh, the sun-god of the Moabites. He is called Chemosh-Moloch just like Baal-Moloch. Molech means king, as Satan is ruler of this wicked world. His consort is Ashtar the moon goddess. Together they are called Astar-Chemosh. She is called Ashtoreth by the Zidonians. Milcom is the Ammonite name of Molech. Moab and Ammon are the incestuous sons of Lot, the nephew of Abraham. [Jeremiah 48:7,13 Judges 11:24 1 Kings 11:5-7 2 Kings 23:4-13] The LORD is going to destroy Shemash and his followers just as He is going to destroy Amon of No (Thebes) and his followers. [Jeremiah 46:25] As both are aspects of Satan.

The Masquerade of Marduk

In the Babylon fable, Marduk created the heaven and earth from the corpse of Tiamat (Apophis the sea serpent of Upper Egypt). This is nonsense. Marduk the Devil, created nothing but chaos (disorder). It was the

Lord (Atum-Ra-Horus in Egypt) who created order in the cosmos from the chaos. The Babylonians have corrupted all the stories including the Creation and Flood stories that everyone was aware of at the Tower of Babel. Marduk is the counterpart to Amen-Ra, the evil sun-god who battles the sea serpent. The sun-god tears his way out of the watery womb of Mut. In the Canaanite version, Baal, the sun-god, defeats Yamm (the sea) and Mot (the underworld or sea of space) and is reborn.

What Marduk did do is wound Tiamat. Tiamut is the second heaven filled with stars called Mut. Marduk divided the stars by rebelling against the Lord's authority. One third of the stars fell from God's favor when they followed him. The constellations are clearly defined in the zodiac. The zodiac is divided. Taurus, Ares, Scorpio and Draco the Dragon are his. That makes Marduk the Dragon who caused one third of the suns of God or angels to fall from heaven. [Revelation 12:3-9] Marduk means "Bull calf of the Sun". Marduk is the star Hades in the constellation of Taurus. Bel-Marduk is the Bull of heaven. The twelve signs are also called houses. A house divided (against the Lord) shall fall.

Marduk even stold the title Asari (Osiris) in his attempt to usurp the throne as king of the gods. Marduk is Molech (king-god) in the Bible. Marduk is king of chaos, antithesis of Mel-chizi-duk (King of Righteousness). Bel-Marduk wore the domed crown of Upper Egypt. {the rule is: l = r, k = ch, and vowels are interchange} In later times, Marduk usurped the central position of the pantheon in Babylon, just as Amen did in Egypt. Compare Marduk to Set's birth. Set was prematurely born on the third intercalary day. He tore himself violently from his mother's womb (Mot). He was rough and wild, his skin was white and his hair red. The Bible says Lucifer, the Daystar was created on the fourth day. He is the white sun during the day, but red at sunrise and sunset. In the Assyrian version, Marduk is the sungod riding in his fiery chariot. The Greeks called him Typhon. Phoenicians called him Ba'al Tsaphon. Satan is Prince of the power of the air. [Ephesians 2:2] The Romans called Marduk; Mars of duk (the Great Mother). Likewise, it was Shiva, in Hinduism, who divided the heavenly Ganga river into seven streams on earth. He forced the Great Mother nature to submit to himself.

The Underworld

Under the earth, beyond the abyss of the Apsu, lay the infernal dwelling place to which men descended after death. It was the "land of no return" and "the house from which he who enters does not come out." "In the house of dust live lord and priest. Live the wizard and the prophet...live those whom the great gods have anointed in the abyss. Dusk is their nourishment and their food is mud." They have combined two ideas here. The house of dust is the grave (Amenta). The abyss of the underworld is the deep darkness of outer space that the Egyptians called Nun.

Enki or Anki is Lord of heaven and earth. Ea-Ankh is the living waters that rain down from heaven. Ea, with the Roman suffix, is Jesus. Apsu is the Egyptian Apsi or Apis (Heavenly Waters) and source of the Nile. Tiamat is the salt waters and also the sea of space containing the sea serpent called Apophis in Egypt. This is the sea serpent (Leviathan) who swallowed Jonah. The dead remain buried at sea or in the dust of the earth until the day of Judgment. To Adam the LORD said: "Till you return to the ground; for out of it you were taken; for dust you are, and to dust you shall return." [Genesis 3:19,20] Earthlings return to the earth, not to heaven! It is Mother Earth (Ki) who labors to give birth. [Romans 8:19-29] Ki is Keb or Geb (Earth) of Egypt.

Anu is Nun, the deep dark abyss from which the suns of God were born. Apophis is the sea serpent or sea of space surrounding the earth. It is the great Asp with many attributes: Hydra, Draco the Dragon, Serpens the Serpent of Old. [Revelation 12:1-6] So the LORD God said to the serpent: "And you shall eat dust all the days of your life. And I will put enmity between you and the woman, and between your seed and her Seed; He shall bruise your head, and you shall bruise His heel." The woman is Nut or Mot the Great Mother of all living. [Genesis 3:14,15,20] We must be born from above, spiritually begotten by the Father in heaven.

Babylon the Great-Harlot

The city-kingdom of Babylon was like the modern day Los Vegas. A place of harlots, lady luck, violence, drugs including alcohol, and atheists. Vegas has made a mockery of the pyramids and holy places of Egypt. It is a place of fairy tales and deceptions, legal prostitution, marriage in a moment that only last a minute, drugs, alcohol, and all sorts of perversions. Babylon represents all the evils of the world that have spread throughout the social system of the New World Order. The New Age movement is promoting psychic advisors, spiritualists, the I am God dogma, and Rapturing to heaven lies, etc... They will readily accept the antichrist Jesus as the true Christ.

Babylon was the merchants who sold at the market places. Just as today they promote man-made holidays, traditions and customs so as to profit from the commercial sales. It is the capitalists who keep the fables and fairy tales alive. The modern Easter is a direct descendant of Istar. She is the great harlot and Babylon is the capitalists who perpetuate the lies. [Revelation 18] Free enterprise means freedom to exploit. To sell people what they do not need and should not have.

The root of the word Market is Mark. As the Mark of the Beast is his logos or tradeMark. Satan puts his mark on all that is his. His Mark is the Satanic star or pentacle. For Satan is the great fallen star who fell from God's favor. Revelations 13:16,17 says, "And he causes all, both small and great, rich and poor, free and slave, to receive a mark in their hand or in their foreheads, and that no one may buy or sell except one who has the mark or the name of the beast, or the number of his name." Soon you will not be able to buy any product without the mark on it. Once you pick up that product, it is in your hand and in the forefront of your mind. Do NOT accept it as yours.

Modern Babylon is the men of capitalism who sell to women at home watching TV. As it is the women who do the buying. And TV is the most powerful "medium" in the world. The men of big business sell the compulsive consumers on the materialistic dream. Television gives the illusion that everyone is participating in the rituals of Babylon. With the desire to conform and fear and ridicule, many participate in the Babylonian religion. They purchase the costumes and things that go with each ritual of these heathen holidays. Such as Halloween, the Day of the Dead and Chrismas the birthday of Chris Cringle (Santa).

TV is broadcast on the air waves and Satan is the prince of the power of the air. [Ephesians 2:2] TV is his spiritual medium. The images it broadcast are not alive even though they claim so. The image of the Beast was given the power to speak and cause many to worship the Beast (Rome). [Revelation 13:15] TV is the black box illuminated by artificial light. [2 Corinthians 11:13-15] Originally Movies were silent but now it has a voice that moves the masses. The power of persuasion is unsurpassed. Tel-evangelists sell their brand of religion to the masses 24 hours a day. Evolutionists sell their monkey to man "theory" as if it were a proven fact. Tele-vision attempts to look into the future with "science fiction". Television is the prophet of Babylon, seeking to profit from their ignorance.

Mystery of Babylon; the Great Mother of harlots

Mystery of Babylon; the Great Mother, mother of harlots. In Babylon, the Great Mother (Mot-ur) was Inanna. Later, she was worshipped in Asia Minor as Dianna. Then Madonna (Great Mother Mary) by the Christians. Madonna is MaDianna, the Great Mother of the Catholic church. The denominations of Christendom are her daughters. They are harlots who live in sin with Satan. Just as Jezebel who worshipped the Great Mother and her consort Baal. Baal is the Devil. [Revelation 2:20-23] To this day Christians practice pagan customs such as eating things sacrificed to idols like the Easter bunny (Ishter) and Santa (Satan). [Exodus 34:15 1 Kings 16:31]

Beware of the babel of Babylon. Including those who say they speak in tongues, but actually babble a satanic chant. Do not conform to the ways of the world. [Romans 12:2] If it is popular among the masses, it is probably of the Devil; who rules this wicked world. Beware of a brother who says he loves Jesus, yet hates his fellow man. [1 John 4:20] And most of all beware of the false church called Christendom. She is mother of god (Mot-ur) and the consort of the Roman sungod, Mithra (Moth-Ra). Together they unite in unholy matrimony as the unholy Roman Catholic empire. Catholicism is the mother church that gave birth to her daughters; the denominations of Christendom. They have nothing to do with Christ or the Word of God.

It was the Babylonians and the Romans who corrupted the story of the constellations of the Zodiac. Astrology means "study of the stars" not worship of the stars. They believed that the planets were stars and they controlled our personalities and destinies. They corrupted the word Horoscope into meaning seeing into the future. Horo-scope comes from the all seeing eye of Horus (Jesus). Only God and His sons can see into the future. Anyone claiming to predict the future is a prophet of God or a false prophet getting information from evil spirit-beings. Diviners, Spiritualists, and psychic advisors get their information from familiar spirits (demons) and are condemned by the Word of God. [Deuteronomy 18:10-14] The Babylonians and Romans were astro-diviners.

Only the good Sun of God can make the voyage through the stars of the Zodiac and return back here on earth. He is the Morning star (Sirius) that shall overthrow the evil sungod (Satan) and take rule over God's kingdom on earth. He is the only one who can ascend into the stars of heaven. He showed us the way to God's kingdom was through resurrection, not ascension into heaven. Humans being transformed into angels who fly in heaven is a fable of Babylon. The Mystery of Babylon is corrupt version of the Ancient Mysteries of Egypt. They tell the stories but have reversed the roles so that the Devil is the hero and savior. They made Ra in his solar bark the savior who takes his followers to heaven to live for millions of years.

In ancient Mesopotamia the king and high priestess performed a fertility ritual in a chamber inside the stepped-pyramid ziggurats. It involved the fertility of Ishtar who was identified with the planet Venus. They called it the Eastern star or Easter. The New Year commenced with the Helical rising of Venus and the fertility of the land brought by the flooding of the Euphrates. Venus, deva of sex and violence, is Ishtar's Roman counterpart. This is a corruption of the original Egyptian theology. The dawn rising of Sirius as the Morning star coinciding with the flooding of the Nile represents Isis (Ist or Ast) being fertile. The Great Pyramid is the Temple or House of the Lord. It is the primordial mount where Osiris was reborn as Horus and ascended to Heaven. Easter is Ishtar's day, while Passover (spring equinox) is the time of the Lord's death and resurrection. Ast-ur (Great Isis), not East-er, was the day she recovered the body of Osiris. Easter sunday was chosen as the day of the sun-god.

Zoroaster

The Word of God came to Zoroaster...

Zoroaster was the prophet of God sent to Persia. In his book the Avesta, he taught that God the Father is the Creator called Zurvan meaning Infinite Time. And the Father had twin suns. The good Sun was called Ahura Mazdah meaning Holy spirit-being and Wise Lord. He is the one we call the Sun of Righteousness and Lord of light. The other Sun is his adversary called Angra Mainyu or Ahriman meaning Destructive spirit and lie. This was Lucifer the Day Star who fell from favor and became Satan the Adversary. He is the author of deception and death.

Plutarch says, "The Persians also tell many fabulous stories about their gods, such, for example, as the following: Oromazes (Aura Mazda), born from the purest light, and Areimanius (Ahriman), born from the darkness, are constantly at war with each other; and Oromazes created six gods, the first of Good Thought, the second of Truth, the third of Order, and, of the rest, one of Wisdom, one of Wealth, and one the Artificer of Pleasure in what is Honourable. But Areimanius created rivals, as it were, equal to these in number." The twelve houses of the Zodiac. "Then Oromazes enlarged himself to thrice his former size, and removed himself as far distant from the Sun as the Sun is distant from the Earth, and adorned the heavens with stars. One star he set there before all others as a guardian and watchman, the Dog-star (Sirius). Twenty-four other gods he created and placed in an egg. But those created by Areimanius, who were equal in number to the others, pierced through the egg and made their way inside; hence evils are now combined with good."

Notice he connects Aura Mazda with Sirius, not the Sun (Ra). Just as Atum-Horus is connected to Sirius. The Cosmic Egg is the birthplace of Atum-Horus called Anu. The bad suns of God invaded his space as Taurus the bull. These shall be cast out as the fallen stars. [Rev.12] Jesus, the Bright Morning star, said, "the kingdom of heaven suffers violence, and the violent take it by force." [Matthew 11:12] The kingdom of Osiris (Anu) is the kingdom in the heavens (Nun). In Egypt, these six gods are called Maat (Law and Order) and Thoth (Truth and Justice). Plutarch, Pythagoras, and Zoroaster were initiated into the ancient Egyptian Mysteries.

Zoroaster is Sar (Osiris) + Aster = Star (Sirius). [Signs & Symbols of Primordial Man by Albert Churchward page 11]

The Bounteous Immortals are the other angels who are not archangels. Some are daivas (demons) and some ahuras (good spirit-beings or angels). The daivas are the fallen angels (fallen stars) who followed Lucifer. [Revelation 12:4 Jude 6 1 Peter 3:19 2 Peter 2:4] They were the ones (sons of God) who witness Satan seducing Eve and decided to try it themselves. [Genesis 6:2] They are the familiar spirits who pretend to help mankind. They are sometimes called Watchers. As Shakespeare said, "The world is a stage" and the angels are the audience or watchers.

Two of Ahriman's attributes are Sauru (Shiva in Hinduism) and Aeshma Daeva. Aeshma is Asmodeus, the one who was responsible for the deaths of the husbands of Sara in the Apocryphal, Book of Tobit. Shiva is the Destroyer. In India, he is Aryaman (Aryan-man). As it was the Aryans who brought the Rig Vedas to Hinduism. Ahriman is also called Angra (Angel-Ra) Mainyu. Ahriman is Ahura-Aman which parallels Egypt's Ra-Aman (Amen-Ra). He is the evil brother of Ahura Ahura is Heru (Horus). Mesta means born of the earth.

Zoroaster retired to a cavern where he wrote his book called the Book of Abraham. It parallels the books of the Old Testament. His desire was to restore the religion of the patriarchs. Compare that to Muhammad, a descendant of Abraham, writing the Quran in a cave. The cave represents conception and new birth. Zoroaster's cave ceiling was ornamented with the constellations of the Zodiac. Showing the roots of his religion were in Egypt. Remember, Egypt ruled over all the Middle East until the Persian empire conquered Egypt during the age of Aries.

Zoroasterism ruled the Middle East from 600 years before Christ to 600 years after Christ. Until the prophet Muhammed was given the Koran and reformed Islam. Cyrus, King of Persia, followed Zoroaster's doctrine and obeyed the Word of God followed Zoroaster's doctrine. Cyrus, king of Persia, obeyed the Word of God. [2 Chronicles 36:22,23] In fact, the title Cyrus comes from O-sirus. Also Zoroaster was born almost in the middle of the days of mankind. 3,400 years were before his day and 2,600 have passed since.

Chronicle of the Cosmos-Cosmic Cycle of the Creation

The preordained time of the cosmos is 12,000 years-which is divided into four periods, each lasting three millennium. Compare to the 12 ages of the Zodiac. For the first three thousand years Armazd (Aura Mazda) was alone. (10000–7000 BC). At about 11000 BC, the age changed from Virgo to Leo and the first begotten Sun of God was born. The Egyptians call him Atum. Zodiac = Zodak (Righteousness) in Hebrew, as Armazd is King of Righteousness (Melchi-Zodak). Then Ahriman emerged from the darkness and the battle of good vs. evil shall continue for nine thousand years. (This is the age of Gemini the Twins) The second period of three thousand years was the age of creating beings by both Armazd and Ahriman. (7000–4000 BC). Notice man was created by the sons of God (clohim) during the age of Taurus. The third period is the time of the human race; between the first man and Zoroaster. (4000–1000 BC) The age of Aries. The fourth period is the age of victory of Armazd and the last judgment. (1000 BC–2000 AD). This is the age of Aquarius.

According to the Zend Avesta, there are six epochs called Gahanbars. These represent the six creative periods as well as the six festivals. In the first epoch Aura Mazda (Ormuzd) created the heavens; during the second he made the waters; in the third, the earth; in the fourth, the vegetation; in the fifth, the animals; and finally, in the sixth, man was born. "Ahura-Mazda produced illumination between the sky and the earth, the constellation-stars and those not of the constellations, then the moon and afterwards the sun." After these six, sixty day periods, Ahura-Mazda rested for 5 days. This is a total of 365 days. Compare this to the five holy days of Egypt added to make 365 total.

Compare this to Genesis. On the first day God created the heavens. On the second day God separated the sea of space from the sea on earth. Also he separates the waters of the sky from the waters of earth. On the third day God separates the earth or land from the seas. He also created the vegetation. On the fourth day God created the stars, the sun and moon. On the fifth day God created the animals of the sea and air. Then on the sixth day, God created the mammals including man. [Genesis chapter one] Only one is out of sequence. The accuracy validates the story.

Aura Mazda (Atum) creates the garden paradise. Then Ahriman (Aman) descends from heaven to earth in the shape of an adder (serpent). He seduces the first man, Meshiah (Messiah?), and the first woman, Meshiane. "He crept over their thoughts, he overthrew their minds, and said to them: It was Ahriman who gave the water, the earth, the trees and the animals. Thus Ahriman fooled them at the very begining, and until the end this cruel one endeavored to seduce them." [Zend Avesta, vol.III, p.351 and 378. The first Adam was a human being the second was the Messiah. [2 Corinthians 15:45]

Devi (Devil), whose speech is all lie (Ahriman), becoming still bolder, came a second time and brought them (the first couple) fruit of which they ate, and thus only the advantage of all advantages was left to them." Our first parents, seduced for the third time, then drank (serpents) milk. They did not drink God's milk. [Hebrews 5:12-14] At the fourth time, they went hunting, ate the meat of the animals and made for themselves garments from the skins, just as the Lord made coats for Adam and Eve. They then discovered iron, made an ax, felled trees and made tents for themselves; they finally united carnally (sexually) and their children inherited their misery. It was Cain's descendants who discovered iron and lived in tents. [Genesis 4:20-22] The Persian Bundahish says before the coming of the Destroyer vegetation had no thorns on it. [Genesis 3:18]

Book of Kings (Shah-Nameh)

In the Book of Kings, Hoshang was the son of Siyamek. He avenged his father's death by the hand of Div (the Devil). Compare to the book in the Bible under the same name. Hoshang = Hoshiah = Joshuah = Jesus. All mean Savior. In Egypt, Hoshang would be Horus who avenged his father Osiris. The Demon was D'amon (ie. Set-amon). Hoshang, like Osiris, went on to civilize the world by preaching peace and justice. He taught men; agriculture and how to domesticate animals.

Zoroaster taught of the day when men would be refined, in the fire, as metal. Purged in God's fire. [Zechariah 13:7-9 2 Peter 3:10-13] The good separated from the bad. The good are resurrected in the kingdom of God. The bad are rendered unconscious forever. Those who keep the law of God are saved. For God is law and order. The Sun of God who ruled over creation on the Sabbath day, stood still over head. That Sun did not set until Adam and Eve choose to follow the bad Sun of God. The good Sun shall rule over the Re-creation on the Lord's day. Ironically, Re of Re-creation is the Sun of God in Egypt. Other related words are: Re-born, Re-generate, Re-new, Re-surrection, Re-store. Zoroaster also used the winged sun disk to represent the Sun of God like the Egyptians. Which means the Sun of God ascends into the heavens to be at the Father's side.

On the day the Lord comes is a Feast day and celebration of a new day. The Word of God says that is the Feast of Tabernacles or Ingathering. [Zech.14:16-19] When the Lord returns to Earth to gather the elect from the ends of the Earth. The dead will be resurrected and transformed. They used the Haoma plant to symbolize the Tree of life that heals the sickness of sin. [Revelation 22:2,3] The Tree transforms white light into green growth. Of which, all living things are dependent upon that vegatation and the oxygen it produces. It is called the breath of life or spirit of life. In the garden of God, all the creatures were originally vegetarians.

At the Creation, Zurvan (God the Father) decided the firstborn would be heir. So Ahriman the evil son of God ripped open the womb and presented himself saying, "I am Ahura Mazdah." Therefore, the Devil has ruled the Earth as king ever since (6,000 years). Just as the Antichrist will say he is Jesus the Savior of the world and will rule the United Nations of Infidels. Satan is the great impostor pretenting to be the Angel of light. [2 Corinthians 11:13-15] Compare this to Set's evil birth. And to Jacob and Easu's birth.

Meanwhile, Ahura Mazdah was made high priest. He became the firstborn of the Re-creation. [Colossians 1:15-18 Romans 8:29] by being the only Son of God born (begotten) of a woman. For he was born of the line of Zadok and in the order of MelchiZadok. [Hebrews 6:20 7:1-28] He is head of the body of believers in the church of God. Satan the serpent seduced the first woman, who inturn seduced the first righteous man. Their sons were twins. Cain is son of Satan and Abel son of Adam. Cain was the first murderer and Abel the first martyr of the Lord.

Zoroaster taught the Word of God including the law. They did not build statues of God or His suns. They worship the Creator not the creation. [Romans 1:25 Exodus 20:1-17] They pray and sacrifice at the foot of mountains like the Hebrews. Prostitution is condemned. A menstruating woman is unclean. [Leviticus 15:19] A dead body is unclean. [Numbers 6:2,6] Adultery, cheating, dishonesty, homosexuality are all sins. [1 Corinthians 6:9,10 Galatians 5:19-21 Ephesians 5:5] Only the obedient ones who have learned discipline shall enter God's kingdom. No liars shall enter in. [Revelation 21:8,27 22:15] The lawless ones shall be destroyed by the Sun of Righteousness. [2 Thes. 1:5-12 2:1-10]

The Devil is described as an evil horned dragon to be slayed by the Lord with the Sword. The battle takes place in the cosmic sea of space (heaven). The dragon, cast down to Earth, will devour one-third of the men and animals. [Revelation 12:7-12] Then the Creator will resurrect the Sun of God to slay the serpent and save mankind. Just as described in Revelation 12 & 13. When Zoroastrians refer to the forces of good they speak of the head, the hand, speaking and dying, but when they refer to forces of evil they speak of the skull, the claw, howling and perishing. For perishing is permanent death; consumed by God.

Last days

The four periods of time according to Zoroaster: 1) gold (Zoroaster's day) 2) silver (follower's of Zoroaster) 3) steel (for Sasanian period) 4) iron (for present time when religion is declining) Daniel's icon of gold, silver, brass and iron & clay parallels: [Daniel 2:31-45] 1) gold is Babylon kingdom 2) silver is Persian kingdom 3) brass is Greece and Rome 4) iron & clay is Rome resurrected (10 nations that make up United States of Europe). The final kingdom is God's.

In the times of trouble; the sun will darken, earthquakes, droughts and famine, and wars. families will break up. [Matthew 24:7 Revelation 6:5,6]

The Savior's first coming as born of a virgin of the line of Zoroaster (meaning son of the star). Ironically, Christ is born of the line of Zorobabel (meaning son of Babylon). [Matthew 1:12 Zechariah 4:10] For he was born in Babylon. The Son of God shall be impregnated in his mother by the water (Holy Spirit). At thirty the Sun of God will stand straight up and en-lighten people. [John 1:1-14] They will live in harmony for three years. The length of his ministry.

During the times of tribulation, the dragon will kill one-third of man and animals. [Zechariah 13:7-9 14:1-5 Revelation 6:8] Then the Lord with the Sword will slay the devil beast in the last blood sacrifice. [Revelation 19:11-21] The dead will rise and be judged. [Revelation 20:11-15] The white sheep will be separated from the black kids. [Matthew 25:31-46] He will resurrect the dead Saints who will go to paradise (Gotatman). Gotatman is the garden of Atum of Anu. (Sekhet-Aanru) This is the seventh epoch of the creation or the Sabbath of the Parsees. [Zend Avesta, vol.III, p.337] Because this occurs on the seventh divine day (7,000th year) called the Lord's Day.

During the millennium there will be no wolves in sheep's clothing and no snakes (devils) to trick the people. [Matthew 7:15] Satan is bound up for a thousand years (one divine day). Following the millennium is the fourth divine day. The souls face judgment. Ahura Mazda weighs the soul's good and evil deeds. The good are refined in the Lake of fire raining down from God, but the bad are incinerated. [Zechariah 13:9] Satan is thrown into the Lake of fire. [Revelation 20:10] Everyone will be vegetarians eating spiritual food of the Tree of life. [Genesis 1:30 Revelation 22:2] There will be no death. The Garden of God is restored by Re (Atum), the Sun of God. [Revelation 21:23] Atum-Ra being the Egyptian name.

A later part of Zoroasterism is the mythology of Mithra. Originally Mithra was not the sun-god but became associated with it after he defeated it. Just as Horus took on the name of Ra after defeating it. Jesus is Sun of Righteousness, but he is not the sun of our solar system. Mithra is the One (Lord with the Sword) who slays the Bull (Baal). Much of the story is symbolic. The Europeans liked it so much, they adopted versions into their mythology. In fact, Mithra parallels Michael's slaying of the dragon in Revelation chapter 12. The story of the evil Minotaur comes from Upper Egyptians who worshipped the Apis or sacred Bull as an aspect of Min. Min is Amon, Amen, Amon. Just as the Apis is also the Asp (Serpent of Old). Apopis is the sea Serpent of space. Another attribute of Satan.

The problem is the story has been corrupted over time. Mithra is said to be born on Dec.25th. This is the birth day of Tammuz, Sol, Helio, Apollo, and Amen-Ra. These are the names of the evil sun of God who dies out during the winter solstice and revives during Easter. The Romans called him Sol Invictus, the Unconquered Sun. Mihr means Sun in Persian. This version competed against the cult of Christendom for dominance in the Roman empire. Finally, Christendom merged as the state religion of the unholy Roman kingdom and Mithraism died out. Just as the sun dies in its day. In fact, Sunday is sun-dies in Latin.

The followers of Mithra would fast for penitence and for expiation of sins; a ritual act of purification. Just like the Catholic penitence and absolution. While the followers of Zoroaster, maintain that true fasting is the abstinence of sin. This parallels the teachings of the Lord who said, God does not desire sacrifice, but obedience to His Commandments. God wants repentance (stop sinning), not penance (payment for offenses). "I desire mercy and not sacrifice. For I did not come to call the righteous, but sinners, to repentance." [Matthew 9:12,13] The Lord wants us to be healed of the sickness of sin. Remission comes from repentance. The cure comes from repenting from sin, not repeating the sin.

Muhammad, Founder of Islam

The Prophet was born Muhammad Al Amin. His father was Abdullah and his mother Amina. Who were pagan Arabians. Muhammad was given the family name of Al Amin. Al is El meaning GOD. They are named after Amon-Ra, the evil sun of God of Upper Egypt. Min (Amin) is one of his attributes. Just as Abraham was called by the Lord to separate from is family who worshipped Amin-Baal. Likewise, Akhenaton was given the name Amonhotep IV, by his father Amonhotep III. When he became Pharaoh, he changed his name to Akhen-Aton to show he worshipped Aton-Ra, the sun-disk. Tutankhamen did the reverse. He changed his birth name of Tut-ankh-Aton to Tut-ankh-Amon to show what family he belonged to.

Muslims like Christians end their prayers with Amin or Amen. Amin is a word that cannot be translated (because it is a proper name). It is always spelled the same and capitalized. The Christians say it means: So be it, or Truly, or Verily, or Assuredly, etc... The Jews say it means; Multitude. [Jer.46:25] The Muslims say it means; Faithful or Trustworthy. Egyptians say it means; the Hidden One. No one can agree on its definition because it is a proper name of the Egyptian deity. In fact, Ra is translated to mean exactly the same things! Amen is the universal mantra of Christians, Jews and Muslims.

Muslims take the name of Muhammad as their sur name; as in Muhammad Ali. A tradition they took from Egypt where the body members of Osiris received Osiris as their family name or sur-name; as in Osiris-Ani. Sur was later corrupted into Sir; as in Sir Wallis Budge. Sir and Sur are the root of Asar (Osiris). The Lord said his followers, who overcome evil, will receive a new family name as children of God. [Revelation 2:17 3:12] Prophet is Nuzur in Arabic. N-asar is Asar and the root of Nasarene. Likewise, the root of Saracen is Sar.

A minaret near a mosque, like a Christian church steeple, originated in Upper Egypt as an obelisk. The obelisk was erected by Min's minions and points up to that sun god. Manar in Arabic means "lighthouse". In fact, the Pharos of Alexandria (one of the Seven Wonders) was a lighthouse converted into a mosque. Many minarets were originally erected near Roman temples worshipping the sun god, which were converted to mosques. The obelisk, like the Min-aret, is a phallic symbol for Min the fertility deity who is portrayed with an erect penis. The Lower Egyptians never built obelisks. The Bible condemns Watch Towers. [2 Kings 17:9]

The Qur'an speaks of the bright Morning Star (Sirius) and of the Zodiac signs. Allah is Lord of Sirius. [Surah 24:35 52:49 53:49 85:1,2 86:3] Sirius, in Egypt, represents the virgin Isis and her child, Horus. Horus is Atum-Ra, the good Sun of God. The Lord who rules over the two lands. As he is the Sun who set in the west and rose again in the east. Pharaoh Osiris dies and resurrects as Horus. For 3,000 years, the Egyptian empire had a strong influence on the nomadic tribes of Asia. It is obvious that they only partly understood the Egyptian Mysteries. The four archangels Michael, Gabriel, Azrael and Israfl are the four sons of Horus. Or attributes of Horus himself.

Muhammad was given a Message in Arabic, but he could not read it because he spoke a foreign language. It is a known fact that he was scholared by Christians, and therefore, spoke the Helenistic tongue. He was not illiterate. He was taught from the Lost Books of Eden and other non-canonized books. [Surah 16:103 44:14] Compare this to Moses who did not speak eloquently. Moses did NOT have a speech impediment! People and animals with physical defects were not allowed in the Lord's presence. The Qur'an says Muhammad is the first Muslim, not Abraham as the Muslim's claim. [Surah 39:12]

Muhammad was enlightened by an angel of God between the ages of 35-52; 570-622 AD. Much like Buddha in 560 BC. He did not become a prophet until the age of 40. Which is considered the minimum age of a prophet. When Muhammad was given the choice of being a prophet-king or prophet-servant, he chose prophet-servant. For the heads of state are ruled by the ruler of this world, Satan (Azazel/Iblis). This is the same temptation Satan put to both Christ and Buddha. [Matthew 4:8,9] The poor and humble shall enter God's kingdom, not the rich and powerful. Christ is head of the church.

Muhammad is founder of Islam which means; to peaceably submit. Muslim means to submit. Moslam means; peacemaker. Shalom means: peace be with you. JeruSalem means; possession of peace. The Jews named it that after they took possession of it. Originally it was called Salem, city of peace. [Hebrews 7:2] Islam's most sacred site. They all have the same root word. Islam represents the place of God's peace and rest. Rest from the world of unRest. "Jihad" means self-sacrifice in the submission of the human will to the will of God and martyrdom. It means to die for God, NOT to kill for God. Our struggle is a spiritual NOT physical battle. [2 Corinthians 10:3-5]

The Temple Mount at JeruSalem is the counterpart to the Egyptian primordial mound at Anu (Heliopolis) from which the Sun of God (Atum) first rose. Originally, Muhammad said his followers should pray towards JeruSalem. Later, he changed his mind and said to pray toward Mecca the birthplace of the Prophet. If it is that easy to change, its not very important in the first place. The only holy land is the place where the Lord stands. [Exodus 3:5 Joshua 5:15] Why not pray towards Heliopolis (Anu), the original birthplace of the Sun of God?

Muhammad had 72 assistants called Ansar (Anti-Sar) on his arrival at Medina. Compare this to the 72 Sami who assisted Set in usurping King Osiris (Sar). Muhammed had 12 Imams, just as there are 12 houses in the Zodiac. Osiris is the house of Ham (Africans). Abraham was of the house of Shem. But Abraham's descendants through Hagar, the Egyptian princes, make Muhammad of the royal line of both Shem and Ham. Muhammad usurped the throne from the Egyptians when he conquered Egypt. Nevertheless, this was not the age of Ham or Shem. It is the age the Lord was working with the sons of Japheth (the Gentiles).

Muhammad's one mistake was to declare war against merchants of Mecca. The war, of which, he lost. A war, I believe, they pressured him into declaring. Only when they preached love and became peacekeepers, did they have victory and peace. Muhammad started out as a warrior, but soon learned the error of his ways much like Elisha. Moslem means peacemaker. No warrior shall enter God's kingdom. The root Islam & Moslam is Lamb or Ram. The age of Aries the Ram, the age of war, is passed away. It is replaced by Pisces, the age of Peace.

The Middle East had always been the middle men trading between the Chinese and the Europeans. Until Muhammad put an end to it. Merchants dealing in forbidden merchandise is not allowed. The caravans sold everything, including slaves. The Word of God says the Common Market, called Babylon, shall be destroyed. [Rev.18:9-13] Canaanite means Merchant and no Canaanite shall enter God's house. [Zechariah 14:21] Capitalism is condemned by God. Muhammad cleaned out the Ka'ba at Mecca just as Jesus cleaned the Temple in JeruSalem. [Matthew 21:12-13]

The Word of God calls the capitalists Babylon and the harlot is the Queen of Babylon. She sells her soul for the love of luxury. Babylon is the business men and she is the compulsive consumer. She buys whatever he sells. Including his fables and wives-tales. She desires the worldly dream and he provides the materialistic things of that fantasy. She prostrates herself before him as a prostitute. The modern version or vision is television. The men of business make the commercials that promote their product and their customs. She buys into the traditions and buys the things necessary for the rituals of that tradition. The costumes and offerings that goes with the man-made traditions like Chrismas and Easter that produce big money for big business.

The Muslims are the grave robbers of the Egyptian tombs and temples. Like Christians, they will do anything for a buck! It was the Muslims like Caliph Al Mamon (m-Amon), who damaged the Great Pyramid, defiling the temple of the Lord, in search of Mammon (Wealth). Muslims stripped off the outer skin of the pyramid temples for their mosques. The Muslim claim that the Pyramids and Sphinx at Giza are pagan idolatry that must be torn down. If this is so, than the Kaba in Mecca is also a pagan idolatry that must be torn down. The Black Stone at the corner of the Kaba is idolized as something divine that fell from heaven. Just as the image of Diana which fell from heaven. [Acts 19:35] "All things shall be settled in the last days." What you do to others shall be done to you.

But even worse than desecrating and destroying ancient treasures, is the stealing of their heritage. These Arabians claim to be descendants of the Egyptians. This is a LIE!!! Arabs are Arabians of the Middle East and the descendants of Shem, son of Noah. Egyptians are sons of Ham (Khamet) and are ALL black people of the Negroid race. Arabians are Semitics of the Mongoloid race. The Egyptian religion predated Islam by 4,000 years and Abraham by 2,000 years. Lies have been spread that the Arabians or the Jews built the Pyramids! No liar shall enter the kingdom of God!

In 641, Amru, general of Omar, second in succession to the Prophet, completed the holocaust started by Julius Caesar. Amru fed the furnaces of the 4000 baths of Alexandria for six months with the Bruchion's priceless treasures (sacred scriptures). Likewise, the Christians stormed the Serapeum in 387 AD and destroyed irreplaceable scriptures. Just as Hitler burned books, and people, in his day. The military mind and ignorance seem to go hand and hand. The Lake of fire awaits you who love the darkness and who seek illumination and warmth by lighting fires to Bell (Beel-zebub) in honor of Beltane! {See the Sirius Connection page 119}

Parts of the Qur'an are a Military Manuel. The Muslim warriors, like their Viking counterparts, believe in a place called Vallhallah for the dead war heroes. Vallhallah (Vall-Allah) is the Hall of Allah. Where the dead warriors rise every morning to do mock battle with each other. In the evening they return to the Great Hall and refresh themselves by feasting and drinking cups of heavenly mead presented to them by the celestial maidens, called Houris. This is a obvious corruption of Horus with the bread of life. The Vikings called the maiden, Valkyries. This life/death cycle continues until Armageddon, the War to End all Wars that will be the death of all warriors! These big eyed maidens and the heavenly mead are described in the Qur'an. The main difference is the Vikings feast on boar (wild pig), a animal detestable to Muslims, Jews, and Egyptians.

According to the Qu'ran, those who would not fight, go to Perdition. Like the Christian crusaders, they claim that the killers who fight for their cause shall by-pass jail and go straight to heaven. On the contrary, the Word of God says that the Lord with the Sword is going to gather the armies of the world to be executed. [Surah 36:75] It is called Armageddon. [Revelation 16:16 19:11-21] Those who fight against the Lord will go to perdition (their destruction). Satan is the son of perdition because he is the Warlord of the world. 'Vengeance is the Lord's, not man's.' [2 Thessalonians 1:7-10 2:2-10]

Warriors vs. Warners

I have a few things against the Muslims who came after Muhammed. It was the Muslims who nearly exterminated the followers of Zoroaster, the prophet of God in Persia (peace be unto him). It was the Muslims who nearly exterminated the followers of Buddha, the prophet of God (peace be unto him). It was the Muslims that took vengeance on the Caucasian cults (Christians and Jews). In doing so, you are just as guilty as the paleface predators. "Vengeance is the Lord's." It is the Saints who are martyred, not the ones who murder, who shall enter God's kingdom.

In Islam there are many sects or denominations just as in Christendom. The Shittes and Sunnies are the major two who hate each other. The Lord said a house divided shall fall. The banner of Christendom is the Cross. The very instrument that killed Christ. The flag of the Muslim states bear the Satanic star (pentacle) and crescent moon. Knowing full well that they are the symbols of the Devil and his consort, the moon goddess. They are holdovers from the time the pagan Arabs worshipped Venus (Ishtar deva of sex and violence) and Inanna (Diana). In Egypt five is the evil number.

"There is no god but God, and Muhammad is his prophet." is the creed. Paralleling the first commandment: "You shall have no god besides God." [Exodus 20:3] "God has no partners." God the Father is not betrothed to Israel. The daughter of Israel was betrothed to the Lord Jesus, (Jehovah), Son of God. God the Father was to give away the bride, but they were later divorced for spiritual adultery. As the Israelites lived in sin with Satan (Baal of Babylon). The greatest of all sins, shirk, is to associate partners with God. The Creator is Not part of the creation. God is Spirit not physical.

Allah (Ellah) means God Lord or Lord God. 'El' means 'God' and 'ah' means 'Lord'. The Hebrew word is Eliah or Eloah. Allah is also found in the word Alleluia or Alleluiah which means 'Praise the Lord.' Muhammad taught that you should learn to read. You need to read the Holy Scriptures given by God: the Torah, the books of Jesus, and the Quran (Koran). Muhammad even gave prisoners their freedom if they taught ten Muslims to read. We are to seek the knowledge of God's kingdom where ever it is. The Quran calls the Jews, the People with the Book (Bible) who do not do what it says. Likewise, Christians do not do what Christ said to do. Christ called them hypocrites. They shall answer for it on Judgment day. The ignorant infidels shall be eliminated. Buddha said the pig of ignorance is slayed. The pig is the sacred animal of Set/Satan/angel of darkness.

The First and the Last Adam

The Qu'ran says God breathed His Spirit into Adam, giving him life. The Qu'ran says that Christ was born of a virgin begotten or fathered by the power on High (God). The Qu'ran says that Christ spoke from birth. He said to his mother to keep silent, point to him, and he will answer any questions. Surprising, but fitting. For the Word of God should be able to speak at birth as a sign of who he was. The Qu'ran says that Christ is a prophet and that he is "a spirit from God" who was not killed because and spirit-being cannot die. He was lifted up by God and is the One to return in the last days to set up God's kingdom. According to the Qu'ran; Miriam, sister of Moses, is mother of Jesus. This makes sense when you know that Miriam means Mary, Mother with Child.

The Qu'ran says that Mary asks, "O my Lord! How shall I have a son when no man hath touched me?" He said: "Even so: God createth what He willeth: when He hath decreed a plan, He but saith to it, 'Be,' and it is!" [Surah 3:47] So the Muslims believe in the virgin birth of Christ. But they firmly deny that God had mated with Mary. Likewise, they say God would not allow His prophet, let alone His Son to be murdered. Therefore, they contend that Judas appeared like Christ and they crucified him instead. Then Jesus was taken to heaven. Which is of little consequence since the Son of God is a spirit-being who can Not die.

The Quran 19:27-34 says: "Mary came to her people carrying him (Jesus). They said: Oh Mary, certainly you have come with a thing unheard of. Oh sister of Aaron, your father (Amran) was not a wicked man nor was your mother (Hanna) a harlot. So she (Maryam) pointed at him (Jesus). They said: How can we speak to one who is still a child in the cradle (manger)? <Jesus said> And <Allah> made me blessed wherever I maybe, and He (Allah) has enjoined on me the worship and charity (love) for as long as I live and he (Allah) has made me honorable to my mother and didn't make me insolent, unblessed. And peace be upon me on the day I was born, and the day I die and the day I am raised to life (resurrected). This is Jesus son of Mary speaking the fact beyond any doubt which in they dispute." The Messiah predicted his death and resurrection as a new born. Compare Jesus son of Mary of Hanna, to Horus son of Isis of Anu (Hanna).

The Qur'an says; "When the angels said, 'Mary, God gives you good tidings of a Word from Him whose name is Messiah, Jesus, son of Mary; high honored shall he be in this world and the next, near stationed to God. He shall speak to men in the cradle, and of age, and righteous he shall be." [Sura 3:38-64] "And We sent, following in their footsteps, Jesus, son of Mary, confirming the Torah before him; and We gave to him the

Gospel, wherein is guidance and light, and confirming the Torah before it, as a guidance and an admonition unto the god-fearing." [Sura 5:48-55] The Torah is the Instruction manuel for all god-fearing people.

The Qur'an speaks of the Day of Judgment, the Day of Resurrection, the Day of the Lord. On that day, the Angel with the Voice of the Lord will call and the righteous shall rise from the grave to enter the garden of delight with the river of living waters, but the lawless infidels shall go to the Lake of fire. Only those who believe in God, repent, and work righteousness shall find salvation. [Surah 28:67 50:41,42] The Word of God says that Angel is the Word of God who is the Judge. Either he is your Savior or Executioner. [John 5:25-30 1 Thes.4:13-16-17]

Muhammad taught that Judgment day would be accompanied by the blowing of trumpet; in every nation will rise up a witness against it; every man will be given a book with his deeds written in it; the wicked will be condemned and sent in troops to Jehinna, and the righteous will be vindicated and sent in troops to Paradise. [Surah 27:87 36:51] The trumpets are in [1 Thessalonians 4:16 Matthew 24:31 Revelation 8:6,8,10,12,13 11:15] and the books are in Revelation 20:12. The Judge will divide good from evil. [John 5:22-30] The trumpets refer to the Day of Trumpets that announce the Lord's coming to judge the nations by their deeds, based upon God's Ten Commandments. [Surah 17:13-34]

Jehinna (Gehinna) he borrowed from Judaism and Christianity. The Valley of the Son of Hinnom was changed to the Valley of Slaughter where the Israelites burned their children in fire to Baal. [Jeremiah 7:9,30-34] It is an incinerator for unwanted things. No where does it say they tormented forever. Not in the Old or New Testament. Only Satan, the false prophet and the beast torment forever in the Lake of fire because they are spirit-beings. The incorrigible sinners who will not repent shall be incinerated in the volcanic lava (Hellfire).

Hades is a Greek concept: a place named after the Greek god Hades. Who is god of the under-world. Under the world not inside the world. Hades ruled the dark side of the planet. Just as Osiris is Orion in the darkness of space. Hades would be Azrail the Angel of Death, not Iblis (Satan). Satan does not have the power of death. Arazil is the archangel Lucifer who would not bow down to Adam. Arazil became Iblis (Satan) when he fell from favor. [Rev.12:9] Azrail is an anagram of Arazil. Azrail is the Angel of Death preceding the Exodus from Egypt called the Angel of God (Archangel Michael). This Angel sets in the west but rises again at the sunrise in the form of Sirius. Known as Atum-Ra in Egypt.

The Word of God says they shall go into the Lake of fire and exist no more. Death and hell (the grave) gave up the Dead. Then death and hell (not Hades) will be thrown into the Lake of fire. [Revelation 20:14] Satan and his angels will go into the Lake of fire. There is No torment for the wicked humans. God is Not a terrorist nor a sadist! The children of God live forever with their Father and brother Christ in the garden of God.

Some claim that Muhammad ascended to heaven at his death, but this is not so. When God took Enoch and Elijah, their bodies were Not left behind. They were translated into sons of God or spiritual beings. [Hebrews 11:5] There was no trace of them to be found. [2 Kings 2:12-18] Forty days after his resurrection, Christ ascended to heaven. He did Not leave his body behind. He was translated or transfigured from Son of Man (human being) to Son of God (spirit being). [Acts 1:9-11] The Lord did not leave the bones of Moses behind, as he was later resurrected and ascended so he could be with Elijah and Christ at the transfiguration. [Matthew 17:1-3 Jude 9]

Elijah was transported by a whirlwind (Ruach the holy Spirit). The chariot of fire is the same as the solar bark of Ra. It represents Lucifer the sun god. The chariot of the sun separated Elijah in heaven from Elisha on earth just as the fiery cherubim keep sinners out of the garden of God. [Genesis 3:24] No sinner shall enter God's kingdom.

The bones of Muhammad and Abraham are in the Ka'ba. Physical proof they never went to heaven. Just as the Catholics claim that Mary ascended to heaven. The day they call the Assumption. They assume she went. And Catholics have been seeing apparitions or hallucinations ever since. Fact is: Mary is dead and buried in her grave to this day just as David is in his tomb. [Acts 2:29-34] When the metamorphous of a caterpillar to the butterfly, no body is left behind. It is transformed into a new form. Osiris was reborn from the cat-pillar. Cat meaning Chat-hor, the womb of Horus. Pillar = the Tet

The Word of God says the Saints will be resurrected and transformed from human beings into spiritual beings when the Lord returns. This metamorphous from the mortal to the immortal is for the children of God. They shall enter the paradise of God's kingdom on Earth. [Surah 21:105] The house of God is filled with the children of God. [Ephesians 2:11-18-22] The church or body of Christ shall be adopted into that house of God.

Perhaps Mohammad had a vision like that of John in Revelation. The Qu'ran says that Mohammad does not ascend to God's throne, but meets with Jesus, the one nearest to the throne, at which time Mohammad asks Jesus to intercede to God for him. [Anacalypsis volume 2 page 378] Only the Son at the right hand has ever seen God. [John 1:18]

The Muslims say the Lotus tree of Paradise contains as many leaves as there are human beings in the world and that on each leaf the name of one human being is written. The lotus represents rebirth. The Egyptians say Thoth writes the name of those found innocent on the leaves of the Tree of life. The Bible agrees. The Lord told Moses that the lawless will have their names blotted out of the Book of life. [Exodus 32:33,34 Revelation 22:19]

They claim the Qur'an is the Word of God, yet it is fragmented excerpts often contradict the Bible. It is a well known fact that the Qur'an was burned and rewrote from memory. The Qur'an recognizes parts of the Bible as the Word of God yet continuously claims Christ is not God's son. They say that the fiery Angel in the midst of the bush who talked to Moses is Allah. Therefore, Allah is an Angel. [Surah 20:9-14] It uses the same terminology and concepts as Paul and Luke even though they claim Paul is a false prophet and Luke his disciple. It is strange that the same angel Gabriel is the one in Luke as in the Qur'an.

The Qur'an says that men and women will mate in the hereafter. Some claim that each (dead) man is given 72 black-eyed maidens called Houris and each one's virginity is eternally renewed. This is obviously a misinterpretation. Horus is the virgin of 72 dodecans of the Zodiac in a 24 hour day. The Jews and other Semitics believe that the spirit stays in the body 72 hours or 3 days before being born new. Christ waited 4 days before resurrecting Lazarus to dispel this silly superstition. [John 11:17] It is God's Spirit that reactivates the corpse. [Ezekiel 37]

The Word of God says, "For in the resurrection they neither marry nor are given in marriage, but are like angels of God in heaven." [Matthew 22:29-32] These angels are sons of God (males). The fairytales of female angels comes from the pagan Arabs and the Catholic cult. Sex is carnal knowledge from the Tree of knowledge of good and evil. The forbidden fruit is Satan (Iblis) seducing and taking Eve's cherry. [2 Corinthians 11:2,3] The sin of the fallen angels was to have sex. [Genesis 6:2] The Qur'an says "children don't know the shame of sex." [Surah 24:31] Sex is an animalistic act that defiles the men of God. [Surah 4:43 Exodus 19:15] The children of God will have no interest in: money, sex, power, anger, or hate. Monks and ascetics are celibate in preparation of God's kingdom where there is no fornication.

When the Angel speaks to Muhammad, he speaks in the plural "We". Just as the Bible says, "Let Us create man in Our image". This We is "Elohim" in Hebrew. Which means "God's sons". Man is created in the image of the angels. They are also Messengers. That's why all the angels appear just like men. Michael, Gabriel and Lucifer are all sons of God. Yet God the Father has no partners. God created His sons through verbal intercourse. Just as God is going to re-create us as sons of God. Not through sexual intercourse.

In Islam, the sacred number is nineteen. One of the reasons is the Solar and Lunar year coincide every nineteen years. Every 235 lunar month or nineteen solar years, the moon and the sun mate during an eclipse. Compare this to Diana and Apollo matings. This is worship of the creation, not the Creator. Nine in the number of the Great Mother; the matrix or Cosmic Egg from which the Sun of God was born. Eight is the number of the Infinite Father and Creator. Seven is the number of his good Son. Six is the number of man. Five is the number of the evil son of God. The number nineteen is of O (zero) importance.

The Qur'an says the People with the Book (Jews) broke Allah's Covenant when the built the Golden Calf. [Surah 65-68] Which was really an

Apis-Bull which the Upper Egyptians held as the sacred bull. The Apis was the living image on earth of the Bull of heaven (Taurus). Taurt the divine cow gave birth to the babe Bull, Baal-Amen. The Pagan Arabians use the bull as symbol of Baal. By breaking the law, the Israelites shattered the dream of paradise (the Promise land). These Sabbath breakers are portrayed as primates (apes). [Surah 4:47] The Egyptians portray man's animal behavior with a baboon, lacking self-control. The scientific name for primates is simian. At Thebes, the priests of Amen (Baal) are called 'sem' and 'ian' refers to a follower of Pan or Baal. Only the law abiding shall enter God's garden paradise on the divine Sabbath day. The Sabbath is a place in time made for man to live in peace and harmony with his Creator.

Dead Sea Scrolls

The books of Qumran were classified into four categories: Torah (Genesis, Exodus, Leviticus, Numbers, and Deuteronomy), Former prophets (Joshua, Judges, 1 & 2 Samuel and 1 & 2 Kings), Latter prophets (Isaiah, Jeremiah, Ezekiel, and the twelve minor prophets), and writings (Psalms, Proverbs, Job, Song of Songs, Ruth, Lamentations, Eccesiastes, Daniel, Ezra-Nehemiah, and 1 & 2 Chronicles. The book of Esther and its celebration called Purim is conspicuously absent. Obviously, the massacre of 70,000 Persians and its celebration was seen as detestable.

They left the scared scriptures open ended. Willing to accept any new Word of God: such as the Testament of Jesus. They did not have a closed canon or closed mind to new revelations like the Jews and Christians. Even the Muslims claim the Quran is the last message and Muhammad is the seal of the prophets. Should God dictate a new message or prophecy, in these last days, they would reject it. Limiting the infinite power and mercy of God.

The community at Qumran may have been Essences. A commune where they shared all things in common, therefore, Communism. [Acts 2:44] The Essences seem to be much like the Nazarenes. John the Baptist was likely an Essence. Paul was called leader of the sect of Nazarenes. [Acts 24:5] Could John have been the Teacher of Righteousness in the Dead Sea Scrolls? Some believe it was James the Just, brother of Jesus. Yet the Teacher of Righteousness speaks words from the mouth of God (i.e. a prophet). And the Wicked Priest is Ananas the high priest of Jerusalem. And the liar is Paul, creator of Christianity. Who taught the Law was done away with. The Man of Lies rebuked the Teacher of Righteousness and rejected the Torah.

Manuel of Discipline 8:13-15 "....from the dwelling-place of the men of perversion [the Jerusalem authorities] in order to go to the wilderness to prepare the way of Him, as it is written [quoting Isaiah 40:3]: "In the wilderness prepare the way of ....[the divine name is marked in this scroll by four dots], make straight in the desert a road for our God!"-this [way] is the search of the Law. Compare to Mark 1:3.

Pesher Habakkuk-The Wicked Priest who was called by the name of truth at the beginning when he arose. But when he ruled over Israel, his heart became haughty and he abandoned God, and he rebelled against the laws for the sake of wealth. And he stole and gathered the wealth of the men of violence who had rebelled against God. And he took the wealth of the nations to add to it the guilt of transgression. And he conducted himself according to abominable ways will all impurity. The Wicked Priest who watched out for the Teacher of Righteousness and sought to put him to death. He pursued the Teacher of Righteousness to swallow him up in his intense anger at the place of his (the Teacher's) exile. And at the time of the festival of their abstention from labor he appeared before them to swallow them up and to make them stumble on the day of the fast of the Sabbath of their abstention from labor.

COMMENTARY: This describes Christ's death on Passover, the day before the Feast of Unleavened Bread. Which is a Sabbath high day. The disciples were scattered and their faith stumbled. The Shepherd was arrested and sheep were lost without him. [Mat.26:3-5 Mark 14:1,2] The Passover, at the spring equinox, is paralleled by the Day of Atonement at the fall equinox. The sacrificial lamb is also the scape-goat that takes away the sins of the people. It is the only day the Priest enters the Most Holy Place of the temple. [Hebrews 9:11,12-28] The Son of God is a spirit-being and did not die. Only the physical Son of Man died on the cross. Then God took vengeance against them by turning them over to the ruthless Romans.

Qumran text 5:13-14 "They shall not enter the water to partake of the pure Meal of the Saints, for they shall not be cleansed, unless they turn from their wickedness: for all who transgress His word are unclean." [Compare to 1 Corinthians 11:17-34 Matthew 26:26-29] The Essences were Saints soon to be sons of God; not Christians! Christians are the Lawless ones.

Temple Scroll 51:19-52:3 Do not do in your land as the nations do: everywhere they sacrifice, and plant for themselves Asherot, and erect for themselves pillars, and set up for themselves figured stones to bow down to (or on to) them... You may not plant [for yourself any tree as an Asherah next to my altar which you shall make for] yourself. Nor may you erect for yourself a pillar [which I despise], n[or] shall you make for yourself (anywhere) in your entire land a [fi]gured [st]one to bo[w] down to (or on).

COMMENTARY: You are Not to make graven images as the Romans make statutes to their gods. Nor like the Roman Catholics make statutes to Mary and the Saints which replaced the Roman deities. Ramsees II, king of Egypt, built stone pillars called obelisks to Amen-Ra (the Devil). The Catholics have one of these pillars at the Vatican. The obelisk is a phallus pointing up to the sun who is supposed to be the potent fertility deity. There is another one in Washington DC along with the goddess of Freedom. The lawless lady libertine. Stonehenge is pillars to Baal in honor of the solar solstice. The Canaanites and the Druids worshipped mother nature (Asherah) and her mate the sun-god (Baal). They brought the symbol of their deva into their houses with the modern Chrismas tree. [Jeremiah 10:1-5]

Qumran-"He shall be great upon the earth, O King! All shall make peace, and all shall serve him. He shall be called the son of the Great God, and by his name shall he be named. He shall be hailed the Son of God, and they shall call him Son of the Most High..., and his kingdom will be a kingdom forever." Compare to Luke 1:35 Daniel 2:34-45

Manuel of Discipline 3:18-21-"He [God] has created man to govern the world, and has appointed for him two spirits in which to walk until the time of His visitation: the spirits of truth and falsehood. Those born of the truth spring from a fountain of light, but those born of falsehood spring from a source of darkness. All the children of righteousness are ruled by the Prince of Light and walk in the ways of light, but all the children of falsehood are ruled by the Angel of Darkness and walk in the ways of darkness. Compare to 1 John 1:5-7 & 4:1-6 By these the generations [walk] of all the sons of man; by their divisions all their hosts inherit a share from age to age. In their paths they walk, and all the reward of their deeds is according to the divisions of (these two spirits)... For God has set these (two spirits) with equal influence until the end time and has put eternal hatred between their divisions{{ellipsis}}. That they may know good [and evil, that] lots may be cast for every creature according to his spirit within [him until the season for vis]itation. [1 QS 4:26]

COMMENTARY: It is the angels who fight in the battle of the Sons of Light vs. the Sons of Darkness. "Behold My Angel shall go before you. Nevertheless, in the day when I visit for punishment, I will visit punishment upon them for their sin." [Exodus 32:33-34] This Angel who Zoroaster called Ahura Mazda is diametricly opposed to the evil angel, Ahiman (Ahura Aman). The Egyptian called him Ra-Aman (Amen-Ra). The Word of God is based on the dualism of good vs. evil. From age to age refers to Zodiac ages. The Teacher of Righteousness came to Qumran just at the change from the Age of Aries to the Age of Picses (166 BC).

Qumran-"And they [those who curse] will be for death [while] the One who gives life will raise to life the dead of his people." Compare to 1 Corinthians 15:45

COMMENTARY: They called Christ the Devil (Baal-zebub) and hanged him on a tree as if he were that Old Serpent. [Matthew 12:24 John 3:14 Galatians 3:10-13] Yet they were the outlaws who murdered an innocent man. They shall receive the curse of sin, which is the death penalty.

Ephraim is a code word for the Pharisees who are the builders of the wall between themselves and the saints. The Old Testament uses Ephraim to describe the northern part of Israel that separated from Judah in the south. Manasseh designates the Sadducees.

4 Qumran 521-[... The Hea]vens and the earth will obey His Messiah, [...and all th]at is in them. He will not turn aside from the Commandments of the Holy Ones. Take strength in His service, (you) who seek the Lord. Shall you not find the Lord in this, all you who wait patiently in your

hearts? For the Lord will visit the Pious Ones and the Righteous will He call by name. Over the Meek will His Spirit hover, and the Faithful will He restore by His power. He shall glorify the Pious Ones on the Throne of the Eternal Kingdom. He shall release the captives, make the blind see, raise up the do[wntrodden.] For[ev]er will I cling [to Him...], and [I will trust] in His Piety (Grace), and [His] Goo[dness...] of Holiness will not delay... And as for the wonders that are not the work of the Lord, when He...then He will heal the sick, resurrect the dead, and to the Meek announce glad tidings. ...He will lead the [Ho]y Ones; He will shepherd [th]em; He will do ... and all of it..."

Compare to Matthew 5:5,9. The Meek shall inherit the earth, not heaven. The peacemakers shall be the sons of God, not the warriors.

COMMENTARY: He is coming to save the Saints who keep the Commandments of God and have the testimony of Jesus. [Revelation 12:14 14:12 22:14] The Spirit of God is the power of God that resurrects the dead back to life. [Ezekiel 37:1-14] 4 Qumran 385-389 is the same as Ezekiel 37. "a blasphemous king will arise among the Gentiles, and do evil things...Israel from (being) a people. In his days I will break the kingdom of Egypt...both Egypt and Israel will I break, (and) give (them) over to the sword."

COMMENTARY: The Gentiles are the Greeks and Romans who conquered Egypt and Israel. The wonders that are Not the Lord's are of the Devil's. [Rev.13:13] The Devil is called Belial. The angels of Mastemoth are the fallen angels. The sons of God mated with human women. [Genesis 6 2 Peter 2:4,5 Jude 6] These fallen ones are of the Elohim. Their sons are called Nephilim or Nop-elim in Hebrew. "Elim" is the same word as Elohim. Which is plural of El. Their sons are demi-gods or half god and half human. They were supernatural beings. The sons of light follow the Angel of light. The sons of darkness follow the ways of the angel of darkness (Satan). The fallen angels are also called the fallen stars. [Rev.12:3,4,7-9] The sons of God are suns of God.

Pesher Nahum-["Deme]trius, king of Greece, who sought to enter JeruSalem with the counsel of the interpreters of false laws, [but God had not given JeruSalem over] into the hand of the kings of Greece from Antiochus until the rise of the rulers of the Kittim... but (later) the city was given into the hand of the rulers of the Kittim. [....Demetrius who made war] against the Lion of Wrath so that he smote his nobles and the men of his council....against the interpreters of false laws in that he hanged men alive [which was never done] in Israel before..."

COMMENTARY: The book of Daniel prophesied this event. [Daniel 11:20-45] The Kittim is the code word for the Romans. The Greeks and Romans are called the Gentiles. Demetrius III Eukerus (95-88 BCE) is king of Greece. Antiochus III the Great (223-187 BCE) was of Alexander the Great's rule. The Lion of Wrath was the Jewish king Alexander Janneus (104-76 BCE), great-grandson of Judah the Maccabee. Who crucified 800 rebel Jews. A detestable practice never before done by the Jews. Not long after, the Romans conquered Greece and occupied Israel. The evil ones who crucified thousands of others besides Christ. The cross is the Roman symbol of death.

The members believed there to be three temples: the one desecrated and later destroyed in 70 AD, the "temple of man", and the temple of God build from the foundation of the world (i.e. New Jeru-Salem coming from heaven). [Ezekiel 40] [Revelation 11:19 15:5 21:10] The one in heaven is the original. [Hebrews 9:24] They moved from Jerusalem because they knew Jerusalem would be destroyed in the last days.

Pesher Nahum 3-4 II,8 [Its] interpretation [con]cerns those who lead Ephraim astray, whose falseness is in their teaching (talmud), and whose lying tongue and dishonest lip(s) lead many astray.

COMMENTARY: Ephraim is the code word for the Pharisees who taught the oral traditions which later became the Talmud. The Lord condemned this teaching. [Matthew 15:1-9 23:13-15 Mark 7:1-13] Manasseh is the code word for the Sadducees who taught the Torah or written law.

War Scroll 1:1-2,5-7 And th[is is the book of the disposition of] the war. The first engagement of the Sons of light shall be to attack the lot ot the Sons of Darkness, the army of Belial, the troop of Edom and Moab, and the sons of Ammon and the army [of the inhabitants of] Philistia and the troops of the Kittim of Assyria, and in league with them the violators of the Covenant... [That shall be] a time of deliverance for the people of God, an appointment time of dominion for all men of His lot, and eternal annihilation for all the lot of Belial. There shall be [great] panic [among] the sons of Japheth, Assyria shall fall, and no one will help him. And the dominion of the Kittim shall depart, so that wickedness will be subdued without a remnant, and none shall escape of [all the Sons of] Darkness.

COMMENTARY: The Kittim is the Romans. Kittim of Assyria refers to the Romans being the descendants of the Assyrians or Aryans. Daniel 11:20-23 speaks of his League of Nations or one world system lead by Belial the Antichrist. The original Europeans are the sons of Japheth called the Gentiles. They are Gomer (Germany), Magog, Tubal, Meshech, Torgarmah, and Javan (Greeks). The battle of the armies of Edom, Moab, Ammon, Philistia, Rome, etc... is described in Ezekiel 38. It is commonly called Armageddon, but takes place at JeruSalem. Gog is the prince of Magog and leader of the rebellion. He leads All nations to their annihilation. [Rev.16:12-16 20:7-9] He is also called prince of Tyre. [Ezekiel 28:2-19] And the head of the Beast who makes war with the Saints. [Rev.13:7] Who he will murder. It is the Angels who are the Sons of light who shall destroy the armies of Belial. [Revelation 17:14 19:11-21] The Lord with the Sword will slay the dragon-beast.

The battle moves from a time of birth pains to deliverance in the age of redemption. [1 QH 3:7-10] Secrets of the Dead Sea Scrolls by Randall Price p.211 Compare this to Romans 8:21,22]

Zadokite Fragments 9:1 Any man who shall condemn (or destroy) any man according to the laws of the nations is to be put to death. Compare to Levi.27:29 and Genesis 9:6. "whoever sheds the blood of man, by man shall his blood be shed,"

COMMENTARY: Anyone who kills, even during time of war, is a murderer who shall receive the death sentence. "You shall NOT kill." "Vengeance is the LORD's."

Josephus says, "Holding righteous indignation in reserve, they (the Essenes) are masters of their temper, champions of fidelity, the very ministers of peace."

4 Qumran 529-"The words of the book that Michael spoke to the angels of God [after he had ascended to the Highest Heaven.] He said 'I found troops of fire there... [Behold,] there were nine mountains, two to the eas[t and two to the north and two to the west and two to the so]uth. There I beheld Gabriel the angel... I said to him, '...and you rendered the vision comprehensible.' Then he said to me...It is written in my book that the Great One, the Eternal Lord... the sons of Ham to the sons of Shem. Now behold, the Great One, the Eternal Lord...when...tears from... Now behold, a city will be built for the Name of the Great One, [the Eternal Lord]... [And no] evil shall be committed in the presence of the Great One, [the Eternal] Lord...Then the Great One, the Eternal Lord, will remember His creation [for the purpose of Good]...[Blessing and honor and praise be to] the Great One, the Eternal Lord. To Him belongs Mercy and to Him belongs... In distant territories there will be a men...he is, and He will say to him, 'Behold this...to Me silver and gold...'

COMMENTARY: The mon-arch-angel Michael is the heavenly name of the Messiah. Who ascended to the first heaven where God dwells alone. He shall descend with the voice of an Archangel. [1 Thessalonians 4:16] He comes in the holy city New JeruSalem that shall settle on the holy Mt. Zion. [Matthew 16:27,28 Rev.21:10] The troops of fire are the fiery angels (seriphim). The angels fight the battle between the sons of light and the sons of darkness called Armageddon. [Revelation 19:11-21] Michael and his angels shall defeat Satan and his angels. [Rev.12:7-9] Then the sons of God (good angels) shall defeat the evil humans. [Mat.13:41 16:27,28 25:31] In Dead Sea Scrolls "sons of God" always refer to the angels. LORD is substituted for the Tetragrammaton YHWH or YHVH. And Michael is God's mediator. In the Bible, Yahweh is the Angel with God's name. [Exodus 23:2—21] He is the ambassador who represents God's kingdom. Yahweh or Jehovah is LORD Jesus who comes in the God given name. [John 17:11,12] The name that no one knows except those who possess it. [Rev.2:17 3:12] Jehovah is Jesouas in Greek. Drop the excessive vowels and you have Jesus. Just as the Hebrew Mashiah is Messias or Messiah. The h becomes an s and the v an u in the Greek. Jesus Christ = Jehovah the Messiah. In the Apocalypse of Abraham, the Angel of God is called Yahoel meaning Lord + God. The Son of God is the Godhead bodily or the head of the body of believers. [Colossians 2:9,17] The many membered body of believers who shall also shall be sons of God. Those incarnate in the physical world. While God the Father is the Godhead of that body. He is head over All His sons. [1 Corinthians 11:3 15:28]

4 Qumran 246-"[the king. And when the Spirit] came to rest upo[n] him, he fell before the throne. [Then Daniel arose and said,] 'O [k]ing, why are you angry; why do you [grind] your teeth? [The G]reat [God] has revealed to you [that which is to come.] It shall indeed all come to pass, unto eternity. [There will be violence and gr]eat [evils.] Oppression will be upon the earth. [Peoples will make war,] and battles shall multiply among the nations, [until the King of the people of God arises. He will become] the King of Syria and [E]gypt. [All the peoples will serve him,] and he shall become [gre]at upon the earth. [...All w]ill make [peace,] and all will serve [him.] He will be called [son of the Gr]eat [God;] by His Name he shall be designated. He will be called the son of God; they will call him son of the Most High. Like the shooting stars that you saw, thus will be their Kingdom. They will rule for a given period of year[s] upon the earth, and crush everyone. People will crush people, and nation (will crush) nation, until the people of God arises and causes everyone to rest from the sword. His Kingdom will be an Eternal Kingdom, and he will be Righteous in all his Ways. He [will jud[ge the earth in Righteousness, and everyone will make peace. The sword shall cease from the earth, and every nation will bow down to him. As for the Great God, with His help he will make war, and He will give all the peoples into his power; all of them He will throw down before him. His rule will be an Eternal rule, and all the boundaries...

COMMENTARY: "Now when all things are made subject to Him, then the Son himself will also be subject to Him who put all things under him, that God may be all and all. [1 Cor.15:20-28] The Lord Jesus is Judge. He is either your Executioner or Savior. But God the Father is head of him. [John 5:22-30] The Sun of God is the Morning star coming with the clouds. [Daniel 7:13 Mat.24:27-31 Rev.14:14] Coming to be King of God's kingdom. [Dan.2:34-45]

War Scroll 17:6-8 He has exalted the authority of Michael with eternal light to enlighten with joy the h[ouse of I]srael, (with) peace and blessing for the lot of God, to increase among the angels the authority of Michael and the dominion of Israel over all flesh.

COMMENTARY: Michael is Prince of light and the Great Prince who stands watch over the sons of your people. [Daniel 12:1 9:25 10:21]

Rule of Congregation 2:11-22 [The ses]sion of the men of renown, [invited to] the feast for the council of the community when [at the end] (of days) the messiah [shall assemble] with them. [The priest] shall enter [at] the head of all the congregation of Israel, and [all his brethern the sons of] Aaron, the priests, [who are invited] to the feast, the men of renown, and they shall sit be[fore him, each] according to his importance.

Afterwards, [the messiah] of Israel [shall enter] and the heads of the [thousands of Israel] shall sit before him, [ea]ch according to his importance, according to [his station] in their encampments and their journeys. And all of the heads of the [households of the congrega]tion, [their] sag[es and wise men,] shall sit before them, each according to his importance. [When they] mee[t at the] communal [tab]le, [to set out bread and win]ne, and the communal table is arranged [to eat and] to dri[nk] wine, [no] one [shall extend] his hand to the first (portion) of the bread and [the wine] before the priest. Fo[r he shall] bless the first (portion) of the bread and the win[e and shall extend] his hand to the bread first. Afterwa[rds,] all the congregation of the community [shall ble]ss, ea[ch according to] his importance. [They] shall act according to this statute whenever (the meal) is ar[ranged] when as many as ten [meet] together.

COMMENTARY: This is the Feast of Ingathering or Feast of Tabernacles. [Zechariah 14:16-21] "But I say to you, I will not drink of this fruit of the vine from now on until that day when I drink it new with you in My Father's kingdom." [Matthew 26:26-29] Bless should be "give thanks". You can not bless an inanimate object.

Halakhic letter B 58-59 And one may not bring dogs into the holy camp because they eat some of the bones of the Tem[ple while] the meat is (still) on them.

COMMENTARY: The dogs are canines or Canaanites. [Zech.14:21 Mat.15:22-28]

11 Qumran Melch-Melechizedek is the favored Angel of God. Melchizedek is identified with the "Elohim" of Psalm 82:1. Elohim means God and his sons. Melchizedek is the priest of Jeru-Salem, the priest of God who destroys the forces of evil and liberates the Sons of light. [Genesis 14:18 Psalms 110:4]

The book of Enoch speaks of the angels mating with human women and then teaching them to make swords of iron and breastplates of brass. Compare to [Gen.4:16-22 & 6:1-4] This is where the Greeks got their Prometheus myth.

In the Parables of Enoch, he is portrayed as the first incarnation of Christ. In the Bible, Enoch is too perfect to be mere mortal. [Gen.5:22-24] He was translated and ascended to God's kingdom. The Lord said, "No one has ascended to heaven but He who came down from heaven, that is, the Son of Man. Hebrews 7:1-3 says Melchizedek was "made like the Son of God". Was this one of many incarnations? John 1:18 says the Son of God was incarnated "the Word became flesh".

Enoch is a type of Christ. He proclaimed the Messiahic message: The Lord is coming with ten thousand of His Holy Ones (angels). To execute Judgment on the lawless ones, the sons of darkness. Then God's kingdom is coming. [Jude 14,15] The book of Jubilees speaks of the observance of the Laws and the holy days. It also speaks of the coming of the Lord to destroy the lawless ones. Jubilees 1:2-5 "And Moses went up to the mountain of the LORD... And God revealed to him both what [was] in the beginning and what will occur [in the future]... And He [the Angel of God] said, "Set your mind on every thing which I will tell you on the mountain, and write it in a book..."

The Genesis Apocryphon says Noah observed the laws of the Torah. Just as Abraham did. [Genesis 26:5]

The Samuel A Scroll says: [And Nahash, king of the children of Ammon, sorely oppressed the children of Gad and the children of Reuben; and he gouged out all their eyes and struck terror and dread] in Israel. There was no one left among the children of Israel beyond the Jordan whose right eye was not gouged out by Nahash, king of the children of Ammon; except for seven thousand men who had fled from the children of Ammon and entered Jabesh-gilead. About a month later...

COMMENTARY: This story obviously originated in Egypt. Ammon is Set-Amon who gouged out the right eye of Horus during the battle for the two lands of Egypt. Now we are told that the children of Ammon and Israel are battling for the lands of Israel. Israel (Asarel) is Asar-el. Asar is Osiris and el is god. Osiris, the first Pharaoh, was murdered by his evil brother, Set. Osiris resurrected as Horus and ascended to heaven. Horus shall one day return to defeat Set-Amon. The children of Israel are the children of God-Osiris.

Damascus Document (CD B. 19:12) says: "These [people] shall escape in the time of the visitation, but they that hesitate shall be given over to the sword when the Messiah of Aaron and Israel shall come. As it happened in the epoch of the visitation of the forefathers, which He said by the hand of Ezekiel: 'to set the mark (ha-Taw) upon the foreheads of such as sign and groan.'" [Ezekiel 9:4]

COMMENTARY: The Semitic Taw, Greek Tau and Latin T are all originated with the Egyptian Messiah, Tem (Atam). The Greek X (Chi) became the abbreviation for Christ. It is the root of the Christian cross (+ or X). It refers to two intersecting lines. As when Sirius crosses the celestial meridian and descends into the underworld. When Sirius rises again, it is reborn from the sea of space. Mes-iah means the 'Lord reborn from the water'. Sirius is the Morning star of Tem-Horus. This T is the mark of God in their minds (in their foreheads means in their forethoughts). [Revelation 7:3 22:4]

Hittite Mythology

The Hittites were one of the 11 tribes of Canaanites. They are the sons of Heth. All were Caucasians. [Genesis 10:15-20] The northern border was the Caucasus mountains where other Caucasians dwelled. The Canaanite mythology is basically the same except the names are changed. Likewise, the Israelite stories are identical. The land of the Hittites is called the land of Hatti or Hades. (t and d are interchangeable, as are the vowels). To the east is the Taurus mountains that divided the Hittites from the Phoenicians (i.e. Syria/Lebanon). Here is where Zeus-Amen transformed into a Bull and carried Europia to Crete. The Greeks considered the Taurus mountains to be the land of Tartarus were their enemies lived. It was linked to the constellation of Taurus. The star cluster Hades is the head and horns of the Bull. The Greeks believed Hades ruled over the Asians, their adversaries (satan means adversary).

Kumarbi, the father of the gods, is the counterpart of Zeus. He is Enlil in Sumeria. However, Kumarbi was not the first god. Before him, Alalu (Uranos) was king of heaven and he was deposed by Anu (Cronus). Then Kumarbi (Zeus) made war on Anu and bit off his penis. Anu's sperm impregnated Kumarbi and produced three terrible gods. These are the three parts of Kumarbi's personality: Teshub (Baal) the fertility god, the Sea (Poseidon), and Hades lord of the underworld. Teshub is known as Hadad, Baal, and Min in Egypt. All are portrayed wearing the domed crown of Amen-Ra. At this point the tablet is mutilated, it is obvious that Teshub overthrows Kumarbi.

In the second scene, the Song of Ullikummi, Kumarbi seeks revenge on Teshub who has deposed him. With the help of the Sea, the personified chaos, Kumarbi fathers a son, Ullikummi, who is then placed on the shoulders of Upelluri, a giant who lives in the midst of the sea. Ullikummi grows to huge size, to alarm of Teshub, who organizes the gods to attack him. But the enterprise fails and Ullikummi forces Teshub to abdicate. Then Teshub resorts to the wise god Ea, who devises a means to detach Ullikummi from his source of strength in Upelluri. Ea summons the gods to renew the struggle. Ea with the Roman suffix us is Jesus.

There is little doubt that the Greeks got their version from their neighbors the Hittites. This is obviously the battle of the gods vs. the Titans. It is a corrupt version of the story of Horus vs. Set for the right to rule the world. This is the ancient battle of good vs. evil. The evil one rules this wicked world for the time being, but good shall triumph in the end.

In Hinduism, Indra is king of the gods, who loses his testicles for seducing a human woman. Shiva is the fertility god whose phallus (penis) is severed and worshipped as the sacred Linga. He is also the sungod who is lord of the dead. Shiva appears in the trimurti (trinity), the sacred grouping of three, as the destroyer. Shiva has a trident (three pronged spear) just as Poseidon. All of Satan's aspects are portrayed as being impotent. In Egypt, Horus castrates his Adversary, Set-aman.

The Hittite empire (Turkey) is the nativity of Christendom, Uncle Sam the circus clown, and Santa Claus. Constantinople was the capital and home of Constantine, the founder of Christendom. St.Nicholas was one of the council of Nicaea. Nicholas played the devil's advocate. The dictionary says Old Nick is the devil. In Egypt, Nika is the evil one. Not to mention; Nicholas is the Latin spelling of Nimrod, who stood against the Lord. All the churches in Revelations, except JeruSalem and Rome, are in the land of the Hittites. Ephesus is the home of the pagan goddess Diana. Satan's (Zeus-Amen's) throne is at Pergamos. Satan's synagogue is at Smyrna. Thyatira is the home of the mother of harlots, Jezebel. Laodicea is the home of Luke and his lukewarm followers. It seems strange that these heathen Hittites are the very same enemies of the ancient Egyptians. The sins of the fathers are passed down to the sons.

The Hittites had a god named Santa. It seems a little more than coincidence that St. Nicholas lived in Anatolia (Modern Turkey), the land of the Hittites. Anatolia is the 'land of Anat', goddess of moisture, the counterpart of Nephthys of Egypt. Anat was the daughter of Asherat, the Great Mother of Baal. Asherat is counterpart to Ashtoreth, goddess of groves (especially ever-green trees). From there we got Santa and the X-mas tree. The Mother and Child, called Chris kringle, is in reality Asherah and Baal. The cradle of Christianity is in the home of the heathen. Baal is actually the anti-chris kringle or anti-christ child who shall rule the wicked world in the last days. [Larousse Encyclopedia of Mythology page 85]

Children of God

The Saints are the children of God (to be). To be born again with a new start to do things right this time. They do NOT purposely sin. The Children of God keep all God's Commandments the best they are able. Giving 100% , not giving up. The reformed Saints are transformed into children of God at the Lord's coming. Then they become the priests of God during the Sabbatical Millennium. Revelation 20:6 In the Old Testament they were called Saints also. The Saints must be resurrected mentally from "the walking dead" before they will be resurrected physical. Those who sleep walk through life must be awakened by the light of truth. Those who are spiritually risen have heard the Word of God, shall recognize his voice when he comes again, and shall be physically risen, like the Son of God. Those who rise from the darkness of ignorance will rise from the darkness of the grave. [John 5:22-30 1 Thessalonians 4:13-17]

According to the Grolier Encyclopedia of Knowledge, 'In the New Testament the word Saint refers to any baptized followers of Jesus Christ'. It has nothing to do with the spurious Catholic saints who are worshipped as Roman gods. The canonized Catholic saint is rare because it is rare to find one that has read the Word of God and even more rare to find one that understands the Word of God and even more rare to find one that obeys the Word of God. They have mutated the immutable Word of God.

The children of God do Not believe in vicarious atonement through transference of sin. Sacrificing an innocent animal does not absolve us of sin, therefore, sacrificing the Lamb of God does not atone for sin. Transferring the sins to a scapegoat infers that the goat (Azazel) is your savior. If your savior is the Serpent who died on a tree, your god is the Serpent. [John 3:14] Set-Typhon was the boar (swine, pig, serpent, goat) banished for his sin. He did not take away mankind's sins. If he took away sin, why is it still here worse than ever? [The Golden Bough by James George Frazer page 668] Don't confuse the One who exposes sins with the Evil One. Don't look upon the Lamb as a Scapegoat. He did not cause you to do evil. Don't slay the Messenger who delivered the message, but has not delivered the people. (No one has been saved yet!).

Only God can forgive sins and only He can pardon on judgment day. Meanwhile, Baptism represents our spiritual death and rebirth. Giving us opportunity to start again, free of sin, innocent as a new born. Whether we remain spotless is up to us. Christ did NOT die so you could continue to sin. He lived a sinless life and then sacrificed himself to set an example for us to follow. If Christ death absolved everyone's sins, then Hitler is in heaven. God forbid! The blood on Hitler's hands (and all sinners) is the Lamb's. And the Lamb's blood does not wash away sins deliberately committed after your conversion. [Hebrews 6:4-6 10:26-29]

The members of the body of Christ are called Nazarenes. [Acts 24:5] Christ is called a Nazarene. [Matthew 2:23] As prophesied in Judges 13:5, "the child shall be a Nazirite to God from the womb;" The laws of the Nazirite are described in Numbers chapter 6. The doctrine they taught was called the Way. It is the Way that leads to God's kingdom. [Acts 16:17 18:25,26 19:9,23 22:4 24:14] "Enter by the narrow gate; for wide is the gate and broad is the way that leads to destruction, and there are many who go in by it. Because narrow is the gate and difficult is the Way which leads to life, and there are few who find it." [Matthew 7:13,14] The pagans called them "Christians" as a mockery. Christ-ian means Christ-Pan (Satian) in Hebrew or Christ-yin (anti-christ) in India. Pan, like Mendes of Egypt, was a goat or ram posing as the Lamb of God. This Satyr (goatman) is the spurious Savior. [Revelation 13:11] [A Book of the Beginnings Vol.2 by Gerald Massey page 9]

Jesus was raised in Galilee in Samaria. Sa-maria means Son of Mary. There is no known city called Nazareth. Modern Christians changed the name of a local city, renaming it Nazareth, so to verify their version of the story. A Nazarene is a citizen of God's kingdom, not the kingdom's of this wicked world. Jesus flatly refuse to be King of Israel.

The cult of Christianity was created by Constantine who coined the term Christian. This cult Christened instead of Baptism. They honored the mother of Christ more then the Son of God. Even though he was considered a god, she was Mother of god. Under Christendom, the woman is head of the household in honor of Mary, mother of god. Under their matriarchal system, the matrix or womb called Maya (Mary) gave birth to god. They call her queen of heaven and represent Christ as a helpless baby or dead on the cross, which in itself is a graven image. The church of God has no statues or idols. God has NO partners. Mary is NOT a goddess. Mary is dead!

The followers of Christ went underground to escape death at the hands of the Roman Catholic crusaders. The Catholic's built their church on the bones and ashes of the martyrs. When the Lord returns, he will resurrect the true church from the catacombs and tombs. He will expose the living lies of Christendom and send them to hell (their graves). Vengeance is the Lord's and we patiently await the Lord's Day.

The church of God assembles on the Sabbath as instructed by the Commandment of God. The Sabbath is the sign you are a child of God. [Ex.31:17] The Lord of the Sabbath is the high priest of God's church. He teaches the Word of God on the Lord's day. [Mark 6:2] Just as Paul taught the Sacred Scriptures on the Sabbath. [Acts 13:14,42,44 17:2 18:4,11] The Sabbath represents God place of Rest. [Hebrews 4:1-13] The Sabbath day was created for all mankind. [Mark 2:27,28] The Sabbatical Millennium is a Divine Day when the Lord will teach his followers.

The Sabbath commemorates the original Creation. The Sabbath starts at sunset just as in the beginning God created the light from the darkness. That light is the Morning star Sirius that rises at night. This is the virgin birth of Atum-Horus (Jesus), the light unto the world that ascended to the right hand of God. It was not till half way through the creation that God created the sun (Amen-Ra/Lucifer). Therefore, 12 hours of night precedes 12 hours of daylight. The sun was created on the fourth day of creation. We were a binary solar system until the seventh day when the Sun of Righteousness left because of man's rebellion. With him went God's kingdom and all its benefits. In seven divine days (7,000 years) the King of kings shall return with the kingdom.

The children of God do NOT purposely lie, steal, kill, covet, commit adultery, worship idols, or other gods. [Matthew 5 & 6] It is the lawless infidels who break God's Commandments. These outlaws are not followers of Christ. [Mat.7:21-23] They are banished from God's kingdom and the Sabbath (Rest). They create a place of unrest. [Hebrews 4] They reject God's laws, yet gladly obey Caesar's laws. [2 Thes.2:1-10] Christ's sacrifice showed us how to avoid the fatal sickness of sin, but since God gave us free will, there is nothing stopping us from committing spiritual suicide. The result of intentionally sinning is to permanently perish.

The children of God seek the knowledge of God wherever they can find it. While the Christians conceal the truth. They teach lies about the Bible and other books of God. It was Christians who burned the great library of Alexandria. They would have burned the Gospel of Thomas if it was not for the Egyptians preserving it. And it was Christians who killed anyone who tried to translated the Bible into any other languages. It is Christians who teach lies about the eastern sacred scriptures. While they teach fables and fairy tales from pagans and heathens. The children of God do not fear to seek truth in the unknown. To the Christians, "ignorance is bliss". They dwell in the darkness of ignorance. The Prince of darkness is their guide.

The Saints believe in the Theory of the Rapture. They believe the lost sheep will be raptured away by the false shepherd. The Saints are well aware that the Antichrist Jesus will come before the true Christ Jesus. He will rapture away the masses who are ignorant of the holy scriptures. [Matthew 24:23-31, 36-44] They will be deceived as Adam and Eve were. [2 Cor.11:2,3,13-15] The Antichrist will claim to be able to save the world through science and technology. This is science fiction. The Antichrist will lead the masses into making war with the Saints. [Revelation 13:7]

Then he will attack the Muslims at JeruSalem. For killing Jews and Muslims is the way of the Christian crusaders of Christendom. Then the Lord will come to put an end to the blood-shed by sacrificing all the soldiers. [Revelation 19:11-21] Don't confuse God's Saints (Sant-ified) with Catholic's canonized pseudo Saints.

The children of God love God and keep His Commandments. They love their fellow man and try to convert through teaching the Word of God and setting a Christ-like example. [1 John 5:1-3] Christ is our perfect example to follow. He never sinned. Love conquers all. [1 John 4:17-21] All men are our brothers. For all are children of Adam (Atum).

Christians live in fear; paranoid of losing possession or life. They conquer through shedding blood; sacrificing humans to their Christian demi-god just as the pagan Aztecs did to their sungod. Their unholy wars shall be the death of them. War is the word people use to cover the nakedness of blood-shed and man-slaughter. Cowards kill out of fear of bodily harm. Ignorant kill out of fear of the unknown. ALL warriors will die at the battle of Armageddon, including the Commanders-n-chiefs. [Revelation 19:11-21]

The Saints fight a spiritual warfare in their minds. They battle the evil forces in their own thoughts. [Eph.6:10-20 2 Cor.10:3-5] Self-improvement is the primary objective in order to prove ones-self worthy to become a child of God. If we can't control our own carnal nature, how can we ask others to do so. God does not want rebellious incorrigibles in His kingdom. When we walk in the steps of Christ, then we find grace in God's eyes. [Genesis 6:8,9] Then and only then, will God transform the reformed into immortal souls like His Son.

The native people around the world believe that there are spirits in all living things. And they are right. God's spirit is the life-force or spirit of life in all living things. There was no life until God's spirit started moving across the waters of the sea of space. When any entity dies, the spirit returns to God. That Spirit is not the personality of the person or entity. They do NOT become ghosts. The conscious state becomes the unconscious state of deep sleep until the day of Resurrection. Then the mortal is transformed into an immortal. If man already possessed an immortal soul, there would be no need of a redeemer or savior.

Judeo-Christian vs. Children of God

Christianity is a sect of Judaism. The Church of God was never called Judaism. They were the Children of God or Children of Israel. They both mean the same thing as Israel (Asarel) is Asar-el. Asar is Osiris the son of God. Osiris' body of believers make up the Church of God that will be redeemed.

PS To hell with Amen, the Devil. Refrain from praising the evil one. At the Church of God, the Logos has the last Word... praise Jesus the

Christ...praise Yoshua the Messiah...Halleliah...Her Ra...Hur Ra...praise Heru-Ra-Atum (Horus-Ra-Atum).

Guide to God

Every belief or religion is based on the same principles. There is One God the Father and His two sons. One son is good and one son is bad. This is an universal theme. The names many be changed, but the story is the same. God the Father transcends all thought. The only way to know of Him is through His good Son called the living Word of God. [John 1:18 5:37] We must seek the knowledge of God's kingdom in order to find our destiny. The search for the truth is our quest. The Word of God may turn up in the most unexpected places. There are several books mentioned in the Bible that are lost: the book of Nathan the prophet [2 Chronicles 9:29] the Prophecy of Ahijah the Shilonite [2 Chronicles 9:29] Visions of Iddo the Seer [2 Chronicles 13:22] The Book of Enoch [Jude 14,15] the book of Abraham, the book of Jasher [Joshua 10:13], etc.... Plus there is the newly discovered Dead Sea Scrolls and Gospel of Thomas. In the quest for truth, we must ask ourselves one question. Can we handle it? As we all know, Truth hurts!

Ignorance is NOT bliss! You must actively seek the knowledge of God's kingdom in order to find God's kingdom. Seek and you shall find the truth that will set you free. The light of enlightenment will deliver you from the darkness of ignorance. The bad sun of God is the ruler of darkness. He is the Warlord who wants to take as many followers as possible into the abyss and then to the Lake of fire. Knowledge is the key that opens the one-way Door of the dual dimension of God's kingdom. And the Word of God is the Archangel Michael who guards the Way. He is the Archangel who guards the gate to the garden of God east of Eden. Only those with the Law of God in his heart may pass through. [Hebrews 8:10 10:16 Revelation 22:14,15] Sinners are forbidden passage into the holy city of God.

Either you follow the Good Son of God into the kingdom of light or you follow the bad son of God into the dark abyss of non-existence. Those who think they shall ascend to the heavens shall end up in the bottomless pit with the fallen angel, Lucifer. [Isaiah 14:12-15] The exalted shall be brought down low. Only the reformed Saints shall be transformed into sons of God like Christ. Therefore, do not conform to the wicked ways of the world, but transform your thoughts and your actions to be like the good Son of God. [Romans 12:2] As Satan is ruler of this wicked world that dwells in darkness until the Lord of light comes to dethrone him.

Why is Christ called the Bright Morning star? [Revelation 22:16] Why is he called the Sun of Righteousness? [Malachi 4:2] Why is the Sun of God coming from the east in the clouds? [Matthew 24:27-31 Rev.1:7, 12-16 14:14] Why is his face like the sun? [Revelation 10:1] Who is Satan pretending to be as the Angel of light? [2 Corinthians 11:14] Lucifer means Day star or sun of God.

The answer is found in the Egyptian Bible of Death and Resurrection. The Bible says God said, "Let there be light." and it was good. This light is the good Sun of God who the Egyptians called Atum-Ra-Horus. The other stars or suns of God were created on the fourth day. [Genesis 1:14-19] Lucifer is the chief of the insurrectionists or fallen angels. Also called fallen stars. [Revelation 12:3-9] The Egyptians call Lucifer; Amen-Ra-Set, the evil sun of God.

In our star quest, Sirius is the guiding light in the dark empty outer space. Space is void of life, except the sentient beings represented by the stars or suns of God. Sirius represents the star-god or sun of God, Atum. He is the extra-terrestrial astro-naut who will navigate the Ark (ship) through the sea of space in time to save the righteous from the flood of fire that shall rain down from heaven. As Sun of God and Lord of the Earth, he shall reign over the earthlings. He shall sit upon the throne of Osiris (David?) here on earth after all things are made new. While God the Father shall rule the heavens.

Jasher is Isr in Hebrew and Asr is Asar (Osiris) in Egypt, therefore, the Book of Isr is the Book of Osiris. Jasher means Savior, just as does Joshua and Jesus. Seek the knowledge at its source!

All the original disciples and followers of Jesus the Christ believed him to be Jehovah incarnated. Jehovah = Jehovas (Greek) = Jeshuas = Jesus. Jesus, Son of the Father, is Horus, Son of Patah (Father). [Anacalypsis by Godfrey Higgins, ESQ volume 1 page 582]

Constellations of the Zodiac

Astro-divination; the believe that the stars (planets) influence man's destiny has nothing to do with the Zodiac. God condemns the star gazers (day-dreamers), pseudo-astrologers, diviners and monthly prognosticators who teach lies. [Isaiah 47:13,14 Deuteronomy 18:14] The idea that being born under certain "signs" produces certain personalities is superstitious nonsense. The astrologers claim if you are born in March that you are born under the influence of the sign of Aries. This is a lie! March 20 in the year of 1996 was the spring equinox and is also the Hebrew new year. The sign in the heavens is Pisces. The age changed from Ares to Pisces 2,000 years ago. The age we are born under is calculated in this way. We are all in the age of Pisces and shall remain there until the dawning of Aquarius about 2010 AD. Everyone since BC (Before Christ) has been born under this sign.

It was the pagan Babylonians and Romans who worshipped the sun, moon and planets as gods. They didn't know that the planets were not stars. They didn't even know there were nine planets. Most horoscopes are based on only seven planets. The stars that influenced these infidels were the fallen stars (fallen angels). [Revelation 12:3-9] These were their gods. It was the Romans who named the days of the week after these gods: Monday = Moon's day, Tuesday = Mars' day, Wednesday = Mercury's day, Thursday = Jupiter's day, Friday = Venus' day, Saturday = Saturn's day, and Sunday is Sun's day. The sun (Helio) was supreme as it traveled through the heavens in its chariot. The Egyptians paid little attention to the planets and little to the sun.

It is the followers of Ra the sun who perceive the sun traveling through each of the 12 Zodiacs at a rate of one for each of the 12 months in a solar year. This is what the pseudo-astrologers use to forecast "horror-scopes". This is astro-divination, not astrology. These frauds from Thebes claimed to predict the future. The bad Omens come from Amen's (Ra's) descent or ascent. Following this method, the Zodiac goes in reverse; from Aquarius to Pisces to Aries to Taurus to Gemini to Cancer to Leo to Virgo, etc.

The Lower Egyptians were well aware that the sun and stars are fixed and do not move. They only appear to move as the earth rotates and wobbles around the sun. The angle of projection changes our perception of the sun in relation to the constellations. The followers of Horus used the spring equinox to calculate the time on the cosmic clock. This Great Year takes 25,920 solar years to complete. Each age being 2,160 years. This divine clock turns in the opposite direction of the solar cycle. The sun-god Ra in his solar bark goes contrary to God's plan and is, therefore, Satanic. Ra is the counterpart of Lucifer the Daystar; the sun being the only star we see in the day-time.

God created the host of heaven. [Psalms 147:4] God named each of the angels; as each star represents a sun of God. God created the stars in heaven as signs. The sun and the moon are for calculating the seasons, months and years. [Genesis 1:14] God formed the constellations of the Zodiac (Mazzaroth in Hebrew). [Job 38:31,32] The signs of the zodiac change every 2160 years, not every month. It is called the precession of the equinoxes. We have been in the age of Pisces since before the birth of Christ, Sun of Righteousness and Morning star (Sirius). Compare Zodiac to Zodak. Melchi-Zodak means King of Righteousness. Astronomy is the study of celestial or extra-terrestrial bodies. Astro-nomy starts with Ast (Isis) who shares the star Sirius with her Son. Astro means Star and nome means region. Astronomy is the region of the stars.

According to Arabic and Jewish tradition, recorded by Josephus, the signs of the zodiac came from Adam, Seth and Enoch. Enoch is seventh for Adam and walked with God. He taught the true meaning of the zodiac. [Jude 14,15] Seth resurrected in the place of Abel. In Egypt, Adam would be Atum the Son of God. Abel would be Osiris the first king of God's kingdom who was kill by his brother. Seth would be Horus who ruled in the place of or instead of Osiris. Adam, Seth, Enoch is the pure line or pedigree of Noah. The only Branch of the family tree worth saving. Atum named all the animals on earth and in the heavens.

All peoples were present at the Tower of Babel. All were given the same knowledge before they were dispersed by confounding the languages. This explains why the same twelve Zodiac symbols are found in Egypt, Judah, Persia, India, China, North and South America, Scandinavia, and the Islamic world. Likewise, all nations were gathered together, at the anniversary of Pentecost, by the transcending of tongues. [Acts 2:1-11] At the dawning of Aquarius, the Spirit of God (Water of life) shall be pour out on all flesh. [Acts 2:17-21] The word Zodiac means the Way or the Path. Zodiac is "zoad" in Hebrew and "sodi" in Sanskrit meaning "animal". Zoe means life and diakos means wheel. Therefore, Zodiac means wheel or cycle of life. The circus of animals going through the circuit. Ironically, Pet is the Egyptian word for Heaven. The Egyptian Book of 12 Ways portrays Horus, Sun of God, as voyaging in a bark (boat-ark) around the sea of space. First the twelve hours of the day and then twelve hours of night. The word Hours is an anagram of Horus. The Morning star, Sirius, goes through the twelve stages of dying and rising again.

The Way of Salvation to through rebirth. As in the day of Noah, only the righteous and obedient were saved aboard the ark. We shall be judged by the things we do in our "day". The righteous will be reborn sons of God like the Morning star.

The Egyptians knew that a sphere has 360 degrees. They saw two hemispheres; the night sky (Nut) and the day sky (Nu). The 180 degrees of the night sky they divided into; the lower heaven (Tuat) from the southern horizon to the Tropic of Cancer and the upper heaven (Taurt) from the Tropic of Cancer to the North Pole star. The Egyptians then divided the night sky into quadrants by intersecting the horizon with the north/south meridian. This divides the night sky into 4 equal parts, 90 degrees each, with the North Pole star the center. The 12 Zodiacs are divided into 4 books with 3 chapters in each and 3 decans in each house (age/sign). Just as the year is divided into 4 parts; spring equinox, summer solstice, autumn equinox, and winter solstice. Each part is 3 months or 90 days. 12 months x 30 = 360 days or degrees.

The key to unlock the mystery of the zodiac is in the sphinx with its lion body and man's head. At the Temple of Esneh in Egypt, the painting on the ceiling shows the constellations of the zodiac. Between Virgo the Virgin and Leo the Lion is a carved figure of the sphinx with its head facing the virgin and the lion's tail pointing at Leo. This tells us to start at Leo and end at Leo. As the Lion of Judah said, "I am the beginning and the end." Now let's take a journey back in time. Traveling through the signs in reverse. The Zodiac is the star map for skilled sailors to navigate the sea of space. Our maiden voyage starts at Virgo the Virgin.

First Book
#1 Virgo the Virgin

In the beginning, about 11,000 years ago, GOD created the light or Sun of God. The sphinx points to the age of Leo rising on the horizon. This is the immaculate conception and virgin birth of the good Sun of God (Atum-Ra-Horus) as represented by the sign of Virgo the Virgin (Anu). The Morning star (Sirius) was born in Nun. About 9,000 years later, during the age of Pisces, he would incarnate as Son of Man born of the tribe of Judah. There are 12 houses in the zodiac just as there are 12 tribes or sons in the house of Israel. [John 1:1-14 Revelation 12:1 Genesis 37:9,10]

As Pisces ascends, Virgo descends-representing the death of the Virgin. Each tribe has its own banner or flag with its sign of the zodiac. [Numbers 2] Judah is the sign of the lion. [Genesis 49:9 Ezekiel 1:10] Issachar is the sign of Cancer. [Genesis 35:23] Zebulun is the sign of Virgo. [Genesis 35:23] Reuben is the sign of Aquarius. [Genesis 30:14 49:3,4] Simeon his the sign of Pisces. [Genesis 35:23] Gad is the sign of Aries the warriors. [Genesis 35:23 49:19] Levites sign is Libra. [Genesis 49:5-7] Ephraim and Manasseh are the two horns of Taurus the bull. [Genesis

48:14-20] Benjamin is the sign of Gemini. [Genesis 49:27] Dan is the sign of Scorpio the scorpion. He is both the eagle and the serpent. Both being carnivorous predators. [Genesis 49:17] Asher (Archer) is the sign of Sagittarius. Naphtali is the sign of Capricornus. [Genesis 49:21]

The Virgin holds in her right hand a branch and in her left hand some seeds of grain. This Seed of Eve would crush the seed of the serpent. [Genesis 3:15] This Branch of God's family tree is Christ. [Zechariah 3:8 6:12] Compare to the Greek story about Persephone eating the pomegranate seeds of Hades.

Each zodiac has three decans. Within the house of Virgo is the decan of Coma. It is a woman sitting in a chair sucking her son. Coma means the "Desired One". The Egyptians call her Isis and the child is Horus. In the Greek version, it is Demeter nursing Demophoon.

Ancient tradition says that the star of Bethlehem was in the constellation of Coma. Zoroaster, God's prophet to Persia, was a student of Daniel when he was in Babylon. He learned from Daniel that the star would appear in the constellation of Coma when the One whom it foretold was to be born. This would explain the wise men from the east. In fact, we had just gone into the age of Pisces when Christ was born. The precession of one zodiac sign to the next takes 2160 years. The next sign is the dawning of Aquarius in 2010 A.D.+/-.

The second decan in Virgo is the Centaur. The bad centaurs are half bull and half man or half goat and half man. In Hebrew his name is Bezeh which means "the despised one". Bull is synonymous with Baal the bad lord or Devil. The Centaur is pictured as a hunter with a spear slaying "the Victim". The Victim is Christ dying on the cross. "Many bulls have surrounded Me." [Psalms 22:12] This is the Roman Centurians (Centaurians) that crucified and pierced Christ with a spear. Christendumb holds that spear as sacred. The star Lupus (Wolf) is the ancient symbol of Rome. The she-wolf suckled Romulus and Remus. The Egyptians depicted it as a Lioness, the antithesis of Leo the Lion. She is the Yin to his Yang. Set is Lion-King of the south. [1 Peter 5:8]

Herakles was mortally poisoned by the blood of the Centaur (Nessus) contaminated with the poison of the Hydra. Nessus was the Centaur who molested Heracles' wife Deianeira. Heracles killed him with arrows dipped in Hydra's poison. Later, Deianeira had poured the centaur's blood on a purple robe for Heracles, believing Nessus' lie that it was a love potion that would make him burn with passion for her. When exposed to the sunlight, it activated the poison that burned Heracles' skin. He built a pyre and set himself on fire. He ascended in a cloud of smoke out of his companions' sight. [Acts 1:9] Like the Phoenix reborn from its own ashes. Then Hera adopted him in the ceremony of rebirth. He entered the company of the gods (elohim). See "The Greek Myths 2" by Robert Graves.

Compare the Centaur's purple robe to the Centurion's scarlet robe placed on Christ just before he died. [Matthew 27:28] His death is called the "Passion". The sun is Helios, the adversary of Herakles. Deianeira hanged herself for her part in his death. Just as Judas hanged himself for betraying Christ, while possessed by the Devil. Both stories represent Satan having a hand in killing the Son of God. Just as Lucifer, the Serpent, used Eve's passions to deceive her and cause the shedding of Adam's blood. Also as Delilah betrayed Samson.

In Greek mythology, centaurs are heaven-begotten sons of the gods. They are half spirit-being and half human-being. They were hated by the gods and men. They were driven to the mountains where they were exterminated. These sons of the gods are the sons of the fallen angels who followed Satan. [Revelation 12:3,4,7-9 Genesis 6:1-4] It was Satan who seduced Eve and produced the half-bred, Cain. Cain was the first murderer and son of Satan. [John 8:44 1 John 3:12] Cain's descendants made weapons for war from metals. [Genesis 4:21,22] The fallen angels followed their leader and mated with humans producing more half-breeds. [Genesis 6:2-4] The final decan in Virgo is Bootes. He is a man holding a sword or scepter in his right hand and a sickle in his left. He is the archangel coming to save the good fruits before the fallen angel or Grim Reaper squashes the bad fruits. [Revelation 14:14-20] The Egyptians call him Smat, which means "One Who Rules, Subdues and Governs." Bo in Hebrew means "To Come." The star in his head is Beta (Nekkar) which means "The Pierced".

Fourth Book
#12 Libra the Scales

The next house in the zodiac is Libra, the Scales. In Latin Libra means "The Scales" and in Hebrew it is Mozanaim "The Scales Weighing." This is the scene of the Judgment Day as pictured by the Egyptians. Osiris is Son of Man who died and resurrected as Horus. Now he is worthy to be Judge. The dead are brought before him and weighed in the balances. Their heart is weighed against a feather. If they are burdened with sin and guilt, the scale will tip and their heart will be consumed by the behemoth-beast, Ammit. Ammit (Taurt) is the composite beast: hippo, crocodile and lioness. It is the northern stars called Am-Smen.

The first decan is called the Southern Cross. It is located under the Centaur holding a spear. In Hebrew it is called Adom which means "The Cutting Off." [Daniel 9:26] Also spelled Adam. The first Adam sinned and brought death into the world, while the second Adam did not sin so he could destroy the curse of death. He defeated death by his resurrection. The Cross is the instrument that killed Christ. The cross is also a grave marker. The Cross is used as a superstitious good luck charm or talisman. Christ on the cross is a graven image condemned by God. Constantine used the symbol of the Hooked Cross or swastika (as an omen) to kill the western Romans and create Christendom. He worshipped the sun-god, Satan.

The Egyptians depict Lupus and Centaurus as a lioness. She is the antithesis to Leo. She is the Yin to Leo's Yang. She is queen of heaven and mother of the Lion-King, Amen. Satan is the lion looking for a victim to devour. The Greek name for Lupus is Thera meaning a Beast.

The second decan in the house of Libra is The Victim. The Arabian figures show it as Sura The Lamb. At the Dendereh zodiac, it is portrayed as a child. Christ is the Lamb of God sacrificed for sin. Christ was the victim of the Roman cross and the spear of the Centurion (Centaur). [John 19:34] Egyptians call the Victim, Osiris, who was reborn Horus the Child. He has his finger to his mouth signaling silence to his mother Isis. And he was "as a sheep before her shearers is dumb, so he opened not his mouth". [Isaiah 53:7] The Greeks called him Harpocrates, meaning "Justice" or the "Victim of Justice."

The third decan in the house of Libra is Cornone Borealis, the Northern Crown. Like the Northern Lights (Aura Borealis). Boreas the North Wind had twin sons, Zetes and Calais where were Argonauts. The Crown is called Al Phecca which means "The Shining." He is crowned with the glory of God and his aura is as brilliant as the Sun. [Revelation 1:16] This Sun of Righteousness has traded in his crown of righteousness for a crown of life. [Revelation 2:10] Zoroaster called him Aura Mazdah (Enlightened Lord). His arch-enemy is the sun-god Lucifer who wears the halo of Helio. He is the great impostor trying to impersonate the Angel of light. [2 Corinthians 11:13-15] The statue of Rhodes, one of the Seven Wonders of the World, is the graven image of Helio.

#11 Scorpio the Scorpion

Next is the house of Scorpio the Scorpion. "And they had tails like unto scorpions, and there were stings in their tails; and their power was to hurt men five months. And they had a king over them, which is the angel of the bottomless pit, whose name in the Hebrew tongue is Abaddon, but in the Greek tongue his name is Apollyon (Destruction). [Revelation 9:10,11] Apollyon is Apollo the sun-god who we know as Satan. The main star in the heart of Scorpio, is Antares means "The Wounding" in Arabic. The Sword of the Lord shall wound the beast. [Revelation 13:3,12,14] The Upper Egyptian Scorpion goddess is Serqet. Mesopotamia countered with Ishara-tamtim (Ishtar in the sea of space?). Both are deadly adversaries.

Both ancient Mexican and Egyptian mythology tell of the story of the evil scorpion (Set or Satan). The Mother (Isis) and Child hid from the pursuit of the scorpion in the papyrus swamps in the Delta. Seven friendly scorpions escort them to a safe haven. They probably represent the seven stars of the constellation of Canis Major in which Sirius is part of. They were prisoners in a house. The scorpion stings the child (Horus), he dies, but is brought back to life again. It is the words of power brought by Thoth (the holy Spirit) that revives Horus. Horus is filled with the holy Spirit and becomes the Word of God. The Bible says, "the dragon stood before the woman who was ready to give birth, to devour her Child as soon as it was born. And she bore a male Child who was to rule all nations with an iron rod. And her Child was caught up to God and to His throne." [Revelation 12:4,5] Pharaoh Menes, founder of Upper Egypt, was known as the "Scorpion King." On the celestial level: as Scorpio ascends Orion-Sirius descends. And vice-versa.

The first decan in Scorpio is Ophiuchus which means "the Serpent-Holder". Ophiuchus is pictured as holding a serpent while standing on a scorpion. Compare this to Horus the child holding two serpents in each hand while standing on two crocodiles. Or Herakles strangling two serpents as a child. In Greek, it is Aesculapius the son of Apollo. This demi-god created the medical profession. The caduceus with two serpents entwined on a staff or Aesculapius staff with one serpent is still their logo. This is the antichrist imitating Christ's healing powers. It is a hold-over from the serpent in the Tree of Knowledge of good and evil. In the Hippocratic oath, doctors pledge their allegiance to their god Apollo.

The second decan in Scorpio is Serpens. This is the serpent that Aesculapius is holding. This is that Old Serpent the Devil. This constellation is mentioned in the book of Job 26:13. In Greek mythology, it is the python. This is the sign of the tribe of Dan, the descendants of Cain, son of the Serpent of Old. [1 John 3:12 John 8:44] He is father to the Romans who's sign is the eagle. In antiquity, the eagle was always associated with Scorpio. The Danites ruled the seas and left a bloody trail wherever they would go. [Genesis 49:17] See Companion Bible-footnote for Numbers 2:25

The third decan is Heracles. He is a demi-god; half god and half man. Which describes the Son of God incarnating as Son of Man. He has in his hand Cerberus, the three-headed dog that guards the gates of Hades (in Greek myth). In his right hand he has a club ready to bruise the head of the monster. This represents Heracles (Horus) going to Hades in the constellation of Taurus and defeating the three monsters; Taurus the bull, Ares the Ram, and Cetus the sea monster. Just as Horus defeated Set (Typhon), Ra-Amun the Ram and the Apopis monster during his voyage in his bark.

The brightest star is in the forehead of Hercules and is called Ras-Al-Gethi, "the Head of Him Who Bruises." Hercules' foot is on the top of the head of the dragon. The second brightest star is "The Branch Kneeling." The "Twelve Labors of Herakles" (in Greek myth) were obviously taken from the Egyptian Book of "Twelve Hours of Horus". The Egyptian Heraktes means Horus on the Horizon.

#10 Sagittarius the Archer

The next sign is Sagittarius the Archer (Kesheth). Kesil is Orion. In Akkadian he is called Nun-ki which means "the Prince of heaven and

Earth." In Sumeria, he is Enki or Ea (Jesus). The LORD is prince or ruler of heaven (En, Nun, An) and earth (ki). [Micah 4:13 Isaiah 54:5 Revelation 11:4] He is the man on a horse drawing a bow and aiming an arrow at Antares, the heart of the Scorpion. [Psalms 21:12 45:5] "And I saw, and behold a white horse: and he that sat on him had a bow; and a crown was given unto him: and he went forth conquering, and to conquer." [Revelation 6:2] The word "bow" is rainbow, the same word in Revelation 4:3 and 10:1. His face was like the sun as he is the Sun of God coming in the clouds.

This rider changes to a red horse and was given him a great Sword (which is the Word of God). [Revelation 6:2] This is in reference to the battle of Armageddon when the blood shall be up to the horses' bridles. [Revelation 14:20 19:11-21] The first decan is Lyra, The Harp meaning "Praise for the Conqueror." [Revelation 5:8] There is also an eagle rising with the harp. The eagles shall feast on the flesh of the dead military men. [Matthew 24:27-31] They shall mourn their sons who died for their country.

This centaur is Chiron the King Centaur with bow in hand. [Revelation 6:2] Chiron was the foster-father of Heracles (Horus) and Jason (Jesus). Chiron taught Jason the knowledge of the stars (Zodiac) and wisdom that had to do with the ways of the gods. Chiron (Sir of On or Osiris of Heliopolis) is half horse (Horus) and half man (Osiris). This means Chiron was half spirit-being and half human-being just as Jesus was Son of God and Son of Man. After Chiron trained Jason, he took him across the great river Anaurus back to earth. Ana-urus: Ana or Annu is the heavenly birthplace of Horus and urus or uranus is the heavenly birthplace of Zeus. In the New Testament, the word "heaven" is translated from the Greek word "uranus". When Herakles accidentally wounded Chiron, the pain was so great that he yielded up his immortality. Compare this to Christ who was pierced by a bad centaur.

The Jason child was sent away to escape the wrath of King Pelias. Joseph, the foster father of the Christ child, was sent away to Egypt to escape the wrath of King Heriod. The Horus Child went to the Nile Delta swamps to escape the wrath of King Set. Both Joshua and Jesus crossed the river Jordan to enter the Home-land.

The second decan in the house is Ara, The Altar. Ara means "Consuming Fire Prepared for His Enemies." This is the Lake of fire prepared for those who follow the Beast. [Revelation 19:20 Psalms 21:8,9] The warriors are sacrificed as a sin offering so the saints can live in peace.

Legend says that the Phoenix flies from Arabia to Heliopolis, Egypt every 500 years. There it sacrifices itself on the altar of fire and rises again from the ashes. It represents Osiris dying and resurrecting as Horus the Hawk. Also at Heliopolis, the Bennu bird did alight on the Benben stone which represents the capstone on the Great Pyramid. This headstone is the all-seeing eye of Horus. The Word of God says when the Lamb of God open the seven seals, the twenty-four elders played harps. [Revelation 5:5,8 14:1-3]

The third decan is Draco, The Dragon. The first book ends with the Dragon being cast down into the abyss. [Revelation 9:1 12:9-11] The second book ends with Cetus, The Sea Monster, Leviathan, being bound. [Revelation 20:1-3] The third book ends with Hydra, that Old Serpent being destroyed in the Lake of fire. [Revelation 20:10] The brightest star in the Dragon is called Thuban which means "The Subtle". He is the subtle serpent that deceive and seduced Eve. In the serpent's head is the star Rastaban, "The Head of the Subtle" or "Head of the Serpent." In the Egyptian, Rastan is the Kingdom of Seker (Death). The third brightest star is Ethanin, "The Long Serpent" or "The Long Lived Serpent." Athanasia means Deathless in Greek. Sagittarius is the Hero on the white horse who defeats the Dragon.

The Dragon is in the center of the zodiac just as the sun (Ra) is center of our solar system. Lucifer is that sun the is red at sunrise and at sunset. Satan is the Red Bloodthirsty Dragon and also the Great Fallen Star. Lucifer means Daystar and the only star visible in the daytime is the sun. The evil sun of God rules over the earth for the time being. [Revelation 12:3,4,7-9,12] The Egyptians depicted a dog for the North Pole star (in Ursa Minor) and called it the Dog star. This is the antithesis of the Dog star Sirius.

The Dragon has scales because it swims in the sea of space. It has wings because it flies through space. It breaths fire because it is a star or seraphim (fiery sun of God). It guards a golden treasure; (the Tree that bears the forbidden fruit). This is the taboo totem pole (celestial pole) with the Satanic star on top.

Third Book
#9 Capricornus the Goat

The twelve signs of the zodiac are divided into three books with four signs in each book. The first sign in the second book is Capricornus, The Goat. It is pictured as a Sea Goat. The front half is a goat and the back is a fish. The Hebrew name is Gedi, which means "A Kid; a Goat". The Word of God says that the beast that rises out of the sea is the Roman Empire ruled over by the Dragon. Who is Satan. The beast has two horns like a ram or goat. [Revelation 13:1,11] Witches worship the Devil in the form of a goat. Satanists kiss the goat under the tail as a sign of submission. The Romans called him Pan. The satyrs were half goat and half men; and wholly horny. Sat (or Set) is the root of satyrs. Satyrs are Satan's minions.

On the most high day of Atonement, the scapegoat that bears the sin of the people is banished into the wilderness, but the goat (sin offering) is taken by the high priest and slain. [Leviticus 16:7-9,15,16] Just as Christ was taken by the high priest and slain. Even though he is the Lamb of

God they looked upon him as if he was the Goat of God. Because he did bear the sins. [Galatians 3:13 John 3:14] It is he who shall return immediately following the day of Atonement to separate the lambs of God from the goats or kids of Satan. [Matthew 25:31-46] The day of Trumpets announces the coming of the Lord during the Feast of Ingathering. [Matthew 24:31 1 Thessalonians 4:16 Leviticus 23]

The first decan is Sagitta, which means "The Arrow". One of the definitions of Sin is "to miss the mark". But those walking the Straight and Narrow are sure to hit the target. In Hinduism, Krishna is pierced by an arrow while hanging on the cross. Sagit-taurus is hitting the Bull's eye.

The second decan is Aquila, The Eagle who is pierced, wounded by the Arrow and falling. Arcas was an Argonaut who brought the eagle down with one bronze-tipped arrow. Heracles shot the Vulture that was punishing Prometheus with one arrow. That Vulture was the offspring of Typhon (Set of Egypt). The eagle could represent the Roman Empire. It was their official symbol. The Roman Beast was fatally wounded by the Word of God. [Revelation 13:3,14] That was the original Fall of the unholy Roman Catholic Empire. The wound was healed in 1993 when the Catholic church reunited the 12 European nations and formed the neo-Roman Catholic Empire.

One legend say Zeus (Jupiter) was fed ambrosia and nectar by Aquila when hiding from Cronos. Another says the goat Amaltheia nursed Zeus-Amon. The goat's horn of plenty became the cornupopia. From which we get Capri-cornus.

The third decan is Delphinus the Dolphin swimming in the sea of space. Delphinus means the dead One rising again. Represented by the baptism in water. [1 Peter 3:20-22 Romans 6:3,4-11] The Sun of God will rise in the east out of the primordial sea of space and set foot on the island called Earth. Oannes, like Jonas (Jonah) died and rose again out of the water. Oannes' was half man and half fish. Jason, like Jonah, is depicted as being vomited up by a large fish. In Hinduism, Vishna is depicted as coming forth from a large fish.

#8 Age of Aquarius

Just before Christ came into the world, we moved into the sign of Pisces. We shall remain in this age until the dawning of Aquarius about 2010 A.D.+/-. This represents the age of the Millennium. The day of the Lord that shall never end. Aquarius, The Water-Pourer, is when God pours out his Spirit onto His sons. [Acts 2:17] The sons of God will be filled with the water of life. [John 7:29-37 Revelation 22:1,2,17] The first decan of Aquarius, is Piscis Australis, The Southern Fish. The second decan is Pegasus, the winged horse. Pegasus in Greek means "Fountain Horse." He represents the Lord on the white horse who will lead his followers to the fountains of the waters of life. [Revelation 7:17 Zechariah 14:8]

The last decan is Cygnus, The Swan. The brightest star in Cygnus is Deneb which means "The Lord or Judge to Come". The star Azel means "He Who Goes and Returns Quickly". Fafage, which means "The Glorious Shining Forth." Lucifer is the fiery seraphim. Smen is the sacred goose of Set-Amen. It is called the Great Cackler. There is a black hole in Cygnus that the Sumerians call "the abode of the demon bird of Marduk" or "open jawed dragon". Marduk was obviously perceived as the "evil one".

#7 Pisces-Phisches-Fishes

In the house of Pisces there are two fishes, one moving toward the center of the circle toward the Pole-star; the other swimming in the path of the ecliptic or sun's path. The two fishes are united by a band tied around the tail. The band is also attached to the back of the head of Cetus, the Sea-Monster, and Aries, the Ram. One of the stars is Okda in Hebrew, meaning "The United". The evil are gathered together at one place [Revelation 16:16] and the good are gathered together at another. [Matthew 24:31] In Hebrew the name for Pisces is Dagim, the Fishes, which is related to the word for multitude. As a great multitude shall be saved. [Revelation 7:9] In ancient Egypt this constellation was called Pi-Cot Orion or Pisces Hori, which means "The Fish of Orion Who Comes" or "The Fish of Horus". For the constellation of Orion represents Osiris who died and resurrected as Horus. They believed that the two fish, Abtu and Ant, were pilots that guided the Bark (boat-ark) to safety. It was the Son of Man who said, "Come after me, and I will make you fishers of men." [Mark 1:15-17] The Lord taught his school of fishes, the Word of God and filled them with the water of life. He turned them into fishers of men.

The fish swallowed Osiris' penis (sperm and Seed). This Seed is Horus. Osiris was the age of Taurus, Horus the age of Aries. The age of Horus (H-aries) was swallowed up the Pisces. Pisces will soon be swallowed by the age of Aquarius. In Hinduism, Hari means Creator!

The first decan of Pisces is Band (the band or bridle which connects the two fishes). The fishes are tied to the neck of Cetus, the Sea-Lion. There are two types of fish: those that sacrifice themselves so the body (of Christ) can grow and those who fight against the fisher of men. They represent the bride that is bonded to the Lord and the bride that is bridled to the Antichrist (Satan). The false church lives in sin with Satan. [Revelation 2:20-23] They learned what they know from the Tree of Carnal knowledge. The dragon shall be bound for a thousand years while the priests of God's kingdom teach the Word of God to the masses. [Revelation 20:1-6]

Two of the statutes on Easter Island are called Dagon (Fish) and Taurus (Bull). These are the ages of mankind. The statutes placed on a round island in the middle of the sea obviously represent stars that make up the 12 constellations moving through the cosmic cycles in the sea of space. [Anacalypsis page 38]

The second decan in the house of Pisces is Andromeda, The Chained Woman. Andro-meda means "Man-Ruler". Princess Andromeda was going to be sacrificed to the sea monster of Poseidon because her mother, Cassiopeia, had bragged she was as beautiful as the Sea-Nymphs. It is Perseus, in Greek mythology, who comes to save her. Perseus, son of Jove (Zeus), has the great sickle-Sword in his hand and the head of Medusa under his arm. He slays the sea monster with his sickle-sword just as the Grim Reaper slays the body of believers of the Beast. [Revelation 14:14-20] This is obviously the Lord with the Sword of God. Argos was the kingdom founded by Perseus' grandfather, therefore, he is heir to the throne. Per-seus means House of Seus (Zeus, Iesous, Jesus, Horus).

The third decan is Cepheus, the Crowned King of Ethiopia and father of Andromeda. He is pictured as a bearded man wearing a crown and seated upon a throne. He holds a scepter in one hand and possibly a winnowing fan in the other. The symbols of Pharaoh. His right foot is on the Pole-star, the most northern and central point. Cepheus means "The Branch or the King". This is King of kings and Lord of the Earth. He is willing to sacrifice himself and as the father, he was willing to sacrifice the one he loved in order to save his kingdom. The age of Pisces had just begun when Christ died, resurrected and ascended to the right hand of God. Andromeda (like Jason's bride Medea) represents the bride of Christ.

In Egypt, this constellation is known as Per-Ku-Hor, "Horus Comes to Rule." Compare to Per-T-Em-Hru, the Book of Coming Forth by Day. The brightest star is called Al Deramin (in Arabic) which means "Coming Quickly." The second brightest star at his midriff is Al Phirk, "The Redeemer". At his left knee is a star named Alrai, meaning "He Who Bruises or Breaks." The word Alrai is El-Ra which means Sun of God. El is God and Ra means Sun Rays. Atem-Ra-Horus means "The Sun of God Horus." Horus is Egyptian for Savior, just as Jesus is Latin for Savior.

Second Book
#6 Aries the Ram

Aries is the Ram of Revelation 13:11 that looks like the Lamb of God, but is not. It is the false church headed by the false prophet. The Beast has two parts; the head of state and head of church. They unite in unholy matrimony and become one Unholy Roman Catholic Empire or the United States of Europe. Then they make war on the saints. [Revelation 13:7] Aries is the Greek god of war. Aries, Cetus and Taurus unite in a Satanic trinity against Orion. These are the three evil spirits that rise from the river and lead the masses to the battle called Armageddon. [Revelation 16:12-16] In Latin, Aries means "Head." Satan is the eighth and final Head of the Roman Beast. [Revelation 17:7-11] Amen was the eighth in the Theban Pantheon.

The name in the Zodiac of Denderah is Tametouris Ammon, meaning the rule of Ammon. In Egypt, Ammon is Amen, the evil sun of God.

Amen-Ra-Set rules the land of Upper Egypt which includes the cities of Thebes (On), Luxor, and Karnak. [Jeremiah 46:25] On the heavenly plain, they are Taurus, Aries and Cetus. "As in heaven, so on earth." Ramoses II was Pharaoh during the Exodus who worshipped Ra-Amen. The Ram was his symbol. The Greeks named one of their cities after Thebes in Upper Egypt out of reverence and Zeus took on the name: Zeus-Ammon. Ares the Ram is Amen the Ram. [see Zodiac assigned to the second Hermes]

In Greek mythology, there is a woman named Nephele (the Cloud). She has two children Phrixus and Helle by King Athamas. They are threatened with death by their new stepmother, Queen Ino. Nephele warns them to flee to Asia Minor. A Ram with Golden Fleece is provided by Hermes (Horus) to carry them to safety. This is the bark of Horus with a ram's head at the prow. Along the way, Helle, the girl child, loses her hold and falls into the sea and drowns. This spot came to be known as Helle's Sea or Hellespont. Phrixus continues on to the city of Colchis, "The City of Refuge." A city of refuge is where a fugitive goes as a safe haven. Phrixus sacrifices the lamb to Jupiter or Zeus. Compare this to Abraham commanded to sacrifice his son, but given a Ram in his place. [Genesis 22:13] Jesus is the Lamb of God. Zeus is Greek for Hey-seus or Jesus. Phrixus and Jason have the same great-grand-father, Chryses (Christ). Chryses means Golden. The Golden Fleece was his skin.

Consider the alternative scenario. The Ram could represent Ra-Amen the ram god moving into the area. It is well documented that Colchis are descendants of Egypt. Herodotus says Rameses II sent his army to Colchis between 1301-1234 BC. and some settled there. This is the age of Ares the Ram. They brought with them the priests of Ra-Amen. The death of Helle represents the death of Hellenism. The Argonauts returning with the golden fleece represents the cult of Amen moving into Greece. The cult went from Thebes, Egypt to Colchis to Thebes, Greece. Mt. Ararat, resting place of Noah's ark, and Mt. Tomaros, resting site of Deucalion's Ark (the Greek Noah), and starting place of the Argo, are on the same 40 degree meridian. When connected to Thebes, Egypt they form a perfect 60 degree equilateral triangle. {See the Sirius Mystery by Robert Temple} This would explain why the Greeks have most of the story backasswards. They got their story from the wrong source: Upper Egypt. This would also explain the worship of Ares the Ram at Colchis. It would also explain how the Zodiac originated in Egypt, yet the "heroes" have Greek names. On their return, the Argonauts are detoured through Africa, where they visit the garden of Hera! Imagine that. The Greek paradise (Eden) is in Africa!

The first decan in the house of Aries is Cassiopeia, a woman enthroned in a chair lifted high. In the ancient Denderah zodiac in Egypt, her name is Set, which means "Set Up as a Queen". This is the Queen of Ken-set (Ethiopia) who conspired with Set to kill Osiris. This is the Harlot who sits as a queen. Set, in Egypt, is Satan. Amen-Ra-Set is the evil Sun-of-God-Set. Set is a corruption of Ast (Isis) queen of Egypt. Cassiopeia is living in sin with Satan. She is called Queen of Heaven, which is the title of Mary mother of god. The Lord says he shall destroy this Queen of Heaven who is the mistress of Baal. [Jeremiah 7:9,18, 30-34 Jeremiah 44:17-19] Her body of believers shall become food for the fowls. [Revelation 19:11-21] They shall burn in the Lake of fire just as they sacrificed their children to fire.

The second decan in Aries is Cetus, The Sea-Lion who devours the fish. This is spurious lion-king, Satan. [1 Peter 5:8] One of the brightest stars is called Mira in Hebrew, which means "The Rebel". Rebel or Re-Baal is the Devil causing insurrection against God. Mira is aMin-Ra, which is another spelling of Amen-Ra. Min in Egypt is one of the attributes of Amen. Min is the root of the Minotaur (Bull or Baal). The brightest star located in the nose, bears the Hebrew name Menkar, "The Bound" or Chained Enemy." The second brightest star in his tail, bears the Hebrew name Diphda, "The Overthrown." The Kabbalah says the sea-monster who swallowed Jonah was Cetos (Cetus). A similar story says it was Heracles who saved Heione from the sea-monster. He broke her bonds then built a wall to protect the city Joppa (also in the Middle East). When the monster poked its head over the wall, it opened its great jaws and Heracles leaped down its throat. He spent 3 days in the monster's belly, then emerged victorious, although the exhausting struggle had cost him every hair on his head. This symbolizes rebirth as in the Nazarite vow. Perseus, Herakles, and Horus are one and the same. They represent Atum being born from the sea of space as the star Sirius. This sea often has an Apophis serpent, a Cetus or a Leviathan within because this is the battle of the light (Sirius) vs. the darkness. Jesus was also 3 days in the belly of mother earth (sheol or hell). [Jonah 2:2]

The final decan in Aries is Perseus, "The Breaker". [Micah 2:13] He was one of the Argonauts. He is pictured with a Sword in one hand and the head of Medusa in the other hand. The constellation of Medusa is called Caput Medusa which means the head of Medusa. In Hebrew Medusa means "the Trodden Underfoot." The brightest star in her head is Al Ghoul meaning "The Evil Spirit or Ghost" the star is named that because it is said to 'wink'. Another star in her head is Rosh Satan, which in Hebrew mean's "Satan's Head". Therefore, Perseus has severed the head of the Beast in an effort to save the body. He represents the Lord with the Sword.

#5 Taurus the Bull

In the Egyptian mythology, Taurus is Upper Egypt, the land of Set (Satan). The bad-lands of Baal the Bull. It is directly above the constellation of Orion which represents Lower Egypt, the land of Osiris/Horus. The head and horns of Taurus is called Hyades (Hades), land of the dead.

The chief star in Taurus is Al Debaran, located in the bull's eye, and means "The Leader" in Arabic. It is Set who leads the body of believers (in Taurus, Aries and Cetus) to rebel against Osiris. The stars Sirius and Al Debaran were the two eyes of Horus, NOT the sun and the moon. Set took one eye during their battle for rule of Egypt. This represents the division the two lands of Egypt. Sirius represents the capital of Heliopolis, Lower Egypt and Al Debaran is Thebes, Upper Egypt. When the Lord returns, Orion's arrow will hit that "bull's eye" with his spiritual arrow and restore the two eyes or two lands to Horus, the rightful heir.

In Greek mythology, Taurus, the white bull, was a form assumed by Jupiter (Zeus-Amen) for the purpose of carrying away (rapturing) his loved one, the beautiful Europa (Europe) across the seas to the island of Crete. Taurt the northern stars represent the northern nations. Taurt is the consort of Taurus. Crete is where they worship the Mino-taur, ruler of the underworld. The Argonaut, Theseus, slayed the evil Minotaur. In the Christian era, they would say, "we pray in the name of Jesus Amen." Amen and Min are the Devil.

The first decan in Taurus is Orion. Orion means "The Brilliant," "The Swift," or "He Who Comes Forth as Light." As Horus is good the Sun of God. In Hebrew, the word is Chesil meaning "A Strong One" or "A Hero." He is the Great Hunter who slays the evil lion, Satan, who goes about seeking whom he may devour. [1 Peter 5:8] The star Rigel found in the foot of Orion means, "The foot that Crushes." This is the Seed of the woman who crushes the head of the seed of the serpent. Set is also an abbreviation for Serpent.

In Orion's belt are three stars called the Three Kings. These are the three pyramids at Giza built by the Kings or Pharaohs of Egypt in honor of the Great King Osiris/Horus. In Orion's shoulder is the star Bellatrix, which means "Quickly Coming" or "Swiftly Destroying". This is Horus (Jesus) who is coming to destroy Set (Satan). The Greeks define Horoscope as the hour the ascending star is visible on the horizon at sunrise. This describes the dawn rising of Sirius, the star of Horus. Horu-scope is the sighting of the Morning star. Both Orion-Osiris and Sirius-Horus are in the Argo or Ark, the constellation directly below their feet.

The second decan of Taurus is Eridanus, The River of Adon (Lord). The fiery river flows out of the foot of Orion, goes past Cetus, the Sea-Lion, and disappears into the outer darkness. Eri-dan-us is the River Jordan in Hebrew. You must cross the river to get to the Promise land. The Egyptians say you must cross this fiery river to get to the Island in the Lake of Fire where Osiris dwells. The incorrigible infidels will be incinerate in the fire, while the righteous will be purged and purified. For them this is the river of life that runs under the White Judgment Throne of Osiris. The Judge is either your savior or executioner.

To the Egyptians, the Milky Way beside Orion represents the Nile river beside the kingdom of Osiris on earth. The Nile is seen as the life source of food and water. That Milky Way is made of fiery stars burning like a river of light. Orion is Osiris the Judge. Under his throne runs the River of life that waters the Lotus. In the Bible, the river of life runs under the throne and waters the Tree of life. In Greek mythology, you must cross the river Styx to get to Elysian Fields. This is the same as crossing over the river Jordan to get to the Promise land. Likewise, the Egyptians believed Herfhaf (Horus) ferried the righteous souls to the Island of fire where Osiris reigned. They must cross the Nile to get to the City of the Sun (Anu/Heliopolis). They were refined and made ready for the Fields of Peace which is the garden of God. The water represents the pouring out of the holy Spirit (God's supernatural force) that has the power to give or take life. To the Upper Egyptians, the Milky Way was divine milk from the heavenly heifer, Hather.

The final decan is the constellation of Auriga, The Goatherd. He is pictured as a man seated on the Milky Way. In the zodiac of Dendera there is a scepter, the upper part shows the head of a goat. The lower part of the scepter is shaped like a cross. Auriga means Charioteer. Helio (Apollo) is the sun-god who rides on the fiery chariot. [2 Kings 23:11] The evil sungod and Warlord rides across the sky in his chariot or solar bark. The brightest star is Alioth meaning She-Goat. The next is Menkilinon meaning a band of goats. The goats are kids of Satan, the false shepherd. [Matthew 25:32-46]

#4 Gemini the Twins

The name of Gemini in the Zodiac of Denderah is Clusus. Patulcius (to open) and Clusus (to close) the Door with the Key. [Revelation 3:7,8] Clusus (Claustrum) Hori means "the place of Horus Who Comes". Herfhaf (Horus) is the Door to God's kingdom. Knowing the Word of God is the Key to unlock the mystery. Santa Claus is Satan coming to close the door in our face. Herfhaf is also the ferryman who takes the souls of the righteous to the Island of Fire (camp of the Saints) where Osiris reigns. [Revelation 20:9] The Egyptian Heraktes (Horus) is Herakles. Compare the twelve labours of Herakles to the twelve hours in the Book of the Dead.

The Twins in Latin were Castor and Pollux (Polydeuces). Pollux is the immortal who like Buddha, would not accept immortality until his mortal brother achieved it too. Their sister is the famous Helen of Troy. Gemini represents man's duality (yin/yang). Castor and Pollux are also the names of the two bright stars found in the heads of each of these two figures. Castor means "the Ruler" as Satan is ruler of this earth for the time being. Pollux means "The Strong One Coming to Labor or Suffer." In Greek mythology they were Apollo and Herakles (Christ).

The star in the left foot of Herakles is Al Henah, meaning "The Afflicted." Christ bruising his foot on the head of the serpent. The star at the waist of Apollo is Wasat (Arabic) meaning "Set". Set is Amen-Ra-Set the evil sun of God. The Hebrew name of Gemini is Thaumin, (Thomas) meaning "Double". Apollo is the dark side of the duet of the Yin / Yang. Both the ancient Mexicans and Egyptians portrayed the good son of God (Horus) and the bad son of God (Set) back to back. The light side and the dark side. Enlightenment vs. Ignorance. Osiris (Horus) and Set were born twins along with Isis and Nephthys. Just as Lucifer (Satan) is the counterfeit clone of the Lord of Light. [2 Corinthians 11:13-15] Apollo and Herakles are sons of two sets of twins fathered by Jupiter (Zeus). Apollo and Artemis are one set of twins. Heracles and Iphicles are the other. Iphicles is a mortal. The old Coptic name of this sign is Pi Mahi, meaning "The United," as in brotherhood. Zoroaster said that the Twin Morning stars are sibling rivals. This is Lucifer the daystar and Michael the Morning star. In the great battle, according to the Dead Sea Scrolls, Lucifer leads the sons of darkness and Michael leads the sons of light. These are the heavenly host of angels. [Revelation 12:7-9 Matthew 16:27 25:31]

Zeus descended one night to the city of Thebes where he assumed the appearance of Amphitryon and did lay with his wife, Alcmene. Shortly afterwards Amphitryon himself returned from a victorious expedition and did lay with his wife. From the two unions Alcmene conceived twins: Hercules and Iphicles.

Herakles is said to be the virgin born son of God (Zeus). He is the Savior of those suffering. The one who betrayed him (Judas), killed himself. He died among his disciples and his mother. His last words were, "It is done." He descended to hell and then resurrected in bodily form. Before his work was finished, he was taken to heaven. Therefore, it is necessary for him to return. This story was 200 years Before Christ.

The first decan of Gemini is Lepus, The Serpent. The brightest star in Lepus is Arnebo, meaning "The Enemy of Him That Comes." Other stars are: Nibal, "The Mad"; Sugia, "The Deceiver"; and Rakis, "The Bound". In Arabic it is "Bound, as with a Chain." Orion is standing on the Serpent showing he has overcome. Lepus and Lupus (Wolf) are unclean animals of Satan. Set-Typhon is the Leprous outcast.

The second decan is called Canis Major, meaning "the Greater Dog." But in the Denderah zodiac in a temple in Egypt, he is called Apes, which means "The Head." He is pictured as a hawk, the natural enemy of the serpent. The name of the star is Naz, meaning "Caused to Come Forth." and "Coming Swiftly Down." Naz as in Nazarene or Nazirite. Mes in Egyptian means "to Come forth" as in rebirth. Mes is the root of Messiah. The Hawk is the symbol of Horus who came forth from his mother Isis. The Hawk is the protector of the child, just as the Dove is the symbol of the power on high coming down to Christ the Nazarene.

The brightest star in the night sky is Sirius A, which in Hebrew means "Prince." Sirius represents Isis with child. Isis dies after child-birth and the star Sirius becomes the firstbegotten Sun of God, Horus. The Son of God said, "I am the bright Morning star." [Revelation 22:16] Since Isis and Nephthys are twins, Sirius B represents Nephthys and her son Anubis the Jackal-headed one. Since a jackal is in the dog family, the star was called the Dog star. Anubis is one of the many aspects or attributes of Horus.

The root of Sirius is Sar, meaning "To Make Oneself a Prince" and Seir, the Prince of the Earth. Sar is also another spelling for Osiris the King. When combining Naz and Seir we get Naz-Seir or Naz-seir-ene. "He shall be called a Nazarene." has nothing to do with a city named Nazareth. [Matthew 2:23] Paul also was called the leader of the Nazarenes. [Acts 24:5] Another spelling is Seer; Horus is the Seer with the all-seeing eye pictured on the pyramid on the back of the USA one dollar bill. Anu is the birthplace of the Sun of God. Anu in heaven is Sirius. Anu on earth is Heliopolis. "As above, also below."

The third decan is Canis Minor, The Lessor Dog. But in Denderah zodiac, it is pictured as a human figure with a hawk's head and is called Sebak. Sebek is the crocodile headed one. Khonsu and Montu are the hawk and ram headed impostors trying to appear like Horus. All three are his adversaries. The brightest star in the body is Procyon, meaning "the Redeemer." This is the fake Horus. Set's Dog star in the constellation of Ursa Minor is the spurious Dog star imitating Sirius. Satan is the Great Impostor pretending to be the Angel of Light.

First Book {continued} #3 Cancer the Crab (sCaRAB)

The next sign is Cancer, the Crab. The Egyptian name is Klaria, meaning "The Folds," "The Resting-Places." The original Egyptians must have been shepherds since the Pharaohs are always pictured holding a shepherd's staff. The Syriac name is Sartano, which means "The One Who Holds". According to the Romans Cancer means "The Traveler's Resting Place for the Encircled." This is the camp of Christ. The star Tegmine, in the tail of the crab means "The Sheltering". Another star in Arabic Al Himerein, "The Kids or Lambs". The Babylonian name of Cancer is Nangar (Carpenter). Just as Christ, Noah, Horus and the Argonauts were carpenters of a supernatural ship.

Originally this sign was the scarab. It is easy to see how it got corrupted from scarab to crab. Just drop the "s" and "a" and you have crab. The Europeans were not familiar with the scarab, so they substituted the crab. The sacred beetle appears in the month before the inundation of the Nile. It rolls the dung ball backwards with its hind legs, into its home in the earth. This represents the force behind the heavenly bodies, including the earth's rotation. The beetle lays one egg in the dung ball and then dies. At the rising of the Nile waters, the dung-ball is the ark that saves the new beetle, which rises from the earth as if reborn. This represents the new birth or resurrection from the grave. The cycle of life continues as the old dies and is recycled new. [A Book of the Beginnings by Gerald Massey page 6] [From Fetish to God in Ancient Egypt by Wallis Budge p. 246]

The Egyptian name for the sacred scarab is Khepera. The Hebrew word for the Mercy Seat is Caphoreth. The 'eth' suffix means 'the'. They are pronounced very similar. The Mercy-Seat is the cover of the Ark of the Covenant, with two cherubs spreading their wings like scarabs. Egyptians used scarabs instead of cherubs. The beetle on the right of the Ark represents the good Son of God, Kheper-Ra or Atum-Ra. The beetle on the left is the bad sun of God, Amen-Ra. In antiquity, Cancer was often depicted as the Horus Child.

Ursa Major is commonly called the Great Bear (i.e. Big Dipper). In Latin, it is Arcturus (Bear) or the Polar Bear of the Arctic Circle. The Egyptians called it Urth (north) and depicted it the same as the Ammit monster who devours the dead of Amenti. It is the behemoth of the Bible. Urth is a composite of a hippopotamus, lion, crocodile and bear. Urt standing at the Mooring Post is Ursa Major turing around the celestial Pole. 'Ring around the May Pole.' May is Maya or Mary or Ma the Great Matrix. She gave birth to the babe Bar (Baal-Typhon). The Egyptians depicted the North Pole star as the Dog-Star of Sut. When the sun reaches its northern peak at summer solstice, it is called the 'Dog Days of Summer'. Compare this to the Beast of Revelation 13: a composite of a leopard, bear, lion and dragon. The dragon being the head or leader. The seven heads are the seven stars of Urth. [Revelation 12:3,4] These northern stars represent the northern nations of the United States of Europe or neo-Roman Catholic empire. The two parts united are Roman state and the Catholic church. [Revelation 13:11] The Mother Church rules over Rome and Rome sits on seven hills. [Rev. 17] It is the same composite beast and kingdom of the north in the Book of Daniel 7:3-28.

In Meso-America, Tezcatlipoca (the sun god) was depicted as sitting on the celestial North pole and his dismembered foot is Ursa Major. In Babylon, the evil Enlil is represented as Arcturus (Polar Bear of the Arctic celestial circle).

To many people, the hibernating bear represents death in the winter and resurrection in the spring. The bear sleeping in the cave or den and rising again from the earth, parallels the sun-god's death and revival. The Polar bear, like the imperishable constellations of Ursa Major and Ursa Minor, do not fall into the deeps of the underworld. Compare the Kodiak bears (Ursus arctos/arctic bears) to the Zodiac bears.

Ursa Major is also known as "The great Sheepfold". The Arabic name is Al Naish which means "The Assembled Together." Sami also means united together under the Antichrist. The Sami are the evil minions of Set-amen who capture their victims with a net. Hyades also means congregation, (in the synagogue of Satan). One of the brightest stars in Ursa Major is Dubheh, which means "Herd of Animals". These are the goats following the false shepherd. [Matthew 25:31-46] In Arabic it means "Purchased." Other stars in Ursa Major are El Alcola, "The Sheepfold"; Cab'd al Asad, "Multitude of the Assembled"; El Kaphrah, "The Protected," or in Hebrew, "The Redeemed." Ursa Minor would be "The Little Flock". The second brightest star in Ursa Minor is Kochab which means "Waiting Him Who Comes". Another star is Alpherkadain which means the "Redeemed Assembly." This is the camp of the Smens (sons of Amen), faithful followers of Set. Urt is also called Taurt, the consort of Taurus the Bull. The Egyptians pictured an Ox pulling a plough. This is Orion-Osiris ploughing the sea of space with Taurus the bull and planting his Seed (Sirius). Compare this to Jason taming the bulls and ploughing the rocky ground of Aeetes (Hades). Then planting the teeth of the dragon (Draco) that grew into dog soldiers (sons of the devil). Jason tossed a stone in the midst of them and they beat themselves to death. It was the Rock (Christ) who defeated those warriors. [Daniel 2:34-45] In the Bible, the bad seeds are called Tares (sons of Taurus). [Matthew 13:37-43]

Ursa Minor is the dog Up-uat. It is Sothis or Sept (S-Apt), the seven stars or suns of Ursa Major (Great Matrix). Upuat or Apuat is the antithesis of Anup (Anti-upuat). Anup or Anubis is the dog star Sirius in Canis Major. The righteous sons of God come forth from Am-Tuat, not Am-Smen or Am-Tuart.

The third decan of Cancer is Argo. Argo means "The Ship" which was named after its builder Argus. The Argo's prow was made from the Ark of Deucalion (the Greek Noah) which rested on Mount Tomaros at Dodona. Tomaros is the Greek version of the primeval Mount at Anu (Heliopolis) created from Nun, the sea of space. It is the birthplace of Tom-Horus. Notice Deucalion ends in "lion" which was the animal on the prow of the Argo and the form of Khepra-Horus, the Sphinx at Giza. Pictured is pilgrims safe at last in harbor. The sails are rolled up, the ship is not in the midst of a journey. The ship has completed its voyage and is at rest in a safe harbor at home. This is describing Noah's ark, filled with those who are saved, coming to rest on Mount Ararat after a year at sea. The Ankh (symbol of life) became the Ankhor. Arbor is the tree (of life) taking root. It is also Atum-Ra-Horus in his bark (boat-ark) reaching his final destination, God's kingdom on earth. He is Sirius going full cycle and rising on the east horizon on the day of the Lord. [Matthew 24:27-31] From Argonauts we got the word Astronauts; men who sail to the Stars (Astro) in the sea of space (naut). Naut is Nut of Egypt.

In the Greek mythology, Jason and the Argonauts went on a quest in the ship Argo in a quest to recover the Golden Fleece from Aeetes, son of the sun (Ra). This Sun is none other than Set-amen or Lucifer. Aeetes is king in the land of the Caucasians next to the Caucasus mountains. During the voyage the Argonauts released a dove, like Noah, to tell them if the Way is safe. Jason battles the guardians; the never-sleeping serpent and the fire-breathing bulls (Taurus). Jason puts a yoke and plow on the bulls.

Jason, with the help of Medea, defeated the sleepless serpent, born of the blood of Typhon (Set), in the grove of Aries, god of war. Just like Herakles, son of Zeus, slayed the dragon in the garden of Hera and tamed the bull of Minos. And Horus, son of Isis, defeated the serpent (Apopis) and subdued Set the bull. The sleepless serpent coiled around the Tree of Knowledge of good and evil, in the garden of Eden, is Satan. The voyages of Sinbad the sailor is the counterpart to Jason's. The sorceress Maeve (Ma-Eve) is the sorceress Medea.

Jason recovered the Golden Fleece from the oak tree in the grove of Aries. Which represents the white wool of the Lamb of God hanged on an Asherah tree. It is the Lord shedding his skin at death and then covering himself with the golden glorified body at his resurrection. [Luke 24:39] Jason is Jesus who only becomes King after he returns from his voyage through the sea of space. Which is the right hand of God in heaven. Medea, daughter of Aeetes, sees Jason as, "like the bright star Sirius rising out of Ocean," Legend says that Medea became the mother of the Medes. Could it be that Perseus was founder of the Persians? When Perseus cut off the head of Medusa, did it represent Persia conquering and uniting the two kingdoms into Mede-Persia?

Herakles completed one of his 12 Labours while he was an argonaut. He killed the vulture that was tormenting Prometheus and freed him from his bondage. Zeus concurred. Meanwhile, the argonauts had Labors of their own. Of the original 17 Argonauts, 12 returned home. Two died, one was held prisoner, and Heracles left on his own quest. Twelve is the universal number meaning Family: twelve tribes of Israel, twelve disciple brothers, etc... The earth labors to give new birth to the suns of God. [Romans 8:19-30] The bride of Jason is the same as the bride of Christ or body of believers. [Revelation 19:7-9] Herakles and Jason are aspects of Jesus who has many offices and many titles. The stories of Theseus, Horus, Dionysus, and Perseus are similar because they different versions of the same story. Jason, like Jesus, never cut his hair.

Perseus and his mother, Danae, being placed in a chest and thrown into the sea by her father is the antitype of Osiris killed by Set. [1 Peter 3:20,21] Noah, Moses, Sargon, Romulus & Remus all share the same story of being saved from being swallowed by the sea. Compare Danae and Perseus in the ark to Isis and Horus sharing the same star Sirius in the sea of space. Perseus' voyage beyond the Ocean that surrounds the earth is the sea of space called heaven. Perseus, Theseus, Jason and Horus were Princes and heirs of a Kingdom.

On their return, the Argonauts got detoured to Africa. Where they had to carry or pull the Argo across the desert. Compare this to the placing the Bark of Atum on the divine Sledge and pulling it by ropes across the dry land as described in the Egyptian Book of the Dead. This demonstrates that the Bark starts on earth and ends on earth. It also echoes Christ's words, "He who does not take his cross (yoke) and follow after Me is not worthy of Me." [Matthew 10:38 11:29] The Argonauts found paradise (Hera's garden) in Africa, but could not enter because they were mortals? This represent Paradise Restored to the righteous (and resurrected) followers of Horus. The garden of Heru (Horus) is on earth. God's kingdom come, His will be done on earth.

Jason's father was King Aeson. Jason's uncle was the evil Warlord Pelias who threaten to kill his peaceful brother and took the throne as king. Compare this to the Warlord Set who killed his brother Osiris and took the throne of Egypt. The rightful heir is Horus (Jason) who shall one day return to take his throne. Horus went on his 12 Hours in the Underworld, which was actually 12 months. See the Egyptian Book of the Dead. This is the dawn rising of the Morning Star, Sirius, at the autumn equinox. Also compare this to King Herod attempting to kill the Christ child who is rightful heir to God's kingdom on earth. Pelias is a combination of King Herod and Pontius Pilate who crucified Christ. The evil king Pelias could not kill Jason on the Feast day because he feared the crowds. Compare this to Jesus during the Feast of Unleavened Bread. [Matthew 26:2-5] The Morning star shall return to sit on the throne of David, his forefather.[1 Chronicles 17:11-15 Revelation 22:16 Luke 1:32,33 Psalm 89:35-37] The story of Jason, Horus and Jesus are the same. The Gospel has gone out to all nations, translated in their own tongue. Sometimes it is mistranslated or misinterpreted and the story becomes corrupted by the mistakes of mortals.

An interesting thing about the ship is the prow displayed the head of a lion. Usually the head faces forward, but on Argo the head is facing inward, watching over the sailors. The Lion-King watches over his body of believers. The Egyptians called him Herfhaf (Horus) who will allow no sinner on his Bark (Boat-Ark). Compare to Noah's ark. He took the righteous souls from Dead-land (Amenta) to the Island of Truth. The Greeks called him Charon, who ferried souls across the river Styx to the Promise Land of Elysian Fields. Both Egyptians and Greeks believed that the Island of the Blessed is the Field of Firstfruits where the Saints resurrected from the dead. This Island in the sea of space is God's garden paradise on Earth. Herfhaf (Horus) is also the Doorkeeper of God's kingdom. In the Bible, the ship Paul sailed in had Gemini (Castor & Pollux) on its prow. They sailed safely into Rome. [Acts 28:11] C-astor means star.

Juggarnaut is the moving of the mill-stone, the turning of the wheel of time, the cycle of the cosmos, the continuum of the celestial procession that no mortal can stop. In Hinduism, the Jaggornaut is the same as the Argonaut. Within Jaggor is the word Argo. Jaggor = Jason as G = C = Ch = Sh = S. Jaggornaut is Jach-chor-nut or Jah-Horus-Nut (Lord Horus son of Nut). The Jagan-nath temple is called Sri Krishna. Sri is Osiris. [Anacalypsis by Godfrey Higgins volume 1 page 765] Plutarch says the commander of the Argo was Osiris or Ysiris. This is the bark of Osiris in the sea of space. It was carried by 72 men. These are the 72 dodecans.

#2 Leo the Lion

The constellation Leo the Lion, means "He That Rends, That Tears Asunder." The king of the beasts is coming to destroy the Beast. The true Lion is coming to dethrone the false lion-king. [Revelation 13:2] The King of kings is coming to kill all heads of state and their armies. [Revelation 19:11-21 Zechariah 14:1-5] The stars of Leo are Regal, which means "Treading Underfoot"; Denebola, "The Judge"; "The Lord Who Comes Quickly" ; Zosma, "The Shining Forth" the "Epiphany"; Minchir al Asad "The Punishing" or "Tearing of Him Who Lays Waste"; Al Defera "The Putting Down of the Enemy."

Now we have gone full cycle, back to the beginning. Just as it is God's desire to re-create man and place him in the garden of God on the Sabbath.

The Lion of Judah has reversed the sin and death of Adam by not sinning and therefore not being worthy of death. The slain Lamb is worthy to open the book of life for his great deed. The Son of God is heir to his own Will as Lord of the Earth called God's kingdom.

The zodiac is divided into 12 houses and each house has 3 decans or rooms which equals 36. 360 degrees is the cycle of life to death. The lunar calendar is 12 months with 28-30 days each, which equals 360 +/ -. While the Sothic year is 365 days. This represents Atum-Ra, the good Sun of God, going beyond the cycle of life as depicted in the Book of the Dead; which is really the Book of the Living. Enoch walked with God for 365 years and was translated into a son of God. Sirius is the Morning star that is reborn once a year in the autumn.

The first decan of Leo is the sign of Hydra the great serpent. The Lion is pouncing on the head of the serpent. The Egyptians portray this as a large cat cutting off the head of the sea serpent that is attempting to swallow the rising sun, Atum-Ra-Horus. This represents the Lord overcoming evil and therein, defeating death. It is the Seed of woman standing on the seed of the serpent. It is Hercules standing on the head of The Dragon, Draco. Hercules destroyed the multi-headed Hydra by cutting off the heads and searing the wounds with a red hot iron to prevent them from multiplying again. This is the iron rod or scepter which the Lord uses to cast the Hydra into the Lake of fire. [Revelation 12:5]

The Hydra is outside the great circle of the ecliptic as he is cast into the darkness of the bottomless pit or abyss for a thousand years. He is chained or put on a leach to keep him from deceiving the masses during the Millennium. The head of the Beast shall be severed from the body of believers. This is the age of teaching the Word of God without any Satanic influences. Immediately following the Millennium, the Devil will be released to unite the lawless ones ie. Sami in an insurrection against the

Lord and his saints. Then the Lake of fire will rain down on those rebels and they will be no more. [Zechariah 14:12] The name Hydra means "He Is the Abhorred." The brightest star in this constellation is located in the neck and is called Al Phard, meaning "The Separated," "The Put Out of the Way." Another star in the constellation is Minchir al Sugia, meaning "Tearing to Shreds of the Deceiver." The star located in the eye of the Raven is Al Chiba, which is Hebrew for "The Curse Inflicted." The curse of sin is death.

The second decan in this sign is Crater, The Cup. This is the Cup of Wrath poured out on the lawless ones. [Revelation 14:10 16:1-21 Psalms 11:6 75:8] Satan tempts people to sin, then accuses them of sin to God, and God allows him to punish the sinners. These are similar to the plagues poured out on Egypt before the Exodus. Even the righteous, like Job, are plagued to test their faith.

The third decan in Leo is Corvus, The Raven. Chorvus + Horus The Raven is pictured attacking the body of the Hydra. For the Egyptians, the serpent is the natural enemy of the Hawk, which represents Horus defeating Set (Satan). The Raven, like the eagle and vulture, are unclean carnivorous predators. They are the fowls that shall feed on the flesh of the Beast (the heads of state and their military men). [Revelation 19:11-21] The battle of Armageddon is the sixth cup of wrath being poured out. [Revelation 16:12-16]

Set (Satan) has ruled the earth for 6,000 years through the dark ages of Taurus, Aries, and Pisces. The Lord worked with Egypt, Israel, and then the Gentiles (Greeks/Romans) each for 2,000 years. The seventh thousandth year is the dawning of Aquarius when the Sun of God will end the reign of evil. The Lion-King will retake his throne as King of God's kingdom.

The seventh cup signals the coming of the Lord with the Sword to slay all the warriors. [Revelation 16:17-21 Zechariah 14:1-5] One third shall die by the Sword, one third by plagues, and one third shall be refined in the fire. [Zechariah 13:7-9 Ezekiel 5:12] These are the ones who will replace the one third of the fallen sons of God. [Revelation 12:4] Then the LORD shall be King over all the earth. [Zechariah 14:9]

Noah released a Raven and it never returned, as it is a scavenger feeding on the dead bodies. It was the homing pigeon or dove that returned home. In its mouth was the olive branch, the symbol of peace & life. Just as the power on high will lead the peacemakers home to the garden of God and fill us with that Spirit of life. Those that hunger and thirst for righteousness shall be filled. The peacemakers shall be called the sons of God. The meek shall inherit the earth. [Matthew 5:3-9] The warriors who create unrest shall be executed while the peacemakers shall enter God's Rest (Sabbath). [Hebrews 4:1-12]

Sacrificed for Sin

We are all familiar with the Lamb of God sacrificed to take away the sins of the world, but in Mithra's day the Bull's blood was shed to take away the sins of the world. When the age of Taurus was ending, the bull was perceived as the embodiment of evil. The bull represented the devil Baal. Mithra slayed the bull, just as Michael slays the dragon. [Revelation 12] During the age of Aries the Ram, the Ram became the embodiment of Ra-Amen. The Ram or Lamb became the animal to be sacrificed. The Lamb was the scape-goat, Azazel. Sheep and goats are of the same species. They are the same kind or kin to one another. One goat was sacrificed as a sin offering, while the other did bear the sins into the Wilderness of Sin. [Leviticus 16:6,8-22] This dualism may be a remnant of the age of the Gemini twins. Azazel is the devil who is often depicted as a goat. Azrael is the angel of death. The death of the devil made Atonement for the world. But, before the goat was sacrificed, a bull was sacrificed as a sin offering.

When the age of Aries started to change to that of Pisces, Christ became the Lamb sacrificed. [Isaiah 53:6,11,12] "Then Aaron shall cast lots for the two goats; one lot for the LORD and the other lot for the scapegoat. And Aaron shall bring the goat on which the LORD's lot fell, and offer it as a sin offering. Its blood shall be sprinkled on the Mercy Seat. But the goat on which the lot fell to be the scapegoat shall be presented alive before the LORD, to make atonement upon it, and to let it go as the scapegoat into the wilderness." [Leviticus 16:8-10,15] Christ was perceived as the serpent in the Wilderness of Sin crucified on the pole. [John 3:14 Numbers 21:9] Christ was perceived as the embodiment of evil (as he took on the sins of the world), therefore the Jewish priests sacrificed him. But only after he was tempted in the Wilderness of Sin for 40 days. The LORD's lot was to be offered up as sin and hung on a pole. "Cursed is everyone who hangs on a tree". [Hebrews 3:13 Deuteronomy 21:22,23]

When the ages changed from Leo the Lion to Cancer, Herakles (Horus) slayed the adversary the devil who walks about like a roaring lion, seeking whom he may devour. [1 Peter 5:8] Herakles slayed the lion and then put on its skin. In other words, he became the Lion who himself was later sacrificed. Likewise, Samson slayed the lion. This represents the sun (Shamesh or Shamson) rising in the sign of Cancer during the spring equinox. Cancer is the two scarab (cherub) facing each other on the Mercy Seat on the Ark of the Covenant. One cherub is Azazel and the other is Asarel (Osiris-el). Judge Osiris is either your Savior or Executioner. When the age changed to Taurus, the Bull broke the twin eggs of Gemini with his two horns. These are the 'horns' on the altar. [Leviticus 16:18]

The point is Christ did not die for your sins, He died because of your sins! When he took on the sins of the world, he became a sinner and was perceived as the Devil. The spotless lamb now has blemishes on his record. Therefore, the more you sin, the more evil he appears. He is made up of his body of believers; some good but mostly bad. By the Day of Judgment, you are going to think it is Hades sitting on the Judgment Throne. The throne being the Mercy Seat of the Ark. When the new age dawns, you may be the animal sacrificed!

"He then would have had to suffer often since the foundation of the world; but now, once at the end of the <Zodiac> ages, He has appeared to put away sin by the sacrifice of Himself. And as it is appointed for men to die once, but after this the judgment, so Christ was offered once to bear the sins of many. To those who eagerly wait for Him He will appear a second time, apart from sin, for salvation." [Hebrews 9:26-28] When he returns, he will be the spotless (sinless) Savior and righteous Judge. [John 5:22-30] He will separate the righteous lambs of God from the lawless rams of Amen. [Matthew 25:31-46]

Ra-Amen the Ram of Aries was sacrificed so the age of Pisces could be born. The school of the fishermen shall teach the Word of God that had been corrupted by the priests of Amen during the age of Aries. God's Word is God's law and the foundation of God's kingdom. The Ten Commandments are our new Covenant written in stone. [Deuteronomy 4:13 Hebrews 9:4]

Osiris did not die for your sins. He died because his brother Set-amen (Satan) was evil. He resurrected as Horus to avenge his murder. 'Vengeance is mine,' says the Lord. Abel did not die for your sins, he died because his brother Cain was of the wicked one. Abel was righteous, Cain was lawless. [1 John 3:12] 'He who sins is of the devil, for the devil has sinned from the beginning. For this purpose the Son of God was manifested (re-incarnated), that He might destroy the works of the devil. Whoever has been born (begotten) of God does not sin.' [1 John 3:8-10] He came to stop people from doing evil. He preached, repent from sin, not repeat your sin.

Modern Mythology

The myth of modern man is the Big Bang theory of creation. In the beginning, there was a great explosion from the fiery furnace. This fireball filled the universe. In fact, was the universe. All that was is inside that explosion of light. Astronomers can see that light from the edge of our universe 20 billion light years. It is just now reaching us.

The Big Bang theory is like a balloon expanding. The light is outside the balloon. Inside the balloon is the darkness of outer space. Once that balloon reaches its expandable limit, time will stop. Then it will reverse and start collapsing. It will return to the state from which it started.

This theory parallels the Bible theology, which says God is a consuming fire. In the beginning, God the Father was alone in the first heaven. He conceived and created the darkness of outer space from nothing. This is the second heaven. God created His Sun or Morning star to rule over the earth. Our atmosphere is the third heaven. God, the Creator, is not part of the creation. He is the light beyond the darkness of space. Which was void of life until God created all living things with His supernatural powers called His holy Spirit.

When God comes to earth in the Last Day, He will consume all the darkness of outer space and all the stars will flee from His fiery face. The darkness will be consumed by the light. The stars or suns of God will be refined in the fire or consumed. The first heaven will replace the second and third heavens and become our new heaven here on the renewed earth. The earth will have gone full cycle back to the garden of God. God's saints will go from life to death to life. Reborn children of God replanted in the restored garden on the Sabbath day (Seventh divine day).

Many people think they will, one day, exodus this terminally ill terra-firma. This is escapism, denial and avoidance. Compare this to the Rapture theory: Christians hoping to escape this sick world they helped to create. Needless to say, no terrestrial is going to dwell in the habitation reserved for the extra-terrestrials (angels). [Jude 6] Christians are Not going to escape the Times of Tribulation. No Egyptian is going to fly in a star ship for millions of light years. In fact, God is coming to earth to dwell with His children.

The problem with the Big Bang theory is: where did the law of gravity come from that pulled together the gasses to form the stars and planets? Did a law create itself from nowhere? It is obvious that God created all the laws; both supernatural and natural (including the laws of physics).

Scientists say people only use 10 % of their brains. This explains why people are so ignorant. Christians know little about the Bible. Americans know little about their history and almost nothing that is going on in the rest of the world. Personally, I use 100% of my brain. Seeking knowledge is the meaning of life; both here and now and in the hereafter. Usually, using common sense is all that is needed to figure things out–whether they be worldly or spiritual.

Use your brain—think for yourself—do NOT let someone do your thinking for you!

The Roots of the Bible; Book of Death and Resurrection

Consider for a moment that the Bible is rooted in Egyptian mythology. The Bible says Adam is the son of God. [Luke 3:38] Compare this to Atum being the Son of God. Adam and Eve had two sons Cain and Abel. Atum and earth (Geb) had two sons Set and Osiris. Let us imagine that the names are wrong. In Egypt, the sons are Osiris and Seth who married their sisters Isis and Nephthys. These were the first earthlings; children of Geb (Earth). One day Seth kills Osiris his brother. The Bible says Cain killed Abel. Then God decides to make a new man in the place of the dead Osiris (Abel). The Egyptians say Osiris was reborn as Horus who the Bible calls Seth. Could it be that the Bible got the names turned around? Cain should be called Seth and Abel should be Osiris. This second son of Adam should be Horus not Seth. Horus is the Seed of Atum (Adam). As Horus (Jesus) is the second Adam or Atum. [1 Corinthians 15:45] In the Egyptian language, the letters "T" and "D" are interchangeable, as are all vowels. Atum is the father of Mankind in Egypt, just as Adam is in the Bible. [A Book of the Beginnings by Gerald Massey volume 2 pages 288 & 289]

Now, if Mary gave birth to the Second Adam then it makes sense that Eve gave birth to the First Adam. Especially since Mary is Eve in Latin. Yet, the Bible says contrary. This may explain the legend of Lilith. The Jewish Talmud says Lilith was a nocturnal specter who assumed the form of a beautiful woman (nymph) in order to beguile and destroy the first man. She was an apparition (like Mary) who existed before Eve. She represents the dark womb from which Adam was born. She is dark sea of space, void of life, until the mouth of God implanted the spiritual Seed in her. Eve + lil is evil, as Enlil is the evil one of Babylon. She is also the Water Lily or the Lotus that represents death and rebirth. Compare to Hera, antagonist and adversary of her son, Herakles. Hera also had a Garden with forbidden fruit. The Jews obviously added Lilith as an after thought, realizing something was missing.

This may sound terribly confusing, but it is not. Just the names have been changed to protect the innocent....and the not so innocent. Yet the story stays the same.

The Bible says Eve is Mother of all living. In Egypt, she would be Nun who gave birth to everything living. Therefore, Adam (Atum) came from inside her, she did not come from his side. She is his flip-side; Yin/Yang. According to the original Greek texts: When Eve gave birth, she said "I have gotten a man, even the Lord." This is obviously Nun, the Great Mother, giving birth to Atum or Adam, the Son of God. Artemis is Eve's dark side that gave birth to Cain and his kind (Am-Smen). Anu is the light side that gave birth to Abel and his kind (Am-Tuat). The Bible never says Eve died. That is because she never really lived. She is the deep dark sea of space, the abyss void of life, the virgin of immaculate conception. Now the two earthlings; Cain and Abel would be Set and Osiris. Osiris, being the incarnation of Atum. Set is the incarnation of Satan. Horus the Child is Osiris reborn as Son of God (Jesus).

According to the Kabbalah, Lilith had a son Hormiz (Horus) or Ormuzd (Aura Mazdah). Hormiz is the Greek Hermes. Her second son and mate was Samael (Set-amen). [Kabbalah by Gershom Scholem page 356] In Egypt, it was Amen who mated with his mother, Mot Neter. Lilith is translated night owl in Isaiah 34:13-15. She is the Great Harlot. In verse 7, Re-amen is translated unicorn or bull. The dragon is the Beast of Revelation 13 & 17. [Companion Bible] Set-amen is the head of the Beast with horns and she is the body members. Together they represent the universal church and state.

In the Egyptian mythology, Atum was the first begotten Son of God who dwelled in heaven. [Genesis 1:3 John 1:1-18] Atum was the Morning Star Sirius. [Revelation 22:16] Nut and Geb created mankind. Nut is the stars or sons of God. Atum and the other elohim or gods created mankind (Osiris, Isis, Set and Nephthys) from the earth (Geb). Set killed Osiris and then was exiled to Upper Egypt and Nubia (Ken-set). Cain went to Nod. Nod may be No (Thebes) or Nubia. Set-Cain killed his righteous brother because he is the son of Satan the evil one. [1 John 3:12] Osiris resurrected as Horus and took his place as king over Lower Egypt. Just as Seth replaced Abel in the Bible. "Then began men to call themselves Lord (Jehovah)." The line of Pharaohs called themselves sons of Osiris and vicars of Horus. It was Atum (Adam) who named all things, including the billions of stars.-

[Genesis 2:19 and the Egyptian texts]

Originally, Atum was clothed in light, but after his 'fall', he was clothed in skin. [Genesis 3:20] This represents Atum descending to earth and incarnating in the flesh as Adam (Osiris). He came because of man's sin to personally show them the Way to life, as opposed to death for sin. The Sun of God became the 'light of men' who enlightened them on God's laws. [John 1:4-11]

Egypt was the garden in the region of Eden where it never rained, yet was abundantly fertile. Egypt was divided between Horus, Lord of Lower Egypt in the north, and Set, ruler of Upper Egypt in the south. Cain was banish to the land of Nod (the sleep walkers or walking dead). Now the original sin is the taking of the life of the Son of God! It is not the taking of the forbidden fruit, but the death of the firstfruit. It is the taking (leading astray) the firstfruits of the Lord. Set lead his followers to the dark continent of deception.

Abel offered to sacrifice the spotless Lamb of God (himself). Cain (Set) offered to sacrifice the god of grain (Osiris/Abel). Osiris/Abel becomes the first human sacrifice or martyr. He is the firstfruit of the earth and firstborn of the resurrection. [1 Corinthians 15:20-28 Colossians 1:15-18] Ab-el means Father + god as Osiris is father of Horus, the son of god. Set is the bull who tramples the grain (Seed of Atum and Eve). Then Set tries to take the place of Horus as heir apparent. Set claims to be the firstborn of Eve. Just as Cain is firstborn in the Bible. In Upper Egypt, they pretended that Set was the Angel of Light. [2 Cor.11:13-15] Set tried to take the throne of all of Egypt. Yet, Thoth (Truth) declared Horus (Seth) the rightful heir, as the Seed of Osiris. And the Seed of Abraham. "Before Abraham, I am". Ab-ra-ham = Ab (Father) ra (sun of god) and Ham is the father of the Africans including Egypt. Khamat or Kemet is Land of Ham. Horus was the antechrist or BC (Before Christ).

The Africans have no concept of Original Sin, as it was the Great Mother (Eve) and her pale faced son (Cain) who committed the original sin. Their descendants inherited the symptoms of sin; pale skin, sickness and death. Original sin only applies to the red race; the white race that blushes from embarrassment.

Adam (Atum) does NOT mean Red or Man, as the scholars say. Atum, Osiris, and Horus are depicted as green or colored. Aman means 'a man'. Amen is Men. Hu means White and Human means white men. Set-Amen is the white faced, red haired sun-god. Aman has the ruddy complexion. Cain is the son of the evil one and the father of the Caucasians. [1 John 3:12] Compare the Mark of Cain to that of Set. Set ripped his way out of the womb of Nut. He was an awful creature with a white face and red hair. Cain's mark and Set's are one and the same. Albinism, or as the Bible calls it Leprosy, is the hereditary mutation of Cain's descendants, the Kenites. Men also means Cattle and Cain's descendants were cattlemen. [Genesis 4:20] Cowboys are sons of Taurt and Taurus the Bull. [A Book of Beginnings vol.2 by Gerald Massey p.289 & 374 & 415]

There is a story where Set tries to rape Isis. Isis has taken the form of Hathor. Hathor means House of Horus. When Set tries to rape her his seed goes to his head and drives him crazy. Compare this to Satan trying to seduce Eve. [2 Corinthians 11:3] He was cursed to be bruised in the head by the Seed of Eve (i.e. Isis). [Genesis 3:15] The serpent that walks on two human legs, in the Egyptian myth, is called Sata! Later it is Horus who emasculates Set. Set has commit the crime, not Eve (Isis). In Egypt, Set is lord of darkness as the serpent Apep. Set is the evil sun of God called Amen-Ra.

Now Atum incarnated as Osiris (Abel) then died and was reborn as Horus (Seth in the Bible). It was Horus who had the knowledge of the kingdom of God. Of which, he passed down to his heirs when he ascended back to heaven. One of those heirs was Enoch who had words of prophecy. [Jude 14,15] Could he be Imhotep, the architect of the Pyramids? The Pyramids at Giza were covered with polished limestones that were cemented into place. They were completely sealed. Could the Pyramids predate the flood? Could there be secrets locked inside until the end times?

Enoch is seventh from Adam. Seven is the number of day in a week. Enoch lived 365 days which is the number of days in a year. Enoch walked with God for 300 years. The Turin Papyrus says Horus ruled Egypt for 300 years. Noah and the seven in his family were later known as the seven sages or followers of Horus (Shem-su Heru). Coincidentally, one of the sons of Noah is Shem. Who line leads to Abraham. Which is the line that leads to Christ. Who said, "Before Abraham was, I AM." [John 8:58] The Seed of Atum and the Seed of Abraham is Jesus (Horus). [Gen.3:15] Compare Shem-su-Heru to Shem's sons, Hebrew. There is an Arabian legend that Seth (Horus) and Enoch built the Pyramids before the flood to preserve the sacred knowledge of the universe called the Ancient Mysteries. If Seth refers to Horus and Enoch to Imhotep or Thoth, this makes sense.

Noah was tenth from Adam. In the Mesopotamia story there were 10 kings who ruled for 432,000 years before the flood. All agree that there was a royal line that ruled for a long period of time before the flood. At the same time their was an evil counterpart in the line of Cain (Set). Both have 10 and some of the names are even the same. In fact, the father of Noah and Naamah are both Lamech. Noah had three sons just like Lamech. One of Noah's grandsons is Tubal. Now if they lived in different places, how could this be?

Adam	Cain
Seth	Enoch
Enosh	Irad
Cainan	Mehujael
Mahalaleel	Methushael
Jared	Lamech
Enoch	Jabal (son of Lamech)
Methuselah	Jubal (son of Lamech)
Lamech	Tubal-Cain (son of Lamech)
Noah	Noamah (daughter of Lamech)

I propose the reason for this is that Satan is the great impostor who mimics all that the Lord does in order to cause confusion. Nimrod was son of Cush (Nubia) from the land of Nod. Canaan the uncle of Nimrod is really Cain of the land of Nod. Both were cursed. Cain's curse was a mark on his skin (leprosy or albinism). Compare this to Set who it is said violently tore his way out of his mother's womb. Set has a white face and red hair. This is odd since the Egyptians and Nubians are dark skinned. Set is the evil sun of God who is red at sunrise and sunset. Canaan is the father of the Canaanites who are the Caucasians. These Canaanites were always the enemies of the Egyptians.

In Egypt, 5 intercalary days were added to the antediluvian (before the deluge) year, which was 360 days. They were named after the 5 gods and made up the 13th month called emboli-mary (embryo of Mary) or Son of Ma. Compare them to the beings of the Bible who lived before the flood:

1) Adam	Osiris (Atum incarnate)
2) Eve	Isis
3) Cain	Set
4) Abel	Nephthys
5) Seth	Horus (Atum reborn)

Nimrod built the Tower of Babel which became Babylon. From there the people and the nations were divided. Nimrod and his uncle Canaan built Nineveh the capital of Assyria. Cain's descendants gave their knowledge of iron weapons to all their allies. Then, I believe Nimrod, the Nubian, built Thebes the capital of Upper Egypt. He many be the one called Menes (or Narmer) the Scorpion king. Narmer from Naamah descendant of Cain. Ta-mera (upper-land) is the Egyptian name for Upper Egypt. Nimrod was a mighty hunter against the Lord Osiris. Osiris is represented by the stars as Orion the hunter. Now Orion is the bull-fighter in the constellation of Taurus. Nimrod united all the people just as Menes did. He is that Bull who trampled Lower Egypt in 3100 BC. Who built the district of Memphis (named after Menes). Where they worshipped the Apis and Menvis bulls. Maybe Menes is Set (Cain) himself. Who was later worshipped as Amen, the bull of heaven. Nimrod is Nicolas in Latin. Neka is the Devil in Egyptian.

The Lower Egyptian were divided from the Upper Egyptians. The Upper Egyptians took the pantheon of Lower Egypt and corrupted it. They replaced Atum with Amen, Nut with Mut and Horus with Khonsu. They have made Amen the head of the 9 gods. They combined Osiris with Amen to produce Osiris-Amen. Isis has become Hathor, the mistress of Amen. Amen, Mut and Khonsu became the Setanic trinity. Amen of Thebes is the diabolical adversary of Atum of Heliopolis. Just as Seth (or Suth) in the South is the opposition of Horus in the north. Amen and Set are one and the same. While Atum and Horus are one and the same.

Cain was cursed from the earth, for murdering the first martyr, Abel-Osiris. This means he can't return to dust, therefore, he can't die. [Genesis

4:11] In Egypt, Set was ruled against by Geb (Earth) and the rule of all of Egypt (God's kingdom) was given to Horus. Who is Seth in the Bible. In the last days, Cain shall unite all his warriors to battle at Armageddon. They will used their iron instruments of war. Horus will slay all the warriors and shall bound Cain in a Great Chain. Cain being the bloodthirsty beast called Set by the Egyptians and Typhon by the Greeks. Cain is Satan incarnated in the flesh.

Abraham was born Abram, but later was spiritually reborn Abraham. Compare Abraham (Ab-Ra-Ham) and Sarah (Sar-ah) to Lord Osiris (Sariah) and Isis. Ab means Father, Ra is Atum-Ra and Ham is the father of the African nations. They have a son Isaac (Isa = Iusa = Iesus = Jesus = Savior). Previously Abraham and Hagar (Hathor?) had a son Ishmael. Their son is called a wild man (Anubis?). Hagar is Egyptian. [Genesis 16:1,12] Hathor is one form of Nephthys (mother nature's wild side and mother of Anubis). Could Ishmael be the wild man like John the Baptist, the forerunner of Jesus? John was the cousin of Jesus just like Horus and Anubis. During Abraham's day, the land of Canaan was ruled over by Egypt. When Abraham died, his wife and sons buried him in a cave in the land of Heth (a province of Egypt). Just as Isis, Nephthys and Anubis embalmed Osiris and entombed him in the land of Seth (South or Upper Egypt). Ish-ma-el means Man of God's law or Covenant. Maat is Egyptian for law. Ishmael was the first of the Covenant.

The Jews say Abraham was too good to be true. (Especially, when compared to Jacob and his descendants.) They believe him, and all the patriarchs before him, to be fiction. On the contrary, he is Mythology written as history. "This is the history of the heavens and earth..." [Genesis 2:4] When God form eth-ha' Adham (the first Adam). Compare to ether (the air). Atum is the root of Atm-o-sphere.

Now Jacob and Easu are twins. Jacob swindles Easu out of his birthright and his blessing. Because Easu sells his birthright, his descendants are cursed forever by God. Does this sound like a merciful God? What did Easu sell anyway? If the things of this world are materialistic and we are told to hate the things of this world, why would he be cursed for giving up a piece of the Promised land that he had never even seen? If Easu understood the birthright to be Palestine, the land from which the Lord later banished All the Jews, what is the big deal? They all lost their birthrights when the Lord divorced or separated from them. Add to this that Easu means Iesus or Jesus. Who said his kingdom is not of this world. The truth is: Jacob should have been cursed for swindling Easu. Yet, years later, when Easu ran into his evil brother, he forgave him. Which one is more Christ like? Jaca in Singhalese means the devil. Raca in Hebrew means the devil. In Egyptian, Kaka means the evil one. Naka is the serpent that deluges. All are roots of Jacob, the swindler.

The Jews say that when the Babylonians destroyed JeruSalem, they burned All the copies of the Bible. The Jews claim Esra rewrote the Bible from memory during the Babylonian captivity. Does that seem feasible that he could rewrite it without error? Did he have a photographic memory? The truth is, it was the Jews who rewrote the Bible and switched the names to protect their guilty ancestor. The Babylonian Bible is almost identical. Careful examination of the Bible exposes the Caucasian Jews as Canaanites and Kenites! The God of the Jews is Baal. Their own scriptures says that from Aaron to Solomon, they all worshipped the Warlord Baal.

[1 Kings 11:4-8 16:31 2 Kings 23:4,13] To this day, they murder in the name of their god. In fact, the Jews murdered the prophets who exposed their evil ways. Jesus (Esau) says that Abraham, Issac and Jacob shall enter God's kingdom, but their children shall be cast out! The god of the Jews is not the father of Jesus! They created their god in their own "corrupt" image. The Jewish Cabalists say that Jehovah is the devil.

An interesting note: after Muhammad finished compiling the Qu'ran and had died, it was burned by his number one disciple! Then it was rewrote completely from memory by his other disciples. Yet it is still called the Word of God. Did anyone ever question, what power on high is causing these books to burn? Esau's descendants are called Edom. According to the scholars, both Edom and Adam mean Red. Therefore, Edom is a direct descendant of Adam, the dark red or brown people. As Adam was created from Adamah, the brown earth. Caleb, the true ancestor of Jesus, was said to be of Edom (or Atum). Caleb, Joshua and Eleasar are the only ones who crossed over to the Promise land. It is well documented that the so-called Israelites who entered the land of Canaan were really Canaanites. Pharaoh Merenptah, son of Rameses II, says he exterminated the people of Israel. Joshua, son of Nun literally means; Yoshua or Jesus son of Nun. Nun is the Egyptian name of the watery womb that gave birth to the firstborn Sun of God. It is the sea of space that gave birth to the Morning star Sirius. Jesus/Horus crossed the celestial river to come to earth. Caleb means Dog. He is the Dog star Sirius. Eleasar is El (God) + asar (i.e. Osiris). Eleasar was high priest of the Zadok of the order of Melchi-Zakok. [Hebrews 6 & 7] Osiris, as Pharaoh, was high priest and king of the house of God. Just as Melchizedek is King of Righteousness and King of Peace (Salem). Melchizedek is made like the Son of God just as Osiris is an incarnation of Atum-Horus, the Sun of Righteousness. This Eleazar is not the son of Aaron who worships the Bull cult. Here is another irony. The Levite priests, like Esau, have no inheritance in the Promise Land. In fact, their founding fathers; Moses and Aaron were not allowed to crossover to the Promise Land.

Joseph has a dream where his father is the sun (Ra) and his mother is the moon and the 12 sons of Israel are stars. They represent the twelve houses of the Zodiac. Joseph says the sun, moon and eleven stars bowed down to him. [Genesis 37:9,10] Later, when he was sold into slavery into Egypt and became right hand man to Pharaoh, this was physically fulfilled. Joseph was schooled in the ancient mysteries, including the meaning of the signs of the Zodiac, while in Egypt. He was well aware that his house was Taurus the bull and his two sons were the horns of the bull. [Deuteronomy 33:13-17] From out of the House of Taurus shall come a Shepherd (Orion the Bull tamer). [Genesis 49:22-26] Yet the Lion of Judah comes from Shiloh (Galilee). [Genesis 49:8-12] At this time in On, they were worshipping the sacred bull, Menvis. Menves is Amen, the Bull of Heaven, from Thebes. He is Menes, the scorpion king, who lead the Upper Egyptians into conquering Lower Egypt. Crossing over into the Promise Land, the Kingdom of Osiris. Legend says a scorpion killed the Horus child. Or killed off the Horus worship in its prime. Joseph taught the "Gospel according to the priests of Amen" to the rest of his family. This is why the Bible ends its sayings with "Amen". The Jews worship the evil sun of God rather than the good Sun of God called Atum of On. The Lord (Atum) says, "Behold, I will bring punishment on Amon of No (Amen of Thebes), and Pharaoh and Egypt, with their gods and their kings-Pharaoh and those who trust in him. And I will deliver them into the hand of those who seek their lives.... Afterward it shall be inhabited as in the days of old." [Jeremiah 46:25] In the ancient times, the Egyptians worshipped God through his good son, Atum-Horus.

This explains why their Lord (Baal) loved: Jacob the swindler, bigamist, adulterer and liar; Moses the murderer; Judah the fornicator and father of bastards, [Genesis 38] David the murderer, adulterer; Solomon the murderer, idolater, sorcerer and adulterer. Solomon is a combination of Sol and Amon, of which, both are the evil sun of God. If these are the chosen of God, this is one sick God! Besides, who said they were the beloved of God? They did! David said it about himself???? The Jewish Moses is portrayed with two horns on his head like a bull. The Latin Vulgate says, "And when Moses came down from Mount Sinai, he held two tablets of the testimony, an he did not know that his face was horned from conversation with the Lord." Revelations 13:11 says the false prophet has two horns and speaks like a devil.

Revelations chapter twelve (as in the 12 Zodiacs) says the woman was clothed by the sun and stood on the moon. Twelve stars or twelve constellations are over head. She is mother earth who gives birth to the Sun of God (Horus/Jesus). The dragon causes a third of the stars to fall in an attempt to devour the child. The dragon is the Daystar Lucifer (Amen-Ra). The evil Sun is trying to swallow the Morning star Sirius. Yet, the dawn rising of Sirius is preordained. The dragon and his angels had left their domain in the constellations, as suns of God. The head and horns of Taurus the bull is called Hades! Menes is the scorpion king of Scorpio. The woman fled into the Wilderness of Sin. She represents the House of Israel following the bull cult of Baal and making the Golden Calf (baby bull). In unison, they all praise Amen-Baal (Amen the Bull of heaven). "God turned and gave them up to worship the host of heaven." [Acts 7:42] Then the Dragon makes war with the true followers of Horus/ Jesus/Easu. These are the Saints who keep God's Commandments, unlike the Jews and Christians. It was the Jews who murdered God's prophets and the Christians who murdered the followers of Horus/Jesus.

The Lord was going to destroy Israel but Moses talked him out of it. Then the "Zionist" Moses decided he had a thirst for blood. The Levite priests murdered 3,000 of their relatives. No wonder they don't have an inheritance in the Promise land. How soon they forgot that the Lord said, "You shall not kill." "I will destroy your enemies." But the Jews demanded that they get to shed blood! The Jews say Hitler was evil for burning them in the holocaust. Yet, it's OK when they burn their children in fire to their god, Baal? [Jeremiah 7:30-34] And attempt to commit genocide on the Canaanites!

"Moses was educated in all the wisdom of the Egyptians (both sacred and profane), and was mighty in the words and deeds." [Acts 7:22] Yet, he rejected the doctrine of Amen, the prince of Thieves, preached by the priests of Thebes. Forty years after his exile for murdering an Egyptian, the fiery Archangel Atum appeared to Moses to reveal the true Sun of God. According to Josephus, Moses was also called Osar-siph (Joseph). Perhaps he was born Joseph and renamed Moses when born again from the water. Just as Abram became Abraham and Jacob became Israel. Osar-siph means; child Osiris! Joseph was also the foster-father of Jesus. Just as Osiris was the father of Horus. Moses or Meses means "brought forth from water" and is the root of Messiah. Moses had two mothers; one natural and one adopted (Egyptian). Just as Horus had two mothers; Isis (mother earth) and Nephthys (mother nature). According to Josephus, in the Ethiopian version; the king's daughter who raise Moses was Thermutis (Ta-Ur-Mut) the Old Great Mother. Ta-Urmut is Ta-Urt the northern stars of Ursa Major. This means he was nursed by the unholy cow. The milk that tastes sour compared to God's. He was weaned from the udder (The-Utter-ences) of Ta-Urt. (R and T are interchangeable) [Hebrews 5:12-14 11:24-29]

The truth is; the books of Moses were taken from the original 42 Books of Thoth, the true Word of God. Moses wrote them down from memory to the best of his understanding. The Torah (Taurus) is a corruption of the Word of Thoth. Thoth is an attribute of the Word of God (Horus). Yet, the Bible or Bable was not compiled until after the Babylon captivity about 900 years later. This explains the Egyptian and the Babylonian influence.

The Book of Joshua is eschatology not history. Joshua, son of Nun, is none other than Jesus. In Egypt, Nun is the womb that gave birth to the firstborn Son of God. Joshua crosses the Jordan river, with the help of the Ark, and enters the Promise Land. Compare this to Horus in his bark, going west on the sea of space and returning to earth in the east. Revelations 11:19 says the Ark of the Covenant is in heaven, therefore, Joshua is in heaven. Jordan in Egyptian is Iurutana (Eridanus). Eridanus is the river in heaven running from the foot of Orion that divides the living from the dead. For the righteous it is the water of life that runs under the throne of Osiris. For the incorrigible sinner it is the river of fire. [Daniel 7:9-11 Psalms 97:3-5 50:3 Habakkuk 3:5 Isaiah 30:27-33 66:15,16 Nahum 1:5,6 2 Thessalonians 1:7,8]

God's power in the Ark causes the walls of Jericho to fall. "And war broke out in heaven." [Revelation 12:7-12] Michael (Joshua/Jesus) casts Satan and his angels to the earth (not Hades). Therefore, hell is on earth. Hades is the head and horns of the constellation of Taurus the bull, just as Satan is the head of the fallen stars. The Lord of the Earth must exterminate all evil in the land of Canaan so the good can live in peace. This is the same Ark as in Noah's day. Only those who keep the righteous requirements of the Covenant shall cross over to the dry Promise land (Eden restored). The walls of Jericho shall be replaced by the walls of new JeruSalem, the city coming down from heaven. God's kingdom on earth. [Revelation 21] The twelve angels (suns of God) at the gates are the 12 houses of Israel and the Zodiac. The dawning of Aquarius will be the dawning of the Sun of God in the Ark of Salvation.

Now Joshua commanded the sun to stand still. [Joshua 10:11-13] This might sound supernatural, yet it is very simple. Since it is the earth that moves not the sun, it is easy to command it to stand still. Therefore, if you are not on the earth, the sun stands still. Obviously, this is part of the war in heaven. In the last days, hail will fall from heaven. The sun will go supernova. It will brighten then darken causing the moon to darken. In that day, the Sun of Righteousness shall eclipse the sun of unrighteousness. [Matthew 24:27-31 Malachi 4:2 Rev.16:8,10,21] The Lord will command the evil sun to 'stop' leading men astray. The sun-god (Lucifer, Amen-Ra, Sol, Helio, Apollo, Baal) shall become impotent. The Lord with the Sword shall slay All warriors so that the rest can live in peace. There will be no sun or moon in God's kingdom to deceive the children of God. The one pretending to be the Angel of light will be stopped in his tracks. [2 Corinthians 11:13-15] The true Angel of Light is the original light when God's said, "Let there be light." This is Atum-Horus (Jesus) the Morning star, Sirius. [Revelation 21:23 22:5,16]

Now Moses represents the Messiah, Joshua the Savior, and Eleazar the high priest in the order of Melchi-Zadok. The Jews and the Essenes believed the Messiah, Savior and high priest to be three separate beings. This leaves no son of David to be king. This is were Caleb comes in. Only Joshua, Eleazar and Caleb crossed over to the Promise land. Caleb, son of Judah, is the true line of David. Yet, Caleb is called a son of Esau (Jesus). In Egypt, Atum (Son of God) incarnated as Osiris (Son of Man) who died and rose again as Horus (Jesus the Son of God). Esau is Osiris and Jacob is his evil brother Set! The Devil is God inversed. And the Jews have reversed the roles of the sages in their saga.

David was son of Jesse (Jesus). Jesse (Ishi) is Ash tree of life in Egyptian. Sharash (Sar-Ash) is the Hebrew for 'the shoot of Jesse' (i.e. the

Messiah). Jesus said, "I am the root and offspring of David, the Bright Morning Star." [Rev.22:16] Just as Horus is the root and offspring of Osiris (Sar). "And there shall come forth a sprout out of the stump of Jesse, and a shoot shall grow out of his roots." [Companion Bible-Isaiah 11:1] Osiris was cut down in the prime of his life, but new life sprouted from the root. Horus returned to his roots as Atum-Horus. The coffin of Osiris became the cradle of Horus. The Sun of God did 'Come Forth by Day' (Am-Tuat) from the Ash Tree of life. Just as Jesus, Son of God, incarnated as Son of Man and died on a tree. Then returned to being the Son of God. Sharash is Osiris in the Ash tree of life. As son of Jesse, the Ephraimite of Bethlehem-Judah; [1 Samuel 17:12] David fulfilled the prophecy of Genesis 49:8-12 & 22-26. He is the descendant of Judah and Joseph through Ephraim. He is the Lion of Judah in the house of Leo and Orion the shepherd in the house of Taurus.

Compare David, the shepherd boy, striking Goliath between the eyes with a stone, to Odysseus striking the giant Cyclop Polyphemus in his eye and escaping under the belly of a rams or sheep. Odysseus and his 12 men are the 12 months. After six are swallowed by the Cyclop in the cave (sun's six months in darkness in the underworld) the remaining six come forth into the light under the age of Ares the ram. The Three Cyclopes of Greek myth are the suns of God or stars (constellations). We are now in Pisces and on the verge of Aquarius.

According to the Bible, David defeated the she lion (antithesis of Leo) and the Great Bear (Ursa Major) and now beheads Goliath the Giant. [1 Samuel 17:36] The Targum on 1 Samuel 17:4 makes Samson (Shamesh the sun-god) the father of Goliath. Go-liath is 'son of Lilith'. Goliath must be Samson reborn. If Samson represents the solar year, Lilith is the Apophis serpent (sea of space) that swallows and then gives birth to Ra, the sun, every morning. The blind Samson turning the grinding Mill is the darkened sun moving through the underworld of the Zodiac. [Matthew 24:29] The 'jawbone of an ass' is the 'mouth of the sun' or the oracle of the sun-god, as an ass represents the sun in Egypt. Samson going between the two pillars is the sun setting in Manu; the western gateway into the underworld.

The 'Brass' Goliath represents the sun (Ra) trying to swallow the star of Bethlehem (Sirius) at the dawn rising. Like, the red Dragon tries to swallow the divine child. [Revelation 12:4,5] 'The Philistines stood on a mountain on one side and Israel on a mountain on the other side: and a valley between them.' This is Bekha, the place of sunrise in the eastern horizon. Am means come forth from, same as 'mes'. Bethlehem (Beth-s-hem-esh) is the birthplace of David and Jesus. It is the Egyptian Bekha-Anu (Heliopolis). Bethlehem is called the House of David; as in House, Sign or Age of the Zodiac. Bethlehem means House of the rising sun. Meaning the sun rising in the House of Pisces during the spring equinox.

Bethlehem also means House of Bread. The astrological House of Virgo is a woman holding a stalk of wheat. Ast (of astrology) is the Egyptian spelling of Isis. She bears the Seed of David. David is Duat and Divide. The Zodiac is divided into 12 ages. The Duat or Tuat is Lower heaven south of the North Pole Star. Bekhama is hippopotamus in Egyptian and Behemah in Hebrew. It is the birthplace of the evil suns of God (the circumpolar stars). It is the Ammat beast (composite of a hippo, lion and crocodile) who devours its young.

Goliath presented himself in the valley (Bekha) forty days. By this time, Orion-Sirius had reached its peak on the celestial meridian and David his maturity. David the shepherd boy is now Horus, the avenger of his father. David did Not wear the brass armor of a sun-god. He took the scepter (staff) of a man of God. He defeats Amen-Set with the spiritual Sword of Truth and the evil sun does set for the last time. The red Dragon, Set-Typhon is down and out.

The Bible says Satan is the Lion seeking whom he might devour. The Great Bear is birthplace of Bar or Baal. The Philistines worshipped Dagon. Could this be Dragon (Draco)? This composite Beast in Revelation 13 is a leopard, bear, lion and dragon. The same Beast is found in Daniel 7:4-8 which represents the unholy Roman empire. David defeated the giant with a Rock. Compare that to the Rock destroying the great image. [Daniel 2:31,45] Duat also denotes Dual; as in heaven so on earth. David's kingdom was divided (North and South) just like Egypt. The temple and the Ark was originally in the north (Shiloh) just like Egypt (Heliopolis). Heliopolis = Heru-polis (City of Horus). The power in the Ark destroyed the image of Dagon. David and the Ark is the counterpart of Jason and the Argo or Horus in his Bark. The signs in the heavens foretell of the destruction of the Beast (neo-Roman empire) by the heir of King David.

At the so-called Battle of Armageddon, Gog of Magog is Goliath. He leads his followers to their death. The Lord with the Sword will rise in the east and slay all the warriors and feed their flesh to the fowls. [1 Samuel 17:44-46 Revelation 16:12-16 19:11-21 Matthew 24:27-31] David is rightful heir to the throne. King Saul is Sultan Set. David spiritually emasculated Saul. Saul tries to kill David but is powerless (impotent). Just as Set tries to kill Horus. [Revelation 12] David plays the lyra to soothe the evil spirit (Dragon) within Saul. The lyra and Draco are two deacons of Sagittarius. Sagittarius is the archer on the white horse who slays the scorpion of Scorpio. It was Set in the form of a scorpion who killed the Horus child. Yet Horus triumphs by defeating death and resurrecting. "O Death, where is your sting? O Hades, where is your victory?" [1 Corinthians 15:55] The stars of Hades in the constellation of Taurus is home of Set-amen.

Jesus is the rightful heir and Sun of Righteousness. The Seed of David (Duat) shall be the Seed of God. [1 Chronicles 17:11-14] The Seed of Eve (Nun) is Atum (Jesus). [Genesis 3:15] He is the Sun of God begotten before time itself. Solomon is the evil sun of God. [1 Kings 11:4-13] Solomon is Sol-amon the evil solar deity. Just like Samson (Shamesh) the sun-god. Solomon is son of Bathsheba. Beth-Sheba means the House of the Seven north stars (Ursa Major) that gave birth to Set-Typhon. He is the Golden Baby Bull, sun of the Ammot (Amen & Mot) monster. Amen being the Bull of heaven (Taurus). Then Solomon mated with his mother, Sheba, Queen of heaven. Just as Mot is Amen's mother and mate. Sheba is identified with Lilith. [Kabbalah page 325] In Hinduism, Bathsheba is Bath-Shiva or House of Shiva (Satan). She is not the ancestor of Jesus!

Then Solomon went after Ashtoreth in the high places. Ashtoreth's stars were the same stars of the Arctic circle. Arc-turus is Latin for Ursa Major. Ashtoreth (Ash-Taurus-t) and Ashtart (Ash-Taurus-t) is the Egyptian Ta-urt, the consort of Taurus. The T suffix denotes feminine. Ta-urt is the Great Mother who gave birth to the evil son. Sheba or Sebau are the earthly (Seb) followers of Set. Also called Sami (Sam's sons), Menat, Smen (Sons of aMen), and minions of Amen. Solomon and Sheba's son was Menolek (Men is Molech, king of the gods).

Because of Solomon's evil, God divided the kingdom of Israel (north and south) just like Egypt. Solomon got Judah in the south just as Sut is King of Southern (Upper) Egypt. [1 Kings 11:4-8, 31-43] Solomon built the Temple made of stone. Jesus was the Temple made without human hands. King Solomon was the slavemaster who forced his people into slave labor in order to build his empire. Just like the kings of Upper Egypt. In Solomon's Temple the priests worshipped the sun-god, Tammuz. [Ezekiel 8:13-16] Solomon's defiled temple was destroyed by decree of the Lord. It was rebuilt twice and destroyed twice more. The temple rebuilt by Herod was a copy of the Temple of Amen at Karnak, right down to the holy of holies. It was destroyed 500 years, to the day, of the destruction of the second temple. The Lord's Temple was destroyed only once and resurrected (metaphysical) as a perpetual memorial.

After Solomon built the temple to his god, he created the cults of the Masons and Templars. Mason is Ma + son (the Great Mother and her evil sun, Amen). Solomon called them Ashtorah and Baal. Templars are the temple builders in the house of Baal. The pentacle is their sacred star and five their number. {Adelphi Quarterly, 1992 and Hidden Secrets of the Eastern Star page 115}

The Gospel of Jesus is his birth, life and death. So when was his birth and death? If you don't know this, you don't know the whole story. In every religion, the Son of God's birth and death is the same. Krishna, Buddha, Quetzalcoatl, Horus/Osiris, Jesus, were all born at the autumn equinox and died during the spring equinox called Passover. The evil sun of God always dies Dec.25th and is new born on New years. This is Sol, Apollo, Helio, Baal, Shamesh, Tammaz, Santa, Set-Amen, and Lucifer. And again, when will the Sun of God return? The Egyptian and Hebrew

New year is the autumn equinox when the Sun (Sirius) shall be reborn. The dawning of the Age of Aquarius is near at hand.

Now Joseph (Osar-siph), foster father of Jesus, is Osiris. He is not the father of Jesus/Horus. Osiris is Horus. He was reborn as Son of God. This is why his genealogy is listed in the Bible. He is the roots of mankind as well as the offspring of mankind. In other words, Atum created man and was then born Son of Man (Osiris). He is the first and second Adam.

Mary, called Queen of Heaven and Mother of god, gave birth to four sons (James, Joses, Judas, and Simon) and two daughters. [Mark 6:3] Compare this to Mot (Nut) and Geb (Earth) giving birth to Osiris, Set, Isis, Nephthys, Horus. Set would be Judas, the betrayer, or even Simon (Set-Amon) the denier. Peter Simon was the Devil's advocate. [Matthew 16:21-23] Simon Bar Jonah means Simon Baal Jonah. Simon the sorcerer usurped the name Peter and founded the church of Rome. Pater means Father as does Pope. Joses (Hosea) means Salvation. Hoseus, Joshua and Jesus are all from the same root. Joses is obviously Jesus and Horus of Egypt. James is a form of Jacob. James was one of the 12 disciples and became the head of the church in Israel. Jacob was father and head of the 12 tribes of Israel. There is no record of Mary's or Eve's deaths. The matrix or primordial watery womb is void of life. Mary means Eve in Latin. Eve (Evening or Darkness) gave birth to the first Adam and Mary to the second Adam. In Egypt, Nun gave birth to the firstborn Sun of God, Atum (Horus the Elder). Isis gave birth to the second Horus the Younger.

According to Christian lore the four gospel writers are: Matthew the Lion, Mark the Bull, Luke the Man, and John the Eagle or Hawk. Compare these to the sons of Horus; Tuamutef the Canine, Hapi the Bull, Amset the Man, and Qebhsenuf the Hawk. Compare to Revelation 4:7. They are also four signs of the Zodiac. There are 12 disciples and 12 sons of Israel, 12 Zodiac signs. There are 72 deacons in the Sanhedron. There are 36 decans and 72 dodecans in the Zodiac.

Steven was the first martyr following the death of Christ. Compare Steven to Abel the first martyr who was reborn as Seth, son of Eve. Steve = Set+eve. The cycle of time keeps turning, millennium after millennium, age after age. The Mill-en-nium is the 'Mill turning in Nun' or the continuum of the Zodiac ages continually retelling the gospel story. When the Lord returns, his faith followers will escape the cycle of life to death. They will receive a continuum of life that never ends.

Now let's return to the roots of some words. First the garden of Eden. Eden is Adon or Adonai, therefore, it is the garden of the Lord (Adon). The Elm is the tree of the Elohim. The forbidden fruit of the Tree of life is nectar of the neter (food of the gods). Ivy is the serpent entwined in the Tree of carnal knowledge (worldly wisdom). Ivy = Eve = Heva = Sheva. Heva is Serpent in Hebrew. In Hinduism, Eve = Maya (meaning Illusion) who is mother of Mara, the Great deceiver. Eve represents the dark side of the Great Mother that gave birth to the son of deception. 'Evening' is the darkness of night-time. At the same time, Maya is mother of the ENlightened One (Buddha). The Great Matrix is neither good nor bad. Just as darkness is neither good or bad. In fact, to those living in the desert, the sun and drought are bad.

The Ark

Did the Lord rain down his wrath upon the Pharaoh of Egypt just to save the wicked Israelites who He knew would rebel against him? Of course not. The Egyptians possessed the Ark of Atum-Ra for 2,000 years. Now it was time for the people of Israel to possess the Ark. After the ten plagues the Pharaoh told Moses the secret location of the Ark. The Israelites entered the Great Pyramid and plundered the treasures of Egypt. The so called king's coffer is the table of the Ark. As long as the people of Israel possessed the Ark they were protected by the Spirit or power of God. They needed no military men, but had one anyway.

The Ark protected the Ancient Egyptian priests from all invaders. They had no need of a standing army. But the time that the Lord was working with Egypt was over. The cosmic clock changed from the age of Taurus to the age of Aries the Ram. The Ram or Lamb being the sacred animal of the Semitics. About 2,000 BC, the evil Hyksos (Arabians) invaded and oppressed the Lower Egyptians. Then about 1500 BC the evil Upper Egyptians invaded and oppressed Lower Egypt. The priests of Thebes took over the temples and taught the worship of Amen-Ra. Amen's sacred animal was the Ram. Rameses II worshipped Amen the Ram. The Bark of Amen-Ra is the solar bark. His empty promises are: his followers shall be transformed into beings of light and together they shall sail the sea of space forever. He promises a Rapture and habitation in heaven. "You will not die. For God knows that in the day you eat of it your eyes will be opened, and you will be like God, knowing good and evil," hissed Satan. [Genesis 3:4,5]

It was God's power in the Ark that parted the Sea turned Red with the blood of the Egyptian soldiers. It was the Ark that Rameses II would not let go. He was glad to be rid of the trouble making Jews! It was God's power in the Ark that parted the Jordan River and destroyed the fortified city of Jericho. When the Lord returns with His Ark, it shall part the good from the evil. All military men shall die so the remnant can live in peace.

The Israelites possessed the Ark for a short time before it disappeared! While the Philistines had it, they were plagued. The whereabouts of the Ark is one of the Mysteries of the world. The Ethiopians claim they have it, but that is probably a copy. The Bible says the Ark is in God's temple in heaven. [Revelation 11:19] When the Lord returns to the earth, the Mercy Seat of the Ark will be his throne from where He will judge the nations. [Ezekiel 1:26-28 Revelation 4:3] The Egyptian judge is Osiris, King of kings.

The Ark of Atum was made from the wood of the Tree of life and was gilded with gold. It possessed the power of life and death. On the top was two scarabs (sacred beetles), not cherubs (angels), facing each other. They represent good vs. evil, Atum vs. Amen, Michael vs. Lucifer. Inside the Ark is the food of the gods, the King's scepter, and God's contract or Covenant with man. The covenant has certain stipulations called Commandments. This contract shall be opened on Judgment day to see if man has fulfilled his conditions. The penalty for breaking the covenant is death.

Atum's Ark was also a Bark. Bark is a boat-ark. It represented the same thing as the Ark of Noah. Those righteous souls who shall be saved will enter the Bark of Atum. The evil incorrigible sinners will die in the Lake of fire. They shall breathe their last and breath of life or spirit will return to God. The followers of Osiris shall die and lay in their tomb/womb until the time of the Resurrection (rebirth) from the womb of Mother Earth. Osiris and his body of believers will rise from the grave together. They shall dwell on earth in the garden paradise created for them. Just as Adam was created from the soil of Mother Earth and placed in God's garden.

Question: Did the Egyptians build the Great Pyramid for the purpose of containing the awesome powers of the Ark? Did the kings of the Old Kingdom (2400 BC) seal the Ark in the Great Pyramid for safe keeping? Did Rameses finally reveal the secret by showing Moses the how to enter the Great Pyramid and carry off the Ark? GP = Great Pyramid or God's Power.

The Ark was taken by Joshua to Shiloh in northern Israel. Shiloh = Sar (Osiris). The Ark remained there until Samuel took it into battle against the Philistines. Israel was defeated and the Philistines captured the Ark. After the power within the Ark had plagued them, they sent it back. Later after David defeated the Philistines, he moved the Ark to the City of David in Judah. Solomon placed it in the Temple he built. Soon after, the Babylonians conquered Judah and the Ark disappeared! "The scepter shall not depart from Judah, nor a lawgiver from between his feet, until Shiloh comes; and to Him shall be the obedience of the people." [Genesis 50:10] Shiloh is Osiris, the Judge returning on Judgment Day.

Compare this to the original story. The Ark was at Anu, northern Egypt for thousands of years. It protected the people of God. When the Upper Egyptians conquered Lower Egypt, they carried the Ark to Thebes. It is strange that the Hebrew word for Ark is Thbe or Thebes. Karnak or

Karnach is an anagram for Ark-Noah. Legend says: When the priests of Amon opened the Ark, the power or spirit of God ascended and flew away in the form of a dove! The moral of the story: God only allows His people to possess His Holy Spirit.

Rules of Grammar

Rules of Grammar q = k or c example: Zedec = Zedek = Zedeq = Zodok = Zodak{{ellipsis}} Kenite = Kainite = Cainite (sons of Cain). Quran = Kuran C sometimes equals G Draco = Dragon s = z 'us' is used as a suffix in Greek to say Zeus' just as 'el' is used in Hebrew to say God's 'le' is used the same in French i = y example: the suffix iah means Yah or Yahweh. Sophia is the root of Philo-sophy, the love of wisdom. Y = j example: Yahweh = Jehoveh. j = i example: Jesus = Iesus = Easu (Aramic). j = h example: Yoshua = Joshua = Hoshua = Hosea = Hayseus. i, j and y are vowels. A E I O U and Y are all vowels. w = v example: Yahweh = Iahweh = Jehoveh. u = v example: Anu = Avon = On and l = r example: Baal = Bar = Bull = Beel-zebub = Bell Greek polis = per of the Egyptians. Both mean city.
t = d example: Atum = Adam Theos (Greek) = Deus (Latin) = Dis = Dios = Deva (Indian) = Deity = Deify = God In Chaldean the Sigma = Tau and Tur = Sur. Thur is Horus and Sur is Sar or Osiris. Since Horus and Osiris are one and the same, Tur = Sur.
sh = s or h example: Shatan = Satan and Seth = Set-amen. Joshua = Jeshuas = Jesus Sheol = hell (grave) Pisces = Pishes = Phisches = Fishes. The sch is the beginning of a school of fishes.
ch = c or h example: Hathor = Cathor = Cathol-ic Christ = hrs-t = Horus-Tem All vowels are interchangeable. They are injected when pronounced. That's the reason we don't know how to pronounce ancient words; such as YHWH. Yahweh = Iahueh = Iaue (minus the silent h) or Jehovah = Iehouah = Ieoua (a,e,i,o,u,y). And since there are no vowels in the Hebrew, it would be _ _ _ _ _ _ . In other words, No one knows God's name! The Tetragrammaton of the Pythagoreans was ieue. The Jewish Targum says the Creator's name is ii.

Double vowels and prefixes (H and M) are used to conceal and confuse: Adonai = Adonis of Greece. Mythology and Mytheology are the same. Hammon, Ammon, Mammon and Amen are the same.
Does anyone understand why receive has a double vowel, yet reception does not? Why does conceive have a double vowel, yet conception does not. The same goes for deceive and deception. This is confusing and insane.

The Mazoretic texts or Massorah is a modern concoction of the Jews to insert 'their' vowels into the Hebrew that had no vowels. Just as the Egyptian writing had no vowels. Compare this to our abbreviations like: USA, or IBM or AT&T. We shorten it is to it's by dropping the vowel. Through becomes thru.

Deo Patre Natus is Latin for Deity Peter Natal or Born of God the Father. Theopator is Greek for Theo-Peter or Son of God the Father. Peter means God the Father. It is Patah is Egyptian.

In Hebrew, the suffix 'im' makes the word plural. Cherub = Angel & Cherubim = Angels. El is God & Elohim = Gods In Aramaic, 'i' or 's' suffix, makes the word plural. Adon is singular Adonai or Adonis is plural. In Greek, 'i' or 's' suffix, makes the word plural. Theo is God & Theos is Gods. 'e' or 'a' suffix makes the word feminine and 's' makes it masculine. In Egyptian, 't' suffix makes the word feminine. From the word Ta meaning Land, as in Mother Earth. 'u' suffix makes the word plural: as in neter (god) and neteru (gods). The Hebrew suffix 'ah' becomes 'as' in Greek. Judah = Judas = Judea = Jude Elijah = Elias = Helios (H prefix) = Heru = Horus.

The Hebrew, Aramaic, Phoenician, Syriac, Chaldean, Coptic and Greek are essentially the same. They were invented by the Egyptians. See Rosetta stone. The spoken tongues were divided at the Tower of Babel, but the written languages are rooted in Egypt. When Abraham traveled to Canaan and Egypt, they communicated easily! The original alphabet went from A to T, with M or MN in the middle. MN is the monogram of Mon or Amen. Now, in Egypt, it is said Amen is the middle or noon day sun, Atum is the setting sun and Tem is the rising Sun of God. Atum is the firstborn Sun of God who passed away, but shall rise again as Tem in the last days. He is the first and the last, the beginning and the end. Both Mut and Nut are names of the Great Mother. M stands for Ma the Great Mother and her evil sun, Mon. Ma and Mon mated, producing their son of incest, Khonsu the Moon deity. The English alphabet goes from A to Z with MN still the middle letters. A = Atum and Z is Zar or Sar (Osiris) the Judge in the last days.

Bibliography

The New King James Open Bible by Thomas Nelson Publishers
{the root of bibliography is biblio or bible which means book}
The Companion Bible by Kregel Publications
The Jewish Book of Knowledge The Pentateuch and Haftorahs edited by Dr.J.H.Hertz, C.H.
The Interlinear KJV-NIV by Alfred Marshall
The Nubian Islam Communitee Publications
The Apocrypha translated by Edgar J. Goodspeed.
The Encyclopaedia Britannica 1962 edition
The Grolier Encyclopedia of Knowledge
The Qu'ran (Koran)
Persian Mythology by John R. Hinnells
Hinduism by V.P. (Hemant) Kanitkar
The Greek gods by Evslin, Evslin, and Hoopes
The Greek Myths by Robert Graves
Bulfinch's Mythology by Thomas Bulfinch
The Mythology of the Romans
A Guide to the gods by Richard Carlyon
The World of Myth by David Adams Leeming
New Larousse Encyclopedia of Mythology by the Hamlyn Publishing Group
The MacMillan Illustrated Encyclopedia of Myths and Legends by Arthur Cotterell
Ancient Egypt by National Geographic Society
Egypt and the Pyramids
The Great Pyramid by Piazzi Smyth
Our Inheritance in the Great Pyramid by C. Piazzi Smyth
The Legendary Past: Egyptian Myths by George Hart
The Ancient Egyptian Pyramid Texts by Raymond Faulkner
Discovering Ancient Egypt by Rosalie David
The Orion Mystery: unlocking the secrets of the pyramids by Robert Bauval and Adrian Gilbert
The Message of the Sphinx by Graham Hancock and Robert Bauval

The Sirius Mystery by Robert K.G. Temple
The Sirius Connection by Murry Hope
Finger-prints of the Gods by Graham and Hancock
The Book of the Dead by E.A. Wallis Budge
Osiris; the Egyptian Religion of Resurrection by E.A. Wallis Budge
The Gods of the Egyptians, volume 1 & 2 by E.A. Wallis Budge
From Fetish to God in Ancient Egypt by E.A. Wallis Budge
The Book of Coming Forth by Day by Maulana Karenga
Egyptian Book of the Dead and the Ancient Mysteries of Amenta by Gerald Massey Pharaohs and Kings by David M. Rohl
The British Museum Book of Ancient Egypt
A Book of the Beginings (vol.1 and 2) by Gerald Massey
Gerald Massey's Lectures by Gerald Massey
The writings of Herbert Armstrong, founder of Worldwide Church of God
Divine Plan of the Ages
Doctrine of the Seventh Day Adventists
Man, Myth, and Magic encyclopaedia by Marshall Cavendish corp. (a set of 20+ books)
The Dictionary of Symbols by Carl G. Liungman
Dictionary of Subjects and Symbols in Art by James Hall
The Dictionary of Festivals by J.C. Cooper
Signs and Symbols of Primordial Man by Albert Churchward
Mysteries of the Unknown series:
The Mystical Year by Time-Life Books
Cosmic Duality by Time-Life Books
Ancient Wisdom and Secret Sects by Time-Life Books
Power of Myth by Joseph Campbell
Historical Atlas of World Mythology by Joseph Campbell
World Mythology by Roy Willis
The Sacred texts of the World, an Universal Anthology by Smart & Hecht.
The Religions of Man by Huston Smith
Mysteries of Atlantis Revisited by Cayce, Schwartzer and Richards
Atlantis the Eighth Continent by Charles Berlitz
The Illustrated Guide to the Supernatural by Richard Cavendish
The Mapping of the Heavens by Peter Whitfield
The Kabballah by Adolph Franck
The Dead Sea Scrolls Uncovered by Robert Eisenman & Michael Wise
Understanding the Dead Sea Scrolls edited by Hershel Shanks
Josephus the Man and the Historian by H.St.John Thackeray
Flavius Josephus by Mireille Hadas-Lebel
The Complete Gospels by Robert J. Miller
The Book of Enoch the Prophet translated by Richard Laurence
From Sabbath to Sunday by Samuele Bacchiocchi
The Real Meaning of the Zodiac by D.James Kennedy, Ph.D.

The Golden Fleece and the Heroes Who Lived Before Achilles by Padraic Colum Gospel of the Stars by Peter Lemesurier
Astrology by Mailly Nesle
The Astrological Foundation of the Christ Myth by Malik H. Jabbar
The History of Hell by Alice K. Turner
From the Browder File by Anthony T. Browder
Deceptions and Myths of the Bible by Lloyd M. Graham
Pagan Origins of the Christ Myth by John G. Jackson
The Golden Bough by James George Frazer
Hamlet's Mill by Giorgio de Santillana & Hertha von Dechend
The Illuminati 666 by William Josiah Sutton
The Word of God by the Holy Spirit of God. The spiritual gift of understanding the knowledge of God's kingdom.